THE LIBRARY
ST. MARY'S COLLEGE OF MARYLAND
ST. MARY'S CITY, MARYLAND 20686

# LOWLAND MAYA CIVILIZATION
IN THE EIGHTH CENTURY A.D.

# LOWLAND MAYA CIVILIZATION IN THE EIGHTH CENTURY A.D.

A Symposium at Dumbarton Oaks
7TH AND 8TH OCTOBER 1989

Jeremy A. Sabloff and John S. Henderson,
*Editors*

Dumbarton Oaks Research Library and Collection
Washington, D.C.

Copyright © 1993 by Dumbarton Oaks
Trustees for Harvard University, Washington, D.C.
All rights reserved
Printed in the United States of America

*Library of Congress Cataloging-in-Publication Data*

Lowland Maya civilization in the eighth century A.D. : a symposium at Dumbarton Oaks, 7th and 8th October 1989 / Jeremy A. Sabloff and John S. Henderson, editors.
    p.    cm.
Includes bibliographical references and index.
ISBN 0-88402-206-4
    1. Mayas—Politics and government—Congresses. 2. Mayas—Social conditions—Congresses. 3. Mayas—Economic conditions—Congresses.
    I. Sabloff, Jeremy A. II. Henderson, John S. III. Dumbarton Oaks.
F1435.3.P7L68   1993
972.81′016—dc20                                       92-8249

# Contents

FOREWORD vii

PREFACE xi

## I. OVERVIEW AND BACKGROUND

1. Introduction 1
   JEREMY A. SABLOFF AND JOHN S. HENDERSON

2. Eighth-Century Physical Geography, Environment, and Natural Resources in the Maya Lowlands 11
   DON S. RICE

## II. ORGANIZATION OF ANCIENT MAYA SOCIETIES

3. The Economics of Social Power and Wealth among Eighth-Century Maya Households 65
   PATRICIA A. MCANANY

4. The Social Organization of the Late Classic Maya: Problems of Definition and Approaches 91
   ROBERT J. SHARER

5. Ancient Maya Political Organization 111
   JOYCE MARCUS

6. The Topography of Ancient Maya Religious Pluralism: A Dialogue with the Present 185
   GARY H. GOSSEN AND RICHARD M. LEVENTHAL

*Contents*

## III. TOPICS AND THEMES

7. A View of Ancient Maya Settlements in the Eighth Century    219
   GAIR TOURTELLOT

8. Pottery, Potters, Palaces, and Polities: Some Socioeconomic and Political Implications of Late Classic Maya Ceramic Industries    243
   JOSEPH W. BALL

9. Analytical Approaches to Late Classic Maya Lithic Industries    273
   DANIEL R. POTTER

10. Architecture and Social Change in Late Classic Maya Society: The Evidence from Mundo Perdido, Tikal    299
    JUAN PEDRO LAPORTE

11. Historical Inscriptions and the Maya Collapse    321
    DAVID STUART

12. On the Eve of the Collapse: Maya Art of the Eighth Century    355
    MARY ELLEN MILLER

13. The Study of Maya Warfare: What It Tells Us about the Maya and What It Tells Us about Maya Archaeology    415
    DAVID WEBSTER

## IV. SUMMARY

14. Reconceptualizing the Maya Cultural Tradition: Programmatic Comments    445
    JOHN S. HENDERSON AND JEREMY A. SABLOFF

INDEX    477

# Foreword

IN 1967 DUMBARTON OAKS initiated its series of symposia in Pre-Columbian Studies with the Conference on the Olmec. The impetus was an accumulation of archaeological data from a number of recent excavations in the Gulf Coast and elsewhere in Mesoamerica that warranted assessment and comparison, for which Elizabeth P. Benson and Michael D. Coe gathered together several dozen specialists to consider the new evidence and discuss the Olmec cultural manifestation. The idea, if not formally stated, was to reach a sense of the Olmec in light of what had recently become known. Twenty-two years and twenty symposia later, Jeremy Sabloff and John Henderson have addressed a similar need with respect to the Maya, organizing and chairing the conference on the eighth-century lowland Maya, of which this publication is the result.

In the intervening years, the Dumbarton Oaks Pre-Columbian symposia have become annual events and have grown from relatively small one-day gatherings of experts to day-and-a-half meetings of a dozen or so presentations delivered to an audience of two hundred. They have given up the sometimes easy, sometimes intense, give-and-take of informal discussion among specialists to accommodate more voices and broader participation. Throughout, however, participation has been international and multi-disciplinary, with archaeologists and art historians talking to each other and to cultural anthropologists, linguists, physicists, and historians. The atmosphere has remained broadly humanistic in keeping with Dumbarton Oaks' fundamental humanities focus and with the commitment of the Pre-Columbian program to foster interdisciplinary communication and perspectives. The results of the meetings characteristically have warranted publication.

Over the years the kinds of topics addressed have expanded to focus variously on a culture, an area, a period, or a cultural connection. Most of the symposia have been broadly topical: looking, for example, at the phenomenon of ritual human sacrifice throughout Mesoamerica, at Mesoamerican writing systems, at the cult of the feline, or at early ceremonial architecture in the Andes. Others have focused on a single city (Teotihuacan) or a single site (the Aztec Templo Mayor). Only a few, such as the conferences

*Foreword*

on the Olmec and on the Chavin, have considered a range of material for an entire culture.

This Maya symposium, like its Olmec and Chavin predecessors, is culturally rather than topically focused. Sabloff and Henderson's decision to look broadly at the Maya was governed by the need to assess a rapidly mounting quantity of new information from a variety of sources, which called for a comprehensive rather than a topical look. Then the temporal focus on the eighth century directed the effort to the period of greatest overall complexity and brought in the fullest range of information. Together they create a fabric—an idea of Maya culture—that is variegated and richly contoured.

One of the notable features of the symposium and this volume is a marked insistence throughout the papers on regional diversity, separate rates of change and stability in different areas, and local ways of doing things. It is clear that our understanding of the Maya is shifting. We are seeing now that there was not a monolithic program of cultural development among the Maya but instead a more complex process marked by great variability from region to region. Instead of presenting Classic Maya society as a united conception, this volume forces us to see lowland and highland Maya societies in the plural.

Elizabeth Hill Boone<br>
Dumbarton Oaks

Dumbarton Oaks Pre-Columbian Conference Proceedings

| | |
|---|---|
| 1967 | Dumbarton Oaks Conference on the Olmec |
| 1968 | Dumbarton Oaks Conference on Chavín |
| 1970 | The Cult of the Feline: A Conference in Pre-Columbian Iconography |
| 1971 | Mesoamerican Writing Systems |
| 1973 | The Junius B. Bird Pre-Columbian Textile Conference (with The Textile Museum) |
| 1973 | Death and the Afterlife in Pre-Columbian America |
| 1974 | The Sea in the Pre-Columbian World |
| 1975 | Pre-Columbian Metallurgy of South America |
| 1976 | Mesoamerican Sites and World-Views |
| 1977 | The Art and Iconography of Late Post-Classic Central Mexico |
| 1978 | Falsifications and Misreconstructions of Pre-Columbian Art |
| 1979 | Ritual Human Sacrifice in Mesoamerica |
| 1980 | Highland-Lowland Interaction in Mesoamerica: Interdisciplinary Approaches |
| 1981 | Painted Architecture and Polychrome Monumental Sculpture in Mesoamerica |
| 1982 | Early Ceremonial Architecture in the Andes |
| 1983 | The Aztec Templo Mayor |
| 1984 | The Southeast Classic Maya Zone |
| 1984 | Mesoamerica after the Decline of Teotihuacan, A.D. 700–900 (Summer Research Seminar) |
| 1985 | The Northern Dynasties: Kingship and Statecraft in Chimor |
| 1985 | Huari Administrative Structure: Prehistoric Monumental Architecture and State Government (Roundtable) |
| 1986 | Aztec Imperial Strategies (Summer Research Seminar) |
| 1986 | Latin American Horizons |
| 1987 | Wealth and Hierarchy in the Intermediate Area |
| 1988 | Art, Ideology, and the City of Teotihuacan |
| 1989 | Lowland Maya Civilization in the Eighth Century A.D. |
| 1990 | Collecting the Pre-Columbian Past |

# Preface

THE IDEA FOR THE OCTOBER 1989 Dumbarton Oaks symposium from which this volume derives was first discussed by the editors two years earlier in the context of planning for interchanges between the University of Pittsburgh and Cornell University as part of their active Latin American consortium. With the support of Elizabeth Boone and the Senior Fellows in Pre-Columbian Studies at Dumbarton Oaks, we developed our original idea into what turned out to be one of the best-attended annual symposia to date in the Pre-Columbian series.

We are particularly grateful to Elizabeth Boone for all her assistance and helpful suggestions throughout the preparations for the symposium and subsequently for this volume. We also thank Don Rice for his assistance in the planning of the symposium. Through the good offices of George Stuart, we were able to obtain financial support from the National Geographic Society to allow us to bring several scholars from Latin America and several additional discussants to the symposium. We thank both George and the Society for their help.

Earlier versions of all the papers in this volume were presented at the symposium, with the exception of David Webster's paper on warfare, which was added at the editors' request. The papers in this volume also benefitted from the extensive discussion that took place during the symposium and at a seminar attended by participants the day after the close of the symposium. We tried to foster more discussion than at other Dumbarton Oaks conferences with the addition of several formal discussants and with additional time for the audience to have greater opportunities to interact with the speakers. E. Wyllys Andrews V, Fernando Robles C., Ricardo Agurcia, and David Webster all provided stimulating formal discussions during the symposium, and we are deeply appreciative of their efforts. In addition, we would like to thank Diane Chase, Arlen Chase, Arthur Demerest, and Norman Hammond, who joined the discussions after the symposium. We are grateful, as well, to two anonymous reviewers who provided extensive and useful comments on earlier drafts of the papers.

In the *Devil's Dictionary,* Ambrose Bierce, in a typically cynical vein, defined "discussion" as a "method of confirming others in their errors."

*Preface*

Fortunately, we found that both the formal and informal discussions at Dumbarton Oaks were far more productive than that, and we fervently hope that these discussions and the papers they helped strengthen still serve to propel the field to new understandings of Classic Maya civilization in the eighth century A.D. in particular and the development of ancient Maya civilization in general.

Jeremy A. Sabloff
University of Pittsburgh

John S. Henderson
Cornell University

# I

# Introduction

## JEREMY A. SABLOFF
UNIVERSITY OF PITTSBURGH

## JOHN S. HENDERSON
CORNELL UNIVERSITY

IT IS A TREMENDOUSLY EXCITING TIME TO BE studying the ancient Maya. New data abound as a multitude of field projects have just been completed or are in the midst of supplying fresh information about Maya civilization. The concentration of work in the translation of Maya hieroglyphic writing is transforming our understanding of the major Maya rulers, their lives, and their interactions. Stimulating ideas as to how all these data are to be interpreted appear in the literature seemingly with every new journal issue and in a continuous stream of edited volumes about the Maya.

However it also is a frustrating time for Maya scholars. The growing specialization within the discipline of archaeology makes it difficult to develop a holistic view of the Maya, while the sheer mass of information is increasingly hard to control. Moreover, the time lag between fieldwork and publication is too often regrettably long, making it exceedingly difficult to synthesize current trends and thoughts.

Nearly ten years ago, Joyce Marcus (1983) perceptively argued that Maya archaeology had reached a crossroads. While there were sharp disagreements about the specific nature of the choices facing the field, few disputed her basic contention. Yet in the past few years the field appears in some respects to have stalled at this critical junction. On the one hand the appeal of older approaches remains strong, in some cases even though their utility and validity have been persuasively questioned, so that the field often appears to be retreading already well-traveled roads; on the other hand, although many new theoretical and methodological paths have opened up, there are few clear markers as to which will prove most productive. Thus, with so many options, the field seems to be unsure of what direction to take, while the lure of the comfortable, familiar road—the traditional emphasis on primary centers, public architecture, and elites, for example—remains a potent, frequently unconscious, force that is influencing the decision-making process.

Obviously, Maya archaeology is being pulled in different directions. But it would be reasonable to predict that there will be no immediate shift, since it takes no great insight to observe that the mills of scholarly change grind relatively slowly in Maya studies. Such conservatism is particularly clear with regard to the "New Archaeology" (see Binford 1972, 1983, 1989), which has had relatively less impact on Maya archaeology than it has had in other areas. While from some perspectives the relatively minor influence of this school of thought on the field is cause for celebration, Maya studies unfortunately has been slow to accept significant innovations in method and theory developed elsewhere in the discipline of archaeology. The field also suffers from a relative lack of appreciation of comparative data on complex societies (see Sabloff's recent book *The New Archaeology and the Ancient Maya* [1990] for a broad discussion that puts Maya studies in the larger context of general trends in archaeological thinking).

Pioneering archaeological research carried out first at Barton Ramie (Willey et al. 1965), then at Tikal (Jones, Coe, and Haviland 1981) and Dzibilchaltun (Andrews IV and Andrews V 1980) in the 1950s and 1960s (see Fig. 1), along with Tatiana Proskouriakoff's (1960) initial breakthroughs in decipherment, brought about the dismantling of the traditional model of ancient Maya civilization that had been so successfully synthesized by Sylvanus Morley in *The Ancient Maya* (1946) and Eric Thompson in *The Rise and Fall of Maya Civilization* (1954) (also see Sabloff 1990). Dynamic new models emerged (see, for example, Henderson 1981; Hammond 1982; Morley, Brainerd, and Sharer 1983), but at the same time new field and analytic techniques that had proved effective elsewhere—such as piece-plotting artifacts in households and flotation, to name only two—were slow to filter into general use, hampering the more rapid advancement of Maya archaeology (Marcus 1983).

Moreover, two fundamental aspects of the New Archaeology (but far less heralded than its more polemical concerns) also were slow to be incorporated into Mayanist thinking. The first is the emphasis on cultural variability. Non-Mayanists were much quicker to recognize the futility of simply digging a pit in a spot just because it looked interesting (the biggest, the smallest, etc.). As archaeologists' conceptions of culture shifted from traditional views of homogeneous traits shared by groups to systemic views of diverse subsystems organized into whole systems, their research strategies underwent comparable transformations. If archaeologists had to be concerned with synchronic variability, which had often been seriously underestimated in the Maya area, then they had to pay careful attention to sampling. Under the traditional view it did not really matter where archaeologists dug

## Introduction

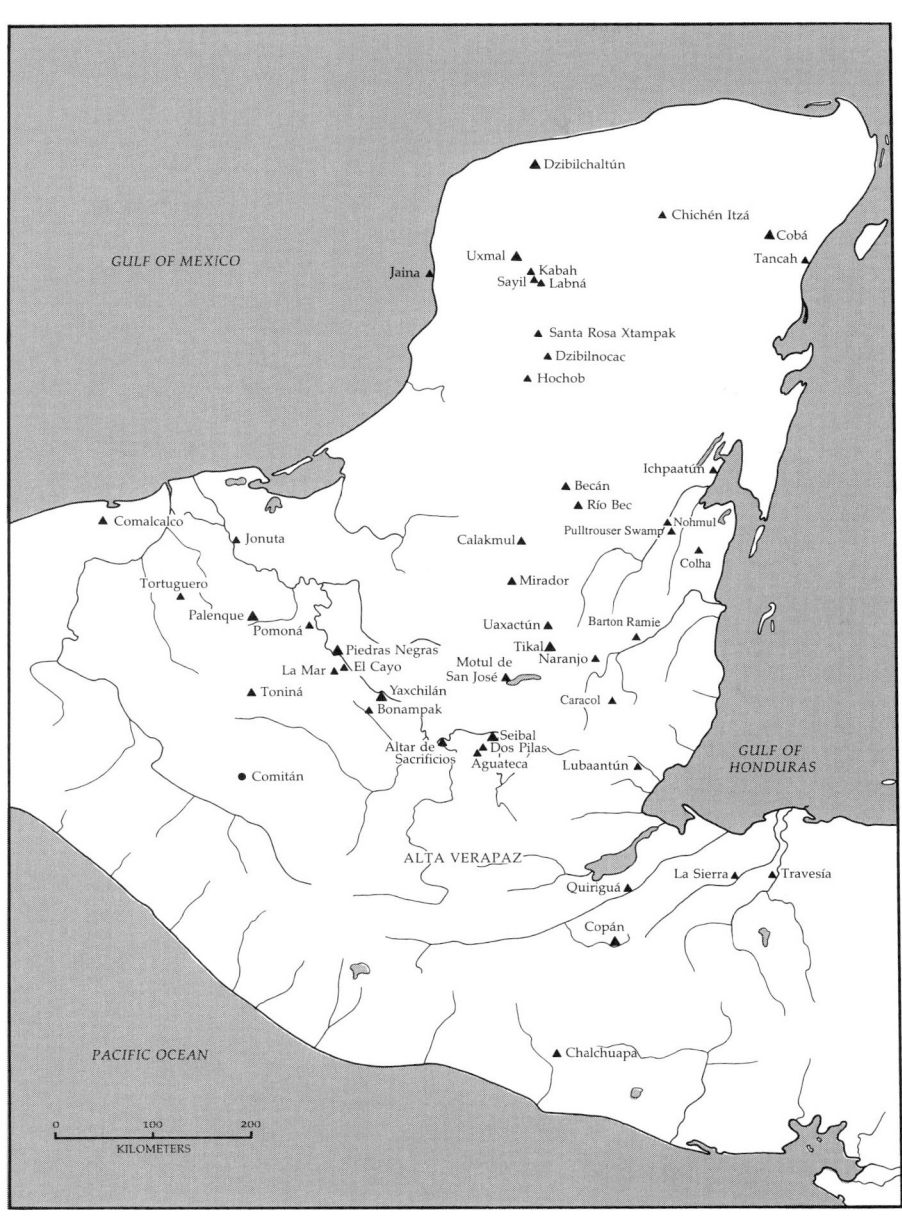

Fig. 1   The Maya world.

their test pits or what structures they excavated, but under a systems view the need to comprehend variability and control-sampling strategies was critical.

The second aspect is the building of regular procedures for the validation of hypotheses about the nature of ancient Maya civilization. Speculation, unsupported assertions, and free associations are no longer considered convincing no matter who makes them, and careful testing designs have replaced them. However, because the latter practices have entered the picture only recently, Maya scholars still have the lamentable tendency to focus their judgments and criticisms on people, rather than their ideas. Although, as Raymond Thompson (1956) pointed out some years ago, there is an inescapable subjective element in archaeological inference, Mayanists need to shift the emphasis from personalities to concepts and the logical structure of arguments.

Nevertheless, new interest in rigorous use of appropriate analogies (how are markets to be recognized, for example), concern with the boundaries and contexts of field studies, attention to the archaeological definition of "Maya" (along with attempts to isolate signatures for such identifications), research in frontier zones and what may have been multiethnic communities, and a more overt concern with theory (as reflected in many of the papers in this volume) all bode well for the immediate future of Maya research (cf. Sabloff 1983, 1986). The emergence of a carefully controlled "conjunctive approach" with hypothesis formulation and testing that rigorously combines information from archaeology, epigraphy, iconography, and ethnohistory (see Culbert 1988) is equally encouraging. As theories about the developmental trajectory of Maya civilization become more explicitly formulated, assessments of the productivity and utility of widely divergent research strategies that move from household to region or vice versa can be made more rational.

We believe that this volume, with its broad thematic but narrow temporal focus, might be a small but productive means of pushing Maya studies a little further away from the crossroads along what we hope will prove to be a productive path. We feel that a comprehensive review and synthesis of the very rich archaeological, artistic, and historical information from the Maya lowlands during the eighth century should provide the foundation for a fresh reconstruction of the Maya world at a time of great complexity. In turn, this new view of the organization of ancient Maya societies will provide a baseline for the kinds of comparative analyses that are essential for an understanding of such key issues as the extent and significance of regional variability within the Maya world, the nature of the developmental processes that produced Maya civilization, and the nature of the processes that began to transform it at the end of the eighth century.

Certainly the period between A.D. 700 and 800 is critical for understanding Classic Maya civilization. This pivotal century, on the eve of a radical transformation of the cultural landscape of eastern Mesoamerica, saw the culmination of developmental trends that had been under way for a millennium. Far-reaching trade links and networks of political and social alliances stretched across the Maya world. Many centers, particularly in the southern lowlands, reached individual peaks of size, internal complexity, prosperity, and political influence. At the same time, important centers in the northern lowlands were just beginning to rise to prominence. The corresponding proliferation of civic architecture, with its associated art and hieroglyphic texts, and of domestic installations representing every social level from commoner/farmer to ruler, has been the focus of considerable archaeological, iconographic, and epigraphic research, so that the eighth century is easily the best-documented period in the history of many centers.

In the past this century would have been viewed as the last gasp of Maya greatness prior to the collapse of Classic Maya civilization at the century's close. With new data, a lowlands-wide perspective, better control of chronology in the north, and new views of the Maya world, the "collapse" currently does not loom as large as it used to, because scholars now recognize many peaks and many "collapses" over the millennia (the 1986 School of American Research Advanced Seminar on Maya Polities [see Culbert 1991] is but one example of such new thinking).

It now appears that at the same time that many cities in the southern lowlands were declining, cities in the Puuc region of the northern lowlands, as well as the great urban center of Chichen Itza, were taking off, increasing in population, wealth, and political power. Some southern lowland cities, particularly those situated along natural transportation routes and located in regions that produced high-demand commodities such as cacao, continued to prosper. Examples would include Seibal, Altar de Sacrificios, Nohmul, and Lamanai. In addition, new evidence uncovered by David Webster and his colleagues at Copan indicate that while the urban core collapsed, much of the rural population continued to thrive (Webster and Freter 1990). Whether these important new conclusions can be generalized to other major cities remains to be demonstrated by careful fieldwork and solid research designs.

It should also be emphasized, as has been previously pointed out (Sabloff 1985; Andrews V and Sabloff 1986), that the late eighth-century florescence in the north shows strong continuities with the Late Classic of the southern lowlands, and that the break between the Classic and Postclassic traditions arguably occurs between the fall of Chichen Itza and the rise of Mayapan around A.D. 1200 rather than during the ninth century.

Nevertheless, despite mounting evidence that the southern lowland collapse was not as severe or as widespread as had been assumed in the past and that the seeds of this decline had been planted well before it took place, current data still indicate that the eighth century A.D. was a period of florescence in terms of lowland-wide population (see Culbert and Rice 1990), architectural construction, and elite cultural achievements. Although Maya civilization continued until the Spanish Conquest with large urban centers (see, e.g., Andrews et al. 1988), sophisticated political systems (Pollock et al. 1962), and widespread economic integration (Sabloff and Rathje 1975; Freidel and Sabloff 1984), lowland Maya societies of the eighth century were in many ways more complex.

In sum, in spite of the plethora of data on eighth-century Maya civilization, the potential of this rich and varied body of information has yet to be properly exploited. We hope that the papers in this volume will provide significant new insights into this world. As a means of providing as systemic a synthesis as possible from a large symposium with many participants, we have organized the papers into three major groups. The first one includes this chapter and one that provides a general environmental context for the eighth-century developments and shows that the environment cannot be considered a neutral backdrop to culture history. The second addresses traditional cultural foci: economics, social organization, politics, and religion. These papers are then crosscut by papers in the third grouping, which focus on topics, themes, and data that we deemed best suited to throw light on the cultural developments of the period. These essays on settlement patterns, ceramics, lithics, architecture, epigraphy, art, and warfare look at the general foci from the perspectives of their individual topics. Some of these papers are quite broad in coverage, while others are anchored in particular sites or regions. A concluding essay by the editors attempts to draw all the themes and topics together; it does not attempt to impose theoretical consistency retrospectively. The most striking common theme in all of the essays is variability, both in the societies of the eighth-century Maya lowlands and in the analytical methods and theoretical perspectives of the authors. It would have been inappropriate (and probably impossible) in the context of a symposium with such a broad theme and so many participants with such varied perspectives to impose a uniform approach or to insist that each essay assess the validity of a few approved models of Maya societies. The disconcerting but healthy result is a set of essays that are thoroughly diverse in their variable emphases on empirical and theoretical concerns and in the particular models they address.

As always, the papers raise more questions than they answer. Yet, as data control has improved and considerably broadened, so have the questions Maya scholars are asking about ancient Maya civilization. Samuel Butler once said that "Life is the art of drawing sufficient conclusions from insufficient premises." At least in relation to the lowland Maya of the eighth century A.D., our premises are no longer as insufficient as they were even a decade ago. Therefore, we can hope—with some degree of confidence—

*Introduction*

that our conclusions are more substantial than the artfully drawn ones of the past.

*Acknowledgments* We wish to thank the symposium participants for their helpful comments. We are particularly grateful to Joyce Marcus, Elizabeth Boone, and two anonymous reviewers for their many useful suggestions.

*Jeremy A. Sabloff and John S. Henderson*

# BIBLIOGRAPHY

ANDREWS, ANTHONY P., TOMAS GALLARETA NEGRON, FERNANDO ROBLES CASTELLANOS, RAFAEL COBOS PALMA, AND PURA CERVERA RIVERO
    1988   Isla Cerritos, an Itza Trading Port on the North Coast of Yucatan, Mexico. *National Geographic Research* 4: 196–207.

ANDREWS IV, E. WYLLYS, AND E. WYLLYS ANDREWS V
    1980   *Excavations at Dzibilchaltun, Yucatan, Mexico.* Middle American Research Institute, Pub. 48. Tulane University, New Orleans.

ANDREWS V, E. WYLLYS, AND JEREMY A. SABLOFF
    1986   Classic to Postclassic: A Summary Discussion. In *Late Lowland Maya Civilization: Classic to Postclassic* (Jeremy A. Sabloff and E. Wyllys Andrews V, eds.): 433–456. University of New Mexico Press, Albuquerque.

BINFORD, LEWIS R.
    1972   *An Archaeological Perspective.* Seminar Press, New York.
    1983   *Working at Archaeology.* Academic Press, New York.
    1989   *Debating Archaeology.* Academic Press, San Diego.

CULBERT, T. PATRICK
    1988   Political History and the Decipherment of Maya Glyphs. *Antiquity* 62: 135–152.

CULBERT, T. PATRICK (ED.)
    1991   *Classic Maya Political History.* Cambridge University Press, Cambridge.

CULBERT, T. PATRICK, AND DON S. RICE (EDS.)
    1990   *Precolumbian Population History in the Maya Lowlands.* University of New Mexico Press, Albuquerque.

FREIDEL, DAVID A., AND JEREMY A. SABLOFF
    1984   *Cozumel: Late Maya Settlement Patterns.* Academic Press, New York.

HAMMOND, NORMAN
    1982   *Ancient Maya Civilization.* Rutgers University Press, New Brunswick.

HENDERSON, JOHN S.
    1981   *The World of the Ancient Maya.* Cornell University Press, Ithaca.

JONES, CHRISTOPHER, WILLIAM R. COE, AND WILLIAM A. HAVILAND
    1981   Tikal: An Outline of Its Field Study (1956–1970) and a Project Bibliography. In *Supplement to the Handbook of Middle American Indians* 1: Archaeology (Victoria R. Bricker and Jeremy A. Sabloff, eds.): 296–312. University of Texas Press, Austin.

MARCUS, JOYCE
    1983   Lowland Maya Archaeology at the Crossroads. *American Antiquity* 48: 454–488.

MORLEY, SYLVANUS G.
    1946   *The Ancient Maya.* Stanford University Press, Palo Alto.

MORLEY, SYLVANUS G., GEORGE W. BRAINERD, AND ROBERT J. SHARER
    1983   *The Ancient Maya,* 4th ed. Stanford University Press, Stanford.

*Introduction*

POLLOCK, HARRY E. D., RALPH L. ROYS, TATIANA PROSKOURIAKOFF, AND A. LEDYARD SMITH
    1962   *Mayapan, Yucatan, Mexico.* Carnegie Institution of Washington, Pub. 619. Washington, D.C.

PROSKOURIAKOFF, TATIANA
    1960   Historical Implications of a Pattern of Dates at Piedras Negras, Guatemala. *American Antiquity* 25: 454–475.

SABLOFF, JEREMY A.
    1983   Classic Maya Settlement Pattern Studies: Past Problems, Future Prospects. In *Prehistoric Settlement Patterns: Essays in Honor of Gordon R. Willey* (Evon Z. Vogt and Richard M. Leventhal, eds.): 413–422. Peabody Museum, Harvard University, and University of New Mexico Press, Cambridge and Albuquerque.
    1985   Ancient Maya Civilization. In *Maya: Treasures of an Ancient Civilization* (C. Gallenkamp and R. Johnson, eds.): 34–46. Harry N. Abrams, New York.
    1986   Interaction among Classic Maya Polities: A Preliminary Examination. In *Peer Polity Interaction and Socio-Political Change* (Colin Renfrew and John F. Cherry, eds.): 109–116. Cambridge University Press, Cambridge.
    1990   *The New Archaeology and the Ancient Maya.* Scientific American Library, W. H. Freeman, New York.

SABLOFF, JEREMY A., AND WILLIAM L. RATHJE (EDS.)
    1975   *A Study of Changing Precolumbian Commercial Systems.* Monographs of the Peabody Museum 3. Harvard University, Cambridge.

THOMPSON, J. ERIC S.
    1954   *The Rise and Fall of Maya Civilization.* University of Oklahoma Press, Norman.

THOMPSON, RAYMOND H.
    1956   The Subjective Element in Archaeological Inference. *Southwestern Journal of Anthropology* 12: 327–332.

WEBSTER, DAVID, AND ANNCORRINE FRETER
    1990   The Demography of Late Classic Copan. In *Precolumbian Population History in the Maya Lowlands* (T. Patrick Culbert and Don S. Rice, eds.): 37–62. University of New Mexico Press, Albuquerque.

WILLEY, GORDON R., WILLIAM R. BULLARD, JR., JOHN B. GLASS, AND JAMES C. GIFFORD
    1965   *Prehistoric Maya Settlements in the Belize Valley.* Papers of the Peabody Museum 54. Harvard University, Cambridge.

2

# Eighth-Century Physical Geography, Environment, and Natural Resources in the Maya Lowlands

## DON S. RICE
SOUTHERN ILLINOIS UNIVERSITY

ANY ANALYSIS OF THE PALEOENVIRONMENTAL characteristics of a region and the human ecology of a prehistoric cultural group is a complex undertaking. While research and personal experiences may provide insights into the natural components and processes of a landscape, it is often difficult to recreate the human perceptions of that environment, or the motivations that led from perceptions to behavioral responses. This difficulty suggests that there are at least two approaches for discussing the ecological character of the Maya lowlands in the eighth century A.D.: one position would be informed largely by the ideological structures and beliefs of the Classic Maya, while the second relies on the tenets of twentieth-century natural science.

I am not an epigrapher or an art historian, and while images reflective of Maya perception of environment are known to me, it would be folly for me to attempt an analysis exclusively from the perspective of the Maya themselves. Therefore, I must admit at the outset that this presentation is biased in favor of modern and paleoenvironmental research and data. My goal is to achieve a brief and selective summary of the eighth-century natural environment, a review that can serve as both a context for the other chapters of this volume and an introduction to issues of debate about Maya modes of resource utilization.

### ABIOTIC FACTORS

*Geology and Physiography*

The lowland Maya occupied the Yucatan Peninsula and adjacent regions of Mesoamerica, a zone that today includes the modern political units of eastern Mexico, northern Guatemala, Belize, and northern Honduras (Fig.

Don S. Rice

Fig. 1  The region of the Maya lowlands.

1). The peninsula, and adjacent submerged shelf to the north, is a limestone platform (often referred to as either the Yucatan or Campeche platform) that extends into the Gulf of Mexico and comprises a total of 350,000 km² (Lopez Ramos 1975: fig. 1; Maldonado-Koerdell 1964: 22, 24; West 1964: 70–73). Approximately half of that total is terrestrial. Surrounded by water on the west, north, and east, the platform is delimited to the southwest by the Tabasco-Campeche alluvial plain of the southern Gulf Coast, and bounded on the south by the Sierra Madre del Sur and Sierra de Chiapas in southern Mexico, and the mountains of central Guatemala and western Honduras.

There is an incremental progression in both absolute elevation above sea level and geological age as one moves from north to south on the peninsula.

*Physical Geography, Environment, and Nature Resources*

The Tabasco-Campeche plain, and the immediate Gulf and Caribbean coasts of northern Yucatan, Quintana Roo, and Belize are low strips of sand, marl (*sascab*), and gravels of marine terraces, and coastal alluvium of Quaternary age (Lopez Ramos 1975: fig. 2). Along the northwestern and northern coasts, barrier beaches enclose extensive lagoons and tidal swamps (Brady 1974). Much of the peninsula's northern east coast is configured somewhat differently, with low cliffs and headlands separated by isolated beaches.

Situated off the peninsula's east coast is a barrier reef of coral, stretching from the northeast corner of the peninsula to the Bay of Honduras and supporting sand cays along its length of more than 650 km. This reef-island system embays an extensive area of shallow-water lagoons along the coast of Belize, creating mangrove swamps on both the island and mainland shores (High 1975).

Anthony Andrews has documented that the eighth-century Maya exploited the coastal lagoons of northwestern and northern Yucatan for making salt (either through solar evaporation of sea waters, or by the manufacture and cooking of salty brine), notably at the sites of Emal, El Cuyo, La Providencia, and Xcambo (1983). And recently J. Jefferson MacKinnon and Susan Kepecs have reported Late Classic salt manufacture at Placencia Lagoon on the coast of southern Belize, although their available obsidian hydration and radiocarbon dates fall in the ninth- through twelfth-century range, and outside of the immediate concerns of this paper (1989).

In addition to resources for salt manufacture, the peninsular coasts, lagoons, and cays offered the eighth-century Maya access to marine fauna. While Joseph Ball and Jack Eaton have reported a decline in littoral occupations between Isla Aguada in southwestern Campeche and Isla Cancuen in northeastern Quintana Roo into the Late Classic, suggesting that the coasts were relatively marginal zones during this period (1972), there is evidence for eighth-century exploitation and movement of marine fauna. Remains of marine mollusks and piscifauna have been recovered for all cultural periods in coastal regions, and in contexts suggesting eighth-century subsistence and ritual use at sites as variable in distance from the coast as Dzibilchaltun, Lubaantun, San Felipe, and Tikal (Hamblin n.d., 1984, 1985; McKillop 1984, 1985; Moholy-Nagy 1963, 1985; Pohl n.d.a; Sorayya Carr 1985; Wing 1975, 1977, 1981; Wing and Steadman 1980). Unfortunately, variable research designs and variable preservation conspire to make it difficult to determine the degree to which eighth-century populations might have relied on marine fauna, and for what purposes.

Interior to the coasts (Fig. 2), the northern third of the Yucatan platform consists of Tertiary (Eocene and Miocene Pliocene) limestone, marl, and gypsum, with elevations rising to approximately 40 m above sea level (Lopez Ramos 1975: figs. 2, 7, 8; West 1964: 70, fig. 18). Southward this

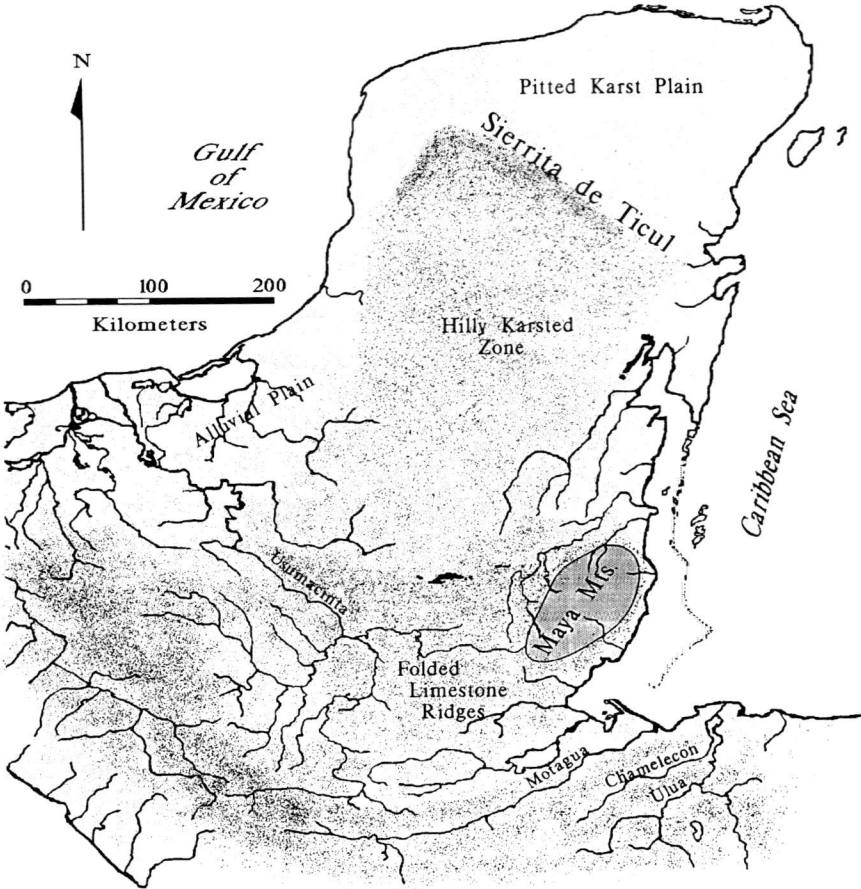

Fig. 2 The physical geography of the Maya lowlands (after West 1965: fig. 18).

zone rises to a line of limestone hills, the "Sierrita de Ticul," a remnant of a Miocene littoral that has undergone subsequent folding, creating a low cuestaform (characterized by a steep escarpment on one side and a long, gentle slope on the other) ridge some 50 m in elevation above the surrounding plain (West 1964: 70). The Sierrita de Ticul demarcates the relatively level northern zone of the Yucatan platform from the karsted (an area of carbonate rock with subsurface drainage), hilly Tertiary (Eocene) limestones, and sandy marls of modern states of Campeche and Quintana Roo to the south. The highest terrain of the interior peninsular landscape lies in eastern Campeche, reaching elevations approximately 350 m above sea level before sloping off south and east (West 1964).

## Physical Geography, Environment, and Nature Resources

Continuing to the south, the Department of Peten, Guatemala, and western Belize are characterized geologically by a series of occasional east-west folds and ridges of limestone, which form low and uneven surfaces varying between 100 m and 300 m in elevation above sea level. These low anticlinal ridges are composed of Mesozoic marine and continental sediments: Triassic shales, and Cretaceous and Jurassic limestones (Lopez Ramos 1975: fig. 2; West 1964: 72). The rolling hills and ridges of these deposits are covered by Cretaceous to Miocene dolomitic limestone. In the central Peten, these folded east-west ranges abut the hilly karsted region to the immediate north and form a line of depressions or troughs on an east-west fault fracture roughly coinciding with 17° north latitude (Vinson 1962).

The broken topography of the southern Peten and the Maya Mountains of southern Belize are a product of the Antillean orogenic belt, a region of geological thrusting and mountain-building that sweeps east from the Guatemalan highlands into the lowlands (Ower 1928). The Belize mountains themselves are a horst of Tertiary igneous and metamorphic rock, a block of the earth's crust that has been uplifted along faults relative to the rocks on either side, reaching 800 to 1,000 m above sea level, and they exhibit extensive outcrops of underlying crystalline rock. Geologically, then, southern Peten and Belize are more akin to Chiapas and the Central American highlands than to the northern Yucatan peninsula (West 1964: figs. 2, 3, 4).

In southern Guatemala and northern Honduras the folded and faulted ranges of marine clastics and limestones of the Yucatan platform give way to older Paleozoic and Cenozoic metamorphic schists, gneisses, and granites exposed in the Chiapas-Guatemalan Depression, a major tectonic zone on the northern edge of the volcanic tablelands of northern Central America (West 1964: 74, figs. 3, 4). The eastern half of this depression, dominated by the Motagua fault, is characterized by highly broken and folded surfaces, and steep slopes of deeply cut valleys.

The Motagua, Jocotan-Chamelecon, and Ulua valleys to the south are part of this wide fault zone, which sits at the Central American portion of the Caribbean-North American tectonic plate boundary and the Honduras Depression (Dengo 1975: figs. 4, 6; Uchupi 1975: fig. 17). This zone of discontinuous grabens (blocks of the earth's crust that have been downthrown along faults relative to the rocks on either side) is primarily composed of old metamorphic rock arranged in a northeast-southwest structural trend, with topographic depressions separating rugged ranges that may reach 2,500 m above sea level in elevation.

There is a tendency to think of the geological substrate of the Maya lowlands as stable or inert, but it is worth noting that the Motagua fault has been subject to Quaternary displacements (Martin and Case 1975: fig. 15; Schwartz, Cluff, and Donnelly 1979). It is not possible to confirm that eighth-century Maya populations actually experienced the tremors associated with crustal shifts or earthquakes, but Robert Sharer has suggested that heavy architectural buttressing at Quirigua may result from efforts to support earthquake-weakened walls (1978). Similar eighth-century effects have been hypothesized for regions as far north as the Belize River Valley (MacKie 1961).

While tremors are potential short-term threats to the safety of populations, they can have unexpected and longer-term impacts. The 1976 earthquake and aftershocks in Guatemala, which were felt at the sites of Quirigua and Tikal and injured or killed as many as 100,000 persons in the highlands, have been implicated in the subsequent dramatic rise of lake levels in the central Peten (Edward Deevey, personal communication, 1986). The rapid shifting of basin sediments is suspected to have effectively sealed lacustrine waters from subterranean aquifers, thus reducing seepage, and the suspected tilting of the southern shores of lakes Peten-Itza and Quexil is thought to have increased magnified water flow to the basins and altered the water table. This earthquake is a specific event without documented parallel in the eighth century A.D. Nonetheless, its occurrence suggests that eighth-century tectonic activity in the vicinity of the Maya lowlands would have had the potential to be both dramatic and far-reaching in impact.

From the northern coasts of the Yucatan Peninsula to the uplands of northern Honduras, the geological mosaic described above offered varied lithic resources to the eighth-century Maya and contributed to highly variable water flow. The surficial rocks of the Yucatan platform are all carbonates, and cut limestone was the basic material for construction and sculpture. The limestone matrix was also the source for siliceous nodules of chert and flints, and for calcareous sands. The former were important to Maya populations for the manufacture of cutting implements, while the latter, together with calcined limestone and water, was a constituent of mortar and plaster. In the Maya Mountains of Belize, outcrops of granites were exploited for the production of ground stone tools.

The entire Yucatan platform displays karst features (sinks, or karst holes interspersed with abrupt ridges and irregular protuberant rocks; usually underlain by caverns and underground streams), and the degree of karstification and local relief can be correlated with the elevation of the region and the depth to the water table (Finch n.d.). North of approximately 19° north latitude the platform is a karstic surface characterized by subsurface drainage (Siemens 1978; Tamayo 1964). Rainwater rapidly infiltrates the carbonate rock and seeps into subterranean aquifers. Most of the discharge of this region occurs in the coastal and near-shore areas as submarine springs. Human access to the water table is most often in the vicinity of sinkholes or cenotes (Back and Hanshaw 1978; Doehring and Butler 1974).

Farther south, in the hilly karsted terrain of Campeche, Quintana Roo, and Peten, drainage is increasingly surficial. There, numerous disappearing

Physical Geography, Environment, and Nature Resources

Fig. 3  Wetland areas in the Maya lowlands (after Pope and Dahlin 1989: fig. 1).

streams, small sinkholes, and inland marsh or swamp wetland areas are found (Fig. 3). These latter *bajos* are poljes, flat areas that form in broad flood plains or basins of residual clays, between the folded and eroded ridges of the upland terrain (Sweeting 1972: 193, cited in Siemens 1978: 136).

Other surface flow follows the course of superficial fracture zones and fault channels, to discharge ultimately in either the Gulf of Mexico or Caribbean Sea (Tamayo 1964). While much stream flow is seasonally intermittent, navigable perennial rivers do drain the eastern and western peripheries of the region. In Peten, the fault depression that lies at approximately 17° north latitude filled with water at the end of the Pleistocene to form the central Peten lake system, or "Comarca Lacustre" (Tamayo 1964: 101).

The tectonic zone of volcanic and metamorphic rock on the southeastern periphery of the Maya zone is markedly different in structure from the Yucatan platform to the north (West 1964: 69–70). This is not substrate of limestone bedrock. Rather, outcrops of sandstone, marble, schist, and rhyolite provided stone for masonry, construction fill, and sculpture, while schists and rhyolites could be fashioned into ground stone implements. Jadeite deposits are known from the upper Motagua Valley, and serpentine, marble, and chert or chalcedony were available for the manufacture of stone sculptures and chipped stone tools (Instituto Geografico Nacional de Guatemala 1972).

The fault lines and uplifted terrain of this relatively mountainous region govern water flow. Perennial rivers in southern Guatemala, the Polochic and Motagua, and in the Honduras Depression, the Chamelecon and Ulua, originate in adjacent highlands and drain those slopes, flowing through structural depressions to the Gulf of Honduras. Within the lower portions of their respective depressions they form extensive flood plains of alluvial soils. The Polochic empties first into Lake Izabal, which is situated at the eastern end of the Polochic depression, and the lake then drains to the sea via the Rio Dulce. While the Rio Dulce-Izabal-Polochic system is navigable, navigation of the southern rivers is made difficult by considerable sediment deposition toward their deltas and the formation of shifting point bars within their lower channels.

*Climate*

The position of the Maya lowlands south of the Tropic of Cancer makes for reduced seasonal variation in temperature, and as part of the Central American isthmus the Yucatan platform is dominated by the northeast trade winds and humid tropical air masses (Vivo Escoto 1964: 192–193). In the Koeppen climate classification, based on averages of temperature and precipitation, the lowlands are characterized as having a humid tropical climate with the mean temperature of any month not less than 18° C (Vivo Escoto 1964: 213–214, fig. 14; Koeppen and Geiger 1930–39). The temperature range is between 18° and 35°C. Two seasonal fluctuations in temperatures are noticeable in most regions: November to February tends to be cool (for example, the average temperature is 25.5° C in Peten, Guatemala), and May through August is warm (Peten's average temperature is 28.2° C). The mean average temperature difference (between maxima and minima) in most zones may be greater for any single month than are the differences around the coastline of Chetumal Bay is "clear evidence of the subsidence of the shoreline since prehistoric occupation" (1990: 242). Mary Pohl and her co-workers, on the other hand, suggest that marine transgressions may have drowned the lower portion of the Hondo River, Belize, beginning in the Late Preclassic period, with ponding and sedimentation covering aboriginal wetland agricultural fields by Late Classic times (Pohl, Bloom, and Pope 1990; Stein 1990). We cannot project specific events or conditions for the eighth century, however, and it remains to verify the exact mechanisms of the inundation, its timing, and its ramifications for local habitat change.

It should be remembered that the projection of cooler moist conditions in the Late Classic period is by necessity a regional climatic model. Local atmospheric conditions, microtopography, and conditions of ground cover would create variability in these parameters across the lowland landscape. In particular, deforestation for modern architecture and agriculture is known to increase surface albedo (the ratio between the light reflected from a surface and the total light falling upon the surface) in the tropics, which in turn reduces surface absorption of solar energy, causing surface cooling, reduced evaporation, and reduced sensible heat flux from the surface (Lean and Warrilow 1989; Potter et al. 1975). These changes ultimately reduce local convective activity and rainfall.

### BIOTIC FACTORS

*Vegetation*

The pattern of vegetation cover in the Maya lowlands is an expression of the region's geological, topographic, and climatic variation, and the history of human occupation. In the absence of human interference, vegetation patterns for the most part reflect the relative fertility and moisture status of soils.

Given the relative geological and topographic uniformity of much of the lowland platform, soil moisture is often the critical factor in classification schemes for modern lowland vegetation. L. R. Holdridge, for example, published a scheme in which vegetation types parallel average annual rainfall patterns, with very dry tropical forest, dry tropical forest, subtropical forest, and moist tropical forest arranged approximately north-to-south on the peninsula (Holdridge et al. 1971, and Tosi Jr. and Voertman 1964, cited in Dahlin n.d.a: 23; see also Miranda 1958: fig. 44 and Wagner 1964; fig. 1). Within any specific zone, however, there is a marked segregation of plants according to their specific soil-condition requirements, with both soil development and soil moisture the keys to plant variation. Depending on the progression of soil development in different regions, the range of vegetation composition within any region may be from high forest to grassland (Fig. 5).

Broadleaf forest is the typical vegetation type on most well-drained soils

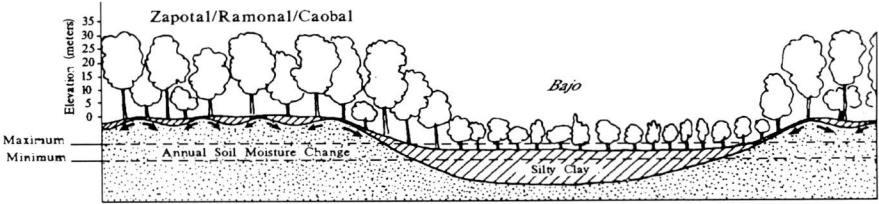

Fig. 5  Generalized vegetation profile for lowland tropical forest, showing high forest vegetation stature relative to that of *bajo* vegetation and the range of ground water fluctuation (after Miranda 1958: fig. 46).

in the Maya lowlands, and variation within this forest is manifest in constituent species diversity, and in variable growth characteristics of the representatives of those species: relative canopy height, number of stems (trunks or individuals), and biomass (total mass or amount of living organisms in a given area or volume). Various special subclimaxes account for nonbroadleaf vegetational variability. The lowland climax forest has been called a quasi-rainforest or mesophytic broadleaf forest because of the presence of a large number of deciduous species. Although the forest is primarily evergreen, the degree of deciduousness of tree species reflects the annual variability of rainfall. This deciduousness makes for variable nutrient cycling within the forest, as a result of varying amounts of dry-season litter production.

In its climax state, the lowland forest is generally characterized by the arrangement of three or more mature tree stories, with the tallest trees standing out as emergents above the closed canopy of the next lowest story (Wagner 1964: 230). The arrangement of stories reflects the enormous amount of variation and competition that characterizes tropical forests, with the lower stories representing adaptations to microenvironments created in part by upper-structure vegetation. The canopies are integrated by the downward movement of dust-laden air and water, and by life forms that transcend and utilize the various niches of the vegetation structure. These include the woody climbing plants and the epiphytes.

Mature climax forest associations are often named for the dominant species in the community. In Peten, for example, a major association is *Zapotal*, so named because of the predominance of sapodilla (*Achras zapote*). Here the emergent story includes *Calophyllum*, *Swietenia*, *Sideroxylon*, and *Lucuma*, while *Achras* shares a closed middle canopy with *Vitex*, *Cecropia*, *Bursera*, *Spondias*, *Aspidosperma*, *Brosimum*, *Pseudomedia*, *Leguminosae*, and *Lauraceae*. A second recognized climax is *Ramonal*, named for the abundance of ramon (*Brosimum alicastrum*) in the middle canopy, while a third, *Caobal*, is named after the caoba or mahogany (*Swietenia*) (Lundell 1937; Wagner 1964: 228).

All three dominants exist in association with the same basic floristic components in the closed vegetation story, and because these are relatively stable vegetation communities common to fertile, well-drained soils, the species often serve as markers to modern farmers of soil suites that are potentially productive for agriculture. The variation in dominants from one such community to the next may be due to varying conditions of nutrients or drainage, or to the history of human interference with the floristic structure of local vegetation (Lundell 1937; Wagner 1964: 230–231).

Interspersed with high forest throughout the lowlands are a number of subclimax associations, such as various species of *palmaceae,* which tend to grow in groves and are quite stable as a vegetation phase. *Bajo* or swamp vegetation also varies greatly from upland forest, in that component species must endure both seasonal inundation and moisture deficiency. Generally, *bajos* exhibit higher species diversity and lower biomass relative to climax forest. Sedges and low xerophytic vegetation tend to be characteristic of central *bajos,* with the height and mesophytic nature of the stands increasing as the terrain rises toward the better-drained uplands.

Savanna, or grassland, is the vegetation subclimax considered indicative of either minimal soil development or extremes in the progression of soil degeneration. Savanna soils are relatively impoverished in both nutrient status and structure, and they suffer extended periods of being either waterlogged or compacted. Grassland vegetation consists of perennials that are adapted to conditions of nutrient stress, annuals that pass their entire vegetative cycle during the wet season, and xerophytic trees and shrubs. While some upland species do occur within small islands of trees that are interspersed in the savannas, the diversity and biomass of the vegetation community are low, and the boundary with the tropical forest is sharp and conforms closely to soil distribution (Brenner, Leyden, and Binford 1990; Hammond 1980; Lundell 1937).

It was at one time thought that the savannas of Peten were products of Classic Maya deforestation and degradation induced by intensive agricultural practice, but archaeological surveys belie this notion. Maya settlement was typically sparse and late, for the most part datable to the eighth and ninth centuries A.D., and phytoliths recovered from beneath Maya structures suggest that the buildings were constructed in grasslands (D. Rice and P. Rice 1979; Rice and Stanish n.d.; P. Rice and D. Rice 1979). Rather, edaphic factors are thought to account for the existence of savannas, with grasses successfully colonizing hydromorphic, red-brown oxisols in the early Holocene, and maintained today by fires and cattle grazing (Brenner, Leyden, and Binford 1990).

Thus, in spite of the stereotypic view of tropical forests as homogeneous, the vegetation of the Maya lowlands demonstrates considerable spatial diversity. The distribution of associations is a mosaic that reflects the nonrandom arrangement of topography, soil fertility, and soil moisture. The diversity of this forest, and the faunal species that it harbors, in turn influence the character of human exploitation of natural resources in the region.

Barbara Voorhies has documented 150 species of plants and 25 faunal species representing potentially exploitable lowland forest products that share relative imperishability and transportability (Voorhies 1982: 72–80, 82–83). These commodities include dyes, fibers, food, fuel, incense, medicine, oils, pelts, and plumage. While the primary production and species diversity of the forest is high, suggesting potentially large amounts of energy and a wide range of resources to be exploited, Voorhies points out that the organizational and processual characteristics of tropical forests can constrain human exploitation of these resources.

The vertical organization of plant and animal biomass, concentrated as it is in the upper forest canopies, makes many resources difficult to obtain. The widely spaced horizontal distribution of plants and animals also requires that human patterns of procurement be spatially diffuse. Reinforcing diversification as an appropriate strategy for exploiting an unaltered forest system is the complex channelization of energy flow among constituent species, with relatively small amounts of energy in any given channel or resource component, and a general failure of the reproductive periodicities of plant and animal species to be closely synchronized (Voorhies 1982: 84–86; see also Longman and Jenik 1974; Odum 1959; Richards 1952). While these attributes of the forests may well have conditioned early Maya subsistence and economic activities, as Voorhies suggests, it was not a pristine tropical forest environment that the eighth-century Maya exploited.

## HUMAN DISTURBANCE AND HABITAT TRANSFORMATION

With the climatic transition from an arid late Wisconsinan period to an early humid Holocene, temperate forests succeeded xeric Pleistocene vegetation, and were in turn supplanted by mesic tropical forest similar to that encountered today. Extant tropical forests in the Maya lowlands are, therefore, no more than 10,000 to 11,000 years old (Leyden 1984). This pre-Maya forest structure cannot be assumed as a context or resource for the eighth-century Maya, however.

The history of Maya occupation of the lowlands is a history of human alteration of the abiotic and biotic components of the ecosystem, and paleoecological data pertinent to the reconstruction of these environmental changes come largely from geomorphological reconstructions and paleolimnological studies. Geomorphological reconstructions assume a constant relationship between geomorphology and soils, and rely on paleogeomorphological maps as a basis for the characterization and mapping of soil distributions, and for the inference of stability and/or instability in natural vegetation. Paleolimnological investigations recover quantitative evidence

*Physical Geography, Environment, and Nature Resources*

of the sequence of sedimentary, palynological, chemical, and macro- and micro- botanical and zoological inputs into lakes.

There are difficulties with reconstructions based on either methodology. The abiotic and biotic components, and ecosystemic processes, are unobserved, but rather extrapolated from partial data. In addition, absolute dating of the environmental record is difficult and relative chronologies are gross, often relying on correlations with social histories and the relative dating of archaeology. Furthermore, both human occupation and climatic change can impact biotic components of the ecosystem, and the effects of one can mask evidence of the other.

Despite the problems involved, analyses from the northern Yucatan peninsula (Covich n.d.; Covich and Stuiver 1974; Dahlin n.d.b; Dahlin et al. n.d.; Price n.d.), Belize (Bloom et al. 1983; Bloom, Pohl, and Stein 1985; Bradbury et al. 1990; Colena Spross Hansen 1990; Pohl, Bloom, and Pope 1990; Olson 1990, n.d.b, n.d.c; Turner II and Harrison 1983; Wiseman 1990), Peten (Binford et al. 1987; Brenner n.d.; Brenner, Leyden, and Binford 1990; Cowgill et al. 1966; Dahlin, Foss, and Chambers 1980; Deevey 1978; Deevey et al. 1979; Deevey and Rice 1980; Deevey, Brenner, and Binford 1983; Olson n.d.a; Olson and Puleston 1972; Rice, Rice, and Deevey 1985; Vaughan n.d.; Vaughan, Deevey, and Garrett-Jones 1985; Wiseman 1978, 1985), and the Ulua Valley (Pope n.d.), Copan (Abrams and Rue 1988; Rue 1987, n.d.; Wiseman n.d.), and Lake Yojoa (Rue 1987) areas of Honduras contribute to an evolving picture of the Late Classic Maya environment, one that can be generalized to the eighth century.

A major finding of paleolimnological analyses in the lowlands is that the landscape was relatively denuded by the Late Classic period. Regardless of the historical details and pace of the environmental transformations, it is anticipated that deforestation would have reached its maximum extent by the eighth century A.D. If the Maya perceived of their civic/ceremonial centers as consisting of mountains and trees, in the form of temples and stelae, as David Stuart and Stephen Houston have suggested (1989), most immediate site environments appear to have been strikingly devoid of both natural features during this era.

Deforestation, establishment of agricultural crops, field abandonment, and natural succession are all thought to be reflected in the kinds and amounts of pollen that found their way into lakes, ponds, and swamps throughout the lowlands. Relatively speaking, in all cases the pollen percentages of deciduous trees in core intervals attributable to eighth-century activity are low when compared to preceding periods (Fig. 6). Forest clearance for agriculture was apparently one major source of such disturbance and tree loss. Corn pollen (*Zea*) is present, and percentages of the pollen of grasses (*Gramineae*) and of cultivation weeds are high, as are in some cases the incidence of burnt grass fragments. High representation of grasses and ferns

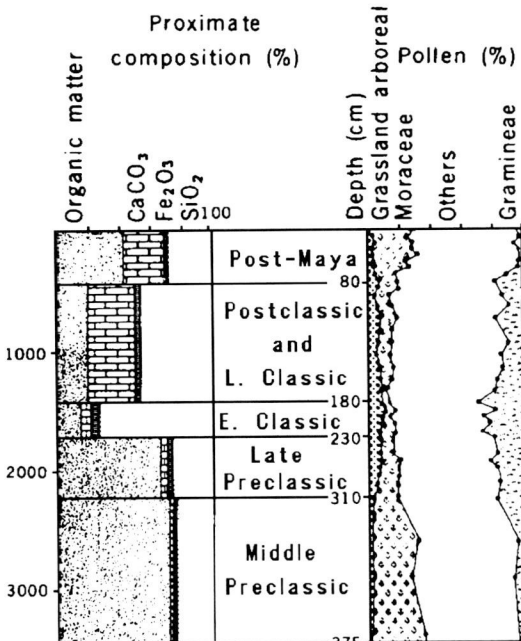

Fig. 6 Sections of chemical composition and pollen profiles measured in lake sediments from Lake Quexil, Peten, Guatemala (after Deevey et al. 1979: fig. 5).

in core segments of assumed eighth-century age from the Copan and Lake Yojoa areas of Honduras suggest to David Rue the existence of intensive (short fallow) cropping, while persistence of a low level of arboreal pollen suggests either periodic succession in agricultural areas, or the maintenance of limited forest refugia (Rue 1987, n.d.).

There are several other likely causes for deforestation that are only occasionally distinguishable from agricultural impact in the paleolimnological record. In the Copan region, low Late Classic percentages of pine (*Pinus*) indicate that even the relatively uncultivable zone of montane forest was stripped of arboreal vegetation. Elliot Abrams and Rue suggest that one use of the pine is for fuel wood (1988), and Frederick Wiseman has pointed to this component of the Maya agroeconomy as a source of conflict between the need to put land into production for subsistence and the need to produce arboreal fuels (1978, 1983). This potential strain is often underestimated.

Approximately one-third of the modern world's population uses wood for fuel, with the majority of users in the tropics, and the average user consumes about one ton (907.18 kilograms or 0.90718 metric tons) of wood per year, or 1.5 m³ per person per year, a figure equivalent to estimates of domestic fuel use in contemporary Latin America (de Montelembert and Clement 1983: 85; United Nations 1967, cited in Lawless 1978: 11). The eighth-century Maya consumption rate may have been comparable, provided arboreal fuels were available.

Forest clearance for architecture also would have diminished the size of standing forests. Not only were clearings required for the placement of civic and domestic buildings, but wood was demanded as structural components and for fuel for the production of lime plaster. Abrams and Rue have hypothesized that in the Copan pocket during the Late Classic as much as 0.13 hectares of forest per year would have been required for lime production, and that 0.026 hectares of forest would have been cut per year for the construction and maintenance of perishable domestic structures (1988: 390–391).

As a landscape is put into production for long periods of time, protracted use and exposure contribute to structural degeneration of soils and altered local water flow, the products of which ultimately find their way into the sediments of lakes and other low catchments. Physical manipulation of a landscape's surface during construction activities further exaggerates erosion and waterborne transport of soils (slopewash). Mechanical breakdown or removal of soils decreases the contextual integrity of surficial organic and inorganic materials, while covering the terrain with impervious architectural surfaces further increases the rates of removal and downhill deposition of those materials.

As a result of these changes, a major characteristic of almost all lake cores analyzed to date in the Maya lowlands is the presence of a thick layer of silty, montmorillonite clay, the major constituent or matrix of the sampled sediments. This layer is an erosional deposit of sediments moved downhill by gravity (as colluvium) or by water (as slopewash) during Maya disturbance. In the central Peten lakes, the differential thickness of these products is thought to reflect the relative degree of human disturbance on their shores (for example, compare the silica curves in Fig. 7, where silicon is being measured because it is a main constituent of soils), but as with palynological changes, it is difficult to determine the relative contributions of agricultural, architectural, or other domestic activities. In situations where there existed a high density of architecture in immediate proximity to a lake, such as in the case of the civic/ceremonial center of Yaxha, it is likely that architectural construction was the major contributor of erosional products.

In the central Peten lakes region it also appears that Maya agricultural and domestic activities released nutrients such as phosphorus from vegetation and concentrated it in surface soils. This process involved the direct release of phosphorus to soils through clearing and burning, as well as through intermediate cycling in which humans consume plant tissues, utilize the captured phosphorus in their organic processes, then cast off excess or incorporated phosphorus through excretion and death. Much of the released phosphorus was then locked in insoluble compounds by limestone-derived soils and removed from the terrestrial environment through erosion, then

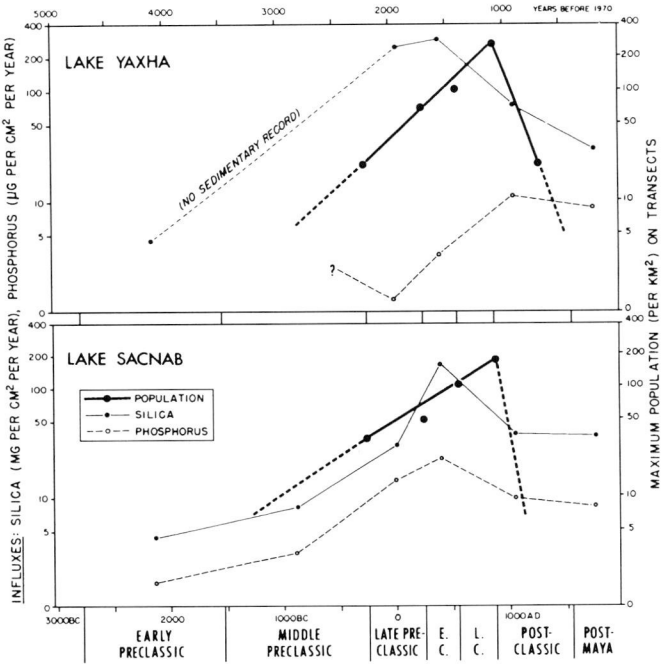

Fig. 7 The relationship between phosphorus and silica influxes, and population growth in the basins of lakes Yaxha and Sacnab (after Rice, Rice, and Deevey 1985: fig. 7.2).

buried in lake sediments (Deevey et al. 1979; Deevey and Rice 1980; Rice and Rice 1984). There it was made permanently unavailable in any form to support forest growth, crops, or human populations (compare the phosphorus curves in Fig. 7).

The evidence for mobilization and deposition of phosphorus is particularly significant because the element is essential to support life in all ecosystems and it is not abundant in the geological materials of limestone regions. In the central Peten paleolimnological studies, however, phosphorus also acted as a voucher for the activity of other nutrients, verifying the processes of nutrient leaching and tracing the loss to "sequestering" in insoluble compounds and nonrecoverable contexts.

### EIGHTH-CENTURY RESOURCE EXPLOITATION AND SUBSISTENCE

As one might expect with limited analyses in a diverse region, there is variation in the degree of landscape alteration measured. For example, Kevin Pope's study of the paleoecology of the Ulua Valley does not suggest to him the degree of eighth-century degradation interpreted in the central Peten and Copan analyses (n.d.; cf. Binford et al. 1987; Rue n.d.). While it is not completely clear whether these differences result from differing analytical methods or differing ecological contexts and cultural histories, the corpus of available data indicate that the Maya did have a transforming impact on the components and processes of their environment, a history of changes that shaped the eighth-century ecosystem and its resource potentials.

Available pollen sequences reflect progressive deforestation in the Maya lowlands, a decline of forest vegetation that is assumed to have peaked in the eighth century A.D. In addition, accelerated removal of soils and deposition of erosional sediments indicate extensive technological manipulation in some of the catchments and zones sampled. These modifications would have diminished natural habitats and affected the availability of lacustrine, riverine, and terrestrial resources for the hunting or collecting of wild food staples or supplements, as well as for the collection of botanical resources for construction, crafts, and fuel. Moreover, by the eighth century a maximum amount of terrain was covered by buildings and plazas, effectively removing much of the well-drained lands from production, in addition to altering local hydrology and promoting erosion (Rice and Rice 1984). Figure 8 presents in schematic form the dynamics of these parallel changes through time, together with an historical trajectory of population size, as conceptualized for the central Peten lakes (see also Binford et al. 1987: 121, figs. 5a and 5b). The question remains, how did the eighth-century Maya utilize this altered landscape?

There are a number of recent publications that have reviewed Late Classic Maya subsistence exploitation of available natural resources, among them the edited volumes assembled by Peter Harrison and B. L. Turner II (1978), Kent Flannery (1982), and Pohl (1985b), and articles by Dahlin (1985), Ray Matheny and Deanne Gurr (1983), Turner II (1983a), Gordon Willey (1989), and Wiseman (1983). It would be unproductive to simply repeat the details of these deliberations here and presumptuous to attempt to improve upon them.

Generally, though, this collection of papers reflects an increasing awareness that the eighth-century Maya landscape was neither a zone of unbounded fertility, nor a homogeneous zone in which cultivation redundancy was in order. The lowlands were diverse in hydrology, soil characteristics, topography, and local weather phenomena, and as a result numerous exploitive responses were possible. A consensus emerges in these publications that there was integrated regional production and that the local centers and populations functioned within a broader pan-Maya community. Implicit in this proposal is the assumption that there was sufficient variability in cropping strategies, cultivars, harvest periods, and productivity throughout the lowlands, that periodic or sustained localized shortfalls could be compensated for by importation of food from other regions.

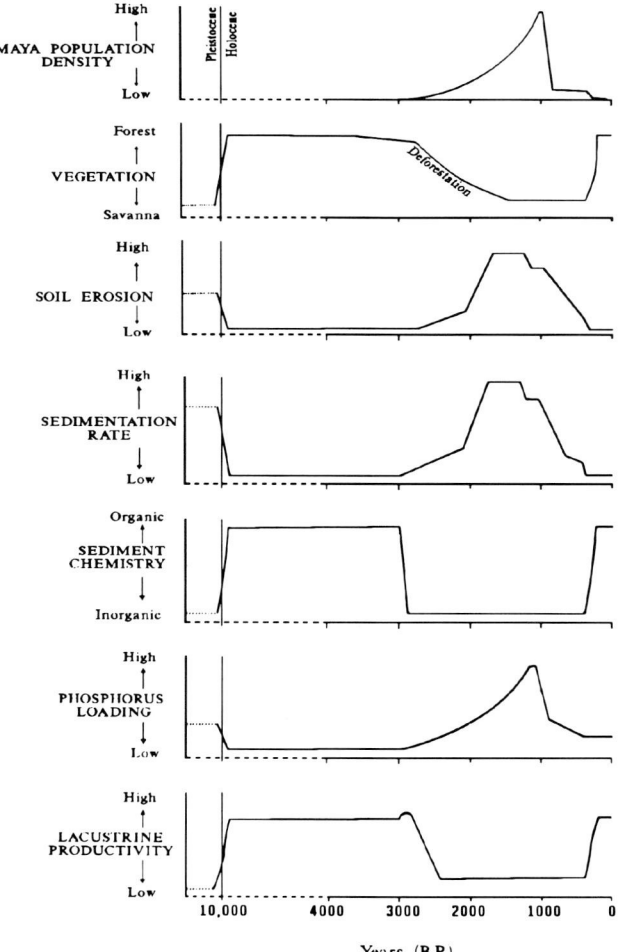

Fig. 8 Impact of long-term Maya settlement on the terrestrial and lacustrine environments of the central Peten lakes (after Binford et al. 1987: figs. 5a, 5b).

The Maya are thought to have been aware of the regional heterogeneity and fragility of their environment, and aware of the impact of their practices on the inherent processes and productivity of the exploited terrain. It has been suggested that this recognition was the basis for labor-intensive, multihabitat, multitechnology subsistence systems that incorporated rainfed agriculture of varying fallow intensities (Fedick 1989; Ford 1986; Sanders 1973, 1979; Tourtellot, this volume), perhaps with crop rotation and/or multiple cropping; gardens and orchards (Chase and Chase 1983; Dunning 1989; Folan, Fletcher, and Kintz 1979; Marcus 1982; Puleston n.d.); intensive terraced-field cropping (Healy et al. 1983; Lundell 1940; Turner II 1974, 1979, 1983b); and raised and drained or channelized fields (Adams, Brown, and Culbert 1981; Gliessman et al. 1983; Harrison 1978; Pohl 1990; Puleston 1977; Siemens 1982; Siemens and Puleston 1972; Turner II and Harrison 1983). The locations of these relic agricultural features are thought to indicate effective use of a number of different local microhabitats, while their structure, contents, and ecological contexts suggest specific cropping procedures instituted as conservation measures within these varied loci (Pohl and Miksicek 1985; Rice 1991; Rice and Rice 1984; Turner 1983a).

Regional integration of these intensive systems has been proposed as the basis for sustained, high-yield agricultural production by the Maya within the fragile tropical lowland environment. *Discover* magazine described the data and proposition as "unraveling another Mayan mystery" (Chen 1987), and *Focus* magazine reported the "Mystery of the Maya Revealed" (Turner II 1986). Despite the evidence and enthusiasm for a multihabitat/multitechnology subsistence system among the eighth-century Maya, however, there are currently debated and unresolved issues regarding the distribution, magnitude, and productivity of these technologies or strategies that should be mentioned.

First, there remains disagreement over the inherent fertility of soils in the Maya lowlands, and over the potential carrying capacity of occupied regions under regimes of corn-based, rain-fed agriculture at various degrees of fallow (cf. Aguilar C. n.d.; Cowgill 1961, 1962; Culbert, Magers, and Spencer 1978; Dumond 1961; Hester n.d.; Reina 1967; Sanders 1973; Schwartz 1985, 1986, 1987). As Gair Tourtellot has argued (this volume), the known distribution of settlement remains leaves open the possibility of a major reliance by eighth-century Maya on swidden agriculture, and the presence of walled field complexes in the Maya lowlands (Adams 1981: 243, 246–247; Turner 1978: 170; Wiseman 1983: 156) implies that the cropping/fallow cycles in some regions were short, perhaps approaching permanency. The question remains: how productive and stable were these systems?

With swidden, or slash-and-burn agriculture, for any given sequence of cropping and fallow on a plot of land, productivity declines from one year of cropping to the next. It is this progressive diminution of yield from year to year that prompts the fallow or rest period in the first place. Local farmers will, therefore, seek a crop/fallow ratio that allows them to rest plots for a prescribed period, then return to cropping these with some assurance of predictable yields that justify their input of labor and sustain the farm family. In the absence of constraints on access to land, the fallow periods may be quite long, and the crop yields high during the several years of the cropping period. Such constraints do exist under conditions of growing population and other economic pressures on environmental resources, however, and regardless of the inherent productive capacity of lowland soils, the extant literature in agronomy suggests that a reduction in soil fertility and degradation of soil structure accompany the shortening of the fallow cycle and the intensification of cropping on any given plot of land.

My own limited observations in the vicinities of Macanche and San Andres, Peten, confirm that transformations in productive capacity of soils contribute to two time frames of human activity and landscape change that should be considered, one short and one long. Regularized, productive cycles of cropping and short fallow are being maintained by many modern farmers in Peten, for example, a cycle of two years of cropping and five to eight years of rest, ratios that allow for similar yields from one cycle to the next with little perceptible deterioration of soil structure or productivity. These short cycles are not sustainable indefinitely in the absence of fertilizers and structural enhancements to the soil, however, and they are embedded in longer periods of change.

Some of the established residents of San Andres who have farmed specific plots for much of their lives, and in some cases who continue to work areas that were cropped by their parents, acknowledge that over the course of multiple cycles there have been declines in the fertility and productive capacity of their fields. They complain that after a generation or more their soils are getting "tired" or "old," that the fallow vegetation does not come back as vigorously from cycle to cycle, and that second-year yields are increasingly unpredictable. Even with access to modern fertilizers and machinery, some farmers of San Andres are abandoning altogether long-used plots within walking distance of the town and taking advantage of modern transportation to travel as many as 40 or 50 km to work new lands. These distances exceed the spacing between many Classic Maya civic-ceremonial centers (Hammond 1974) and, as Tourtellot implies (Chap. 7), such options for movement are unlikely to have been available to eighth-century Maya farmers.

Under conditions of repeated cycles of cropping and short fallow, continuous deterioration requires that plots of land ultimately be rehabilitated, usually through rest. Depending on local population densities, and the production needs of those populations, large segments of the landscape may eventually need to be taken out of circulation and allowed to recoup fertility and structure over extended periods of time, perhaps generations, thus requiring local realignments in arrangements of access to land, and even in residential location. While the shorter agricultural cycle, in terms of the balance of years of cropping to years of fallow, is often built into models of population support capability for the Maya lowlands (the carrying capacity of short fallow vs. long fallow, for example), the impact of the longer, less immediately perceptible cycle of deterioration on local production and settlement has thus far been largely ignored.

## Physical Geography, Environment, and Nature Resources

A second category of interest or topic of debate about Maya subsistence patterns concerns the role of localized gardens and orchards. While there is ethnohistoric and ethnographic evidence for the role of integrated kitchen gardens and tree-cropping in the Maya world, pre-Hispanic evidence is somewhat equivocal and the degree of reliance on these systems remains speculative. Impressive lists of carbonized botanical remains have been reported from Late Classic deposits at Copan (Turner II and Miksicek 1984), Pulltrouser Swamp (Miksicek 1983), and Tikal (Pohl n.d.b; C. Earle Smith, personal communication, cited in Turner II and Miksicek 1984: 185; Miguel Orrego, personal communication, cited in Pohl and Miksicek 1985: 16), demonstrating exploitation of a variety of field, garden, and tree crops in the eighth-century A.D., but most of the nonfield contexts are loci of consumption, not production (see Pohl and Miksicek 1985, and Turner II and Miksicek 1984 for comprehensive lists of subsistence and economic plant species recovered from Maya sites).

Arlen and Diane Chase have discussed the archaeological evidence for possible horticultural production in the center of Ixtutz, Peten (1983), and between the residential groups surrounding epicenter Caracol, Belize (1987). Based on intensive surface collection and a program of soil analysis at Sayil, Yucatan, Nicholas Dunning has suggested that the site's inhabitants pursued intensive plant production on artificially enriched soils between residences (1989; Killion et al. 1989). And Arturo Gomez-Pompa has been investigating the remains of possible garden walls, or *pet kotoob,* in a number of locations in the northern Yucatan peninsula (Chen 1987). Given these considerations, Tourtellot suggests that Maya centers may have been "garden-cities," and proposes that Maya farmers practiced a spatially restricted "garden-infield" system of agriculture consisting of household gardens and fields within easy walk of the center (Chap. 7). Only from the site of Coba, however, is there systematically collected quantitative botanical evidence for a strong relation between Maya settlement and maintenance of gardens and orchards that produce calorically or economically important bark, fibers, fruits, nuts, or resins (Folan, Fletcher, and Kintz 1979).

At Coba, the spatial distribution of such species is concentrically arranged, with the greatest density at the core of the site, and this is thought to reflect the intervention of the Maya and the control of orchard crops by elites. While vegetation surveys have been pursued in archaeological zones elsewhere in the Maya lowlands (Coffin 1990; Darch 1983; Lambert and Arnason 1978; Leino and Pohl 1990; Lundell 1937; Nelson and Rice n.d.; Rice 1978; Rice n.d.), similar micropatterning has yet to be clearly defined. It also remains to be confirmed that such patterning, where identified, is a product of Maya intervention and selection rather than determined by ecological conditions presented by abandoned Maya sites (cf. Puleston n.d.; Lambert and Arnason 1978, 1982).

The degree to which arboreal pollens recovered from archaeological and paleolimnological contexts elsewhere in the Maya lowlands might also represent managed forests, either as sources of vegetable materials and foods, or as habitats for sources of animal protein, remains unclear. With regard to the latter, however, a number of studies have confirmed the eighth-century exploitation of a diverse terrestrial and freshwater aquatic fauna (Covich 1983, 1990; Hamblin n.d., 1984; Healy, Emery, and Wright 1990; Pohl n.d.a, n.d.b; Wing 1975; Wing and Pohl 1990), and Pohl has suggested the possibility of elite privilege in the exploitation of some larger terrestrial vertebrates (1985a). Pru Rice and I have speculated that some semidomesticated fauna may have been maintained, rather than hunted, in circular and "figure 8" structures that we identified in the savannas of Peten (D. Rice and P. Rice 1979; P. Rice and D. Rice 1979). While the phosphorus content of soils sampled within the remains of these low foundation walls was high relative to that of nonstructure samples, it is impossible to determine whether human or other animal species were its source (Rice and Stanish n.d.). Unfortunately, architectural evidences for possible husbandry in the lowlands, and faunal remains generally, are still too few to allow quantification of available protein resources, or of the habitat sizes and characteristics necessary for their maintenance.

A third feature of the multihabitat/multitechnology model that is being debated is the role of intensive agricultural systems in which capital improvements of landscapes are involved, such as rain-fed terraced agriculture and channelized or raised-field complexes that were presumably devoted to production of corn as a staple crop. Confirmed remains of these systems are regionally localized and questions remain regarding their true extent and productive capacity (Fig. 9). While extensive terrace systems are reported from southeastern Campeche and Quintana Roo (Fry n.d.; Harrison 1981, 1982; Turner II 1979, 1983a, 1983b), and the Maya Mountains of Belize (Healy et al. 1983; Lundell 1940), for example, evidence of their construction in the densely occupied central Peten and relatively hilly regions to the south remains somewhat more elusive (cf. Blom 1946: 5, and Turner II 1974: 124, cited in Turner II 1978: 168).

There are several types of agricultural terracing that have been confirmed in the Maya lowlands (Turner II 1979: 106–113, 1983b: 71–89) and the variability in contexts and construction characteristics may contribute to the problems of identifying the extent of eighth-century rain-fed field systems. Dry-field, linear terraces roughly following slope contours exhibit the greatest investment of labor in construction, and they are more likely to be preserved over large areas. Channel-bottom weir terraces are less substantial, however, more subject to erosion, and less likely to be preserved or recognizable in peripheral regions.

A case demonstrating the problems of the latter is my own difficulty in

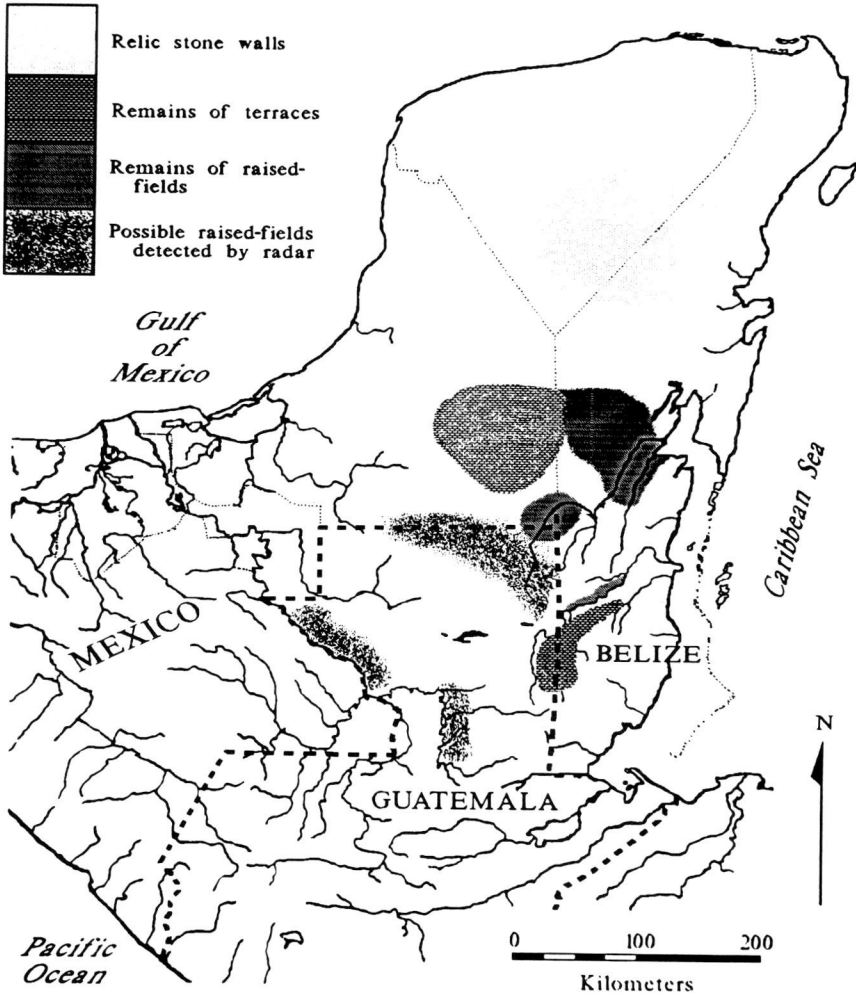

Fig. 9 Distribution of evidence for intensive pre-Hispanic agriculture in the Maya lowlands (after Chen 1987: 44 and Turner II 1986: 3).

identifying and mapping agricultural terracing in the central Peten savanna region (D. Rice and P. Rice 1979; P. Rice and D. Rice 1979). In a finger of savanna south of the modern town of San Francisco, Pru Rice and I found a series of stone lines situated on a land slope of less than 2°, in association with a late Late Classic community. Every indication is that the recovered

Don S. Rice

lines are the collapsed remnants of dry-laid terrace walls that functioned like channel-bottom weirs, to capture silt-laden runoff from surrounding higher terrain.

Initial surveys in the region missed the presence of the terracing completely because the walls had collapsed to a single layer of debris and the grass was high during the period of the surveys. Only with the serendipitous natural burning of the grasslands during a return visit did the system become obvious. In the more broken upland terrain of Peten, similar dry-laid stone constructions would be almost impossible to recover. While it can be argued that such ephemeral terracing does not reflect the concerted investment in sustained improvement and use of landscape that is evident in Campeche or the Maya Mountains, I think that it would be an error to dismiss totally the notion of capital improvements to landscape in Peten during the eighth century A.D.

The geographic and temporal distribution of agricultural terracing in the Maya lowlands therefore remains to be determined, but we must also ask the degree to which such terraces, regardless of their extent, helped to prolong cropping intervals. With respect to the latter, it must be remembered that terraced soils suffer the same processes of fertility and structural degradation that affect unmodified planting surfaces, and that intensive subsistence systems are increasingly susceptible to vicissitudes of climate, predation of pests, and plant diseases (Brewbaker 1979; Turner 1974: 123; Wiseman 1978: 113). While it is generally assumed that the act of terracing implies constant improvement of soil status through green manuring or application of night soil by the Maya, this assumption is presently unsubstantiated.

Similar questions are being asked about the evidence for Late Classic channelized and raised fields in the Maya lowlands. Fields that are assumed to have been constructed and/or used in the eighth century A.D. have been confirmed at Albion Island and in Pulltrouser Swamp in northern Belize (Pohl 1990; Turner II and Harrison 1983); in the upper Belize River Valley (Kirke 1980); in the Rio Candelaria, Campeche (Siemens and Puleston 1972); in the *bajos* Morocoy and Acutuch, Quintana Roo (Fry n.d.; Harrison 1981, 1982); and at Rio Azul, Peten (Adams 1986; Black 1987; Culbert, Levi, and Cruz 1989). In addition, remote sensing work by archaeologists and the Jet Propulsion Laboratory, reported by Adams, Walter Brown, Jr., and T. Patrick Culbert in 1981, suggested the existence of zones of some 125,000 to 250,000 hectares of fields in Belize and Peten. This discovery added hope and persuasion to the argument that wet-field agriculture was both widespread in the Late Classic period and integral to the successful maintenance of Late Classic populations, although it remained to acquire ground-truth for the majority of agricultural systems indicated in the imagery.

Pope and Dahlin published a revisionist view, however, based on their interpretation of available remote sensing and ecological research (1989).

They fail to find potential canal-field patterns in available radar imagery and they suggest that a lack of field verification reinforces the likelihood that such systems were not extensive, and that much of the reported lattice arrangements may represent electronic anomalies. This belief and their analysis of environmental data lead them to conclude that many wetland habitats are unsuitable for productive and predictable sustained agriculture. It is their feeling that wet-field agricultural systems were confined to perennially inundated areas.

Also important for our considerations here, Pope and Dahlin express concern over the assignment of a Late Classic date to the majority of the known systems; they see them as generally earlier in construction and use-life. Similar concerns about dating have been raised by Pohl and her colleagues, specifically for the field systems in northern Belize (1990). While these arguments are acknowledged to be counterintuitive, in light of reconstructions that would have agricultural intensification attendant to peak periods of population size and density (e.g., Boserup 1965; Sanders 1973)—that is, the Late Classic—the work of Pope and Dahlin, and Pohl et al., give pause that perhaps wetland cultivation was of relatively minor importance in the eighth century A.D.

Adams, Culbert, Brown, Peter Harrison, and Laura Levi have responded to Pope and Dahlin with the suggestion that the latter's inability to detect lattices in radar imagery results from a failure to follow similar procedures of analysis and a lack of consultation with the original researchers (1990). They take issue with Pope and Dahlin's ecological classifications of wetlands, in particular the identification of seasonally and perennially inundated regions, and they offer field observations to verify the presence of agricultural systems in both. They also rightly acknowledge the main problem upon which much of the debate hinges, that there is little detailed research from the wetlands of the Maya lowlands, and much need for microscale archaeological and environmental data.

If there are concerns over the extent and production of rain-fed fallow agriculture, gardens and orchards, and terraced or raised-field intensive systems, the model of spatially diverse, labor-intensive, multihabitat, multi-technology subsistence systems also begs questions of the degree of regional economic and political integration in the eighth century A.D. (Marcus, Chap. 5; McAnany, Chap. 3). Despite art and recorded histories that give considerable evidence for Late Classic intersite warfare (Culbert 1991), did the Maya have mechanisms by which differences in regional subsistence demands and output could be equalized or shared?

Pru Rice and I have suggested that major centers would have been better able, through control of resources, entrepreneurial initiatives, and alliances, to buffer against temporary losses of productive landscape and other subsistence stresses than more rural populations (1990). In turn, success at such "spatial energy averaging" (Isbell 1978) may well have promoted population growth, aggregation, and stability in the vicinity of some major centers in the eighth century A.D. It is arguable, though, the degree to which political mechanisms also could have moderated what Robert Tainter has described as the relative redundancy of products and synchrony of agricultural production cycles, and problems, throughout the Maya lowlands (1988: 170; cf. Voorhies 1982).

These observations remain speculative at best because variability in regional population histories and its potential causes are only now beginning to be investigated (Culbert and Rice 1990). The resolution of questions about eighth-century subsistence production becomes all the more important, however, in the context of accumulating estimates of the relative densities per $km^2$ of Late Classic site populations in the Maya lowlands (Table 1).

TABLE 1. ESTIMATES OF LATE CLASSIC POPULATION DENSITIES FOR MAYA SITES AND REGIONS (ESTIMATES COMPUTED FROM DATA IN RICE AND CULBERT 1990: TABLE 1.3)

| | |
|---|---|
| Copan—Urban Core | 9,662–15,773 |
| Copan—Rural portion of the Copan pocket | 400–497 |
| Copan Valley—Rural areas outside the Copan pocket | 6–8 |
| Copan Valley—Total | 37–50 |
| Quirigua—Center | 394–526 |
| Macanche/Salpeten Basins | 260 |
| Yaxha/Sacnab Basins | 212 |
| Quexil/Petenxil Basins | 163 |
| All lake Basins | 222 |
| Tikal–Central 9 $km^2$ | 805 |
| Tikal–Next 7 $km^2$ | 495 |
| Tikal—Total Site Within Boundaries | 385 |
| Tikal—Rural Within 10 km | 139 |
| Tayasal—Spine | 858–1,040 |
| Tayasal—Outer Ring | 428–611 |
| Tayasal—Periphery | 115–175 |
| Tayasal—Total | 244–359 |
| Nohmul—Whole Site | 150 |
| Sayil—Whole Site (based on mound counts) | 2396–2938 |
| Sayil—Whole Site (based on chultun counts) | 1441–2941 |

The implications of these figures for Maya exploitation of natural resources lie in the conversion of estimated population densities to per capita availability of land, and correlation of that availability with the land requirements of agricultural systems. In 1978 I projected what I called feasibility ratios for the Yaxha-Sacnab region of the central Peten lakes, ratios of land availability per person to the land required to support a person under a specified cropping frequency with a particular cultivar (Table 2). These

TABLE 2. FEASIBILITY RATIOS FOR ESTIMATED LATE CLASSIC POPULATIONS IN THE YAXHA-SACNAB REGION (AFTER RICE 1978: TABLE 4.8).

| Land Categories | Land Required per Person (in hectares) ||||||||||||||
| --- | --- | --- | --- | --- | --- | --- | --- | --- | --- | --- | --- | --- | --- | --- |
| | Subsistence Only ||||||| Assuming Surplus |||||||
| | Maize |||| Root Crops ||| Ramon | Maize |||| Root Crops ||| Ramon |
| | 1:6 | 1:3 | 1:1 | 1:6 | 1:3 | 1:1 | Permanent | 1:6 | 1:3 | 1:1 | 1:6 | 1:3 | 1:1 | Permanent |
| TU | .16 | .21 | .32 | .39 | .53 | .78 | 1.24 | .11 | .14 | .22 | .27 | .35 | .51 | .80 |
| TU & MS | .26 | .34 | .52 | .64 | .85 | 1.25 | 2.00 | .18 | .22 | .35 | .43 | .57 | .83 | 1.30 |
| TU, MS, & SF | .34 | .44 | .68 | .83 | 1.10 | 1.63 | 2.59 | .23 | .29 | .45 | .56 | .73 | 1.07 | 1.69 |
| TU, MS, SF & ST | .38 | .49 | .75 | .92 | 1.23 | 1.81 | 2.88 | .26 | .32 | .51 | .62 | .82 | 1.20 | 1.88 |

economic densities were figured for successive increments of different land categories (tall upland forest, moist slope forest, swamp forest, and swamp thicket), categories that are assumed to have presented the Maya with different potential productivities and different management problems.

If the ratio of land availability to land required falls below one, then there is a land shortage and some compensation must be made. Given estimates of Late Classic population size for the combined Yaxha-Sacnab basins, the feasibility ratios for corn-based agriculture grown at 1:6, 1:3, and 1:1 fallow cycles are 0.38, 0.49, and 0.75, respectively, if the farmer considered only subsistence needs and if the total landscape was considered productive and so utilized. If surplus production (here approximated as one-third yield, following Sanders 1973: 342) was required as a hedge on losses, for future seeding, and for social and political overhead, the ratios are 0.26, 0.32, 0.51. If terrain of all classes was not put into production, and undoubtedly it was not, the ratios are smaller still. The magnitude of land shortage would be reduced with the primary or supplementary production of cultivars that have a higher caloric yield than corn, in this simulation root crops (Bronson 1966) and ramon (Puleston n.d.), but we have no evidence for the extent of Maya reliance on such crops.

While one can argue about the precision of the population estimates and productivity figures used in the calculations, if they are accurate in their order of magnitude then the message is clear. The eighth century A.D. was a period when there appears to have been a shortage of resources at Yaxha-Sacnab, at least in the form of arable land. A comparison of population density estimates for contemporary sites and settlement areas (Table 1) suggests that such strains may have been considerably worse elsewhere.

These estimates represent projected Late Classic populations for a number of sites situated in very different geographical locations and habitats. Thus, while there is variation, broad sample distribution removes some suspicion that particular sites or regions may be anomalous in their high densities as a result of specific environmental or cultural factors. There are large areas of unsurveyed terrain in the Maya lowlands, however, and we do not yet control the variation in regional population sizes in the eighth century A.D., nor the magnitude of Late Classic lowland population.

A very different set of data indicates the potential negative impact of imbalances between population and available arable land. Nutritional and health problems have long been proposed as a potential cause for the Classic Maya collapse (see Sabloff 1973 for a review of past hypotheses). Analyses of skeletal materials from the Belize Valley (O. Elliot and H. K. F. Bleibtreu, in Willey et al. 1965), Tikal (Haviland 1967), and Altar de Sacrificios (Saul 1972, 1973) have implicated poor nutrition in decreasing stature and robustness, vulnerability of populations to epidemic diseases, and decreased capacity for work, but the samples have been small and they have generally been recovered from elite contexts. Stephen Whittington has just completed an analysis of 149 Late Classic rural or lower-class burials from Copan, however, and his results also portray a population suffering considerable nutritional impoverishment (n.d.).

Whittington's conclusion is that the Copanec population was highly stressed and unhealthy during the periods leading up to the political collapse of the center. During the eighth century A.D., when the population growth rate reached its maximum and population size approached its peak, high incidence of hypoplasia shows that childhood stress was greater than during preceding phases. Frequencies of anemia and subadult caries were higher than at any other time. Infection is thought to have increased significantly in response to rising population density, and poor diet is implicated in producing a high frequency of iron-deficiency anemia and enamel hypoplasia through its synergistic relationship with infectious diseases and parasites. Preliminary analyses by Rebecca Storey of center, or elite, burial populations from Copan during the same period offer similar results (David Webster, personal communication, 1989). Nutritional stress does not appear to have affected the center and rural populations differentially.

## SUMMATION

Archaeological, paleolimnological, and pedological data from the southerly regions of the Maya lowlands attest that by the eighth century considerable landscape had been dramatically transformed as a result of more than a millennium of human occupation. These data imply a diminution of natural terrestrial habitats, a degradation of adjacent lacustrine and riverine ecosystems, and a concomitant loss of constituent floral and faunal resources. The parallels of environmental change, increasing population densities, and subsequent societal collapse are seductive in their suggestion that Maya construction, extraction, and subsistence activities undermined the productivity of much of the lowland environment. These correlations raise the question: was the carrying capacity of regional subsistence systems substantially surpassed in the eighth century A.D.?

Classic Period Maya society appears to have flourished throughout the lowlands until the eighth and ninth centuries, and in the north occupation is sustained somewhat unabated into the Postclassic periods (Chase and Rice 1985; Culbert 1973; Sabloff and Andrews V 1986). Such apparent successes speak positively for the technological sophistication of Maya agricultural practices (Rice and Rice 1984) and their coordination, and breeds skepticism over possible environmental limits to Maya population and polities.

While it seems clear that the eighth-century Maya were being forced to consider and cope with a changing environment, the magnitude, timing, and ultimate impact of these changes is obviously still a matter of debate. Resolution of these issues does not appear to be immediately forthcoming, for want of regionally representative data on Maya natural and social histories.

In 1981 Dennis Puleston made the point that settlement studies had sampled less than one-fifth of one percent of the total area of Peten, Guatemala (Rice and Puleston 1981: 137), and the coverage of environmental analyses was even less. The quantity of available survey information for Peten is largely unchanged and other regions of the Maya lowlands suffer similar neglect. It should come as no surprise, then, that a remaining order of business in Maya studies is the microscale documentation of regional cultural and environmental variability.

If we are to understand eighth-century subsistence and nonsubsistence production, and the impact of Maya population upon these resources, then there are several questions or categories of data that are critical to our deliberations and with which we must continue to grapple. At the broadest level is the issue of climate. What is the status of Late Classic climatic stability or change? Were there global or regional trends that affected local productive potentials within the Maya lowlands? What is the timing and magnitude of subsidence or sea-level rises, and what is the degree to which such changes altered marine and fresh-water habitats along the lowland coasts? Were wetlands channeled or raised in response to changing water tables, rather than in response to population pressures in upland zones, or to sociopolitical demands for increased production? Is there evidence for localized or regional climatic fluctuations that would have put subsistence systems under stress?

A second area of concern is the magnitude of landscape modification by humans, through time, in the lowlands. Recognizing that regional habitats were inherently variable in terms of their geological parent materials, topography, and soil characteristics, were the per capita impacts of Maya population equally variable and to what degree did different agricultural technologies delay or counterbalance processes of degradation?

The identification of climatic fluctuation and human-induced modifications as sources of environmental change present difficulties for research agendas. A primary problem for archaeologists and paleoecologists is to distinguish between the two.

To date, models of Holocene climate change developed by climatologists have largely been global in scale, while the data suggesting environmental change are local. The correlation of local environmental sequences with global climatic designs, as well as with local social histories, requires adequate absolute dates by which to compare data.

Unfortunately, there are few absolute dates for geomorphological sequences in the Maya lowlands and carbonate error has rendered a number of the available radiocarbon dates from lacustrine sediments useless. As a result, most environmental histories are relative sequences, or are anchored to absolute dates through rather convoluted and suspect sets of assumptions. And as indicated earlier, the problem of chronology is compounded by the fact that human perturbations can obscure evidence of climate change, and vice versa, because the data signatures of each can be virtually the same.

What is required are programs of environmental research that can control the critical variables of time and the Maya. Sequences must be recovered from contexts where chronological distortions can be minimized, and from settings that sample the environmental heterogeneity of the lowlands. Within the latter, however, there must be experimental controls on the quantity and quality of Maya occupation.

Such was our intent when we designed the paleolimnological research in the lakes region of Peten in the late 1970s. But while we successfully extracted lacustrine sediments representing pre-Maya, Maya, and post-Maya chronological intervals in a number of physiographically and culturally distinct basins, we failed to recover similar sequences from comparable lake systems that had not been impacted by the Maya. Only through comparison of environmental histories under experimental conditions that do control the presence of Maya populations, and in turn through correlation of these with global climate models, can we hope to distinguish between local climatic perturbations and the differential effects of human activity.

A third factor or category of data that is important to our understanding of Maya use of natural resources is the variability in eighth-century regional demography within the lowlands. Increasing numbers of settlement surveys, in different geographic settings, point to the presence of large eighth-century populations throughout the Maya zone. There are considerable tracts of unsurveyed land, however; the northwestern and Petexbatun regions of Peten are examples. And most settlement analyses do remain centered or focused on large architectural centers. Until we have comparable data from all habitats of the lowlands, arguments about pan-Maya productivity and consumption are moot.

If we are to make sense of population estimates, in the context of debates over the carrying capacities of environments and technologies, we also need to continue to verify the distribution, function, and age of Maya efforts at intensive subsistence production. For example, which habitats actually supported or required some form of channelized or raised-field agriculture? What was the productivity of these fields and to what degree were they subject to degradation? The same should be asked of Maya efforts to terrace upland fields. Equally important, to what degree was there local manipulation of the distributions and quantity of exploitable floral and faunal resources, such as is implied for the site of Coba?

Finally, and perhaps the most difficult question of all with respect to prevailing models of Maya resource exploitation: What is the degree to which specific sites or regions were capable of producing surpluses, and under what systems of organization and motivation could such production have been managed? Was an integrated multihabitat/multitechnology system even possible, given eighth-century Maya culture, institutions, and events?

None of these concerns has an easy solution and all require a magnitude of fieldwork that is difficult to envision in the immediate future. The challenge is to recognize lacunae and to build into manageable (and fundable) small-scale research the kinds of data-collection strategies that will ultimately contribute to testing of large-scale models.

## BIBLIOGRAPHY

ABRAMS, ELLIOT M., AND DAVID J. RUE
    1988    The Causes and Consequences of Deforestation among the Prehistoric Maya. *Human Ecology* 16 (4): 377–396.

ADAMS, RICHARD E. W.
    1981    Settlement Patterns of the Central Yucatan and Southern Campeche Regions. In *Lowland Maya Settlement Patterns* (W. Ashmore, ed.): 211–257. University of New Mexico Press, Albuquerque.
    1986    The Rio Azul Archaeological Project: Introduction and Summary. In *Rio Azul Reports, No. 2: The 1984 Season* (R. E. W. Adams, ed.): 1–17. The Center for Archaeological Research, University of Texas, San Antonio.

ADAMS, RICHARD E. W., WALTER E. BROWN, JR., AND T. PATRICK CULBERT
    1981    Radar Mapping, Archaeology, and Ancient Maya Land Use. *Science* 213: 1457–1463.

ADAMS, RICHARD E. W., T. PATRICK CULBERT, WALTER E. BROWN, JR., PETER D. HARRISON, AND LAURA J. LEVI
    1990    Rebuttal to Pope and Dahlin. *Journal of Field Archaeology* 17: 241–244.

AGUILAR C., MARIO A.
    n.d.    Indices de Complejidad de los Bosques Humedo y Muy Humedo Subtropical de El Peten, Guatemala. Tesis de Grado Magister Scientiae, Instituto Interamericano de Ciencias Agricolas de la OEA, Turrialba, 1974.

ANDREWS, ANTHONY P.
    1983    *Maya Salt Production and Trade.* The University of Arizona Press, Tucson.

ANDREWS, ANTHONY P., TOMAS GALLARETA NEGRON, FERNANDO ROBLES CASTELLANOS, RAFAEL COBOS PALMA, AND PURA CERVERA RIVERO
    1988    Isla Cerritos, An Itza Trading Port on the North Coast of Yucatan, Mexico. *National Geographic Research* 4 (2): 196–207.

BACK, WILLIAM, AND B. HANSHAW
    1978    Hydrochemistry of the Northern Yucatan Peninsula, Mexico, with a Section on Mayan Water Practices. In *Geology and Hydrogeology of Northeastern Yucatan* (W. C. Ward and A. E. Weidie, eds.): 229–260. New Orleans Geological Survey, New Orleans.

BALL, JOSEPH, AND JACK D. EATON
    1972    Marine Resources and the Prehistoric Lowland Maya: A Comment. *American Anthropologist* 74: 772–776.

BARRERA, ALFREDO, ARTURO GOMEZ-POMPA, AND C. VASQUEZ-YANES
    1977    El manejo de las selvas por los Mayas: Sus implicaciones silvicolas y agricolas. *Biotica* 2 (2): 47–61.

BELTRAN, ENRIQUE
    1958    *Los Recursos Naturales del Sureste y Su Aprovechamiento.* II Parte, Estudios Particulares, Tomo 2°. Ediciones del Instituto de Recursos Naturales Renovables, A. C., Mexico.

BINFORD, MICHAEL W., MARK BRENNER, THOMAS J. WHITMORE, ANTONIA HIGUERA-GUNDY, AND EDWARD S. DEEVEY
    1987    Ecosystems, Paleoecology and Human Disturbance in Subtropical and Tropical America. *Quaternary Science Reviews* 6: 115–128.

BLACK, S. B.
    1987    Settlement Pattern Survey and Testing, 1985. In *Rio Azul Reports, No. 3: The 1985 Season* (R. E. W. Adams, ed.): 183–221. The Center for Archaeological Research, The University of Texas, San Antonio.

BLOM, FRANZ
    1946    Apuntes sobre los ingenieros Mayas. *Irrigacion en Mexico* 27: 5–16.

BLOOM, PAUL R., MARY POHL, CYNTHIA BUTTLEMAN, FREDERICK WISEMAN, ALAN COVICH, CHARLES MIKSICEK, JOSEPH BALL, AND JULIE STEIN
    1983    Prehistoric Maya Wetland Agriculture and the Alluvial Soils Near San Antonio, Rio Hondo, Belize. *Nature* 301: 417–419.

BLOOM, PAUL R., MARY POHL, AND JULIE STEIN
    1985    Analysis of Sedimentation and Agriculture along the Rio Hondo, Northern Belize. In *Prehistoric Lowland Maya Environment and Subsistence Economy* (M. Pohl, ed.): 21–34. Peabody Museum of Archaeology and Ethnology, Harvard University, Cambridge.

BOSERUP, ESTER
    1965    *Conditions of Agricultural Growth: The Economics of Agrarian Change Under Population Pressure.* Aldine Publishing Company, Chicago.

BRADBURY, J. P., R. M. FORESTER, W. ANTHONY BRYANT, AND ALAN P. COVICH
    1990    Paleolimnology of Laguna de Cocos, Albion Island, Rio Hondo, Belize. In *Ancient Maya Wetland Agriculture. Excavations on Albion Island, Northern Belize* (M. Pohl, ed.): 119–154. Westview Press, Boulder.

BRADY, MICHAEL J.
    1974    Sedimentology and Depositional History of Coastal Lagoons, Northeastern Quintana Roo, Mexico. In *Field Seminar on Water and Carbonate Rocks of the Yucatan Peninsula, Mexico* (A. E. Weidie, ed.): 148–175. New Orleans Geological Society, New Orleans.

BRENNER, MARK
    n.d.    Paleolimnology of the Maya Region. Guatemalan Lakes. Ph.D. dissertation, University of Florida, Gainesville, 1983.

BRENNER, MARK, BARBARA LEYDEN, AND MICHAEL BINFORD
    1990    Recent Sedimentary Histories of Shallow Lakes in the Guatemalan Savannas. *Journal of Paleolimnology* 86: 1–14.

BREWBAKER, J. L.
    1979    Diseases of Maize in the Wet Lowland Tropics and the Collapse of the Classic Maya Civilization. *Economic Botany* 33 (2): 101–118.

BRONSON, BENNET
    1966    Roots and the Subsistence of the Ancient Maya. *Southwestern Journal of Anthropology* 22: 251–279.

CHASE, ARLEN, AND DIANE CHASE
    1983    Intensive Gardening among the Late Classic Maya: A Possible Exam-

ple at Ixtutz, Guatemala. *Expedition* 25 (3): 2–11.

1987   *Investigations at the Classic Maya City of Caracol, Belize: 1985–1987.* Pre-Columbian Art Research Institute Monograph 3. San Francisco.

CHASE, ARLEN, AND PRUDENCE M. RICE (EDS.)

1985   *The Lowland Maya Postclassic: Questions and Answers.* University of Texas Press, Austin.

CHEN, ALLAN

1987   Unraveling Another Mayan Mystery. *Discover,* June: 40–49.

COFFIN, BARBARA ANN

1990   A Modern Vegetation Transect of a Prehistoric Maya Wetland Field and Canal Complex. In *Ancient Maya Wetland Agriculture. Excavations on Albion Island, Northern Belize* (M. Pohl, ed.): 79–85. Westview Press, Boulder.

COLENA SPROSS HANSEN, BARBARA

1990   Pollen Stratigraphy of Laguna de Cocos. In *Ancient Maya Wetland Agriculture. Excavations on Albion Island, Northern Belize* (M. Pohl, ed.): 155–186. Westview Press, Boulder.

COLLIER, ALBERT

1964   The American Mediterranean. In *Handbook of Middle American Indians, Volume 1: Natural Environment and Early Cultures* (R. C. West, ed.): 122–142. University of Texas Press, Austin.

COVICH, ALAN

1983   Mollusca: A Contrast in Species Diversity From Aquatic and Terrestrial Habitats. In *Pulltrouser Swamp. Ancient Maya Habitat, Agriculture, and Settlement in Northern Belize* (B. L. Turner II and P. D. Harrison, eds.): 120–139. University of Texas Press, Austin.

1990   Appendix 8.3. Freshwater Gastropod Assemblages. In *Ancient Maya Wetland Agriculture. Excavations on Albion Island, Northern Belize* (M. Pohl, ed.): 269–278. Westview Press, Boulder.

n.d.   Stability of Molluscan Communities: A Paleolimnologic Study of Environmental Disturbance in the Yucatan Peninsula. Ph.D. dissertation, Yale University, New Haven, 1970.

COVICH, ALAN, AND MINZE STUIVER

1974   Changes in Oxygen 18 as a Measure of Long-term Fluctuations in Tropical Lake Levels and Molluscan Populations. *Limnology and Oceanography* 19: 682–691.

COWGILL, URSULA

1961   Soil Fertility and the Ancient Maya. *Transactions of the Connecticut Academy of Arts and Sciences* 42: 1–56.

1962   An Agricultural Study of the Southern Maya Lowlands. *American Anthropologist* 64: 273–286.

COWGILL, URSULA, G. EVELYN HUTCHINSON, A. A. RACEK, C. E. GOULDEN, RUTH PATRICK, AND MATSUO TSUKADA (EDS.)

1966   The History of Laguna de Petenxil: A Small Lake in Northern Guatemala. *Connecticut Academy of Arts and Science,* Memoir 17: 1–126.

CULBERT, T. PATRICK (ED.)
- 1973 *The Classic Maya Collapse.* University of New Mexico Press, Albuquerque.
- 1991 *Classic Maya Political History.* Cambridge University Press, Cambridge.

CULBERT, T. PATRICK, MARA SPENCER, AND PAMELA C. MAGERS
- 1978 Regional Variability in Maya Lowland Agriculture. In *Pre-Hispanic Maya Agriculture* (P. D. Harrison and B. L. Turner II, eds.): 157–162. University of New Mexico Press, Albuquerque.

CULBERT, T. PATRICK, LAURA J. LEVI, AND L. CRUZ
- 1989 The Rio Azul Agronomy Program 1986 Season. In *Rio Azul Reports, No. 2: The 1984 Season* (R. E. W. Adams, ed.): 189–214. The Center for Archaeological Research, The University of Texas, San Antonio.

CULBERT, T. PATRICK, AND DON S. RICE (EDS.)
- 1990 *Precolumbian Population History in the Maya Lowlands.* University of New Mexico Press, Albuquerque.

DAHLIN, BRUCE H.
- 1983 Climate and Prehistory on the Yucatan Peninsula. *Climate Change* 5: 245–263.
- 1985 La geografia historica de la antigua agricultura Maya. In *Historica de la Agricultura Epoca Prehispanica-Siglo XVI* (T. Rojas Rabiela and W. T. Sanders, eds.): 125–196. Coleccion Biblioteca del Instituto Nacional de Antropologia e Historia, Mexico.
- n.d.a Ecological Inference and Ancient Maya Agricultural Systems. Unpublished manuscript, 1979.
- n.d.b Project to Reconstruct Holocene Environments on a Karstic Plain, Yucatan, Mexico. Request for FY90 incremental funding from the National Space and Aeronautics Administration, Minority Institution Programs NAG 2-585. Department of Sociology and Anthropology, Howard University, Washington, D.C., 1989.

DAHLIN, BRUCE H., JOHN E. FOSS, AND MARY ELIZABETH CHAMBERS
- 1980 Project Akalches. In *El Mirador, Peten Guatemala: An Interim Report* (R. Matheny, ed.): 37–58. New World Archaeological Foundation, Pub. 45. Provo.

DAHLIN, BRUCE H., WITH CONTRIBUTIONS FROM THE RESEARCH STAFF
- n.d. Reconstructing Ancient Maya Adaptive Patterns on the Northern Plains of Yucatan, Mexico: 1986 Interim Report. Department of Sociology and Anthropology, Howard University, Washington, D.C., 1986.

DARCH, JANICE P.
- 1983 Vegetation Associations at Pulltrouser Swamp. In *Pulltrouser Swamp: Ancient Maya Habitat Agriculture, and Settlement in Northern Belize* (B. L. Turner II and P. D. Harrison, eds.): 21–30. University of Texas Press, Austin.

DEEVEY, EDWARD S.
- 1978 Holocene Forests and Maya Disturbance near Quexil Lake, Peten, Guatemala. *Polskie Archiwum Hydrobioloqii* 25: 117–129.

DEEVEY, EDWARD S., DON S. RICE, PRUDENCE M. RICE, HAGUE H. VAUGHAN, MARK BRENNER, AND MICHAEL S. FLANNERY
    1979    Mayan Urbanism: Impact on a Tropical Karst Environment. *Science* 206: 298–306.

DEEVEY, EDWARD S., AND DON S. RICE
    1980    Coluviacion y retencion de nurtrients en el distrito lacustre del Peten, Guatemala. *Biotica* 5: 129–144.

DEEVEY, EDWARD S., MARK BRENNER, AND MICHAEL BINFORD
    1983    Paleolimnology of the Peten Lake District, Guatemala, III. Late Pleistocene and Gamblian Environments of the Maya Area. *Hydrobiologia* 103: 211–216.

DE MONTELEMBERT, M. A., AND J. CLEMENT
    1983    *Fuelwood Supplies in the Developing Countries.* FAO Forestry Paper 42, United Nations, Rome.

DENGO, GABRIEL
    1975    Paleozoic and Mesozoic Tectonic Belts in Mexico and Central America. In *The Ocean Basins and Margins, Volume 3: The Gulf of Mexico and the Caribbean* (A. E. M. Nairn and F. G. Stehi, eds.): 283–323. Plenum Press, New York.

DOEHRING, DONALD O., AND JOSEPH H. BUTLER
    1974    Hydrogeologic Constraints on Yucatan's Development. *Science* 186 (4164): 591–595.

DUMOND, DON E.
    1961    Swidden Agriculture and the Rise of Maya Civilization. *Southwestern Journal of Anthropology* 17: 301–316.

DUNNING, NICHOLAS P.
    1989    *Archaeological Investigations at Sayil, Yucatan, Mexico: Intersite Reconnaissance and Soil Studies during the 1987 Field Season.* University of Pittsburgh Anthropological Papers No. 2. University of Pittsburgh, Pittsburgh.

FEDICK, SCOTT L.
    1989    The Economics of Agricultural Land Use and Settlement in the Upper Belize Valley. *Research in Economic Anthropology,* Supplement 4: 215–253.

FINCH, W. A.
    n.d.    The Karst Landscape of Yucatan. Ph.D. dissertation, University of Illinois, Urbana, 1964.

FLANNERY, KENT V. (ED.)
    1982    *Maya Subsistence. Studies in Memory of Dennis E. Puleston.* Academic Press, New York.

FOLAN, WILLIAM J., LARAINE A. FLETCHER, AND ELLEN R. KINTZ
    1979    Fruit, Fiber, Bark, and Resin: Social Organization of a Maya Urban Center. *Science* 204: 697–701.

FOLAN, WILLIAM J., JOEL GUNN, JACK D. EATON, AND ROBERT W. PATCH
    1983    Paleoclimatological Patterning in Southern Mesoamerica. *Journal of Field Archaeology* 10: 453–467.

FOLAN, WILLIAM J., AND BURMA H. HYDE
    1985   Climatic Forecasting and Recording among the Ancient and Historic Maya: An Ethnohistoric Approach to Epistemological and Paleoclimatological Patterning. In *Contributions to the Archaeology and Ethnohistory of Greater Mesoamerica* (W. J. Folan, ed.): 15–48. Southern Illinois Press, Carbondale and Edwardsville.

FORD, ANABEL
    1986   *Population Growth and Social Complexity: An Examination of Settlement and Environment in the Central Maya Lowlands.* Arizona State University Anthropological Research Papers, No. 35. Tempe.

FRY, ROBERT
    n.d.   Settlement Systems in Southern Quintana Roo, Mexico. Paper presented at the 41st International Congress of Americanists, Mexico City, 1974.

GLIESSMAN, STEPHEN R., B. L. TURNER II, F. J. ROSADO MAY, AND M. F. AMADOR
    1983   Ancient Raised Field Agriculture in the Maya Lowlands of Southeastern Mexico. In *Drained Field Agriculture in Central and South America* (J. P. Darch, ed.): 91–110. BAR International Series 189, Oxford.

GRAHAM, ELIZABETH, AND DAVID M. PENDERGAST
    1989   Excavations at the Marco Gonzalez Site, Ambergris Cay, 1986. *Journal of Field Archaeology* 16: 1–16.

GUNN, JOEL, AND RICHARD E. W. ADAMS
    1981   Climatic Change, Culture, and Civilization in North America. *World Archaeology* 13 (1): 87–100.

HAMBLIN, NANCY L.
    1984   *Animal Use by the Cozumel Maya.* The University of Arizona Press, Tucson.
    1985   The Role of Marine Resources in the Maya Economy: A Case Study from Cozumel, Mexico. In *Prehistoric Lowland Maya Environment and Subsistence Economy* (M. Pohl, ed.): 159–174. Peabody Museum of Archaeology and Ethnology, Harvard University, Cambridge.
    n.d.   Animal Utilization by the Cozumel Maya: Interpretation through Faunal Analysis. Ph.D. dissertation, Department of Anthropology, University of Arizona, Tucson, 1980.

HAMMOND, NORMAN
    1974   The Distribution of Late Classic Maya Major Ceremonial Centres in the Central Area. In *Mesoamerican Archaeology: New Approaches* (N. Hammond, ed.): 313–334. University of Texas Press, Austin.
    1980   Prehistoric Human Utilization of the Savanna Environments of Middle and South America. In *Human Ecology in Savanna Environments* (D. R. Harris, ed.): 73–106. Academic Press, New York.

HARRISON, PETER D.
    1978   Bajos Revisited: Visual Evidence for One System of Agriculture. In *Pre-Hispanic Maya Agriculture* (P. D. Harrison and B. L. Turner II, eds.): 247–254. University of New Mexico Press, Albuquerque.

## Physical Geography, Environment, and Nature Resources

    1981    Some Aspects of Preconquest Settlement in Southern Quintana Roo, Mexico. In *Lowland Maya Settlement Patterns* (W. Ashmore, ed.): 259–286. University of New Mexico Press, Albuquerque.

    1982    Subsistence and Society in Eastern Yucatan. In *Maya Subsistence. Studies in Memory of Dennis E. Puleston* (K. V. Flannery, ed.): 119–130. Academic Press, New York.

HARRISON, PETER D., AND B. L. TURNER II (EDS.)
    1978    *Pre-Hispanic Maya Agriculture.* University of New Mexico Press, Albuquerque.

HAVILAND, WILLIAM A.
    1967    Stature at Tikal, Guatemala: Implications for Ancient Maya Demography and Social Organization. *American Antiquity* 32: 429–433.

HEALY, PAUL F., KITTY EMERY, AND LORI E. WRIGHT
    1990    Ancient and Modern Maya Exploitation of the Jute Snail (*Pachychilus*). *Latin American Antiquity* 1 (2): 170–183.

HEALY, PAUL F., JOHN D. H. LAMBERT, J. T. ARNASON, AND R. J. HEBDA
    1983    Caracol, Belize: Evidence of Ancient Maya Agricultural Terraces. *Journal of Field Archaeology* 10: 397–410.

HESTER, JOSEPH A.
    n.d.    Natural and Cultural Bases of Ancient Maya Subsistence Economy. Ph.D. dissertation, University of California, Los Angeles, 1954.

HIGH, LEE R.
    1975    Geomorphology and Sedimentology of Holocene Coastal Deposits, Belize. In *Belize Shelf: Carbonate Sediments, Clastic Sediments, and Ecology* (K. W. Wantland and W. C. Pusey III, eds.): 53–96. American Association of Petroleum Geologists, Tulsa.

HOLDRIDGE, L. R., W. C. GRENKE, W. H. HATHEWAY, T. LIANG, AND J. A. TOSI JR.
    1971    *Forest Environments in Tropical Life Zones: A Pilot Study.* Pergamon Press, Oxford.

INSTITUTO GEOGRAFICO NACIONAL DE GUATEMALA
    1972    *Atlas Nacional de Guatemala.* Ministerio de Comunicaciones y Obras Publicas, Guatemala.

ISBELL, WILLIAM H.
    1978    Environmental Perturbations and the Origin of the Andean State. In *Social Archeology: Beyond Subsistence and Dating* (C. Redman, M. J. Berman, E. V. Curtin, W. T. Langhorne, Jr., N. M. Versaggi, and J. C. Wanser, eds.): 303–313. Academic Press, New York.

KILLION, THOMAS W., JEREMY A. SABLOFF, GAIR TOURTELLOT, AND NICHOLAS P. DUNNING
    1989    Intensive Surface Collection of Residential Clusters at Terminal Classic Sayil, Yucatan, Mexico. *Journal of Field Archaeology* 16: 273–294.

KIRKE, C. M. ST. G.
    1980    Prehistoric Agriculture in the Belize River Valley. *World Archaeology* 11 (3): 281–286.

KOEPPEN, W., AND R. GEIGER (EDS.)
1930–1939   *Handbuch de Klimatologie.* Berlin.

KONRAD, HERMAN W.
1985   Fallout of the Wars of the Chacs: The Impact of Hurricanes and Implications for Prehispanic Quintana Roo Maya Processes. In *Status, Structure, and Stratification: Current Archaeological Reconstructions* (M. Thompson, M. R. Garcia, and F. J. Kense, eds.): 321–330. Archaeological Association of the University of Calgary, Calgary.

LAMBERT, JOHN D. H., AND J. T. ARNASON
1978   Distribution of Vegetation on Maya Ruins and Its Relationship to Ancient Land-use at Lamanai, Belize. *Turrialba* 28: 33–41.
1982   Ramon and Maya Ruins: An Ecological, Not an Economic Relation. *Science* 216: 298–299.

LAWLESS, ROBERT
1978   Deforestation and Indigenous Attitudes in Northern Luzon. *Anthropology* 2 (1): 1–17.

LEAN, J., AND D. A. WARRILOW
1989   Simulation of the Regional Climatic Impact of Amazon Deforestation. *Nature* 342: 411–413.

LEINO, PHILIP, AND MARY POHL
1990   Rio Hondo Botanical Catalog. In *Ancient Maya Wetland Agriculture. Excavations on Albion Island, Northern Belize* (M. Pohl, ed.): 85–110. Westview Press, Boulder.

LEYDEN, BARBARA W.
1984   Guatemalan Forest Synthesis after Pleistocene Aridity. *Proceedings of the National Academy of Sciences* 81: 4856–4859.

LONGMAN, K. A., AND J. JENIK
1974   *Tropical Forest and Its Environment.* Longman Group, London.

LOPEZ RAMOS, E.
1975   Geological Summary of the Yucatan Peninsula. In *The Ocean Basins and Margins, Volume 3: The Gulf of Mexico and the Caribbean* (A. E. M. Nairn and F. G. Stehi, eds.): 257–282. Plenum Press, New York.

LUNDELL, CYRUS
1937   *The Vegetation of Peten.* Carnegie Institution of Washington, Pub. 478. Washington.
1940   The 1936 Michigan-Carnegie Botanical Expedition to British Honduras. In *Botany of the Maya Area,* Miscellaneous Paper 14, Carnegie Institution of Washington, Pub. 522. Washington, D. C.

MACKIE, E. W.
1961   New Light on the End of the Classic Maya Culture at Benque Viejo, British Honduras. *American Antiquity* 27 (2): 216–224.

MACKINNON, J. JEFFERSON, AND SUSAN M. KEPECS
1989   Prehispanic Saltmaking in Belize: New Evidence. *American Antiquity* 54 (3): 522–533.

*Physical Geography, Environment, and Nature Resources*

MALDONADO-KOERDELL, MANUEL
    1964    Geohistory and Paleography of Middle America. In *Handbook of Middle American Indians, Volume 1: Natural Environment and Early Cultures* (R. C. West, ed.): 3–32. University of Texas Press, Austin.

MARCUS, JOYCE
    1982    The Plant World of the Sixteenth- and Seventeenth-Century Lowland Maya. In *Maya Subsistence. Studies in Memory of Dennis E. Puleston* (K. V. Flannery, ed.): 239–274. Academic Press, New York.

MARTIN, RAY G., AND J. E. CASE
    1975    Geophysical Studies in the Gulf of Mexico. In *The Ocean Basins and Margins, Volume 3: The Gulf of Mexico and the Caribbean* (A. E. M. Nairn and F. G. Stehi, eds.): 65–106. Plenum Press, New York.

MATHENY, RAYMOND T., AND DEANNE L. GURR
    1983    Variation in Prehistoric Agricultural Systems of the New World. *Annual Review of Anthropology* 12: 79–103.

MCKILLOP, HEATHER I.
    1984    Prehistoric Maya Reliance on Marine Resources: Analysis of a Midden from Moho Cay, Belize. *Journal of Field Archaeology* 11: 25–35.
    1985    Prehistoric Exploitation of the Manatee in the Maya and Circum-Caribbean Areas. *World Archaeology* 16 (3): 337–353.

MIKSICEK, CHARLES H.
    1983    Macrofloral Remains of the Pulltrouser Area: Settlements and Fields. In *Pulltrouser Swamp. Ancient Maya Habitat, Agriculture, and Settlement in Northern Belize* (B. L. Turner II and P. D. Harrison, eds.): 94–104. University of Texas Press, Austin.

MIRANDA, FAUSTINO
    1958    Estudios acerca de la vegetacion. In *Los Recursos Naturales del Sureste y Su Aprovechamiento*. II Parte, Estudios Particulares, Tomo 2° (E. Beltran, ed.): 215–271. Ediciones del Instituto de Recursos Naturales Renovables, A. C., Mexico.

MOHOLY-NAGY, HATTULA
    1963    Shells and Other Marine Material from Tikal. *Estudios de Cultura Maya* 3: 63–83.
    1985    The Social and Ceremonial Uses of Marine Molluscs at Tikal. In *Prehistoric Lowland Maya Environment and Subsistence Economy* (M. Pohl, ed.): 147–158. Peabody Museum of Archaeology and Ethnology, Harvard Univerity, Cambridge.

NATIONAL ACADEMY OF SCIENCES
    1975    *Understanding Climatic Change. A Program for Action*. United States Committee for the Global Atmospheric Research Program, National Research Council, National Academy of Sciences, Washington, D.C.

NELSON, WILEY, AND DON S. RICE
    n.d.    Vegetation in the Residential Periphery of Caracol, Belize. Unpublished manuscript, 1991.

Don S. Rice

OBSERVATORIO NACIONAL DE GUATEMALA
    1964    *Mapas Climatologicos de la Republica de Guatemala.* Ministerio de Agricultura, Instituto Agropecuario Nacional, Guatemala City.

ODUM, EUGENE P.
    1959    *Fundamentals of Ecology.* Saunders, Philadelphia.

OLSON, GERALD W.
    1990    Soils of Albion Island. In *Ancient Maya Wetland Agriculture. Excavations on Albion Island, Northern Belize* (M. Pohl, ed.): 53–78. Westview Press, Boulder.
    n.d.a    Description and Data on Soils of Tikal, El Peten, Guatemala, Central America. Mimeo 69-2, Department of Agronomy, Cornell University, Ithaca, 1969.
    n.d.b    Field Report on Soils Sampled around San Antonio in Northern Belize (British Honduras). Mimeo 74-23, Department of Agronomy, Cornell University, Ithaca, 1974.
    n.d.c    Study of Soils in the Sustaining Area around San Antonio in Northern Belize (British Honduras). Mimeo 75-1, Department of Agronomy, Cornell University, Ithaca, 1975.

OLSON, GERALD W., AND DENNIS E. PULESTON
    1972    Soils and the Maya. *Americas* 24: 33–39.

OWER, LESLIE H.
    1928    The Geology of British Honduras. *Journal of Geology* 36: 494–509.

POHL, MARY
    1985a    The Privileges of Maya Elites: Prehistoric Vertebrate Fauna from Seibal. In *Prehistoric Lowland Maya Environment and Subsistence Economy* (M. Pohl, ed.): 133–146. Papers of the Peabody Museum of Archaeology and Ethnology 77. Harvard University, Cambridge.
    n.d.a    Ethnozoology of the Maya: An Analysis of Fauna from Five Sites in Peten, Guatemala. Ph.D. dissertation, Department of Anthropology, Harvard University, Cambridge, 1976.
    n.d.b    The Terminal Late Classic Period Economy at Tikal. Paper presented at the 45th Annual Meeting of the Society for American Archaeology, Philadelphia, 1980.

POHL, MARY (ED.)
    1985b    *Prehistoric Lowland Maya Environment and Subsistence Economy.* Papers of the Peabody Museum of Archaeology and Ethnology 77. Harvard University, Cambridge.
    1990    *Ancient Maya Wetland Agriculture. Excavations on Albion Island, Northern Belize.* Westview Press, Boulder.

POHL, MARY, PAUL R. BLOOM, AND KEVIN O. POPE
    1990    Interpretation of Wetland Farming in Northern Belize: Excavations at San Antonio, Rio Hondo. In *Ancient Maya Wetland Agriculture. Excavations on Albion Island, Northern Belize* (M. Pohl, ed): 187–254. Westview Press, Boulder.

POHL, MARY, AND CHARLES H. MIKSICEK
    1985    Cultivation Techniques and Crops. In *Prehistoric Lowland Maya Environ-*

POPE, KEVIN O.
  n.d.   *ment and Subsistence Economy* (M. Pohl, ed.): 9–20. Papers of the Peabody Museum of Archaeology and Ethnology 77. Harvard University, Cambridge.

POPE, KEVIN O.
  n.d.   Paleoecology of the Ulua Valley, Honduras: An Archaeological Perspective. Ph.D. dissertation, Geological Archaeology, Stanford University, Stanford, 1986.

POPE, KEVIN O., AND BRUCE H. DAHLIN
  1989   Ancient Maya Wetland Agriculture: New Insights from Ecology and Remote Sensing Research. *Journal of Field Archaeology* 16: 87–106.

POTTER, GERALD L., HUGH W. ELLSAESSER, MICHAEL C. MACCRACKEN, AND FREDERICK M. LUTHER
  1975   Possible Climatic Impact of Tropical Deforestation. *Nature* 258: 697–698.

PRICE, L. G.
  n.d.   Ostracod Communities from Lake Chichancanab, Yucatan, Mexico. M.A. thesis, Washington University, St. Louis, 1974.

PULESTON, DENNIS E.
  n.d.   *Brosimum alicastrum* as a Subsistence Alternative for the Classic Maya of the Central Southern Lowlands. M.A. thesis, University of Pennsylvania, 1968.
  1977   The Art and Archaeology of Hydraulic Agriculture in the Maya Lowlands. In *Social Process in Maya Prehistory: Studies in Honour of Sir Eric Thompson* (N. Hammond, ed.): 449–469. Academic Press, New York.

REINA, RUBEN E.
  1967   Milpas and Milperos: Implications for Prehistoric Times. *American Anthropologist* 69: 1–20.

RICE, DON S.
  1978   Population Growth and Subsistence Alternatives in a Tropical Lacustrine Environment. In *Pre-Hispanic Maya Agriculture* (P. D. Harrison and B. L. Turner II, eds.): 35–62. University of New Mexico Press, Albuquerque.
  1991   Roots: Resourceful Maya Farmers Enabled a Mounting Population to Survive in a Fragile Tropical Habitat. *Natural History* 2: 10–14.
  n.d.   A Comparison of Approaches for Investigating the Heterogeneity and Potential Productivity of the Lowland Maya Environment. Paper presented at the 42nd Annual Meeting of the Society for American Archaeology, New Orleans, 1977.

RICE, DON S., AND T. PATRICK CULBERT
  1990   Historical Contexts for Population Reconstruction in the Maya Lowlands. In *Precolumbian Population History in the Maya Lowlands* (T. P. Culbert and D. S. Rice, eds.): 1–36. University of New Mexico Press, Albuquerque.

RICE, DON S., AND D. E. PULESTON
  1981   Ancient Maya Settlement Patterns in the Peten, Guatemala. In *Lowland*

*Maya Settlement Patterns* (W. Ashmore, ed.): 121–156. University of New Mexico Press, Albuquerque.

RICE, DON S., AND PRUDENCE M. RICE
    1979    Introductory Archaeological Survey of the Central Peten Savanna, Guatemala. In *Studies in Ancient Mesoamerica IV* (J. A. Graham, ed.): 231–277. Contributions of the University of California Archaeological Research Facility, No. 41. Berkeley.
    1984    Lessons from the Maya. *Latin American Research Review* 19 (3): 203–215.
    1990    Population Size and Population Change in the Central Peten Lakes Region, Guatemala. In *Precolumbian Population History in the Maya Lowlands* (T. P. Culbert and D. S. Rice, eds.): 123–148. University of New Mexico Press, Albuquerque.

RICE, DON S., PRUDENCE M. RICE, AND EDWARD S. DEEVEY
    1985    Paradise Lost: Classic Maya Impact on a Lacustrine Environment. In *Prehistoric Lowland Maya Environment and Subsistence Economy* (M. Pohl, ed.): 91–105. Peabody Museum of Archaeology and Ethnology, Harvard University, Cambridge.

RICE, DON S., AND CHARLES STANISH
    n.d.    Grassland Anthropogenesis in Peten, Guatemala. Unpublished manuscript, 1984.

RICE, PRUDENCE M., AND DON S. RICE
    1979    Home on the Range: Aboriginal Maya Settlement in the Central Peten Savannas. *Archaeology* 32: 16–25.

RICHARDS, P. W.
    1952    *The Tropical Rain Forest: An Ecological Study*. Cambridge University Press, Cambridge.

RICKLEFS, ROBERT E.
    1973    *Ecology*. Chiron Press, Portland.

RUE, DAVID J.
    1987    Early Agriculture and Early Postclassic Occupation in Western Honduras. *Nature* 326 (6110): 285–286.
    n.d.    A Palynological Analysis of Pre-Hispanic Human Impact in the Copan Valley, Honduras. Ph.D. dissertation, Pennsylvania State University, 1986.

SABLOFF, JEREMY A.
    1973    Major Themes in the Past Hypotheses of the Maya Collapse. In *The Classic Maya Collapse* (T. P. Culbert, ed.): 35–40. University of New Mexico Press, Albuquerque.

SABLOFF, JEREMY A., AND E. WYLLYS ANDREWS V (EDS.)
    1986    *Late Lowland Maya Civilization*. University of New Mexico Press, Albuquerque.

SANDERS, WILLIAM T.
    1973    The Cultural Ecology of the Lowland Maya: A Reevaluation. In *The Classic Maya Collapse* (T. P. Culbert, ed.): 325–366. University of New Mexico Press, Albuquerque.

n.d.   Ecological and Archaeological Pollen Analysis at Copan, Honduras. In *Habitat and Agriculture in the Rio Copan Zone,* by B. L. Turner II, W. C. Johnson, G. Mahood, F. M. Wiseman, B. L. Turner, and J. Poole. 1980 report to the Proyecto Arqueologico Copan, C. Baudez, Director, 1980.

ZONNEVELD, J. I. S.
1968   Quaternary Climatic Changes in the Caribbean and N. South America. *Eiszeitalter und Gegenwart,* 19: 203–208, Ohringen/Wurtt., 31. Oktober.

3

# The Economics of Social Power and Wealth among Eighth-Century Maya Households

PATRICIA A. McANANY
BOSTON UNIVERSITY

INTRODUCTION

One then has a picture of this whole lowland area, excluding savanna, swamp, and other sections unsuited to settlement, studded with countless ceremonial centers, varying in size from those comprising four thatched hut-temples atop simple platforms enclosing a courtyard scarcely fifty feet in each direction to vast masses of platforms and pyramids, palaces and temples, rising jaggedly like granaries in Iowa or grouped with the architectural harmony of an Andalusian city. The country around, one visualizes as a patchwork of forest, cleared areas, and land reverting to forest . . . and here and there the thatched huts of the peasants grouped in fours and fives in clearings shaded by fruit trees. (Thompson 1966: 99)

DUE TO THE TREMENDOUS BURST of new research, this evocative, descriptive picture of Classic Maya society has changed dramatically over the past twenty-five years. Named kings of entrenched dynasties now reside in the "Andalusian" cities, more "thatched huts" have been added to the landscape, the size of forested areas reduced, and some of the uninhabitable swampland converted to raised fields and the hillslopes to terraces. Yet despite this new information about the Maya, these "facts" have not been integrated into a coherent, revised interpretation of Classic Maya society. At this time, we have only very rudimentary notions about the economic organization of the eighth-century Maya household and polity. This state of the art, in part, is due to the fact that we simply haven't been aggressively asking questions or structuring focused programs of inquiry regarding the Classic Maya economic system—the topics of society and politics having a longer history of sustained inquiry in the Maya lowlands.

*Patricia A. McAnany*

The Maya economy was conceptualized by J. Eric Thompson as a relatively simple system, its main components being *milpa* agriculture and long-distance trading networks. The vivid images of the Maya landscape as composed of "a patchwork of forest, cleared areas, and land reverting to forest" conveyed by Thompson's (1966: 99) description endured until recent investigations (Harrison and Turner 1978) demonstrated the subtle complexities of Classic Maya agriculture. Likewise, the presumed dominance of long-distance trade and the virtual absence of local production and exchange systems during the Classic period has only recently been revised in the face of evidence for brisk lowland trade in pottery and stone tools (McAnany 1989a). Furthermore, there is now some question as to whether long-distance trade is really an economic process or whether it should be conceptualized in terms of social power—an issue I discuss in great detail below. Finally, the much expanded settlement data base available to us twenty-five years after Thompson wrote that "here and there the thatched huts of the peasants [were] grouped in fours and fives in clearings shaded by fruit trees" (1966: 99) indicates that there were many more households than simply a few "here and there"; the implications of these densities for systems of land tenure, specialized production, and the process of household fissioning is only now receiving attention (Wilk 1988). In the pages to follow, I will focus on the potentially heterogenous economic and social composition of eighth-century Maya households, examining factors, such as land disenfranchisement, which could have brought such a heterogeneous structure into existence, as well as the implication of a heterogeneous model for the analysis of the archaeological record.

Recent interpretation of Classic Period iconography and texts (Miller, Chap. 12; Stuart, Chap. 11) has reinforced the notion that the elite class forged a cosmology that was all-encompassing, politically integrative, and manifested in the display of material symbols of social power. Below, I discuss the production of the instruments of social power and royal authority by elite artisans and examine the implications of this production not only on the taxation base of the Maya polities but also on the distribution of power and wealth throughout society.

If we are to replace the vivid descriptive brilliance of Thompson with a deeper, more profound understanding of Classic Maya society, then we need to generate analytical constructs of Late Classic Maya society that address the organizational properties of the Maya economic system as a complex, multilayered fabric. This paper is a contribution to such research. I begin by examining past and prevailing theoretical constructs; this is followed by a critical dissection of concepts used to analyze noncapitalistic economies. Finally, a revised construct of eighth-century Maya economy, which attempts to synthesize the topics of social power, economic wealth, and household heterogeneity is presented.

*The Economics of Wealth among Eighth-Century Maya Households*

### SALIENT FEATURES OF PREVIOUS CONSTRUCTS

During the past decade or so a few archaeologists have tackled the thorny questions of Classic Maya economic organization. While there has been an interesting plurality of approaches, most constructs have emphasized one of three factors: (1) environmental forces subsumed within a cultural ecology model, (2) vertical obligations within the construct of a political economy, or (3) forces of commodity production and exchange subsumed within a purely economic and sometimes a market economy model.

Historically, attention to environmental factors, that is, a distinction between the semiarid Mexican highlands and the humid, tropical lowlands (Sanders 1973, 1977; Sanders and Price 1968) resulted in the first truly comparative framework for all of Mesoamerica. In this sense, the cultural ecology model was truly revolutionary. Unfortunately, the inherent typological ranking of sites within this environmental framework (Sanders and Webster 1978) resulted in the propagation of notions that the Maya economy was somewhat underdeveloped in comparison with the highland economies, which were asserted to be more complex and more hierarchically organized. Regardless of the accuracy of these assertions (which I have discussed in further detail elsewhere [McAnany 1989a]), I think that it is realistic to ask just exactly how powerful environmental factors or the forces of production are in explaining variability among complex societies? I return to this point below.

The second construct, that of the political economy, provides a different perspective on the Maya. Essentially a feudal model of organization as proposed by R.E.W Adams and Woodruff Smith (1981), this construct stresses the vertical obligations of the producing or dominated class to the dominant or elite class in the form of material transfers through taxation. Variations on this model, while powerful in characterizing the relations between classes and the authority and legitimized power base of the elite stratum, often lack the comprehensive scope to consider the structure of autonomous production among the lower economic strata of society.

The third major construct that has been proposed emphasizes specialized production and marketing mechanisms (Freidel 1981; Rice 1987a; Blanton et al. 1981). These models generally deal essentially with production of items such as ceramic pots or stone tools at the household level; elite involvement in production and marketing is favored by some (Freidel 1981, 1986a) and not by others (Rice 1987b; de Montmollin 1987). This construct is both a product of settlement studies of the past two decades and a stimulus to further household-level research. As such, this research has been largely inductive in character and, more and more, stands apart from the more deductive approach taken to studies of Maya political economy. Currently, there is a need to synthesize our ideas about these different sectors of the Maya economy in order to generate holistic models of eighth-century Maya

67

political organization. In this chapter, I present a model of Maya economy that is actually a hybrid of political economy and household production models.

## THEORETICAL CONSIDERATIONS

Assumptions and basic postulates of our theoretical models require careful scrutiny. For instance, many analyses of past Mesoamerican economies have been carried out using the framework of a capitalist or market economy and thus have incorporated some basic assumptions that are not necessarily warranted for eighth-century Mesoamerica such as the commodification of labor, the interdependence of classes in the production process, the equivalency between social power and economic wealth, and expansion of the forces of production and monopolistic control of raw-resource extraction as a major power source (see Santley 1984 for a particularly striking example of a capitalist model of Teotihuacan obsidian production). At the root of all this conceptual borrowing are two basic and fundamental questions that simply will not go away: first, is the basis of power, authority, and class domination in noncapitalistic societies the same as it is in capitalistic societies? Specifically, is it based on the management of nonagrarian resources? Second, shouldn't we examine our analytical variables and methods and, when necessary, work to generate approaches to the study of complex economies that are neither ethnocentric nor capital bound? Here I am not attempting to resurrect the moribund debate between formalists and substantivists nor to necessarily promulgate a structuralist perspective, I am simply advocating self-scrutiny of the conceptual foundations of our models and an examination of the appropriateness of our analytical methods to the study of the past.

Anthony Giddens (1981), for example, has criticized the use of a Marxist perspective to explain the structure of noncapitalist class-stratified societies. In brief, he has argued that expansion of the forces of production (raw-resource extraction and the development of technology) are simply not the primary basis of power in noncapitalist or nonmarket economies. Rather, he suggests that power is generated and maintained through the domination of authorization structures (Giddens 1981: 47), that is, control of the social world rather than of the technological-resource realm. While Giddens may be painting an overly nonmaterialistic view of the past, his critique is timely in the sense that the role of technology and the capture of raw resources, per se, should be deemphasized as primary factors in the generation and maintenance of power structures. Mesoamerican elites were not incipient captains of industry or managers of craft production; their power base lay elsewhere. This argument is not new to the study of Mesoamerican economies (see interchange between Carrasco [1981] and Offner [1981]) and, given the sparse number of previous studies of Classic Maya economic organization,

## The Economics of Wealth among Eighth-Century Maya Households

Mayanists cannot be said to be particularly culpable on this issue. Important fundamental organizational differences do exist between the economic organization of capitalist and noncapitalist complex societies, particularly in the following four areas: (1) organization of agricultural production, (2) bases of economic wealth and social power, (3) economic role of nonagrarian specialists, and (4) relationship between economic status and residential location. Since these topics are fundamental to the design of economic research and should be kept in mind when analyzing archaeological data, I discuss each topic below in the hope of crystallizing a consensus or sparking a debate regarding economic process among the Classic Maya.

### Organization of Agricultural Production

From the perspective of class relations, the organization of production in a noncapitalist, class-based society such as the Maya differs from that of a capitalist society. The struggle between classes in a capitalist society is played out within a production framework in which both the bourgeoisie and the proletariat are vitally intertwined and really need each other to complete the trajectory of production (Giddens 1981). In an agrarian-based, stratified society, on the other hand, the underclass of producers generally do not really need the dominant class to complete the cycle of production. While the producers may need the political clout and military strength of the dominant class to protect their agricultural holdings, that dependency is contingent upon the relative stability of the macropolitical climate and does not necessarily extend to the organization of agricultural production. Consequently, in a noncapitalistic setting, such as the class-divided Maya society of the eighth century, there may have been few structural linkages between the elite and producer blocs and a significant degree of economic autonomy within the agrarian class as one moved beyond the political economy (appropriation of a stimulated surplus or corvée labor). Although we have no direct information regarding Classic Period Maya land tenure, the large residential groupings so typical of the lowland cities and hinterland suggest that they functioned as the organizational nexus of agricultural production. Overall, the Maya economy may be profitably conceptualized as a pluralistic one that included sectors organized by the multifaceted ties of kinship imbedded within the vertical tethers of kingship (see Gailey 1987 and Wolf 1982 for further discussion of contrasts between kin- and king-organized modes of production).

### Economic Wealth and Social Power

To continue the contrast of noncapitalist with capitalist societies as it pertains to our understanding of eighth-century Maya, I examine the distinction between economic wealth and social power in a noncapitalist society. For the sake of this discussion, I draw a distinction between *economic wealth*, which I define as the by-product of control of land or labor, and *social power*, which was derived from genealogical depth and privileged access to esoteric knowledge regarding sidereal-based ritual. Social power was manifested in the authority to control social relations (through extending favors and calling in debts), to act as mediator between humans and gods, and in the possession of material, protean symbols of social power. These two entities are practically interchangeable in our society where money "meshes together an indefinite range of otherwise incommensurable phenomena" (Giddens 1981: 55), but in noncapitalist societies, social power and economic wealth may be generated and maintained through separate but intersecting spheres of activity and exchange. Much of the time social power and economic wealth are highly correlated particularly in a hierarchical society such as the Maya, however they are two distinct variables, albeit interdependent. For instance, in discussing the colonial situation in the Yucatan, Ralph Roys (1972: 34) describes the great internal variability in wealth within the class of commoners and specifically notes mechanisms by which wealthy commoners might be blocked from positions of social and political power due to their lack of a certain body of esoteric knowledge which was possessed only by the noble class—a clear example of economic wealth with real restrictions on social power. Correspondingly, since the wealth base of any given Maya polity was finite, the economic wealth even of the highest ranking lineages was likely concentrated in the hands of a few. Many younger sibs who enjoyed a position of great social power and access to esoteric knowledge, nevertheless may have very limited direct access to economic wealth. Below, I suggest that it is just this tension that results in the diversion of these socially powerful individuals into roles of "palace artisan" or into the priesthood—the latter a trajectory noted by Roys (1972: 87).

Systems of long-distance trade that moved raw materials such as jade may have been linked more directly to the maintenance of social power rather than to the accumulation of economic wealth. This may seem like a very fine, perhaps overly fine, distinction to draw, but let us not forget that, as Bohannon (1955) has noted, many noncapitalist economies have clearly differentiated spheres of conveyance. Thus, the conversion of items such as jade (or brass rods among the Tiv [Bohannon 1955]) into food, land, or labor may not have been socially sanctioned or even desirable. Certain items such as cacao beans and red shells, which served as media of convertibility in the pan-Mesoamerican trade networks of the Postclassic, appear to have woven together separate spheres of conveyance and thus ameliorated, to a limited degree, the distinction between social power and economic wealth. The eighth-century Maya polities, however, were primarily a tapestry of local agricultural systems and, hence, of local wealth bases with interpolity exchange of foodstuffs, pots, or chert tools being a secondary consideration. In contrast, items acquired from exotic places—jade, shell, and perhaps obsidian—were high-value, low-bulk items of prime, intrinsic value (Appadurai 1986) that were badges of status and not necessarily wealth generators in any directly convertible sense.

In the past "exotic" artifacts have been analyzed from a slightly modified capitalist perspective with emphasis on the expansion of control over the extraction of raw materials that could be used, over the long run, to amass capital wealth. But could items of prime intrinsic value such as jade be used to amass wealth? The high-status Maya individuals pictured on polychrome vases and stelae as dripping with jade and shell ornaments symbolize all the social power, political authority, and esoteric knowledge of the dominant class, but ironically and perhaps counterintuitively, those jade ornaments may not be convertible into anything else and so, strictly speaking, have little direct economic value. To use the term "banking" in relation to these symbols of social power is a true misnomer (but cf. Renfrew [1986a] for a contrasting view). One of the more interesting by-products of social complexity is the tendency for the conflation of economic wealth with social power, but this by-product must not be construed analytically to be a monolithic causal factor.

## Economic Role of Nonagrarian Specialists

Even more germane to our understanding of Classic Maya economy and deserving of closer scrutiny is the role and status of nonagrarian specialists. Within the capitalistic mode of production, which is justly famous for the commodification of time and labor, we have seen historically an explosion of specialists who are able to transform their nonagrarian labor into food, shelter, and clothing through the medium of money and market exchange (Arnold 1980; Cook 1982). Today, some of these specialists, especially the artistic specialists, can be so successful that they amass large amounts of capital wealth and become part of the elite class. But really how successful is a specialization such as pottery or stone-tool production, as a long-term life strategy, in the absense of labor commodification and a money-based economy? Even within traditional economies that are partially integrated into national monetized economies, such as contemporary Mesoamerica, several ethnographic case studies (Howry 1978; Parsons 1936; Tax 1952) have pointed to a strong correlation between craft specialization and economic deprivation, generally land-disenfranchisement. If it is so difficult to survive as a craft specialist in a monetized economy, then it must have been almost impossible for a landless specialist living in eighth-century Yucatan to maintain a stable livelihood much less accrue wealth within the vagaries of an economy based on barter exchange within and between small political units. Below, I discuss two kinds of specialists: elite specialists operating out of royal and nonroyal elite households, and "supplemental" specialists whose production is organized under the umbrella of large, economically and socially heterogeneous households.

Patricia A. McAnany

*Economic Status and Residential Location*

In a class-based society, such as the eighth-century Maya, a diverse array of asymmetrical relationships of dependency can develop between the land-poor and the land-rich. Graded in the extent to which they are compulsory or "volunteer," these relationships include slavery (well-documented for the Postclassic period and suggested by Classic period iconography), tenancy, servitude, and clientage. Most of these forms are cemented by residency within the household of the land-rich. Thus, as Richard Wilk (1988) has suggested, the potential for social and economic heterogeneity, particularly within land-wealthy Classic Maya households, is great. As I suggest below, this concentration of diverse economic and social roles under one roof has implications for the division of labor, organization of agrarian and craft production, and more immediately for the analysis of assemblage composition and for our archaeological models of urban structure. Specifically, while the concentric zonation model (first described by Landa [Tozzer 1941: 62] and later reviewed by Marcus [1983]) may, on occasion, be an accurate architectural description, it does not capture spatial trends in the range of variability in social status and economic roles among and within households (also see Millon [1976] for critique of this model as applied to Teotihuacan). For instance, the formation of class-based neighborhoods is linked integrally to the urbanization process within the capitalistic mode of production in which the wealthy live in one sector of town, the middle class in another, the poor in yet another, and the utterly disenfranchised huddle somewhere on the outskirts of the city. But if we seriously entertain a model in which slaves and members of the underclass lived in wealthy elite and nonelite households, then we must grapple analytically with the implications for our current methods of assigning meaning to architectural and assemblage variability among Maya residential units.

REVISED CONSTRUCT OF EIGHTH-CENTURY MAYA ECONOMIC ORGANIZATION

Attempting to incorporate some of the ideas and critical thoughts discussed above, we can envision, in a new light, the complex, textured quality of the eighth-century Maya economy, particularly in respect to two key organizational forces: social power and household production.

*The Production and Maintenance of Social Power*

At the heart of each political unit, and probably the primary criterion by which it was identified, was the city. In the heart of the city, royal power and authority was concentrated in a central sector of monumental architecture that is so well-known, familiar, and comfortable to most Maya archaeologists. This core was materially supported by direct appropriation of labor and agricultural products from producers who lived in dispersed compounds around the more concentrated zone of core architecture. In addition, the elite corps of each city (both the royal dynasties and minor elite lineages) undoubtedly had direct control of large tracts of rich arable land upon which maize and "elite-consumption" crops such as cacao and cotton were grown wherever soil and rainfall conditions permitted, the agricultural labor on these lands being supplied by corvée labor or agricultural servants. From the overwhelming evidence of monumental architecture, it is clear that the ruling class was certainly able to muster corvée labor. Traditional analyses have stressed the time and labor spent on the construction of the magnificent Maya edifices, using it as a criterion of social complexity. Quantitative labor estimates, recently by Elliot Abrams (1987) and earlier by Charles Erasmus (1965), have helped us to put this aspect of Maya society in a more realistic perspective; I have suggested (McAnany 1989b) that the real labor demands within the Maya cities were not associated with the sporadic construction of new edifices, but with the constant need to maintain and refurbish monumental architecture and public spaces.

In addition to the labor requirements of building construction and maintenance, taxation in-kind would have been necessary to support the entourage (including a possible military component) of the royal households. There has been much discussion about the size of the elite class during the Late Classic period; the essential proposition underlying much of this discussion is that a burgeoning elite class might have placed unrealistic demands on agricultural production, thus facilitating environmental degradation and the collapse of the agricultural system (see Santley, Killion, and Lycett 1985 for an evaluation of the thesis of a burgeoning elite class). While no quantitative estimates exist for the size of the Late Classic elite population, the construction of large plaza-focused residential units, generally described as "elite," is well-documented at Maya cities throughout the lowlands from Palenque to Copan during the Late Classic. Volumetrically, Late Classic construction of monumental structures forms the bulk of architecture at Maya epicenters such as Tikal and Copan. The dramatic increase in the number of dated inscriptions (Lowe 1985: fig. 5), the bulk of which detail the exploits of ruling dynasties, also supports the thesis that the ruling or elite class expanded during the Late Classic. Finally, settlement data synthesized by B.L. Turner (1990) for the central Peten suggests wholesale expansion of all social strata during the Late Classic. Armed with this evidence, it seems reasonable to examine the social and political mechanisms through which the size of the elite class may have been able to expand and still maintain, and in fact enhance, its social power.

The spatial geometry of eighth-century Yucatan was one of spatially bounded polities. In such a milieu, the following two responses to the expansion of the elite class are probable: (1) establishment of cadet lineages in the form of royal households spatially removed from the founding household, and (2) the channeling of elite offspring who are not in direct line of inheritance into high-status military, ritualistic, or artisan roles. This second response could include positions within a sanctified priesthood or a "college" of scribes: roles that were restricted to members of the nobility during the Postclassic and Colonial periods (Roys 1972: 87). The establishment of cadet lineages spatially removed from the founding lineage has also been suggested for the Postclassic (Fox 1987) and, in this regard, the Classic period settlement data from southern Belize (Dunham, Jamison, and Leventhal 1989) is particularly provocative due to the affinities in architecture and iconography between the sites in southern Belize and those of the central Peten. In the competitive context of already highly populous eighth-century Maya polities, however, the viability of this option may have been diminishing. The channeling of elites into artisan, religious, and scribal roles may be responsible to a great extent for what we term, from an art historical and iconographic perspective, the florescence of Maya civilization.

Specialists within elite households are generally assumed to have worked raw materials of prime intrinsic value (Appadurai 1986), such as feathers, jade, and shell. Emergent complex societies of Mesoamerica and elsewhere (Renfrew 1986a) had an affinity for exotic items that could be worn or displayed as badges of status or indicators of prestige. The demand for prestige goods appears to have become very pronounced during the Middle Formative, at which time long-distance trade networks circulating jade, serpentine, shell, and magnetite, among other items, are solidified in the Gulf Coast lowlands and highland Oaxaca. During the Classic period, the association of materials of prime intrinsic value with social power appears to become strengthened and, in fact, institutionalized in the Maya lowlands; surviving monuments and painted vases depict highly redundant imagery of jewelry and ritual paraphernalia worn exclusively by elites and manufactured from these prime materials. No doubt, these symbols of social power were often highly curated and inherited heirlooms, nevertheless, the repeated occurrence of jade and shell in elite burials indicates the ritualized disposal of these materials and, correspondingly, the need to maintain supply lines to bring in additional raw material.

Paradoxically, in perusing any reconstruction of the spatial geometry of Late Classic political units it becomes clear that these materials ultimately destined for the display of social power had to travel across multiple polity boundaries before arriving at any particular Maya city. Given the iconographic and hieroglyphic evidence of political and military disputes during the Late Classic (see Miller, Chap. 12, and Webster, Chap. 13), is it not reasonable to ask how materials that symbolized status and territorial authority moved across the very boundaries that may have been under dispute? Phrased in terms of peer-polity interaction (Renfrew 1986b), could heightened levels of warfare coexist with a steady flow in the exchange of goods? Perhaps coexistence was possible if the goal of Maya warfare was the taking of captives (as Freidel [1986b] has suggested) rather than territorial expansion. Nevertheless, it is likely that there was frequent trouble along these supply lines—a situation that Roys has documented for Postclassic interpolity trade (1972: 53). The formation of regional hierarchies during the Late Classic as suggested by Marcus in this volume provides one possible solution to these potential supply problems. Another solution is suggested by William Rathje's (1973) analysis of Late Classic burial goods, which indicates that an increasing proportion of burial items were manufactured locally from readily available materials. These items, such as polychrome vessels, were often made from mundane and ubiquitous materials and were imbued with social power through the application of hieroglyphic and esoteric iconographic images. A trend that can be clarified by further research may have existed in the Late Classic, then, away from the use of raw materials valued due to their scarcity and toward the working of mundane materials that accrued social power as a result of the labor process.

The expansion of the roles of "palace artisans" went hand-in-hand with the increasing emphasis on power symbols that were created by the amalgamation of clay, water, paint pigment, or local limestone, with a corpus of esoteric knowledge. It is, thus, reasonable to conclude that many of the artisans were, themselves, members of the elite class who had been schooled in the Maya orthodoxy. The presence of "palace schools" of design has been suggested by Clemency Coggins (n.d.) for Tikal, and more recently by Joseph Ball (Chap. 8) for Buenavista. David Stuart (1988) reports on the famous cacao pot from Rio Azul, which bears what has been interpreted as the maker's signature argued to be that of an elite individual. These examples suggest that highly skilled elite labor residing within elite households were producing items that supplemented or replaced the more traditional symbols of social power manufactured from materials of prime intrinsic value.

In this model, the manufacture of symbols of social authority, either from jade or clay, occupied the time and talents of certain members of the elite class who may have been politically powerless and perhaps without an economic wealth base, thus demonstrating the interplay among political, social, and economic variables. At this point a hypothetical proposition may be put forth: the florescence of Classic period Maya society—in terms of an intensification of the production of esoteric imagery, inscriptions, monumental architecture, and other sumptuary goods—is directly related to the increased size of elite households and, in particular, to the expansion of royal households that occupied the core of Maya cities. This accommodation to the growth of the elite class, represented by the expansion of the role of highly skilled specialists, maintained the essential exclusivity of the elite class, intensified class divisions, and expanded the realm of social power for elites who may compete for, but probably never would gain, a significant amount of political power.

Patricia A. McAnany

The production of social power was undoubtedly a major concern of the elite class, and the correct interpretation of these protean symbols is a major concern of most Maya archaeologists, since these trappings of elite society comprise some of the most salient characteristics of ancient Maya society. Nevertheless, in demographic terms, the elite represented a small percentage of the overall Maya populace, most of whom lived in dispersed groupings loosely focused on areas of core monumental architecture. We now turn our attention to the social and economic organization of these household groupings.

*Heterogenous Households of the City and Hinterland*

Due to the hard labor of countless Mayan *brecheros* and students of Maya archaeology—who have squinted through the lens of a transit in order to shoot "a line" into yet another residential platform—we are increasing by geometric proportions the tally of Late Classic Maya households. True, their density relative to modern cities is low, and they are almost never arranged in any orderly gridlike pattern, but there are few habitable, arable places in the Maya lowlands that were not colonized by the Late Classic. Even the Puuc Hills, where there is a decidedly "user-unfriendly" rainfall regime, contains ample evidence of Late and Terminal Classic population (Tourtellot, Sabloff, and Smyth 1990; McAnany 1990). T. Patrick Culbert (1988) has estimated that the overall settlement density in the Late Classic lowlands ranges from a rural density of 168 persons per sq km to an intrasite density of 300 to 500 persons per sq km. For the central Maya lowlands alone Turner (1990) has suggested a population density of 150 persons per sq km or an overall population estimated to be near 3.4 million people. In this discussion, the topic of population levels is not focused on a quantitative determination of the number of Maya living in the lowlands during the Late Classic, but rather is directed toward an examination of the implications of these empirically demonstrated high population levels upon the social composition and economic organization of Maya households.

Don Rice (Chap. 2) describes in demographic terms the "filling in" process that occurred throughout the lowlands as both dry-land and swamp were utilized for cultivation, settlement, or the construction of monumental architecture. Focusing on the interplay between environment and culture as revealed in the resultant palaeoecological record, Rice characterizes the eighth-century Maya lowlands as a "built landscape." From this depiction, certain conditions pertaining to the system of land tenure in effect among the Classic Maya can be derived. Specifically, if the lowlands were a built landscape, then it is highly probable that areas of prime agricultural land were already claimed by established families or lineages and passed down through the generations to their heirs. "New" families (that is, recent immigrants to an area, or younger siblings who were not in line to inherit all or even a portion of the family's land holdings) may have found it very difficult to establish independent households and an agricultural wealth base by budding off from existing households. Despite the evidence for high population levels during the Late Classic as cited above, overall population levels really need not be staggeringly high in order for this process of competitive exclusion to manifest itself; in fact, within a hierarchical society such as the Maya, unequal access to basic resources such as land is almost axiomatic. The presence of coresidential but separate households residing within one complex, even among the so-called elite residences of Copan, as suggested by the presence of multiple food preparation areas (Hendon 1989), indicates that the oldest known solution to a limited resource base—that of family fissioning—may not have been an option during the Late Classic.

If certain segments of the Late Classic Maya population were excluded from access to agricultural lands either as a result of population growth or elite monopoly over arable tracts, then certain structural changes in the organization of labor and household composition would have occurred. Limited evidence of this process comes from the ethnohistorical record of the Yucatan Peninsula of the Postclassic period. In other, more populous, areas of Postclassic Mesoamerica, such as Morelos, however, Pedro Carrasco has documented the presence of "joint households [in which] the different married couples lived together in a landlord-tenant relationship" (1976: 54). Census records collected from the *calpulli* of Molotla in 1540 (just twenty years after the Spanish Conquest) indicate that approximately one-third of the population was grouped into large, socially and economically heterogeneous compounds (Carrasco 1976: table 8) with one head family and two to ten dependent couples with or without children. Only half of the dependent families were kin-related to the head of the compound, the other half being bound by strictly economic ties. The head of the compound possessed greater wealth and status than the heads of minor constituent households, the latter of which were dependent upon the compound head for access to plots of land and, most importantly, were obliged to assist in tribute and services. Michael Smith (n.d.: table 1, fig. 3) has archaeologically documented this type of residential compound at the Late Postclassic Morelos sites of Capilco and Cuexcomate. The casual plaza arrangements and mixture of structures with differing degrees of architectural elaboration are strongly reminiscent of Late Classic Maya settlement configurations.

Focusing more narrowly on the variables of land exclusion and social adjustment, we can examine the interaction of these variables using a case study from seventeenth-century rural Japan (T. Smith 1959; also discussed in Wilk 1988). While fully realizing that the macropolitical climate of Tokagawa period Japan is not directly analogical to the eighth-century Maya, I intend here not to "pin the tail on the donkey" by employing a direct analogy but to focus on the interaction of two variables that produces a certain kind of household structure. The applicability of the thesis of heterogeneous household structure to the Classic Maya may be validated or dismissed through further fieldwork and analysis; the goal here is to examine the relationship between social and economic organization and its resultant pattern in the archaeological record. The effect of land shortages upon the social composition of households in preindustrial seventeenth-century rural Japan has been vividly described by Thomas Smith (1959), who has studied the system of land tenure. There the countryside was so packed and land-tenure systems so rigid that new families were forbidden to even establish independent households much less acquire a parcel of land. Today, in countries such as Mexico where land disenfranchisement is a real economic problem, families often pack their bags and travel to the nearest regional center where they can sell their labor or craft items produced with their labor. This dynamic has established Mexico City as the fastest-growing city on the face of the earth. In the absence of the commodification of labor and money as exchangeable commodities, however, land-disenfranchised components of society have severely limited options. In the case examined by Smith, families locked out of the agricultural landscape responded by establishing relationships of dependency with the wealthy households. Variously described as agricultural or domestic servitude, tenancy, and even slavery, these arrangements involved residence within the household, that is, a physical attachment of oneself and/or one's family to a wealthy (and oftentimes related) head of a household. In return for the food, clothing, and shelter that was provided, the individual or family rendered agricultural, domestic, and craft services.

The examples of large socially heterogeneous compounds provided by Carrasco (1976) for sixteenth-century Morelos and by Smith (1959) for seventeenth-century Japan suggest that large successful households did, in effect, absorb some portion of the underclass who otherwise might have been excluded from access to arable land. Smith (1959) stresses the social obligations embedded within such a relationship of dependency. Essentially, the relationship is perceived by the participants in noneconomic terms, that is, as an all-encompassing social bonding that includes everything from the adoption of the ancestral family deity to the use of fictive kinship terms. Of course, in analytical terms, the economic implications of this manipulation of labor are overwhelming; through paternalistic adoption of the land-disenfranchised, the powerful heads of households are able to increase their labor force and productivity and thereby maintain control of a disproportionate amount of prime agricultural land. In such situations, when new families can gain a foothold, it is usually because they are willing to open up marginal lands, even if it means intensive labor investment in land reclamation. The striking thing about the large, established households of rural, Tokagawa period Japan is their occupational stability. Villagers were said to comment on the fact that the old households that controlled much of the prime agricultural land had been established several hundred years ago (Smith 1959: 191).

The thesis of socially heterogeneous households can be tested with settlement survey and large-scale excavation data from eighth-century Yucatan. This thesis would be supported by evidence of (a) long-term trends in settlement location from highly arable to less arable lands; (2) the presence of large, architecturally diverse compounds; and (3) a long occupational duration for the large, diverse compounds. In fact, many areas of the Maya lowlands do show a pronounced temporal trend in settlement location, with early settlement on the prime agricultural lands and later settlement filling in the areas of secondary and tertiary productivity or areas requiring reclamation. The residences of K'axob, which is located on the southeastern side of Pulltrouser Swamp, for instance, displays a distinct spatial and temporal pattern whereby residences built during the Late Classic are located in proximity either to tracts of less arable land or to the swamp itself. Scott Fedick (1989) has documented a similar pattern of successive settlement expansion onto less desirable agricultural lands in the Belize River Valley and, in a surveyed transect from Tikal to Yaxha, Anabel Ford (1986) found predominantly Late Classic settlement in the low-lying *bajo-tintal* regions. Regarding platform size and internal diversity, Gair Tourtellot (Chap. 7) notes a correlative trend in the decrease in platform size, complexity, and occupational depth with increasing distance from the fertile soils of major centers such as Copan. At Rio Azul, Jack Eaton (1987) has documented a large, diverse, residential compound with stone buildings and low platforms, which he suggests housed servants as well as elite bureaucrats.

The issue of occupational duration has always been a slippery one for Mayanists. On the one hand, households observed on an ethnographic time scale follow rather predictable cycles of growth and decline, on the other hand, Maya residences observed on an archaeological time scale often show a steady accumulation of construction units that may span 1,500 to 2,000 years. Even if a 2,000-year accumulation of cultural material does not represent a single bloodline, nevertheless the conclusion that certain places in the Maya landscape were continuously occupied for long periods of time is inescapable. In a gallant attempt to reconcile ethnographic and archaeological time scales, Tourtellot (1988) analyzed household size and elaboration at Seibal from the perspective of the life cycle and age development of households. Although some of the households were apparently built big from the start, much of the variability he observed could be explained by differences between older, larger, more architecturally heterogeneous households and younger, smaller, less diverse households. The dimension of time and factor of occupational stability, therefore, are important to the determination of the social and economic composition of Maya households, many of which may have had a temporal stability on the order of a *baktun* or about 400 years.

If, by the eighth century, large Maya households (both elite and non-elite) were absorbing excess land-disenfranchised labor and possibly acquiring slaves through military raids and conquests, then household compounds would have developed into very heterogeneous entities. Individuals with vastly different social status and economic roles would have been living side by side in many urban elite and large, rural non-elite households. Small, internally homogeneous non-elite residential units would have existed alongside the larger compounds. In the southern part of K'axob, for instance, many small patio groupings and single platforms are situated within 500 meters of the large, focal, and architecturally diverse plaza group (McAnany n.d.). The social and economic relationship between the large plaza group and the "satellite" structures is not clear; however, the smaller platforms may be linked closely in a relationship of dependency or the entire cluster may represent a macroresidential level of integration similar to the *calpulli* of Postclassic Morelos (Carrasco 1976; Smith n.d.).

The model of heterogeneous household composition has tremendous implications for the development of theories of household structure and, more urgently, for specific programs of analysis of site structure, assemblage composition, and household formation processes. A logical corollary of the model of internally heterogeneous households is the thesis that variation in social status within many households (particularly elite households) was equal to that which existed between households. Clearly, we run the risk of ignoring significant social variability when we attempt to assign a single social ranking to a Maya household compound based on its size and elaboration. It is interesting to note that the analysis of social class based upon supposed elite goods such as polychrome pots and obsidian has been confounded by the ubiquitous, low-density presence of these items at many residential compounds, even those located distant from major epicenters of monumental architecture (Adams n.d.; McAnany n.d.). Perhaps we should be conceptualizing these artifacts as polythetic sets diagnostic of socially heterogeneous household units, rather than flagging a domestic unit of a particular homogeneous class.

The possibility that a significant portion of the large Late Classic Maya households were internally heterogeneous has implications for the division of agricultural labor and also for the residential location of craft production. As more Maya residences are excavated and arrayed along a continuum of architectural complexity, we have increasing documentation of deep deposits of lithic debris or sherd wasters found adjacent to platform complexes. Mayanists are increasingly asking questions about the role and status of the individuals who produced these largely utilitarian pots or stone tools. Were they land-disenfranchised individuals as Rice (1987a) has suggested or were they members of wealthy non-elite households? In light of the distinctions discussed above between craft specialists in capitalist and noncapitalist settings, it seems logical to envision these specialists as attached to a household through which the basic necessities of life, such as food, clothing, and shelter are supplied and, in most cases, to consider craft production as supplemental to agrarian production.

It is, therefore, more likely that intensive lithic or ceramic production will be one of several production foci of large, successful households. The activity would have taken place within the organizational framework of a large compound although the actual production may have been undertaken by individuals of low status who were residing at or near the complex. The conditions under which this type of intensified production (Rice 1987a) took place were very different from those under which the elite artisans created sumptuary goods. In spatial terms, this organization of craft production implies that separate wards of land-poor, craft specialists were not a common feature of Maya cities; the archaeological records from Sayil (Killion et al. 1989) and Copan (Webster and Freter 1990) provide some support for this model (but see Pyburn [1989] for a contrasting view).

Evidence of intensified production has surfaced in diverse types of residential contexts throughout the lowlands. Chert stone tool debris at Colha (Shafer and Hester 1983; E. King, personal communication, 1989) and obsidian debris at Quirigua (Ashmore 1988) are found associated with a range of residential types that crosscut structure size and architectural complexity. Wendy Ashmore (1988), Rice (1987a), Robert Rands and Ronald Bishop (1980), Robert Fry (1980), and Arlen Chase (personal communication, 1989) have also noted the tendency for evidence of craft production, particularly pottery production, to occur at households that are located outside of the monumental architectural cores of Quirigua, sites of the Peten lakes district, Palenque, Tikal, and Caracol respectively. This evidence points toward a situation in which production (agrarian and nonagrarian) was organized within the domestic unit, although in the instances of joint family compounds these units may not have been closely kin-related.

When households are perceived as socially heterogeneous units with long-term temporal stability, clear implications for site-formation processes and assemblage analysis emerge. For instance, small communities such as K'axob and Tibaat—which are located around Pulltrouser Swamp and are composed of multiplatform groupings, most of which were non-elite residences—have revealed differences in the intensity of chert tool use and recycling. The differences exist between the large and small residential complexes. There is no chert near Pulltrouser Swamp and most of the knappable stone enters the households as finished bifaces; the production locale was most likely at Colha, which is located about 30 km to the south (McAnany 1989c; Potter, Chap. 9). After breakage, tool fragments were used for the production of expedient flake tools. At the larger residential complexes, which through test excavations also have greater occupational depth, there is proportionately much more recycling of broken tool fragments than at the smaller complexes. Assuming that this pattern is not a function of sampling error or site-structural characteristics peculiar to large complexes, two possible explanations for this pattern can be suggested: (1) large households were, in fact, not wealthy and therefore could not secure replacements for their broken tools; and (2) large, wealthy households, for one reason or another, produced less hard-fraction garbage. In the context of a contemporary study of household garbage-disposal patterns in Tuscon, Rathje (1974: 240) notes that "high-income residents are associated with the discard of very little waste of either food or tools." But why should wealthy households necessarily be more conservative or less wasteful in their disposal habits, either in modern-day Tucson or in the eighth-century Yucatan? Coincident with the premise that a heterogeneous economic structure existed at large, wealthy compounds of the ancient Maya, I would maintain that this pattern indicates that a wider array of activities was undertaken by a larger number of people over a longer period of time. Broken tool fragments scattered around the large households were used, again and again, to produce sharp-edged flakes needed for a suite of activities from woodworking to matmaking, and the provisional dumps were simply mined more frequently for core material. Essentially the same dynamic may be operating in Tucson, where the waste stream has been protracted by the transfer of unconsumed food and used tools from the larders of the wealthy to the spatially separated residences of their day-servants. Among the Maya, however, this example demonstrates that duration of occupation and diversity of production activities may directly affect residential assemblage composition, and these variables need to be controlled when domestic assemblages are analyzed.

## CONCLUSIONS

Our interpretations of eighth-century Maya economy are dependent, of course, on the models we generate to structure this inquiry. Therefore, assumptions and basic postulates of our theoretical models require careful scrutiny, particularly in the areas of critical structural disjunctures between capitalist and noncapitalist societies. These disjunctures are most salient in the organization of agrarian production, the economic role of nonagrarian specialists, the distinction between wealth and social power, and the relationship between economic status and residential location. I have suggested that the production and maintenance of social power was a primary and active concern of elite households and that this concern was related synergistically to the expansion of the elite class; together, the two resulted in the increased breadth of the role of the elite artisan, who transformed mundane raw materials into objects of social value.

## The Economics of Wealth among Eighth-Century Maya Households

The organization of the Classic Maya household, a topic of increasing interest to Mayanists, was a product of agricultural production and, as I have suggested, exclusion of certain population segments from agrarian land holdings. The occupational stability of many Maya residential compounds may be viewed as indicative of their intrinsic social and economic heterogeneity as these established households, that had already laid claim to the agricultural landscape, absorbed as economic dependents the increased population so well-noted for the Late Classic period. The resultant diversity in economic roles and social statuses within the large residential complexes has profound implications for our archaeological analysis of these cultural features. By suggesting that some of the Late Classic Maya households were socially heterogeneous and economically diverse, I have tried to show that we need to focus our analytical methods on techniques suitable for exploring inherent variability rather than forcing a typology of social status and architectural elaboration upon Late Classic Maya households.

Recent developments, both in the decipherment of hieroglyphs and tragically in the accelerated looting of Maya cities, have resulted in a resurgence of research focused on the elite stratum of Maya society. If we are to understand the transformation of this sector of society at the end of the Classic period, then the organization of production within the royal compounds and the role of specialists must be approached on an analytical rather than a descriptive level. Concepts of wealth and status need to be rigorously defined in such analyses and not loosely used as synonyms.

Archaeologists and anthropologists have yet to discover the "yellow-brick road" of comparative economic analysis. The diversity of economic arrangements, even within a single society, has proven difficult to conceptualize much less quantify. Nevertheless, we now possess more information relevant to the Late Classic Maya economy than ever before and so we are in a position to isolate the important variables and driving forces behind this complex, multilayered economy. The Maya political economy meshed with the domestic economy while both maintained a separate sphere within which largely different organizational principles operated. The eighth-century Maya were a prime example of a pluralistic economy and deserve to be studied as such.

GAILEY, CHRISTINE WARD
    1987    *Kinship to Kingship: Gender Hierarchy and State Formation in the Tongan Islands*. University of Texas Press, Austin.

GIDDENS, ANTHONY
    1981    *A Contemporary Critique of Historical Materialism, Vol. 1: Power, Property and the State*. University of California Press, Berkeley.

HARRISON, PETER D., AND B.L. TURNER II (EDS.)
    1978    *Pre-Hispanic Maya Agriculture*. University of New Mexico Press, Albuquerque.

HENDON, JULIA A.
    1989    Elite Household Organization at Copan, Honduras: Analysis of Activity Distribution in the Sepulturas Zone. In *Households and Communities, Proceedings of the 21st Annual Chacmool Conference* (Scott MacEachern, David J.W. Archer, and Richard D. Garvin, eds.): 371–380. Chacmool, the Archaeological Association of the University of Calgary.

HOWRY, JEFFRY C.
    1978    Ethnographic Realities of Mayan Prehistory. In *Cultural Continuities in Mesoamerica* (David L. Browman, ed.): 239–257. Mouton Publishers, The Hague.

KILLION, THOMAS W., JEREMY A. SABLOFF, GAIR TOURTELLOT, AND NICHOLAS DUNNING
    1989    Intensive Surface Collection of Residential Clusters at Terminal Classic Sayil. *Journal of Field Archaeology* 16 (3): 273–294.

LOWE, JOHN W. G.
    1985    *The Dynamics of Apocalypse: A Systems Simulation of the Classic Maya Collapse*. University of New Mexico Press, Albuquerque.

MARCUS, JOYCE
    1983    On the Nature of the Mesoamerican City. In *Prehistoric Settlement Patterns* (Evon Vogt and Richard Leventhal, eds.): 195–242. University of New Mexico Press, Albuquerque.

MCANANY, PATRICIA A.
    1989a    Economic Foundations of Prehistoric Maya Society: Paradigms and Concepts. In *Prehistoric Maya Economies of Belize* (P. A. McAnany and B.L. Isaac, eds.): 347–372. Research in Economic Anthropology, Supplement 4. JAI Press, Greenwich.
    1989b    Introduction. In *Prehistoric Maya Economies of Belize* (P. A. McAnany and B.L. Isaac, eds.): 1–13. Research in Economic Anthropology, Supplement 4. JAI Press, Greenwich.
    1989c    Stone-Tool Production and Exchange in the Eastern Maya Lowlands: The Consumer Perspective from Pulltrouser Swamp, Belize. *American Antiquity* 54: 332–346.
    1990    Water Storage in the Puuc Region of the Northern Maya Lowlands: A Key to Population Estimates and Architectural Variability. In *Precolumbian Population History in the Maya Lowlands* (T. Patrick Culbert and Don Rice, eds.): 263–284. University of New Mexico Press, Albuquerque.

n.d. K'axob: A Formative and Classic Period Settlement at Pulltrouser Swamp, Belize. Manuscript in author's possession.

MILLON, RENE
1976 Social Relations in Ancient Teotihuacan. In *The Valley of Mexico* (E.R. Wolf, ed.): 205–248. University of New Mexico Press, Albuquerque.

OFFNER, JEROME A.
1981 On the Inapplicability of "Oriental Despotism" and the "Asiatic Mode of Production" to the Aztecs of Texcoco. *American Antiquity* 46: 43–61.

PARSONS, E. C.
1936 *Mitla: Town of Souls*. University of Chicago Press, Chicago.

PYBURN, K. ANNE
1989 *Prehistoric Maya Community and Settlement at Nohmul, Belize*. BAR International Series 509. Oxford.

RANDS, ROBERT L., AND RONALD L. BISHOP
1980 Resource Procurement Zones and Patterns of Ceramic Exchange in the Palenque Region, Mexico. In *Models and Methods in Regional Exchange* (Robert E. Fry, ed.): 19–46. Society for American Archaeology Papers 1. Washington, D.C.

RATHJE, WILLIAM L.
1973 Classic Maya Development and Denouement: A Research Design. In *The Classic Maya Collapse* (T. Patrick Culbert, ed.): 405–454. University of New Mexico Press, Albuquerque.
1974 The Garbage Project: A New Way of Looking at the Problems of Archaeology. *Archaeology* 27: 236–241.

RENFREW, COLIN
1986a Varna and the Emergence of Wealth in Prehistoric Europe. In *The Social Life of Things: Commodities in Cultural Perspective* (Arjun Appadurai, ed.): 141–168. Cambridge University Press, Cambridge.
1986b Introduction: Peer Polity Interaction and Socio-Political Change. In *Peer Polity Interaction and Socio-Political Change* (Colin Renfrew and John F. Cherry, eds.): 1–18. Cambridge University Press, Cambridge.

RICE, PRUDENCE
1987a Lowland Maya Pottery in the Late Classic Period. In *Maya Ceramics: Papers from the 1985 Maya Ceramic Conference*, Part II (P.M. Rice and R.J. Sharer, eds.): 525–543. BAR International Series 345(ii). Oxford.
1987b Economic Change in the Lowland Maya Late Classic Period. In *Specialization, Exchange, and Complex Societies* (Elizabeth M. Brumfiel and Timothy K. Earle, eds.): 76–85. Cambridge University Press, Cambridge.

ROYS, RALPH L.
1972 *The Indian Background of Colonial Yucatan*. University of Oklahoma Press, Norman.

SANDERS, WILLIAM T.
1973 The Cultural Ecology of the Maya Lowlands: A Reevaluation. In *The Classic Maya Collapse* (T. Patrick Culbert, ed.): 325–366. University of New Mexico Press, Albuquerque.

1977 Resource Utilization and Political Evolution in the Teotihuacan Valley. In *Explanation of Prehistoric Change* (James N. Hill, ed.): 231–257. University of New Mexico Press, Albuquerque.

SANDERS, WILLIAM T., AND BARBARA J. PRICE
1968 *Mesoamerica: The Evolution of a Civilization.* Random House, New York.

SANDERS, WILLIAM T., AND DAVID WEBSTER
1978 Unilinealism, Multilinealism, and the Evolution of Complex Societies. In *Social Archaeology: Beyond Subsistence and Dating* (Charles Redman et al., eds.): 249–302. Academic Press, New York.

SANTLEY, ROBERT S.
1984 Obsidian Exchange, Economic Stratification, and the Evolution of Complex Society in the Basin of Mexico. In *Trade and Exchange in Early Mesoamerica* (Kenneth G. Hirth, ed.): 43–86. University of New Mexico Press, Albuquerque.

SANTLEY, ROBERT S., THOMAS W. KILLION, AND MARK T. LYCETT
1985 On the Maya Collapse. *Journal of Anthropological Research* 42 (2): 123–159.

SHAFER, HARRY J., AND THOMAS R. HESTER
1983 Ancient Maya Chert Workshops in Northern Belize, Central America. *American Antiquity* 48: 519–543.

SMITH, MICHAEL E.
n.d. Houses and the Settlement Hierarchy in Late Postclassic Morelos: A Comparison of Archaeology and Ethnohistory. In *Household, Compound, and Residence: Studies of Prehispanic Domestic Units in Western Mesoamerica* (Robert S. Santley and Kenneth G. Hirth, eds.). CRC Press, Boca Raton, Fla.

SMITH, THOMAS C.
1959 *The Agrarian Origins of Modern Japan.* Stanford University Press, Stanford.

STUART, DAVID
1988 The Rio Azul Cacao Pot: Epigraphic Observations on the Function of a Maya Ceramic Vessel. *Antiquity* 62: 153–157.

TAX, SOL
1952 Economy and Technology. In *Heritage of Conquest* (Sol Tax, ed.): 43–75. The Free Press, Glencoe, Ill.

THOMPSON, J. ERIC S.
1966 *The Rise and Fall of Maya Civilization.* University of Oklahoma Press, Norman.

TOURTELLOT, GAIR
1988 Developmental Cycles of Households and Houses at Seibal. In *Household and Community in the Mesoamerican Past* (Richard R. Wilk and Wendy Ashmore, eds.): 97–120. University of New Mexico Press, Albuquerque.

TOURTELLOT, GAIR, J. A. SABLOFF, AND M. P. SMYTH
    1990    Room Counts and Population Estimation for Terminal Classic Sayil in the Puuc Region, Yucatan, Mexico. In *Precolumbian Population History in the Maya Lowlands* (T. Patrick Culbert and Don Rice, eds.): 245–261. University of New Mexico Press, Albuquerque.

TOZZER, ALFRED M. (ED. AND TRANS.)
    1941    *Landa's Relacion de las Cosas de Yucatan* (1566). Papers of the Peabody Museum 18. Harvard University, Cambridge.

TURNER II, B. L.
    1990    Population Reconstruction for the Central Maya Lowlands: 1000 B.C. to A.D. 1500. In *Precolumbian Population History in the Maya Lowlands* (T. Patrick Culbert and Don S. Rice, eds.): 301–324. University of New Mexico Press, Albuquerque.

WEBSTER, DAVID, AND ANNCORINNE FRETER
    1990    The Demography of Late Classic Copan. In *Precolumbian Population History in the Maya Lowlands* (T. Patrick Culbert and Don Rice, eds.): 37–61. University of New Mexico Press, Albuquerque.

WILK, RICHARD R.
    1988    Maya Household Organization: Evidence and Analogies. In *Household and Community in the Mesoamerican Past* (Richard R. Wilk and Wendy Ashmore, eds.): 135–151. University of New Mexico Press, Albuquerque.

WOLF, ERIC W.
    1982    *Europe and the People Without History*. University of California Press, Berkeley.

# 4

# The Social Organization of the Late Classic Maya: Problems of Definition and Approaches

ROBERT J. SHARER

THE UNIVERSITY MUSEUM
UNIVERSITY OF PENNSYLVANIA

## INTRODUCTION

THE DELINEATION AND UNDERSTANDING of human organizations has long been one of the cornerstones of the social sciences. Certainly the study of non-Western social organizations has been fundamental to the growth of anthropology over the past century. The reasons for this are obvious—the ways and means of human organization define the fabric and boundaries of all societies, make collective action possible, and provide for the transmission of cultural tradition through time. Thus the study of human organizations is no less than the study of human culture.

Within anthropological archaeology, the reconstruction of ancient social organizations is a somewhat more recent phenomenon; it has been no less important, however, to the growth of the discipline and to our understanding of our origins. But in attempting to reconstruct the social organization of any past society, scholars immediately confront several problems, ones widely recognized but nonetheless requiring explicit (if brief) acknowledgment here.

The first and perhaps most immediate of these is the fundamental threshold between the observable ethnographic present and the unobservable archaeological past. Archaeology reconstructs past behavior from the residues of that behavior. But archaeology is a science without the means for direct scientific verification of its interpretations. What the material remains from past behavior allow us to reconstruct about the social past must be rigorously tested, but our reconstructions will always remain the most plausible, most economical, most consistent explanations, rather than proven fact.

This paper assumes that the delineation of the social organization of the Classic Maya is fundamentally an archaeological problem. While it is widely acknowledged that historical sources—whether deciphered Classic texts or retrospectively applied ethnohistoric documents—greatly enrich our perceptions of the ancient Maya, for better or for worse, archaeological data provide the core of our direct evidence for reconstructing Classic period social organization. Contemporaneous Classic texts deal mostly with politics and ritual, but even when they record specific kinship and marriage information this is restricted to the uppermost echelons of Maya society—the vast majority of the population, the non-elite, are not even mentioned. Classic period sculpture, painting, and other iconographic evidence can greatly enrich our insights into social relationships, but once again this information pertains almost exclusively to the Maya elite. The rich ethnohistoric sources provide far more complete information about Maya social organization, but because of their closer temporal links, have been far more useful in studies of Postclassic Yucatan (Smith 1962; Freidel and Sabloff 1984) and the Postclassic Maya highlands (Hill and Monaghan 1987). It is useful to keep in mind that the Classic lowland Maya are as far removed in time from the Conquest period as we today are from the Middle Ages; thus the uncritical use of ethnohistoric sources for the Classic Maya interjects all the potential problems stemming from undocumented change within the intervening centuries. The most useful means for applying ethnohistoric sources to the Classic era will be outlined at the conclusion of this paper.

Having made these points, however, we should remind ourselves that no archaeological inquiry would be possible without input from documentary or observational sources (history, art history, and ethnography). This is seldom more obvious than in the Maya case. The greatest strides in reconstruction of the ancient Maya stem from an interdisciplinary approach—the combined and interdependent application of history, art history, epigraphy, ethnohistory, ethnography, and archaeology.

But archaeology remains the mainstay in this endeavor. In attempting to reconstruct ancient social organization, archaeology relies primarily on inferences based on a series of overlapping data sources—artifact patterning, burials, architecture, the recently defined specialty of household archaeology, and settlement patterning (Ashmore 1981; Wilk and Ashmore 1988). Nonetheless, archaeological studies of Classic Maya social organization have traditionally been heavily weighted toward the elite, although a recent increase in the investigation of non-elite domestic remains promises eventually to yield a more balanced perspective (Webster and Gonlin 1988).

Before venturing further, the precise subject of this paper should be made clear. This paper is about two things: one is the problem of defining and describing Classic Maya social organization, and the other is a suggested approach for confronting this problem. This paper is explicitly *not* about the history of studies of Maya social organization, nor is it a survey of all genres of such organization. Its stated domain is, of course, Classic Maya social organization, but since human organizations ultimately encompass all aspects of behavior, the subject of this paper necessarily overlaps with that of other papers in this volume that detail Maya economic, political, and religious realms. It also invokes such other forms of organization as military orders or secret societies. To give the subject a practical boundary, and because of space limitations, this paper will be concerned with the basic organization of human social interaction as traditionally defined by anthropologists. Studies of ancient Maya demography and resulting population reconstructions are prime examples of the successful application of archaeological methods (see Culbert and Rice 1990), and provide the necessary foundation for our attempts to define aspects of past social organization. Discussion here will therefore treat the following narrowly defined categories concerning the organization of these populations, including reference to groups and relationships defined by both involuntary and voluntary criteria: social stratification, marriage and family, residence, and descent. As all specialists know, many of these topics have proved to be among the most difficult areas to document archaeologically.

The basic premise that underlies this discussion is that there is no such monolithic entity as "Classic Maya social organization"—as in other aspects of Maya civilization variation rather than uniformity characterized Classic society (see Haviland n.d.; Becker n.d.; Willey and Leventhal 1979; Rice and Rice 1980; Webster 1980; Ashmore 1984; Sanders 1986; Tourtellot 1988a; Webster and Gonlin 1988). Differences in time (even within the eighth century), space (meaning both geographic distance and ethnic variation), and societal scale led to gradients and contrasts in organizational forms. Indeed, diversity in the past should come as no surprise, given the considerable variability in contemporary and ethnohistoric Maya social organization (see Wilk 1988; Weeks 1988). As archaeologists have found in other domains, it is ultimately not sufficient to seek simply the central cultural norms to which all social groups ideally adhered. Rather, we should try to discover the varieties of social life, in all their dynamic flux, and to assess the conditions under which particular forms occur.

Now that the necessary preliminaries have been addressed, the remainder of the paper will survey some of the important issues raised by studies of Classic Maya social organization.

### SOCIAL STRATIFICATION

There is near universal agreement among Mayanists that Classic society was stratified into two classes—usually termed the elite and non-elite. This conclusion is based on an overwhelming assemblage of broadly familiar evidence from archaeological (e.g. Freidel 1979; Haviland 1970; Schortman 1986), art historical (e.g., Miller 1985; Schele and Miller 1986), epigraphic (e.g., Marcus 1983; Schele and Miller 1986), and ethnohistoric (e.g., Roys 1939, 1943, 1965; Tozzer 1941; Hellmuth 1977) realms. There is also a wealth of data from related Mesoamerican societies that can be used to supplement the Maya sources (e.g., Marcus 1978, 1983, n.d.).

Apart from this, however, there is a great deal of uncertainty and even confusion regarding the nature of social stratification among the Classic Maya. Archaeologists usually define social stratification on the basis of differential access to basic resources. The social determinants of such differential access to resources include inheritance, marriage, and social rank. Although most agree that the extant archaeological data reflect the broad distinctions between Classic Maya elite and non-elite, it is often difficult to use such evidence to define actual patterns of inheritance, marriage, and rank. Molloy and Rathje (1974) used burial data to propose a shift in the pattern of inheritance from achieved status during the Early Classic to ascribed status during the Late Classic. The degree to which the Classic Maya elite were endogamous or exogamous remains a matter of debate, although some scholars see a broad pattern of endogamy within Mesoamerican elites (Marcus 1983).

The traditional and often best indicator of these distinctions is wealth. But the definition of wealth and wealth distinctions in preindustrial societies has been another area of considerable debate. Smith (1987) has addressed this issue and has provided a very useful framework for the definition of wealth distinctions in the archaeological record. The criteria used by Smith include both architectural and artifactual remains (Smith 1987: 301–320). Optimum evidence for such determinations lies in uncovering direct associations of artifacts in primary context with domestic architecture. But while such associations have been found in many highland areas of Mesoamerica (see Winter 1976; Flannery and Winter 1976), they have thus far been difficult to locate in the Maya lowlands where most household remains appear to have been swept clean of artifacts and debris.

In viewing the gradations within Late Classic archaeological remains, however, the definition of the actual dividing line between elite and non-elite is seldom explicit (e.g., Willey and Leventhal 1979). More often than not, in assessing each category of artifacts archaeologists are confronted by a continuum rather than a well-defined dichotomy, probably reflecting internal ranking gradations within the elite stratum. Burials and architecture have been the most commonly used criteria for defining an elite/non-elite distinction in the archaeological record. But even here the situation is seldom clear-out. For example, at Seibal, the results of what surely is the most sophisticated study to date of lowland Maya residential architecture contradict the traditional assumption that size of dwelling reflects wealth or status (Tourtellot 1988a: 362). Overall, the Seibal data show that structures classed as dwellings exhibit no clear dichotomy, except between those built with stone walls and those built without stone walls, although the latter can be divided into some four subcategories based on location and platform volume/floor area ratios (Tourtellot 1988a: 366).

Given the difficulties in using any single category of data to delineate Late Classic social stratification from the archaeological record, it would seem that an analysis integrating all data classes at a given site, with adequate temporal controls, might provide a better means of approaching this problem. Of course such a study would still be plagued by the difficulty in establishing the contemporaneity of such data, along with the already mentioned paucity of primary context artifacts in association with residential architecture.

When Classic Maya social stratification is approached by using nonarchaeological evidence, specifically ethnohistoric and ethnographic studies, we immediately confront one of the most important contrasts between Pre-Columbian and Post-Columbian society—and one of the major problems with applying the direct historic approach using Maya ethnography to reconstruct Classic Maya society (cf. Vogt 1983)—the virtual disappearance of the Maya elite class during the Spanish Colonial era (see Farriss 1984). While there is direct ethnohistoric evidence and considerable archaeological support for the existence of these two classes among Pre-Columbian Maya, there is less agreement in the definition of the finer gradations within Maya society—the nature and number of subdivisions within these two classes—and the means by which membership in such groups was defined, whether by voluntary criteria such as occupation, or involuntary criteria such as kinship (see Adams 1970; Becker n.d., 1973; Haviland 1970, 1977).

More importantly, perhaps, scholars have tended to fall into two camps in assessing the degree of similarity in the organization of elite and non-elite. For example, some hold that both classes were internally ranked, while others see a ranked elite and a non-elite without internal ranking (see Demarest 1989). It seems clear, based on epigraphic evidence and consistent with Conquest period ethnohistoric accounts in both Yucatan and the Maya highlands, that the Late Classic Maya elite were ranked. Ranking seems to be reflected in the gradations in the architectural and burial data. But the most direct support for ranking comes from a series of titles recently deciphered from Classic texts (Schele and Miller 1986; Freidel and Schele 1988). As might be expected, individual rulers usually monopolized the inventory of these titles, but by the Late Classic a case can be made for at least three ranks within the ruling hierarchy (Schele and Miller 1986; Stuart 1989; Houston 1989): *Kul Ahau* ("supreme ruler"), *Ahau* ("ruler"), and *Cahal* ("subordinate ruler").

Marcus (1983) cites considerable ethnohistoric and epigraphic evidence for the separate and dissimilar organizations of elite and non-elite classes within Maya society. On the other hand, Haviland (1985: 41), using both archaeological and epigraphic data to reconstruct the social organization of one elite residential group at Tikal (Group 7F-1), states that this "provides us with a model to test against data from lower class residential situations." Such a proviso assumes, however, that there was a close similarity in organization between the two classes. Haviland's procedure for making inferences about the past based on testing models against new data is laudable. He also has some support for the specific approach he recommends, since at Tikal a similar pattern of burials is associated with residential constructions in both elite and non-elite situations (Haviland 1965, 1970). But we must be cautious about presuming how far such evidence of similar burial patterns can take us, given other information that reflects significant *differences* in the structuring of elite and non-elite classes (see below). Indeed, given what we are beginning to realize about the degree of internal variation within Maya society, it may be that the archaeological evidence mustered by Haviland reflects a Tikal pattern of social organization that will turn out to be only one of several such patterns typical of the Classic Maya lowlands. For instance, Tourtellot (1988a) notes several formal distinctions between dwellings at Seibal and those at Tikal and other lowland sites.

In sum, therefore, we have only begun to recognize the existence of variability within these two basic Maya classes. Furthermore, we have too little knowledge about the lowest stratum of Maya society. For example, Conquest period documents in Yucatan describe "slaves," but we still know very little about this social stratum in ancient Maya society, let alone its distribution in time and space. Cases such as this point to the need to design and execute research to delineate the degree and nature of variability in ancient Maya social organization, and especially to secure more information about the non-elite (see Webster and Gonlin 1988).

## MARRIAGE, FAMILY, AND RESIDENCE

The life of every individual among the contemporary Maya is intimately intertwined with the immediate family, kin groups, community, and the supernatural. The life cycle—birth, acquisition of names, puberty, marriage, and death—is marked by ritual, as it was in Bishop Landa's day. Obviously, however, there are severe limits on the degree to which we can infer the details of domestic life from Classic period archaeological evidence. Thus, in this area especially, we are heavily dependent on ethnohistoric and ethnographic accounts to define the domain of Classic period domestic life.

In the sixteenth-century, marriages were often arranged between families. Monogamy was and remains the rule, incest taboos being extended to anyone with the same surname (patronym), with a more limited extension on the maternal side (mother, mother's sister, mother's daughter). Polygyny was and is permitted, and was probably much more widespread among the Classic elite than the non-elite; today, in traditional Maya communities, it is often determined by the wealth of the individual (cf. Roys in Tozzer 1941). Cross-cousin marriages were allowed, and in fact have been proposed as an ancestral form of preferential marriage, with kinship terminology cited as evidence for same (Eggan 1934). The decipherment of texts from Piedras Negras has led Fox and Justeson (1986) to hypothesize that cross-cousin marriage was the basis of Classic period dynastic succession. It may well be that this form of marriage was utilized in specific instances to assure a successful dynastic line (see below)—and thus may be further evidence for variation within the Late Classic social system. But there is little evidence for the practice elsewhere—either from the Classic texts at other sites or in the later ethnohistoric and ethnographic data (Haviland 1967; Fox and Justeson 1986), and at least one investigator has mustered a convincing argument against this interpretation, based on the decipherment of the crucial kinship relation glyph at the crux of Fox and Justeson's thesis (Hopkins 1988: 98–99).

Among the Maya today, the most frequent residence pattern is an initial uxorilocal phase, followed by patrilocal residence, with each son establishing a new nuclear household, or neolocal residence, adjacent to that of his father (Wilk 1988). Patrilocal residence tends to form generationally extended family residential groups, which, based on frequent occurrence of archaeological housemounds arranged in "patio clusters" at lowland sites, was seemingly a basic characteristic of Classic Maya society as well (Haviland n.d., 1988; Tourtellot 1988a, 1988b; see below). In fact, Tourtellot's Seibal study offers some cautious support for a Late Classic pattern of patrilocal residence. The support is provided by an ethnographically based cross-culturally validated measure (at the 95% confidence level) of dwelling floor size by which the relevant Seibal data match the patrilocal range (Tourtellot 1988a: 356). This latter case offers an example of how specific questions of social organization can be addressed archaeologically—based on statistically valid correlations from ethnographic studies that can be tested against factors visible in the archaeological record.

### DESCENT

It is important to keep in mind that descent systems refer specifically to the transmission of social-group membership and must be distinguished from related systems of inheritance ("descent" of property) and succession ("descent" of power, usually through "political" and/or "religious" offices). There is a general consensus, based primarily on historical and ethnohistorical data, that patrilineal descent was a basic organizational principle among the Classic Maya. Ethnohistorically, the primary source has always been Landa's description of the Yucatec Maya (Tozzer 1941). A series of investigators have concluded that Landa's account is most consistent with a system of nonlocalized, exogamous, patrilineal clans (Beals 1932; Nutini 1961; Hopkins 1988).

Clan in this sense defines a social group where membership is assumed to be based on sharing a common surname, rather than by establishing actual kinship links to define lineages (see Hopkins 1988). In addition, it seems certain that these Maya kin groups were without the corporate characteristics typical of African descent groups. Technically, therefore, as Haviland (1968: 100) points out, they would more closely fit the definition of a sib as given by Murdock (1960: 1). Nonetheless, these nonlocalized kin groups seem to have been identified with patron deities and various social obligations (Eggan 1934; Roys 1940; Tozzer 1941).

A basic nonlocalized patrilineal clan organization for the Maya is supported by analysis of Maya kinship terminology (Eggan 1934); other Conquest period accounts, such as that of Las Casas (1909) describing the Verapaz region of Guatemala; and ethnographic data from the Lacandon (Tozzer 1907) and other Maya groups (Nutini 1961; Wilk 1988; Hopkins 1988: 100–106). The inheritance of wealth seems to have been patrilineal as well (Eggan 1934; Roys 1940; Tozzer 1941).

There is, of course, good support for patrilineal descent groups during the Late Classic within specific ruling families at many lowland Maya sites. Deciphered texts in these cases document the succession of rulers through time, sometimes specified as from father to son, forming what can only be termed ruling lineages or dynasties (see Haviland 1977; Hopkins 1988: 107–115). At Copan, for example, Altar Q offers a dramatic iconographic summary of that site's dynasty, with the portraits and name glyphs of sixteen male rulers, spanning some four hundred years, the sequence being completed by the sixteenth ruler, Yax Pac, seated facing the dynastic founder, Yax Kuk Mo, from whom he is shown receiving emblems of office (Stuart and Schele 1986).

Evidence for regional variation in the pattern of dynastic rule and succession is ample in the Classic period inscriptions (see Hopkins 1988). At some sites accounts of descent through both the male and female lines is stressed, as at Palenque (Mathews and Schele 1974), while at other sites the male line is emphasized, as at Tikal (Haviland 1977) and Copan (Stuart and Schele 1986). There are prominent portraits of elite women in association with rulership—as at Piedras Negras (Proskouriakoff 1960), Coba (Marcus 1976), Yaxchilan, and Palenque (Schele and Miller 1986), or paired male/female portraits, as at Calakmul (Marcus 1987). At other sites, including Tikal, Quirigua, and Copan, depictions of women are rare or nonexistent. While there is no evidence that women ruled at these later sites, there is good evidence for women rulers at Palenque and several of the Usumacinta sites. This pattern of variation within the uppermost echelons of elite society is consistent with other evidence for diversity in Classic Maya social organization. There may have been additional advantages for flexibility in determining the lines of succession for Maya rulers, for the availability of more options for succession allow for a more successful transmission of power and may help avoid potentially disastrous power struggles. But even with this evidence of diversity, there is no compelling evidence for anything other than a patrilineal system of descent among the ruling houses of the Late Classic Maya lowlands.

Of course, in working with the deciphered accounts of ruling genealogies, like all such examples of historical texts, archaeologists seek independent evidence in an attempt to separate fact from fiction. In the case of citations of founders and early members of ruling dynasties in much later inscriptions, there is often reason to suspect retrospective "creative history" on the part of Late Classic rulers. But, there are several cases where a little digging has produced hard evidence to support and/or refine these later claims, as at Tikal (Coggins n.d.; Jones 1977; Schele and Freidel 1990), Quirigua (Sharer 1978; Ashmore 1984), and Copan (Fash n.d.; Schele and Freidel 1990). At Copan, for example, ongoing excavations in Structure 16 and the adjacent Acropolis have produced architectural, sculptural, and textual evidence contemporary with the reign of Yax Kuk Mo, including the discovery this year of the earliest dated stela known at the site (Fash n.d.; Williamson n.d.), apparently dedicated by Yax Kuk Mo's successor to his illustrious predecessor (Stuart et al. 1989).

The lines of evidence from our excavations in the Acropolis East Court suggest that the Acropolis itself was established as the ritual and residential compound for Copan's rulers during the lifetime of the dynastic founder, adding additional support for the claims in later texts. These findings include the discovery of several fifth-century structures under the East Court—with one being of particular interest since it is a palace-type building with a fragmentary painted glyphic inscription on an interior wall, datable to the very period of Yax Kuk Mo's reign (Sharer, Sedat, and Miller n.d.).

Regardless of how well such specific cases can be documented by combining historical and archaeological evidence, we must remember that within each polity the ruling lineage represents only one family among many such elite families. And beyond the elite level, the archaeological evidence for the existence of descent groups among the Late Classic non-elite is indirect at best. The case for such organizations in the later ethnohistoric record (and among some contemporary Maya groups, such as those of highland Chiapas) is highly suggestive, but once again one must be wary of many potential pitfalls in applying the direct historic approach to the Classic Maya.

Even with the overwhelming evidence for a patrilineal pattern of descent, there have been a number of interpretations that propose other descent systems among the Maya. A case for a complementary matrilineal system, including a special term for the matriline and the inheritance of the matronym, was advanced a number of years ago (Roys 1940, 1965). An ances-

99

tral bilateral or double-descent system has been reconstructed from analyses of kinship terms (Eggan 1934; Edmonson 1979). Haviland (1968) has argued against these as earlier forms, presenting a case for an ancestral cognatic system in which descent-group membership was through *either* the male or female line, based on individual choice. In fact, Haviland (1968: 104) points out that cognatic organizations can be documented for the colonial period Chontal (Scholes and Roys 1948) and the present-day Chorti (Wisdom 1940).

The existence of matrilineal and/or double descent among the Maya was the subject of a flurry of comments nearly two decades ago (Haviland 1971; Adams 1972). The principal advocates of these alternative positions, in addition to Roys, have been Coe (1965), who proposed that double descent was *the* norm for the Classic lowland Maya, along with Joyce (1981), Thompson (1982), and Fox and Justeson (1986). Marcus (1983: 470) suggests that bilateral descent may have been more likely among the Maya elite as a means to distinguish this group from the non-elite, while the latter was probably more firmly associated with patrilineal descent (see also Edmonson 1979). While it is impossible to rule out the possibility that some form of bilateral or double descent operated in varying ways and with varying importance within many Maya groups, including the Lacandon (Edmonson 1979) and even as possible variations among the Classic lowland Maya, the ethnohistorical and ethnographic evidence remains strongly on the side of patrilineal descent. In fact, the cases for matrilineal and double descent have been effectively critiqued by Haviland (1971, 1977) and Hopkins (1988).

### APPROACHES TO RECONSTRUCTING CLASSIC MAYA SOCIAL ORGANIZATION

As should be clear from the foregoing, and as in all archaeological interpretation, Mayanists are reliant on analogical models to reconstruct the varieties of Classic social organization. In this effort we find two basic approaches—those based on general analogies drawn from comparable non-Maya sources or those based on specific analogies drawn from Maya sources (cf. Demarest 1989). Both approaches have merit—general analogies are necessary to test the full range of possibilities, while specific analogies certainly provide more precise possibilities in evaluating the archaeological record. Thus, it should be obvious that the application of both forms of analogies are desirable, although as stated previously (Marcus 1983; Sharer n.d.), the rich resources provided by the Maya themselves have been relatively underutilized by archaeologists seeking analogies to interpret the past.

Regardless of the source of the analogy, the most critical aspect in deriving archaeological inferences lies in the evaluation of models so as to arrive at the most likely reconstruction of the past. The basic procedures for doing this were described a number of years ago by Binford (1967): generating models from secure analogies, followed by defining a series of tests for such models based on how the archaeological record should appear under the conditions described by the model.

It is hardly surprising that there have been so few archaeological studies involving the organization of Classic Maya society that are based on this procedure—given the general difficulty in correlating archaeological evidence with social factors, and the specific problems of preservation and transformations of the archaeological record faced by Maya lowland archaeologists. But progress is being made as the entire field of Maya archaeology has adopted increasingly sophisticated methodological and theoretical frameworks over the past few decades (see Sabloff 1990). Some of the best examples of innovative research aimed at ancient Maya social organization deal with non-elite household organization. For example, two recent studies evaluate the utility of a generationally extended family model to explain a common pattern of domestic settlement found at lowland Maya sites—specifically the function and growth of the patio groupings of residential structures—one by Tourtellot (1988b) at Seibal, the other by Haviland (1988) at Tikal. Both studies conclude that the generationally extended family model provides the best explanation for the archaeologically observed patterns. While the source of the model is a general ethnographic analogy (Goody 1958), Tourtellot does anchor some of his tests in data from lowland Kekchi Maya ethnographic studies by Wilk (1983). In addition, as mentioned previously, in his analysis of the Seibal settlement data, Tourtellot (1988a) correlates specific cross-cultural ethnographic studies with the archaeological record to suggest the most plausible forms of social organization, including indications of a pattern of patrilocal residence.

In several related papers, Wilk (1983, 1984, 1988) has presented household organizational models drawn from both general analogies (feudal Japan) and specific ones (the Kekchi Maya). His ethnographic study of the lowland Kekchi found that wealth and larger houses were associated with heads of household clusters (Wilk and Wilhite n.d.). There are basic differences between this ethnographic analogy and the Classic lowland Maya, given the pioneering context of the modern Belizean Kekchi settlements (Wilk, Reynolds, and Wilhite n.d.). Therefore, this specific analogy has been more helpful in reconstructing the organization of the initial (Preclassic) settlers in the eastern lowlands. But given Tourtellot's Seibal study that found a lack of correlation between dwelling size and wealth or status (Tourtellot 1988a: 362), it may be possible to propose a testable hypothesis that links the largest dwellings with heads of household clusters, provided we can derive indicators of such status that survive in the archaeological record.

At this point in the study of Classic social organization, it seems to me that Maya archaeologists are just beginning to meet the challenges posed by the need to define rigorous and testable models from relevant analogies. In attempting to do this we are confronted by something of a paradox. While the inherent limitations of the archaeological record have always made reconstruction of ancient social organizations extremely difficult, Maya archaeologists are in a unique position to utilize an unusually rich resource of epigraphic, ethnohistoric, and ethnographic data dealing with many aspects of past social life. While the Classic textual record helps considerably in reconstructing specific aspects of ruling-elite society, our major problem remains linking the broader Conquest period resource base to the Classic period. But, provided that we can successfully span the intervening centuries (see Rice [1988] for an example of the Classic-Postclassic transition in lowland households), we will be in an excellent position to make better use of established procedures to apply this ethnohistoric resource base to generate testable models of the past. Once such models are defined, we can then begin archaeological research specifically designed to test and refine these models, and thus begin to delineate the various forms of social organization that characterized the Classic Maya. In the meantime, despite some excellent studies that provide an effective starting point, we will have barely begun to attack the problem of describing and understanding Classic Maya social organization.

## BIBLIOGRAPHY

ADAMS, RICHARD E. W.
- 1970 Suggested Classic Period Occupational Specialization in the Southern Maya Lowlands. In *Monographs and Papers in Maya Archaeology* (W.R. Bullard, ed.): 487–502. Papers of the Peabody Museum of Archaeology and Ethnology 61. Harvard University, Cambridge.
- 1972 Reply to Haviland. *American Antiquity* 37: 140–141.

ASHMORE, WENDY A. (ED.)
- 1981 *Lowland Maya Settlement Patterns.* University of New Mexico Press, Albuquerque.

ASHMORE, WENDY A.
- 1984 Quirigua Archaeology and History Revisited. *Journal of Field Archaeology* 11:365–386.

BEALS, RALPH
- 1932 Unilateral Organizations in Mexico. *American Anthropologist* 34: 467–475.

BECKER, MARSHALL J.
- 1972 Plaza Plans at Quirigua, Guatemala. *Katunob* 8 (2): 47–62.
- 1973 Archaeological Evidence for Occupational Specialization among the Classic Period Maya at Tikal, Guatemala. *American Antiquity* 38: 396–406.
- n.d. The Identification of a Second Plaza Plan at Tikal, Guatemala, and Its Implications for Ancient Maya Social Organization. Ph.D. dissertation, Department of Anthropology, University of Pennsylvania, 1971.

BINFORD, LEWIS
- 1967 Smudge Pits and Hide Smoking: The Use of Analogy in Archaeological Reasoning. *American Antiquity* 32: 1–12.

COE, MICHAEL D.
- 1965 A Model of Ancient Community Structure in the Maya Lowlands. *Southwestern Journal of Anthropology* 21: 97–114.

COGGINS, CLEMENCY C.
- n.d. Painting and Drawing Styles at Tikal: An Historical and Iconographic Reconstruction. Ph.D. dissertation, Department of Art, Harvard University, 1975.

CULBERT, T. PATRICK, AND DON RICE (EDS.)
- 1990 *Precolumbian Population History in the Maya Lowlands.* University of New Mexico Press, Albuquerque.

DEMAREST, ARTHUR A.
- 1989 The Olmec and the Rise of Civilization in Eastern Mesoamerica. In *Regional Perspectives on the Olmec* (R. Sharer and D. Grove, eds.): 303–344. Cambridge University Press, Cambridge.

EDMONSON, MUNRO
- 1979 Some Postclassic Questions about the Classic Maya. *Estudios de Cultura Maya* 12: 157–178.

EGGAN, FRED
    1934   The Maya Kinship System and Cross-Cousin Marriage. *American Anthropologist* 36: 188–202.

FARRISS, NANCY
    1984   *Maya Society under Colonial Rule: The Collective Enterprise of Survival.* Princeton University Press, Princeton.

FASH, WILLIAM L.
    n.d.   Sociopolitical Evolution in Copan: Correlations and Contradictions in the Material and State Records. Paper presented at the 88th Annual Meeting of the American Anthropological Association, Washington, D.C., 1989.

FLANNERY, KENT V., AND MARCUS WINTER
    1976   Analyzing Household Activities. In *The Early Mesoamerican Village* (K. Flannery, ed.): 34–47. Academic Press, New York.

FOX, JOHN, AND JOHN JUSTESON
    1986   Classic Maya Dynastic Alliance and Succession. In *Supplement to Handbook of Middle American Indians,* Vol. 4 (V. Bricker and R. Spores, eds): 7–34. University of Texas Press, Austin.

FREIDEL, DAVID A.
    1979   Culture Areas and Interaction Spheres: Contrasting Approaches to the Emergence of Civilization in the Maya Lowlands. *American Antiquity* 44: 36–44.

FREIDEL, DAVID A., AND JEREMY A. SABLOFF
    1984   *Cozumel: Late Postclassic Settlement Patterns.* Academic Press, Orlando.

FREIDEL, DAVID A., AND LINDA SCHELE
    1988   Kingship in the Late Preclassic Maya Lowlands: The Instruments and Places of Ritual Power. *American Anthropologist* 90: 547–567.

GOODY, JACK (ED.)
    1958   *The Developmental Cycle in Domestic Groups.* Cambridge University Press, Cambridge.

HAVILAND, WILLIAM A.
    1965   Prehistoric Settlement at Tikal, Guatemala. *Expedition* 7 (3): 14–23.
    1967   Stature at Tikal, Guatemala: Implications for Ancient Maya Demography and Social Organization. *American Antiquity* 32: 316–325.
    1968   *Ancient Lowland Maya Social Organization.* Middle American Research Institute, Publication 26 (5). Tulane University, New Orleans.
    1970   Tikal, Guatemala and Mesoamerican Urbanism. *World Archaeology* 2: 186–198.
    1971   Entombment, Authority, and Descent at Altar de Sacrificios, Guatemala. *American Antiquity* 36: 102–105.
    1972   Principles of Descent in Sixteenth Century Yucatan. *Katunob* 8 (2): 63–73.
    1977   Dynastic Genealogies from Tikal, Guatemala. *American Antiquity* 42: 61–67.
    1981   Dower Houses and Minor Centers at Tikal, Guatemala: An Investigation into the Identification of Valid Units in Settlement Hierarchies. In

*Lowland Maya Settlement Patterns* (W. Ashmore, ed.): 89–117. University of New Mexico Press, Albuquerque.

1985    Population and Social Dynamics: The Dynasties and Social Structure of Tikal. *Expedition* 27 (3): 34–41.

1988    Musical Hammocks at Tikal: Problems with Reconstructing Household Composition. In *Household and Community in the Mesoamerican Past* (R. Wilk and W. Ashmore, eds): 121–134. University of New Mexico Press, Albuquerque.

n.d.    Excavation of Small Structures in the Northeast Quadrant of Tikal, Guatemala. Ph.D. dissertation, Department of Anthropology, University of Pennsylvania, Philadelphia, 1963.

HELMUTH, NICHOLAS

1977    Cholti-Lacandon (Chiapas) and Peten Ytza Agriculture, Settlement Pattern and Population. In *Social Process in Maya Prehistory* (N. Hammond, ed.): 421–448. Academic Press, London.

HILL, ROBERT M., AND JOHN MONAGHAN

1987    *Continuities in Highland Maya Social Organization: Ethnohistory in Sacapulas, Guatemala*. University of Pennsylvania Press, Philadelphia.

HOPKINS, NICHOLAS

1988    Classic Mayan Kinship Systems: Epigraphic and Ethnographic Evidence for Patrilineality. *Estudios de Cultura Maya* 17: 87–121.

HOUSTON, STEPHEN D.

1989    *Maya Glyphs*. British Museum Publications, London.

JOYCE, R.A.

1981    Classic Maya Kinship and Descent: An Alternative Suggestion. *Journal of the Steward Anthropological Society* 13 (1): 45–57.

JONES, CHRISTOPHER

1977    Inauguration Dates of Three Late Classic Rulers of Tikal. *American Antiquity* 42: 28–60.

LAS CASAS, B. DE

1909    *Apologética historia de las Indias*. Serrano y Ganz, Madrid.

MARCUS, JOYCE

1976    *Emblem and State in the Classic Maya Lowlands*. Dumbarton Oaks, Washington, D.C.

1978    Archaeology and Religion: A Comparison of the Zapotec and Maya. *World Archaeology* 10: 172–191.

1983    Lowland Maya Archaeology at the Crossroads. *American Antiquity* 48: 454–488.

1987    *The Inscriptions of Calakmul: Royal Marriage at a Maya City in Campeche, Mexico*. University of Michigan Museum of Anthropology, Technical Report 21. Ann Arbor.

n.d.    Royal Families, Royal Texts: Examples from the Zapotec and Maya. In *Mesoamerican Elites: An Archaeological Assessment* (D. Chase and A. Chase, eds.). University of Oklahoma Press, Norman. (in press)

MATHEWS, PETER, AND LINDA SCHELE

1974    Lords of Palenque: The Glyphic Evidence. In *Primera Mesa Redonda de*

Palenque (Part 1): 63–76. The Robert Louis Stevenson School, Pebble Beach, CA.

MILLER, MARY ELLEN
1985  Tikal, Guatemala: A Rationale for the Placement of the Funerary Pyramids. *Expedition* 34: 6–15.

MOLLOY, J.P., AND WILLIAM L. RATHJE
1974  Sexploitation among the Late Classic Maya. In *Mesoamerican Archaeology: New Approaches* (N. Hammond, ed.): 431–444. University of Texas Press, Austin.

MURDOCK, GEORGE P.
1960  Cognatic Forms of Social Organization. In *Social Structure in Southeast Asia* (G. Murdock, ed.). Viking Fund Publications in Anthropology No. 29. New York.

NUTINI, HUGO G.
1961  Clan Organization in a Nahuatl Speaking Village in the State of Tlaxcala, Mexico. *American Anthropologist* 63: 62–78.

PROSKOURIAKOFF, TATIANA
1960  Historical Implications of a Pattern of Dates at Piedras Negras, Guatemala. *American Antiquity* 25: 454–475.

RICE, DON S.
1988  Classic to Postclassic Maya Household Transitions in the Central Peten, Guatemala. In *Household and Community in the Mesoamerican Past* (R. Wilk and W. Ashmore, eds.): 227–248. University of New Mexico Press, Albuquerque.

RICE, DON S., AND PRUDENCE M. RICE
1980  The Northeast Peten Revisited. *American Antiquity* 45: 432–454.

ROYS, RALPH
1939  *The Titles of Ebtun*. Carnegie Institution of Washington, Publication 505. Washington, D.C.
1940  *Personal Names of the Maya of Yucatan*. Carnegie Institution of Washington, Publication 523, Contribution No. 31. Washington, D.C.
1943  *The Indian Background of Colonial Yucatan*. Carnegie Institution of Washington, Publication 548. Washington, D.C.
1965  Lowland Maya Society at Spanish Contact. In *Handbook of Middle American Indians*, Vol. 3. (R. Wauchope and G. Willey, eds): 659–678. University of Texas Press, Austin.

SABLOFF, JEREMY A.
1990  *The New Archaeology and the Ancient Maya*. W. H. Freeman and Company, New York.

SANDERS, WILLIAM T. (ED.)
1986  *Excavaciones en el Area Urbana de Copan*. Instituto Hondureño de Antropologia e Historia, Tegucigalpa.

SCHELE, LINDA, AND MARY ELLEN MILLER
1986  *The Blood of Kings: Dynasty and Ritual in Maya Art*. Perpetua Press, Los Angeles.

SCHELE, LINDA, AND DAVID A. FREIDEL
    1990  *A Forest of Kings*. William Morrow and Company, New York.

SCHOLES, FRANCE V., AND RALPH L. ROYS
    1948  *The Maya Indians of Acalan-Tixchel: A Contribution to the History and Ethnography of the Yucatan Peninsula*. Carnegie Institution of Washington, Publication 560. Washington, D.C.

SCHORTMAN, EDWARD M.
    1986  Interaction between the Maya and Non-Maya along the Late Classic Southeast Maya Periphery: The View from the Lower Motagua Valley, Guatemala. In *The Southeast Maya Periphery* (P. Urban and E. Schortman, eds.): 114–137. University of Texas Press, Austin.

SHARER, ROBERT J.
    1978  Archaeology and History at Quirigua, Guatemala. *Journal of Field Archaeology* 5: 51–70.
    n.d.  From Prehistoric to Historic Perspective: The Meaning of Our Concept of Maya Civilization. Paper prepared for the School of American Research Advanced Seminar on the Maya, 1986.

SHARER, ROBERT J., DAVID W. SEDAT, AND JULIA MILLER
    n.d.  Toward an Architectural History of the Eastern Acropolis, Copan, Honduras. Paper presented at the 88th Annual Meeting of the American Anthropological Association, Washington, D.C., 1989.

SMITH, A. LEDYARD
    1962  Residential and Associated Structures at Mayapan. In *Mayapan, Yucatan, Mexico* (H. E. D. Pollock, ed.). Carnegie Institution of Washington, Publication 619. Washington, D.C.

SMITH, MICHAEL E.
    1987  Household Possessions and Wealth in Agrarian States: Implications for Archaeology. *Journal of Anthropological Archaeology* 6: 297–335.

STUART, DAVID, AND LINDA SCHELE
    1986  Yax-K'uk-Mo', The Founder of the Lineage of Copan. *Copan Notes*, No. 6. Austin.

STUART, DAVID, N. GRUBE, LINDA SCHELE, AND F. LOUNSBURY
    1989  Stela 63, A New Monument from Copan. *Copan Notes*, No. 56. Austin.

THOMPSON, PHILIP C.
    1982  Dynastic Marriage and Succession at Tikal. *Estudios de Cultura Maya* 14: 261–287.

TOURTELLOT, GAIR
    1988a  *Peripheral Survey and Excavation and Settlement and Community Patterns. Excavations at Seibal* (G. R. Willey, general ed.). Peabody Museum, Memoir 16. Harvard University, Cambridge.
    1988b  Developmental Cycles of Households and Houses at Seibal. In *Household and Community in the Mesoamerican Past* (R. Wilk and W. Ashmore, eds.): 97–120. University of New Mexico Press, Albuquerque.

TOZZER, ALFRED
    1907  *A Comparative Study of the Mayas and Lacandones*. New York.

1941 (ed.) *Landa's Relación de las cosas de Yucatan* (translated and edited with notes). Papers of the Peabody Museum 18. Harvard University, Cambridge.

VOGT, EVON Z.
1983 Some New Themes in Settlement Pattern Research. In *Prehistoric Settlement Patterns: Essays in Honor of Gordon R. Willey* (E. Z. Vogt and R. M. Leventhal, eds.): 3–20. University of New Mexico Press, Albuquerque.

WEBSTER, DAVID
1980 Spatial Bounding and Settlement History at Three Walled Northern Maya Centers. *American Antiquity* 45: 834–844.

WEBSTER, DAVID, AND N. GONLIN
1988 Households of the Humblest Maya. *Journal of Field Archaeology* 15: 169–190.

WEEKS, JOHN
1988 Residential and Local Group Organization in the Maya Lowlands of Southwestern Campeche, Mexico: The Early Seventeenth Century. In *Household and Community in the Mesoamerican Past* (R. Wilk and W. Ashmore, eds): 73–96. University of New Mexico Press, Albuquerque.

WILK, RICHARD R.
1983 Little House in the Jungle: The Causes of Variation in House Size among Modern Maya. *Journal of Anthropological Archaeology* 2: 99–116.
1984 Households in Process: Agricultural Change and Domestic Transformation among the Kekchi Maya of Belize. In *Households: Comparative and Historical Studies of the Domestic Group* (R. Netting, R. Wilk, and E. Arnould, eds): 217–224. University of California Press, Berkeley.
1988 Maya Household Organization: Evidence and Analogies. In *Household and Community in the Mesoamerican Past* (R. Wilk and W. Ashmore, eds): 135–151. University of New Mexico Press, Albuquerque.

WILK, RICHARD R., AND WENDY A. ASHMORE (EDS.)
1988 *Household and Community in the Mesoamerican Past.* University of New Mexico Press, Albuquerque.

WILK, RICHARD R., L. REYNOLDS, AND H. WILHITE
n.d. The Settlement Area Sampling Project at Cuello, 1980. Paper presented at the 45th Annual Meeting of the Society for American Archaeology, Philadelphia, 1980.

WILK, RICHARD R., AND H. WILHITE
n.d. The Settlement Area Sampling Program at Cuello. Unpublished manuscript, 1982.

WILLEY, GORDON R., AND RICHARD M. LEVENTHAL
1979 Prehistoric Settlement at Copan. In *Maya Archaeology and Ethnohistory* (N. Hammond and G. Willey, eds): 75–102. University of Texas Press, Austin.

WILLIAMSON, RICHARD
n.d. The Founder's Temple and Stela; Excavations Beneath Copan Structure 26 First. Paper presented at the 88th Annual Meeting of the Ameri-

can Anthropological Association, Washington, D.C., 1989.

WINTER, MARCUS
    1976    The Archaeological Household Cluster in the Valley of Oaxaca. In *The Early Mesoamerican Village* (K. Flannery, ed.): 25–30. Academic Press, New York.

WISDOM, CHARLES
    1940    *The Chorti Indians of Guatemala*. University of Chicago Press, Chicago.

5

*Ancient Maya Political Organization*

JOYCE MARCUS

UNIVERSITY OF MICHIGAN

FOR HALF A CENTURY, ARCHAEOLOGISTS have noted the apparent homogeneity of lowland Maya culture over an area of approximately 300,000 km$^2$, and have wondered how it achieved such regional uniformity while retaining local diversity (Fig. 1; Morley 1946; Morley and Brainerd 1956: 436; Thompson 1954). Through what form of political and territorial organization was such uniformity achieved? Did powerful, centralized states, whose administrative hierarchies controlled large numbers of interdependent units, give the Maya "organic" solidarity? Or were the Maya composed of hundreds of small, independent units, whose sameness gave them a kind of "mechanical" solidarity?

Archaeologists have changed their minds repeatedly on the topic, often returning to positions they had rejected decades before. In the 1950s, J. Eric Thompson (1950: 7; 1954: 81) and Sylvanus Morley and George Brainerd (1956: 434, 437) imagined the Classic Maya as a theocracy, where priests had complete control and religion was the basis for power. Maya sites were not considered to be multifunctional cities, but "religious centers to which the Maya resorted only for ceremonies" (Morley and Brainerd 1956: 261). They saw no evidence for large-scale warfare or fortifications, only for "occasional raids" undertaken to obtain sacrificial victims. As for unity, Thompson (1954) asked himself the question on page 77 and answered it on page 81:

> Q. Does this unity with local diversification indicate a system of city states, such as existed in Greece or mediaeval Italy, with political independence but a fairly uniform culture and a common language, or does it point to a single state?
> A. I am inclined to think of the Maya lowlands during the Classic Period as a loose federation of autonomous city states, the government of which was largely in the hands of a small caste of priests and nobles, related by blood and dominated by religious motifs.

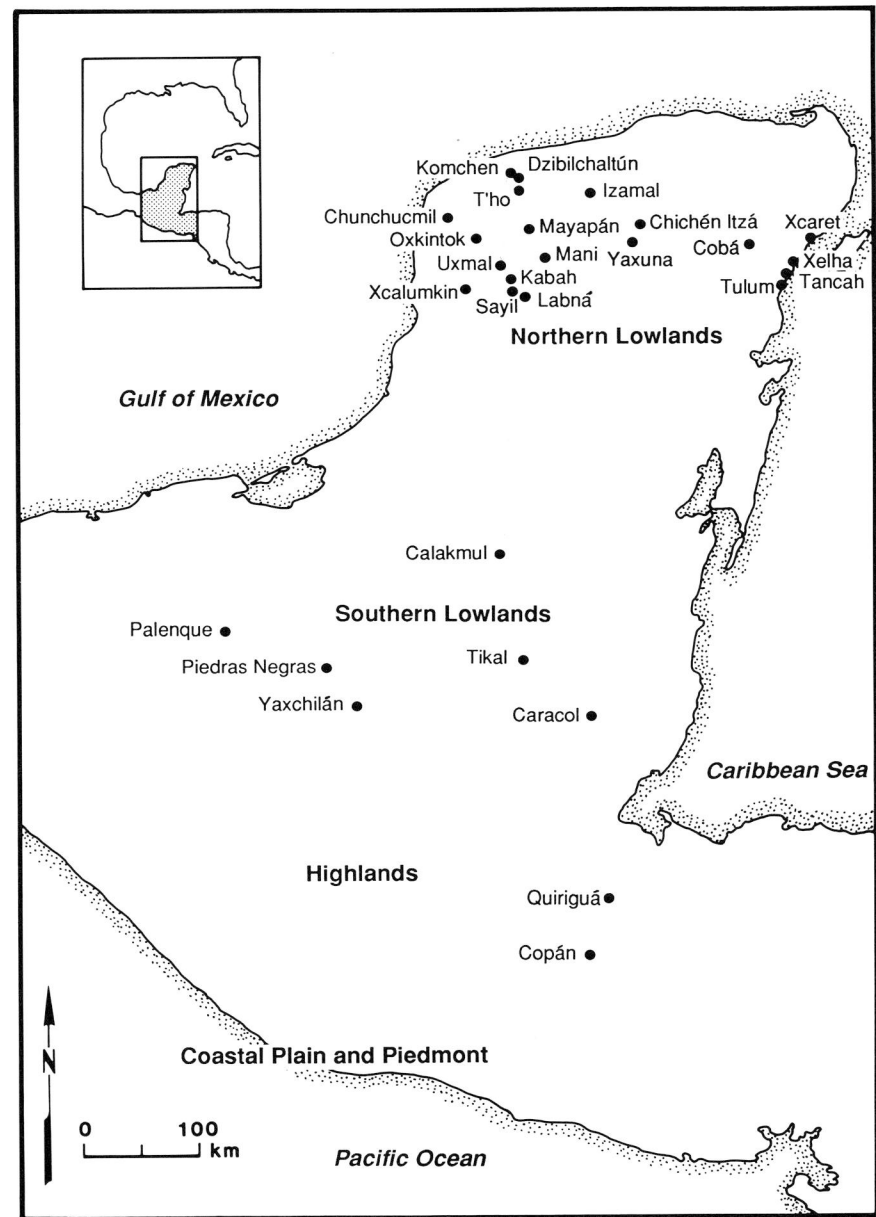

Fig. 1 The Maya area, showing its three principal subregions—the northern lowlands, the southern lowlands, and the highlands. Although significant local and regional diversity exists, the area as a whole shares a common cultural heritage and linguistic ancestry.

While this was a reasonable answer for its time, there already were inconsistencies in Thompson's scheme. In the same book in which he declared Maya centers autonomous, he made it very clear that he felt Bonampak was administratively under Yaxchilan (Thompson 1954: 82). He omitted mention of the fact that the Greek city-states, to which he had drawn comparisons, lost their autonomy under the powerful Mycenaean state and only regained it after the Mycenaeans fell (Marcus 1989; Taylour 1964; Snodgrass 1977, 1980).

In the 1960s, there was a move away from Thompson's city-state model, due largely to extensive mapping and excavation at the site of Tikal (Carr and Hazard 1961; Haviland 1966, 1967, 1970; W. R. Coe 1962, 1965a, 1965b, 1967). The University of Pennsylvania's Tikal project (1956–1970) yielded evidence for a city of perhaps 60,000 people during the Late Classic period (A.D. 600–850). Tikal's areal extent, architectural monumentality, Cycle 8 stelae, central location within the Peten, and large population estimates changed everyone's mind. When I began graduate school in the late 1960s, Tikal was considered to be *the* capital—the *only* capital—for the entire southern lowlands. Thus, for a time Thompson's alternative model of a single state, with its promise of organic solidarity, had the upper hand.

Several other discoveries followed rapidly. Tatiana Proskouriakoff's (1960) revelation that Maya texts referred to actual rulers' exploits, not simply astronomical events, was followed by discoveries and excavations of defensive works at Tikal (Puleston and Callender 1967), Becan (Webster 1976), Cuca (Fig. 2), Chaccob, Dzonot Ake (Webster 1978, 1979), and Muralla de Leon (Rice and Rice 1981). These discoveries led to the reconsideration of scenes of warfare on the Bonampak murals and Yaxchilan stelae, all of which suggested that Maya warfare was much more than "occasional raids for sacrificial victims."

The 1970s brought gradual awareness that Tikal had not been the only capital of the whole southern lowlands. In the 1970s, as a result of combining Central Place models with Berlin's (1958) definition of Emblem Glyphs, I proposed a model in which Tikal was one of four major centers dominating the southern lowlands at A.D. 731 (Marcus 1973, 1976, n.d.d); Copan, Tikal, Calakmul(?), and Palenque were seen as primary centers ruling secondary centers, tertiary centers, and villages. Not long after this, Adams and Jones (1981) agreed that there had been large regional states in the southern and northern lowlands, and Bove (1981), in a trend surface analysis for the lowlands at A.D. 800, also found evidence for regional states.

More recently, in the late 1980s, there has been a return to Thompson's 1954 view. Peter Mathews (1985) has applied Thiessen polygons to the Maya lowlands on the assumption that all sites with Emblem Glyphs were completely autonomous, which would imply that the Late Classic was a time of mechanical solidarity among small, loosely affiliated polities. In-

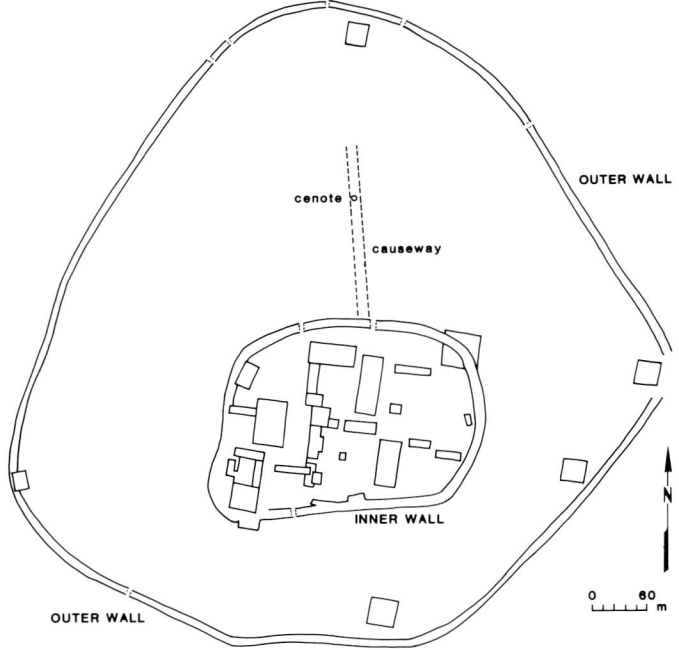

Fig. 2 Concentric walls define two zones at the northern Yucatan site of Cuca. The inner zone—an area of less than 5 hectares—contains most of the impressive civic and residential Puuc-style architecture. The outer wall encloses a total area (*including* the inner zone) of 33 hectares. A similarly dense occupation continued outside of the walled inner and outer zones. The walls were apparently constructed during the Puuc period and served to protect members of the upper stratum from outside attack. Although Cuca was not founded as a fortified center (as Chaccob was), the Cuca elite apparently responded effectively to competitive pressures by constructing a defensive system (redrawn after Webster 1979: map 1).

deed, since Bonampak's polygon is separate from Yaxchilan's in Mathews' scheme, the city states he suggests would have been even smaller than those in Thompson's model.

What I will do in this paper are four things. First, I will argue that a problem shared by all these models—including my own in 1973—is that they are *static,* rather than *dynamic.* We need a new model that allows for change over time, and we need to consider the underlying processes that bring about such change.

Second, I will argue that models from classical Greece, medieval Italy, or feudal Europe are less useful than the eyewitness accounts of the Maya from the Spaniards who conquered them. I will use those sixteenth- and seventeenth-century accounts, in Maya and Spanish, to construct a dynamic model for Maya political organization at the time of the Conquest.

Third, I will evaluate that dynamic model in relation to the Classic Maya—first to see how well it fits, and later to see if we can use it to organize and explain the political events of the period. In the process, I will reveal which earlier models I think are probably right, and which are probably wrong.

Fourth, I will argue that our dynamic model may fit a number of archaic states in both the New World and the Old, making the Maya seem more the result of nomothetic regularities than of tropical mysteries.

### THE MAYA AS AN ARCHAIC STATE

From at least A.D. 534 onward, the Maya displayed the archaeological manifestations of what anthropologists have called an "archaic state": a stratified, highly centralized, internally specialized society with a professional ruling class. As a political system, the archaic state is seen as having more institutionalized power than the ranked but unstratified societies that preceded it, particularly in the areas of waging war and exacting tribute (Flannery 1972; Marcus 1976, 1983a, 1992; Flannery and Marcus 1983: 80–83). In general, the state's control of *information* and *manpower*—whether for coordinating public construction projects, warfare, or tribute collection—was much more impressive than that displayed by rank societies (or "chiefdoms").

Significant differences between rank societies and states include: (1) a change in the settlement (and administrative) hierarchy from three levels to four; (2) an escalation in the ideology that linked rulers to a sacred supernatural origin, thereby giving them the divine right to rule; (3) a severing of the kinship bonds that formerly linked the rulers to the ruled; (4) the construction of a palace as the ruler's official residence; (5) the emergence of full-time specialization; and (6) the change from a single centralized authority figure (a "chief" for want of a better term) to a government that employed *legal* force while denying its citizens the use of *personal* force (Fried 1960, 1967; Service 1962, 1975; Flannery 1972; Sanders 1974; Marcus 1974b, 1976: 22–27, 1978, 1987, 1992; de Montmollin 1989; Wright 1977; Wright and Johnson 1975; Flannery and Marcus 1983: 79–83).

Most archaic states in Mesoamerica, including the Late Classic Maya, shared four important features: (1) two class-endogamous strata ("nobles" and "commoners"),[1] whose members were distributed unevenly within a

---

[1] Note, however, that *within* each stratum there are several ranks (Marcus 1992), such that we can speak of a continuum of ranks or categories within the noble stratum and a continuum within the commoner stratum.

single site and throughout the hierarchy of sites; (2) a well-developed ideology of stratification in which a belief in separate descent distinguished lower-stratum commoners from upper-stratum nobles; (3) a four-tiered hierarchy of settlements, the upper three of which had administrative functions, with the fourth being simple villages; and (4) a hierarchy of decision-makers within settlements, through at least the three upper levels of the settlement hierarchy; these decision-makers were also differentially distributed.

All or most of these features, including the four-tiered site hierarchy, appeared in the southern lowlands by A.D. 534 (Marcus 1974a, 1983a, 1992, n.d.d). Particularly significant is the Maya palace, which appears by the fifth or sixth century A.D. Maya rulers' palaces were built for them by their subjects and reflect the institution of kingship; for although "chiefs frequently can summon considerable numbers of workers for sustained periods of time for the construction of such public buildings as tombs and temples, they cannot amass such levels of manpower for the construction of residences for themselves" (Sanders 1974: 109).

A key concept in understanding archaic states is that of *hierarchy*, because no state lacked it. State hierarchies were multilevel, and, as we shall see, they could be very dynamic over time. There were hierarchies of political personnel, of military personnel, of religious personnel, and so on, along with abundant evidence to suggest that these different hierarchies were not isomorphic (Marcus 1983a: 466). In fact, one of our future goals should be to distinguish these different kinds of hierarchies in archaic states, and to compare them—political hierarchy vs. site-size hierarchy, religious hierarchy vs. economic hierarchy, and so forth (Marcus 1983a: 464–466, 1983b, 1984). Furthermore, accumulating evidence indicates that the Maya had a hierarchy similar to that discussed by Lösch (1954), in which settlements of the same size need not have all of the same functions, and in which the larger settlements need not have all of the functions of smaller places (Marcus 1976: 24–25). In particular, smaller sites sometimes retained special functions not shared by larger centers (Marcus 1976: 25, 1983a: 477).

## A MODEL BASED ON THE LOWLAND MAYA THEMSELVES

It has always struck me as odd that archaeologists and art historians have drawn so many of their models for the Classic Maya from medieval Europe, the Greeks and Romans, southeast Asia, or the twentieth-century United States. Do we really need to go that far afield when we have eyewitness accounts of the lowland Maya, written by the first Europeans to contact them?

In this section I will present a model for Maya political and territorial organization drawn from three sources. The first source consists of sixteenth and seventeenth-century Spanish descriptions of Maya life in Yucatan and El Peten. The second includes *pepet tsibil,* the circular paintings or

*Ancient Maya Political Organization*

"maps" on which the Indians depicted their territories. The third source consists of the terms the Maya themselves used for their own political and territorial units, drawn from dictionaries of the early Colonial period. I believe this model accounts for more features of the eighth-century Maya than could any model drawn from the Old World.

*Sixteenth-Century Yucatan*

When the Spaniards first contacted the Itza Maya who lived around Lake Peten Itza in northern Guatemala, they were told by those Indians that their neighbor to the north was a "nation" or "kingdom" called Yucatan. Not only did their neighbors to the south view them as a "nation" ("polity" would be a better term), that is also how the Yucatec Maya viewed themselves.

According to sixteenth-century sources (Chi 1582 in Tozzer 1941; Ciudad Real [1588] 1873, Book 2: 470–471; Landa 1566 in Tozzer 1941; López de Cogolludo [1688] 1867–68, Book 2, Chap. 1; Noyes 1932: 354–355), Yucatan had twice been united into one "empire," which viewed itself as a single people. The first time such centralized administration, called *mul tepal* or "joint rule," occurred was when Chichen Itza was the capital of Yucatan (ca. A.D. 1000–1221). The second time was when Mayapan served as the capital (ca. A.D. 1250–1450). In the *Relaciones de Yucatán* (Vol. 11: 118), written in the 1580s, Mayapan is reported to have been the last true city of the Maya.

Ethnohistoric data (Tozzer 1941: 26, 36; López de Cogolludo 1867–68, Book 2, Chap. 1; Ciudad Real 1873, Book 2; Noyes 1932; Roys 1957, 1962) indicate that Mayapan was co-ruled by a group of lords who had been drawn into the capital from different provinces of Yucatan. This apparently voluntaristic confederation lasted about two hundred years before Mayapan collapsed and Yucatan broke up into sixteen provinces. Members of the Xiu lineage (helped by the Itza and other lineages at Mayapan) conspired against the Cocom lineage and killed all but one of the male Cocom leaders. This act of treachery led to the sacking and abandonment of Mayapan (Noyes 1932; Landa in Tozzer 1941).

It is not yet clear how comparable Mayapan's rise and decline was to that of Postclassic Chichen Itza, which is said to have undergone its renaissance "when the four divisions were called together" (Tozzer 1941: 21). Ralph Roys (1933: 139) suggests that "this method of organization was the result of amalgamation of four different peoples into one (Itza) nation" (see below). At any rate, this account of a voluntaristic confederation that lasted two hundred years and then broke up into more balkanized units reminds us of Richard Blanton's (1978, 1983) model for the earlier rise and fall of the Zapotec state at Monte Alban.

Less than one hundred years before the arrival of the Spaniards, and certainly related to the abandonment of Mayapan, the Yucatec Maya "kingdom" or regional state had split into at least sixteen territorial units. Each of

*Joyce Marcus*

these units was called a *cuchcabal,* a term variously defined as "territory," "jurisdiction," "province," "region," and "all the subjects of one ruler." Helping to provide the last meaning of *cuchcabal* was the term *cuch,* which meant "responsibility," "the load on one's back," or "people one controls as subjects" (Martínez Hernández 1929: 205–209). Therefore, it seems clear that *cuchcabal* referred both to the territorial/geographic unit and to a group of people who were the subjects of one ruler (Marcus 1983b). This last meaning of *cuchcabal* was a very ancient and essential aspect of the Maya concept of territory and hierarchy.

In a series of important publications, ethnohistorian Roys (1943, 1957, 1965) identified three types of territorial organization that characterized the sixteen provinces that existed in Yucatan following the breakup of Mayapan. Let us look at these three types of organization carefully, for they allow us to construct our model for Postclassic Maya political organization.

*Type A.* One type of province (Fig. 3) was ruled by a *halach uinic,* a member of the hereditary nobility who held the title of *ahau* ("lord") of the province. In addition to ruling the entire province, he was also the *batab* (local ruler, governor) of the town where he lived. Below him were a series of towns ruled by *batabob*[2] or local rulers, who were important members of the hereditary elite but subordinate to the *halach uinic.* The *halach uinic* had the right to exact tribute from all the towns of his province, and in times of war he could call up the entire male population for military service (Roys 1957: 6). The town where the *halach uinic* resided in his palace was called *holcacab* or *hol cah* (*hol* = head; *cah* = town)—the "head town," or capital, of the province.

The office of territorial ruler or *ahau* was hereditary. After the death of a territorial ruler, brothers or sons followed him in office. Roys identified the provinces of Ah Kin Chel, Cochuah, Mani, Hocaba, Sotuta, and Cehpech as examples of this type of territorial organization.

*Type B.* Roys' second type of province (Fig. 3) had no single individual, or *halach uinic,* at the top. Rather, most of the local lords (*batabob*) were members of the same lineage, and that lineage held control even though different brothers and relatives administered different towns. In other words, a web of kin ties linked the towns and provided cohesion. Examples of this type of rule characterized the provinces of Ah Canul and Cupul. In both cases there is evidence of significant competition and jockeying for power among lineage lords. In fact, with the arrival of the Spaniards, some Ah Canul lords allied with the Spaniards, while others fought against them. The province of Cupul also provides many examples of intraprovincial strife. However, when an outside threat was felt by the Cupul, the lords of various towns banded together, forgot their differences, and fought together against the Spaniards.

[2] The suffix "*ob*" indicates a plural in Maya.

# Ancient Maya Political Organization

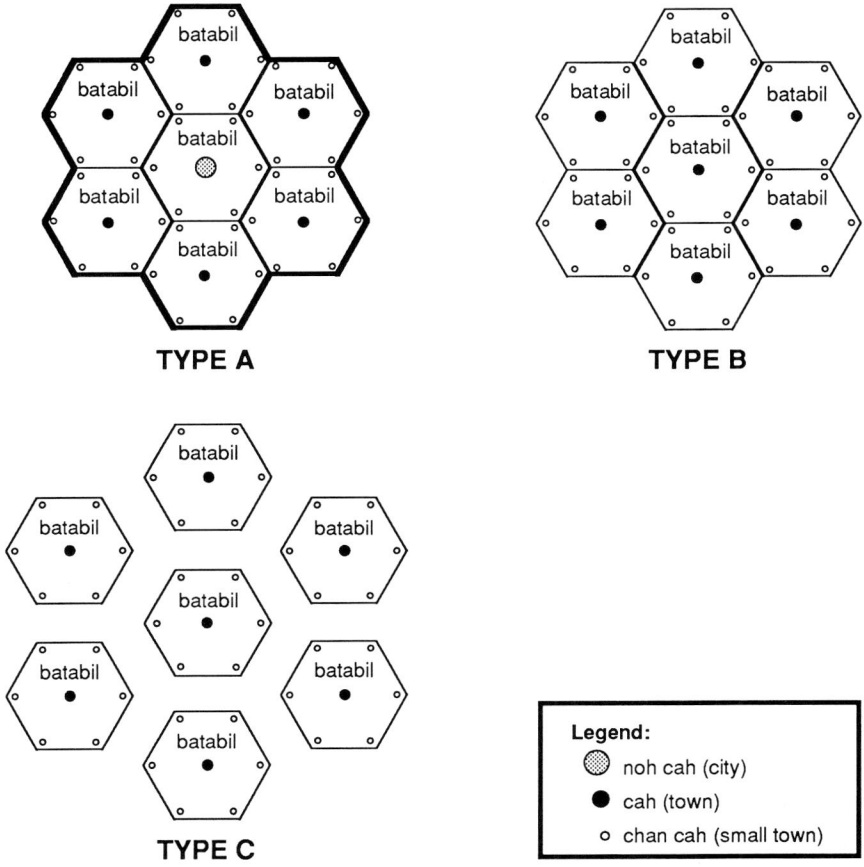

Fig. 3 Schematic representations of Roys' three types of provinces (*cuchcabalob*):

*Type A.* A centralized polity with a territorial ruler (*halach uinic*) who resided in the *noh cah* or city (stippled circle) of the province. The *halach uinic* also ruled a series of dependencies (*batabil*) administered by local rulers (*batabob*). Each *batab*'s town is shown as a black dot; his villages are small white circles.

*Type B.* This type of province had no overall territorial ruler. Instead, the province was co-administered by related *batabob*, usually members of the same lineage, each of whose towns is shown as a black dot.

*Type C.* This type of province was administered by a loose affiliation of towns (black dots) headed by unrelated *batabob*, each of whom controlled a set of smaller villages (white circles).

*Type C.* The provinces of Ecab, Uaymil, Chakan, and Chikinchel provided Roys (1957: 6) with a third type of territorial entity (Fig. 3), one he hesitated to label "organization" because it consisted of loosely allied groups of towns. These groups of towns were temporarily independent because they had been able to avoid incorporation into more powerful provinces. In contrast to the provinces ruled by a *halach uinic,* which tended to occur near the old capital of Mayapan, these loosely united provinces tended to occur nearer the outskirts of the Yucatec system. Had the Spaniards not arrived when they did, it is likely that these units eventually would have been incorporated into more powerful provinces. Thus, had the Yucatec Maya had more time to reorganize themselves following the collapse of Mayapan, we would probably have examples of only Roys' first two types of provinces. In the sixteenth-century documents there are numerous cases of more aggressive groups, like the Xiu, moving to take towns from the Itza (Roys 1957).

It is significant that warfare and competition existed *within* provinces as well as *between* provinces. In other words, when we find evidence for warfare, we cannot assume that the parties involved were separate polities, for it may have been capital vs. dependency. Within northern Yucatan such strife took place between lords at the same hierarchical level and between lords at different levels of the regional hierarchy. For example, in the Cupul province, different rulers of relatively equal status declared war on each other. The Cupul ruler of Ekbalam took captives from the town of Nabalam, where another Cupul lord ruled (*Relaciones de Yucatán,* Vol. 13: 161). The elimination of a brother, an uncooperative relative, or potential threat probably occurred much more often than it was recorded.

What all three types of provinces described by Roys had in common were the *batabob,* or hereditary local lords who governed the towns. In provinces that had a *halach uinic,* he was the one who mediated all interaction with other provinces. In cases where a *halach uinic* was lacking, the *batabob* of a province tried to reach some consensus before acting. The lack of a supreme ruler in such provinces led to dynamic instability, since hereditary lords at the level of *batab* were continuously concerned with where they ranked relative to their noble kinsmen. Many battles were "battles of ranking," which contributed volatility to the regional hierarchy. Having a *halach uinic* gave a province greater stability, but with loss of autonomy by the *batabob;* having no *halach uinic* gave the *batabob* more autonomy, but at the cost of greater volatility. Having only loose alliances left a province continually vulnerable to takeover.

Before moving on to discuss El Peten, let me emphasize what I believe to be the most important lessons of Roys' work. First, it appears that the *province* was the most stable political unit through time. No matter what happened to a province, whether it joined a confederacy or was subsumed under a more powerful unit, it retained its integrity.

*Ancient Maya Political Organization*

  Second, Roys' Type A, B, and C polities should *not* be considered alternative static models of how the Maya were organized. Rather, they were stages in the breakup of the regional state or "empire" formerly centered at Mayapan. In other words, they were all part of a *single, dynamic model,* one that changed over time as it swung between high centralization and relative decentralization. First, four Maya territorial units are said to have come together to make Chichen Itza their "capital." This centralized system lasted for perhaps two hundred years, and when it broke down, it almost certainly broke into units like Roys' Types A, B, and C. Later, these multiple units again reunited to form a regional state whose capital was Mayapan. This highly centralized state lasted for two hundred years, and when it broke down it left the Type A, B, and C provinces seen by the Spaniards. Had the Spaniards not arrived, it seems likely that a new centralized regional state, with a new capital, would have formed eventually. What would be interesting to know is whether the sixteen provinces left after the collapse of Mayapan were the same units that had come together to form the *mul tepal.* If so, the boundaries of these provinces might have been the "cleavage planes" along which the regional state was likely to break up when the time came (Marcus 1989: 206).

  A third point made clear by the sixteenth-century Yucatec data is that the system was *never* egalitarian; it had both sociopolitical and settlement hierarchies. In provinces with an *ahau* (or *halach uinic*), his town was the capital and he was administratively over the *batabob* of the other towns, even though those towns were important places with well-known names. And that was the situation *after* the breakup of Mayapan; we have evidence that allows us to reconstruct even more impressive hierarchies when Mayapan was at its peak, and the provincial head towns were just secondary centers below the capital (Roys 1957; Proskouriakoff 1962; Marcus 1989).

*Seventeenth-Century El Peten*

  One of the groups that may have left Yucatan, either after the collapse of Chichen Itza (López de Cogolludo 1867–68, Vol.2, Book 9, Chap. 14; Villagutierre Soto-Mayor 1933: 326) or after the collapse of Mayapan (Landa in Tozzer 1941: 37), were the Itza who settled in the northern Guatemalan Department of El Peten (Fig. 4). In A.D. 1696 the Spaniards entered the region of Lake Peten Itza and reached Tayasal (or Tah Itza), capital city of the Itza, believed to have been located on the island called Flores today (Jones, Rice, and Rice 1981). The Spaniards were told that before their arrival, the regional polity of the Ytzaes had a strong political hierarchy, headed by a principal ruler and consisting of territorial subdivisions governed by local lords who owed him allegiance. These early accounts of Itza territorial organization (Avendaño y Loyola 1696a, 1696b; Villagutierre Soto-Mayor 1701, 1933; Means 1917; Thompson 1977) are interesting because that same region was once the heartland of the Classic Maya state.

Joyce Marcus

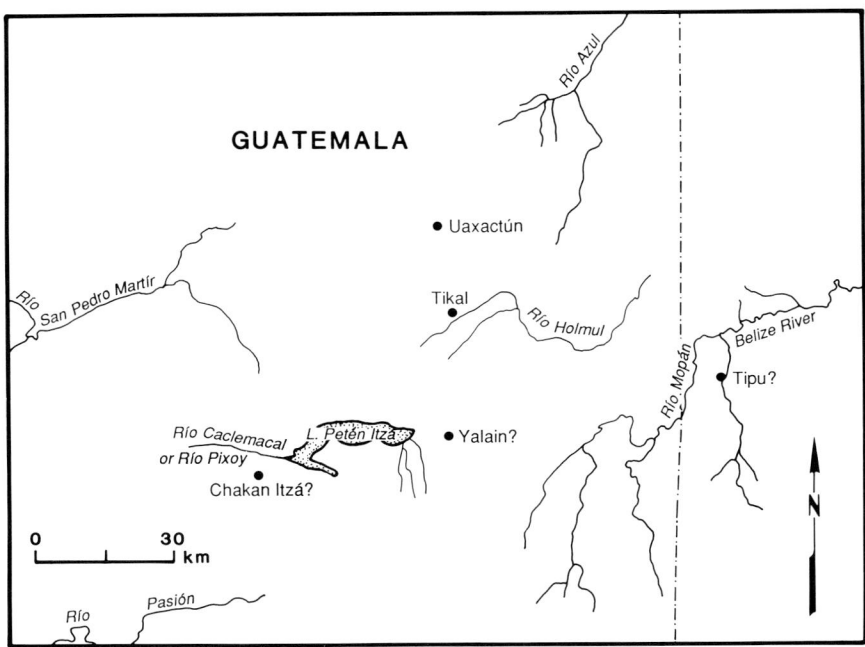

Fig. 4 The ruler Ah Canek—whose capital was located on an island in Lake Peten Itza—was able at various times to dominate other nearby ethnic groups located around the lake, as well as other more distantly located groups. Until 1697, this powerful Itza nation successfully maintained its independence, withstanding the attempted takeovers by the Spaniards (redrawn with modifications from Jones, Rice, and Rice 1981: fig. 1).

The Spaniards explained the geographic location of the Itza as follows: "In the north lies the kingdom of Yucatan; toward the south the road which the men of Guatemala have opened, starting from Vera Paz; on the west Cha Kan Ytza [administered by the ruler Ah Can] and the Cehaches; on the east and slightly north is the nation of Tipu [in western Belize]" (Avendaño y Loyola 1696a, 1696b: folios 41v–42r).

If all that territory were controlled by the Itza "kingdom," it would have been a rather large polity. The Itza polity was composed of different Itza groups surrounded by non-Itza groups, all of whom spoke a dialect of Yucatec. Determining the degree of autonomy each "group" possessed at different times in the prehispanic and Colonial eras will be important in determining what kind of polity operated in the center of El Peten. Thompson (1977) has proposed that the Itza, the Mopan Maya, the Cehach, the Chinamita, and the Lacandon should all be regarded as the "Chan subgroup," a group that had more in common with each other than with other Maya speakers.

## Ancient Maya Political Organization

In 1696, the Spaniards found one supreme ruler in the Lake Peten Itza area. This ruler, named Ah Canek,[3] is described as a "great king" who lived on the main island in the lake. In addition to the main island, Canek ruled four other islands and a series of communities on the mainland, as well as other "ethnic groups" such as the Tuluncies or Chinamita (Avendaño y Loyola 1696a, 1696b: folio 42v). Like the *halach uinic* or *ahau* in Roys' Type A province, Canek was simultaneously the governor of his own island and of the whole province. Each of the other four islands was a dependency with a local lord (*batab*) who owed allegiance to Canek. West of the Lake Peten Itza were the Chakan Itza, who were also under Canek's control (Villagutierre Soto-Mayor 1701, 1933).

The main island alone consisted of twenty-two districts or towns, each bearing the name of the *batab* who governed it, and each owing allegiance to Canek.

> Peten Ytza is situated in the middle of a great lake and there is not only this one on which the King [Canek] lives, but also four other *petens*, or islands, which also lie in the same lake. (Avendaño y Loyola 1696a, 1696b: folio 41r–v)

> The largest and best calculation which I can make of this nation was from the account which the King and his chiefs gave me, and this was that the island or *peten* in which we stopped consisted of 22 districts or towns, and they did not know how to give me the count [census] of each town, since they know how to count only up to 20 towns, and in going beyond many 20s, they do not know how to explain it, for it appears to them an infinite number. (Avendaño y Loyola 1696a, 1696b: folios 41v–42v)

> Each of the other four *petens*, although smaller in size, had the same number of districts, and the same number of people . . . . at most there were about 24,000–25,000 people of all ages and both sexes on the 5 islands, without counting the villages and the hamlets in the forest, which were innumerable. (Villagutierre Soto-Mayor 1933: Book 7, Chap. 4, p. 312)

The "kingdom" administered by Canek was divided into four divisions (Brinton 1882: 183), perhaps corresponding to the four islands or some larger units—each with its own *batab,* with whom Canek consulted before important undertakings (Villagutierre Soto-Mayor 1933; Thompson 1977). We will have more to say about this quadripartite organization in a later section.

This "great king" Canek promised the Spaniards that he would deliver to

---

[3] Ah Canek can be translated as "Lord Black Serpent." *Ah* = the "masculine prefix," "he," or "lord"; *Can* = serpent (probably his matronym); *Ek* = black, star (probably his patronym).

them all his islands and what he called "the nation of the Ytzaes," if, in return, they would execute his enemies (Avendaño y Loyola 1696a, 1696b: folio 48r). Unlike Fray Andrés de Avendaño y Loyola (1696b: folio 42v), who indicates that the Tuluncies were part of the Itza polity administered by Canek, Juan de Villagutierre Soto-Mayor (1933: Book 8, Chap. 11; Book 9, Chap. 3) indicates that the Itza rulers considered them enemies, referring to them as *ma uinicob* ("not men"), and eating them when they could capture them. The large Chinamita town of Tulumci ("Wall of Agave") was fortified by a palisade of agaves and a moat that protected 8,000 people. (Moats [and probable palisades] had been used earlier at Classic sites such as Calakmul and Becan). Just as we saw in Postclassic Yucatan, intraprovincial strife was apparently a widespread feature.

If Canek's whole kingdom consisted of the five islands (the main island plus the four islands administered by *batabob*) and some lakeshore settlements, his kingdom would have been far smaller than Tikal's in the early eighth century. If, however, his kingdom included the territory of the Chakan Itza (Thompson 1977: 24) and other ethnic groups (such as the Tuluncies, as Villagutierre Soto-Mayor's account indicates), it would have extended far beyond the lake and immediate vicinity. Utilizing Avendaño y Loyola's (1696a, 1696b) and Villagutierre Soto-Mayor's (1701, 1933) accounts, it is difficult to calculate the exact size of Canek's territory, primarily because it is not always clear if the Chakan Itza, Coboxes, Tuluncies, and many other ethnic groups were his temporary or long-term subjects.

Now let us look at the twenty-two "districts or towns" on the great island that were subject to Canek. Avendaño y Loyola (1696b: folio 38r–v) lists them as follows:

| | |
|---|---|
| that of King Ah Canek | that of Ach Cat Baca |
| that of Noh Ah Chata | that of Ach Cat *halach uinic* |
| that of Ah Dzec Dzin *batab* | that of Ach Cat Mulcah |
| that of the *cacique* Nohche | that of Ach Cat Kinchil |
| that of Ach Chatan Ek | that of Ach Cat Kinchan |
| that of Ach Cat Cixban | that of Ach Cat Kayom/Kayan |
| that of Noh Dzo Can Punab | that of Ach Cat Cit Can |
| that of Noh Dzo Can Noh | that of Ach Cat Ytza |
| that of Dzo Can Dzic | that of Ach Cat Pop |
| that of Ach Cat Matan Cua | that of Ach Cat Camal |
| that of Ach Cat Batun | that of Ach Cat Mas Kin |

Several points emerge from the list. First, as in the case of Roys' Type A Yucatec provinces, Canek was considered governor (*batab*) of his own capital city. Second, the term *ach cat* seems to have functioned as a title. We also find *batab, halach uinic,* and *cacique* used as titles (the last term being an Antillean word introduced into Mesoamerica by the Spaniards). The listing of a *halach uinic* as subject to "King" Canek is a bit surprising; if correct, it could mean that that particular lord had once governed one of the other islands or quadrants of the Itza, and that Canek had had a still grander title. Or, if one of Canek's brothers or sons ruled one of the districts, that could perhaps account for the expression "Ach Cat *halach uinic*." Finally, many of the names (e.g., Noh, Camal, Kin) are also known from Yucatan (Roys 1940).

Unfortunately, the Spaniards do not often give us the biological relationships among these *batabob* and Canek. We do know that Canek's first cousin was the priest called Kin Canek,[4] who had a great deal of power and was sometimes referred to as a "king" (Villagutierre Soto-Mayor 1933). Canek's sister married a man from Tipu, a town on the Macal River in western Belize. She and her husband lived in Yalain, to the east of Lake Peten Itza, a dependency controlled by Canek (Avendaño y Loyola 1696a, 1696b: folios 49v–50v; Villagutierre Soto-Mayor 1933: 353).

What do we learn from this El Peten case? First, we learn that in 1696, Canek ruled a polity or kingdom that was at least as centralized and hierarchically organized as Roys' Type A provinces. There was a definite capital, a royal family residing there, clear authority of "great king" over *batabob*, and perhaps a quadripartite regional organization at the level above the "district or town." We learn that Canek was related by blood to the ruler of another part of the Itza polity, the Chakan Ytzaes, whose territory lay on the other side of the "River Caclemacal" (Rio Pixoy). We also learn that Canek had enemies of whom he had apparently been unable to rid himself (Villagutierre Soto-Mayor 1933: 380); this is very reminiscent of the atmosphere of volatility we saw in some Yucatec provinces.

Despite the fact that our Peten Itza case comes from the period following the collapse of Mayapan, we do not have an egalitarian structure. Every *batab* of every district on the main island, and every *batab* who ruled his own island, was hierarchically below Canek's rule—and this in spite of the fact that Canek's power over distant places was probably far less than that of the rulers of major Classic cities. Bear this in mind as we critique some recent models for the Classic Maya in a later section of this paper.

*Pepet Tsibil*

How did the sixteenth-century Maya view their own territories? To answer this question we need to look at their native maps, or *pepet tsibil*, many of which were drawn by the Indians to make sure the conquering Spaniards knew which lands each native ruler controlled. Maya maps tended to be round, with the capital placed at the center and the dependencies sometimes linked to it by lines. Alternatively, the dependencies may be shown surrounding the capital in concentric rings, with the outermost ring giving the

---

[4] Sometimes spelled Quincanek.

names of border towns and natural landmarks separating one province from another. Like other Mesoamerican groups, the Maya regarded the east-west path of the sun as the most important axis, and frequently placed east at the top of the map, where we would usually place north (Roys 1933; Marcus n.d.d, 1976, 1983a, 1983b).

The so-called Land Treaty of Mani (Stephens 1843, 2: 264; Roys 1943: Figs. 1–3) is a 1557 document, accompanied by a map showing the province controlled by the *halach uinic* of Mani in northern Yucatan. The Tutul Xiu royal family presented a copy of this map (Fig. 5), along with a copy of their family tree, to the Spaniards to show them the extent of the province they once ruled (Morley 1946: pl. 20, 22).

The capital, Mani, is shown at the center. Lines link the capital to nearby subject towns. Around the perimeter are the names of more distant subject towns and natural landmarks such as cenotes (natural wells) and springs, as well as "boundary mounds" that were established to "show accurately how the borders of our forest lands were marked off" (Roys 1943: 192).

As early as 1545, the ruler of the province of Mani had surveyed the limits of his province along with his *batabob* (Roys 1943: 178). However, part of the territory he claimed as his realm was also claimed by his neighbors, the Xiu on the west and the Cupul on the east. Therefore, on 15 August 1557, the *halach uinic* Don Francisco de Montejo Xiu and his *batabob* from several towns (Ticul, Oxkutzcab, Tekax, Muna, Mama, Tekit) met in Mani: "There they assembled and deliberated as to the advisability, they said, of marking off [the boundaries], fixing the corners and placing crosses at the borders of the fields of the towns of their subjects, for each [town] separately. . . . After they had deliberated together, they said it was advisable to bring in the governors [*batabob*] of the towns. We answered that they should come here to the center of the town of Mani and that they should each bring two regidores with them to witness the marking off of the borders of the forests, the borders of the lands" (Roys 1943: 185).

Each *batab* of a dependency who attended the boundary marking received five 400-piece lots of cacao, five cotton mantles of "4 breadths each," a string of red beads "as long as one's arm," and twenty green stones (Roys 1943: 186).

A second map, purporting to show northern Yucatan, was included in the Chilam Balam of Chumayel (see Fig. 6; Roys 1933: 125). This map, too, is circular, with west at the top. At the center is Tihoo, the capital (now known as Merida); there is an outer ring, but it contains no border towns. Most interesting is the fact that east-west and north-south lines divide the circle into four quadrants, with subject towns in each. Mani and Campech lie in the west, Calkini and Cumkal in the west, Itzmal in the east, and Zaci in the east. In other words, the entire Mani map we saw earlier would fit into this one as a small "inset" in the southwest quadrant.

## Ancient Maya Political Organization

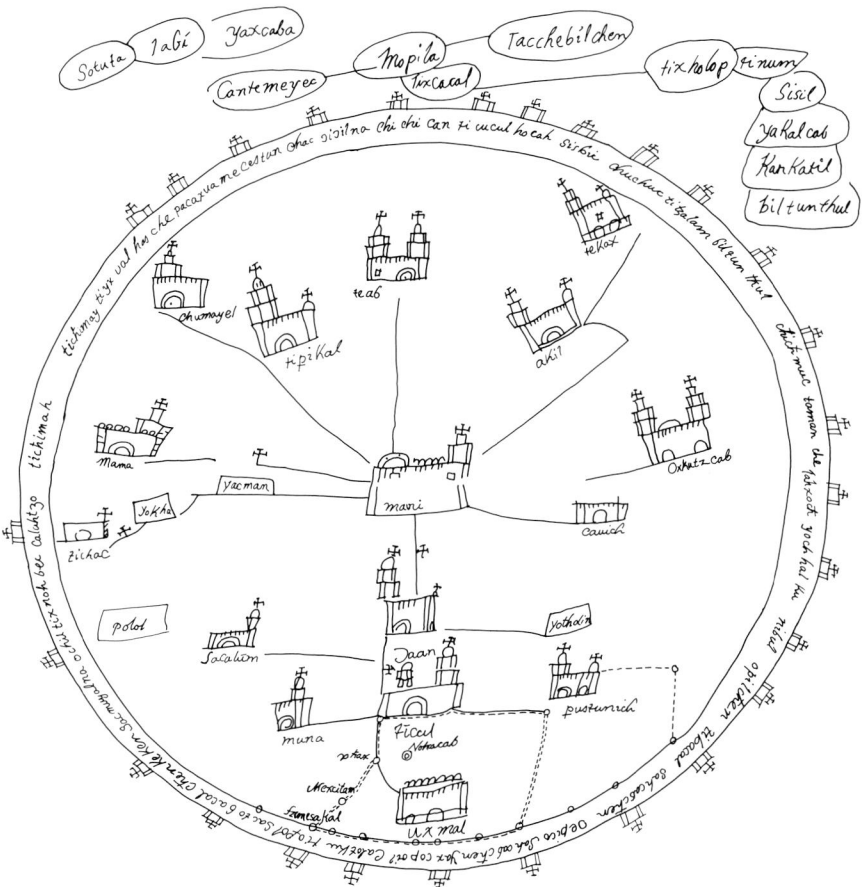

Fig. 5   This A.D. 1557 map once belonged to the Xiu lineage who administered the province of Mani. At the center is the principal town, also called Mani. Linked by lines to Mani are dependencies such as (moving clockwise) Akil and Tekax, Cauich, Yotholin, Dzaan, Ticul, the ruins of Uxmal, Muna, Sacalum, Yacman and Yokha, Mama, Chumayel, and Teab(o). The still-inhabited towns are designated by Catholic crosses, while the ruins of Uxmal are marked by the drawing of a pre-Hispanic temple. On the periphery is a ring of border landmarks—towns, cenotes, or springs—that define the limits of the province of Mani. Drawing by Kay Clahassey (after black-and-white photo in Roys 1943: fig. 1).

What we learn from the *pepet tsibil* is that—*regardless of the realities of geography as we see them*—the Maya envisioned a large territory, such as the regional state of Yucatan, as circular but with quadripartite divisions. The smaller "provinces" within a regional state were also seen as circular, with

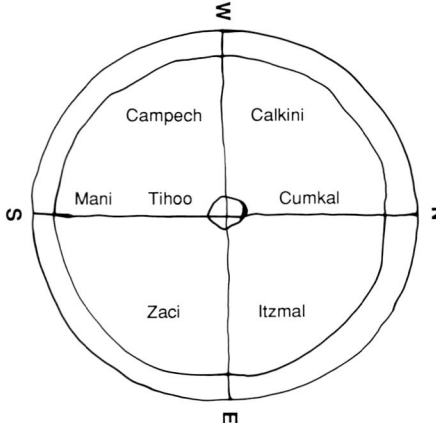

Fig. 6 Indigenous 16th-century map showing the division of northern Yucatan into four equal quadrants. At the center is the capital Tihoo (now called Merida). Surrounding Tihoo are places and provinces, such as Mani, Campech (Campeche), Calkini, Cumkal, Itzmal (Izamal), and Zaci (now called Valladolid). Map was included in the Chilam Balam of Chumayel (redrawn with modifications after Roys 1967: fig. 27).

the capital viewed as the center and the dependencies seen as smaller places encircling it. These smaller provinces could lack the quadripartite division.

*Sixteenth-Century Terms for Territory and Hierarchy*

A continuing problem in the analysis of Pre-Columbian cultures is our struggle to fit Indian concepts into terms drawn from English, Latin, and Greek. The sixteenth- and seventeenth-century Spaniards collected many Maya words for territorial units and political offices, and while they also struggled with their definitions, it can be helpful to look at these terms. We will look first at the indigenous categories the Spaniards called "nation" (polity), "province," "capital," and "dependency." The indigenous categories provide a hierarchy of size (from large to small) and inclusivity (from most to least inclusive).

"Kingdom" or Polity. Various Maya terms were translated by the Spaniards as "nation," "kingdom," "polity," or "homeland." One Yucatec Maya term for "kingdom" was *ahaulil*. Other terms were *baalcab, baalcah,* and *cab,* which could mean "world," "region," or "town." Derived from *cab* was the related term *cabil,* "polity" or "kingdom," which was used in expressions such as "*Tabx cabil ech?*," "What 'kingdom' or polity do you belong to?" (Martínez Hernández 1929: 162). Other broadly inclusive terms were *luum,* "land," and *luumil,* "one's fatherland or homeland or where one lives" (Martínez Hernández 1929: 570–571).

Province. When referring to a unit smaller than the regional state, Maya speakers used a variety of terms for "province"—a rich, well-developed category. Province names were derived from: (1) the name of its ruler, (2) the ethnic group residing there, (3) the capital within it, or (4) some prominent geographic landmark (hill, body of water, etc.).

There were at least three frequently used terms for "province": *cuchcabal*, *tzucub*, and *peten* (Martínez Hernández 1929; Beltrán de Santa Rosa 1898; Pío Pérez 1898; Solís Alcalá 1949; Barrera Vásquez et al. 1980). In some contexts, these terms were used as *synonyms* by the same ethnic groups; in other contexts, it appears that different groups preferred to use one term over another.

The use of the term *cuchcabal* seems to have been restricted to the Yucatan Peninsula. Yucatec Maya speakers used it to mean "province" and "the subjects administered by a head town." The head town administered dependencies within the province.

The second term for province was *tzucub* (*tzuc* = part, division; a group of towns, or lineages; a numerical particle used to count towns). This term seems to emphasize that each province was made up of a group of towns, and that the *tzucub* itself was part of a larger whole. In other words, the province was just a part of the "empire" once administered by Mayapan, or the larger whole, "the regional state."

The term *tzucub* was frequently employed in the Yucatan Peninsula. For example, the "province for Ziyan" was designated as *tzucubte ziyan*. The "province of the Ceh Pechs [Cumkal and Mutul]" was designated *u tzucub ah ceh pechob* (Pío Pérez 1898; the Chilam Balam of Mani[5]); in this case, the province was named after the ethnic group residing there. The *Diccionario de Motul* (Martínez Hernández 1929: 268) gives additional examples in which the name of the ruling lineage or the name of the principal ethnic group was sufficient to convey the name of the province; examples include: (1) *u tzucub ah canulob*, "the province of the Canul [Calkini]"; (2) *u tzucub ah cocomob*, "the province of the Cocom [Zututa]"; (3) *u tzucub ah xiuob*, "the province of the Xiu [Mani]."

The third term for province, *peten*, was most frequently employed in the lake district of northern Guatemala, but it was also used in Yucatan (Roys 1967: 51). *Peten* could also mean "island" as well as "territory," "district," or "province." *Peten* seems to have been used for any province that had *definite boundaries*, suggesting that when the Maya used the term *peten* they were referring to a province whose boundaries were as clear as those of an island (Brinton 1882: 122).

*Capitals and Dependencies.* Capitals within provinces were called "head towns," *hol cahob* or *hol cacabob*. Beneath these head towns was a hierarchy of dependencies.

---

[5] The *Books of Chilam Balam* were sacred books kept by the priest in various towns of Yucatan during the fifteenth and sixteenth centuries. They were written in the Yucatec Maya language, but using European script. A number of these books have been preserved and are now named after the town from which they originated. Thus, the books from Mani and Chumayel are known as the Chilam Balam of Mani and the Chilam Balam of Chumayel. *Chilam* (*chilan*) referred to the priest or "speaker," and *Balam* (Jaguar) was a common last name for Maya nobles and priests from Classic times (A.D. 250–900) onward. Roys (1933: 3) called each book "The Book of the Prophet Balam."

There were a number of Maya terms for "dependency," including *cuchteel, hatsal,* and *mek'taan cahil. Cuchteel* was derived from *cuch,* "burden, obligation, cargo, responsibility." *Cuchteel* referred to the towns and people who were the responsibility of a ruler. *Hatsal* referred to a subject town, a term derived from *hats,* "to divide, to split up." *Mek'taan cahil* was another term for "subject town." A related term, *mek'elte,* referred to "the people held or controlled by the ruler." Both *mek'taan* and *mek'elte* were derived from *mek,* "control, hold, or grasp in one's hand." Other expressions that relate to subjugation include *culaan yalan oc hunpay,* "one who is subject to another," and *cultal yalan yoc,* "to subjugate someone or to be a subject" (Martínez Hernández 1929: 210, 211).

*Site Size Hierarchies.* At the top of the size hierarchy were "cities," or *noh cah* (*noh* = big, great; *cah* = town, place). For example, *noh cah* was used to describe Ichcanzihoo, the native name for Merida (Roys 1933: 73, 126).

Some cities or towns were "capitals" or "head towns" (*hol cacabob, hol cahob*—derived from *hol* = head; *cah* = town, place; or *cab* = region, place). Below the "head towns" were subordinate towns, distinguished from *hol cacabob* both on the basis of size and the ruler's authority. Indigenous terms for these subordinate units were *cah* (town), *chan cah* (small town), *chanchan cah* (very small town), and *pet cah* (village or hamlet, literally "round town or place") (Marcus 1983a: 469). The settlement hierarchy by size would thus be designated as follows: (1) *noh cah* (usually a head town, *hol cah*); (2) *cah;* (3) *chan cah;* (4) *chanchan cah;* and (5) *pet cah.*

Within a newly conquered province, towns would be divided up among the victorious rulers so that they could receive tribute from them. This distribution of towns to different rulers was designated *toxol cahob.*

Cities and towns of reasonably large size usually displayed subdivisions. The most general term for a sector of the town was *hun huntzuc ti cahob* (literally "each division of the town"). Many towns were divided into wards called *china* or *chinateel,* often four in number. Making up the ward were houses (*na*) and households (*nalil*).

*Hierarchies of Political Personnel.* In addition to the size hierarchy of settlements, there was a definite hierarchy of political personnel. At the top was the territorial ruler or *halach uinic,* who carried the title of *ahau.* One of the terms for the territory he controlled was *ahaulil* (*ahaulel*), probably most like our term "realm." Below the *ahau* were local lords or *batabob* who administered second- and third-level dependencies. The realm administered by each *batab* was called a *batabil.* One kind of assistant to the *batab* was called an *ah kulel,* "deputy"; another of his assistants was called an *ah can,* "he who speaks." Most *batabob* had three or more *ah kulelob* and *ah canob.* Also aiding the *batab* was a special war lord, called the *nacom,* and a group of *holcanob,* men who would "call up" adult men from the *batab's* district to bear arms. Each of the (usually four) ward heads within a town was called an *ah cuchcab.* For those provinces that had a *halach uinic,* all towns within the province were subject to him, and all *batabob* owed him their allegiance (*Relaciones de Yucatán* 1898–1900, Vol. 2: 89).

This hierarchy of lords was of great importance. Maya rulers were careful to indicate in their statements to the Spaniards whether they were the *batabob* serving a *halach uinic,* or whether they were the *halach uinic* who directed many *batabob*. Lords within polities acknowledged allegiance *up* the hierarchy, and lords at the top of the regional hierarchy gave orders that passed *down*. Lords lived in palaces, and as is the case in other archaic states, the Maya ruler used corvée labor to construct his palace. Commoners constructed "at their own expense" the houses of lords (Landa in Tozzer 1941: 86). Among the Chontal Maya the commoners raised cacao and maize for their lord, and they cut timber and sent it to Tixchel as ordered by their ruler (Scholes and Roys 1948: 207).

What we learn from these definitions—and from the descriptions of the realm of Ah Canek we examined earlier—is that just because a town or district had a name of its own does not mean that it was autonomous or independent. Many "districts or towns" were named for an important *batab,* but that *batab* in turn owed allegiance to a *halach uinic* at a *hol cah* some distance away. We will return to this important point when we discuss the Emblem Glyphs of the Classic period.

In addition to the multilevel size hierarchies of settlements and the hierarchies of political personnel, there is significant evidence that economic hierarchies existed and that there was specialization among towns. The *halach uinic* at the top of the regional hierarchy received tribute[6] from his dependencies (Roys 1957: 75). Within the provinces of northern Yucatan, some specialization by towns is documented in sixteenth-century *relaciones* (*Relaciones de Yucatán* 1898–1900). These documents make it clear that both the *kind* and the *amount* of tribute varied significantly from town to town. For example, some towns were required to pay twenty-five bushel baskets of salt a year, while other towns even closer to the sources were not required to deliver any salt. Some towns were responsible for 2,000 pounds of dried fish per year, while others delivered none. Still others were responsible for delivering more than 6,000 square yards of cotton cloth, and other towns were responsible for bushels of maize, turkeys, and honey. Only part of these variable tribute demands can be explained by site location and by size of population (Roys 1957). Position in the provincial hierarchy, kin ties to the ruler, and alliances also played important roles in determining the kinds and quantities of goods demanded.

Subordinate towns and small dependencies were often specialized. Special-

---

[6] Warren Barbour (personal communication, 1989) has suggested that the term *tribute* be restricted to payments from conquered ethnic groups, with the term *taxes* used for payments from one's own ethnic group. While I agree with the distinction, I have used *tribute* throughout because the term used in the Spanish documents is *tributo,* and ethnic affiliation is not always clear.

ization by lower-order centers was only possible because a specialist town's other essential needs were met by the other towns administered by the same regional hierarchy. Thus, the state not only maintained such specialization, but also fostered it. This economic interdependence *within a province* is another important integrative feature of the regional hierarchy. Between provinces, much of the exchange that took place was controlled by the *halach uinicob* from their provincial capitals.

## The Ethnohistoric Evidence for Quadripartite Organization

Let us briefly consider one more aspect of Maya organization, a concept that pervaded their cosmology at all levels from heaven to the earthly village. At the highest level, the sixteenth-century Maya believed that the cosmos was divided into four great world quarters, each associated with a color, a bird, and a tree, as well as one of the four mythical brothers (*bacabob*) who held up each corner of the sky. Many sources reveal the importance of these four world quarters as an important organizing principle among ancient and modern Maya (e.g., Roys 1933, 1967; Thompson 1934; Redfield and Villa Rojas 1934). Codices such as the Dresden and Tro-Cortesianus and ethnohistoric sources convey the importance of the four world quarters, the four corners of the sky, and the four sky-bearers (Roys 1933: 170–172; 1965: 9; Landa in Tozzer 1941: 135–137; Thompson 1934).

At a lower level, the Maya often used this quadripartite model as a basis for territorial organization, calling it *cantzuc* or *cantzucul cab* (*can* = four; *tzuc* = division; *cab* = land, territory). This principle of quadripartition operated on several territorial levels, from large geographic units (e.g., the Yucatec lowlands) to the sixteenth-century town, and down to some twentieth-century Maya villages. Ethnohistoric data and indigenous documents report that four "provinces" came together to found Chichen Itza; it involved a "calling together of the four divisions, the four territories as they were called" (Brinton 1882: 181; Roys 1933, 1967: 139).

We have already seen an indigenous map that divided Yucatan into four quadrants (Fig. 6); in the same document (the Chilam Balam of Chumayel), in the chapter called "The Ritual of the Four World Quarters," there is a discussion of the ideal world order, and the colors, animals, stones, and ethnic groups that settled the four quarters (Roys 1933: 63–66). We have also seen Avendaño y Loyola's (1696a, b) and Villagutierre Soto-Mayor's (1701) reports that Lord Canek in the Lake Peten Itza region administered a territory divided into four parts (Brinton 1882: 183).

Four divisions were also characteristic of many towns. For example, when Mayapan fell, the supreme ruler Tutul (Xiu) is said to have left with "the lords and the four divisions of the town" (Tozzer 1941: 37, footnote 180). Fray Diego de Landa (in Tozzer 1941: 37) has reported that Yucatec towns were often divided into four wards. Scholes and Roys (1948: 54–55)

# Ancient Maya Political Organization

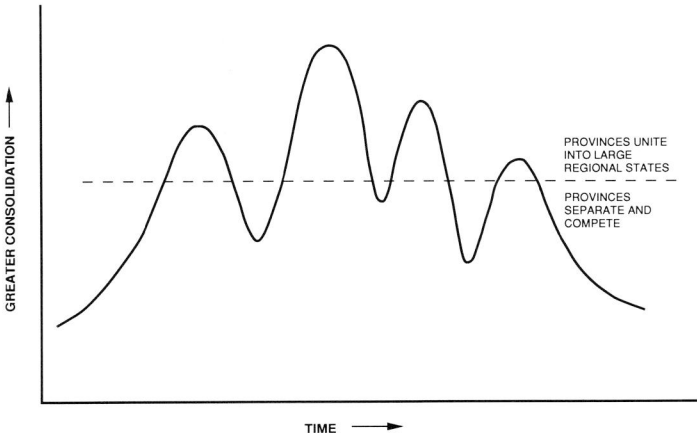

Fig. 7 Schematic depiction of the dynamic model. Peaks represent periods when provinces united into large regional states. Troughs represent periods when large states broke down into autonomous provinces again.

reported that the Acalan town of Itzamkanac was also divided into four quarters, designated *chan tzucul cab* in the Chontal text. Landa (in Tozzer 1941: 139) stated, "It was the custom in all the towns in Yucatan that there should be two heaps of stone, facing each other at the entrance of the town, on all four sides of the towns, that is to say, East, West, North, and South. . . ." Landa lists east, then west, the same order we will see used in a Late Classic text on Copan's Stela A. Tozzer (1907: 39) reported that a Lacandon town "has four trails leading to it, corresponding to the four cardinal points." In the modern village of Chan Kom, Robert Redfield and Alfonso Villa Rojas (1934: 114) also report that the community was divided into quadrants by the four roads leading in. Even the four sides of an Early Classic tomb at Rio Azul, Guatemala, were correctly labeled; each side bore the appropriate hieroglyph for the corresponding world direction (Adams 1987).

## THE DYNAMIC MODEL

Now let us see what model of political and territorial organization we can derive from the sixteenth-century descriptions of the Maya themselves.

First and foremost, the model will have to be *dynamic*. A description of Yucatan at A.D. 1400, during the height of consolidation at Mayapan, would not match the descriptions of the sixteen provinces found by the Spaniards in A.D. 1550. Our model must therefore present a series of oscillations over time like the ones shown in Figure 7, with the *peaks* representing moments of consolidation and the *troughs* representing dissolution.

Second, our model must have hierarchies of units—large regional state, province, head town, dependent town, village, and hamlet—not all of which were stable over time. It appears that the largest unit with long-term stability was the *province,* which seems to have weathered all the oscillations.

At moments of peak unification, large numbers of provinces came together to form the units the Spaniards called "nations," and which we might call "large regional states." A single city—Chichen Itza at A.D. 1150 or Mayapan at A.D. 1350—served as the capital for such a unit, and in some cases it appears that elite representatives from each province were drawn into the capital. The former *hol cahob,* or head towns, of the participating provinces then served as secondary administrative centers. They were governed by (and sometimes named for) *batabob* who were themselves hereditary rulers, and who often controlled considerable manpower. At the height of unification, the boundaries between provinces were less visible, but they were there nonetheless. They were the potential cleavage planes along which the regional state would break up when the time came, for regional states do not seem to have been long-term stable units (Marcus 1989).

Inevitably, even after a few centuries of apparent success, each regional state began to dissolve into its constituent provinces. Some of these provinces, close to the old capital, retained a lot of hierarchical structure: they had a single head town with a *halach uinic,* many dependent towns governed by *batabob,* and a pattern whereby orders passed down from the head town and tribute passed up from the dependencies. Other provinces, farther away and harder to control, consisted of loosely allied towns that only came together for mutual defense. The farther the system broke down in the direction of these more weakly integrated provinces, the deeper the trough in our oscillating model.

The third thing our dynamic model needs is a set of processes bringing about the consolidation or dissolution of regional states. In this paper I will restrict myself entirely to *processes demonstrably present in the ethnohistoric data.*

Archaic states can be shown to form in at least three ways: coercion, voluntary confederation, or some combination of the two. We have examples of coercive states elsewhere in Mesoamerica—like the one the Mixtec ruler 8 Deer "Tiger Claw" put together by conquest around A.D. 1046—but that is not how the documents describe Chichen Itza or Mayapan. Both of the latter seem to have been voluntaristic (*mul tepal*) confederacies. One of the advantages of coming together as a regional state is that it makes it easier to keep peace among formerly warring provinces. If Ah Canek was willing to deliver his subjects and dependencies to the Spaniards in return for their "executing his enemies," one can only imagine how great the pressure to end such warfare was.

As for the process of dissolution, the key word used in the documents is either "treachery" or "disloyalty." If keeping the peace is an advantage of confederacy, one disadvantage is having to pay tribute. As soon as one of the strongest members of a regional state decides he will pull out and keep the products of his province for himself, the fatal weakening process has begun. In the case of Mayapan, the Xiu were angry with the Cocom because the Cocom ruler was very arrogant and he "began to covet riches and for this reason he arranged with the troops of the garrison, which the rulers of Mexico kept at Tabasco and Xicalango, to hand over the city to them" (Landa in Tozzer 1941: 32). Later, "among the successors of the house of Cocom was a very haughty man, an imitator of Cocom, and he made another league with the men of Tabasco, and he introduced more Mexicans into the city, and he began to play the tyrant and to make slaves of the poorer people. On this account the nobles joined with the faction of the Tutul Xiu, who was a statesman like his ancestors, and they conspired to put Cocom to death. And this they did, killing at the same time all his sons, except one who was absent" (Landa in Tozzer 1941: 36–37).

The quarrels between the Xiu and the Cocom lasted for so long that they both abandoned Mayapan around A.D. 1450 "and left it in solitude, each party returning to his own country" (Landa in Tozzer 1941: 37). The Xiu went to Mani, while the Cocom settled in Zotuta. In 1536 the Xiu requested and received permission from the Cocom to pass through Cocom territory to reach the Sacred Cenote at Chichen Itza. Since Nachi Cocom—great-grandson of the Cocom ruler killed at Mayapan—regarded Xiu treachery as responsible for his ancestor's death, he was able to gain a measure of revenge by killing forty Xiu nobles in his own territory (after he had wined and dined them!).

Prior to becoming the capital of a centralized state, Chichen Itza was one of several centers in northern Yucatan whose interactions oscillated between being relatively peaceful and being quite competitive. Among these centers were those flowering from A.D. 800 to 950 in the Puuc region (Oxkintok, Uxmal, Mul-Chic, Kabah, Sayil, Sabacche, Labna, Kom, Chacmultun, Xlabpak, and Xcalumkin) as well as other important sites to the north, east, and south (Dzibilchaltun, Coba, and Becan) (Fig. 8). According to Jeff Karl Kowalski (1987: 238), "Warfare seems to have been occurring sporadically at the time the House of the Governor (at Uxmal) was built," or between A.D. 850 and 920. Evidence of conflict includes epigraphic accounts, the construction of walls to protect the "downtown" zone of various sites such as Uxmal, and the painting of murals and carving of stone sculpture that depict warriors and bound captives.

Some time after A.D. 950 it appears that Chichen Itza became the centralized capital, and that conflict among centers was reduced for a while. Part of Chichen Itza's increased power came at the expense of many Puuc cities that were abandoned around A.D. 950 (Andrews V 1979). "Some centers may have resisted and were depopulated forcibly, while others, realizing that the

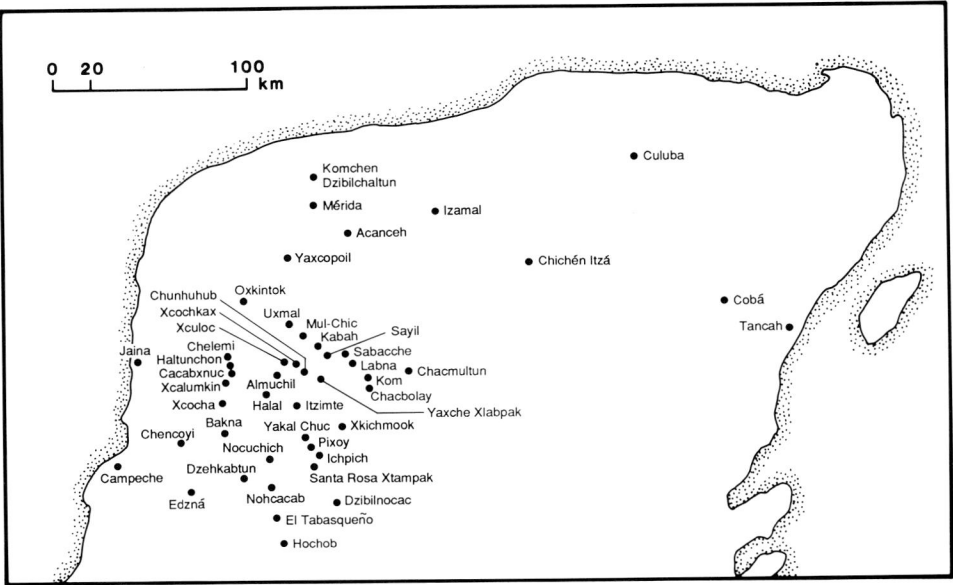

Fig. 8 Map of northern Yucatan showing the location of several sites within the Puuc region—Kabah, Sayil, Labna, and Xlabpak—as well as others outside.

political situation was shifting radically, may have collaborated with the new rulers at Chichen Itza" (Kowalski 1987: 238). Some alliances forged among important lords and lineages apparently brought about the centralized state centered at Chichen Itza. These northern lowland events took place at the same time that many of the dynasties administering southern lowland cities (particularly in the Peten) were losing their political power and were abandoning the "downtown" areas of their cities.

Taking into account the political collapse of some southern lowland dynasties, the *average size* of polities in the southern lowlands decreased, but that decrease was somewhat offset by the increase in polity size by Chichen Itza in the northwest and by Coba in the northeast, and the florescence of the Puuc sites. Thus a period which would look like a trough in our dynamic model if we viewed only the southern lowlands, would look like a peak if we viewed only the Puuc region. With the emergence of the Mayapan Confederacy, much of the territory once administered by Chichen Itza was unified again, although Fernando Robles and Anthony Andrews (1986), relying primarily on differences in architecture and ceramics, have inferred that the eastern territories of Ecab and Cozumel Island remained unincorporated.

This, then, is our dynamic model—one of stable but competitive provinces, periodically consolidating into large regional states to reduce competition at the cost of their autonomy, and periodically breaking down again into autonomous (but warring) provinces. At the peaks of consolidation, polities had the manpower to construct great cities with impressive public works; in their troughs of dissolution, they resembled Roys' Type A, B, and C provinces.

It has been customary for Mayanists to think of the Classic as a long, stable plateau of greatness, followed by a mysterious collapse, followed in turn by a Postclassic that was very different. But what if the Postclassic was not so different? What if the peaks and troughs we see at Chichen Itza and Mayapan were simply the latest in a long series of peaks and troughs, stretching back to the fifth century A.D.? Might a dynamic model help to resolve some of our disagreements over what we see in the Classic?

In the next section, I apply our dynamic model to the Classic period in an attempt to find evidence for four of its most important features: (1) a series of peaks, during which there were large regional states with a hierarchy of capitals, secondary centers, tertiary centers, and villages; (2) moments during which secondary centers pulled away from capitals, helping to cause the eventual breakdown of that regional state to a lower level of integration; (3) provinces of loosely allied towns, one of which eventually rose to become the capital of that region; and (4) evidence that provinces were stable for longer periods than regional states.

## APPLYING THE DYNAMIC MODEL TO THE CLASSIC PERIOD

We can begin with Cycle 8 in the Maya calendar (A.D. 292–434), a period preceding the first clear evidence for a Maya state. During Cycle 8, as I wrote in 1976, ". . . there were apparently no regional capitals, no four-tiered hierarchy [of sites], and no hexagonal lattices of secondary centers around capitals" (Marcus 1976: 191).

I see nothing that has happened in the last fourteen years to change this assessment of the period A.D. 292–434. I would therefore compare Cycle 8 to the periods that immediately *preceded* the establishment of a Yucatec regional state centered at Chichen Itza and the establishment of a *mul tepal* capital at Mayapan. Such periods were probably characterized by a whole series of autonomous provinces, each with Roys' Type A or B organization, but not yet united into a regional state with a supreme capital.

Tikal and Uaxactun were probably two of the most powerful Cycle 8 centers, accounting for 50% of all Cycle 8 monuments (Marcus n.d.d). Tikal and Uaxactun are logical candidates for "head towns" of Type A provinces—towns in which an *ahau* served as the *batab* for his own town, and was owed allegiance by lesser *batabob* at dependent towns. At one point during Cycle 8, Tikal dominated Uaxactun. Later, Uaxactun regained its independence. Still later, Tikal again gained the upper hand. During Cycle

Joyce Marcus

Fig. 9 The "Toothache" hieroglyphic expression, whose general meaning—"accession to office"—was determined by T. Proskouriakoff (1960) and whose name was coined by J. E. S. Thompson (1962). These four hieroglyphic expressions are variants of a similar phrase probably derived from the verb *hoktal,* "to be seated," whose first syllable is depicted as a "knot," *hok,* or as "tied up item," *hok'(a'an).*

8, as in Roys' Type A provinces, there were only three levels in the site hierarchy—the *ahau*'s town, the dependencies ruled by *batabob,* and simple villages.

I find it significant that during Cycle 8, Tikal's rulers were using the Toothache glyph (T-684; Thompson 1962: 289) to record their accessions to rulership (for example, on Stela 4 [at A5], erected ca. A.D. 378). This glyph for accession is often associated with second-order sites, such as Piedras Negras, El Cayo, Aguateca, and Naranjo (Fig. 9). Its use is further evidence that Tikal was still only the *hol cah* of a Type A province.

Early in Cycle 9 (A.D. 514–534), important changes occurred in the southern lowlands (Fig. 10). The "uniformity" noted by Thompson made its appearance as a more standardized symbolic system on monuments over a wide geographic area. Indeed, during Cycle 9, Classic Maya monuments reached their maximum areal extent; never again would they be distributed over so wide a region. The palace—that architectural manifestation of kingship—became a common feature of major sites, along with standardized temple plans (Marcus 1983b). A four-tiered hierarchy of sites replaced the earlier three-tiered one, suggesting a new level of political administration at the top. And when the positions of secondary centers are plotted, they form hexagonal lattices around major centers, like those predicted by Central Place Theory for a hierarchy that optimizes administration (Marcus

## Ancient Maya Political Organization

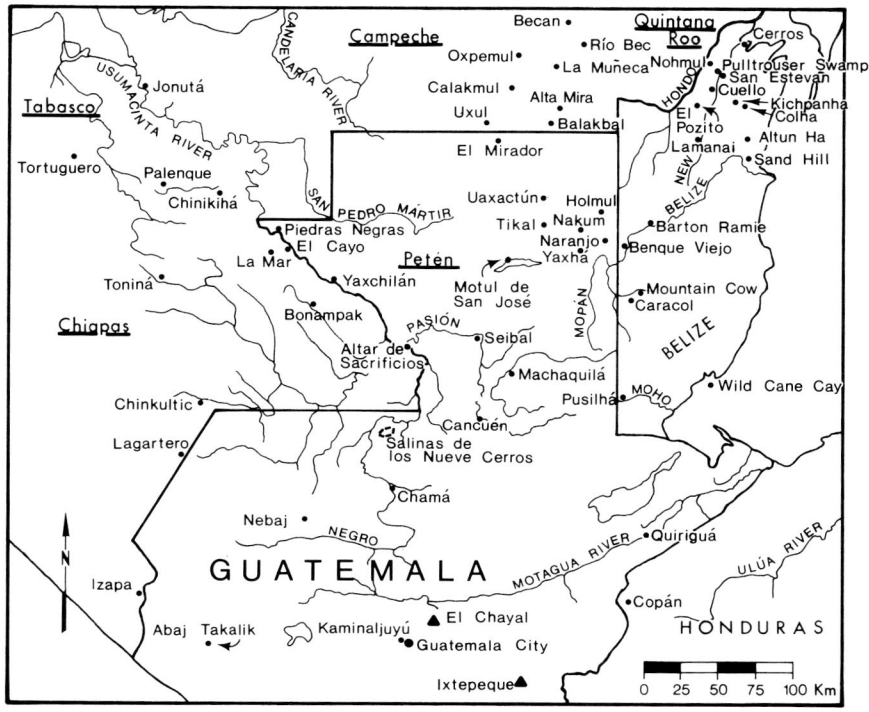

Fig. 10  Important Preclassic and Classic period sites in the southern lowlands.

1973, 1974a, 1976). All these changes indicate that the Maya had become an archaic state.

In terms of our dynamic model, this period represents the consolidation and centralization of the lowland Maya into the kinds of large units that the sixteenth-century Spaniards described as "nations." Indeed, judged by their size and public works, they were very large polities, as large as or larger than the one later centered at Mayapan. Some of these polities may have been formed by the voluntaristic coming together of formerly autonomous provinces, just as Chichen Itza and Mayapan are said to have been formed, but on a larger scale.

Of course, some large Maya states may have been formed by coercion, like the polity established in the eleventh century by the Mixtec ruler 8 Deer "Tiger Claw" (Caso 1977; Smith 1973; Marcus and Flannery 1983: 218–219). Still other capitals may have used royal marriage alliance to bring additional provinces within their hegemony (see below). One clue that some early regional capitals may have been of *mul tepal* type is the fact that some of the largest Classic Maya cities (such as Yaxchilan) had two or more

139

*Joyce Marcus*

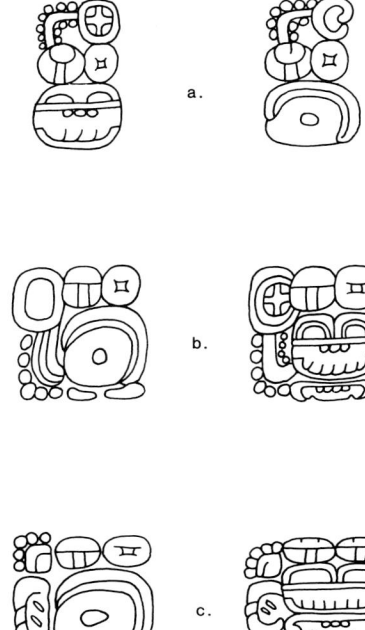

Fig. 11 Yaxchilan's "paired" Emblem Glyphs. The use of these dual Emblem Glyphs may be the result of a confederacy of two lords, lineages, or polities: (a) shows T-562★ + T-511, Yaxchilan, Lintel 56; (b) shows T-511 + T-562, Yaxchilan, Stela 11; (c) shows T-511 + T-562, Yaxchilan, Lintel 2.
★ The T-number refers to the number assigned to the glyphic main signs by Thompson (1962).

Emblem Glyphs. Heinrich Berlin (1958), who first identified these "geographical referents," suggested they might represent the name of a city, titular deity, or its royal dynasty. The significant patterning in the distribution and use of Emblem Glyphs that we have noted is in no way affected whether we opt for a geographic designation, a dynastic name, or a title as the principal meaning for the Emblem Glyph. In fact, Floyd Lounsbury (1973, 1989) has achieved a compromise position by reading the Emblem Glyph superfix (*ah po*) as "lord" or *ahau* (a title) and the main sign as the place (geographic referent). An Emblem Glyph might then be understood as the title + place associated with a particular ruler. Furthermore, the use of dual Emblem Glyphs (Fig. 11) might be read as "*ahau* of x" and "*ahau* of y," signifying that two lords from two specific places had come together at a new capital, in this case at Yaxchilan.

We have stressed that all states have hierarchies, so let us now look at some evidence for the hegemony of major centers over secondary centers. We can begin with a change in the glyph used by Tikal to record the accession of its rulers to power. We have seen that before the formation of the Maya state, Tikal did this with the Toothache glyph. During Cycle 9, however, as Tikal rose to be one of the largest and most powerful Maya

## Ancient Maya Political Organization

Fig. 12 The "Seating" hieroglyphic expression—whose general meaning is "seated in office"—can now be read as *chuma'an* or *cumaan*. Six variants are illustrated, drawn from the texts of Palenque and Tikal (redrawn after Thompson 1950: fig. 19).

cities, it began to use the "Seating" glyph (Fig. 12) to record rulers' accessions (Thompson 1962: 252–253).

Thompson (1950: 119–120, 1962: 253) and Berlin (1968, 1977) did the first important work on the differential distribution of these two accession glyphs; Berlin, in fact, suggested that they might reflect different types of office or accession. More recently, these glyphs have been restudied by William Ringle (1985) and Victoria Bricker (1986). It now appears that major regional capitals such as Tikal, Palenque, and Copan used the Seating glyph in an expression that can be read *cumaan/chumaan*, "has been seated [in office]" (Proskouriakoff 1960; Roys 1933; Bricker 1986). In contrast, Naranjo—which I consider to have been a secondary center below Tikal—used the "Toothache" accession glyph. There are at least two possible explanations for this asymmetric relationship: (1) The ruler of Tikal was to the ruler of Naranjo as the *halach uinic* of a Type A province was to the *batab* governing one of his dependencies; or (2) The ruler of Naranjo was like the *halach uinic* of a Type A province, while the *ahau* of Tikal was a "great king" who ruled a "nation" of many such provinces.

Further evidence for the inequality of Tikal and Naranjo comes from a marriage recorded in the hieroglyphic texts of Naranjo. In A.D. 682, a woman from the royal house of Tikal arrived at Naranjo to marry the local ruler (Fig. 13). Approximately five years later she gave birth to a son, who went on to become ruler of Naranjo (Marcus 1973, 1976: 165–169). The son, "Scroll Squirrel," emphasizes his Tikal mother, while his Naranjo father is not even named. His mother's bloodlines were worth stressing, because they raised the status of Naranjo from a tertiary to a secondary center below Tikal.

This is a familiar process in many chiefdoms and states, where the giver of the bride takes on higher status and the recipient lower status (Marcus 1974a). For example, among the Kachin of highland Burma, the giver of the bride becomes *mayu* (higher status) while the recipient becomes *dama* (lower status). Edmund Leach ([1954] 1964: 151) has remarked: "We have seen that a crucial element in the structure of *gumsa* society is that when an individual marries out of his or her own social class it is normally the man who marries up and the woman who marries down . . . a powerful chief [is able] to pick and choose among potential suitors for his daughters and to use their marriage as direct instruments of political alliance."

This process of women "marrying down" is called *hypogamy,* and it was used by the early Aztec state in trying to bring formerly autonomous Basin of Mexico towns under its control (Motolinía 1971; Carrasco 1984). Farther from home, the Aztec king Ahuitzotl ended a war with the Zapotec of Oaxaca by sending his daughter Coyolicatzin to marry the Zapotec ruler Cociyoeza (Marcus 1983c: 303). Cociyopii, the son resulting from this marriage, went on to rule the Zapotec. In addition to reinforcing the inequality of primary and secondary centers within the regional hierarchy, hypogamous marriage alliances were designed to strengthen the loyalty of lower-order towns. Often it worked, but in some cases the offspring of the marriage—emboldened by his royal ancestry—tried to break away and establish his town's autonomy.

In addition to the Tikal-Naranjo marriage already mentioned, ca. A.D. 785 a woman from the royal house of Yaxchilan married the lord of Bonampak, a secondary center within Yaxchilan's realm (Marcus 1976). It is worth noting that although both Naranjo and Bonampak were important sites with their own Emblem Glyphs, that fact in no way made them "autonomous" or "equal in stature" to Tikal or Yaxchilan. Just as the towns in Lord Canek's realm had their own names—drawn from the *batabob* who governed them—we can expect Classic secondary centers to have had Emblem Glyphs because they were ruled by important lords (Marcus n.d.a, 1976). However, those lords' inaugurations were usually only important enough to merit the Toothache glyph, not the Seating glyph, and those lords were the recipients, not the donors, of hypogamous brides.

Another archaeological clue to the asymmetric relationship between primary and secondary centers is the "meddling" of higher-order rulers in the

Fig. 13 Stela 24, Naranjo, Guatemala. This monument portrays a royal woman from Tikal who stands on the body of a captive; the two incised hieroglyphs in the captive's midsection represent "western land." The marriage of this royal woman to a local Naranjo lord, and the subsequent birth of her son, named Scroll Squirrel (who went on to rule Naranjo), gave Naranjo a status it had not formerly enjoyed. Her son's reign witnessed a major program in building construction and stelae carving. Photo courtesy of the Peabody Museum, Harvard University, Cambridge.

Fig. 14 Lintel 3, Piedras Negras, Guatemala. Bat Jaguar, an emissary from Yaxchilan, arrived at Piedras Negras via canoe. Here he is shown seated on a throne holding an audience, presumably to discuss the next ruler of Piedras Negras. Among those in the audience are secondary lords subject to Yaxchilan and tertiary lords subject to Piedras Negras. Photo courtesy of the University Museum, University of Pennsylvania, Philadelphia.

affairs of their dependencies (Flannery 1972). An example comes from Piedras Negras, a secondary center below Yaxchilan. In A.D. 757, the ruler of Piedras Negras lay dying. The ruler of Yaxchilan dispatched an emissary (a noble named Bat Jaguar) down the Usumacinta River to Piedras Negras, where he is shown on Lintel 3 holding an audience with the nobles of that site (Fig. 14). Eighteen days after the conference, the Piedras Negras ruler died. Because of the timing, it seems likely that this discussion centered on who the next ruler of Piedras Negras would be, probably because there were several competing candidates. It was not until five years later that a new ruler was inaugurated (with the Toothache glyph) at Piedras Negras (Marcus n.d.d, 1976: 85–87). It seems that the ruler of Yaxchilan influenced the choice, and in fact, his emissary may have governed Piedras Negras during the five years that it was temporarily without a ruler. In turn, similar meddling characterized Piedras Negras' relations with El Cayo (a still-lower-order center that was one of its dependencies), and so on down the hierarchy.

Further evidence for hierarchic relationships among Classic Maya cities comes from the use of Emblem Glyphs in the hieroglyphic texts of various cities. Major centers such as Tikal, Palenque, and Copan rarely mention the lords and Emblem Glyphs of the lower-order centers below them. Secon-

## Ancient Maya Political Organization

dary centers, on the other hand, do mention the lords and Emblem Glyphs of the primary center above them, but not the lords and Emblem Glyphs of the tertiary centers below them. In turn, tertiary centers mention the secondary centers to which they owed allegiance (Marcus 1973, 1974a, 1976, 1983a, 1984, 1987). Thus, third-order El Cayo mentions Piedras Negras, and second-order Piedras Negras mentions first-order Yaxchilan; second-order Naranjo mentions first-order Tikal, but Tikal does not mention Naranjo. This is not the behavior of autonomous provinces, but of *batabob* who owed allegiance to a supreme *ahau*.

Asymmetric and hierarchic relationships are also conveyed in an iconography of Classic power (Marcus 1974b) in which Maya rulers are shown standing on the backs of scantily clad, bound captives. In some cases the captive seems to represent an individual important enough to have his name carved on his thigh (Fig. 15), but in other cases it appears that the captive stands for an entire subject population, town, or territory (Marcus 1976: 162–163). For example, the incised glyphs shown on the body of the captive in Fig. 16 can be read as *chikin cab,* "western land." The first sign, *chi,* has an inset *kin* sign; the next sign is *cab,* a sign for "earth" or "land," which can be seen in a number of contexts in later Maya codices.

Still another archaeological clue to the territorial control of lower-order centers by higher-order centers can be found in the rapidly developing field of Maya economic specialization (Fry 1979; Fry and Cox 1974; Gibson 1989; Shafer and Hester 1983; McAnany 1989a,b). In some archaic states, craft specialists were concentrated in the cities, while the villages remained largely agricultural. Such was the relationship, for example, between the city of Ur and the village of Sakheri Sughir in Sumer (Wright 1969). In other archaic states, however, the capital city had such control over the countryside that potters or metalsmiths could be concentrated in villages, leaving the city to the nobles, priests, royal family, and administrators (Marcus 1983b). This was the case in ancient China (Chang 1968) and in the Valley of Oaxaca, where Monte Alban Ic villages like Tomaltepec specialized in reduced-firing ceramics (Whalen 1981). The Classic Maya also appear to have had the latter system; thus, dependencies like Colha could produce the eccentric flints that were used in major centers such as Tikal and El Mirador. Similarly, pottery produced in the smaller centers around Tikal and Palenque satisfied much of their utilitarian pottery needs (Rands 1967; Fry 1979).

### Changes in Hierarchies over Time

Data from the Classic Maya also support our notion of a dynamic system that changed over time, rather than exhibiting long-term stasis. A site's position in the hierarchy could rise or fall, and in this paper I give examples of both processes.

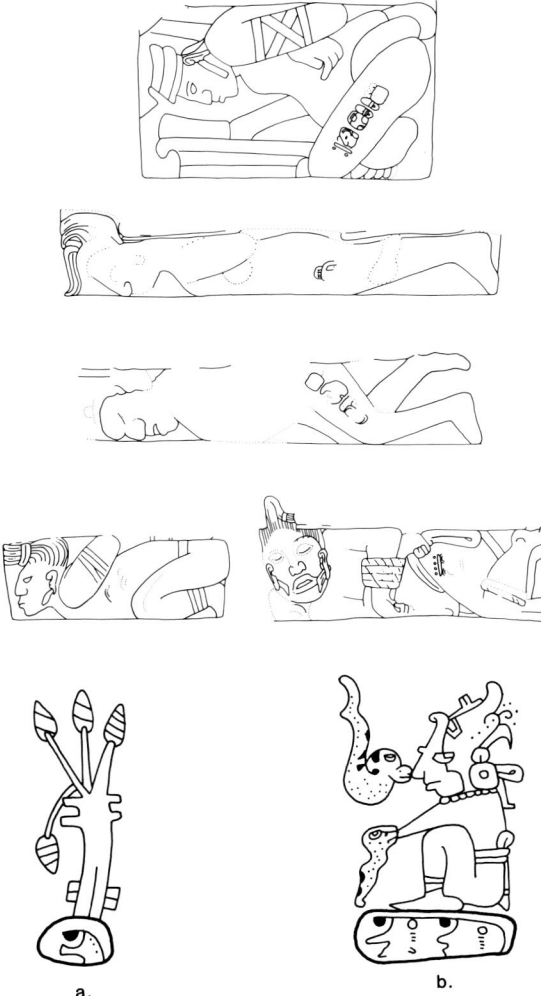

Fig. 15 Prostrate captives from monuments at Naranjo, shown with upper arms or wrists bound with rope, all of whom served as pedestals for reigning rulers. In Figs. 13 and 16c, we see a bound captive who represented "subjugated land" or "subject town." Here we see examples of named individuals, whose hieroglyphic names are usually incised on their thighs (redrawn after Graham and von Euw 1975, 2: 49, 59, 37, 27, 53).

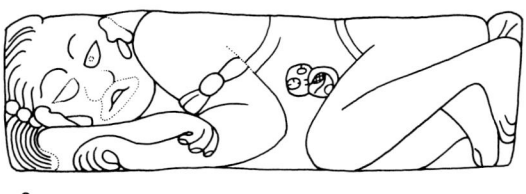

Fig. 16 The sign for "earth" or "land" in various contexts: (a) Vegetation growing out of the sign for earth (Madrid Codex); (b) Maize deity seated on the sign for earth (Madrid Codex); (c) Hieroglyphs for *chikin cab*, "western land," grace the midsection of this captive depicted in the lower register on Naranjo's Stela 24 (see Fig. 13).

*Ancient Maya Political Organization*

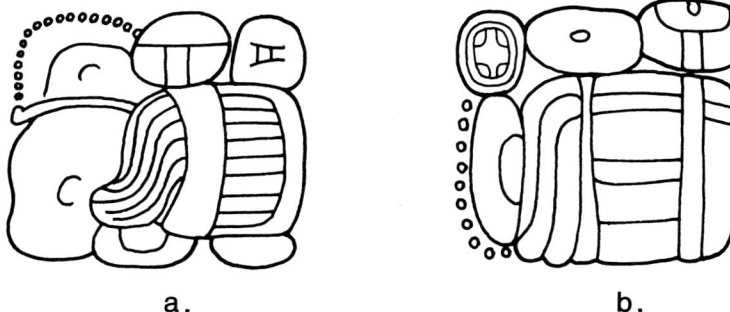

Fig. 17 Emblem Glyph shared by members of the Petexbatun Confederacy, co-administered by Dos Pilas and Aguateca in the 8th century: (a) La Amelia, Stela 2, A9; (b) Dos Pilas, Stela 16, C6 (redrawn after Marcus 1976: fig. 4.11 c, d).

At A.D. 751 there was one region of the Peten that may provide an analogy for Roys' Type B provinces. Those provinces, as we have seen, had no capital and no *halach uinic,* but were closely integrated because most principal towns were governed by *batabob* drawn from the same lineage. During the Classic period the Pasion River region was organized as the Petexbatun Confederacy, which consisted of a series of neighboring sites such as Aguateca, Dos Pilas, Tamarindito, La Amelia, and Seibal. One of the reasons we believe this cluster of sites was a confederacy is that they shared the same Emblem Glyph at one time or another (Fig. 17). Perhaps because some of their rulers were members of the same lineage, or linked through marriage, these sites considered themselves all part of the same province. I would suggest that they alternated over time between Roys' loosely allied Type C provinces, and his more closely allied Type B provinces.

The towns of the Petexbatun Confederacy spent a great deal of the Classic period jockeying for power among themselves; this is a region where I predict future archaeological work will uncover substantial evidence for warfare. My 1974 hunch—based on their hieroglyphic texts, ceramic evidence, and geographic location—was that this group of towns had formerly been secondary and tertiary centers within the large regional state headed by Tikal (Marcus n.d.d, 1976: 63–74, 1983a, 1984). Over time, some of these sites seem to have shifted from secondary to tertiary status. It appears that when they were closely united, they had the power to break away from Tikal; however, when they were warring with each other, Tikal could again dominate them. When they broke away it appears that Dos Pilas became dominant for a while, to be joined later by Aguateca as a co-dominant center (A. Demarest, personal communication, 1989). Together they expanded and annexed additional towns, but could not control them permanently.

The Petexbatun evidence illustrates a point already made for the Postclassic by Roys, and confirmed by almost every archaic state we know: *the lords of secondary centers are almost always the major source of trouble for primary centers.* Just as the *batabob* in Roys' Type A provinces were potential threats to undermine the power of the *halach uinic,* so also were the lords at secondary centers in the large Classic Maya regional states. Two of the major reasons for the rebellion of secondary centers were probably: (1) a desire to keep the tribute/taxes they collected from tertiary centers, rather than passing it on to the capital; and (2) a wish to utilize their labor forces for their own purposes, not someone else's.

I suspect that we will find that most Maya warfare occurred at this secondary center level—as a result either of secondary centers jockeying for power among themselves, or of secondary centers fighting to free their province from a regional capital. Significantly, I see no evidence that major centers, such as Tikal, Palenque, Copan, or Yaxchilan, fought wars against each other.

The Petexbatun area also presents us with a nice example of how a lower-order center could rise in the hierarchy. Prior to A.D. 751, Seibal was a fairly small tertiary center in the Dos Pilas political sphere. After that date, it displayed a newly gained Emblem Glyph and was elevated to secondary-level status. Seibal's rise in the hierarchy continued, until it could claim to be one of the four powerful dynastic seats of power in the lowlands by A.D. 849.

One secondary center that apparently succeeded in breaking away from its capital was Quirigua. In the early eighth century Quirigua was an important secondary center below Copan, a regional capital. In A.D. 738, the Quirigua ruler variously called "Two-armed Sky" (Marcus 1976: 134), "Cauac Sky" (Sharer 1978), or "Two-legged Sky" (Kelley 1962) claimed to have won a military victory over the Copan ruler 18 Jog;[7] as a consequence, Quirigua achieved a degree of autonomy for a while. Perhaps not surprisingly, this event is mentioned at least four times at Quirigua, but only once at Copan (Marcus 1976: 130; Sharer 1978).

Robert Sharer (1978) has demonstrated that during its period of autonomy, Quirigua enjoyed a flurry of building construction, perhaps diverting much of its labor force into its own aggrandizement instead of serving Copan. This "disloyalty" by Quirigua recalls the later "disloyalty" of the Xiu against the Cocom, which brought down Mayapan.

Some groups of Puuc sites in northern Yucatan might also have resembled the towns in Roys' Type B provinces, linked by marriage alliances and

---

[7] I use 18 Jog rather than 18 Rabbit for two reasons: (1) 18 Jog has precedence in the literature; and (2) the animal known as *ba* in Maya is a rodent (paca, agouti, or gopher), not a lagomorph.

## Ancient Maya Political Organization

Fig. 18 "The Four on High" at A.D. 731 according to the Copan ruler 18 Jog. Line 1 gives a phrase that refers to the four lordly titles, dynasties, or places listed in Line 2. Line 3 gives east (*lakin*), west (*chikin*), south (*nohol*), and north (*xaman*) as the four world quadrants or directions (redrawn after Marcus 1973: fig. 3).

governed by members of the same lineage. Chichen Itza, prior to becoming a centralized capital, appears to have had some of the characteristics of the head town of a Type A province, and when more work has been done in the area we may have examples of Type C provinces as well.

*Changes Between A.D. 731 and 849*

The timing of Quirigua's rebellion against Copan—A.D. 738—may be significant in light of a second development, suggested by hieroglyphic monuments at A.D. 731 and 849, and in the context of our new dynamic model.

An interesting three-clause passage occurs on Stela A at Copan, a monument dedicated in A.D. 731 by the ruler 18 Jog (Fig. 18). I originally read the first clause as *can caanal*, "the four on high" (Marcus 1976). The second clause lists the Emblem Glyphs of Copan, Tikal, Calakmul(?), and Palenque, in that order (Berlin 1958; Barthel 1968; Marcus n.d.a, 1973). The third clause gives the four great world quarters of the Maya—east, west, south, and north—in that order.

We have already seen that quadripartite organization was a fundamental part of Maya ideology, from the organization of the heavens down to the ward organization of villages. Because of this tendency toward quadripartite organization, I suggested that Copan's ruler viewed these four great dynasties and cities as "four on high," representing the four quadrants of the lowland Maya world. The clauses have a sweeping, global quality, as if 18 Jog were giving his version of the "ideal" world layout; it is cosmology, not history or accurate geography. East was listed first because it was the important direction of the rising sun (Thompson 1934; Redfield and Villa Rojas 1934; Roys 1933; Marcus n.d.b.). Copan was listed first not because it was in the east, but because Copan's ruler was commissioning the monument. Four Emblem Glyphs were listed, not because those were the only four great Maya cities, but because 18 Jog felt that those four cities—or the *four royal houses ruling them*—were the most powerful in each of the four quadrants of the Maya world at A.D. 731.

Although the quadripartite view seen on Stela A was the *Maya* view— more specifically, 18 Jog's view—in the literature I still find references to "Marcus' quadripartite model." Let me make this clear: *my* model was of *large regional states* (Fig. 19) *with primary, secondary, and tertiary centers forming an administrative-optimizing hierarchy* (Haggett 1972: 288–289). The "cosmological, quadripartite model" should be attributed *not* to Marcus 1973, but to 18 Jog, A.D. 731.

Independent analyses by Adams and Jones (1981) led them to conclude that ". . . there certainly seem to have been two regional states at Calakmul and Tikal during the Late Classic. There is every evidence, however, of two or more contemporary regional states north of the central Petén and at least three more centered on Copán, Palenque, and Yaxchilán to the south" (Adams and Jones 1981: 320).

Thus Adams and Jones, on the basis of courtyard counts and other data, find empirical evidence that the southern lowlands might have been organized into five regional states, with other states such as Rio Bec and Chenes occurring in the central and northern lowlands. They also point out substantial differences in absolute size among the "capitals" of those regional states. Palenque, for example, while it was the largest city in its region, was no bigger than some of the secondary centers below Tikal (Adams and Jones 1981: 319).

I see nothing to object to in this, nor am I surprised that five or more regions emerge in the etic view of the field archaeologist. What Copan's Stela A gives us is 18 Jog's emic view of the Maya world, a world he saw as dominated by his royal house and the royal houses of three other great cities. This is such a widespread cosmic view that it should not surprise us.

Ancient Maya Political Organization

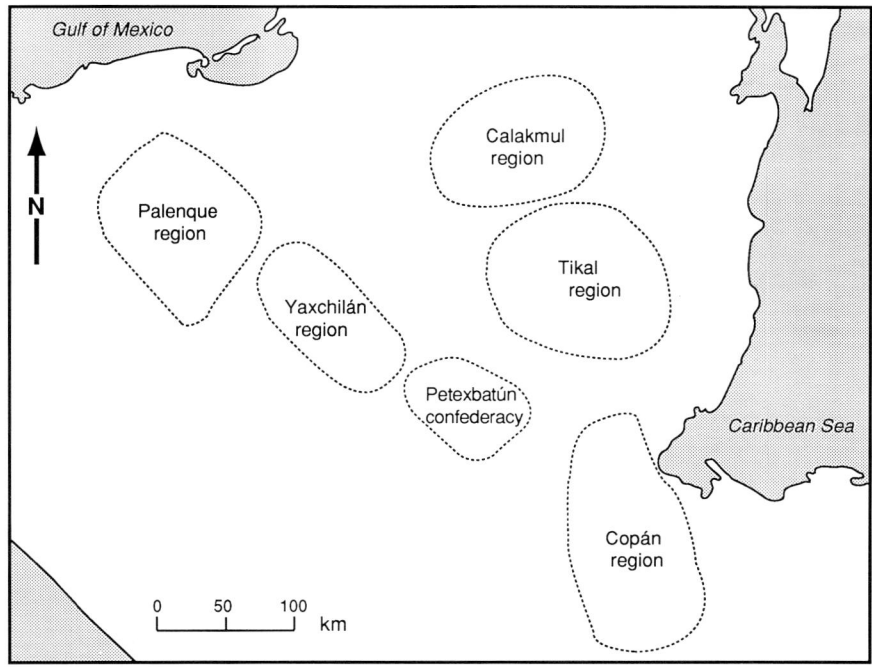

Fig. 19 Large regional states of the southern lowlands. At least four polities had major capitals, such as Palenque, Calakmul, Tikal, and Copan. For a while, after A.D. 752, Yaxchilan administered a similar polity. At various times the Petexbatun region was administered by Dos Pilas, by a confederacy headed by Dos Pilas and Aguateca, or by Seibal (redrawn after Marcus 1984: fig. 6).

For example, the Inca viewed their world as consisting of four *suyus* (Zuidema 1964; Rostworowski 1988), the ancient Chinese saw their capital as "the pivot of the four quarters" (Wheatley 1971), and the Sumerian ruler called himself "the King of the Four Quarters" (Redman 1978: 312). In all three of the latter cases, the etic reality shows that there were more than four important cities.

It is easy to see why 18 Jog singled out the four places he did, for no matter how Maya cities are analyzed, those four emerge as something special in A.D. 731. Beginning in the 1920s, Morley (1920, 1938, 1946) had assigned Tikal and Copan to his "Rank I" category on the basis of size, number of stelae, and monumentality of buildings. Morley (1946: 317, 319) also indicated that "Calakmul should possibly be included . . ."; however, he did not do so ". . . because in spite of its mass production of monuments the individual sculptured stelae are for the most part of little esthetic merit. . . ." Richard Adams and Richard Jones' courtyard study also places

Copan, Tikal, Calakmul, and Palenque in the upper echelon. Significantly, Adams and Jones agree that places like Naranjo were hierarchically below the capitals in their respective regions, a view apparently also shared by T. Patrick Culbert (1988).

But something happened to Copan and Palenque after A.D. 731. Only seven years after the dedication of Stela A, as we have seen, the secondary center of Quirigua broke away from Copan. Perhaps other secondary centers broke away after that; whatever the case, Copan was no longer listed as one of the "four on high" by A.D. 849. Palenque, too, was declining in importance, especially after A.D. 800. In terms of our dynamic model, some states in the southern lowlands were evidently breaking down into less centralized units, like Roys' Type A or B provinces.

Stela 10 at Seibal, carved in A.D. 849, names four lords with associated Emblem Glyphs for Seibal, Tikal, Calakmul(?), and Motul de San Jose(?), in that order (Marcus 1973, n.d.d, 1976). Predictably, the lord of Seibal is listed first because he had commissioned the stela; what is interesting is that the lords of Copan and Palenque are no longer listed among the four. Moreover, the distances among the four places mentioned at 849 were less than half as great as those among the four places mentioned at 731, suggesting a considerable reduction in the size of the territory (and/or population) governed by the southern lowland Maya. The two cities no longer listed are those that had been the farthest out, near the western and southeastern limits of the system.

I have attached question marks to both Calakmul(?) and Motul de San Jose(?) because there are too few occurrences of those Emblem Glyphs to be conclusive. Motul de San Jose is the only site using the fourth Emblem Glyph at that time, but since Motul was relatively small, we must hold out the possibility that it was simply mentioning a primary center to which it owed allegiance. However, a trend surface analysis of the lowland Maya area during Calendar Cycle 10 undertaken by Frederick Bove (1981: 109) has independently confirmed the presence of "political regions" centered on Seibal, Calakmul, Tikal, Motul de San Jose, and Chinkultic. Thus we are left with five regions, defined by etic analysis, which include the four mentioned in the Seibal ruler's emic statement.

Adams and Jones (1981: 302) find it incongruous that between A.D. 731 and 849, ". . . Calakmul, the northern capital (over 5 km$^2$ in extent), is replaced by Motul de San Jose (about .5 km$^2$ in extent) in Marcus' reconstruction." While I understand their concern, it is not the case that Motul "replaced" Calakmul; Calakmul is still listed as one of the four capitals in 849. Moreover, to call Calakmul "the northern capital" implies that 18 Jog of Copan had assigned each of the royal houses and cities to a specific quadrant. In fact, his clause "east, west, south, north" may simply be an expression similar to our "four corners of the earth," or "from Maine to California."

In the context of our dynamic model, the cosmological content of Stela A at Copan and Stela 10 at Seibal is not nearly as important as the evidence they provide for instability and change. Those two monuments, carved only 118 years apart, show us that the area of great regional states was shrinking even before the so-called collapse of centers in the Peten. Most importantly, that 118-year period shows us evolutionary change in two directions. Even as the Copan state began to break up into autonomous provinces, like that of Quirigua, the Petexbatun region was going in the opposite direction. Once a loose alliance of towns resembling Roys' Type B and C provinces, it gradually consolidated first under Dos Pilas and Aguateca, and then (by 849) became a regional state with Seibal as its capital (Marcus 1976).

## THE APPLICATION OF GEOGRAPHIC MODELS

We are now in a position to evaluate Mathews' (1985) contention that there was no political hierarchy in the Classic Maya area, and that every site with an Emblem Glyph was autonomous. While there were clearly periods in which hierarchies broke down, and secondary centers pulled their provinces away from a capital, such an egalitarian model is surely inappropriate for the "peaks" of the dynamic model, such as during the first half of the eighth century. To demonstrate this, I must briefly discuss two techniques of locational analysis used by human geographers. One, Central Place Theory, is appropriate for state-level societies with administrative hierarchies; the other, Thiessen polygons, is appropriate for egalitarian societies where all sites are of equal size or power.

### Central Place Models

As the name suggests, Central Place Theory is based on the assumption that a region includes a central place that serves the needs of a hierarchy of subsidiary towns, villages, and hamlets beneath it (Christaller 1933; Lösch 1954; Haggett 1966). In turn, the subsidiary units provide goods and manpower for the central place, whose needs cannot otherwise be met. While lower-order centers often provide the goods they manufacture, the central place exercises administrative control in decision-making, promises military protection, and displays regional religious control (Lösch 1954; Haggett 1966: 124).

W. Christaller's (1933) Central Place models display the interdependent service functions of lower- and higher-order centers as hexagonal lattices that convey an idealized settlement pattern. This is because, as demonstrated by Peter Haggett (1966: 49), the most efficient settlement system in an isotropic, featureless plain is a hexagonal lattice surrounding a central place.

Christaller's hierarchy of centers was made up of recognizably distinct levels or tiers. August Lösch's hierarchy revealed a continuous sequence of centers rather than distinct tiers, such that settlements of the same size need not have the same function, and larger central places need not necessarily have all the functions of smaller centers. This version (Marcus 1976: 24; Haggett 1966: 124) is more appropriate for the Classic Maya.

Although Christaller's work on Central Place Theory has been available since 1933 and Lösch's on the economics of location since 1938, neither caught the attention of archaeologists until the 1960s. British geographer Haggett (1966) and British archaeologist David L. Clarke (1968) made the techniques of locational analysis widely known. Archaeologists at Chicago and Michigan, among others, turned to these methods. At Michigan, Henry Wright and Gregory Johnson (Wright and Johnson 1975; Johnson 1972, 1973) applied them to Near Eastern sites, while Kent Flannery (1972) was the first to apply them to Maya sites.

Central Place models seem appropriate to the lowland Maya area because, for more than fifty years, archaeologists have argued that large Maya cities were "ceremonial centers" providing services for a wide sustaining area, an area which in turn participated in the construction and maintenance of public buildings at the central place. What was lacking in Flannery's preliminary work was a way of making sure all sites in the model were occupied contemporaneously; monuments dated by the Long Count provide that assurance (Marcus 1973, 1974a, n.d.d).

When one applies Central Place models to the capitals of the major Classic regional states we have discussed (such as Tikal, Palenque, and Calakmul)— and to their secondary centers (such as Naranjo, Uaxactun, Naachtun, and Tonina)—we get immediate confirmation of the appropriateness of the model. Secondary centers form hexagonal lattices of equidistantly spaced sites around capitals, with the hexagonal lattice of sites around Calakmul having a particularly uniform spacing of 30 km, or one day's travel between centers (Fig. 20). *Such a close match to an ideal hexagonal lattice would not be present if the assumption of administrative hierarchy were false.*

## Thiessen Polygons

The second geographic technique borrowed by Mayanists is that of drawing Thiessen polygons; its application to the Maya was pioneered by Norman Hammond in 1972 and 1974, and it has been used more recently by Mathews (1985). The ease with which this technique can be applied has been described by Flannery, somewhat tongue-in-cheek, as follows: "Those of you who may have hesitated to use the Thiessen method because of your weak grades in math can stop worrying. You simply measure the distance between each site and its neighbor, calculate half the distance, and draw a boundary there, at right angles to a straight line between the sites. This is one of the newest approaches . . . and it demands all the rigor of those

## Ancient Maya Political Organization

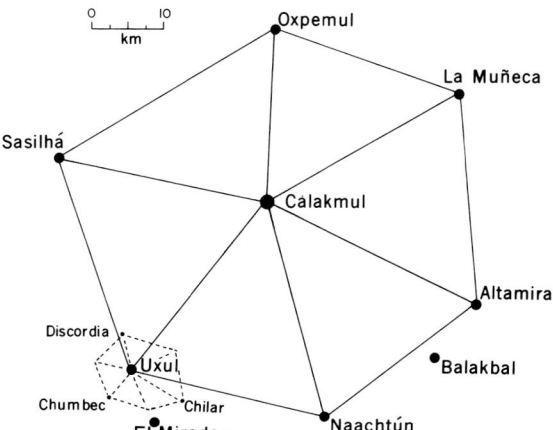

Fig. 20 The hexagonal lattice of subordinate sites around Calakmul displays remarkably uniform spacing, with each subject site located roughly one day's travel from the capital (redrawn after Marcus 1987: fig. 43).

follow-the-dots puzzles you used to work out as a kid" (Flannery 1977: 661).

Perhaps the most important contribution of Hammond's work is the discovery that the "packing" of sites was greatest in the area around Tikal, suggesting that the population density of that part of the Peten was higher than that of other areas, such as the area around Palenque (Hammond 1974: 330). Precisely because of this closer spacing of sites, however, the Thiessen method winds up giving every city in the Tikal region a smaller territory than a city in one of the less densely populated areas (Fig. 21). This fact was noted by Flannery (1977) and by Adams and Jones (1981), who pointed out that the use of Thiessen polygons ". . . leads to the patently absurd result of the very large site of Tikal (16 km$^2$ in extent) being given only as large a territory as the very small center of El Encanto (less than 1 ha in extent). Therefore, the question of hierarchical relationships among the ancient centers becomes crucial" (Adams and Jones 1981: 302).

Hammond himself put his finger on the problem when he noted that the Thiessen method requires one to treat all sites "as being of equal political status," adding, "I am aware that this may not be so, indeed probably is not so . . ." (Hammond 1974: 318). Indeed, Hammond (1975) then turned his attention to the study of site size hierarchies in northern Belize.

Later, Mathews (1985) used Thiessen polygons to model Classic Maya polities by drawing a polygon around each site that had its own Emblem Glyph (see below). This once again resulted in Tikal having a smaller territory than Bonampak or Tonina. Mathews treated each site with its own Emblem Glyph as if it were autonomous, as if all such sites were "equal in terms of political power" (Mathews 1985: 54). I find this surprising in view

*Joyce Marcus*

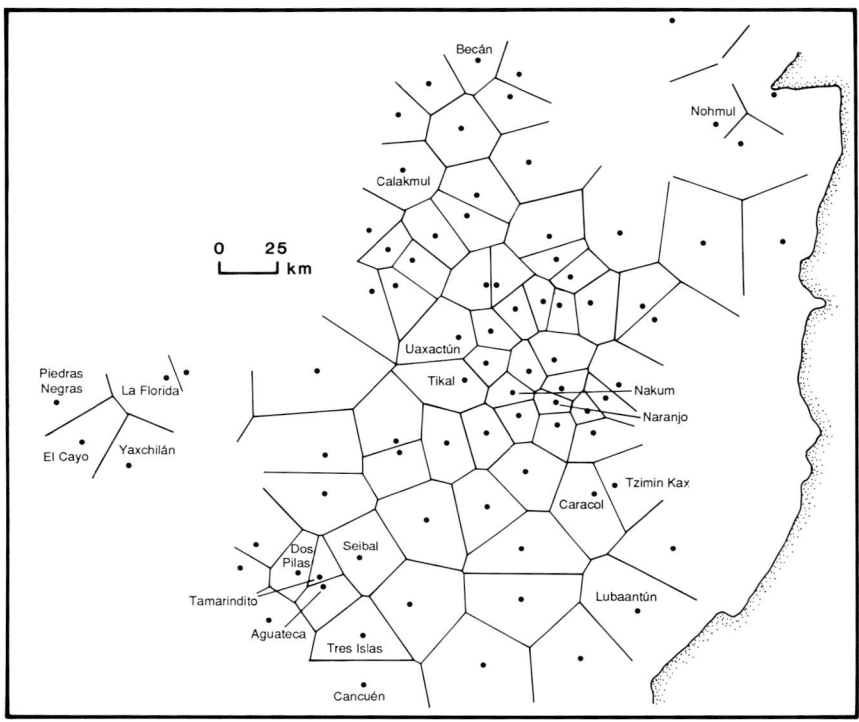

Fig. 21 Hammond's imposition of Thiessen polygons on the southern lowlands (redrawn after Hammond 1974: fig. 3).

of the fact that Mathews himself (1985: 54) states that "Archaeologically, it is clear that this assumption is not a valid one."

The problem with the use of Thiessen polygons, as many investigators have noted, is that the model assumes complete equality of centers. In other words, it is appropriate for egalitarian cultures such as the New Guinea highland societies, where no settlement is administratively under any other. It becomes increasingly inappropriate at the level of chiefdoms, and fails altogether at the level of states, which are *by definition* hierarchical. No archaic state had such an egalitarian organization, and I think most of us agree that the eighth-century Maya were a state.

Prior to state formation there are cases of competing chiefdoms (such as the "peer polity" situation described by Renfrew and Cherry [1986] where there is temporary autonomy among polities. The state forms, however, when one polity begins to gobble up its peers, ending their autonomy by reducing them to provinces within its hegemony.

## THE SIZE OF MAYA POLITIES

Now let us consider the sizes of Classic Maya states and their levels of administrative hierarchy. Studies of early Near Eastern states (Wright and Johnson 1975; Johnson 1973, 1980) and early Mesoamerican states like the one centered at Monte Alban (Kowalewski et al. 1989) show them to consist of hundreds of thousands of people distributed across tens of thousands of square kilometers, and to display a hierarchy of settlements with at least four tiers. This organization contrasts with that of chiefdoms, or rank societies, which generally have only two to three tiers of decision-making and extend over much smaller territories. The pre-state chiefdoms of southwestern Iran (Wright 1977; Johnson 1980) and the Rosario-phase chiefdom of the Valley of Oaxaca (Marcus and Flannery n.d.) would be examples.

The point I intend to make is this: by all the ethnographic, ethnohistoric, and archaeological criteria used by researchers working on the origins of the state, the Maya polities proposed by Mathews (1985) are too small and hierarchically simple to qualify as states. To demonstrate this, I have prepared four maps all to the same scale, and three tables of polity sizes calculated on a Summagraphics Intelligent Digitizer.

Let us begin with the Maya state centered at Mayapan, A.D. 1300–1400 (Fig. 22a). This state covered 85,700 km$^2$ and subsumed a whole series of provinces, each with its own head town. Those head towns, each ruled by an important hereditary noble, formed the second tier of a four-level hierarchy. Below them were smaller towns, ruled by *batabob,* which constituted the third tier of the system; at the bottom were simple agricultural villages.

Now let us look at what happened after Mayapan collapsed and Yucatan broke up into sixteen separate provinces (Fig. 22b). First of all, the top tier of the hierarchy disappeared; Yucatan no longer had a large regional state. Instead, it had a series of "maximal chiefdoms" (Carneiro 1981) corresponding to Roys' (1957) Type A provinces; a series of "minimal chiefdoms" corresponding to Roys' Type B provinces; and a series of loosely confederated Type C provinces, which may have had too little hierarchy even to qualify as chiefdoms.

If we look at the territories covered by these provinces (Table 1) we see that the smallest (Hocaba, Tases, and Chakan) covered about 1,000–2,000 km$^2$; medium-sized provinces (Ah Kin Chel, Chikinchel, and Chetumal) covered about 3,000–6,000 km$^2$; large provinces, such as Mani (Tutul Xiu) and Cupul, covered 10,000 km$^2$; and the largest province (Uaymil) covered about 11,000 km$^2$. It is unlikely that any of these provinces—even Type A provinces such as Mani—qualified as a state.

Now let us look at the sizes of the eighth-century Maya polities proposed by Mathews, based on the notion that every site with an Emblem Glyph was autonomous (Fig. 23a and Table 2). Tikal—once thought to be the capital of the entire southern lowlands—is allowed only 1,081 km$^2$. Yaxchilan—

Joyce Marcus

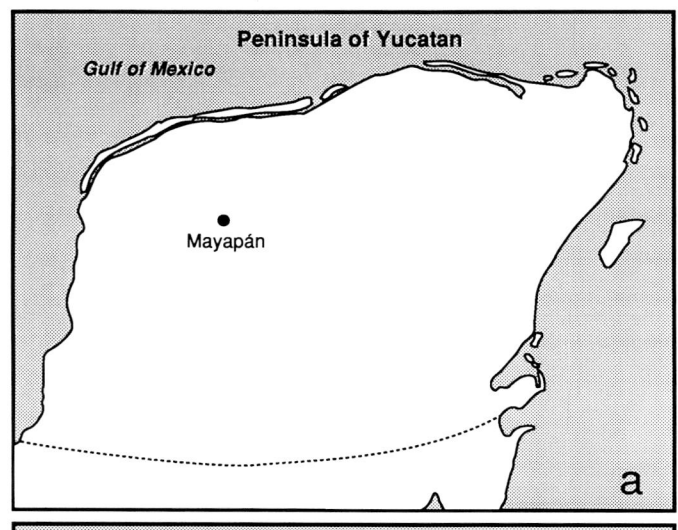

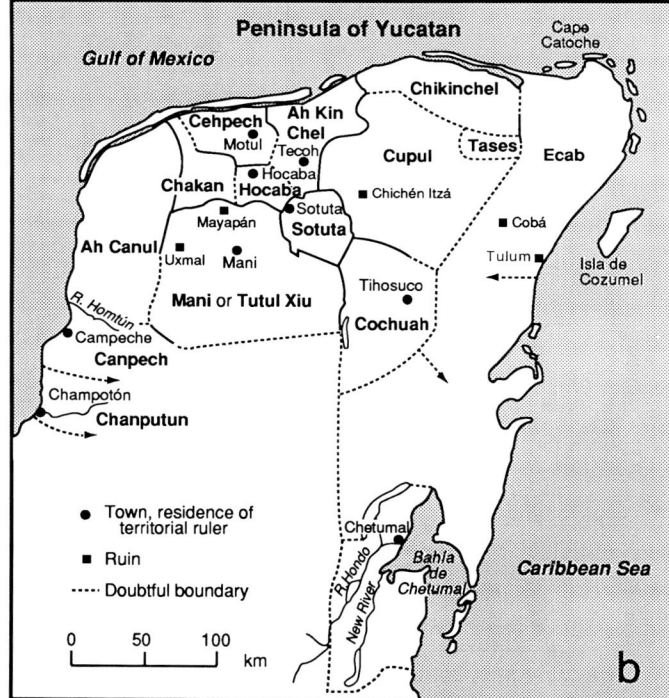

Fig. 22  Maya polities of the northern lowlands: (a) the extent of the territory controlled by Mayapan at its peak is indicated by the dashed line; (b) the sixteen provinces of Yucatan, following the breakup of Mayapan (redrawn after Roys 1957: map 1).

TABLE 1: SIZES OF YUCATEC PROVINCES
AFTER COLLAPSE OF THE MAYAPAN
STATE

| Province | Size in km$^2$ |
|---|---|
| Ah Canul | 7906 |
| Ah Kin Chel | 3427 |
| Cehpech | 2423 |
| Chakan | 1602 |
| Chetumal | 6161 |
| Chikinchel | 3720 |
| Cochuah | 6069 |
| Cupul | 10,046 |
| Ecab | 9479 |
| Hocaba | 1066 |
| Mani (Tutul Xiu) | 10,203 |
| Sotuta | 1869 |
| Tases | 1034 |
| Uaymil | 11,285 |

believed by many to be one of the greatest Maya centers—is assigned 1,846 km$^2$. Seibal gets 1,289 km$^2$. These territories are as small as, or smaller than, those of the tiniest Yucatec chiefdoms following the Mayapan collapse. Indeed, the whole series of territories, with the possible exception of Tonina's, are as small as or smaller than anything seen in Yucatan at the time of the Conquest.

Nor would any of these territories have had the four-tiered hierarchy characteristic of states. In my view, Tikal was the capital of a regional state in which Naranjo, Uaxactun, and other sites would be the secondary tier of administrative centers, that is, the "head towns of provinces." Removing these sites from below Tikal eliminates the second tier of the hierarchy and drops Tikal to the level of a rank society with only three hierarchical levels. In one stroke, a "forest of kings" has been reduced to a "forest of chiefs."

Mathews' view raises an interesting possibility. What if, in the future, a new site midway between Tikal and Naranjo were discovered to have had its own Emblem Glyph? Would we draw more lines, reducing Tikal's and Naranjo's territories still further? In other words, if (as seems likely) more and more monuments with Emblem Glyphs are found, will we see Tikal's territory shrink to 500 km$^2$, or even 250 km$^2$? Could Tikal eventually be reduced to a minimal chiefdom with only two hierarchical levels? I hope not, and I suggest that the polity sizes proposed by Adams and Jones (Fig. 23b and Table 3) make much more sense in terms of what is known about states. Adams (1990: 36) has argued that his rank-size analysis of Classic Maya cities "indicates political units of regional state size." In the case of

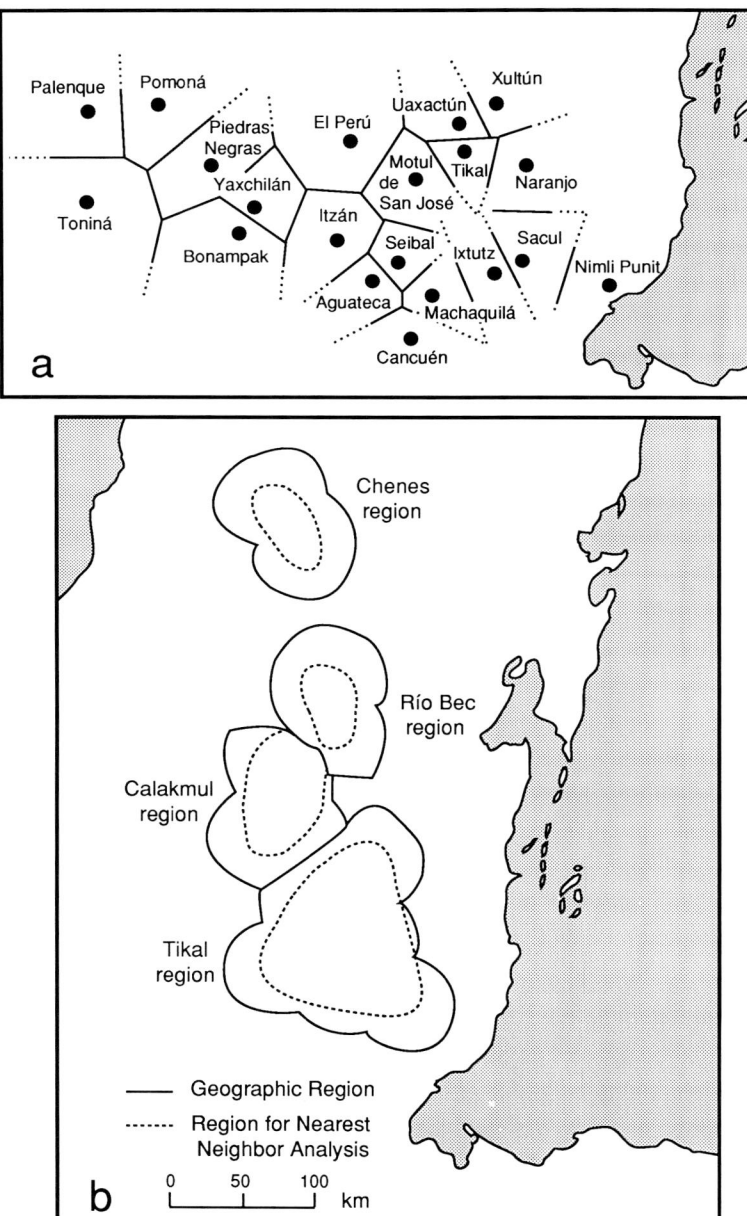

Fig. 23 Maya polities of the southern lowlands: two alternative views: (a) very small territories assigned to 8th-century sites by Mathews (1985); (b) much larger territories assigned to regional states by Adams (1990). (The scale of Figs. 22 and 23 is the same.)

TABLE 2: SIZES OF POLITIES ASSIGNED TO EIGHTH-CENTURY MAYA CITIES BY MATHEWS (1985)

| Province | Size in km$^2$ |
|---|---|
| Aguateca | 2238 |
| Bonampak | 8708 |
| Cancuén | 7193 |
| Itzán | 3585 |
| Ixtutz | 3241 |
| Machaquilá | 1807 |
| Motul de San José | 3067 |
| Naranjo | 4411 |
| Nimli Punit | 5486 |
| Palenque | 9980 |
| El Perú | 7522 |
| Piedras Negras | 4421 |
| Pomoná | 6129 |
| Sacul | 2831 |
| Seibal | 1289 |
| Tikal | 1081 |
| Toniná | 14,128 |
| Uaxactún | 3105 |
| Xultún | 6447 |
| Yaxchilán | 1846 |

TABLE 3: SIZES OF VARIOUS LOWLAND REGIONAL STATES ACCORDING TO ADAMS AND JONES (1981)

| Province | Size in km$^2$ |
|---|---|
| Calakmul | 8907 |
| Chenes | 8632 |
| Río Bec | 7932 |
| Tikal | 21,095 |

Tikal, for example, Adams and Jones (1981: 318) suggest that "at one period in the Classic, [Tikal] may also have dominated the Calakmul and Rio Bec regions to the north, the Belize area to the east, and the Pasion zone to the south. This would be a total area of more than 100,000 km$^2$." It would also be an area some eighteen percent larger than the Postclassic state centered at Mayapan. I do not consider that figure at all out of line for what many regard as the most powerful of the Peten's Classic polities. I also consider it *much* more plausible than the 1,081 km$^2$ proposed by Mathews.

Even for the eighth century, which is the focus of this volume, Adams and Jones would allow Tikal a territory of at least 21,095 km$^2$. Their estimates for Calakmul, Rio Bec, and Chenes are all in the 7,000–9,000 km$^2$ range, *many times larger* than those allowed for Seibal, Tikal, and Yaxchilan by Mathews.

There is real irony in what Mathews has proposed since it would imply that the *peak* of Maya civilization actually came in the Postclassic at Mayapan, when for the first time there was a polity covering 85,700 km$^2$. Indeed, in his model no polity in the Classic southern lowlands would have been a state; our first Maya states would appear in Postclassic Yucatan. I would argue that the Maya state had formed by A.D. 534, and that Mathews' whole model is based on the erroneous assumption that any site with an emblem (whether it represents a place, a title, a patronym, or all three) is autonomous. That assumption is *not* supported by Maya epigraphy or ethnohistory, and it produces polities that are too small, and have too few administrative levels, to be states.

Since Morley's rankings of sites in the 1920s and 1930s, the size and monumentality of capitals such as Tikal, Copan, and Calakmul have been apparent; they have always stood out from their regional landscapes. With new settlement pattern data and increasing information from Copan (Willey and Leventhal 1979; Leventhal 1981; Webster and Freter 1990; Fash 1988), Calakmul (Folan n.d.; Folan and May Hau 1984; Marcus 1987, n.d.c), and Tikal (Carr and Hazard 1961; Puleston 1974; Haviland 1970), it is becoming clear that these first-rank centers (1) had very substantial populations numbering in the tens of thousands, perhaps even 60,000 at Tikal; (2) controlled a lot of manpower in their region; (3) served over time as "magnets" pulling in more people from smaller centers; and (4) had territorial boundaries that shifted over time as some provinces rebelled.

Unfortunately, lower-order dependencies—although more numerous than primary centers—are underrepresented in many excavation reports and settlement-pattern studies. Exceptions include the northern Belize projects of Hammond (1975), Harry Shafer and Thomas Hester (1983), Richard MacNeish (1982), Robert Fry (1989), Patricia McAnany (1989b), and Eric Gibson (n.d.). Confounding our attempt to understand the hierarchy is an unwillingness on the part of some Mayanists to admit that *their* site could have been anything less than a "capital." The result is that we know less than we should about secondary centers, in spite of the fact that they were often the most dynamic level in the system—and even less about provinces, although they were the system's most stable large unit.

Whether we measure the importance of sites through the study of *Emblem Glyphs* (Marcus 1973, n.d.d, 1976; Mathews 1985), *numbers of stelae* (Morley 1938, 1946), *numbers of courtyards* (Adams and Jones 1981), *monumentality of the public buildings* (Morley 1920, 1938, 1946), or *sheer size* (Haviland 1969, 1970), Tikal emerges as a special site at the top of its regional hierarchy. By whichever criterion, Tikal was a site *distinct from all other sites in its region*, which makes it all the more implausible to assign it as small a territory as the Thiessen method does, especially when this occurs as a direct result of the high population density of its region. All the Thiessen model does is separate capitals from their major dependencies.

Identifying some cities as major capitals does not diminish the importance of Maya secondary centers. Indeed, some secondary-center territories may coincide with "manufacturing zones," such as those for the production of utilitarian pottery (Fig. 20). Many of the utilitarian jars and bowls in the Tikal and Palenque region were produced by lower-order centers (Fry 1979; Fry and Cox 1974; Rands 1967). Other lower-order centers such as Colha were producing flint tools of various kinds for the Altun Ha region and well beyond (Gibson n.d.; Marcus 1983a, 1983b, 1984; Shafer and Hester 1983). Some of these goods were distributed within a small province, others were distributed to other provinces headed by secondary centers, and others were produced for consumption at the capital of the regional state itself. To view them all as independent units would obscure this picture of a regional state's internal organization. Finally, some of these goods crossed the regional state's boundaries, and were given as gifts or included in caches, building dedications, and funeral offerings at sites in a more distant regional system (Marcus 1983a, 1984). It is true that the provincial makeup of each state and the distribution network of its products remain to be understood, but progress has been made (Ashmore 1981; Marcus 1982), particularly in the regions of Tikal (Fry 1979, 1989), Palenque (Rands 1967; Rands and Bishop 1980), and northern Belize (Potter, this volume; Shafer and Hester 1983; Gibson 1989; McAnany 1989a, 1989b).

Thiessen polygons might be appropriate for loosely allied, autonomous units. For example, Roys' Type C provinces for sixteenth-century Yucatan, including Chakan and Chikinchel, seem to have had that type of organization (Roys 1957: 6). However, those provinces were largely the breakdown products of Mayapan's collapse, and do not reflect the situation at the peak of Mayapan's power. Central Place Theory is more appropriate for examining the *peaks* of each oscillation in the dynamic model, moments such as A.D. 731 and 849, when there is evidence for large regional states with central places, secondary centers, and tertiary centers.

## DISCUSSION OF RESULTS

Let us now return to the question asked by Thompson in 1954: were the Classic Maya characterized by large, powerful, centralized states that controlled numerous provinces, or did they have loose alliances of small, autonomous city-states? The answer supplied by our dynamic model is *both,* because one is the periodic breakdown product of the other.

Based on multiple lines of evidence, it seems clear that at A.D. 731, Copan, Tikal, Calakmul, and Palenque were the capitals of large regional states, and shortly after A.D. 731 Yaxchilan was also. Those states were made up of provinces, each headed by a secondary center whose ruler (while important in his own right) owed allegiance to the *ahau* at his capital. And below the secondary centers were tertiary centers, each governed by a lesser noble like the *batabob* of Roys' Type A provinces. When there was a problem in succession at a secondary center, as at Piedras Negras in A.D. 757, an emissary from the regional capital was sent to resolve the problem, perhaps even to rule as regent until the matter was settled.

But the lords at secondary centers, who controlled the manpower of a whole province, were the weak link in the whole hierarchy. At certain times, and under certain conditions, they might break away from the capital by force, as Quirigua claims to have done from Copan in A.D. 738. At other times, several secondary centers might ally themselves, as did some sites in the Petexbatun region, so that their combined strength could be used to resist that of a capital like Tikal; it is possible that some Puuc sites also formed this type of confederacy. Capitals had ways of strengthening a province's loyalty, such as sending a royal woman from the capital to marry the lord of a secondary center. We have evidence for all of these processes in the eighth-century data from the southern lowlands (Fig. 24).

None of the great regional states we have mentioned lasted for all of Maya prehistory. Those headed by Copan and Palenque broke down before A.D. 849; the one headed by Seibal took over the secondary centers that had once been the Petexbatun Confederacy, but it fell by A.D. 950. When a great regional state fell, it broke up into its constituent provinces. Those in which secondary centers retained control over tertiary centers probably looked a lot like Roys' Type A provinces. Those in which a group of centers were allied closely enough to share the same Emblem Glyph probably looked like Roys' Type B provinces (Fig. 25). Those in which towns were essentially autonomous, uniting only in response to an outside threat, probably looked like Roys' Type C provinces. Since the dynamic model assumes that unification and breakdown went on continuously, from at least A.D. 534 to the Conquest, at any time there were probably some Type C provinces somewhere in the system. Thus our dynamic model not only resolves the conflict between Thompson's two alternative positions, but also provides us with a model that is more realistic, *since it accounts for the changes we see over time.*

## Consolidation

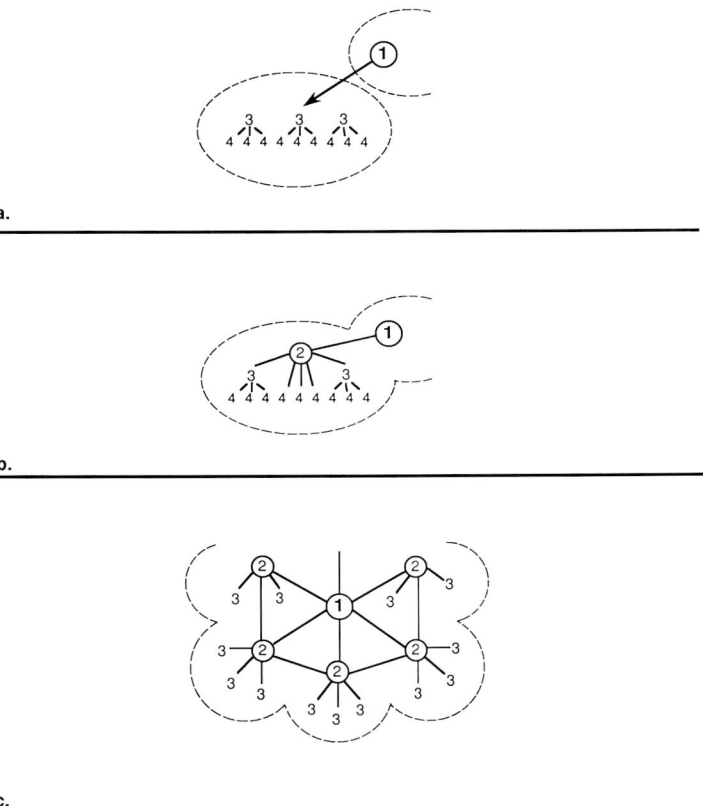

Fig. 24 Diagram illustrating one of several ways that the consolidation of large regional states could take place: (a) a province with several third-order towns and fourth-order villages lying near the border of a territory administered by a large first-order center. The first-order center sends a royal woman to marry the ruler of one of the province's third-order centers (arrow); (b) this royal marriage alliance has raised the status of the third-order center to second-order center, creating a four-level administrative hierarchy and moving the formerly autonomous province into the realm of the first-order center; (c) the kind of large state that can result when this process happens five or six times, linking a whole series of second-order centers (and their provinces) to a first-order center. (Fourth-order villages have been omitted from (c) to simplify the diagram.)

There are three other aspects of the dynamic model which I believe have implications for future Maya research:

(1.) As we have seen, the model suggests that *provinces* were the largest units with long-term stability. This focuses attention on *secondary centers*

Joyce Marcus

**Dissolution**

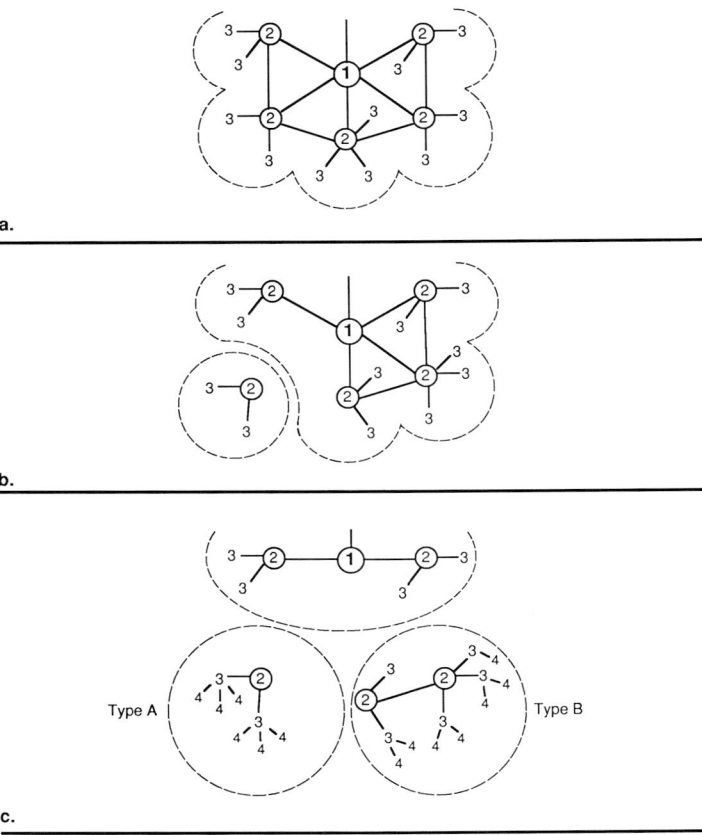

a.

b.

c.

Fig. 25 Diagram illustrating two of the ways that a large regional state could break down into its constituent provinces: (a) a part of the same large regional state we saw in Fig. 24c; (b) the most southwestern second-order center breaks away from the first-order center by warfare, taking its province and its tribute with it; (c) the two most southeastern second-order centers have formed an alliance that gives them the military strength to break away from the first-order center. The southwest province now has a structure like that of Roys' Type A provinces (Fig. 3a), with a single *hol cah* (the former second-order center). The southeast province has a structure like that of Roys' Type B provinces (Fig. 3b), with leadership claimed by a set of allied head towns rather than a single *hol cah*. The territory ruled by the first-order center is now much less powerful than it was in (a). (Fourth-order villages have been omitted from (a) and (b) to simplify the diagram.)

(and their rulers) as the most dynamic level of the system. Sometimes they were the autonomous "head towns" of their provinces; sometimes they were administratively below a regional capital; sometimes they were allied with other secondary centers in a confederacy. Thus the well-preserved secondary center is more likely to show evidence of (a) warfare with a capital or a neighboring secondary center; (b) gaps in succession filled by an emissary from the capital; (c) escalation in monument building following either a battle or a hypogamous marriage; and (d) changes in Emblem Glyph use over time.

(2.) The ethnohistoric data on which the dynamic model is based suggest that we may have underestimated the role of *mul tepal,* or "joint rule," in the rise of Maya regional states. I see evidence of both coercion and voluntaristic confederacies. For the latter, there are documents that discuss the "coming together" of many provinces to form Postclassic Chichen Itza and Mayapan. If *mul tepal* actually began in the Classic, it might explain why some regional capitals have more than one Emblem Glyph. It would also open up a new way to look at the rise of some great regional states.

(3.) Mayanists have tended to view the Classic as a long, stable "golden age" focused in the Peten, followed by a "mysterious collapse"; this in turn was followed by a Postclassic, focused in Yucatan, which was considered too different to be relevant. Recently, however, dissenters to this view have argued that "the *differences* between the southern and northern lowlands have been overemphasised at the expense of the *resemblances*" (Sabloff 1986: 112) and have called for "a much wider perspective in *all* periods in order to do away with the older, restricted viewpoints that have dominated Maya archaeology for so many decades" (Andrews V and Sabloff 1986: 456).

Instead of focusing on the Peten, we should look at the entire Maya lowlands from Dzibilchaltun to Copan. I further propose that, in accord with the dynamic model, we view the whole of the Classic and Postclassic as a continuous series of peaks and troughs as great regional states unify and break down (Fig. 26). In such a model, there is no "golden age" and no "mysterious collapse." Instead, it appears that the concept of a general "Maya collapse," viewed as a unique event that somehow ended an ancient civilization, is an artifact of our narrow focus on the southern lowlands. At the very moment that some large regional states were dissolving in the Peten, others were rising in the Puuc zone. A pan-lowland perspective shows us that one site's peak may coincide with another site's trough. Tikal's rise came at the expense of Uaxactun (Marcus 1976); Rio Azul's hiatus coincides with Kinal's rise (Adams 1989); Caracol's rise .nay have come, for a time, at the expense of Tikal and Naranjo (Chase and Chase 1987).

Setting aside the notion of a single, unique "collapse of the Maya empire"—a romantic event that has fascinated readers and defied explana-

Joyce Marcus

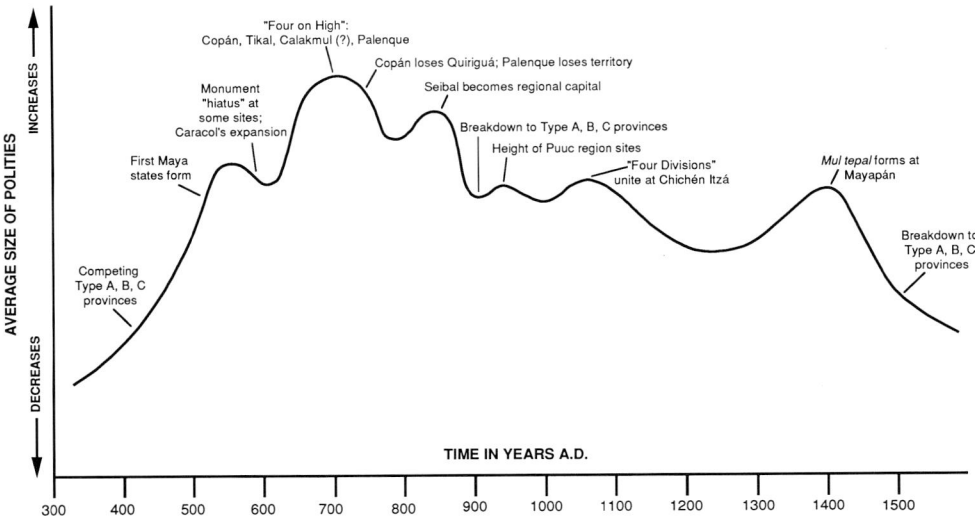

Fig. 26 The dynamic model applied to the Maya lowlands. In this simplified and schematic version, we see some of the many peaks and troughs that occurred throughout the Classic and Postclassic. One site's peak may have been another site's trough; one region's rise may have accompanied another region's demise. One of the principal points of interest is that there were many rises and many falls, rather than a single steep peak and a single abrupt collapse. (The specific trajectory of any single site is not expected to conform to this diagram; rather, the diagram attempts to show how the *average* size of polities, and their degree of consolidation, increases and decreases over time.)

tion for decades—we see instead a rise to a new level of sociopolitical integration early in Cycle 9. An early eighth-century peak in the northern and southern lowlands is then followed by a trough in the southern lowlands in the ninth century, and by a trough in the northern lowlands sometime in the second half of the tenth century. After this came peaks at Chichen Itza and Mayapan. Even in the Peten itself there may have been another peak rising at Tayasal and Topoxte when the Spaniards arrived and put an end to it.

If, as our model suggests, these peaks have to do with the ability of large centers to bring provinces under their control, and the troughs represent periods when provinces were able to break away, the underlying causes are political. We will not find their explanation in soil exhaustion, drought, or changes in the pollen record. It will be found in the machinations of royal dynasties, in their ability to shift supporters from one central place to an-

## Ancient Maya Political Organization

other, and in their ability to defend themselves both from annexation by larger centers and from insurrection by their dependencies.

### WIDER APPLICATIONS OF THE MODEL

Finally, I suspect that this dynamic model may be applicable to other archaic states, far from the Maya region. Consider, for example, what happens if we look at the whole of central Mexico from Tula to the Mixteca. We first see a high peak in A.D. 500 at Teotihuacan, analogous to the one at A.D. 731 in the Peten. With the collapse of Teotihuacan there is a deep trough, followed by the rise of the Toltec capital at Tula. With Tula's fall at A.D. 1168, Toltec nobles dispersed over a wide area. Many Postclassic rulers in the Mixteca claimed descent from them; other Toltec elites are reported to have traveled as far as Yucatan (Roys 1943, 1957). When a major center arose at Azcapotzalco in the Basin of Mexico around A.D. 1300, its rulers also claimed descent from the old Toltec nobility.

One of the ethnic groups subject to Azcapotzalco was the Mexica. In A.D. 1427, their ruler Itzcoatl allied himself with the ruler of Texcoco and succeeded in throwing off Azcapotzalco's rule. Here is another case of two secondary centers forming a confederacy to break away from a capital. Together with Tlacopan and Texcoco, the Mexica of Tenochtitlan went on to form the Triple Alliance from which the Aztec "empire" was directed. Thus this final peak in the central Mexican system, while it is perhaps most famous for its wars with other regions, apparently originated as a voluntaristic alliance.

But the potential applicability of our dynamic model is not limited to Mesoamerica. There were archaic states in the Old World—Egypt, for example—which show the same long-term stability of provinces as the Maya, and the same cycles of unification and dissolution under capitals. After the unification of Upper and Lower Egypt at roughly 3100 B.C.—a date which signifies for many scholars the emergence of the Egyptian state—a single ruler administered those two formerly independent "chiefdoms." As a legacy from that earlier era, the new Egyptian ruler wore a "Double Crown," which combined the Red Crown of Lower Egypt and the White Crown of Upper Egypt.

Called *n-sw-bit*,[8] the Egyptian ruler built a palace at his capital, located initially at Memphis near the border separating Upper from Lower Egypt. Hierarchically below the *n-sw-bit* were a series of secondary centers, each governing a province; we know these provinces by their Greek name, *nomes,* and their governors as *nomarchs.* Each *nomarch* administered the lower-order centers and dependencies within the boundaries of his *nome.* Significantly, each *nome* had its own name, as well as an emblem displayed

---

[8] The title *pharaoh* (derived from the word *per-o,* "great house" or "palace") was not used until Dynasty 18.

by its warriors on a wooden standard when they entered battle, either on behalf of their *nomarch* or the *n-sw-bit* himself. The number of *nomes* varies significantly over time; at one time Upper Egypt had about twenty-two and Lower Egypt about twenty.

One of the important dynamics of ancient Egypt was the changing relationship of the second-level lords, or *nomarchs,* in relation to the *n-sw-bit*. At moments when the Egyptian state was particularly strong, the *n-sw-bit* was all-powerful and the *nomarchs* posed no threat; during other eras (called Intermediate Periods), the *nomarchs* were surprisingly powerful and did pose a serious threat to the *n-sw-bit,* particularly when they formed alliances. At one point, Memphis was abandoned and Thebes was selected as a new capital, but the *nomes* went on as before.

When the state was strong there was not only a political hierarchy, but also a hierarchy of temples and shrines throughout Egypt. There were state-level deities, *nome* deities, and even local village and household deities. There was also considerable mobility of these beings over time. For example, at times a local deity might be selected for state-level worship, or a state-level deity might be demoted (or returned to its former, local status).

In some respects, Egyptian *nomes* behaved like the provinces below a Maya regional capital. Each had its own *nomarch* who, like the ruler of a Maya secondary center, controlled the manpower of his province, but owed allegiance to an even greater ruler at the capital. An Egyptologist excavating at the *nome* capital might locate hieroglyphic inscriptions supplying the site's name and the feats of its *nomarch,* but he would be wrong if he then concluded that the *nome* was autonomous. Even during Intermediate Periods, when *nomarchs* were powerful enough to cause trouble for the *n-sw-bit,* there was a capital at Memphis or Thebes to which they owed allegiance. It is simply the case that relations between the *n-sw-bit* and his *nomarchs* were dynamic, not static.

If we are truly interested in Maya political organization, we should not make the mistake of looking at too small a territorial unit. No hieroglyphic text, no isolated plaza, no single city shows us enough of an archaic state. No settlement pattern survey yet conducted around a Maya capital has extended far enough out to reach all of its secondary centers. Moreover, we must be aware that *all* sites are of equal importance in our goal of understanding the Maya state; in fact, a systematic analysis of lower-order centers may give us a clearer view of how the Maya state actually operated than does our present capitalcentric view. We should not assume that a *batab* or local lord was autonomous just because his monuments boast that he took captives, and we must not assume that all Maya centers were equal in political power. Finally, we cannot assume, as I did in 1973, that the southern lowlands is a large enough unit to reveal the whole picture. The dynamic model proposed here suggests that some patterns only become clear when the *whole of the northern and southern lowlands are combined.*

*Acknowledgments* I would like to thank the conference organizers—John Henderson and Jerry Sabloff—as well as R. E. W. Adams, Joe Ball, Warren Barbour, Kathryn Bard, Elizabeth Boone, Arlen Chase, Diane Chase, Arthur Demarest, Gary Feinman, Gary Gossen, Norman Hammond, Jeff Kowalski, Richard Leventhal, Henry Nicholson, Don Rice, Bob Sharer, and Jennifer Taschek for their comments on this manuscript at different stages.

Very special thanks go to Will Andrews, who encouraged me to incorporate more data on the northern lowlands. Due to page limitations, I was unable to include all of the relevant and abundant information. In fact, given all the data now available, two additional articles of equal length, one for the northern lowlands and one for the highlands, could be written.

Illustrations were drafted by Kay Clahassey, John Klausmeyer, and Mark Orsen.

# BIBLIOGRAPHY

Adams, Richard E. W.
    1987    *Río Azul Reports: Number 3, The 1985 Season. Proyecto Río Azul, Informe Tres: 1985* (Richard E. W. Adams, ed.). University of Texas at San Antonio.
    1989    *Río Azul Reports: Number 4, The 1986 Season. Proyecto Río Azul, Informe Cuatro: 1986* (Richard E. W. Adams, ed.). University of Texas at San Antonio.
    1990    Archaeological Research at the Lowland Maya City of Rio Azul. *Latin American Antiquity* 1 (1): 23–41.

Adams, Richard E. W., and Richard C. Jones
    1981    Spatial Patterns and Regional Growth among Classic Maya Cities. *American Antiquity* 46: 301–322.

Andrews V, E. Wyllys
    1979    Some Comments on Puuc Architecture of the Northern Yucatan Peninsula. In *The Puuc: New Perspectives. Papers presented at the Puuc Symposium, Central College, May, 1977* (Lawrence Mills, ed.): 1–17. Central College Press, Pella, Iowa.

Andrews V, E. Wyllys, and Jeremy A. Sabloff
    1986    Classic to Postclassic: A Summary Discussion. In *Late Lowland Maya Civilization: Classic to Postclassic* (Jeremy A. Sabloff and E. Wyllys Andrews V, eds.): 433–456. University of New Mexico Press, Albuquerque.

Ashmore, Wendy (ed.)
    1981    *Lowland Maya Settlement Patterns*. School of American Research Advanced Seminar Series. University of New Mexico Press, Albuquerque.

Avendaño y Loyola, Fray Andrés de
    1696a    *Relación de las entradas que hize a la conversión de los gentiles Itzaex*. Manuscript in Newberry Library, Chicago, Illinois.
    1696b    *Relación de las dos entradas que hize a la conversión de los gentiles Itzaex y Cehaches (1695, 1696)*. Translation by Charles P. Bowditch. Manuscript in Tozzer Library, Harvard University, Cambridge.

Barrera Vásquez, Alfredo, et al.
    1980    *Diccionario Maya Cordemex. Maya-Español, Español-Maya*. Ediciones Cordemex, Mérida.

Barthel, Thomas S.
    1968    El complejo "emblema." *Estudios de Cultura Maya* 7: 159–193.

Beltrán de Santa Rosa, Pedro (see Pío Pérez 1898)

Berlin, Heinrich
    1958    El glifo "emblema" en las inscripciones mayas. *Journal de la Société des Américanistes* 47: 111–119.
    1968    The Tablet of the 96 Glyphs at Palenque, Chiapas, Mexico. Middle American Research Institute, Publication 26: 135–150. Tulane University, New Orleans.

1977  *Signos y Significados en las Inscripciones Mayas.* Instituto Nacional del Patrimonio Cultural de Guatemala, Guatemala.

BLANTON, RICHARD E.
    1978  *Monte Albán: Settlement Patterns at the Ancient Zapotec Capital.* Academic Press, New York.
    1983  The Founding of Monte Albán. In *The Cloud People: Divergent Evolution of the Zapotec and Mixtec Civilizations* (Kent V. Flannery and Joyce Marcus, eds.): 83–87. Academic Press, Orlando.

BOVE, FREDERICK J.
    1981  Trend Surface Analysis and the Lowland Classic Maya Collapse. *American Antiquity* 46: 93–112.

BRICKER, VICTORIA R.
    1986  A Grammar of Mayan Hieroglyphs. Middle American Research Institute, Publication 56. Tulane University, New Orleans.

BRINTON, DANIEL GARRISON (ED.)
    1882  *The Maya Chronicles.* Brinton's Library of Aboriginal American Literature, No. 1. Philadelphia.

CARNEIRO, ROBERT
    1981  The Chiefdom: Precursor of the State. In *The Transition to Statehood in the New World* (Grant D. Jones and Robert R. Kautz, eds.): 37–79. Cambridge University Press, Cambridge.

CARR, ROBERT F., AND JAMES E. HAZARD
    1961  Map of the Ruins of Tikal, El Peten, Guatemala. Tikal Report, No. 11. University Museum Monographs. University Museum, University of Pennsylvania, Philadelphia.

CARRASCO, PEDRO
    1984  Royal Marriages in Ancient Mexico. In *Explorations in Ethnohistory: Indians of Central Mexico in the Sixteenth Century* (Herbert R. Harvey and Hanns J. Prem, eds.): 41–81. University of New Mexico Press, Albuquerque.

CASO, ALFONSO
    1977  *Reyes y reinos de la mixteca.* Fondo de Cultura Económica, Mexico.

CHANG, KWANG-CHIH
    1968  *The Archaeology of Ancient China,* revised and enlarged edition. Yale University Press, New Haven.

CHASE, ARLEN F., AND DIANE Z. CHASE
    1987  Investigations at the Classic Maya City of Caracol, Belize: 1985–1987. Pre-Columbian Art Research Institute, Monograph 3. San Francisco.

CHI, GASPAR ANTONIO
    [1582]  Relación sobre las costumbres de los Indios, translated by Ralph L.
    1941   Roys. In Tozzer 1941: 230–232.

CHILAM BALAM OF MANI (SEE CRAINE AND REINDORP 1979)

CHRISTALLER, W.
    1933  *Die zentralen Orte in Süddeutschland.* G. Fischer, Jena.

CIUDAD REAL, ANTONIO DE
[1588] *Relación breve y verdadera de algunas cosas de las muchas que sucedieron al*
1873 *Padre Fray Alonso Ponce en las provincias de la Nueva España* . . . 2 vols. Imprenta de la Viuda de Calero, Madrid.

CLARKE, DAVID L.
1968 *Analytical Archaeology.* Methuen and Co., Ltd., London.

COE, MICHAEL D.
1965 A Model of Ancient Community Structure in the Maya Lowlands. *Southwestern Journal of Anthropology* 21 (2): 97–114.

COE, WILLIAM R.
1962 A Summary of Excavation and Research at Tikal, Guatemala, 1956–61. *American Antiquity* 27: 479–507.
1965a Tikal, Guatemala, and Emergent Maya Civilization. *Science* 147: 1401–1419.
1965b Tikal: Ten Years of Study of a Maya Ruin in the Lowlands of Guatemala. *Expedition* 8 (1): 5–56. University Museum, University of Pennsylvania, Philadelphia.
1967 *Tikal: A Handbook of the Ancient Maya Ruins.* University Museum, University of Pennsylvania, Philadelphia.

CRAINE, EUGENE R., AND REGINALD C. REINDORP
1979 *The Codex Perez and the Book of Chilam Balam of Mani.* University of Oklahoma Press, Norman.

CULBERT, T. PATRICK
1988 Political History and the Decipherment of Maya Glyphs. *Antiquity* 62: 135–152.

DE MONTMOLLIN, OLIVIER
1989 *The Archaeology of Political Structure: Settlement Analysis in a Classic Maya Polity.* Cambridge University Press, Cambridge.

FASH JR., WILLIAM L.
1988 A New Look at Maya Statecraft from Copan, Honduras. *Antiquity* 62: 157–169.

FLANNERY, KENT V.
1972 The Cultural Evolution of Civilizations. *Annual Review of Ecology and Systematics* 3: 399–426. Annual Reviews, Inc., Palo Alto.
1977 Review of Mesoamerican Archaeology: New Approaches (Norman Hammond, ed.). *American Antiquity* 42 (4): 659–661.

FLANNERY, KENT V., AND JOYCE MARCUS
1983 The Origins of the State in Oaxaca. In *The Cloud People: Divergent Evolution of the Zapotec and Mixtec Civilizations* (Kent V. Flannery and Joyce Marcus, eds.): 79–83. Academic Press, Orlando.

FOLAN, WILLIAM J.
1985 Proyecto Calakmul. Su Centro Urbano, Estado y Región en Relación al Concepto del resto de la Gran Mesoamérica. *Información* 9: 161–185. Centro de Estudios Históricos y Sociales, Universidad Autónoma del Sudeste, Campeche, México.

n.d. Calakmul Site Map and Survey Results. Manuscript in author's possession, 1989.

FOLAN, WILLIAM J., AND JACINTO MAY HAU
1984 Proyecto Calakmul, 1982–1984: El Mapa. *Información* 8: 1–14. Centro de Estudios Históricos y Sociales, Universidad Autónoma del Sudeste, Campeche, México.

FRIED, MORTON H.
1960 On the Evolution of Social Stratification and the State. In *Culture in History* (Stanley Diamond, ed.): 713–731. Columbia University Press, New York.
1967 *The Evolution of Political Society*. Random House, New York.

FRY, ROBERT E.
1979 The Economics of Pottery at Tikal, Guatemala: Models of Exchange for Serving Vessels. *American Antiquity* 44: 494–512.
1989 Regional Ceramic Distributional Patterning in Northern Belize: The View from Pulltrouser Swamp. In *Research In Economic Anthropology*, Supplement 4, Prehistoric Maya Economies of Belize (Patricia A. McAnany and Barry L. Isaac, eds.): 91–111. JAI Press Inc., Greenwich, Conn.

FRY, ROBERT E., AND SCOTT C. COX
1974 The Structure of Ceramic Exchange at Tikal, Guatemala. *World Archaeology* 6: 209–225.

GIBSON, ERIC
1989 The Organization of Late Preclassic Maya Lithic Economy in the Eastern Lowlands. In *Research In Economic Anthropology*, Supplement 4, Prehistoric Maya Economies of Belize (Patricia A. McAnany and Barry L. Isaac, eds.): 115–138. JAI Press Inc., Greenwich, Conn.
n.d. Diachronic Patterns of Lithic Production. Use and Exchange in the Southern Maya Lowlands. Ph.D. dissertation, Harvard University, Cambridge, 1986.

GRAHAM, IAN, AND ERIC VON EUW
1975 *Corpus of Maya Hieroglyphic Inscriptions, Volume 2, Part 1. Naranjo*. Peabody Museum of Archaeology and Ethnology, Harvard University, Cambridge.

HAGGETT, PETER
1966 *Locational Analysis in Human Geography*. St. Martin's Press, New York.
1972 *Geography: A Modern Synthesis*. Harper & Row, New York.

HAMMOND, NORMAN
1972 Locational Models and the Site of Lubaantun: A Classic Maya Centre. In *Models in Archaeology* (David L. Clarke, ed.): 757–800. Methuen and Co., Ltd., London.
1974 The Distribution of Late Classic Maya Major Ceremonial Centres in the Central Area. In *Mesoamerican Archaeology: New Approaches* (Norman Hammond, ed.): 313–334. University of Texas Press, Austin.
1975 Maya Settlement Hierarchy in Northern Belize. *Contributions of the University of California Archaeological Research Facility* 27: 40–55. Berkeley, California.

HAVILAND, WILLIAM
    1966    Maya Settlement Patterns: A Critical Review. In *Archaeological Studies in Middle America,* Publication 26: 21–47. Middle American Research Institute, Tulane University, New Orleans.
    1967    Stature at Tikal, Guatemala: Implications for Ancient Maya Demography and Social Organization. *American Antiquity* 32: 316–325.
    1969    A New Population Estimate for Tikal, Guatemala. *American Antiquity* 34: 429–433.
    1970    Tikal, Guatemala, and Mesoamerican Urbanism. *World Archaeology* 2: 186–198.

JOHNSON, GREGORY A.
    1972    A Test of the Utility of Central Place Theory in Archaeology. In *Man, Settlement and Urbanism* (Peter J. Ucko, Ruth Tringham, and G. W. Dimbleby, eds.): 769–785. Duckworth, London.
    1973    Local Exchange and Early State Development in Southwestern Iran. Anthropological Papers of the Museum of Anthropology, No. 51. Museum of Anthropology, University of Michigan, Ann Arbor.
    1980    Spatial Organization of Early Uruk Settlement Systems. *Colloques Internationaux de Centre National de la Recherche Scientifique* 580: 233–263. Paris.

JONES, GRANT D., DON S. RICE, AND PRUDENCE RICE
    1981    The Location of Tayasal: A Reconsideration in Light of Petén Maya Ethnohistory and Archaeology. *American Antiquity* 46 (3): 530–547.

KELLEY, DAVID H.
    1962    Glyphic Evidence for a Dynastic Sequence at Quirigua, Guatemala. *American Antiquity* 27: 323–335.

KOWALEWSKI, STEPHEN A., GARY M. FEINMAN, LAURA FINSTEN, RICHARD E. BLANTON, AND LINDA M. NICHOLAS
    1989    Monte Alban's Hinterland, Part II: The Prehispanic Settlement Patterns in Tlacolula, Etla, and Ocotlán, the Valley of Oaxaca, Mexico. Memoirs of the Museum of Anthropology, University of Michigan, No. 23. Ann Arbor.

KOWALSKI, JEFF KARL
    1987    *The House of the Governor: A Maya Palace at Uxmal, Yucatan, Mexico.* University of Oklahoma Press, Norman.

LANDA, FRAY DIEGO DE (SEE TOZZER 1941)

LEACH, SIR EDMUND R.
    [1954]    *Political Systems of Highland Burma: A Study of Kachin Social Structure.*
    1964    Bell and Sons, Ltd., London.

LEVENTHAL, RICHARD
    1981    Settlement Patterns in the Southeast Maya Area. In *Lowland Maya Settlement Patterns* (Wendy Ashmore, ed.): 187–210. University of New Mexico Press, Albuquerque.

LÓPEZ DE COGOLLUDO, FRAY DIEGO
    [1688]    *Historia de Yucatán escrita en el siglo XVII por el reverendo padre Fray Diego*
    1867–68    *López Cogolludo.* 2 volumes, 3rd ed. Manuel Aldana Rivas, Mérida.

LÖSCH, AUGUST
  1954   *The Economics of Location*. Translated by William H. Woglom. Yale University Press, New Haven.

LOUNSBURY, FLOYD G.
  1973   On the Derivation and Reading of the 'Ben-Ich' Prefix. In *Mesoamerican Writing Systems* (Elizabeth P. Benson, ed.): 99–143. Dumbarton Oaks, Washington, D.C.
  1989   The Names of a King: Hieroglyphic Variants as a Key to Decipherment. In *Word and Image in Maya Culture: Explorations in Language, Writing, and Representation* (William F. Hanks and Don S. Rice, eds.): 73–91. University of Utah Press, Salt Lake City.

MACNEISH, RICHARD S.
  1982   *Third Annual Report of the Belize Archaic Archaeological Reconnaissance*. Robert S. Peabody Foundation for Archaeology, Phillips Academy, Andover, Mass.

MARCUS, JOYCE
  1973   Territorial Organization of the Lowland Classic Maya. *Science* 180: 911–916.
  1974a  Reply to Romanov and Hammond. *Science* 183: 876–877.
  1974b  The Iconography of Power among the Classic Maya. *World Archaeology* 6: 83–94.
  1976   *Emblem and State in the Classic Maya Lowlands: An Epigraphic Approach to Territorial Organization*. Dumbarton Oaks, Washington, D.C.
  1978   Archaeology and Religion: A Comparison of the Zapotec and Maya. *World Archaeology* 10: 172–191.
  1982   Review of Lowland Maya Settlement Patterns (Wendy Ashmore, ed.). *American Antiquity* 47 (4): 899–902.
  1983a  Lowland Maya Archaeology at the Crossroads. *American Antiquity* 48 (3): 454–488.
  1983b  On the Nature of the Mesoamerican City. In *Prehistoric Settlement Patterns: Essays in Honor of Gordon R. Willey* (Evon Z. Vogt and Richard M. Leventhal, eds.): 195–242. University of New Mexico Press, Albuquerque, and Peabody Museum, Harvard University, Cambridge.
  1983c  The Reconstructed Chronology of the Later Zapotec Rulers, A.D. 1415–1563. In *The Cloud People: Divergent Evolution of the Zapotec and Mixtec Civilizations* (Kent V. Flannery and Joyce Marcus, eds.): 301–308. Academic Press, San Diego.
  1984   Mesoamerican Territorial Boundaries: Reconstructions from Archaeology and Hieroglyphic Writing. *Archaeological Review from Cambridge* 3 (2): 48–62. Department of Archaeology, Cambridge, England.
  1987   *The Inscriptions of Calakmul. Royal Marriage at a Maya City in Campeche, Mexico*. Museum of Anthropology, University of Michigan, Technical Report No. 21. Ann Arbor.
  1989   From Centralized Systems to City States: Possible Models for the Epiclassic. In *Mesoamerica after the Decline of Teotihuacan: A.D. 700–900* (Richard A. Diehl and Janet Catherine Berlo, eds.): 201–208. Dumbarton Oaks, Washington, D.C.

Joyce Marcus

 1992 Royal Families, Royal Texts: Examples from the Zapotec and Maya. In *Mesoamerican Elites: An Archaeological Assessment* (Diane Z. Chase and Arlen F. Chase, eds.): 221–241. University of Oklahoma Press, Norman.

 n.d.a Naranjo, Tikal, and Territorial Organization. Manuscript in author's possession, prepared for course with Tatiana Proskouriakoff, Harvard University, Cambridge, 1970.

 n.d.b An Analysis of Color-Direction Symbolism among the Maya. Manuscript in Tozzer Library, prepared for course with Evon Z. Vogt, Harvard University, Cambridge, 1970.

 n.d.c An Iconographic and Epigraphic Analysis of the Calakmul Monuments. Manuscript in author's possession, prepared for course with Tatiana Proskouriakoff, Harvard University, Cambridge, 1970.

 n.d.d An Epigraphic Approach to the Territorial Organization of the Lowland Classic Maya. Ph.D. dissertation, Harvard University, Cambridge, 1974.

MARCUS, JOYCE, AND KENT V. FLANNERY

 1983 An Introduction to the Late Postclassic. In *The Cloud People: Divergent Evolution of the Zapotec and Mixtec Civilizations* (Kent V. Flannery and Joyce Marcus, eds.): 217–226. Academic Press, Orlando.

 n.d. Cultural Evolution in Oaxaca: The Origins of the Zapotec and Mixtec Civilizations. In *Cambridge History of the Native Peoples of the Americas* (Murdo MacLeod and Richard E. W. Adams, eds.). Cambridge University Press, Cambridge. (in press)

MARTÍNEZ HERNÁNDEZ, JUAN (ED.)

 [1585?] *Diccionario de Motul: Maya-Español*. Atribuido a Fray Antonio de
 1929 Ciudad Real y *Arte de la lengua Maya* por Fray Juan Coronel. Compañía Tipográfica Yucateca, S.A., Mérida.

MATHEWS, PETER

 1985 Maya Early Classic Monuments and Inscriptions. In *A Consideration of the Early Classic Period in the Maya Lowlands* (Gordon R. Willey and Peter Mathews, eds.): 5–54. Institute for Mesoamerican Studies, No. 10. State University of New York at Albany, Albany.

MCANANY, PATRICIA A.

 1989a Economic Foundations of Prehistoric Maya Society: Paradigms and Concepts. In *Research in Economic Anthropology*, Supplement 4, Prehistoric Maya Economies of Belize (Patricia A. McAnany and Barry L. Isaac, eds.): 347–372. JAI Press Inc., Greenwich, Conn.

 1989b Stone-Tool Production and Exchange in the Eastern Maya Lowlands: The Consumer Perspective from Pulltrouser Swamp, Belize. *American Antiquity* 54 (2): 332–346.

MEANS, PHILIP AINSWORTH

 1917 History of the Spanish Conquest of Yucatán and of the Itzas. Papers of the Peabody Museum of Archaeology and Ethnology 7. Harvard University, Cambridge.

MORLEY, SYLVANUS GRISWOLD
 1920 The Inscriptions of Copan. Carnegie Institution of Washington, Publication 219. Washington, D.C.
 1938 The Inscriptions of Petén, Volume V. Carnegie Institution of Washington, Publication 437. Washington, D.C.
 1946 *The Ancient Maya.* Stanford University Press, Stanford, California.

MORLEY, SYLVANUS G., AND GEORGE W. BRAINERD
 1956 *The Ancient Maya.* 3rd ed. Stanford University Press, Stanford, California.

MOTOLINÍA, TORIBIO DE BENAVENTE
 1971 *Memoriales o libro de las cosas de la Nueva España y de los naturales de ella* (Edmundo O'Gorman, ed.). Universidad Nacional, México.

NOYES, ERNST (ED. AND TRANS.)
 1932 Fray Alonso Ponce in Yucatan, 1588. Middle American Research Institute, Paper 4: 297–372. Tulane University, New Orleans.

PÍO PÉREZ, JUAN
 1898 *Coordinación alfabética de las voces del idioma Maya que se hallan en el arte y obras del Padre Fr. Pedro Beltrán de Santa Rosa, con las equivalencias castellanas que en las mismas se hallan.* Mérida.

PROSKOURIAKOFF, TATIANA
 1960 Historical Implications of a Pattern of Dates at Piedras Negras, Guatemala. *American Antiquity* 25: 454–475.
 1962 Civic and Religious Structures of Mayapan. In *Mayapan, Yucatan, Mexico,* Harry E. D. Pollock, Ralph L. Roys, Tatiana Proskouriakoff, and A. Ledyard Smith. Carnegie Institution of Washington, Publication 619: 87–164. Washington, D.C.
 1963 Historical Data in the Inscriptions of Yaxchilan, Part I. *Estudios de Cultura Maya* 3: 149–167. UNAM, Mexico.
 1964 Historical Data in the Inscriptions of Yaxchilan, Part II. *Estudios de Cultura Maya* 4: 177–201. UNAM, Mexico.

PULESTON, DENNIS E.
 1974 Intersite Areas in the Vicinity of Tikal and Uaxactun. In *Mesoamerican Archaeology: New Approaches* (Norman Hammond, ed.): 303–311. Duckworth, London.

PULESTON, DENNIS E., AND DONALD W. CALLENDER, JR.
 1967 Defensive Earthworks at Tikal. *Expedition* 9 (3): 40–48. University Museum, University of Pennsylvania, Philadelphia.

RANDS, ROBERT L.
 1967 Ceramic Technology and Trade in the Palenque Region, Mexico. In *American Historical Anthropology* (Carroll L. Riley and Walter W. Taylor, eds.): 137–151. Southern Illinois University, Carbondale.

RANDS, ROBERT L., AND RONALD L. BISHOP
 1980 Resource Procurement Zones and Patterns of Ceramic Exchange in the Palenque Region, Mexico. In *Models and Methods in Regional Exchange,*

Society for American Archaeology Papers 1 (Robert E. Fry, ed.): 19–46. Washington, D.C.

REDFIELD, ROBERT, AND ALFONSO VILLA ROJAS
1934   Chan Kom: A Maya Village. Carnegie Institution of Washington, Publication 448. Washington, D.C.

REDMAN, CHARLES
1978   *The Rise of Civilization.* W.H. Freeman & Co., San Francisco.

RELACIONES DE YUCATÁN
1898–   In *Colección de documentos inéditos relativos al descubrimiento, conquista y*
1900   *organización de las antiguas posesiones españolas de ultramar.* 2nd series, Tomos I, II (Vols. 11 and 13). Real Academia de la Historia, Madrid.

RENFREW, COLIN, AND JOHN F. CHERRY
1986   Preface. *Peer Polity Interaction and Socio-Political Change* (Colin Renfrew and John F. Cherry, eds): vii–viii. Cambridge University Press, Cambridge.

RICE, DON S., AND PRUDENCE M. RICE
1981   Muralla de Leon: A Lowland Maya Fortification. *Journal of Field Archaeology* 8: 271–288.

RINGLE, WILLIAM
1985   Notes on Two Tablets of Unknown Provenance. In *Fifth Palenque Round Table, 1983,* Vol. 7 (Merle Greene Robertson and Virginia M. Fields, eds.): 151–158. Pre-Columbian Art Research Institute, San Francisco.

ROBLES C., FERNANDO, AND ANTHONY P. ANDREWS
1986   A Review and Synthesis of Recent Postclassic Archaeology in Northern Yucatan. In *Late Lowland Maya Civilization: Classic to Postclassic* (Jeremy A. Sabloff and E. Wyllys Andrews V, eds.): 53–98. University of New Mexico Press, Albuquerque.

ROSTWOROWSKI DE DIEZ CANSECO, MARÍA
1988   *Historia del Tahuantinsuyu.* Instituto de Estudios Peruanos, Lima.

ROYS, RALPH LOVELAND
1933   The Book of Chilam Balam of Chumayel. Carnegie Institution of Washington, Publication 438. Washington, D.C.
1940   Personal Names of the Maya of Yucatán. Carnegie Institution of Washington, Publication 523, Contribution 31. Washington, D.C.
1943   The Indian Background of Colonial Yucatán. Carnegie Institution of Washington, Publication 548. Washington, D.C.
1957   The Political Geography of the Yucatán Maya. Carnegie Institution of Washington, Publication 613. Washington, D.C.
1962   Literary Sources for the History of Mayapan. In *Mayapan, Yucatan, Mexico,* by Harry E. D. Pollock, Ralph L. Roys, Tatiana Proskouriakoff, and A. Ledyard Smith. Carnegie Institution of Washington, Publication 619: 24–86. Washington, D.C.
1965   Lowland Maya Society at Spanish Contact. *Handbook of Middle American Indians,* Vol. 3 (Robert Wauchope and Gordon R. Willey, eds.): 659–678. University of Texas Press, Austin.

1967    *The Book of Chilam Balam of Chumayel.* University of Oklahoma Press, Norman.

SABLOFF, JEREMY A.
1986    Interaction among Classic Maya Polities: A Preliminary Examination. In *Peer Polity Interaction and Socio-Political Change* (Colin Renfrew and John F. Cherry, eds.): 109–116. Cambridge University Press, Cambridge.

SANDERS, WILLIAM T.
1974    Chiefdom to State: Political Evolution at Kaminaljuyú, Guatemala. In *Reconstructing Complex Societies: An Archaeological Colloquium* (Charlotte B. Moore, ed.). Supplement to the Bulletin of the American Schools of Oriental Research, No. 20: 97–116. Boston.

SCHOLES, FRANCE V., AND RALPH L. ROYS
1948    The Maya Chontal Indians of Acalan-Tixchel: A Contribution to the History and Ethnography of the Yucatan Peninsula. Carnegie Institution of Washington, Publication 560. Washington, D.C. (2nd edition, 1968. University of Oklahoma Press, Norman).

SERVICE, ELMAN R.
1962    *Primitive Social Organization: An Evolutionary Perspective.* Random House, New York.
1975    *Origins of the State and Civilization.* Norton, New York.

SHAFER, HARRY J., AND THOMAS R. HESTER
1983    Ancient Maya Chert Workshops in Northern Belize, Central America. *American Antiquity* 48: 519–543.

SHARER, ROBERT J.
1978    Archaeology and History at Quiriguá, Guatemala. *Journal of Field Archaeology* 5: 51–70.

SMITH, MARY ELIZABETH
1973    *Picture Writing from Ancient Southern Mexico: Mixtec Place Signs and Maps.* University of Oklahoma Press, Norman.

SNODGRASS, ANTHONY M.
1977    *Archaeology and the Rise of the Greek State.* Cambridge University Press, Cambridge.
1980    *Archaic Greece: The Age of Experiment.* J. M. Dent & Sons Ltd., London.

SOLÍS ALCALÁ, ERMILO
1949    *Diccionario Español-Maya.* Yikal Maya Than, Mérida.

STEPHENS, JOHN LLOYD
[1843]    *Incidents of Travel in Yucatan.* 2 Vols. Dover Publications, New York.
1963

TAYLOUR, LORD WILLIAM
1964    *The Mycenaeans.* Frederick A. Praeger, New York.

THOMPSON, J. ERIC S.
1934    Sky-Bearers, Colors and Directions in Maya and Mexican Religion. Carnegie Institution of Washington, Publication 436. Contributions to American Anthropology No. 10. Washington, D.C.

1950 Maya Hieroglyphic Writing: An Introduction. Carnegie Institution of Washington, Publication 589. Washington, D.C. (2nd and 3rd editions printed by University of Oklahoma Press, Norman).
1954 *The Rise and Fall of Maya Civilization.* University of Oklahoma Press, Norman.
1962 *A Catalog of Maya Hieroglyphs.* University of Oklahoma Press, Norman.
1977 A Proposal for Constituting a Maya Subgroup, Cultural and Linguistic, in the Petén and Adjacent Regions. In *Anthropology and History in Yucatán* (Grant D. Jones, ed.): 3–42. University of Texas Press, Austin.

TOZZER, ALFRED MARSTON
1907 *A Comparative Study of the Mayas and Lacandones.* The MacMillan Company, New York and London.
1941 Landa's Relación de las Cosas de Yucatán. A translation edited with notes by A. M. Tozzer. Papers of the Peabody Museum of American Archaeology and Ethnology 18. Harvard University, Cambridge.

VILLAGUTIERRE SOTO-MAYOR, JUAN DE
1701 *Historia de la conquista de la Provincia de el Itzá, Reducción, y Progressos de la de El Lacandón, y Otras Naciones de Indios Barbaros, de la Mediación del Reyno de Guatimala, a las Provincias de Yucatán, en la América Septentrional.* Madrid.
1933 Historia de la conquista de la provincia de el Itzá, reducción y progresos de la de el Lacandón. *Biblioteca "Goathemala" de la Sociedad de Geografía e Historia,* Vol. 9. Tipografía Nacional, Guatemala.

WEBSTER, DAVID
1976 Defensive Earthworks at Becan, Campeche, Mexico. Middle American Research Institute, Publication 41. Tulane University, New Orleans.
1978 Three Walled Sites of the Northern Maya Lowlands. *Journal of Field Archaeology* 5 (4): 375–390.
1979 Cuca, Chaccob, Dzonot Aké. Three Walled Northern Maya Centers. Occasional Papers in Anthropology 11. Department of Anthropology, Pennsylvania State University, University Park, Pa.

WEBSTER, DAVID, AND ANNCORRINE FRETER
1990 The Demography of Late Classic Copan. In *Precolumbian Population History in the Maya Lowlands* (T. Patrick Culbert and Don S. Rice, eds): 37–61. University of New Mexico Press, Albuquerque.

WHALEN, MICHAEL
1981 Excavations at Santo Domingo Tomaltepec: Evolution of a Formative Community in the Valley of Oaxaca, Mexico. *Prehistory and Human Ecology of the Valley of Oaxaca, Mexico* (Kent V. Flannery, ed.) Vol. 6. Museum of Anthropology, University of Michigan, Ann Arbor.

WHEATLEY, PAUL
1971 *The Pivot of the Four Quarters: A Preliminary Enquiry into the Origins and Character of the Ancient Chinese City.* Aldine Press, Chicago.

WILLEY, GORDON R., AND RICHARD M. LEVENTHAL
1979 Prehistoric Settlement at Copan. In *Maya Archaeology and Ethnohistory*

(Norman Hammond and Gordon R. Willey, eds.): 75–102. University of Texas Press, Austin.

WRIGHT, HENRY T.
1969 The Administration of Rural Production in an Early Mesopotamian Town. Anthropological Papers of the Museum of Anthropology 38. Museum of Anthropology, University of Michigan, Ann Arbor.
1977 Recent Research on the Origins of the State. *Annual Review of Anthropology* 6: 379–397.

WRIGHT, HENRY T., AND GREGORY JOHNSON
1975 Population, Exchange, and Early State Formation in Southwestern Iran. *American Anthropologist* 77 (2): 267–289.

ZUIDEMA, R. TOM
1964 *The Ceque System of Cuzco*. Leiden, The Netherlands.

# 6

## The Topography of Ancient Maya Religious Pluralism: A Dialogue with the Present

GARY H. GOSSEN
THE UNIVERSITY AT ALBANY, STATE UNIVERSITY OF NEW YORK

RICHARD M. LEVENTHAL
UNIVERSITY OF CALIFORNIA AT LOS ANGELES

### INTRODUCTION

Now, as we approach the quincentenary of the encounter between the New and Old Worlds, much is known of the religious beliefs and practices of the ancient Maya. Beginning with the great synthetic works of J. E. S. Thompson (1966, 1970), based largely on a careful, if fanciful, reading of the archaeological and ethnohistoric record; and continuing in our time with the incorporation of massive testimony from hieroglyphic texts, rendered by the ancient Maya's own hands (Schele and Miller 1986; Marcus 1976); and the sensitive new translations and interpretations of well-known texts (notably D. Tedlock's Popul Vuh [1985] and Edmonson [1982]), our dialogue with the Maya past is changing significantly. It has shifted from a once-prevailing interpretive framework based upon European analogy (i.e., Maya religion was similar to Greek polytheism), to a more cautious approach that is based upon axiological premises of the Maya themselves.

However, the interpretive tradition in our time continues to regard Maya state religion as homogeneous, omnipresent, and universally embraced by one and all, from princes to peasants, from merchants to farmers, and by inhabitants of all the cities throughout the Maya lowlands (Hammond 1982; Thompson 1966, 1970). We seek in this paper to present an alternative view, one that directly addresses the evidence for religious pluralism, perhaps even competing cult affiliation, among the ancient Maya.

The dialogue we try to generate within this paper between an ethnologist and an archaeologist is not based upon a belief in the direct historical approach (e.g., Vogt 1964, n.d.). We are aware of and accept that change has been dramatic from the eighth century A.D. to the present, but feel that this dialogue will help us identify structural principles that will allow us to make comparisons and to use the present to examine the past and the past to understand the present. By "structural principles," we mean to suggest relational patterns of beliefs, discourse, and practice within whole symbolic systems; a metaphysics of who's who in the social and supernatural universe.

It is essential at this point to clarify a point of terminology that occurs frequently in our discussion. As both ancient and modern Maya societies are state-level societies, consisting of city centers and outlying political and economic dependencies, we are dealing in both cases with two distinct types of moral communities: what Robert Redfield (1941, 1960) called Great Traditions, consisting of official state-level ideology and religious practice, and Little Traditions, consisting of local variants of the state-level ideology and alternative local ideologies and religious practices. We shall attempt to adhere to Redfield's terminology so as to avoid ambiguity and misunderstanding inherent in such distinctions as center/periphery or core/periphery. It is well understood, following Redfield's well-known concept of the folk-urban continuum, that the gradient between the ideal types, while permeable, nevertheless tends to express—in the Little Tradition at the folk extreme of the continuum—a collection of culture traits which are local, circumscribed, and typically conservative; these traits may antedate the advent of the currently prevailing Great Tradition that is associated with the urban centers.[1] We would like to emphasize that, as with Redfield, we are aware of the great variation found along this folk-urban continuum. However, we feel that the identification of the two ends of this continuum, the Little and Great Traditions, provides us with a starting point for our analysis.

Specifically, we utilize modern Maya ethnography as a stimulus for discussing the points of articulation between Classic Maya state religion and the ideologies of the Little Tradition. While the inferential leap is large and potentially cluttered with more than a thousand years of cultural baggage, there is evidence from elsewhere in Mesoamerica that this is not a fruitless strategy. Flannery and Marcus have used such a structure of inference for interpreting the ideational principles of ancient Oaxaca (Flannery and Marcus 1976). The Maya area also has a few powerful case studies (Hunt 1977; Bricker 1981; and Farriss 1984) that show that the intellectual, ideological, and religious spheres of Maya life have, because of their quiet embeddedness in language and esoteric knowledge, proved to be resilient and functional in the Colonial and modern eras.

The general issue of identifying points of continuity and change in the

---

[1] The terms center and periphery refer, within this paper, to only the physical location associated with the layout of ancient and modern Maya settlements.

## The Topography of Ancient Maya Religious Pluralism

New World as it has evolved since contact with the Old World has been argued into a kind of fruitless impasse by the polarization of positions between those arguing for continuity and those arguing for a fundamental transformation of the Indian world into a peasant periphery of the "world system." Within the Maya region of Mexico and Central America, there can be little doubt that both positions have been overstated. Any reasonable discourse on the subject must take as a first premise that both continuity and change are operative today, just as they always have been in the past. It is clear that public economic, religious, and political affairs—even the social organization of Indian communities themselves—have been altered at the convenience of colonial and national interests for more than four centuries (Kendall, Hawkins, and Bossen 1983; Chambers and Young 1979; Wasserstrom 1983). It is also indisputable that such groups as the Mam (Watanabe 1983), Quiché (B. Tedlock 1982) and Tzotzil (Gossen 1974a; Morris 1987; Bricker 1989) preserve in their living Maya languages, beliefs, and related expressive forms clear continuities from earlier periods. The task in establishing a meaningful dialogue between past and present, therefore, becomes primarily one of identifying areas of discourse in the modern Maya world where one is most likely to find beliefs and practices that have proved to be either "unthreatening" to the dominant Hispanic Christian world or relatively "invisible" to its authority structure. Such a cluster of relative immunity from forced intervention and change is to be found in the Little Tradition of the Maya area in the realm of domestic social life and economic production and in the art forms, belief systems, and cosmology surrounding the domestic unit. The most important anchor point of this conservatism of Maya Little Tradition is language itself; more than six million people in contemporary Mexico, Guatemala, and Belize live in Maya-speaking households. It is therefore to the private sphere of modern Maya domestic life, particularly to the local knowledge that is carried in Maya languages, that we turn for the clues to continuity that guide our dialogue between the past and present.

We began considering the issues presented in this paper using a more-or-less formal model based upon the city, bearer of the Great Tradition, and contrasting outlying communities, bearers of the Little Tradition. As the paper evolved, this model began to weaken as we discovered the power and ambiguity of women in ancient and modern societies. In fact, the categories of the model became permeable rather than rigid. It is precisely this permeability and flux, rather than rigidity, that guides us in our central concern, which is the whole configuration of religious belief and practice in ancient Maya society.

Within the limited space of this paper, we have set for ourselves a large task in the examination of ancient Maya religion. We realize that we will not be able to cover all possible subjects and their implications. Rather, we envision this paper as an opportunity to present numerous ideas, their implications, and some of the archaeological and ethnographic material to support these ideas. We will not present these ideas in the form of testable hypotheses with a series of test implications. Rather, below are a series of models that we hope will stimulate others to examine these questions in both the archaeological and ethnographic record.

CYCLICAL AND LINEAR TIME IN THE PEASANT PERIPHERY AND CENTER

Cyclical time as an intellectual and theological artifact of ancient Mesoamerica was first expressed in the Calendar Round in the Preclassic period (Aveni 1989). The 52-year cycle, based on intermeshing cycles of the 260-day and 365-day calendars, preceded the Classic Maya Long Count by about 600 years (Aveni 1989), and has, in its modern permutations, survived the Maya Long Count by more than one millennium (Gossen 1974b, 1989b).

Because the old solar calendar still survives, largely in the domestic, private sector of contemporary Maya communities, the function and logic of sacred cyclical time may be understood in a full ethnographic context. It is significant that the modern Tzotzil solar calendar carries with it a dependent set of corollary cycles, such that the structure of the solar year is homologous with the structure of the day; the human life cycle; the agricultural year; and the four-part cycle of creations, or restorations, of the cosmos. Modern Tzotzil cosmology not only preserves a variant of the philosophy of sacred cyclical time, but also incorporates without dissonance the Gregorian calendar, a linear system with a single anchor point in the past. Therefore, it is possible to examine how a conservative cyclical system of Maya time-reckoning interacts and intermeshes with a more recently introduced linear system.

How can such a case suggest insights into the Maya past? Modern Tzotzil public ritual and administrative life are regulated by the linear Gregorian calendar that was forcibly introduced, as a new "long count," with Dominican missionization in the sixteenth century. The dates of the saints' days and liturgical cycle, particularly those dates of the variable part of the cycle (Ash Wednesday to Pentecost), are published each year as an inexpensive religious and agricultural almanac called *El Calendario del más antiguo Galván*.[2] This linear calendar enjoys a high profile of importance among the religious and political leaders; indeed, it is an indispensable document. Its written form, as with the Maya Long Count inscriptions, contributes to its symbolic power through its association with central administrative authority. In addition to serving as a basis for the public festival calendar and providing the administrative and fiscal schedules of the civil authorities, the Western linear calendar's cumulative and sequential years provide the register of

---

[2] *El Calendario del más antiguo Galván* is a broadside distributed in the central market of San Cristobal de las Casas, Chiapas, Mexico.

future ritual obligations. Waiting lists for individuals who will assume religious offices (involving sponsorship of saints' cults) are kept in this system. For some offices, these waiting lists, kept under lock and key in the town hall, run well into the twenty-first century. Thus, both present and future orchestration of Chamula public life—a current local expression of Mexico's Great Tradition—is focused on the administrative center and depends upon the linear calendar.

Nevertheless, the Western linear calendar is conceived by Tzotzils to be no more than a cumulative reckoning system within the "Fourth Creation," the present epoch in the four-part cycle of creations of restorations recognized in Chamula cosmology. Thus, to summarize, the linear Gregorian calendar, a recent introduction, functions as a subset within a larger Maya system of cyclical time. This four-part cycle subsumes the linear system not only logically, but also historically, for the major cycles of creation and destruction were undoubtedly in place before the Conquest.

At this point, it should be noted that it is primarily male political and religious authorities who need and use the linear calendar to manage the affairs of Chamula public life; indeed, most Chamula women, the large majority of whom have never been to school, do not even use or understand years in the Christian era. The linear calendar, therefore, functions as a symbolic and practical tool of the male-dominated administrative center. In contrast, the cyclical concepts within which the linear calendar is logically embedded are diffused in nearly everyone's collective knowledge (male and female, humble and powerful) and may be said, therefore, to be omnipresent in the sense of both social and physical space.

Just as knowledge of the larger cyclical framework of the linear calendar is diffused in all of the community, so the modern descendant of the old Maya solar calendar (Calendar Round) also survives as an important time-reckoning tool that is widely known and comfortably coexists with the Gregorian calendar. Known in Tzotzil as the *otol k'ak'al* ("counter of days"), the old solar calendar of 18 months of 20 days plus a 5-day 19th month is used for two principal purposes, neither of which involves central statecraft in the Great Tradition. Typically kept in the form of a wooden tablet with charcoal tally marks, the old Maya solar calendar still functions as an agricultural almanac that identifies propitious days for engaging in traditional economic activities ranging from roof-beam-cutting to the planting of maize (Gossen 1974b). It also serves as the schedule for "flower-changing rituals," which must be staged every 20 days by ritual officials who sponsor saints' cults. Unlike the public spectacles of the saints' days, these rituals occur in the privacy of officials' homes and are not open to the general public. Furthermore, unlike the case of the Gregorian calendar, knowledge and use of the old solar calendar is as common among women as among men. In fact, the version of this calendar which has been analyzed came from the home of an elderly woman who is a shaman (Gossen 1974b).

It should be noted for comparative purposes that not only in the Maya area, but throughout the Americas and elsewhere, asymmetrical gender relations have figured prominently in the dynamics of states and the articulation of their patrifocal Great Traditions with their more egalitarian Little Traditions. The Tzotzil-Tzeltal region provides a number of well-documented cases of female instrumentality, esoteric knowledge, and political activity, most of it linked to the nonpublic spheres of life: extensive knowledge of oral narrative and oral history (Laughlin 1977; Karasik 1988) and key roles in subversive religious cult activity (Bricker 1981). In Guatemala, the Mam (Watanabe 1983) and Quiche (B. Tedlock 1982) are well-documented cases of females (and males) as repositories of traditional knowledge regarding cosmology and divination. Elsewhere, in the Andes, females were, apparently by community consensus, actually designated as "keepers" of tradition, even as males were forced during the colonial period to become religious and political agents of the new Indian puppet-state. This arrangement apparently received the unwitting endorsement of the colonial establishment, since women were regarded as irrelevant to its vision of local rule (Silverblatt 1987). Perhaps something comparable was going on in the Maya area.

We believe, therefore, that gender relations, as articulated with time-reckoning, narrative, and cosmology, provide a useful and hitherto unexplored angle from which to consider conceptual parallels between ancient and contemporary Maya religion.

### THE NATURE OF TIME AND HISTORY AMONG THE ANCIENT MAYA

At this point, we would like to summarize several introductory points: (1) ancient and modern Maya cosmologies are strongly linked by a central logical structure based on cycles; (2) both ancient and modern cosmologies emphasize cyclical time as the more dominant and conservative time-reckoning system, and cyclical time is primarily associated with the Little Tradition of both ancient and modern Maya communities; and (3) linear time is the more ephemeral and pragmatic time-reckoning system and is associated with the creation and maintenance of political authority in the Great Tradition. We argue that both ancient and modern political and religious systems and authority in the cities, derived from and recorded in linear time, are in fact subject to the structural rules of the cyclical perception of time and history that preceded these authority systems and ultimately outlived them.

It has long been understood and discussed that the ancient Maya conception of time and history was cyclical in nature (Thompson 1966). A simplistic statement of this principle is that what has occurred in the past is also occurring in the present, and will occur in the future. There is an entire series of cyclical calendars through which the ancient Maya marked time.

These include the 260-day Sacred Round (*tzolkin*), the 365-day Solar or Vague Year (*haab*), a combination of the *tzolkin* and *haab* that forms the 52-year cycle called the Calendar Round, as well as the 9-day Lord of the Night cycle, which cycles every 467 years with the Calendar Round. Other cycles existed, but these were the primary ones used by the ancient Maya. This cyclical nature of time appears to relate specifically to the ritual activity of the Maya.

In contrast to the Calendar Round and the cyclical nature of time is a more linear view of time as presented in the Long Count. We believe that there is evidence that the ancient Maya viewed this calendrical system as being both linear and cyclical in nature. The Long Count is a time-counting system based upon the 360-day "year" or tun. It is cyclical in that it focuses upon a cycle of 13 baktuns or 5,200 tuns. The Maya used this to mark the beginning and the end of the previous and present-day worlds. The creation of the present world for the Maya occurred on 11 August 3113 B.C. and the destruction will come in the year A.D. 2012. Although it is cyclical, the length of the cycle is so long—5,200 tuns (360-day periods)—that the history of the Maya and the present day fall into the same creation of the world, and it therefore presents a more linear view of time than that of the Calendar Round and its components.

There is also evidence that the Maya perceived the Long Count as a linear count of time. The basic components of the Long Count are the kin (a single day), the uinal (a period of 20 days), the tun (a period of 360 days), the katun (a period of 20 tuns), and the baktun (a period of 20 katuns or 400 tuns). However, we have evidence from several monuments that the Maya continued to expand this basically vigesimal system beyond the baktun to include the pictun (a period of 20 baktuns), the calabtun (a period of 20 pictuns), and the kinchiltun (a period of 20 calabtuns). For example, Tikal Stela 10 bears a date of 1.11.19.9.3.11.2.?, which presents a time or time period well beyond the reach of the basic Long Count cycle of 13 baktuns (Jones and Satterthwaite 1982).

However, Coggins argues that, within the midst of what appears to be a predominantly linear calendrical system, the development of the importance of the katun ending or katun completion marks the imposition of a cyclical structure (a 20-year cycle) upon the linear Long Count (Coggins 1979, 1980). Coggins argues that the identification or celebration of the katun ending first appears at Uaxactun at 8.16.0.0.0 and then at Tikal at 8.18.0.0.0, and marks the arrival of Teotihuacanos at Uaxactun and Tikal (Coggins 1980).

Therefore, within the basic calendrical systems of the ancient Maya, we find a combination of the two concepts of time or types of experiences defined by Leach as: (1) a notion of repetition, and (2) a notion of nonrepetition (Leach 1971). Leach argues that within "primitive societies" the notion of repetition predominates due, he argues, to the psychological repugnance to death. Leach continues and states that death and birth are therefore equated, creating a repetitive view of time.

However, within the ancient Maya, we see the continued use and importance of both a nonrepetitive or linear system and a repetitive or cyclical system. How can we begin to understand the correlation of these calendars that represent both a linear and cyclical view of time? Schele and Miller (1986) discuss the calendars as "an overlapping set of cycles, each different in duration and reference." Again, according to Schele and Miller, the primary reason for the use of such a complex set of cycles was, as with other people, to record "the history of human events." However, this does not explain the utilization and interrelationship of the linear and cyclical calendars. Although the Maya did not utilize the Calendar Round as the final cycle of renewal and rebirth as did other groups in Mesoamerica, such as the Aztecs (Schele and Miller 1986), it was a primary method of identifying time and history. The two parts of the Calendar Round have a certain amount of antiquity which cannot be ascribed to the Long Count, which is fairly recent and dates to the seventh baktun.

We argue in this paper that the development and utilization of the Long Count in Mesoamerica, and its widespread utilization throughout the Maya lowlands, is due to the development of a lineage-based kingship within the Gulf Coast, Pacific Coast, and then Maya lowland area. This lineage-based kingship, in order to legitimate not only the living king, but also his successor, needed a linear calendar of time.

The earliest and most secure Long Count dates in Mesoamerica are found on Stela 2 at Chiapa de Corzo ([7.16.] 3.2.13 [6 Ben 16 Xul]); Stela C at Tres Zapotes 7.16.6.16.18 6 Etznab [1 Uo]); and monuments from El Baul, Abaj Takalik, and La Mojarra (Winfield Capitaine 1988). The earliest monuments with a Long Count fall within the beginning of the first century A.D. and relate to developments during the Late Preclassic in Mesoamerica. The societies located within the Gulf Coast, Chiapas and Guatemalan Highlands, and the Pacific Coast have all been characterized as being complex and stratified in their political and social organization. Most often, these societies, such as the Olmec or the Izapa people, have been slotted within the chiefdom level of sociopolitical complexity (Flannery 1982; Sharer and Grove 1989). However, anthropologists have realized that the term chiefdom is rife with possible meanings and cultural interpretations (Drennan and Uribe 1987).

We argue that chiefdom-level society, a developmental phase between egalitarian society and complex state-level organization, can be equated with two forms of control of leadership. Flannery (1972) has argued that within a chiefdom-level society, the institution of chief exists separately from an individual who holds that office. There is no direct succession to the office of chief. We would argue that as some chiefdom-level societies become more complex, a lineage-based succession or descent system develops and it is at this point that the Long Count, or a more linear view of time than had existed previously, is utilized to legitimize this different political system. The appearance of the Long Count at Chiapa de Corzo, at Tres Zapotes, and at La Mojarra, all indicate to us the existence of a lineage-based chiefdom society at these sites and within these areas. We will not argue that full state-level complexity is the next step within these geographic and cultural regions. Rather, it is the lowlands (the Maya area) and some parts of the highlands (the Valleys of Mexico and Oaxaca) that develop into the more complex state-level organizations.

We are not arguing for the preeminence of the Long Count and a linear view of time and history in any of these Mesoamerican societies. Rather, we feel that there is an important integration of linear and cyclical time that provides for a different type of chiefdom-level organization, and possibly even state-level organization within the Maya lowlands. Cyclical structure still provided the basic underpinnings of the society, but this linear construction allowed for a different type of legitimization of power and rulership.

We can identify this same type of integration of cyclical and linear views of time and history within the modern Maya of Chiapas. Gossen has demonstrated that several aspiring historical actors in Chamula central political life—each of whom has proposed radical political and religious transformation of the central authority structure of the community—have in fact been both raised to power and destroyed by logical exigencies that literally existed before they were born. In this sense, the careers of Maya leaders, past and present, are also both constrained and assisted by cyclical time. Structurally and culturally speaking, individual Maya may be said to live before they are born, so powerful is the capacity of the past to structure the present (Gossen 1977; 1988).

One such case is the Chamula revitalization movement of 1867–70, known as the War of Santa Rosa. In this violent religious and political separatist movement, Chamula protagonists behaved not so much as new actors in history, but rather, as re-enactors of the mythological past as they understood it. It is recorded that among the actors was a Tzotzil woman, Augustina Gómez Chechev, who declared, upon receiving sacred images from the sky, that she was the new "Mother of God" (referring to the Moon/Virgin Mary deity), and was commanded by the Sun/Christ deity to form a new Indian religious cult, separate from the Ladino (Mexican-Hispanic) religion (Fig. 1). The climax and ultimate downfall of this cult came with the crucifixion of an Indian youth, Gómez Chechev's relative, who was, through his death and expected rebirth, to become the new Indian Sun/Christ. This bizarre event caused outrage among Ladino church and government officials, and the ensuing separatist movement was destroyed by Ladino troops in 1869–70, but only after its protagonists rose and fell as

Fig. 1 Drawing of Augustina Gómez Chechev and her cult followers by Marian López Calixto of San Juan Chamula.

new representations of old mythological players on the Maya Tzotzil stage (see also Gossen 1977; Bricker 1981: 119–125).

Another case involves a very recent Tzotzil culture hero named Miguel Kashlán, who founded the Chamula Protestant movement in 1965. He was eventually assassinated by traditionalist adversaries in 1981, but only after living a long life that bore striking structural similarities to the life history of the founding creator deity, the Sun/Christ. Thus, even in moments of radical culture change that do not look favorably on Maya traditionalism, the Maya produce actors who are not really modern pragmatists and rationalists, but rather haunting semblances of their mythological forebears (Gossen 1988).

In pursuing the dialogue between the Maya present and the past, this model suggests to us that the Classic Maya dynasties were morally underwritten and legitimated by the Long Count as a divine "historical" genealogy. These dynasties and the use of the Long Count were subject to cosmological exigency to reflect the past as dictated by the more dominant structures of a cyclical view of time and history. There is ample evidence for the importance of the ritual cycle within the structure of the genealogical history of the ancient Maya rulers. Long Count dates on stelae and other monuments within the lowlands are constantly found in association with calendar round dates and other cyclical dates. Although the linear perception of the Long Count is an integral part of the elite/kingship of the Great Tradition, it is intimately tied to the cyclical construct of the Little Tradition.[3]

In the present-day surge of hieroglyphic translations and presentations of the ancient Maya past as presented by the documents and other forms of material culture, it is important to recall an article by Dennis Puleston in 1979. Within this article, Puleston argues that the 13-katun historical cycle (256-year Short Count) was not only a primary factor in the development of historical events during the Postclassic and Colonial periods but also structured history during the Classic period. "It is clear that the Maya conception of historical repetition did not entail an exact repetition of past events but rather a conformance of history to certain underlying, predictable patterns as revealed in the katun prophesies" (Puleston 1979: 63). This concept of the death and rebirth of cycles and of time can be seen with Puleston's argument for the 13-katun cycle, the 13-baktun cycle, or Long Count as it relates to the destruction and creation of the world, and numerous other cycles including the individual katun cycle emphasized by Coggins (1979). This cyclical perception of time and history will therefore have an impact both upon the way events unfold and also, importantly, upon the way these events are perceived and constructed in a written form. This argument goes beyond Puleston's and necessitates new approaches to our "writing of Maya history."

Carlson (1980) raises the issue of what he calls "tampering with history" in terms of the genealogical structure and ritual time of the ancient Maya. We believe, however, that it is not an issue of "tampering with history," for the concept of what is history remains uncertain. We argue that Maya kingship "history" was constructed. What we would like to emphasize is a point presented above of "people who live before they are born." One can argue, as Schele and Miller (1986) or Lounsbury (1980) have, that the historical dates are set in time as records of actual events and that the ritual cycle was utilized to justify or legitimize the actions or activities on these dates. However, we would like to turn this around and argue that the Calender Round and other cycles structured history and provided the framework within which the Long Count could lineally record the construction of history. Mythical ancestor gods, mythical ancestors, and important ancestors such as a lineage founder may have provided the life-cycle structure—perhaps even specific dates—for more recent rulers. This is not "tampering with history." Rather, the ancient

---

[3] Schele and Miller (1986) also mention the importance of the cyclical nature of time in terms of two types of dates: special records of the zero date and Lounsbury's contrived numbers. These numbers "record" the actions of the past, present, and future within a cyclical structure. These special records of zero dates and the contrived numbers emphasize the dominance of cyclical time in relation to linear time—the long count.

Maya world view is structured upon and exists within a long tradition of the cyclical view of time and history. A more recently imposed linear calendar, utilized for kingship, is embedded within this cyclical system.

## MODELS

We have thus far spoken of a highly structured and conservative template of underlying logic of the Maya cosmos that is based upon cyclical time. We have asserted that such a paradigm may account for striking patterns of similarity that exist between the structure of religious authority systems in the Classic Maya and those of the contemporary Tzotzil and other Maya groups. In this section we will sketch the derivation, outlines, and corollaries of the model.

### Derivation

Practice and empirical social life simultaneously derive from and reify belief. To turn it about, as Clifford Geertz has so felicitously phrased it, sacred symbols are models of and for social reality (Geertz 1963: 123). In the context of this discussion that means the structure of everyday Tzotzil domestic life is the wellspring of the social reality of the cosmos. Religion articulates the essential qualities of both spheres. The paradigm we propose, therefore, derives from mythology—the past, and contemporary social life—the present, for each simultaneously sustains, reaffirms, and continually re-creates the other. The model proposed is thus necessarily paradigmatic (pure structure, that is, timeless) and syntagmatic (structure realized in time and history).

### Tzotzil Domestic Life—A Mini Portrait

Tzotzils who are not public officials live in patrilineal compounds scattered in hamlets among the cornfields and sheep pastures. Women traditionally move from their patrilineal compounds of birth to those of their husbands after extensive bride-price transactions and initial matrilocal residence are concluded. Women maintain the household and attached kitchen gardens and small livestock. For many months each year, women run these households in the absence of their husbands, who move about in a more distant orbit of economic activities and public service that takes them frequently to the Chamula Center and to the commercial and political centers of mestizo Mexico. Thus, the peasant periphery and Little Tradition of the Tzotzil world is permanently and primarily occupied by women.

It should be noted that the Tzotzil language itself suggests this association in the term of reference *yahval hna* ("the owner of my house") that a man uses for his wife. This term is used even when (as is the typical case) the house is located on land owned by his own patrilineage. It is also the case that the traditional custom of bride service requires that a newly wedded couple live matrilocally at the wife's home compound for several years before moving to the husband's compound. The labor provided by the husband for the maintenance of the wife's home household is considered part of bride price. Tzotzil men, therefore, live in close association with female-dominated domestic arrangements both as young children and as newly wedded husbands. Both childhood and adult life for men are initiated in the surrounding environment of a female locus. Even death, in particular the preparation of the corpse for burial, is exclusively in the hands of women.

Thus, although males dominate most aspects of modern Maya public life most of the time, and are the customary articulators of the community with Mexico's Great Tradition, it is nevertheless the case that women have occasionally risen to public power as founders and prophets of a new or revitalized Great Tradition. Notable cases that are discussed elsewhere in this paper are María de la Candelaria, founder of the Tzeltal Revolt of 1712, and Augustina Gómez Chechev, founder of the 1868–69 Chamula movement (note that even Ladino history associates this movement with Santa Rosa [Bricker 1981: 125]). On these occasions and others (the 1911 Pajarito movement and the more recent Protestant evangelical movement), women have risen to prominence in public affairs as leaders and symbols of proposed "new" Great Traditions, based on native priesthoods. Their moments in power have been brief, and in all cases they have been preceded and succeeded by male public leaders.

However, to reiterate the point, females and the Little Tradition with which they are associated are foci not only of beginnings and endings but also chief actors in the transitional and critical moments in the life cycle and historical process. Although the female principle is not typically or even consistently high in the public profile, it is nevertheless the permanent force on which this patrifocal community depends for initiation, revitalization, and final marking of cycles. Femaleness is ambiguous and anomalous in Maya society; it is therefore powerful not only in the maintenance of the *status quo* in the Little Tradition, but also powerful in the public arena when the Great Tradition experiences critical moments of transition, revitalization, and renewal.

## Roots in Myth

The pattern of domestic division of labor is reproduced in the interaction of the solar (Sun/Christ) and lunar (Moon/Virgin Mary) deities in the primordial creation myth of the cosmos. It should be noted that Tzotzil mythology assigns primordial sexual identity in the cosmos to the female, who then brings male sexuality into existence only to have it (that is, him) usurp her own primordial power. The following is a paraphrase and synthesis of many narrative versions of the origin myth from Gossen's transcribed corpus of narratives:

Before the First Creation, the world was a single surface of mud and slime and it existed in total darkness. This world was populated by precultural and asexual monkeys, demons, and (thanks to the Dominicans) Jews. Our Mother Moon (Virgin Mary) was alone in this primordial chaos. She becomes pregnant and was aware that the being in her womb was full of heat. The demons were also aware of the potential force in her womb and they pursued her so as to kill her child upon birth. Shortly after he (the future Sun/Christ) was born, the demons and their allies killed him, but he came back to life and fled west to the edge of the earth platform and went into the underworld, pursued by the demons. He spent two days there. On the third day, he began to rise from the underworld to the eastern horizon. On the fourth day, he emerged from the eastern horizon as the nascent sun. When he reached the zenith of the heavens, his heat and light destroyed his enemies. With these events, the world experienced its first day and, simultaneously, the cosmos received its configuration and spatial limits, for these were traced by the Sun/Christ's orbit by day (heavens) and by night (the underworld).

*A Tzotzil Cosmological Paradigm*

Figure 2 is a schematic synthesis of the spatial and temporal categories that are implicit and explicit in the cosmos, according to Tzotzil premises, as revealed in narrative and interviews. Note the homologies that prevail among the daily and annual solar cycles and the cycles of annual agricultural activity and the life cycle. Also note the shifting gender valences of the quadrants of the day and the annual cycle, which are created by the combined values of light/darkness (male/female), on the one hand; and ascending sun/descending sun (midnight to noon/noon to midnight). Chamula belief asserts that female power becomes dominant each day and each year in the descending phase of the sun.

Figure 3 represents the stages of the cosmogonic narrative of the First Creation, which also constitute the logical sequence of major narrative accounts of the three subsequent creations (or restorations). Since the sequence of narrative logic (A1 to A2) is homologous with the pattern of daily life, it becomes a kind of timeless template that generates the possibilities for historical action in the present and future. It is suggested that this pattern (A1 to A2) forms a deep structural backdrop for decision-making (with cognitive accounting) whenever any part of it is expressed historically with new content, new actors, or new challenges. In this manner, mythology provides the pattern for historical action in the present. It is both paradigmatic and syntagmatic.

## The Topography of Ancient Maya Religious Pluralism

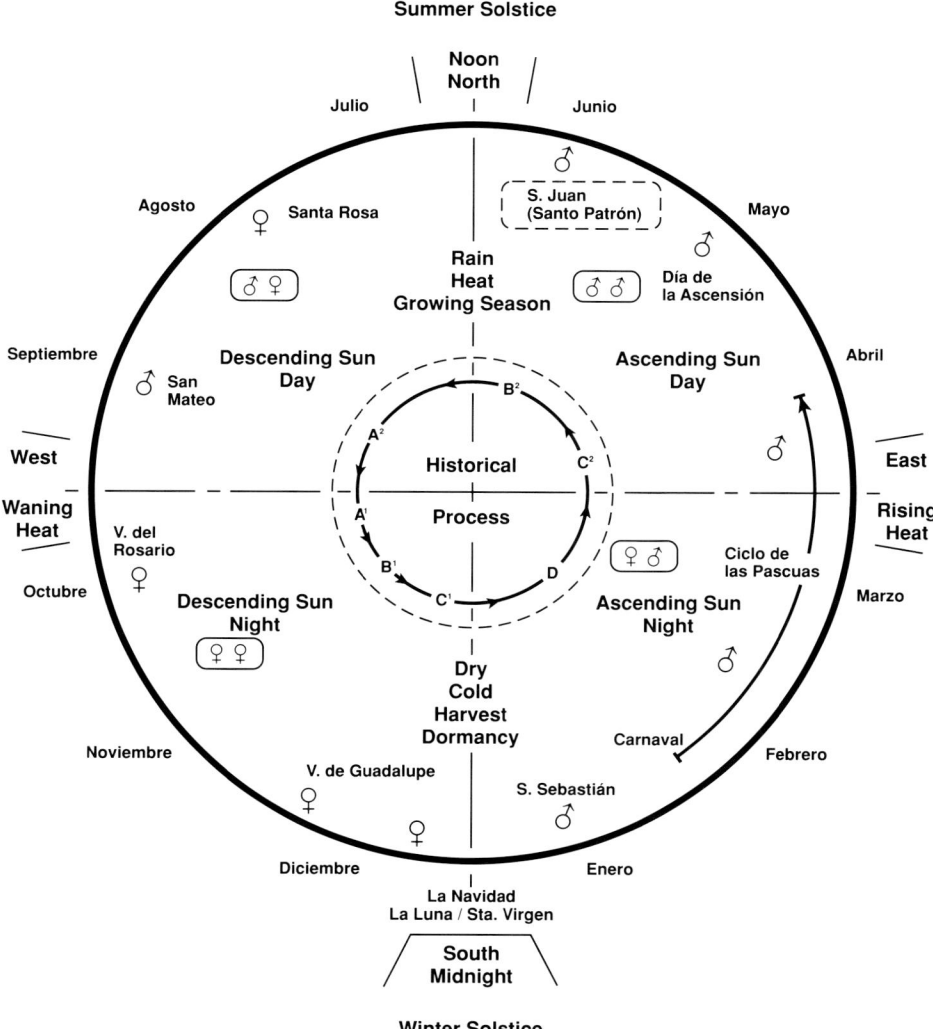

Fig. 2   Scheme of Chamula Tzotzil cosmological categories and paradigm of historical process.

### A Grammar of Narrative and Social Change

The model presented in Figures 2 and 3 has been applied to the interpretation of Tzotzil ethnohistoric texts (Gossen 1977), contemporary biography (Gossen 1988), and ritual drama (Gossen 1986). In each case, human circumstances begin with an initial phase of social uncertainty or ambiguity (see A1

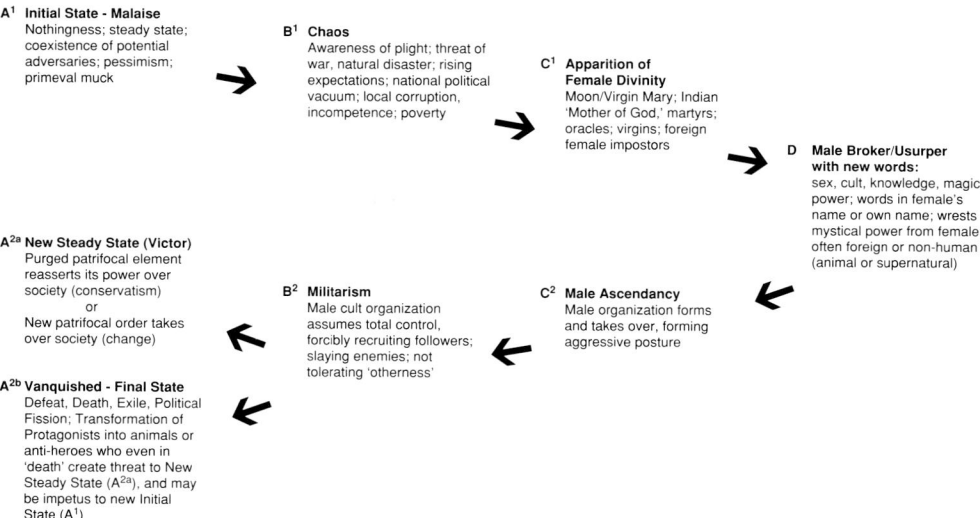

Fig. 3  Toward a Tzotzil Maya theory of history.

and B1 of Fig. 3). This ambiguity is taken away or clarified by means of female mystical force or creative power (see C1 of Fig. 3). In the case of the cosmogonic myth, the Holy Mother Moon has this role as the primordial creative power in the universe, for she is (or is to be) the mother of the Sun/Christ. No sooner is the primordial female power made manifest as a source of new being and creation than a male personage (see D in Fig. 3) appears and attempts to take away or capture the power of the female, be it her reproductive capacity or her mystical power as the "mother of god" or oracle for new cults. Once the woman or her power has been subdued and put away under male patronage (see C2 in Fig. 3, e.g., marriage), male protagonists enter into conflict with other males in order to dominate the flow of events in short or long-term public history. It is at this point (B2 in Fig. 3) in the paradigm of cyclical history that male-dominated periods of linear history may be best accommodated. Some of these male actors win (A2a) and some lose (A2b), the same in local affairs as in the public political and religious forum. This paradigmatic drama begins as a local conflict between the sexes and inevitably becomes a public conflict between male adversaries for political, economic, and religious power. The paradigmatic drama is realized on a small scale in the history of ephemeral but violent revitalization movements or in long-term historical trends. In all cases, the pattern is paradigmatic in that it is simultaneously the pattern of the day, year, and human life cycle, the logic of the cosmos, and historical change.

## The Topography of Ancient Maya Religious Pluralism

### THE GENDER VALENCES OF TIME AND SPACE

The early and concluding phases of narrative and historical sequences involve instrumental female power. The Tzotzil narrative tradition is full of such cases, as is the Western written record of postcontact Tzeltal and Tzotzil history. For example, the Tzeltal Revolt was precipitated by the declaration of María de la Candelaria that she had been designated by the Virgin as spokesperson for a new cult. This led to an effort to establish a separate Indian Church, apart from the Spanish Church and from the authority of the Spanish political authorities (Bricker 1981: 59–66). Again, in 1868, Augustina Gómez Chechev precipitated the Tzotzil separatist movement described above. In 1910, a Chamula Tzotzil woman came to power as the "Holy Mother" of a violent religious and political movement known as the Pajarito Rebellion, which was (in league with conservative Catholic clergy) concerned with purification of Chamula religion against the godless revolutionaries who were soon to produce the Mexican Revolution (Gossen, unpublished field notes; Moscoso Pastraña 1972). Even more recently, the post-1965 Chamula Protestant movement is said to have found its initial success in conversion through sympathy inspired by two sisters. These little Chamula girls became heroines for the cause of Protestant conversion after they survived severe burns inflicted by the ruling oligarchy of Chamula, who ordered the girls' home burned as punishment for their faith (Gossen 1988, 1989a).

In all of the cases just cited, these Maya religious movements began outside the local administrative centers, within the Little Tradition, in periods of rising expectations for local autonomy or local reform that were associated with periods of political malaise or transition in the national society. In 1712, the greater backdrop was the shift from Hapsburg to Bourbon administration of Spanish Crown policy toward the Church in relation to local communities in America. In 1867–70, the Juárez anticlerical and federalist reforms were in full swing in the Mexican national government, giving considerable latitude for expression of local ethnic autonomy. In 1910, the anticlerical forces of the early years of the Mexican Revolution were being felt at the local level, thus diminishing Mexican central church authority over local Indian religion. In the 1960s, the national oil boom had shifted policy priorities to encourage industrial transformation at the cost of continued agrarian reform in peasant communities. Protestantism promised prosperity (that the government was accused of no longer delivering through land reform) to marginal peasants through radical change in their own life styles.

In all of the cases just cited, the initial female impetus, which was fundamental in launching the movements, was captured by a male leader who sought to shift the movement from secondary to primary importance. In all cases, the females faded from view as males brought the movements into violent confrontation with other male-led interest groups.

The point of this discussion is to suggest that the ideology of cyclical time appears to have given to all of these movements a remarkably similar pattern of genesis and development, in spite of their diverse origins and different contexts. Given that all of the movements were of Tzotzil and Tzeltal Maya origin, and that these communities are fundamentally patrifocal in the structure of their political and religious affairs, the female role in founding these new political and religious movements is striking. We believe that this instrumental female role can be understood as an expression of the initial phase of a timeless template of historical process that existed before the events themselves. We further suggest that this is a fundamentally Maya template, based on cyclical solar time. Perhaps it is a very old one.

It is important to note at this point that the pattern of gender associations just proposed appears to bear a strong resemblance to well-worn interpretive themes that associate females with hearth, home, and "nature," and males with the public arena and "culture." Is not the initial primacy of the female principle everywhere dominant in the semiotics, psychology, and biology of the human experience? Is femaleness not universally associated with the domestic sphere, local customs, continuity, conservatism, and with the early phases of ontogenetic development of individuals? Although the apparent answer is "yes" (Ortner 1974), we argue in this paper that a broader view emphasizes the importance and power of women not only during the initial phases of development but also during transitional and terminal phases. It is also during these periods of change where female symbolic dominance is clearly identified in both the ancient and modern Maya domestic sphere (Little Tradition) and, most importantly, within the historical process of the public sphere (the Great Tradition).

For comparative purposes, it is important to note that we are not observing something bizarre or anomalous in the adaptive behavior of the Maya, but rather, a typical response of underclass individuals to their opportunities for political empowerment in stratified, patrifocal, or state-level societies. Instrumental female involvement in political movements that eventually involve the public sector is well-documented cross-culturally, and there is, we believe, good reason to incorporate the politics of gender into our consideration of the ancient Maya theocratic states. Irene Silverblatt (1988: 451–452 [footnotes omitted]) has eloquently summarized this challenge as follows:

> Studies in European and American history remind us that the state is not a monolithic event or institution that merely fulfills functional requirements of power and economy. Western histories, along with the variability of earlier states, have illustrated the com-

plex nature of the relationship between any particular state and the gender relations within. They have also shown that as states contributed to the definition of womanhood, so did women contribute to the definition of states.

Women conspicuously and collectively participated in the political movements protesting the traumatic changes in social relations and circumstances wrought by the expansion of capitalism. From the religious uprisings during the British civil wars, to food riots in France, to religious challenges in Italy, to tax riots in Holland, women noticeably—to eyewitness observers and often belatedly to scholars—clamored against the threatened diminishment of their lives. Women's protests throughout the world assumed varying shapes and were centered on diverse issues. The nature of state power, the organization of work, the character of class divisions and transformations (each including their gender aspects), cultural expectations regarding legitimate standards of living, practice, and gender activities—all tied to specific state-making, colonial, and economic histories—contoured the possibilities of women's alliances and political engagements.

No uniform history of women in the state can account for the complex, often contradictory, histories of how women have engaged their particular political worlds. Some women's movements have been "enlightened" and progressive, while others—like the robust one that was integral to Nazi rule—have not. Justice to progressive feminism requires honest assessment of its limits, as well as of women who passionately embrace fundamentalism, the veil, and the "right to life." Feigning innocence of power, ambiguity, and contradiction ultimately demeans women's struggles, as it denies their potential.

### FEMALES IN THE ANCIENT MAYA WORLD

Women played important roles within the ancient Maya political and ritual world. Little research has focused upon the role of women within the Little Tradition of ancient Maya society. This is an area of research that is lacking in our understanding of the ancient Maya past. However, we can turn to the elite sphere or the Great Tradition and study the role of women within a historical context.

In examining historical figures, there are two areas of discussion we would like to pursue within this paper. The first will be the role of women as powerful figures within the ancient Maya political structure and as rulers. The second is the relationship between women and blood sacrificial rites.

We have emphasized above that within modern Maya communities, women play a multiplicity of roles: first, they are the focus of the conservative folk cult or Little Tradition and can be associated with ancient cyclical concepts of time and history; and, second, they are transitional and initiate change or serve as harbingers for new crises in the system, particularly within the Great Tradition. The power of women within modern and (as will be shown below) ancient communities is the contradictory structure they provide—both conservative and dynamic in their form.

This ambiguous and contradictory nature of women is evident within the hieroglyphic texts and iconographic representations of the elite and rulers of Maya centers. On the one hand, women provide a conservative structure that allows for the maintenance of the ruling lineage. Relationship glyphs or parentage statements, often found on monuments, document the apparent ties of the present ruler to his/her parents (Schele 1982). Another system-maintaining mechanism for women is the utilization of marriage alliances between centers to create connections for political power and growth (Molloy and Rathje 1974; Marcus 1976).

The Popul Vuh is a good place to start in the identification of the role of women within Postclassic/Colonial Maya and possibly within Classic period society (D. Tedlock 1985). Two women figure prominently within the story and provide us with good examples of both the conservative and transitional nature of women in Maya society. The point of intersection between Xmucane, the grandmother of the Hero Twins, and Blood Woman, their mother, clearly identifies the roles of women as we have discussed above. Blood Woman marks the point of transition between many aspects of the world. As the daughter of one of the Xibalban or Underworld Lords, she marks the transition point between the Underworld and the Earth. In addition, within the story of the Popul Vuh the world seems to be in disorder, for the Xibalban Lords have defeated One Hunahpu and Seven Hunahpu; but the story is not finished for Blood Woman is pregnant with the Hero Twins. We would argue that with the birth of the Hero Twins, Blood Woman restores order to the world.

In contrast to her daughter-in-law, Xmucane demonstrates the conservative side of women. She realizes that Blood Woman is her daughter-in-law and pregnant by seeing the mark of the carrying net in the dirt of the corn field. Dennis Tedlock (1985: 40) makes an insightful comment when he states,

> To understand how Xmucane is able to interpret the sign of the net we must remember that she knows how to read the auguries of the Mayan calendar, and that one of the twenty day names that go into the making of that calendar is "Net." . . . The event that is due to come next in the story is the rebirth of Venus as the morning star, which should fall, as she already knows, on a day called Net. When she sees the imprint of the net in the field, she takes it as a

sign that this event is coming near, and that the faces of the sons born to Blood Woman will be reincarnations of the face of One Hunahpu.

Xmucane as a "daykeeper" maintains and understands the past, while Blood Woman signifies change and transition.

At the same time, within the contradictory fashion of women within Maya and other societies, women who have become rulers have caused a dramatic transition within the genealogical structure of the kingship. Women are identified as rulers or powerful elite at numerous sites including Palenque, Naranjo, Copan, and Caracol, to name just a few (Schele and Miller 1986; Chase and Chase 1987).

The Palenque genealogy with its women rulers is one of the best documented in the Maya area and will be discussed here. According to Schele's reconstruction of the Palenque genealogical chart for the ruling lineage at Palenque (Schele 1991), two women come to power within a short span of time. Lady Kanal-Ikal accedes to the throne on 9.7.10.3.8 and dies a little more than twenty years later. She is followed by a male ruler, Ac Kan, who lasts fewer than eight years on the throne. The second woman, Lady Zac-Kuk, then comes to the throne for a short period and apparently steps aside when Pacal reaches the age of twelve and takes on the mantle of power. In terms of relationships, Lady Kanal-Ikal is the grandmother and Lady Zac-Kuk is the mother of Pacal. Schele and Freidel (1990) identify some anomalies with the accession of these women on the monuments of Palenque. First, Pacal portrayed both women twice on his sarcophagus. No other ruler is presented as such and there is no apparent explanation of this anomaly. Second, the identification of Lady Kanal-Ikal's accession to the throne follows the standard pattern according to Schele and Freidel (1990). However, Lady Zac-Kuk is not identified specifically by name but rather by a concept that refers to her as the "mother of the gods" (note the similarity in the role played by Augustina Gómez Chechev, discussed above). Schele and Freidel argue that these two anomalies are Pacal's way of justifying his position on the throne—by emphasizing the importance of his grandmother with two representations and by arguing that his mother is a god. Pacal, himself, becomes a god.

This elaborate manner of justification by Pacal is needed because these two women, with their identifiable positions of rulership, cause a transition or change within the lineage structure at Palenque (Schele and Freidel 1990). In a patrilineal system, when women come to the throne, the accession of their offspring causes a shift or jog within the patrilineage. The offspring of each of these women are tied to their mother's husband's lineage, not to their mother's father's lineage; therefore a shift in descent occurs. It might almost be called a moment of transition or even crisis, caused and perhaps resolved, by these women as rulers. However, as our model argues, once this period of transition or crisis, precipitated by women and even resolved by women, comes to an end, the new structure of the Great Tradition is returned to men. Again, power at Palenque is centered within the hands of the male ruler Pacal.

It is interesting to note that both of these women at Palenque are rulers whose periods of reign are very close to each other in time. This may mark a general period of transition and change within the Palenque community. At the same time, note that this conspicuous clustering of women rulers falls at the end of the "hiatus," another period of change and transition that affects most of the entire lowland Maya area. It might also be possible to speculate that Lady Zac-Kuk and Lady Kanal-Ikal are mythical rulers who were created to justify the genealogical shift to a new or different lineage structure. Such a creation may explain what appears to be an overly energetic justification or presentation of these women as rulers.

We would like to present one more example of an identified female ruler in the Maya lowlands who marks what appears to be a point of transition at a site. The ruler is Lady 6 of Naranjo. Lady 6 has been identified by numerous scholars including Berlin (1968), Marcus (1976), and Closs (1985).

Closs has divided the inscriptions and "history" of Naranjo into three periods: the early period of 9.8.0.0.0 to 9.10.10.0.0; the middle period of 9.13.10.0.0 to 9.14.15.0.0; and the late period of 9.17.10.0.0 to 9.19.10.0.0 (1985: 65). Although he acknowledges a hiatus in the inscriptions, Closs indicates that there is continuity in the dynastic structure between the early and middle periods. There is no such apparent continuity between the middle and late periods at Naranjo. The reign of Lady 6's apparent son, Smoking Squirrel, and of Lady 6 herself marks the end of the middle period at Naranjo—a clear transition point in the history of this site. Naranjo's power as a major center is waning at this time and does not reemerge until about 9.17.10.0.0 or the beginning of the late period.

Whether or not Lady 6 of Naranjo or Ladies Zac-Kuk and Kanal-Ikal of Palenque are real is not the question. The point must be made that at major transition points in the life cycle of an ancient Maya city, women, either real or mythological, were often identified as powerful figures who may have caused this period of transition or even helped resolve the apparent lack of order within the world structure.

Images of women are often associated with the bloodletting ritual. At sites such as Yaxchilan, Bonampak, Piedras Negras, Naranjo, and Nim Li Punit, females are either performing a bloodletting ritual themselves or in conjunction with another person, usually a male, or are associated with the males who are performing this ritual (Schele and Miller 1986). We do not want, within this paper, to get into a discussion of whether such rituals were actually performed. These are iconographic representations of bloodletting rituals; whether real or not is unimportant. The question remains: why are women associated with the bloodletting ritual? We would argue that bloodletting, within Maya culture, is an act which takes place at a transitional period (Schele and Miller 1986), and therefore, women who are transitional actors within the Maya world view are part of this ritual. Bloodletting is transitional on several levels. First, the act was performed or was stated to have been performed at periods of transition within the life of a lord/ruler and within the life of a city. These transitional periods included accession, birth, death, warfare, or even period endings, and are associated with the political world. At the same time, these bloodletting rituals, which mark transition points, are utilized to maintain the *status quo* and legitimize the lineage. Again, we see the ambiguous nature of women within Maya society, both as sustaining symbols and instigators of change.

A bloodletting ritual is also a transitional period from a spiritual perspective. This ritual, which is analogous to shamanic acts, marks the actual transition of a person from a physical body into a spirit, an animal spirit, in order to communicate with the gods. It is a transition from this world to another. Therefore, as a primary transition point or force in religious ritual, women play an integral role in ancient Maya society.

## THE TOPOGRAPHY OF RELIGIOUS PLURALISM

We have asserted that deified cyclical time is the older, latent moral order on which ancient Maya society and its theocratic authority system rested. We have also asserted that linear time was not pansystemic (i.e., subscribed to by all inhabitants of a city's surrounding settlement). Rather, the cults of the Great Tradition based on linear time were relatively short-lived and potentially fragile systems that required periodic genealogical adjustment as dynasties that ruled with the authority and legitimacy of these systems rose and fell. The more fundamental rhythm of cyclical time was the logical underpinning of linear time.

We also contend that the dynasties of kings, similar to Catholic cults and the Mexican civil government in Chamula, were male-focused expressions of the Great Tradition that coexisted with numerous cults of the Little Tradition. The dynasties that ruled through the authority of linear time were tuned to "faster turnovers" and were more malleable, in terms of content, than those of the periphery. The cults of the periphery, on the other hand, were and are today, more conservative and stable than those of the center in that they are concerned with the rhythm and maintenance of domestic social life and domestic economy. The cults of the periphery are tuned explicitly to deified cyclical time and articulate easily—if often in token fashion—with the cults of the center. Why? Because the periphery is logically prior to the center in origin and has consistently, in both the Pre-Columbian world and the modern world, outlasted it.

Gary H. Gossen and Richard M. Leventhal

*Modern Religious Pluralism*

We should now like to sketch the panorama of particular religious cults and supernatural transactions that coexist in the contemporary Tzotzil world of Chamula, in the hope that the logic of their location and function in social space (though not their content) will provide a possible source of inference about the configuration of ancient Maya religion.

The vast majority of all Chamula Tzotzil live in scattered hamlets that lie outside of the administrative center that is the focus of all public civil and religious activity—the local expression of Mexico's Great Tradition. Although all people occasionally visit the central church (there are no outlying chapels) periodically for private petitions to particular saints, virtually all life crisis and curing rituals of a personal or family nature take place in the homes, hamlets, woods, and fields that lie outside of the administrative center. Christian baptism—in effect, a naming ceremony—is the only exception to the pattern in that it requires the presence of a Catholic priest who performs the ritual in the Chamula church. All other ritual markings of the life cycle—birth, first baby-tooth loss, first menses, bride-petitioning, selection of compadres, house-entering ceremonies (i.e., marriage), burials, and annual offerings to ancestors (male and female, who return to visit the living on November 1)—take place in the outlying hamlets. These domestic rituals contrast with public rituals in that they may involve active participation of both male and female lineage elders.

Similarly, male and female shamans, who number in the many hundreds, have equal stature and perform their services of health maintenance in the homes of their clients. The supernaturals invoked in life-crisis rituals are male and female saints, the sun (male) and moon (female) deities, and the all-important animal soul companions of patients. An animal soul companion, of a particular species and of the same gender as the human counterpart, is assigned to each individual at conception. These special animals, known as *chanuletik,* share a tongue-soul (*ch'ulel*) with their human counterparts, and their two aspects, junior and senior, live in a mountain corral (junior home) and in the third layer of the sky dome (senior home) (see Gossen 1975; Linn 1989). The destiny of each animal soul—health, injury and sickness, wealth and poverty, life and death—is shared with its human counterpart and is the object of supernatural intervention on the part of the shamans.

Just as life-crisis rituals, other domestic rituals, and shamanistic practice are located almost entirely in the periphery and involve a strikingly egalitarian participation of male and female practitioners and supernatural beings, so witchcraft is practiced and ritually exorcised on what might be called a gender-blind basis in the periphery, often in the woods and caves. Witches and their victims may be male or female, just as shamans who deal with remedial measures against witchcraft may be male or female. Likewise, there is a widely practiced, though clandestine, tradition of divination that focuses on oracles known as *caxaetik* ("talking boxes"). These boxes or coffers have owners or spokespersons—male or female—who will consult the oracles for a fee if a client has a particular problem or desire for information that cannot be dealt with through regular shamanistic practice.

In addition to the cults just discussed that focus on personal welfare, there is also present in the Little Tradition a complex body of beliefs focusing on the earth lords (*yahval banamil*). The earth lords live in caves and underground passages and are ultimately responsible, in their manifestations as clouds, lightning, and thunder (*anheletik,* "angels"), for rain and the water supply. The earth lords live in families (usually mother, father, and children) in caves and are typically represented as wealthy, white-skinned Ladinos. In addition to their association with water, they are believed to control material wealth in the form of metallic money. Thus, they are the subject of many and frequent transactions between humans and their realm. They are the recipients of a major annual ritual offering that is performed at all local waterholes and springs as a petition for rain; this occurs annually on the festival of Santa Cruz (May 1–3). Furthermore, the earth lords are the subject of many narrative accounts of promises of human loyalty and service to them in exchange for monetary wealth. Significant in these transactions is the role of the daughter of the earth lords as a contact person. This woman typically offers herself as an attractive sexual companion or as a snake in distress. With these guiles, she lures human males into caves and into often catastrophic transactions of labor bondage and marriage in exchange for unlimited money and food supplies. Thus, it is clear that the earth lord complex is heavily linked symbolically with economic aspects of both the Little Tradition of the periphery (i.e., earth, rain, and agricultural productivity) and the Great Tradition of Mexican society (i.e., labor-bondage and money). The earth lord complex is "invisible" or absent from public religious practice, but visible in its realm (the periphery) as an important cult focus that is associated with instrumental female power.

In addition to all of the above, there are numerous minor spooks and supernatural beings, of both sexes and of an asexual nature, who inhabit the periphery and with whom individuals must, on occasion, deal. Among them are male and asexual demons (*pukuhetik:* winged, hairy, black creatures who inhabit underground tunnels and caves), the female wind deity (*me' ik'*), and the female "charcoal-cruncher" (*shk'ush 'ak'al*). All of these creatures cause human misfortune and are, in various ways, ritually placated or tricked so as to protect humans from their malevolent activities.

In summary, Chamula supernatural belief and practice form a multifaceted complex of competing and overlapping cults. The continuum stretches from the highly visible public cults of the center that are, for the most part, dominated by male practitioners, to the nonpublic, even clandestine, cults of the periphery, that are essentially egalitarian with regard to gender of supernaturals and cult practitioners. Many, in fact, are solely female or involve females as the instrumental actors.

The great potential of female supernatural power in the periphery enters and subsumes the central male cults in the great festivals of the period spanning the fall equinox to the winter solstice (the Virgin of Rosario in October and the Virgin of Guadalupe and the Moon/Virgin Mary in December). Temporary female primacy in the center reaches a climax in the Christmas ritual, which is culminated by an all-female procession at midnight on Christmas Eve. Women also enter central political activity when the central male cults are "in trouble" or in transition; it is here that women become the new "mothers of god" and may potentially precipitate experiments with new or revitalized cults in the center, as exemplified by the "rebellions" or the lineage adjustments of the Classic period discussed above. This "intrusive female" role is also ritualized annually in the prominent role of Malinche—actually a male ritual official dressed as a Ladino woman—in the year-renewal ritual of Carnival, which occurs in February (Gossen 1986).

Conversely, periods of crisis in the Tzotzil centers routinely send central male authorities to the "female" domain of the mountains and caves, where both male and female ancestors and earth lords are asked for help. A recent case involved petitions for relief from a major drought in the 1970s.

Thus, the periphery maintains many cults and supernatural complexes that coexist with those of the center. These peripheral cults are more individualistic and egalitarian, with both female and male practitioners and deities. These cults do not compete openly with the cults of the center, for they have different rhythms, functions, and agendas. They do not really depend on the central cults, although they passively acknowledge them. Rather, in the last analysis, the center depends, both cognitively and spiritually, on the periphery for survival and renewal.

## PLURALISM IN THE ANCIENT MAYA WORLD

In developing this section on the ancient Maya world, we wish to emphasize that we do not propose that the Little Tradition of the ancient Maya bears specific resemblance to that of the modern Tzotzil described above. We do, however, propose that the ancient Maya Little Tradition is certain to have existed in some form. A responsible reading of the ancient Maya world must proceed with an appreciation that there was undoubtedly a complex realm of individual and domestic supernatural practice that did not find its way into the formal inscriptions and iconography of the centers. We propose that its content will reveal a cosmos in which state religion was but one of many voices of supernatural vigilance over human affairs.

We can easily begin, as Leventhal and others have argued (Leventhal 1983; Proskouriakoff 1952), that Maya religion on all levels is based upon ancestor worship. Within the centers, ancestor worship is highly complex and structured for it is, *de facto,* the state religion. Outside of the center, within the periphery, ancestor worship is also evident but it is a more localized version, clearly different in each family's case. Within the Little Tradition of the periphery, there is an integration with state religion of the Great Tradition, which provides a canopy under which the individualized ancestor worship can function.

The existence of a complex Little Tradition which exists alongside the state religion of the centers has been argued many times in the past. Probably the strongest proponent of such a model was Stephen de Borhegyi, who identified the existence of what he termed the "folk cult" or "folk tradition" that was omnipresent in the ancient Maya cultures of the highlands and lowlands (Borhegyi 1956). Borhegyi perceived this folk cult as a stable manifestation that survives, relatively unchanged, within the lower strata of society, among the farmers and the peasants. During periods of highly complex, centralized state-level religious and political organization, the folk cult, according to Borhegyi, continues to exist but disappears in terms of its material manifestations. The material culture is controlled by the state religion. During periods when the centralized state religion does not exist, the material remains are dominated once again by the folk cult, similar in form to their previous existence.

We agree with Borhegyi's picture of a complex series of distinct "subcultures" that existed within ancient Maya religious organization. However, we feel that the physical manifestations or remains of these cults did not disappear completely during periods of centralization such as the eighth century A.D. The great number of incense burners, household altars, handmade and mold-made figurines, and family shrines found in direct association with residential structures at numerous ancient Maya sites including Copan (Leventhal n.d.) argues for the existence of localized cults.

These Little Tradition cults are integrated with the centralized state religion within the settlement and outlying hinterland surrounding the Maya cities. For even within these outlying plaza groups, we find evidence of the centralized state religion of each city in the form of shrines, oratories, altars, and caches. These are found at such sites as Seibal (Tourtellot 1988), Copan (Leventhal n.d.; Willey et al. n.d.), and Tikal (Haviland n.d.) to name a few.

The picture of the ancient Maya religion continues to become complex and clouded when one turns to the center and identifies the existence of not only ancestor worship but also the worship of a series of deities tied to the natural world (Schele and Miller 1986). These deities have become formalized with specific features and markings to identify them, and they are used as a setting for the ancestor gods. Good examples include the Celestial Monster, the Cauac Monster, the Jaguar God or the Sun God, and, most importantly, the Maize God. The existence of these formalized "natural" gods within the centers of the ancient world emphasize the differences between the ancient and modern Maya worlds. This is a contrast between the internal, autochthonous, development of ancient Maya complexity and those forms that resulted from imposed conquest situations.

Within the ancient world, the city centers were, at an earlier time, a part of the periphery. They were single family household groups that grew and gradually became the focal points of cities for numerous reasons not to be examined here. The center, therefore, is the periphery transformed, writ large, and formalized. Ancestor worship becomes structured and the animal souls, spooks, and natural deities of the periphery become formalized into a state religion.

## CONCLUSION

To merge beginnings and endings will, we trust, be acceptable in this setting. As we conclude, it should be noted that we have not once defined the phrase, "the topography of religious pluralism," which appears in our title. What, at last do we mean? To read it literally, topography is a representation of what is where in a physical landscape. To extend this, we have attempted to sketch what is where in the supernatural and metaphysical landscape of Maya thought.

Modern and ancient Maya religious organizations are complex systems which both define and organize the surrounding world in the past and present. We have attempted to present what we argue is a deep structural template that allows us to examine the past and the present in relation to one another. The template provides us with a model that emphasizes the conservative periphery and the more fluid center. It is the conservative periphery that allows us to examine the ancient and modern worlds. And, because the fluid centers and Great Traditions of the ancient world are indeed a formalized periphery deriving from the Little Tradition, we are able to gain insights into the entire spectrum of the ancient Maya world at the eighth century A.D.

## BIBLIOGRAPHY

AVENI, ANTHONY F.
    1989    *Empires of Time; Calendars, Clocks, and Cultures.* Basic Books, Inc., New York.

BERLIN, HEINRICH
    1968    Estudios Epigráficos II. Antropología e Historia de Guatemala 20 (1): 13–24.

BORHEGYI, STEPHEN DE
    1956    The Development of Folk and Complex Cultures in the Southern Maya Area. *American Antiquity* 21: 343–356.

BRICKER, VICTORIA
    1981    *The Indian Christ, The Indian King: The Historical Substrate of Maya Myth and Ritual.* University of Texas Press, Austin.
    1989    The Calendrical Meaning of Ritual among the Maya. In *Ethnographic Encounters in Southern Mesoamerica: Essays in Honor of Evon Zartman Vogt, Jr.* (Victoria R. Bricker and Gary H. Gossen, eds): 231–249. Institute for Mesoamerican Studies, State University of New York, Albany.

CARLSON, JOHN B.
    1980    On Classic Maya Monumental Recorded History. In *Third Palenque Round Table, 1978, Part 2* (Merle Greene Robertson, ed.): 199–203. University of Texas Press, Austin.

CHAMBERS, ERVE, AND PHILIP P. YOUNG
    1979    Mesoamerican Community Studies: The Past Decade. *Annual Review of Anthropology* 8: 45–69.

CHASE, ARLEN F., AND DIANE Z. CHASE
    1987    *Investigations at the Classic Maya City of Caracol, Belize: 1985–1987.* Monograph 3. Pre-Columbian Art Research Institute, San Francisco.

CLOSS, MICHAEL P.
    1985    The Dynastic History of Naranjo: The Middle Period. In *Fifth Palenque Round Table, 1983, Vol. 7* (Merle Greene Robertson, general ed., and Virginia M. Fields, volume ed.): 65–77. Pre-Columbian Art Research Institute, San Francisco.

COGGINS, CLEMENCY
    1979    A New Order and the Role of the Calendar: Some Characteristics of the Middle Classic Period at Tikal. In *Maya Archaeology and Ethnohistory* (Norman Hammond and Gordon R. Willey, eds.): 38–50. University of Texas Press, Austin.
    1980    The Shape of Time: Some Political Implications of a Four-Part Figure. *American Antiquity* 45 (4): 727–739.

DRENNAN, ROBERT D., AND CARLOS A. URIBE (EDS.)
    1987    *Chiefdoms in the Americas.* University Press of America, Lanham, Md.

EDMONSON, MUNRO S.
    1982    *The Ancient Future of the Itza: The Book of Chilam Balam of Tizimin.* University of Texas Press, Austin.

FARRISS, NANCY
  1984  *Maya Society under Colonial Rule: The Collective Enterprise of Survival.* Princeton University Press, Princeton.

FLANNERY, KENT
  1972  The Cultural Evolutions of Civilizations. *Annual Review of Ecology and Systematics* 3: 399–426.
  1982  Review of *In the Land of the Olmec. American Anthropologist* 84: 442–447.

FLANNERY, KENT, AND JOYCE MARCUS
  1976  Formative Oaxaca and the Zapotec Cosmos. *American Scientist* 64 (4): 374–383.

GEERTZ, CLIFFORD
  1963  Religion as a Cultural System. In his *The Interpretation of Cultures:* 87–125. Basic Books, New York.

GOSSEN, GARY H.
  1974a  *Chamulas in the World of the Sun: Time and Space in a Maya Oral Tradition.* Harvard University Press, Cambridge.
  1974b  A Chamula Calendar Board from Chiapas, Mexico. In *Mesoamerican Archaeology: New Approaches* (Norman Hammond, ed.) 217–253. University of Texas Press, Austin.
  1975  Animal Souls and Human Destiny in Chamula. *Man* 10: 448–461.
  1977  Translating Cuscat's War: Understanding Maya Oral History. *Journal of Latin American Lore* 3 (2): 249–278.
  1986  The Chamula Festival of Games: Native Macroanalysis and Social Commentary in a Maya Carnival. In *Symbol and Meaning Beyond the Closed Community: Essays in Mesoamerican Ideas* (Gary H. Gossen, ed.): 227–254. Culture and Society Series 1. Institute for Mesoamerican Studies, State University of New York, Albany.
  1988  Vida y Muerte de Miguel Kashlán: héroe Chamula. In *Biografías y confesiones de los indios de América* (Manuel Gutiérrez Estevez, ed.). *Arbor* 131 (515–516): 125–144. Consejo de Investigaciones Científicas, Madrid.
  1989a  Life, Death and Apotheosis of a Chamula Protestant Leader: Biography as Social History. In *Ethnographic Encounters in Southern Mesoamerica: Essays in Honor of Evon Z. Vogt, Jr.* (Victoria R. Bricker and Gary H. Gossen, eds.): 217–230. Culture and Society Series 3. Institute for Mesoamerican Studies, State University of New York, Albany.
  1989b  El tiempo cíclico en San Juan Chamula: ¿mistificacíon o mitología viva? *Mesoamerica* 18: 441–459.

HAMMOND, NORMAN
  1982  *Ancient Maya Civilization.* Rutgers University Press, New Brunswick.

HAVILAND, WILLIAM A.
  n.d.  *Excavations of Small Structures in the Northeast Quadrant of Tikal, Guatemala.* Ph.D. dissertation, University of Pennsylvania, Philadelphia, 1963.

HUNT, EVA
  1977  *The Transformation of the Hummingbird: Cultural Roots of a Zinacantecan Mythical Poem.* Cornell University Press, Ithaca.

Jones, Christopher, and Linton Satterthwaite
    1982    *The Monuments and Inscriptions of Tikal: The Carved Monuments.* Tikal Report No. 33, Part A, University Museum Monograph 44. University Museum, University of Pennsylvania, Philadelphia.

Karasik, Carol
    1988    *The People of the Bat: Mayan Tales and Dreams from Zinacantán* (Robert M. Laughlin, trans.). Smithsonian Institution Press, Washington, D.C.

Kendall, Carl, John Hawkins, and Laurel Bossen (eds.)
    1983    *Heritage of Conquest Thirty Years Later.* University of New Mexico Press, Albuquerque.

Laughlin, Robert M.
    1977    *Of Cabbages and Kings: Tales from Zinacantán.* Smithsonian Contributions to Anthropology 23. Smithsonian Institution Press, Washington D.C.

Leach, E. R.
    1971    Two Essays Concerning the Symbolic Representation of Time. In *Rethinking Anthropology:* 124–136. London School of Economics, Monographs on Social Anthropology 22. The Athlone Press, University of London, London.

Leventhal, Richard M.
    1983    Household Groups and Classic Maya Religion. In *Prehistoric Settlement Patterns: Essays in Honor of Gordon R. Willey* (Evon Z. Vogt and Richard M. Leventhal, eds.): 55–76. University of New Mexico Press, Albuquerque, and Peabody Museum, Harvard University, Cambridge.
    n.d.    *Settlement Patterns at Copan, Honduras.* Ph.D. dissertation, Harvard University, Cambridge, 1979.

Linn, Priscilla R.
    1989    Souls and Selves in Chamula: A Thought on Individuals, Fatalism and Denial. In *Ethnographic Encounters in Southern Mesoamerica: Essays in Honor of Evon Z. Vogt, Jr.* (Victoria R. Bricker and Gary H. Gossen, eds.): 251–262. Culture and Society Series 3. Institute for Mesoamerican Studies, State University of New York, Albany.

León-Portilla, Miguel
    1968    *Tiempo y realidad en el pensamiento maya: ensayo de acercamiento.* Universidad Nacional Autónoma de Mexico, Mexico, D.F.

Lounsbury, Floyd G.
    1980    Some Problems in the Interpretation of the Mythological Portion of the Hieroglyphic Text of the Temple of the Cross at Palenque. In *Third Palenque Round Table, 1978, Part 2* (Merle Greene Robertson, ed.): 99–115. University of Texas Press, Austin.

Marcus, Joyce
    1976    *Emblem and State in the Classic Maya Lowlands.* Dumbarton Oaks, Washington, D.C.

Miles, Suzanne W.
    1952    An Analysis of Modern Middle American Calendars: A Study in Conservatism. In *Acculturation in the Americas, Selected Papers of the 29th*

International Congress of Americanists (Sol Tax, ed.): 273–284. Chicago.

MOLLOY, JOHN P., AND WILLIAM L. RATHJE
 1974 Sexploitation among the Late Classic Maya. In *Mesoamerican Archaeology: New Approaches* (Norman Hammond, ed.): 431–444. University of Texas Press, Austin.

MORRIS, WALTER
 1987 *Living Maya*. Harry Abrams, Inc., New York.

MOSCOSO PASTRAÑA, PRUDENCIO
 1972 *Jacinto Pérez "Pajarito": El último líder Chamula*. Editorial del Gobierno de Chiapas, Tuxtla Gutiérrez, Mexico.

ORTNER, SHERRY B.
 1974 Is Female to Male as Nature is to Culture? In *Woman, Culture and Society* (M. Z. Rosaldo and L. Lamphere, eds.): 67–87. Stanford University Press, Stanford.

PROSKOURIAKOFF, TATIANA
 1962 Civic and Religious Structures of Mayapan. In *Mayapan, Yucatan, Mexico*: 87–163. Carnegie Institution of Washington, Pub. 619. Washington, D.C.

PULESTON, DENNIS E.
 1979 An Epistemological Pathology and the Collapse, or Why the Maya Kept the Short Count. In *Maya Archaeology and Ethnohistory* (Norman Hammond and Gordon R. Willey, eds.): 63–71. University of Texas Press, Austin.

REDFIELD, ROBERT
 1941 *The Folk Culture of Yucatan*. University of Chicago Press, Chicago.
 1960 *The Little Community*. University of Chicago Press, Chicago.

SCHELE, LINDA
 1982 *Maya Glyphs: The Verbs*. University of Texas Press, Austin.
 1991 An Epigraphic History of the Western Maya Region. In *Classic Maya Political History: Hieroglyphic and Archaeological Evidence* (T. Patrick Culbert, ed.): 72–101. Cambridge University Press, Cambridge.

SCHELE, LINDA, AND DAVID FREIDEL
 1990 *A Forest of Kings: The Untold Story of the Ancient Maya*. William Morrow and Co., New York.

SCHELE, LINDA, AND MARY MILLER
 1986 *The Blood of Kings, Dynasty and Ritual in Maya Art*. George Braziller, Inc., New York, and the Kimbell Art Museum, Fort Worth.

SHARER, ROBERT J., AND DAVID C. GROVE (EDS.)
 1989 *Regional Perspectives on the Olmec*. School of American Research, Cambridge University Press, Cambridge.

SILVERBLATT, IRENE
 1987 *Moon, Sun and Witches: Gender Ideologies and Class in Inca and Colonial Peru*. Princeton University Press, Princeton, New Jersey.
 1988 Women in States. *Annual Review of Anthropology* 17: 427–460.

TEDLOCK, BARBARA
    1982    *Time and the Highland Maya.* University of New Mexico Press, Albuquerque.

TEDLOCK, DENNIS
    1985    *Popul Vuh: The Definitive Edition of the Maya Book of the Dawn of Life and Glories of Gods and Kings.* Simon and Schuster, New York.

THOMPSON, J. E. S.
    1966    *The Rise and Fall of Maya Civilization,* 2nd ed. University of Oklahoma Press, Norman.
    1970    *Maya History and Religion.* University of Oklahoma Press, Norman.

TOURTELLOT III, GAIR
    1988    *Peripheral Survey and Excavation: Settlement and Community Patterns.* Memoirs of the Peabody Museum of Archaeology and Ethnology 16. Harvard University, Cambridge.

VOGT, EVON Z.
    1964    The Genetic Model and Maya Cultural Development in *Desarollo Cultural de los Mayas* (Evon Z. Vogt and Alberto Ruz L., eds.): 9–48. Universidad Nacional Autonóma de México, Mexico City.
    n.d.    On the Application of the Phylogenetic Model to the Maya. In *The Social Anthropology and Ethnohistory of American Tribes: Essays in Honor of Fred Eggan* (Raymond J. DeMallie and Alfonso Ortiz, eds.). University of Oklahoma Press, Norman. (in press)

WASSERSTROM, ROBERT
    1983    *Class and Society in Central Chiapas.* University of California Press, Berkeley.

WATANABE, JOHN
    1983    In the World of the Sun: A Cognitive Model of Mayan Cosmology. *Man* 18 (4): 710–728.

WILLEY, GORDON R., RICHARD M. LEVENTHAL, ARTHUR A. DEMAREST, AND WILLIAM L. FASH, JR.
    n.d.    Ceramics and Artifacts from Excavations in the Copan Residential Zone. Papers of the Peabody Museum of Archaeology and Ethnology. Harvard University, Cambridge. (in press)

WINFIELD CAPITAINE, FERNANDO
    1988    La Estela de La Mojarra, Veracruz, Mexico. *Research Reports on Ancient Maya Writing* 16. Center for Maya Research, Washington D.C.

# 7

# A View of Ancient Maya Settlements in the Eighth Century

## GAIR TOURTELLOT
### BOSTON UNIVERSITY

If Winston Churchill had been an archaeologist, he might have said that during the eighth century the greatest number of Maya sites was occupied by the greatest number of people, whose leaders erected the largest number of monuments in the shortest period of time—with, perhaps, the least thanks, since they were so quickly abandoned (Culbert and Rice 1990; Lowe 1985). One certainly has the impression that the Maya were both undergoing a period of explosive population growth and pushing the limits, exploiting all the available environmental and productive niches. Let us look at these common impressions.

In this paper I shall take a bottom-up and outside-in view of lowland Maya society. Data from the northern lowlands will be explicitly included, supplementing the traditional focus on the southern lowlands. Settlement data from the eighth-century Maya are among the prime sources for highlighting inferences on ancient Maya demography, economy, and society, and may encapsulate reflections of ideology as well. I wish to pose and examine several outstanding issues in Maya settlement archaeology that are especially critical for understanding the peak of Classic Maya civilization.

Conveniently for the subject of this symposium, most spatial analyses of Maya settlement patterns perforce deal with Late Classic sites. These sites are often spectacular, possess datable monuments, or comprise the latest and most easily accessible occupation on the surface. In fact, it is rare to find an analysis that examines a settlement system—one consisting of multiple major sites in a single region—that is either earlier or later than this Late Classic period, for such an analysis usually requires deep, expensive excavations at many places.

We often think of the peak of Classic Maya civilization in the eighth century as the culmination of two millennia of development. Yet it is really sobering to realize how few sites actually exhibit substantial occupation throughout the whole sequence. Places with very limited histories of development before the Late Classic include such well-known locales as Palenque, Copan, Lubaantun, Dzibilchaltun, Chichen Itza, and the Puuc region. Many other sites have an ostensibly weak Early Classic occupation despite a strong earlier start (for example, Seibal, Becan, and Edzna, not to mention those, like Mirador and Komchen, that virtually died after the Preclassic). In other words, the history of the Maya in any one region or individual city is far more episodic than is generally acknowledged (cf. Webster 1988: fig. 4). This parochial and historical view of Maya evolution serves as a necessary counterpoint to exciting formulations conflating vast sweeps of data, such as the model presented by Joyce Marcus (Chap. 5; but see also Stuart, Chap. 11).

On the other hand, it is also becoming less and less possible to hold that Classic Maya civilization totally collapsed after the eighth century, even in the southern lowlands (Sabloff 1985). This continuation is particularly the case if "civilization" is not taken only in the sense of elite culture, including writing, or the Great Tradition, and if the supporting (even participating?) populace is included within civilization defined as a system of organization.

## ROLES FOR SWIDDEN AND INTENSIVE GARDENING

The available data show that not only the histories of cities but also the practicalities of everyday life in the eighth century were by no means uniform (see Rice, Chap. 2, for environmental variations). The Maya exploited a very full range of agricultural and settlement practices, whether in fact or arguably so (e.g., Harrison and Turner 1978; Turner 1983). On the one hand, a remarkable number of different subsistence techniques has been discovered, each of which was more or less visibly employed somewhere in the Maya area. On the other hand, in any one place or region, subsistence and settlement are emerging as a crazy quilt of only selected techniques necessitated by local variation. The demonstrable variations in these and other Maya practices are keys to understanding the internal organization of eighth-century polities, which are not all alike (e.g., Tourtellot 1983; Webster 1988). A good question could be the extent to which elite culture—the hallmark of Maya civilization—parallels, or ignores, these distinctions. An answer will depend upon thorough codification and exacting comparison, extending to ceramics, lithics, and house types as well as fine architecture, sculpture, and glyphic systems.

Looking at Maya subsistence, the discovery of intensive and highly productive agricultural techniques once employed by the Classic Maya has generated much justifiable excitement (see Harrison and Turner 1978; Flannery 1982; Pohl 1985). Nevertheless, many Maya must still have depended on swidden techniques to grow their food, even during periods of high population density such as the eighth century.

The justifications for this assertion are as follows. First, there are a variety of techniques of intensified agriculture visible in the archaeological record, among them field walls, slope terraces, raised or channeled fields, and irrigation (see Rice, Chap. 2). Yet each technique has been documented only for largely separate and limited geographic areas, lying principally across the middle of the Yucatan Peninsula (Turner 1983; Pope and Dahlin 1989). Consequently, no single region appears to have exploited the full repertoire. Second, these agrotechnologies are by no means universal, even in the aggregate. In fact, most Maya lowland territory presently lacks evidence for such intensification at any time. (As Rice points out in this volume, sometimes the problem may lie in our low expectations rather than ancient fact.)

For example, in the northern lowlands we have yet to find evidence for significant agricultural constructions. At best, slope terraces not accompanied by house remains seem few and far between. Powerful polities like Uxmal, Chichen Itza, or Mayapan therefore could not have depended on any currently recognized system of agricultural intensification. Consequently, people in the North had few alternatives to depending on extensive swidden agriculture for vegetal food, even during times of maximum population.

One alternative—or better, supplement—to swidden is intensive food gardening in house yards. Although gardening may leave few traces, this is a challenge less to its former existence than to our present ingenuity. We can now show that much of the open area between contemporaneous neighboring house groups is truly vacant, within at least some parts of some Maya settlements. In these open areas it is rare to find either hidden building remains from the eighth century or the patterns of associated artifact scatter that are characteristic of domestic discards and refuse (Killion et al. 1989; cf. Webster and Gonlin 1988). Somewhat paradoxically, these small open areas instead may provide the best evidence for truly widespread agricultural intensification, namely labor-intensive gardening (e.g., Chase and Chase 1983; Santley, Killion, and Lycett 1986: 133–134).

At Sayil in the Puuc, for instance, Nicholas Dunning (1989) chemically distinguished between an area of artificial soil enrichment in the open and areas of ordinary garbage disposal around buildings. (Specifically he found higher values of phosphate Fraction I and lower Fraction III than expected in the open test, compared to the building area; see Rice, Chap. 2, for the vital role of phosphorus.) He suggests this contrast is due to prolonged artificial fertilization in gardens. Ceramics provide a corroboration of artificial soil fertilization, for we discovered much lower sherd frequencies, yet larger average sherd sizes, in the same open area when compared to house refuse (cf. Killion et al. 1989). This deposition pattern can be expected of the "chamberpots" involved in transport, due to accidental breakage in low-traffic areas away from houses (for an analogous case, see Wilkinson 1982).

Judging by the amount of open space inside Maya settlements, gardening would have been more widespread than the actually rare agrotechnologies that involve permanent construction. Gardens may even have been a greater factor in total food production. Also, it is well to keep in mind that permanent agriculture does not require permanent constructions (e.g., silviculture or levee cultivation), although terraces and ditches are certainly easier to identify.

### THE SCOPE OF AGRICULTURAL SYSTEMS

The catchment area for the diversified systems of agriculture of each Maya lowland community was probably spatially restricted. A system would include kitchen gardens and variously cultivated infields within an easy walk out around each town, but not true outfields maybe thirty or forty kilometers away (following the spatial distinctions made by Killion n.d.). The indirect evidence for a spatially restricted garden-infield system includes, first, the almost universal existence of open space around and separating ordinary households. This unimproved open space could have been used for growing food. In a beautiful twist on the usual explanation for residential dispersion, Robert Drennan (1988) argues that the more concentrated the labor resources put into farming, the more dispersed the settlement, because the closer the farmers will want to live to their fields. Thus, the relatively open "garden-city" appearance of Maya settlements is the result of highly intensive agricultural methods, rather than a result of the supposed centripetal effect of swidden on house locations. Although evidence to date shows the quite restricted incidence of expensive agricultural construction, it also shows that quasi-dispersion, arguably due to intensive gardening, could be a nearly universal Maya pattern among the non-elite.

Second, the close packing of civic centers and entire settlements in several regions of the Maya lowlands also speaks in favor of spatially restricted garden-infield systems. These regions include the northern plains, Puuc, northeast Peten, and Petexbatun regions. The distances between minor or major centers are frequently only three to fifteen kilometers. Consequently, there is very little room for distant outfields in these crowded landscapes.

Third, as modern land clearance and archaeological survey proceed (in uneasy union), we are simply running out of unexplored or unoccupied tracts of land. That is, there are fewer and fewer potential locations for productive outfields, over a day's trip from the nearest known ancient settlement, from which large supplies of surplus food might have been obtained. A case in point is the Puuc region, which has in historic times on several occasions been the "breadbasket" of Yucatan (Matheny 1978). Nevertheless, current research shows that during Late and Terminal Classic times population must have been so high and dense in the Puuc that they barely had the technology or distribution system to sustain themselves (Dunning 1989), let alone supply the numerous people at contemporary Dzibilchaltun and elsewhere in the agriculturally more marginal northern plains. In any case, only a few of the largest and most powerful of centers conceivably could have drawn upon foodstuffs from wider tributary areas located more than a dozen kilometeters away, while simultaneously denying full access from settlements closer to those fields. Furthermore, enormous problems of political access, labor scheduling, remote supervision, and jealous defense would have been involved in productively working distant fields. If anything, the well-attested massive building programs of the eighth century not only consumed labor otherwise available for agricultural production (as modeled in the extreme by Hosler, Sabloff, and Runge 1977), but also removed garden space from cultivation, still further exacerbating problems of food supply.

Indeed, difficulty in obtaining food from near or far (Santley, Killion, and Lycett 1986), under alleged conditions of increasing crowding, would be an obvious motivation for political marriage alliances and the crescendo of Late Classic warfare, as documented in the simultaneously expanding politicoreligious system represented by the stela cult (see the papers by Miller, Stuart, and Webster, this volume). Increasing strangulation of land and food could also be a powerful motivation for increased emphasis on craft production and export (cf. McAnany, Chap. 3). What we do not seem to see, however, is evidence for the accumulation of surplus crops in the form of large granaries. So far as one can tell, food stores seem to have been maintained at the household level (Smyth n.d.). If this is so, numerous small storage facilities, rather than a few large or centralized ones, could be an economic basis for the weakness of Late Classic polities (see Stuart, Chap. 11, regarding political instability). Dispersed storage would also make it more difficult for warfare to find a conclusive target or efficiently capture food resources.

### DEALING WITH ALLEGEDLY PEAK POPULATIONS

But really, how good are our current high estimates of maximum populations for Late Classic settlements, the basis for our worry that the Maya could no longer support themselves? Evidence of population peaks during the eighth century is critical to the suggestions just made, and underpin several of the other chapters in this book, as well as the title of the symposium. Populations on the order of 10,000 persons apiece are currently estimated for many major sites—up to 60,000 or more for supercenters like Tikal—with these totals achieved by high rates of apparent population growth during the Late Classic (Culbert and Rice 1990). Could the ancient Maya really have consistently fed such huge and rapidly increasing numbers? My incredulity here stems from the extraordinarily close packing of nucleated sites in parts of the northern lowlands, the seemingly endless blanket of substantial occupation in much of the south, the limited distributions of intensive agrotechnologies, and our difficulty in pinning down free locations for agricultural outfields producing a surplus. Furthermore, apparent evidence for dense populations throughout the lowlands is far more widespread than the evidence for intensive agrotechnologies. Accordingly, we appear to be in the position of 1970 all over again: too many people for the known means of support (then thought to be swidden alone), but now the population numbers are ratcheted up to a higher level.

This quandary can be solved in either of two ways. One is to find evidence for other means or conditions of intensified production. These might include widespread use of fertilizers, future expansion of the areas once cultivated by the archaeologically more visible agrotechnologies, discovery of additional intensification strategies (e.g., fish ponds [cf. Thompson 1974]), identification of major granaries, successful importation of basic foods, or formerly more favorable climatic regimes (Dahlin 1983). One of the surprises may turn out to be that the central part of the Yucatan Peninsula, where most of the intensive agrotechnologies have been documented, was not the area with highest densities of population. A close reading of the population estimates advanced in T. Patrick Culbert and Don Rice (1990) suggests that central urban densities, if not whole-site (community) densities, were actually higher by a factor of four or more at some sites outside the southern lowland core area, as in Copan or the northern lowlands (see also Rice, Chap. 2). Clearly there is potentially much yet to be learned about the interaction between Maya agriculture and settlement.

The other way to handle an imbalance between production and population is to reduce the current high population estimates themselves. Culbert and Rice's book on *Precolumbian Population History in the Maya Lowlands* (1990) examines numerous discount factors that may require cumulative reductions in our previous estimates of maximum site and regional population figures (based on numbers of houses). The deepest discounts, however, occur with the application of temporal standardization, essentially the conversion of total house or population counts per archaeological phase into *average* counts per century per phase. Allegedly this conversion provides better comparison between phases that differ widely in their durations. However, the proposed reductions are far greater for long occupation phases than for the typically short Late Classic phases, approaching reductions of ninety percent for some Preclassic phases. If these drastic reductions for earlier periods are accepted, the net effect is really to forcefully heighten how incredibly rapid and massive was the Late Classic population increase, even if estimates of maximum population levels are ameliorated.

Rapid increases in population, approaching a dire exponential rate of growth (Santley 1990), may have been far more perceptible and immediate a problem to the Late Classic Maya than merely large populations. Instability of population size may have been the greatest problem, rather than the absolute size. If this is the case, then the two central questions will become, first, the role very rapid population growth played in the eventual ninth-century collapse in the heart of the southern lowlands, and second, what changes produced, sustained, and aggravated this huge surplus of survival.

In the eighth-century setting of combined florescence and impending crisis, along with uncertainties regarding maximum absolute population numbers, perhaps we should devote some research to the extreme possibility that the huge number of recorded Late Classic house platforms—not to mention "invisible" or nonplatform houses (see below)—might be the result of rapid flux in population *location* rather than overall increases in numbers of people alone. We know, for example, that the monuments indicate, nay, glorify, the capture of many nobles. Did Maya nobility capture subject commoners as well—the depicted nobles standing in for the larger social groups they represented? Since monuments ignore commoners in other matters, we might assume heuristically that they ignore their capture or movement as well. (This is an argument from parallel evidence, not from negative evidence, although of course no more convincing for that; see Sharer, Chap. 4, for other examples of the same problem.) Forced shifts in residential location are a conceivable outcome of see-saw conflicts and conquests in a time of rapidly shifting segmental political alliances (see de Montmollin's discussion [1989] of forced settlement). Note that these shifts have nothing to do with the old, and false, argument that shifting cultivation requires shifting houses as well (Palerm and Wolf 1957).

Settlement flux could be produced by several events or processes. Agricultural facilities may have been devastated or crops and stores stolen, resulting in famines. The farming population itself may have been periodically laid waste (and perhaps repeatedly rebuilt in a generation on new sites). Or farmers were physically moved along with their conquered masters rather than allowed merely to reorient their trade and tribute to a different political capital, as suggested by the mighty Middle Classic prosperity of Caracol accompanying its defeats of Tikal and Naranjo (cited by Miller, Chap. 12). Alternatively, the farmers might simply have fled, temporarily or eventually permanently, exercising their ultimate mode of institutional resistance, much as their descendants later dispersed to escape the onerous policies of Europeans (Farriss 1984). I can also conceive of few tactics more likely to destroy the productivity of specialized Late Classic farmers and help bring about a collapse. Nevertheless, finding conclusive evidence for or against this hypothesis will be extraordinarily difficult, particularly in view of the difficulties we already encounter just trying to narrow chronology down to those hundred-year phases cited above.

To mention only one project that is applying new tools, Webster and his students on the Copan Project are obtaining really exciting results relevant to both non-elite settlement and population estimates. A most welcome and sensitive new tool for settlement analysis appears to be offered by analyses of the temporal spread of more than 1,500 obsidian hydration dates obtained on artifacts from literally dozens of house groups, the largest corpus of dated houses yet obtained. If basic data, method, and analyses are verified upon full publication, then the remarkable preliminary results destroy some of our easy assumptions about household histories and contemporaneity.

First, it appears that no house locus at Copan was occupied throughout the full 500 years of the nominally Late Classic Coner phase, but instead for only some 100 to 325 years apiece (Webster n.d.a; Webster and Gonlin 1988). This finding is obviously relevant to the question raised above concerning temporal standardization of population estimates.

Second, the delayed formation of some households and the early abandonment of others mean that the maximum number of simultaneously occupied groups is approximately sixty percent of the total (i.e., five of the eight rural loci detailed in Webster and Gonlin 1988). (This reduction must be taken because the average rate at which household loci were formed and abandoned appears to be fairly constant [based on a slide graph accompanying Webster n.d.a]). This drop in percentage would require an approximately forty percent discount to population estimates, when those are estimated from household ruin counts, in what otherwise had looked like formally and ceramically contemporaneous occupation.

### ELITE COLLAPSE VERSUS THE PERSISTENCE OF POPULATIONS

Another disturbing implication of the new Copan analyses, should they prove correct, is that the ceramic chronology apparently misses the main political event: the collapse of the Copan royal dynasty early in the ninth century! Ceramics date most of the Copan collections to the nominally Late Classic Coner phase. However, the temporal distribution of obsidian dates for this phase suggests that it continued, with significant occupation in the Copan Valley, for some four hundred years *after* the eighth century (Webster n.d.a; Webster and Gonlin 1988). If we cannot rely on ceramics, what then? If obsidian hydration dating can be successfully confirmed, then perhaps we can take some of the chronological load off the long-suffering ceramic analysts, and let them explore some anthropologically interesting problems (e.g., Ball, Chap. 8). The preliminary Copan obsidian data surely suggest that we should be more suspicious of early abandonment dates in general: while the installation of dated monuments may coincide well with population growth, it conspicuously fails to track population decline in this and some other cases of overlooked or "analytically invisible" Postclassic people (see papers and references in Chase and Rice 1985; Sabloff and Andrews V 1986; among others).

While the dynasty may have collapsed at Copan, contrarily the bulk of the people living in the valley must have continued along for some time just as they had before (Webster and Gonlin 1988). Although the absence of immediate demographic collapse could mean that a body of (nonroyal?) leaders also continued for some time, clearly they were no longer so brazenly visible as before. It may even be possible to recognize differential survival of the former symbols of rulership, or to follow in more detail the fortunes of individual Copan families (or at least the history of their obsidian consumption), because the occupation spans of individual households apparently can now be more precisely established.

Nevertheless, we might draw a still more shocking implication from this apparent lack of demographic collapse in the Copan Valley: that the Classic elite was significantly irrelevant! If ordinary farmers were indeed able to carry on for several centuries in a genuine absence of royal or noble leadership, then perhaps these leaders, or certainly the particular form their organization and beliefs took, were not essential to the success of ordinary Maya people. This of course is only another light on the vexed question of just what was the relation between noble and commoner in Maya society. While a disconnection between the elite and the peasantry is probably overdrawn, the thought alone suggests that the lifeways of ordinary Maya farmers must be a specific focus of attention if we are to understand their own eventual abandonment of many lowland areas. We have passed the point where it is sufficient to speak of *the* collapse. We must recognize that not only did different regions and sites grow or decline at slightly different times (Marcus, Chap. 5), but that different classes of their inhabitants may also have experienced different kinds of collapse (or liberation).

## THE FUNCTIONS OF STRUCTURES AND THE TYPES OF SITES

A different concern in Maya settlement archaeology arises if we take the new interpretations of Maya texts and images literally, as dealing principally with the myths and rituals of a bloody-minded royal elite (Schele and Miller 1986; but see Stuart, Chap. 11, and Webster, Chap. 13). We could be heading back toward the old idea that the famous Maya cities were vacant ceremonial centers at heart, the loci only for elite civil and religious ritual, from which everyday concerns and ordinary people were perhaps literally banned. Most of the sculpted monuments with the carved texts at issue, for instance, are restricted to central locations. It has also proved remarkably difficult to pin down royal households, because so many different activities are jumbled together in typical Maya site-cores (e.g., Harrison n.d.), and so much domestic refuse was fastidiously removed—or perhaps was never there (but see Ball's revealing discussion of potters' debris, Chap. 8). Because the deciphered documents seem to have so little of popular (as distinct from royal) interest, any new information from settlement studies is pure gain.

A particularly good example of settlement data on the question of functional site differentiation is provided by Jennifer Taschek and Joseph Ball's (n.d.; Ball and Taschek n.d.) underpublicized investigations in the lower

Mopan-Macal river area of western Belize, even though—or, rather, precisely because—spectacular monuments are absent. Instead of concentrating a full spectrum of elite and community activities at a single major center, in this case the administrative city of Buenavista, many of the elite are alleged to have lived in what Taschek and Ball call three residential regal-ritual satellites, each more than five kilometers away. Most commoners, in turn, appear to have been concentrated along the nearby river floodplains in what Gordon Willey once called "ribbon settlements" (Willey et al. 1965). The proximity of major river floodplains severely distorts the apparently usual tendency for population to concentrate radially (or concentrically) around their major centers (but see Arnold and Ford 1980; Ford 1986). This distortion conveniently produces an unusually clear spatial segregation of settlement types. These types are similar to those analytically proposed in the formal-functional hierarchy for Belize developed by Norman Hammond (1974), but here are based on Richard Fox (1977). (An even more extensive functional differentiation was applied to groups and sites on Cozumel Island, although that is Late Postclassic [Freidel and Sabloff 1984].)

Strong contrasts exist between the Mopan-Macal polity—with its allegedly separate settlements for king, nobles, and commoners—and such highly centralized or intermixed places as Naranjo, Tikal, or Copan, with their causeways to organize and express political order. These contrasts remind us that these great sites are not necessarily "typical" of Maya settlements per se. Perhaps they represent only what Maya scholars have "typically" investigated in detail, namely, the highest levels in the Maya settlement hierarchy (cf. Webster, Chap. 13). Conversely, it may be that lower-level political realms like Buenavista's usually exhibit a closer match of people to the agricultural resources of their immediate territory, with also a wider spread of their elite supervisors as well. Or is the Buenavista realm typical only of realms dependent on an agriculture that exploited linearly distributed resources like floodplains or drained-lake margins? Sites located on uplands or in the interior, as in the Puuc region, are instead associated with pockets of good soil (Dunning n.d.) and are consequently more compact and centrally focused.

For both population and settlement analyses, it would be helpful to know if the number of elite compounds in the largest Maya centers corresponds in some more or less one-to-one fashion with the number of subordinate polities controlled from these centers. David Freidel and Jeremy Sabloff (1984: 158–162) identify a distinctive architectural group on the ground at San Gervasio that may concretely express the ancient political quadripartition of Cozumel Island. This is a Late Postclassic rather than Late Classic example, of course, but may inspire us to seek out earlier examples as well. If similar nonhierarchical Classic period correspondences can be found, such duplications would suggest a pattern of dual residence for the provincial elite rather than a necessarily larger and permanent elite population.

Another kind of correspondence suggesting political dual residence might be obtained from matching the number of central elite residences with the sheer number of more peripheral elite buildings within single communities. A more concrete expression of dual residence may be the central and terminal architectural complexes associated with causeways, which often include elite range-type structures. Causeways were one highly visible tool for internally organizing the spatial, and perhaps social, order of central portions of many settlements. Subdivision or quadripartition of Classic settlements may have been achieved by means of linear or cruciform systems of causeways that split sites into halves or quarters, with their associated residences. The grid of causeways at Coba is one extreme example (Folan, Kintz, and Fletcher 1983), while Caracol apparently provides a quite different radial design (Chase and Chase 1987) that accomplishes the same objectives of subdivision and communication. Causeway partition may be a rather late phenomenon, conceptually imposed on recalcitrant preexisting settlements, as at Seibal (Smith 1982), or imposed from the start on new settlements like Terminal Classic Ek Balam (Ringle and Bey n.d.).

More broadly, dual residence may have been practiced for economic reasons, particularly seasonal agriculture. For the Classic period such a suggestion remains speculative, but can be attested historically, as on Cozumel (P. Sabloff 1975). Again, correspondence in numbers might be a key, if we can match the inventory of urban households with field hut remains. One problem here is the frequent lack of survey and excavation in the rural areas far out from major sites, while another is the vexing question of "invisible" nonmound structures wherever they are located (see below).

The question of seasonal residence has hardly been broached. Beyond numbers alone, more sensitive signatures of dual residence might come from comparison of artifact, plant, and animal remains. The search here would be for assemblages of artifacts and ecofacts showing contrasting seasonal activities in structures located in disparate parts of sites. Discovery of artifact "fitters" or stylistic quirks in different loci is frankly unlikely and would not be conclusive. Genetic markers in burial skeletons might be helpful, if rural burials were available for comparison with their urban "relatives." Environmental situations also suggest possible examples of seasonal settlement. One is the simple platforms located in seasonally dry *bajo* swamps, as at Mirador (although Dahlin [personal communication, 1989] attributes their presence to a drier climatic regime). A second example is the simple rural platforms and gravel mounds in the Puuc that frequently lack water cisterns, without which they could not have been continually occupied during the severe dry half of the year (Dunning 1989).

Other transient housing alternatives like hostels, colonnaded reception halls, and mens' houses only further muddle our models of residence and population. Another kind of temporary residence (often called "kitchens") may have housed young couples and children during temporary postmarital brideservice (Tourtellot 1988: 356).

### WHERE DO ELITE PEOPLE RESIDE AND HOW MANY WERE THERE?

How, in fact, do we identify the elite and locate their residences? Did the leaders actually live in the huge multiroom structures commonly called "palaces"? Taking the Central Acropolis at Tikal for an example, Peter Harrison (1986; n.d.) concluded that despite many transient people, no more than a single royal family probably lived full-time within the huge 46-structure complex, in but a single building. Excavation of a supposed royal house, Structure 223 in the center of Copan, showed it lacked domestic refuse and burials, and was also more likely for transients, a house for young men (Webster n.d.b). Mary Ellen Miller's analysis (1988) of the ancient activities on the Main Acropolis at Copan, as read from its sculpture and layout, likewise indicates purely ritual uses. Linda Schele and Miller (1986: 133–134, and footnote 1) have provocatively commented that perhaps the rulers at many sites did not actually reside in their stone palaces, but rather had their quarters in nearby perishable structures! That would put the elite out into the perishable structures that most of us have been assuming were houses for lesser nobility, retainers, or the commoners (cf. Sharer, Chap. 4).

The logic of these interpretations might seem once again to be driving us to consider anew whether the cores of some sites were only what we used to call vacant ceremonial centers, theaters for the play of elite ritual. However, I resist that logic, posing instead the good historiographer's question whether the elite textual sources report the full range of people and activities in the site-core (including the plazas, temples, and palaces plus the interstitial and immediately adjacent settlement). More concretely, ordinary house remains often march right up to the edges of the royal and ritual complexes (see also McAnany, Chap. 3, on the possible mixture of highly disparate social statuses in households). In other words, it is misleading to call a possibly exclusive royal-ritual plaza precinct a "vacant ceremonial center" when it is situated at the center of a densely occupied city like Tikal or Copan. However, Uxmal may be a lonely exception, for the surrounding residential zone appears to stop several hundred meters short of the perimeter wall around the central precinct (Ian Graham, personal communication, 1988).

Comparison among sites throws another light on the question of where the elite resided. If we compare the frequencies of stone-walled, range-type (multiroom) structures from site to site, such remarkable variations emerge that we must question the easy assumption that these masonry buildings are the archaeological signature of elite residences.

For example, as one might expect, masonry buildings are common in the urban core of Copan but not in the distant rural zones (Webster and Gonlin 1988). However, in the Rio Pasion region, there are extremely few masonry buildings in the site-cores, let alone the peripheries, whether in the eighth century or at any time (Tourtellot, Sabloff, and Carmean n.d.). At the other extreme, in the northern lowlands, buildings with stone walls, if not also vaults, are much more common. In fact, at Sayil, for example, masonry buildings with vaults make up nearly nineteen percent of all potential residential structures, representing thirty-six percent of all the room-spaces (Tourtellot, Sabloff, and Carmean n.d.). All told, minimally fifty-two percent of the buildings at Sayil included at least partial masonry walls, in contrast to no more than nine percent at contemporaneous Seibal in the Pasion region.

Now, it is doubtful that the elite were so common or so variable in their numbers at major sites as these architectural figures might indicate. To some extent, then, as in the Rio Pasion drainage, the elite may be significantly invisible to archaeologists, where masonry buildings as a supposed elite marker are significantly rare. Another deranging factor is the greater likelihood that palatial assemblages of masonry buildings contain specialized buildings and rooms, and thus were not thoroughly residential. If specialized uses are a significant component in the number of masonry buildings and rooms at a site (Harrison n.d.; Robertson 1985), then obviously it will be harder to argue directly to the size of either the total or the elite populations. Arguments for identifying public versus private spaces on Late Postclassic Cozumel, based on Conquest sources, may provide a model for resolving some of this ambiguity (Freidel and Sabloff 1984).

It is necessary to approach the identification of elite residential architecture from other perspectives. We might heuristically limit elite residence to only the largest examples of vaulted architecture, the multistoried terrace complexes or the vast courtyard acropoli—but then to whom belonged the many, but not universal, smaller masonry buildings? Or we could try demarcating elite residential sectors, rather than architectural types, using central precinct walls, the vast platforms underlying parts of some sites, or the complexes connected by causeways. Still another perspective derives from the earlier argument that many households sit in a small pocket of space, or house lot, because that land was used for intensive gardening. The palaces of the elite, however, conspicuously lack such house lots. Vacant space rarely surrounds elite structures, particularly unimproved open space. It follows that there was no room for food cultivation. The absence of garden space then implies one of two things. Either these palatial assemblages were not in fact residences at all, since they lacked the kitchen gardens everyone else had, or we need to explore the old but untested idea that elite establishments were supplied food through some form of tribute (see McAnany, Chap. 3).

Because of the number of problems involved in going from architecture to the identification of actual elite residences, we consequently have severe problems when we want to identify the elite on the ground, rather than on their monuments, in their tombs, or in their boastful texts. First, what was their actual domestic lifestyle like, or their interaction with or dependence on craftspeople and farmers? The extent to which elites were directly involved in productive or managerial roles versus parasitic activities is a key question (Rathje 1983; cf. Stuart, Chap. 11; and McAnany, Chap. 3).

A second critical problem is, to what extent did the elite themselves actually increase in numbers and proportions at the eighth-century climax? Answers will not be easy to obtain, as indicated above. Yet the number of elite people is a fundamental measure of the production stresses that allegedly swelling numbers placed on ancient Maya society, to tip it not only into decline but into collapse.

Finally, can we look outward from the central elite and see how their influence extended out over their whole communities? Beyond the scope of causeway systems, in both space (they are commonly confined to the site-core) and function, very little attention has been given to whether the elite and their beliefs mandated the siting and characteristics of non-elite residence located in more peripheral zones of the community, imposing some form of cosmogram or program on nature.

## PRACTICAL CONSIDERATIONS

We need to pay continued attention to several archaeological problems—beyond those already evident to the reader—that may jeopardize our understandings of the eighth century derived from settlement data. One of these research opportunities is the palimpsest problem in archaeological mapping. We have only a limited sample of well-mapped Maya settlements, and not all periods and regions are yet represented. Even fewer settlement maps show exclusively eighth-century remains. Consequently, we need continued studies based on excavations or extensive surface collections in order to identify what was contemporary at each site during each period (or at least the patterns of types and associations based on representative sampling).

Even where mapping is extensive, we currently know the actual limits of few settlements with any degree of certainty (e.g., Tikal, Copan, Komchen, Sayil). In other words, when we speak of Maya settlements, only rarely do we actually know both their entire configuration and the patterns at any one time. It is obviously going to be misleading to construct, interpret, or compare the spatial and functional structures of sites without knowing the location and nature of the site borders. A case in point is our studies at Sayil in Yucatan (Tourtellot et al. 1988). At the end of each field season of mapping, we thought we had a good idea of the limits and extent of the site, based on an initial series of four cardinally oriented long transects and the progressive mapping of the areas between them. Each season, however, revealed numerous additional hectares of heavy settlement beyond the projected limits and another half-dozen or more entirely new types of mappable archaeological features. What is humbling about this experience is that our field survey was designed to supposedly forewarn us. Yet the actual shape of the settlement now more closely resembles a wild amoeba than the simple oval initially suggested from the radial transects. What is frightening is the doubt cast on samples and transects as accurate representations of the total configuration or patterns of sites.

Another major area of opportunity is the reverse of the palimpsest problem: the question of "hidden housemounds" or the "invisible universe," buried or nonplatform buildings that do not show up on our maps. This potentially serious problem has numerous dimensions, and many reasons account for the failure to record all the structural remains, let alone artifacts, that were once left on a site (perishability of material, removal, burial under later features, erosion and aggradation, inadequate or inappropriate recovery methods, scholarly disinterest, expense). The really nagging question, however, is whether we are playing with a full deck when we draw conclusions from the types, frequencies, and distributions of mapped settlement remains. Do we have samples of all the *types* of remains, and their associations, in order to reliably draw conclusions, or does the forest conceal certain invisible "jokers" up its sleeve, so to speak?

We positively know that some structures are indeed hidden, but I think the overall problem is tractable rather than impossible to resolve. One point is that, on present evidence, both buried and nonplatform structures may actually have been rare in the northern lowlands (Kurjack 1974; Killion et al. 1989). Numbers and densities of visible remains are already high, and the soil is too thin to cover much else. If invisible-type structures are restricted specifically to parts of the southern lowlands, their presence might go a long way toward redressing the tremendous disparities in site densities observable when comparing some current site maps from the two subareas. However, my current beliefs are that nonplatform structures are low in frequency and located mostly in peripheral or rural areas rather than in site centers (Tourtellot 1988: 345–350; Pyburn 1989). They may be rarer still in the northern lowlands simply because many sites appear to be relatively nucleated and rural occupation is consequently rare.

A second point is that a majority of so-called invisible structures may not belong to the final occupation of their sites, but to earlier phases (e.g., 67% of Seibal hidden platforms date to the Late Classic Tepejilote phase rather than to the nominally maximal Terminal Classic Bayal phase [Tourtellot 1988: 348]). Since "final" occupation is often ninth century, therefore invisibles may loom as a relatively larger component of the eighth-century settlements under discussion. This century, of course, is already considered the time of maximal occupation at many sites. The addition of any invisibles—if they were actually dwellings rather than ancillary structures—will only exacerbate the question of how still more people could have been supported by an agricultural system apparently already diversified nearly to its maximum capacity.

Invisible and wholly perishable nonplatform buildings may be largely a phenomenon of the margins of sites and sites apparently of low density. I remain unconvinced that the already high density of some sites, and particularly the central areas of many, will have to be further increased to take account of invisible Late Classic dwellings.

## CONCLUSIONS

In my view there are two promising technical developments in settlement analysis and several steps that can be taken in future research. One development is the mass application of obsidian-hydration dating as a key to settlement history and process, for reasons already mentioned. The preliminary results are tremendously exciting, but remain to be fully published and validated. Furthermore, the ease of obtaining obsidian at Copan is unlikely to be matched at sites farther from the sources. Another continuing development is the increasing emphasis on broad horizontal sampling by means of extensive transect mapping, broad surface collection, chemical testing, or areal excavation, abetted in some places by the otherwise lamentable clear-cutting of the tropical forest. These operations can provide much broader information on contexts than testpits, and are particularly suitable to yield data regarding invisible structures if their scope of application is sufficiently catholic. These two innovations will contribute powerfully to picking apart both the temporal trajectories of Maya settlements and the organization of activities, or site structure, within entire communities. Because numerous eighth-century remains are on or close to the surface, these approaches promise rapid increases in our knowledge of settlement and life in the climactic eighth century.

One direction in which to go is the more frequent extension of mapping out over the borders of sites, if we are to speak reliably of the configuration of entire communities and not only their centers. These configurations may differ geographically between northern and southern lowland sites, as regarding density and nucleation, or temporally between walled sites of predominantly(?) the Terminal Preclassic and Terminal Classic periods versus open settlements occupied in other periods. My concern with borders, frustrated at Seibal, has been stimulated by research in the Puuc. Nevertheless, sharp artificial (rather than natural) borders may not exist during the Late Classic, due to population growth and expansion, but only during earlier and later periods, as for example during the pioneer colonization demonstrated at Seibal (Tourtellot 1988: 421–424, maps 5–13). The apparent Puuc nucleation may also be a temporary, pioneer phenomenon, since occupation before the Late Classic seems very light or scattered (Dunning n.d.). In order to determine the parameters of individual Maya settlement systems, we need first to locate site boundaries and boundary features, if they exist, and then to continue our searches into rural areas, if a distinctive form of rural occupation can be identified. Data from such expanded pursuits should be relevant not only to the conformation and function of settlements and their parts, but to further discovery, plotting, and "ground-truthing" of agricultural areas and features as well. While exciting discoveries have been made, it is clear that we are still far from agreeing on the significance and ubiquity of intensive agricultural systems.

Another step to take is the search for ever more rapid means of survey and mapping. We have progressed from relatively uninformative aerial photographs of tropical forest cover to ever broader and more insightful analysis of other remote imagery (e.g., Pope and Dahlin 1989). In this we are abetted by the progressive deforestation of the lowlands, laying bare the skeletal outline of ancient settlement (e.g., Laporte's work in southeastern Peten, Chap. 10). On-the-ground electronic-mapping stations have speeded our work, again most successfully in cleared areas. Soon we may be able to use handheld global-positioning devices to rapidly locate ourselves on the ground with a resolution of a few tens of meters, allowing us to loosen the tyranny of time-consuming trail-cutting. With a small number of judiciously chosen spot readings, extensive or far-flung survey- and sketch-mapping may be able to speed up from the pace at which it has been conducted for over two decades now.

Finally, numerous small sites simply must have existed, and probably many single-period or short-occupation sites as well. Both are ripe for investigation, especially of the lower-level or non-elite stratum of society. Pulltrouser Swamp hamlets, for example, have very limited development of upper-class features and only the most simple elite or ritual architecture (Turner and Harrison 1983). The investigation of small and single-period sites is an opportunity to counterbalance the upsurge in insights gained from major royal centers and our often limited glimpses of appurtenant settlement. Small sites provide a chance to more easily and cheaply acquire a holistic view of a functioning community, its essential parts, and its specializations (cf. Potter, Chap. 9). They provide a conveniently small focus, important in an atmosphere of restricted funding, but potentially encompassing in microcosm a full range of social, economic, and political institutions, not excepting elements of royalty. Small sites may represent a basic building block, or alternatively a kernel, in Maya settlement, whatever the scale. It will be interesting to see whether small sites were more common before the Late Classic, before they expanded into, or were themselves incorporated by, the burgeoning and perhaps more aggressive Late Classic polities.

*Acknowledgments* I gratefully acknowledge the support of a Fellowship in Pre-Columbian Studies from Dumbarton Oaks during the initial preparation of the views expressed here, although the good people of Dumbarton Oaks are not responsible for any of the shortcomings of this paper. The comments of Jerry Sabloff and two acute, but anonymous, reviewers were especially helpful during the final revision of the manuscript.

## BIBLIOGRAPHY

Arnold, Jeanne E., and Anabel Ford
    1980   A Statistical Examination of Settlement Patterns at Tikal, Guatemala. *American Antiquity* 45: 713–726.

Ball, Joseph W., and Jennifer T. Taschek
    n.d.   Secondary Centers and Classic Maya Political Organization: The Mopan-Macal Triangle Project. Paper presented at the 54th Annual Meeting of the Society for American Archaeology, Atlanta, April 1989.

Chase, Arlen F., and Diane Z. Chase
    1983   Intensive Gardening among the Late Classic Maya. *Expedition* 25 (3): 2–11.
    1987   *Investigations at the Classic Maya City of Caracol, Belize: 1985–1987.* Monograph 3. Pre-Columbian Art Research Institute, San Francisco.

Chase, Arlen F., and Prudence M. Rice (eds.)
    1985   *The Lowland Maya Postclassic.* University of Texas Press, Austin.

Culbert, T. Patrick, and Don S. Rice (eds.)
    1990   *Precolumbian Population History in the Maya Lowlands.* University of New Mexico Press, Albuquerque.

Dahlin, Bruce H.
    1983   Climate and Prehistory on the Northern Yucatan Peninsula. *Climate Change* 5: 245–263.

de Montmollin, Olivier
    1989   *The Archaeology of Political Structure: Settlement Analysis in a Classic Maya Polity.* Cambridge University Press, Cambridge.

Drennan, Robert D.
    1988   Household Location and Compact Versus Dispersed Settlement in Prehispanic Mesoamerica. In *House and Household in the Mesoamerican Past* (Richard Wilk and Wendy Ashmore, eds.): 273–293. University of New Mexico Press, Albuquerque.

Dunning, Nicholas P.
    1989   *Archaeological Investigations at Sayil, Yucatan, Mexico: Intersite Reconnaissance and Soil Studies during the 1987 Season.* University of Pittsburgh Anthropological Papers 2. Pittsburgh.
    n.d.   Prehispanic Maya Settlement in the Puuc Region of Yucatan, Mexico: Preliminary Analysis of Water and Soil Resources. Paper presented at the Annual Meeting of the Association of American Geographers, Minneapolis, May 1986.

Farriss, Nancy M.
    1984   *Maya Society under Colonial Rule: The Collective Enterprise of Survival.* Princeton University Press, Princeton.

Flannery, Kent V. (ed.)
    1982   *Maya Subsistence: Studies in Memory of Dennis E. Puleston.* Academic Press, New York.

FOLAN, WILLIAM J., ELLEN R. KINTZ, AND LARAINE A. FLETCHER
  1983   *Coba: A Classic Maya Metropolis.* Academic Press, New York.
FORD, ANABEL
  1986   *Population Growth and Social Complexity: An Examination of Settlement and Environment in the Central Maya Lowlands.* Arizona State University, Anthropological Research Paper 35. Tempe.
FOX, RICHARD G.
  1977   *Urban Anthropology: Cities in Their Cultural Settings.* Prentice-Hall, Englewood Cliffs, New Jersey.
FREIDEL, DAVID A., AND JEREMY A. SABLOFF
  1984   *Cozumel: Late Maya Settlement Patterns.* Academic Press, Orlando.
HAMMOND, NORMAN
  1974   Maya Settlement Hierarchy in Northern Belize. *Contributions of the University of California Archaeological Research Facility* 27: 40–55. Berkeley.
HARRISON, PETER D.
  1986   Tikal: Selected Topics. In *City-States of the Maya: Art and Architecture* (Elizabeth P. Benson, ed.). Rocky Mountain Institute for Pre-Columbian Studies, Denver.
  n.d.   The Central Acropolis, Tikal, Guatemala: A Preliminary Study of the Functions of Its Structural Components during the Late Classic Period. Ph.D. dissertation, University of Pennsylvania, 1970.
HARRISON, PETER D., AND BILLIE LEE TURNER II (EDS.)
  1978   *Pre-Hispanic Maya Agriculture.* University of New Mexico Press, Albuquerque.
HOSLER, DOROTHY J., JEREMY A. SABLOFF, AND DALE RUNGE
  1977   Simulation Model Development: A Case Study of the Maya Collapse. In *Social Process in Maya Prehistory* (Norman Hammond, ed.): 553–584. Academic Press, London.
KILLION, THOMAS W.
  n.d.   *Agriculture and Residential Site Structure among Campesinos in Southern Veracruz, Mexico: Building a Foundation for Archaeological Inference.* Ph.D. dissertation, University of New Mexico, Albuquerque, 1987.
KILLION, THOMAS W., JEREMY A. SABLOFF, GAIR TOURTELLOT, AND NICHOLAS P. DUNNING
  1989   Intensive Surface Collection of Residential Clusters at Terminal Classic Sayil, Yucatan, Mexico. *Journal of Field Archaeology* 16 (3): 273–294.
KURJACK, EDWARD B.
  1974   *Prehistoric Lowland Maya Community and Social Organization. A Case Study at Dzibilchaltun, Yucatan, Mexico.* Middle American Research Institute, Pub. 38. Tulane University, New Orleans.
LOWE, JOHN W. G.
  1985   *The Dynamics of Apocalypse: A Systems Simulation of the Classic Maya Collapse.* University of New Mexico Press, Albuquerque.
MATHENY, RAY T.
  1978   Northern Maya Lowland Water-Control Systems. In *Pre-Hispanic Maya Agriculture* (Peter D. Harrison and Billie Lee Turner II, eds.):

185–210. University of New Mexico, Albuquerque.

MILLER, MARY ELLEN
1988 The Meaning and Function of the Main Acropolis, Copan. In *The Southeast Classic Maya Zone* (Elizabeth H. Boone and Gordon R. Willey, eds.): 149–194. Dumbarton Oaks, Washington, D.C.

PALERM, ANGEL, AND ERIC WOLF
1957 Ecological Potential and Cultural Development in Mesoamerica. In *Studies in Human Ecology:* 1–37. Pan American Union, Social Science Monographs 3. Washington, D.C.

POHL, MARY (ED.)
1985 *Prehistoric Lowland Maya Environment and Subsistence Economy.* Papers of the Peabody Museum 77. Harvard University, Cambridge.

POPE, KEVIN O., AND BRUCE H. DAHLIN
1989 Ancient Maya Wetland Agriculture: New Insights from Ecological and Remote Sensing Research. *Journal of Field Archaeology* 16: 87–106.

PYBURN, K. ANNE
1989 *Prehistoric Maya Community and Settlement at Nohmul, Belize.* BAR International Series 509. Oxford.

RATHJE, WILLIAM L.
1983 To the Salt of the Earth: Some Comments on Household Archaeology among the Maya. In *Prehistoric Settlement Patterns: Essays in Honor of Gordon R. Willey* (Evon Z. Vogt and Richard M. Leventhal, eds.): 23–34. University of New Mexico Press, Albuquerque, and Peabody Museum, Cambridge.

RINGLE, WILLIAM M., AND GEORGE J. BEY III
n.d. *Preliminary Report of the Ek Balam Project: 1987 Field Season.* Report submitted to the National Geographic Society, 1989. Davidson College, North Carolina.

ROBERTSON, MERLE GREENE
1985 *The Sculpture of Palenque. Volume II: The Early Buildings of the Palace and the Wall Paintings. Volume III: The Late Buildings of the Palace.* Princeton University Press, Princeton.

SABLOFF, JEREMY A.
1985 Ancient Maya Civilization. In *Maya: Treasures of an Ancient Civilization* (Charles Gallenkamp and Regina Elise Johnson, eds.): 34–46. Harry N. Abrams, New York.

SABLOFF, JEREMY A., AND E. WYLLYS ANDREWS V (EDS.)
1986 *Late Lowland Maya Civilization: Classic to Postclassic.* University of New Mexico Press, Albuquerque.

SABLOFF, JEREMY A., AND WILLIAM L. RATHJE (EDS.)
1975 *A Study of Changing Pre-Columbian Commercial Systems: The 1972–1973 Seasons at Cozumel, Mexico.* Peabody Museum, Monographs 3. Harvard University, Cambridge.

SABLOFF, PAULA L. W.
1975 Changing Patterns of Dwelling Distribution (1847–1972). In *A Study of Changing Pre-Columbian Commercial Systems: The 1972–1973 Seasons at*

Santley, Robert S.
    1990    Demographic Archaeology in the Maya Lowlands. In *Precolumbian Population History in the Maya Lowlands* (T. Patrick Culbert and Don S. Rice, eds.): 325–343. University of New Mexico Press, Albuquerque.

Santley, Robert S., Thomas W. Killion, and Mark T. Lycett
    1986    On the Maya Collapse. *Journal of Anthropological Research* 42 (2): 123–159.

Schele, Linda, and Mary Ellen Miller
    1986    *The Blood of Kings: Dynasty and Ritual in Maya Art*. George Braziller, New York, and Kimbell Art Museum, Fort Worth.

Smith, A. Ledyard
    1982    *Excavations at Seibal, Major Architecture and Caches*. Peabody Museum, Memoir 15 (1). Harvard University, Cambridge.

Smyth, Michael P.
    n.d.    Domestic Storage Behavior in the Puuc Region of Yucatan, Mexico: An Ethnoarchaeological Investigation. Ph.D. dissertation, University of New Mexico, 1988.

Taschek, Jennifer T., and Joseph W. Ball
    n.d.    Regal-Ritual Residences and Administrative Hubs: Differential Structure and Function among the Major Centers of the Upper Belize Valley. Paper presented at the 52nd Annual Meeting of the Society for American Archaeology, Toronto, April 1987.

Thompson, J. Eric S.
    1974    "Canals" of the Rio Candelaria Basin, Campeche, Mexico. In *Mesoamerican Archaeology: New Approaches* (Norman Hammond, ed.): 297–302. University of Texas, Austin.

Tourtellot, Gair
    1983    An Assessment of Classic Maya Household Composition. In *Prehistoric Settlement Patterns: Essays in Honor of Gordon R. Willey* (Evon Z. Vogt and Richard M. Leventhal, eds.): 35–54. University of New Mexico Press, Albuquerque, and Peabody Museum, Cambridge.
    1988    *Excavations at Seibal, Department of Peten, Guatemala: Peripheral Survey and Excavation. Settlement and Community Patterns*. Peabody Museum, Memoir 16. Harvard University, Cambridge.

Tourtellot, Gair, Jeremy A. Sabloff, and Kelli Carmean
    n.d.    Will the Real Elites Please Stand Up?: An Archaeological Assessment of Maya Elite Behavior in the Terminal Classic Period. In *Mesoamerican Elites: An Archaeological Assessment* (Arlen F. Chase and Diane A. Chase, eds.). University of Oklahoma Press, Norman. (in press)

Tourtellot, Gair, Jeremy A. Sabloff, Michael P. Smyth, L. Val Whitley, Stanley L. Walling, Tomas Gallareta Negron, Carlos Perez Alvarez, George P. Andrews, and Nicholas P. Dunning
    1988    Mapping Community Patterns at Sayil, Yucatan, Mexico: The 1985 Season. *Journal of New World Archaeology* 7 (2/3): 1–24.

TURNER II, BILLIE LEE
    1983   *Once Beneath the Forest.* Westview Press, Boulder.

TURNER II, BILLIE LEE, AND PETER D. HARRISON (EDS.)
    1983   *Pulltrouser Swamp: Ancient Maya Habitat, Agriculture, and Settlement in Northern Belize.* University of Texas Press, Austin.

WEBSTER, DAVID
    1988   Copan as a Classic Maya Center. In *The Southeast Classic Maya Zone* (Elizabeth H. Boone and Gordon R. Willey, eds.): 5–30. Dumbarton Oaks, Washington, D.C.
    n.d.a  Copan and a Household Model of Mayan Society. Paper presented at the 21st Chacmool Conference, University of Calgary, Alberta, Canada, November 1988.
    n.d.b  Investigating Maya Institutions and Culture History at Copan, Honduras. Paper presented at the 53rd Annual Meeting of the Society for American Archaeology, Phoenix, April 1988.

WEBSTER, DAVID, AND NANCY GONLIN
    1988   Household Remains of the Humblest Maya. *Journal of Field Archaeology* 15: 169–190.

WILKINSON, T. J.
    1982   The Definition of Ancient Manured Zones by Means of Extensive Sherd-Sampling Techniques. *Journal of Field Archaeology* 9: 323–333.

WILLEY, GORDON R., WILLIAM R. BULLARD, JR., JOHN B. GLASS, AND JAMES C. GIFFORD
    1965   *Prehistoric Maya Settlements in the Belize Valley.* Peabody Museum, Papers 54. Harvard University, Cambridge.

# 8

## Pottery, Potters, Palaces, and Polities: Some Socioeconomic and Political Implications of Late Classic Maya Ceramic Industries

### JOSEPH W. BALL
SAN DIEGO STATE UNIVERSITY

DESPITE THE ENORMOUS STRIDES made over the past two decades in such diverse fields of scholarship as epigraphy, iconography, subsistence archaeology, and lithic analysis, pottery vessels and their fragments remain both the most extensive and accessible source of information on virtually every aspect of Classic period Maya civilization. Traditionally relied on to establish local and regional chronologies, date other associated materials and features, and provide some tangible suggestions as to intersite and regional relationships, they have also in recent years been drawn on increasingly to provide data concerning ancient Maya economic systems, political history, ceremonial behavior, ideology, societal structure, and community organization. Perhaps not surprisingly, their most effective contributions to date have involved studies of local pottery production-distribution systems and the derivative inferences concerning ancient Maya economic patterns in general that these make possible.

To consider in even superficial overview the ceramic industry of the late Cycle Nine lowland Maya or the contributions of ceramic studies to our broader perception of their civilization represents an almost overwhelmingly ambitious undertaking, and what I will attempt here is not so much a state-of-knowledge synthesis as a selective review of some ways in which ceramic studies over the last twenty years have contributed to our understanding of Late Classic Maya societal structure and political organization. Another thing I will do is attempt to briefly state some of the sociobehavioral correlates assumed but rarely made explicit by Mayanist archaeologists in utilizing such constructs as the ceramic group, complex, and sphere. While there has been a great deal of consideration given to the analytical merits and even the emic values of types and larger integrative units, scant effort has been made to discuss the likely sociobehavioral correlates of these. In light of the surprising actual spottiness of studies pertaining to the various issues that ceramics have been used to investigate, I will employ an areal rather than region-by-region framework for this review.

## EIGHTH-CENTURY LOWLAND MAYA POTTERY PRODUCTION, DISTRIBUTION, AND LOCAL CONSUMPTION: CERAMIC GROUPS AND PASTE VARIANTS

What were the social and economic circumstances of pottery manufacture in the Late Classic Maya lowlands? What can be said regarding the contexts and mechanisms of pottery distribution at both the local and regional levels, and what in turn can be inferred concerning the socioeconomic structure and political organization of the eighth-century lowland Maya from these data?

In two now classic sets of studies focusing on ceramic distributions in the environs of Palenque and Tikal, Robert L. Rands (1967; Rands and Bishop 1980), Ron Bishop (1976, 1980, n.d.; Bishop, Harbottle, and Sayre 1982; Bishop and Rands 1982; Bishop, Rands, and Harbottle 1979), and Robert E. Fry (1979, 1980; Fry and Cox 1974) have attempted to address these questions. Prudence Rice (1987a; 1987b) has capably summarized their findings in two recent papers, and I can do little better here than reiterate her observations concerning production-siting and likely circulation modes. I will, however, differ somewhat from her in my own interpretations of these data.[1]

In the southern lowlands at least, the manufacture of utilitarian domestic pottery currently appears to have taken place within a context of dispersed households, hamlets, and village communities lying outside the strict limits of the major and minor architectural centers. Vessel production was not a continuous phenomenon across the intercenter landscape, but was spotted irregularly among the satellite communities of the hinterland. Data from both Palenque and Tikal suggest situations associated with agriculturally

---

[1] Rice stresses a dichotomization in production and distribution between so-called serving vessels and other utilitarian wares following a distinction earlier suggested by Tourtellot and Sabloff (1972). This in turn leads to a suggestion of community-level specialization in the production of specific vessel form classes. Neither archaeological nor ethnographic data support such a model, however, Rands and Bishop (1980: 43) observed that:

> the patterned covariation in form class and paste composition in ceramics that were apparently imported to Palenque indicates the existence of specialized production centers *while cutting across the traditional lines of domestic and serving pottery* [emphasis added]. Tourtellot and Sabloff (1972; Sabloff 1975: 237) have seen a dichotomy in ceramic production and exchange between utilitarian and serving vessels, the former being manufactured at several locations surrounding a ceremonial center and distributed only within its sustaining area ("domestic" trade), the latter being produced at a much smaller number of locations and distributed among the elite in the "controlled" trade. Investigating utilitarian and serving vessel exchange at Tikal, Fry (1979: 510) has questioned the likelihood of two wholly separate systems of distribution for these functional classes, a position which is consistent with our understanding of the Palenque data.

marginal or less productive lands may have played a role in the adoption of pottery production as a supplemental economic activity (Rands and Bishop 1980: 42; Fry 1980: 2; see also Arnold 1978a, 1978b: 330–331, 1985: 196–201).

As in the Maya highlands today, utilitarian pottery production is generally assumed to have been a part-time seasonal activity with specialization occurring at the community rather than the individual level (Arnold 1985; Reina and Hill 1978). Rice (1987a; 1987b) has suggested such specialization involved specific shapes or form classes, but neither archaeological nor ethnographic data in fact support this. Both Fry and Rands did emphasize form classes in their analyses for practical reasons, but their findings suggest multiform assemblages more closely corresponding to the typologists' *ceramic groups*[2] as the most likely products of community-level specialization. This is also the pattern documented by Ruben Reina and Robert Hill (1978) throughout Highland Guatemala (Fig. 1). One community may become renowned for a particular shape or form category and market this widely, but its production and local circulation repertoire nonetheless remain varied. Native potters may conceptualize their products in terms of form classes (Arnold 1985; Reina and Hill 1978), but they still produce them as surface-finish groups in many respects actually more amenable to most archaeological manipulations (Fig. 2). I do not mean here to in any way belittle the importance of form-oriented ceramic studies, but to reemphasize the value of the *ceramic group* as an analytical reflection of the individual pottery-producing community. In combination, a specific finish group and paste variant[3] archaeologically fingerprint a single producer community or workshop. Given the continued absence of more direct evidence concerning production loci, this is an important point for the analyst to keep in mind.

Despite impressive independent analyses employing data from both the Tikal and Palenque regions (Bishop 1976, 1980, n.d.; Bishop, Harbottle, and Sayre 1982; Bishop and Rands 1982; Bishop, Rands, and Harbottle 1979; Fry 1979, 1980; Fry and Cox 1974; Rands 1967; Rands and Bishop 1980), the mechanisms of circulation that interlinked individual Late Classic ceramic producer communities with each other, the major centers, and other consumer locales remain far from being satisfactorily understood. In both cases, the distributions identified could result from any of several possibilities, and on one point only, in fact, does there seem to be some general accord: Late Classic Maya centers were consumers rather than producers, exporters, or even major redistributors of utilitarian pottery ves-

---

[2] A *ceramic group* is a set of very similar and closely related pottery exhibiting a distinctive homogeneity in range of variation with respect to base color, surface-finish character, form repertoire, and other allied attributes, but potentially encompassing a variety of secondary decorative techniques and styles and cross-cutting two or more paste variants (cf. Smith and Gifford 1965: 501).

[3] A *paste variant* is a specific, consistent, and distinct preparation of clay body, tempering materials, and firing characteristics as manifest in the freshly broken wall-section of a fired pottery object.

Joseph W. Ball

Fig. 1  Multiform, multitype, household-level part-time specialist pottery production. Rabinal, Guatemala, July, 1970.

Fig. 2  A multiform, multitype, single-firing ceramic group (single-paste variant). Rabinal, Guatemala, July, 1970.

sels.[4] Rice (1987b) has examined some potential ramifications of the Rands and Fry studies as to the likely economic central place roles and organizational influences of the Tikal and Palenque centers. She concludes that "it cannot be clearly demonstrated that political centers exerted any region-wide influence in the production or distribution of most classes of pottery," but that, "elite (or 'wealth') items seem to be the one exception" to this. Rice also observes, as do Rands and Fry, that the multimodality of Late Classic utilitarian pottery distribution graphs suggests that some noneconomic or noncentralized and unmeasured factors were at work in determining the circulation of these wares. Kinship relations and associated mechanisms of redistribution are one possible candidate, as was suggested some years ago by Richard Adams (1977: 147–148, 161).

The apparent production-distribution patterns identified in the case of Late Classic lowland Maya utilitarian ceramics would be equally at home within the varied sociopolitical contexts represented by complex chiefdoms or segmentary states, but not within those of centralized bureaucratic states. Similarly, the reported patterns would fit equally well were Late Classic Maya centers functionally regal-ritual centers, administrative centers, or regal-ritual cities in the urban typology proposed by Richard G. Fox (1977) and recently applied in pure or modified form to Mesoamerican cases by several authors (Marcus 1983; Taschek and Ball n.d.; Sanders and Webster 1988).[5] In each of these cases, concentrations of wealth and sumptuary materials are expected to occur within major central places conjointly with a broader dispersal of productive and distributive activities involving nonsumptuary, utilitarian commodities (see Fox 1977: 24–38, 39–57). Centralized marketing, exchange, or redistribution may or may not also be present, but emphatically need not be. In any case, it is of little matter to the resident elite: their primacy and status and that of their residential settlement is rooted in ideology and, for the Classic Maya, hereditary descent from deified ancestral war-leaders and a shamanistic ability to communicate with these (cf. Freidel and Schele 1988).

I do not believe the now-apparent patterns of ceramic production and distribution are compatible with Fox's administrative city model, whether the urban settlement he conceived of in traditional or "garden-city" terms. Although an administrative city can serve as do regal-ritual centers as "the residence of the state elite and a center of prestige and ritual functions, . . . administrative cities contain and perform many more functions of communication and transportation. *They centralize commerce, crafts, and other occupa-*

---

[4] It should be noted that these analyses in fact involve depositional and therefore circulation/use/discard patterns, rather than true "distributional" ones (cf. Rice 1987b). The derived inferences are assumed to be generally valid, however.

[5] I should note here that I have adopted Fox's typology not as a rigid means of *categorizing* Maya central places, but as a convenient, useful, and appropriate means of *characterizing* them as to functional aspect and attributes.

*tional specialties*" [emphasis added] (Fox 1977: 61). Sharply demarcated both physically and socially from their own hinterlands, administrative cities comprise the political and economic nodes of the highly organized bureaucratic polities with which they are associated. Within their limits are concentrated both the institutions and mechanisms of economic interchange, and the fruits of their highly centralized extractive control over the agricultural and commercial production of their subject rural populations and urban inhabitants. Their correlative archaeological pattern with respect to the production, circulation, and consumption of a utilitarian commodity such as pottery is a clear and unambiguous one, and bears little resemblance to those identified for Tikal and Palenque.

One other functional urban-type/political-form combination also is excluded unambiguously by the ceramic data. This is the mercantile city/city-state. The "city-state" label has been among the most frequently applied to ancient Maya polities, but rarely has it been so with any clear and explicit statement of its meaning or appreciation for its implicit sociofunctional significance on the part of those who have used it. Properly, city-states are urban-based mercantile entities and any usage other than this is incorrect. They are characterized by "the importance of acquired wealth over hereditary status in access to power" (Fox 1977: 111), and a considerable consequent social mobility. In the absence of ascriptive offices, electoral systems typically emerge to resolve political issues. City-states develop where little or no centralized authority exists and a source of wealth and economic autonomy other than control over peasant subsistence agriculture is present. Their wealth may derive from long-distance trade or money-lending activities or from involvement in the large-scale local production of exportable handicrafts such as pottery, stone tools, or cotton cloth. In any event, the city itself "is a place for the production of riches, not merely a consumption center where wealth squeezed from peasant labor is expended by state rulers, or where artisans congregate to supply the needs of resident state administrators" (Fox 1977: 95). Nothing could be farther from the character of Classic Maya cities and centers as the mathematical models of Fry (1979, 1980; Fry and Cox 1974) and Rands (1967; Rands and Bishop 1980) have suggested and extensive recent excavations at Copan (Webster 1988; Sanders and Webster 1988) and Buenavista (Ball and Taschek n.d.) have confirmed. From the ceramics perspective at least, the long popular but inappropriate city-state label together with its implied social and political correlates can and should finally be discarded (cf. Culbert 1988: 136).

It ought to be noted that in all the foregoing cases, what is actually at issue is the nature and extent of managerial involvement by a central place in the day-to-day *economic* affairs of the larger society. With respect to the Late Classic Maya lowlands, this increasingly appears to have been minimal and of a consumptive yet nonexactive character.

To the foregoing studies should be added important new work by Doris J. Reents (n.d.; Reents and Bishop n.d.; Reents-Budet and Bishop n.d.) and Bishop (et al. 1985) involving polychrome-painted archaeological ceramics from the greater Naranjo region on the eastern edge of the Peten and stylistically related unprovenienced vessels from several private and institutional collections. Unlike the Tikal and Palenque analyses, Reents' study focused on a putatively costly decorated fineware of limited availability rather than a high-volume, high-demand basic consumer commodity. The vessels studied by Reents embody considerable iconographic and even epigraphic erudition and reflect varying levels of artistic skill in their execution. Their contextual distributions, where known, suggest patterns of use and circulation that differed significantly from those assumed for utilitarian-ware categories. To a considerable extent, these differences are quite clearly status-related. Like Rands and Fry, Reents sought to identify probable production centers and distribution patterns for her study population, and her findings generally parallel theirs despite the strongly varying characters of those populations. She herself does differ somewhat on some points in interpreting these data, but here I would emphasize the fundamental congruence of her findings with those of Rands and Fry.[6]

The specific vessels considered by Reents all pertain to the cream-field polychrome Zacatel ceramic group. By means of a meticulous and exhaustive stylistic analysis, she first established the existence of two distinct style-groups within the larger Zacatel series. These share common pictorial programs and iconography, but differ in execution sufficiently to suggest the efforts of several different individuals working within two separate schools or traditions. Trace-element paste compositional analyses confirmed the discrete integrity of the two style-groups. Reents then employed a combination of occurrence distributions, compositional comparisons, and even some limited epigraphic data to argue a probable primary distributional and production association of one group with the Holmul center and its environs and the other with the greater Naranjo subregion.

---

[6] Reents (n.d.: 175–181) rejects the correlation between agricultural marginality and pottery-making as an alternative economic pursuit identified by virtually every other student of Maya pottery production whether ancient or modern. In part this reflects the special character of her study population and its likely production by attached or palace-sponsored, if not actual elite, artisans. The economic circumstances of these potters were not comparable to those of the larger populace and inferences concerning them should not be extended thereto. Moreover, Reents' (n.d.: 175) homogenizing characterization of the Holmul-Naranjo area as "one of good agricultural potential" overreaches reality and ignores the actual environmental diversity and soil quality zonation of the east central Peten region (see, for example, Fedick 1989; Birchall and Jenkin 1979). Within the broad territorial limits of any one polity, overall conditions may indeed be "good" or even "excellent." Localized areas of lower-quality marginal lands are nonetheless still likely to be present, and it is at this subregional zonal or community level that pottery production will occur as a supplement or alternative to agriculture; not, as Reents implies, at the macroregional or polity level (cf. Rands and Bishop 1980: 42–43).

Joseph W. Ball

The Zacatel series ceramics recovered from Holmul and Naranjo thus appear to represent the output of two separate and distinct pottery-making communities. Sufficient uniformity of style and homogeneity of paste composition exist within each group to support the existence of a "Holmul School" and a "Naranjo School" of production, each utilizing compositionally distinct paste-clay and temper resources combined in consistent but locally distinctive manners. Within each of the two larger regional groupings, however, enough stylistic and compositional heterogeneity occur to indicate that a number of different artists and pottery-making households or workshops were involved in their production.

In the immediately adjacent upper Belize Valley zone, I have recently identified yet a third Zacatel series style-group quite distinct from, but at the same time clearly related to, Reents' others (Figs. 3, 4). Vessels assignable to this set are heavily concentrated at the major local regal-ritual center, Buenavista del Cayo, and are more lightly represented at secondary rural palaces and plaza groups, such as Cahal Pech and Yaxox. They appear to be all but absent from lower-order settlement units such as rural plazuela groups, patio groups, and isolated mounds, and indeed may prove to be entirely missing from such contexts once analyses have been completed. In other words, there is a strong apparent positive correlation between the occurrence of figure-painted polychrome pottery and progressively higher order central places evidenced in the archaeological distributions of the upper Belize Valley. Whether this is a phenomenon of localized production or restricted circulation is as yet unclear; however, a concentrated deposit containing literally dozens of whole but broken cream-polychrome vases, bowls, dishes, jars, and cups was found associated with one building within the Buenavista palace group (Fig. 5). Study of this collection is only just beginning, but one obvious possibility suggested by its content and location is that of palace-sited polychrome pottery production. An associated termination offering including a carved calcium-carbonate statuette of the twin monkey-god patrons of writing, artists, and artisans perhaps lends some support to this possibility.[7]

Reents also explored the complex question of Late Classic potter-painter relationships and cogently, if somewhat cautiously, concluded that in some cases potter and painter were one while in others two different individuals possibly are represented by the final product (see also Coggins n.d.: 529, 544–545). In either case, she argues, both most probably worked within the same production unit: "an extended household unit specializing in ceramic production, wherein task-specialization was more than likely present" (Reents n.d.: 221).

---

[7] Also associated with this deposit were a variety of materials incontrovertibly evidencing the manufacture of finely carved and inscribed bone ornaments and pressure-reduced projectile points of fine-grain chocolate brown chert. These included partly finished and "rejected" items, bone and chert scrap, worn out craftsman's tools, and broken craftsman's tools.

*Pottery, Potters, Palaces, and Polities*

Fig. 3  *Cabrito cream-polychrome: Guajiro variety.* Principal design-program variants as represented in the Buenavista palace deposit: profile-view seated personage.

Fig. 4  *Cabrito cream-polychrome: Guajiro variety.* Principal design-program variants as represented in the Buenavista palace deposit: full-figure standing personage and accompaniments.

Joseph W. Ball

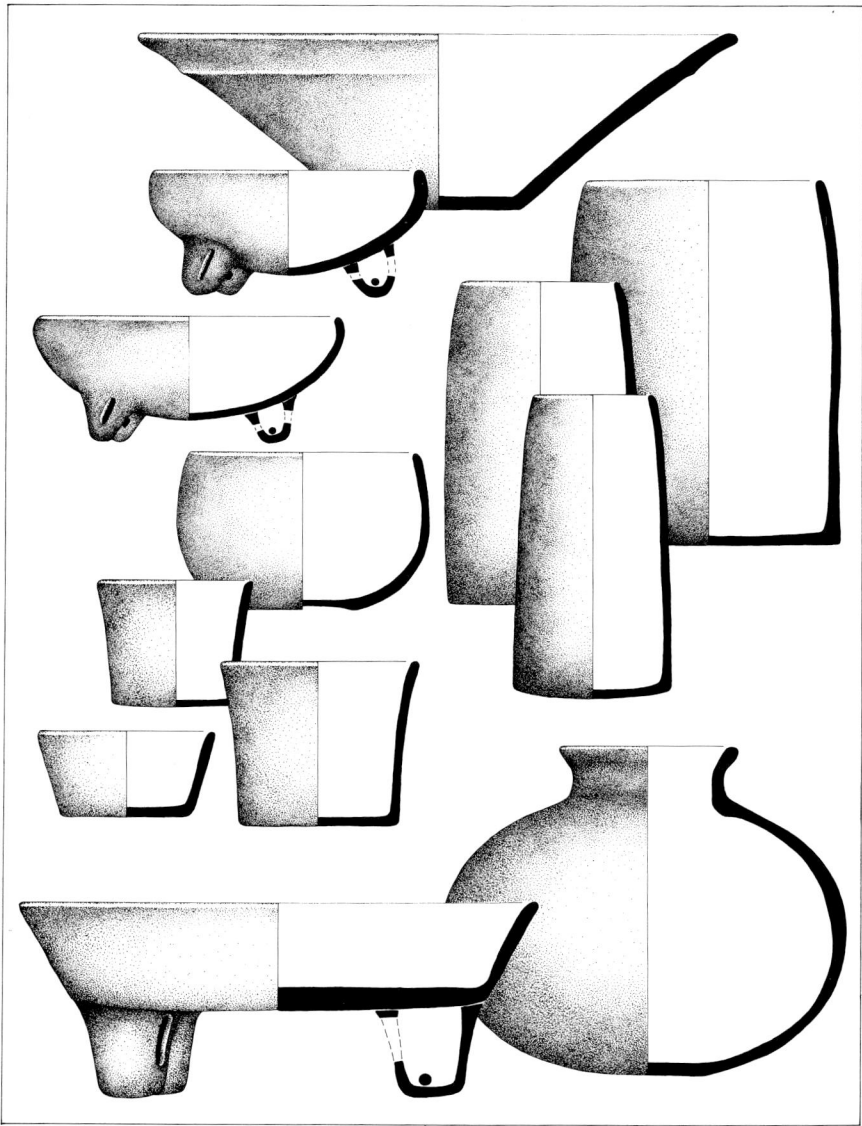

Fig. 5 *Cabrito cream-polychrome: Guajiro variety*. Partial form-set for this figure-painted polychrome variety based on a collection of actual vessels recovered from a single on-floor primary deposit located within the Late Classic palace complex at Buenavista del Cayo. All are of the same paste variant and were without question painted by the same artist. See Figs. 3 and 4 for examples of their decorative program.

*Pottery, Potters, Palaces, and Polities*

Implicit in this reconstruction is the possibility that at least some Late Classic painted fineware production involved a greater degree of producer specialization or labor intensification (see Rice 1987a: 537) than did the manufacture of unpainted service and utilitarian wares. In that this would have involved individuals having considerable familiarity with the most esoteric aspects of elite Maya ideology and courtly lifeways as well as a working knowledge of the hieroglyphic writing system, it raises again the question as to where such fineware manufacture took place and by whom. Logic does indeed suggest production sites within and associated with the major elite centers, but hard data actually bearing on this are both scanty and qualitatively disparate. Based on our own now available data, for example, the Buenavista palace deposit could reflect either localized production or restricted access circulation. At Palenque, specialized ritual wares including cache vessels and incensario stands—although not the censers themselves—appear to have been manufactured within the center along with utilitarian bowls, basins, serving vessels, and some figurines based on compositional data (Rands and Bishop 1980). Similar data suggest the production of polychrome painted pottery and figurines within the bounds of the Lubaantun center in southern Belize (Hammond 1975: 371–374, 1982: 227). Clemency Coggins (n.d.: 406–408, 429–430, 513–514) has argued that site-specific series of both cream Zacatel and orange Palmar group vessels in a variety of forms were manufactured by the inhabitants of patio group 4H-1 on the eastern edge of central Tikal. She also suggests a sponsored or "attached" status for these artisans based on their evident wealth and the ultimate elite funerary disposition of their apparent wares. Marshall J. Becker (1973, 1983: 40) also attributes the production of censers, figurines, whistles, and possibly ceramic masks to the group 4H-1 residents.

Reents' eastern Peten data are not actually applicable to this question, but among the vessels she assigns to her Naranjo group is Grolier No. 47 (Coe 1973: 102–103). David Stuart and Stephen Houston (Stuart 1989: 156–157; Stuart and Houston 1989: 87) note that this vessel was signed by its maker, who identifies himself as a son of the Naranjo *ahaw* and a "Lady of Yaxha," thereby possibly providing the most unequivocal information concerning this question that we now possess.

Overall, what currently can be said regarding the production of Late Classic lowland Maya ceremonial pottery, finewares, and ceramic specialty items such as figurines is meager, but broadly approximates the findings for common household utilitarian wares. Like the latter, the polychrome finewares associated with each major Late Classic Maya center appear to represent the products of geographically local producer-communities consisting of multiple individuals or workshops specializing in multiform, multitype finish groups. In the case of the finewares and ceramic specialty items, there are definite suggestions that production might have been localized at or in immediate proximity to some centers. It is not in all instances entirely certain, however, that what the archaeological distributions reflect are patterns of localized production rather than ones of restricted circulation. In either case, the cited data from Tikal, Palenque, Lubaantun, and Buenavista do conjoin to once again highlight the particular appropriateness of Fox's regal-ritual model to higher order Late Classic lowland Maya central places. I suggest this and the correlative identification of a segmentary state-type political structure for the individual regional Classic lowland Maya polity to comprise the two most important implications to be drawn from our current understanding of eighth-century lowland Maya pottery production and distribution at the local center or community level.[8]

## COMMUNITIES, COMPLEXES, POLITIES, AND SPHERES: CORRELATIONS AND CAVEATS

Individual ceramic group-paste variant combinations represent the output of specific interactive producer units. Do Late Classic Maya consumer units such as communities and polities have similar expressions as ceramic entities?

The integrative units most commonly recognized and employed in ceramics-based considerations of historical and behavioral processes in the Maya area are multigroup *complexes* and *spheres*.[9] Depositionally, these represent systemic consumption units and consumer circulation patterns rather than production units or distribution networks. With respect to these latter, *ceramic complexes* are composite entities, *ceramic spheres* even more so. Both represent circulation systems within which information and ideas moved as well as material goods. This movement involved varying degrees and kinds of access inequalities, but nonetheless took place within and so defined the limits of distinct interaction spheres. Such units, ones distinguished by the intensity of regular interactions among their members, conform reasonably acceptably to most definitions of a community, and, indeed, Mayanist archaeologists have consistently—if almost invariably without discussion or qualification—treated individual ceramic complexes as the correlates of discrete synchronic communities.[10] As in practice actually defined, however,

---

[8] See Demarest (n.d.) and Ball and Taschek (n.d.) for in-depth discussions of the segmentary-state type, its applicability to the Classic lowland Maya, and the archaeological testing of its suitability in their case.

[9] A *ceramic complex* comprises the sum total of pottery and attributes thereof that can be associated as a discrete and readily distinguishable assemblage with a specific geographical locus or zone and a fixed chronological span. Theoretically, at least, its spatial extent should be limited and its temporal duration brief (cf. Gifford 1976: 11–12). "The concept of *ceramic sphere* was defined to emphasize a high degree of content similarity between complexes. A ceramic sphere exists when two or more complexes share a majority of their most common types. Whereas the [ceramic] horizon need imply no more than a few connections at the modal level, the sphere implies high content similarity at the typological level" (Willey, Culbert, and Adams 1967: 306). See Ball (1976: 323–324) for an expanded discussion and suggested quantification of the sphere construct.

[10] The term "community," as employed here, refers to an interacting population of individu-

such complexes do not represent populations that are in any way truly consistent from site to site in functional, social, economic, or other behavioral correlates. They are, instead, often highly selective samplings of the heterogeneous ceramic pools once in circulation at particular localities over the course of variable, but not infrequently relatively lengthy, periods of time. Recognizing the actual potential sociobehavioral heterogeneity, chronological dynamism, and artificiality of these constructs, is it nonetheless still possible to use them to delineate and compare one-time valid synchronic social units such as local communities?

Since 1983, the upper Belize Valley Mopan-Macal Triangle Archaeological Project has expended considerable effort specifically in examining the relationships between Late Classic Maya ceramic assemblages and their sociobehavioral contexts. Our findings clearly document a strong positive correlation between a discrete mid-to-late eighth-century upper-valley local community as inferred from a combination of settlement data, locational models, and other nonartifactual criteria, and a distinct pottery assemblage. Ceramic variations within the hypothesized community can be shown almost without question to correlate with functional, status, and/or wealth factors when chronology is controlled for. Ceramic lots from individual sites as varied as Buenavista (the major local center), Cahal Pech (a rural palace complex), Guerra (a suburban village settlement), Nohoch Ek (a rural manor), and Eden (an isolated hilltop farmstead) all can be assigned to the same local complex. Subcomplex-equivalent social and functional variations occur, but when these are explicitly isolated, correctly identified, and their potential distortions allowed for, a single community-wide assemblage can be defined.

Pertinent comparative data are available from the sites of Pacbitun (Bill n.d.), Baking Pot (Bullard and Bullard 1965), and Barton Ramie (Gifford 1976). Our model places these in two separate communities adjoining, but distinct from, that of Buenavista throughout the eighth-century period during which we believe all three pertained to the same Naranjo polity. The ceramic data identify a close sphere-level relationship among Buenavista, Pacbitun, and Baking Pot-Barton Ramie, but indicate quite definite *minor* distinctions at the complex level that are not explainable as resulting from economic, social, functional, other behavioral, or chronological factors. In other words, recognizably distinct complexes are associated with and can be utilized to identify discrete Late Classic communities.

The data currently available from Naranjo itself are too limited to evaluate as to complex proximity, but do demonstrate a tight sphere-level rela-

---

als residing together in one place. Such a grouping may form part of a larger social system, or comprise a full society in itself. In either case, its members are assumed to compose a discrete, functionally interrelated whole and to interact with each other more regularly or intensely than with outsiders. To some extent at least, they may also share common economic, political, or ideological interests or a common historical background.

tionship with the other three. In contrast, when comparisons are made between the Late Classic Buenavista or Baking Pot-Barton Ramie assemblages and complexes of comparable date from sites known or believed to have pertained to polities other than that of Naranjo, *significant* disparities involving basic utilitarian wares immediately are apparent.[11] These readily distinguish the complexes concerned and likely are of sphere-level magnitude. This is not to suggest that ceramic spheres correspond to regional polities. Spheres were larger and more stable than these fragile, ephemeral entities. Perhaps somewhat complicating matters, however, is the fact that in no known case has any individual Late Classic polity been shown to have extended beyond the limits of a single sphere. Thus, spheres may represent larger bounded social universes within which most polity formation and expansion occurred.

In sum, our findings indicate that ceramic complexes do correspond to individual communities, but they also suggest that no good correlations exist between ceramic spheres or other higher-order integrative units and the territories of identifiable regional polities. I believe there is a fairly simple and straightforward reason for this. The singular mix of ceramic products available within any given community was ultimately a product of the social forces operative in organizing and integrating that community. The local complex conveniently but exclusively crystallizes these specific *local* forces. This is equally true whether the community concerned was associated with a primary regional center—such as Tikal, Palenque, or Chichen Itza—or affiliated with a minor local one like Buenavista or Baking Pot. The absence of larger cohesive ceramic units corresponding to specific Late Classic polities is simply another reflection of the weak politicoeconomic integration characterizing these realms. As observed earlier, major centers appear not to have exercised any real control in the more mundane day-to-day economic affairs of their political territories. Together, the absence of clearly and unambiguously developed economic functions for the major centers and this weak overall socioeconomic (as distinct from socioceremonial or political) integration of the Late Classic realms are in line with their likely correct respective characterizations as regal-ritual cities and segmentary states.

### CERAMIC SPHERES AND REGIONAL TRADITIONS

Ceramic spheres are the products of common cultural traditions. Their content is the result of shared values and information among a populace of both producers and consumers, and the unobstructed flow of both goods and

---

[11] Data from Tikal, Uaxactun, San Jose, Caledonia (Cayo), and Caracol were considered in making these assessments. To the greatest extent possible, these involved personal examinations of the pertinent materials and consultations with their respective analysts. Sources consulted included Awe (n.d.); Culbert (n.d.); Coggins (n.d.); Smith (1955); and Thompson (1939).

ideas among this population. Ceramic spheres do not correspond to single social communities, economic networks, or polities, although their limits may sometimes be coincident with these. In particular, ceramic sphere boundaries may on occasion correspond to those of discrete polities, but this is by no means a necessary or regular situation. Thus, ceramic spheres should not be used casually to map the political geography of the Late Classic Maya lowlands. On the other hand, the systematic definition and plotting of spheres may illuminate, if not explain, major cultural processes transpiring among the eighth-century Maya of far more sweeping significance than the periodic coalescence and dissolution of regional polities.

Across the northern lowlands, from the Chenes subregion on the southwest to the northwestern Caribbean coast, the single most important ceramic development of the eighth century was the appearance and spread of the slateware ceramic tradition. Considerable effort over the last quarter-century has established the staggered early through late eighth-century emergence of slatewares across the northern area from Edzna, Dzibilnocac, and Uomuul to Isla Cerritos, Coba, and Tancah. By the close of the century—essentially the start of the full Late Classic florescence in the north—these low-gloss, "soapy" wares of the Cehpech sphere completely dominated the northern assemblages. Local variations likely correlating with local producer-communities are present, but the overriding impression conveyed by Cehpech is of a monolithic production tradition. As to what the historical, social, political, or economic genesis and ramifications of this development might have been, I offer no suggestions here.[12] What I do wish to point out is that the emergence of a distinct, vital, Late Classic northern Maya cultural tradition is mirrored and can be charted in the appearance and spread of the Cehpech ceramic sphere. Coevally, in the southern lowlands, the increasing regionalization of ceramics and assemblages over the eighth century ultimately leading to a mosaic of subregional spheres in the ninth bespeaks something far more deeply and seriously wrong with the basic fabric of southern Maya society than mere political fragmentation and the collapse of individual political units. What were becoming increasingly alienated in the south were not just rulers and ruling families, elites and their cohorts, but individuals and communities at all levels of society. This, at least, is what I believe the multiplication and regionalization of ceramic spheres to imply.[13]

---

[12] Fernando Robles and Anthony Andrews (1986: 75–87) have examined this issue in some detail, and the interested reader is referred to their excellent treatment for discussions of the most likely historical possibilites. They also provide some basis for recognizing either a subdivision of Cehpech into regionally distinct "Eastern" and "Western" subspheres or, somewhat more likely in my opinion, two typologically separate and distinct regional spheres. This possibility cries out for further investigation.

[13] The progressive regionalization of Late Classic southern lowland ceramic assemblages, and especially polychrome subtraditions, has been noted by several authors (Fry n.d.; Ball 1977; Reents n.d.; Rice 1987b). Fry (n.d.: 242–245), Reents (n.d.: 173–175), and Rice (1987b:

*Joseph W. Ball*

PALACE SCHOOLS AND VILLAGE TRADITIONS: THE CERAMIC SYSTEM AS
INTERACTION TRACER

Still remaining is the question as to whether any ceramic "signatures" for Maya polities exist that can reliably be used in identifying these and their interactions. I suggest an answer lies in the probable existence of distinct "palace schools" of ceramic art as suggested by Reents' (n.d.) study, and the likely use of fine pottery vessels as presentation items and reciprocal gifts among elites, their subordinates, and peers. Archaeologists have been collecting the pertinent data for decades, but have only just recently begun to systematically organize and make use of these. Methodologically, what is involved is the identification of specific polychrome fineware ceramic groups with particular centers; redefinition of these groups as "*palace school*" *subcomplexes;* charting of their zones of high-frequency distribution (the probable internal circuits of the originating polities); and accurate plotting of their wider low-frequency occurrences. The latter should illuminate external interactions of types perhaps better interpreted through frequency distribution and occurrence context criteria than by mathematical modeling (see Ball 1983a for an extended examination of this topic). Significant differences should distinguish the occurrence contexts and frequencies of decorated vessels owing their distributions to homologous production, large-scale interzonal trafficking, or special occasion presentation and reciprocity. Comparative statements regarding Late Classic Maya pottery in general have not paid heed to such matters. Instead, gross distributions are identified and these are regarded as in some way reflecting local production, associated populations, the movements of these, or generic "trade." What is required here among other things is greater attention to discriminating among locally produced and circulated painted wares and their geographically more exotic counterparts. Failure to do this has resulted not only in slow progress toward recognizing the existence of local palace schools and community traditions of painted pottery production, but in perpetuation of one of the most frequently repeated "common knowledge" fallacies of Maya archaeology:

79–80) regard this as evidence for increasing numbers of (part-time) specialist potters through the eighth century, and Rice (1987b: 83) in particular argues an economic motive for this development. In her estimation, the regionalization of styles and localization of paste variants characterizing Late Classic southern lowland ceramic industries likely reflect adaptive diversifications on the part of economically stressed and sociopolitically insecure populations. I would agree with this as it applies to the *internal* heterogeneity of any single community or polity. I question its applicability to the region as a whole, however, and would suggest either decreasing interaction or increasing alienation as the mechanisms of cause at this level. John Henderson (personal communication, October 1989) rightly questions whether "increasing regionalization must imply alienation rather than merely diminished interaction." It need not; but in this case, at least, the point is moot: the eighth-century southern Maya lowlands *were* the scene of steadily escalating warfare, political rivalry, and political instability culminating in the massive regional sociopolitical and conjoined ceremonial collapses of the early through middle ninth century. What we see in the areal ceramic regionalization of this period was ultimately the product of these forces, whatever its actual raison d'etre might eventually prove to have been.

258

in fact, eighth-century polychrome-decorated glosswares, or, for that matter, *any* truly fine ceramic vessels of nonlocal origin are all but absent from the Barton Ramie settlement. They are not, as frequently repeated, almost ubiquitous among the housemounds and patio groups composing the site (e.g., Adams 1970: 496; Reents n.d.: 171). Better represented but still not overly abundant are bowls of Benque Viejo polychrome, a locally produced and circulated type of Vinaceous Tawny Ware. This does not currently appear to have been a palace school product, but more likely a "village tradition" one. I suggest the "village tradition" as a folk-order parallel to the "palace school" concept. Even less has been done to date on this level by Mayanist ceramic analysts, and other than calling attention to its existence and potential importance for examining extrapolitical patterns of ceramic interaction, I will defer its further discussion to another occasion.[14]

The point of all this is simply that both local community traditions and palace schools of ceramic fineware production appear to have coexisted in the Late Classic Maya lowlands. Their products circulated among different populations by means of differing mechanisms at both the local and larger regional levels. Those products can be utilized to identify not only socioeconomic producer communities, consumer communities, and the mechanisms interlinking these, but also the component member-centers of distinct polities and the lines of interaction among these. Ceramics should be able to provide a portable object complement to Emblem Glyph distributions in this respect. For this to be realized, however, will require greater efforts to identify accurately and associate correctly individual production schools and their centers. Greater precision and care in making comparative assessments will be necessary as well. Finally, it should be noted that unprovenienced vessels from private and institutional collections—no matter how finely painted or extensively inscribed—are completely and utterly worthless in this endeavor. Baldly stated, their only possible contributions can be those of distributional obfuscation and misrepresentation resulting from the efforts of dealers and collectors to enhance their cultural "pedigrees" and consequent dollar values or conceal their true origins. All such ascriptions should categorically be treated with unequivocal suspicion.

Clearly, not all Late Classic ceramic distributions result from the mechanisms responsible for the formation of complexes and spheres. John Henderson and Ricardo Agurcia (1987) have recently revived use of the *ceramic system*[15] as an analytical tool for identifying and describing the distributions

---

[14] Some very preliminary work with these two complementary constructs suggests that village tradition polychromes are characterized depositionally by wider geographic distributions, a broader range of contextual occurrences, and much higher actual frequencies than are those produced in palace schools.

[15] A *ceramic system* consists of a geographically continuous series of chronologically equivalent types sharing a significant body of stylistic modes involving such attributes of surface treatment and decoration as decorative designs, design elements, design and design element

*Joseph W. Ball*

of types that do not obviously do so (see also Urban and Schortman 1987). I suggest such systems can also function as ceramic tracers for more specific kinds of interactions than are represented by complexes and spheres.

To date there have been few efforts to employ or even define systems outside the southeastern zone. Impressionistically, it seems probable that one or more Palmar-series style-groups eventually might be tied to the Petexbatun polity and a Zacatel or Palmar-series one to Tikal (Coggins n.d.). Reents' (n.d.) work has likely correctly identified the central palace-school styles of the great regal-ritual city, Naranjo, and at least one affiliated emulator, Holmul. A Petkanche system has been assigned to either Altun Ha or Aventura by several investigators (Ball n.d, 1983b; Clarkson 1978: 97; Fig. 6), and an important Azcorra system encompassing both slipped and unslipped-burnished polychrome vessels has been tied provisionally to El Pozito in northern Belize (Ball n.d.; Fry 1983, 1987). What are involved in all cases are true artworks, the pieces so avidly sought after by both looter and collector today. As Reents (n.d.: 160–162, 170–173) correctly observes, however, these encompass considerable ranges of technical and stylistic quality reflecting highly varying individual abilities and likely varying producer-center wealth and prestige as well.

Although we know of such vessels best from looted burials, and a pathetically small number of archaeologically recovered tombs, there is no real reason to believe their presentation was restricted exclusively to funerary ceremonies (see Adams n.d. and 1971: 159–161; Coggins n.d.: 492, 568–585). I suggest they traveled more frequently on occasions during an individual's lifetime to symbolize and reaffirm ties between elites, their peers, and subordinates (cf. Stuart 1989: 158). The now-apparent restriction of such vessels to mortuary contexts is more an artifact of recovery chance than a reflection of systemic or depositional realities. It is, moreover, without question spurious. At Buenavista, while an exceptionally fine presentation vase apparently belonging originally to Smoke-Squirrel of Naranjo was recovered from a high status burial of early eighth-century date, fragments of several equally fine and finer vessels were recovered from a late eighth-century palace dump (Fig. 7).[16] These do not represent products of either the local Buenavista palace school or village tradition, and indirect glyphic evidence again strongly suggests some association with Naranjo.

The distinctive red-and-orange-on-cream hallmark of the eighth-century Naranjo polity has been recovered not only from centers once probably

---

execution, design field layout, and so on (cf. Gifford 1976: 12; Henderson and Agurcia 1987: 432–433; Urban and Schortman 1987: 341–344).

[16] Similarly, broken and discarded vases of Petkanche Orange Polychrome, a probable product of either the Altun Ha or Aventura Belize coastal plain polity, were recovered from the Bejuco-phase palace dump at Becan in the east central Campeche Rio Bec-Chenes zone (Ball 1977: 72, 177, fig. 29a).

*Pottery, Potters, Palaces, and Polities*

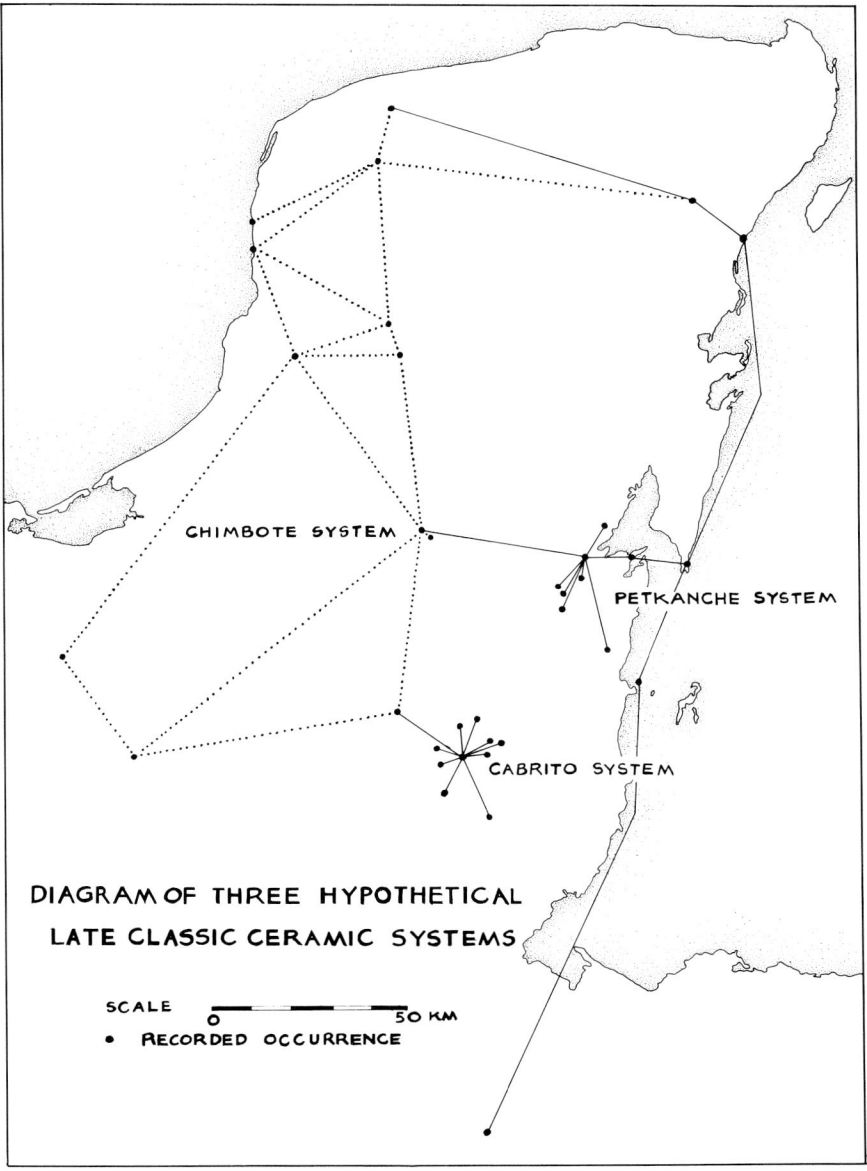

Fig. 6   Diagrammatic representation of three hypothetical Late Classic polychrome ceramic systems. The *Cabrito* and *Petkanche systems* most likely correspond to the distributions associated with two major palace schools. The *Chimbote system* more probably reflects the output and circulation from a number of interactive village traditions.

Joseph W. Ball

Fig. 7 *Chinos black-on-cream: variety unspecified.* Representative vessel fragments from a late 8th-century palace dump, Buenavista del Cayo, Belize.

within that realm, but also from those of neighboring allies such as Uaxactun (Smith 1955: figs. 2b, 73b2; Reents n.d.: 134, 195–196) and even from once-and-future rival Caracol (personal observation, March 1988). The significance of their presence in these cases remains unfortunately ambiguous.

Reemphasizing that ceramic systems have yet to be worked out for the Maya lowlands at large, I believe it nonetheless possible to presage a tentative partial outline of their likely overall traceries. Even now, some interesting parallels to the better-documented spheres emerge from this exercise.

The Late Classic southern lowlands are characterized by the presence of numerous distinct painted fineware systems. I suggest these correspond to numerous discrete palace schools (and village traditions) of production. Their existence and the dendritic networks of their distribution imply a highly fragmented sociopolitical landscape characterized by great need to symbolize local identities and signify formal ties of relation. The palace school style-groups emblematize specific centers: the ceramic systems identify their networks of dependence and alliance.

In the northern lowlands, a very different situation appears to hold true. Complex cross-cutting integrative systems *may* be present among Ticul group thinslate and Teabo redware pottery, but the need to visually distinguish multiple individual centers through the production of distinctive local fineware traditions does not seem to have been so strongly developed.[17] There is even some evidence of a gradual displacement of polychrome ceramic style-group subcomplexes along the southern margin of the Cehpech sphere coincident with its eighth-century emergence and spread. Ceramics provide less evidence of fine-grain regionalization and attempts to counteract this, greater indication of integration on a regional or areal scale.[18]

The northern deemphasis of painted wares may correlate with a lesser need for self-signification on the part of individual polities and centers than existed in the south, but just what the sociopolitical significance of this might be remains to be established. Otherwise, the polychrome systems represented in the northern area, like their ninth-century and later fine pasteware successors, appear largely to reflect long-range ties to production zones clustered on the southeastern and western edges of the southern lowlands. As I have previously commented, the real meanings and mechanisms

---

[17] Recently, however, Nikolai Grube (1990; Riese and Grube n.d.) has demonstrated quite convincingly on epigraphic and iconographic grounds that the so-called Chochola style of modeled-carved vases (see Coe 1973; Tate 1985) very probably originated at the far northern Campeche site of Xcalumkin. I suggest it comprised the Xcalumkin palace-school product and so potentially could be used to partly trace high-level elite Xcalumkin interactions in a manner comparable to that proposed for the southern polychrome traditions.

[18] There is some evidence that Cehpech should be divided into two typologically distinct geographic spheres (see Robles and Andrews 1986: 77–82, figs. 3.4, 3.5). These can be loosely associated with Coba and its neighbors in the northeastern peninsula and with the Puuc constellation of centers and their more northerly neighbors on the western side. See also note 12.

of their occurrence remain to be established through conjunctive assessments of source zones, overall distributions, frequency distributions, and occurrence contexts. Now-available ceramic data could begin to address these; now-available ceramic studies largely have not.

The existence of palace schools of ceramic fineware production and painting is in accord with the kinds of attached specialists and production activities to be expected within the systemic context of regal-ritual cities and centers. On the other hand, the presentation and exchange of emblematic sumptuary items are an important regular aspect of formal integrative and affirmative ceremonies not only in chiefdoms and segmentary states, but among even the most complex modern industrial nation-states. Their occurrence, consequently, is neither necessary nor unequivocally informative as to the nature of those political units within and between which it takes place. In fact, in the absence of broader complementary data, even determining whether patron-client or peer-polity type relationships are so reflected must remain largely speculative.

## SUMMARY

In the foregoing pages, I have examined some of the economic and sociobehavioral inferences to be drawn from what we currently know of Late Classic Maya ceramics, their depositional contexts, and their spatial distributions. Although the data these yield do pertain largely to the economic subsystem of Classic Maya culture, the patterns revealed are sufficiently clear and distinctive to make possible some reliable extrapolations to other interlinked subsystems. Summarized, these patterns conform essentially to what would be expected had Late Classic Maya central places functioned as regal-ritual cities and centers in the terminology of urban anthropologist Fox (1977). They also match the distributions to be expected within the political context of so-called segmentary states (Fox 1977; Southall 1956). Polities of this kind are characterized by weak or poorly developed central political authorities whose position depends largely upon their ideological prestige and correlative social status. They exercise little meaningful control over the more mundane day-to-day economic affairs of their dependent populations. Productive and distributive activities transpire largely outside of and peripheral to major central places, although the latter may enter into these to an extent comparable to that of other communities within their realms. They may also provide a permanent or periodic siting for their occasion (Fox 1977: 51; cf. Freidel 1981). Otherwise, the central places of any segmentary state are primarily economic consumers rather than producers, extractors, or redistributors of the society's wealth. Most production occurring within such centers involves "attached" or sponsored artisans oriented toward servicing the sumptuary needs of the ruling elite. Among the Classic Maya, we now know these sometimes were members of the royal household itself, but I suggest they also included especially adept and well-regarded "commoner" craftsmen. Only thus could have been maintained both the high-quality workmanship *and* the high-volume output clearly required to satisfy Late Classic Maya courtly needs.

Beyond this, our now-in-hand data suggest an industry involving spatially dispersed workshop households, hamlets, or village communities of marginally productive subsistence farmers supplementing their agricultural income by working as part-time potters specializing in the manufacture of workshop-specific ceramic groups. These ranged in nature and quality from unslipped wide-mouthed jars used for both storage and cooking to simple geometric and abstract design polychrome service vessels. By far their greatest numbers comprised plain, "trickled," incised, or otherwise surface-modified monochrome vessels ranging in form from cups, bowls, and vases to plates, dishes, basins, and jars. Such ceramic groups or "workshop traditions" make up the qualitative essence and quantitative bulk of most Late Classic lowland Maya pottery assemblages. Supplementing rather than complementing them are the finer figure-painted polychromes and surface-altered monochromes of what I have earlier in this paper termed "palace schools." In actuality, I suspect these were more inclusive in content than I have above suggested: monochrome serving vessels suitable for formal palace presentation ceremonies such as depicted on so many Late Classic vases (e.g., Coe 1973: 64–75; Coggins n.d.: figs. 119, 124a, 142a) must have been manufactured to specific standards best guaranteed by the patronage of sponsored or supported "attached" potters. Extensive excavations of use-related ceramic refuse associated with the Late Classic palace complex at Buenavista del Cayo clearly indicate that a consistent caliber of workmanship was required of vessels destined for courtly use. Of six spatially discrete and functionally varied Late Classic palace deposits recovered in toto, all reflected exceptionally high quality in both the production technology and external appearance of their ceramic contents. Similarly, vessels ultimately destined for gift-presentation or exchange, based on those few whose recovery contexts are known and so permit evaluation, plainly were created under circumstances other than those of a hungry peasant farmer's front porch and yard.

In sum, Late Classic Maya pottery manufacture comprised a complex and diverse industry with respect to products, producers, intended markets, and modes of distribution. Only now are we beginning to fully appreciate this and the fact that Maya ceramics can be used effectively for purposes other than merely those of dating and identifying intersite relationships. In closing, however, it warrants repetition and, I believe, reemphasis here that while any single data class—whether it be ceramics, lithics, monumental art, or hieroglyphic inscriptions—can individually help build toward an ever-more detailed and accurate understanding of Classic Maya civilization, its potential to do so is greatest and will be most fully realized only when it can be considered in terms of a known archaeological recovery context and so used conjunctively with other data to this end. Unprovenienced Classic Maya vessels, no matter how exquisite their execution or complex their depictive content, provide little other than personal gratification to their individual owners and a very small coterie of less than ethical "connoisseurs." In the interest of preserving at least something of the now rapidly vanishing nonrenewable resource that is the Maya archaeological record, let us condemn the unconscionable traffic in these antiquities that has grown so popular and acceptable in recent years. As with so much else, this resource is ours to use but not abuse: this generation has earned no right to ravage it.

*Acknowledgments* Both the form and content of this paper have benefitted greatly from the comments of my wife, Jennifer Taschek, who also prepared its several illustrations. I would also like to thank John Henderson and Fernando Robles for their helpful comments and suggestions. I hope I have not ill-used these too egregiously in the foregoing essay for which I do take full responsibility. The research reported on was supported in part by grants from the National Science Foundation (Award Nos. BNS-8310677 and BNS-8719157) and San Diego State University. Permission to carry out field work in Belize was graciously extended by Mr. Harriot Topsey (Commissioner) of the Belize Department of Archaeology, and by Sr. Antonio Guerra, on whose lands the Buenavista and Guerra sites are located.

# BIBLIOGRAPHY

ADAMS, RICHARD E.W.
- 1970 Suggested Classic Period Occupational Specialization in the Southern Maya Lowlands. In *Monographs and Papers in Maya Archaeology* (William R. Bullard, Jr., ed.): 489–502. Papers of the Peabody Museum of Archaeology and Ethnology 61. Harvard University, Cambridge.
- 1971 *The Ceramics of Altar de Sacrificios.* Papers of the Peabody Museum of Archaeology and Ethnology 63 (1). Harvard University, Cambridge.
- 1977 *Prehistoric Mesoamerica.* Little, Brown and Company, Boston and Toronto.
- n.d. Implications of a Maya Elite-Class Funeral at Altar de Sacrificios, Guatemala. Paper presented at the 33rd Annual Meeting of the Society for American Archaeology, Santa Fe, 1968.

ARNOLD, DEAN E.
- 1978a Ceramic Variability, Environment, and Culture History among the Pokom in the Valley of Guatemala. In *The Spatial Organization of Culture* (Ian Hodder, ed.): 39–59. Duckworth, London.
- 1978b Ethnography of Pottery Making in the Valley of Guatemala. In *The Ceramics of Kaminaljuyu, Guatemala* (Ronald K. Wetherington, ed.): 327–400. Pennsylvania State University Press, University Park.
- 1985 *Ceramic Theory and Culture Process.* Cambridge University Press, Cambridge.

AWE, JAIME J.
- n.d. Archaeological Investigations at Caledonia, Cayo District, Belize. M.A. thesis, Trent University, 1985.

BALL, JOSEPH W.
- 1976 Ceramic Sphere Affiliations of the Barton Ramie Ceramic Complexes. In *Prehistoric Pottery Analysis and the Ceramics of Barton Ramie in the Belize Valley* (James C. Gifford and Carol A. Gifford, compilers): 323–330. Peabody Museum of Archaeology and Ethnology, Memoirs 18. Harvard University, Cambridge.
- 1977 *The Archaeological Ceramics of Becan, Campeche, Mexico.* Middle American Research Institute, Pub. 43. Tulane University, New Orleans.
- 1983a Teotihuacan, the Maya, and Ceramic Interchange: A Contextual Perspective. In *Highland-Lowland Interaction in Mesoamerica: Interdisciplinary Approaches* (Arthur G. Miller, ed.): 125–145. Dumbarton Oaks, Washington, D.C.
- 1983b Notes on the Distribution of Established Ceramic Types in the Corozal District, Belize. In *Archaeological Excavations in Northern Belize, Central America* (Raymond V. Sidrys, ed.): 203–220. UCLA, Institute of Archaeology, Monograph 17. Los Angeles.
- n.d. Polychrome Pottery and Regional Exchange in the Early Classic Northern Maya Lowlands. Paper presented at the 43rd Annual Meeting of the Society for American Archaeology, Tucson, May 1978.

BALL, JOSEPH W., AND JENNIFER T. TASCHEK
- n.d. Secondary Centers and Classic Maya Political Organization: The

Mopan-Macal Triangle Project. Paper presented at the 54th Annual Meeting of the Society for American Archaeology, Atlanta, April 1989.

BECKER, MARSHALL J.
    1973    Archaeological Evidence for Occupational Specialization among the Classic Period Maya at Tikal, Guatemala. *American Antiquity* 38 (4): 396–406.
    1983    Indications of Social Class Differences Based on the Archaeological Evidence for Occupational Specialization among the Classic Maya at Tikal, Guatemala. *Revista Espanola de Antropologia Americana* 13: 29–46. Madrid.

BILL, CASSANDRA R.
    n.d.    Excavation of Structure 23: A Maya "Palace" at the Site of Pacbitun, Belize. M.A. thesis, Trent University, 1987.

BIRCHALL, C. J., AND R. N. JENKIN
    1979    *The Soils of the Belize Valley, Belize.* Overseas Development Administration, Land Resource Development Centre, Supplementary Report No. 15. Surbiton.

BISHOP, RONALD L.
    1976    Textural and Chemical Variation in a Numerical Study of Western Lowland Maya Ceramic Trade. In *Archaeological Frontiers: Papers on New World High Cultures in Honor of J. Charles Kelley* (Robert B. Pickering, ed.): 1–44. Southern Illinois University, University Museum Studies Research Records, No. 4. Carbondale.
    1980    Aspects of Ceramic Compositional Modeling. In *Models and Methods in Regional Exchange* (Robert E. Fry, ed.): 47–65. Society for American Archaeology Papers 1, Washington, D.C.
    n.d.    Western Lowland Maya Ceramic Trade: An Archaeological Application of Nuclear Chemistry and Geological Data Analysis. Ph.D. dissertation, Southern Illinois University, Carbondale, 1975.

BISHOP, RONALD L., GARMAN HARBOTTLE, AND EDWARD V. SAYRE
    1982    Chemical and Mathematical Procedures Employed in the Maya Fine Paste Ceramics Project. In *Excavations at Seibal: Analyses of Fine Paste Ceramics* (Gordon R. Willey and Jeremy A. Sabloff, eds.): 273–282. Peabody Museum of Archaeology and Ethnology, Memoirs 15 (2). Harvard University, Cambridge.

BISHOP, RONALD L., AND ROBERT L. RANDS
    1982    Maya Fine Paste Ceramics: A Compositional Perspective. In *Excavations at Seibal: Analyses of Fine Paste Ceramics* (Gordon R. Willey and Jeremy A. Sabloff, eds.): 283–314. Peabody Museum of Archaeology and Ethnology, Memoirs 15 (2). Harvard University, Cambridge.

BISHOP, RONALD L., ROBERT L. RANDS, AND GARMAN HARBOTTLE
    1979    A Ceramic Compositional Interpretation of Incense-burner Trade in the Palenque Area, Mexico. Brookhaven National Laboratory Report, BNL-26787. Upton.

BISHOP, RONALD L., DORIS J. REENTS, GARMAN HARBOTTLE, E. SAYRE, AND L. VAN ZELST
    1985    The Area Group: An Example of Style and Paste Compositional Covariation in Maya Pottery. In *Fifth Palenque Round Table, 1983* (Merle Greene Robertson and Virginia Fields, eds.): 79–84. The Pre-Columbian Art Research Institute, San Francisco.

BULLARD JR., WILLIAM R., AND MARY R. BULLARD
    1965    *Late Classic Finds at Baking Pot, British Honduras.* University of Toronto, Royal Ontario Museum, Occasional Paper 8. Toronto.

CLARKSON, PERSIS B.
    1978    Classic Maya Pictorial Ceramics: A Survey of Content and Theme. In *Papers on the Economy and Architecture of the Ancient Maya* (Raymond V. Sidrys, ed.): 86–141. University of California, Institute of Archaeology, Monograph 8. Los Angeles.

COE, MICHAEL D.
    1973    *The Maya Scribe and His World.* The Grolier Club, New York.

COGGINS, CLEMENCY C.
    n.d.    Painting and Drawing Styles at Tikal: An Historical and Iconographic Reconstruction. Ph.D. dissertation, Harvard University, 1975.

CULBERT, T. PATRICK
    1988    Political History and the Decipherment of Maya Glyphs. *Antiquity* 62 (234): 135–152.
    n.d.    *The Ceramics of Tikal.* Manuscript in author's possession. (in preparation)

DEMAREST, ARTHUR A.
    n.d.    Ideology in Ancient Maya Cultural Evolution: The Dynamics of Galactic Polities. In *Ideology and Cultural Evolution in the New World* (A.A. Demarest and G. Conrad, eds.). (in preparation)

FEDICK, SCOTT L.
    1989    The Economics of Agricultural Land Use and Settlement in the Upper Belize Valley. In *Prehistoric Maya Economies of Belize* (Patricia A. McAnany and Barry L. Isaac, eds.): 215–253. Research in Economic Anthropology, Supplement 4. JAI Press, Greenwich.

FOX, RICHARD G.
    1977    *Urban Anthropology: Cities in their Cultural Settings.* Prentice-Hall, Inc., Englewood Cliffs.

FREIDEL, DAVID A.
    1981    The Political Economics of Residential Dispersion among the Lowland Maya. In *Lowland Maya Settlement Patterns* (Wendy Ashmore, ed.): 371–382. University of New Mexico Press, Albuquerque.

FREIDEL, DAVID A., AND LINDA SCHELE
    1988    Kingship in the Late Preclassic Maya Lowlands: The Instruments and Places of Ritual Power. *American Anthropologist* 90 (3): 547–567.

FRY, ROBERT E.
    1979    The Economics of Pottery at Tikal, Guatemala: Models of Exchange

for Serving Vessels. *American Antiquity* 44 (3): 494–512.

1980 Models of Exchange for Major Shape Classes of Lowland Maya Pottery. In *Models and Methods in Regional Exchange* (Robert E. Fry, ed.): 3–18. Society for American Archaeology Papers 1. Washington, D.C.

1983 The Ceramics of the Pulltrouser Area: Settlements and Fields. In *Pulltrouser Swamp: Ancient Maya Habitat, Agriculture, and Settlement in Northern Belize* (B.L. Turner II and Peter D. Harrison, eds.): 194–211. University of Texas Press, Austin.

1987 The Ceramic Sequence of South-Central Quintana Roo, Mexico. In *Maya Ceramics: Papers from the 1985 Maya Ceramic Conference, Part II* (Prudence M. Rice and Robert J. Sharer, eds.): 111–122. BAR International Series 345. Oxford.

n.d. Ceramics and Settlement in the Periphery of Tikal, Guatemala. Ph.D. dissertation, University of Arizona, Tucson, 1969.

FRY, ROBERT E., AND S. C. COX

1974 The Structure of Ceramic Exchange at Tikal, Guatemala. *World Archaeology* 6 (2): 209–225.

GIFFORD, JAMES C.

1976 *Prehistoric Pottery Analysis and the Ceramics of Barton Ramie in the Belize Valley*. Peabody Museum of Archaeology and Ethnology, Memoirs 18. Harvard University, Cambridge.

GRUBE, NIKOLAI

1990 The Primary Standard Sequence on Chocola Style Ceramics. In *The Maya Vase Book, Vol. 2* (J. Kerr, ed.): 320–330. Kerr Associates, New York.

HAMMOND, NORMAN

1975 *Lubaantun: A Classic Maya Realm*. Peabody Museum Monographs 2. Harvard University, Cambridge.

1982 *Ancient Maya Civilization*. Rutgers University Press, New Brunswick.

HENDERSON, JOHN S., AND RICARDO AGURCIA F.

1987 Ceramic Systems: Facilitating Comparison in Type-Variety Analysis. In *Maya Ceramics: Papers from the 1985 Maya Ceramic Conference, Part II* (Prudence M. Rice and Robert J. Sharer, eds.): 431–438. BAR International Series 345. Oxford.

MARCUS, JOYCE

1983 On the Nature of the Mesoamerican City. In *Prehistoric Settlement Patterns: Essays in Honor of Gordon R. Willey* (Evon Z. Vogt and Richard M. Leventhal, eds.): 195–242. University of New Mexico Press, Albuquerque.

RANDS, ROBERT L.

1967 Ceramic Technology and Trade in the Palenque Region, Mexico. In *American Historical Anthropology: Essays in Honor of Leslie Spier* (Carroll L. Riley and Walter W. Taylor, eds.): 137–151. Southern Illinois University Press, Carbondale.

RANDS, ROBERT L., AND RONALD K. BISHOP

1980 Resource Procurement Zones and Patterns of Ceramic Exchange in the

Palenque Region, Mexico. In *Models and Methods in Regional Exchange* (Robert E. Fry, ed.): 19–46. Society for American Archaeology Papers 1. Washington, D.C.

REENTS, DORIS J.
    n.d.    The Late Classic Maya Holmul Style Polychrome Pottery. Ph.D. dissertation, University of Texas at Austin, 1985.

REENTS, DORIS J., AND RONALD L. BISHOP
    n.d.    The Maya Polychrome Ceramics Project. Paper presented at the 1985 Maya Ceramic Conference, Washington, D.C., 1985.

REENTS-BUDET, DORIS J., AND RONALD L. BISHOP
    n.d.    The Late Classic Maya Codex-style Pottery. Paper presented at the Primer Coloquio Internacional de Mayistas, Mexico, D.F., 1985.

REINA, RUBEN E., AND ROBERT M. HILL, II
    1978    *The Traditional Pottery of Guatemala*. University of Texas Press, Austin.

RICE, PRUDENCE M.
    1987a    Lowland Maya Pottery Production in the Late Classic Period. In *Maya Ceramics: Papers from the 1985 Maya Ceramic Conference, Part II* (Prudence M. Rice and Robert J. Sharer, eds.): 525–543. BAR International Series 345. Oxford.
    1987b    Economic Change in the Lowland Maya Late Classic Period. In *Specialization, Exchange, and Complex Societies* (Elizabeth M. Brumfiel and Timothy K. Earle, eds.): 76–85. Cambridge University Press, Cambridge.

RIESE, BERTHOLD, AND NIKOLAI GRUBE
    n.d.    Epigraphy of the Puuc and Chenes Archaeological Regions. Paper presented at the First Maler Symposium on the Archaeology of Northwest Yucatan, Bonn, August 1990.

ROBLES C., FERNANDO, AND ANTHONY P. ANDREWS
    1986    A Review and Synthesis of Recent Postclassic Archaeology in Northern Yucatan. In *Late Lowland Maya Civilization* (Jeremy A. Sabloff and E. Wyllys Andrews V, eds.): 53–98. University of New Mexico Press, Albuquerque.

SABLOFF, JEREMY A.
    1975    *Excavations at Seibal: Ceramics*. Peabody Museum of Archaeology and Ethnology, Memoirs 13 (2). Harvard University, Cambridge.

SANDERS, WILLIAM T., AND DAVID L. WEBSTER
    1988    The Mesoamerican Urban Tradition. *American Anthropologist* 90: 521–546.

SMITH, ROBERT E.
    1955    *Ceramic Sequence at Uaxactun, Guatemala*, 2 Vols. Middle American Research Institute, Pub. 20. Tulane University, New Orleans.

SMITH, ROBERT E., AND JAMES C. GIFFORD
    1965    Pottery of the Maya Lowlands. In *Handbook of Middle American Indians* (Robert Wauchope and Gordon R. Willey, eds.) 2: 498–534. University of Texas Press, Austin.

SOUTHALL, AIDAN W.
    1956    *Alur Society*. Oxford University Press, Oxford.

STUART, DAVID
    1989    Hieroglyphs on Maya Vessels. In *The Maya Vase Book, Vol. 1* (J. Kerr, ed.): 149–160. Kerr Associates, New York.

STUART, DAVID, AND STEPHEN D. HOUSTON
    1989    Maya Writing. *Scientific American* 261 (2): 82–89.

TASCHEK, JENNIFER T., AND JOSEPH W. BALL
    n.d.    Regal-Ritual Residences and Administrative Hubs: Differential Structure and Function among the Major Centers of the Upper Belize Valley. Paper presented at the 52nd Annual Meeting of the Society for American Archaeology, Toronto, May 1987.

TATE, CAROLYN
    1985    The Carved Ceramics Called Chochola. In *Fifth Palenque Round Table, 1983* (Merle Greene Robertson and Virginia Fields, eds.): 123–133. The Pre-Columbian Art Research Institute, San Francisco.

THOMPSON, J. ERIC S.
    1939    *Excavations at San Jose, British Honduras.* Carnegie Institution of Washington, Pub. 506. Washington, D.C.

TOURTELLOT, GAIR, AND JEREMY A. SABLOFF
    1972    Exchange Systems among the Ancient Maya. *American Antiquity* 37 (1): 126–139.

URBAN, PATRICIA A., AND EDWARD M. SCHORTMAN
    1987    Copan and Its Neighbors: Patterns of Interaction Reflected in Classic Western Honduran Pottery. In *Maya Ceramics: Papers from the 1985 Maya Ceramic Conference, Part II* (Prudence M. Rice and Robert J. Sharer, eds.): 341–395. BAR International Series 345. Oxford.

WEBSTER, DAVID L.
    1988    Copan as a Classic Maya Center. In *The Southeastern Classic Maya Zone* (Elizabeth H. Boone and Gordon R. Willey, eds): 5–30. Dumbarton Oaks, Washington, D.C.

WILLEY, GORDON R., T. PATRICK CULBERT, AND RICHARD E. W. ADAMS
    1967    Maya Lowland Ceramics: A Report from the 1965 Guatemala City Conference. *American Antiquity* 32 (3): 289–315.

# 9

## *Analytical Approaches to Late Classic Maya Lithic Industries*

DANIEL R. POTTER

HARVARD UNIVERSITY
AND
THE CENTER FOR ARCHAEOLOGICAL RESEARCH
THE UNIVERSITY OF TEXAS AT SAN ANTONIO

But seeing that they were without metals, God provided them with a ridge of flint near the range of hills, . . . from which they got stones for war and the knives for the sacrifices. (Diego de Landa [Tozzer 1941: 186])

### INTRODUCTION

FOR THE PRESENT PAPER I HAVE BY necessity thrown a "wider net" for my study, chronologically speaking, and as a result have hauled in data falling outside of the one hundred-year period upon which this volume focuses. Such license is perhaps justified by the likelihood that Classic (and particularly Late Classic) lowland lithic industries were well established and durable, and that radical systemic change in lithic economy was probably minimal throughout the period. Also, it is sometimes difficult to subdivide lithic assemblages among relatively fine temporal units, such as the eighth-century lowland Maya. The reason for this difficulty in fine chronological resolution is in part due to the tendency of lithic styles to be rather conservative relative to other artifact forms, such as ceramics. However, the traditional typological analysis approach is only one of many ways to gain understanding of Maya lithic assemblages. It is suggested here that only recently have we truly begun to explore the potential of lithic assemblage analysis in resolving a wide range of problems confronting Maya scholars today.

This study is not intended as an exhaustive summary of what is now known about Late Classic Maya lithic industries. Rather, my intent here is first to outline some of the current modes of analysis within Maya lithic research, and second, to discuss what recent lithic studies have taught us about the Late Classic Maya, particularly regarding the social and economic context in which Maya lithic economies functioned. I use the term lithic economy here as an explicit attempt to perceive stone tool assemblages as more dynamic entities than simple collections of artifacts showing greater or lesser amounts of stylistic consistency. As Landa noted (see above), the Maya were essentially without metals, and thus stone tools were of great importance at the interface between the Maya and their physical, social, and ritual environments. Archaeological tool assemblages passed through a complex system of dynamic stages from procurement of raw material (chert or obsidian) through manufacture, exchange, use, attrition, maintenance, and recycling, to final discard. Thus the important role of stone tools in Classic Maya culture, and the complex system through which tools passed in their functional life histories, can be described as aspects of Maya lithic economy.

Lithics are particularly appropriate to the larger study of Maya socioeconomy. Perhaps to a greater extent than any other archaeological material, lithic remains leave an indelible trail for the archaeologist to follow. From the quarrying of raw material through tool production, exchange, use, maintenance, and final discard, lithic assemblages leave sequentially distinct and characteristic residues at each stage along the way to the midden dump or structure fill context in which they are so often found by archaeologists.

The term "lithics" can apply to a variety of materials, including obsidian, chert or flint (interchangeable terms), jade, groundstone of various types, and limestone artifacts. This chapter has as its focus lowland chipped-stone industries, not because these are necessarily more important than other aspects of lithic economies, but because it is particularly these materials that have received the bulk of recent attention. Obsidian and chert are generally treated as two separate classes of artifact within the chipped stone category. Obsidian, a volcanic extrusive, was a resource prized by Mesoamerican peoples, including the Late Classic lowland Maya, who utilized this material for a range of artifacts including blades, bifacial tools, and eccentrics. Obsidian found in lowland sites has been traced to various sources in the highlands of Mexico and Guatemala, with the latter, less distant region being the more important. Of particular importance during the Late Classic were the Guatemalan sources at El Chayal and Ixtepeque, although other sources, such as Rio Pixcaya (also known as San Martin Jilotepeque), also provided limited amounts of material to the lowlands during the period (Nelson n.d.).

The second class of chipped stone artifact is interchangeably referred to as chert, flint, or chalcedony, which can be generally described as cryptocrystalline siliceous rocks. While the geological ontogeny of chert is still unclear, it occurs in sedimentary contexts and was locally available to many Maya communities in the karstic limestone lowlands (see Rice, Chap. 2). Both chert and obsidian exhibit conchoidal fracture, a characteristic that allowed ancient Mesoamerican peoples to fashion implements through a

## Analytical Approaches to Late Classic Maya Lithic Industries

variety of subtractive or reductive techniques. The reduction process entails the removal of unwanted portions from a mass of material through any of several techniques, including pressure-flaking as well as direct and indirect percussion. Examination of a number of Classic Maya assemblages leads me to believe that direct percussion was the primary technique for chert industries, while the pressure technique predominated in most obsidian blade industries.

### TRACING LITHIC SOURCES AND LITHIC EXCHANGE

*Obsidian*

While only rarely found in large amounts, obsidian is seemingly ubiquitous across the lowland archaeological landscape, most commonly found in the form of prismatic blades or blade fragments. Because obsidian has very limited areas of natural occurrence in the highlands, and can be accurately fingerprinted through compositional analyses such as X-ray florescence (XRF) and Neutron Activation Analysis (NAA), this glasslike material can provide excellent data on Maya exchange systems. Numerous studies in the past thirty years have established that obsidian sources were utilized differentially through time, and that major sources were linked to the lowlands through differing routes (Hammond 1972, 1976; Sidrys 1976; Nelson n.d., 1985). During the Late Classic period, it appears that El Chayal and Ixtepeque, located in the Guatemalan highlands, supplied more obsidian to the lowlands than any other sources. In two recent summaries of long-distance obsidian exchange, Fred Nelson (n.d., 1985) has proposed that El Chayal obsidian reached the lowlands through a riverine/overland route or routes. The general pattern of Nelson's Late Classic period obsidian flow model is dendritic in nature, with a central trunk or main route running south to north from the highlands to major Peten centers such as Tikal (Nelson n.d.: 44–45). From these Peten centers, smaller branch routes carried primarily El Chayal obsidian to the west, north, and east. The large centers of the "Core Area" were thus viewed as redistribution points not only for their own zones of political control, but for all lowland Maya centers. Norman Hammond has offered a contrasting model of "complementary" trade routes, with the riverine/overland route dominated by El Chayal, and an independent Motagua/Coastal Caribbean route that carried Ixtepeque obsidian (1972, 1976; Hammond, Neivens, and Harbottle 1984). He believed the two systems overlapped somewhat in the eastern lowlands, as indicated by sites such as Nohmul, which revealed a workshop with both Ixtepeque and El Chayal obsidian (Hammand, Neivens, and Harbottle 1984).

Recently, in a detailed analysis of obsidian distribution in Belize, Meredith Dreiss (1988) has found that during the Late Classic period Ixtepeque obsidian frequency was unexpectedly high, at 42% of her total sample. El

Chayal material held a small edge with 57%. Sites where Ixtepeque glass was particularly well represented were Colha, Wild Cane Cay, and Nohmul. Wild Cane Cay has become a focal point in obsidian exchange models not for its size or grandeur, as the site is wholly unimpressive in these terms, but rather because of its location, on a small island north of Punta Gorda, off the southern Belize coast. Wild Cane Cay was one of a number of island sites that sat astride the major coastal trade corridor linking the highland lithic resources of Guatemala and Honduras with the Maya lowlands. Surface collection at the site by Hammond revealed nineteen Ixtepeque and four El Chayal blades (Hammond 1976: 72). Dreiss (1988) thus argues convincingly that there were both Ixtepeque and El Chayal materials flowing through the Motagua/Coastal route, although Ixtepeque was dominant. Similarly, sites that are supposedly in the main flow of El Chayal obsidian, such as Tikal (Moholy-Nagy, Asaro, and Stross 1984), Seibal, and Palenque (Johnson 1976) also show a mixture of both El Chayal and Ixtepeque materials, although El Chayal is predominant. Thus it would appear that the "overlap" of El Chayal and Ixtepeque coverage of the lowlands may have been complete in the Late Classic, due to the likelihood that both interior and coastal routes were carrying obsidians from multiple sources, rather than one.

As a richer and more complex lowland obsidian data base emerges, I expect that current obsidian trade models will be deemed too simplistic, particularly as regards actual trade routes involved and the mechanism(s) by which the material was exchanged. Indeed, some researchers, such as Raymond Sidrys (1979), have preferred to utilize linear distance from obsidian sources to archaeological sites, rather than to attempt reconstruction of the turns and twists of intervening trade routes with meager data.

*Technological Analysis in Obsidian Studies*

Current problems in obsidian research are not entirely due to small samples and inadequate data coverage, however. There also exists a problem of analytical approach. For example, most lithic researchers have yet to critically evaluate the seemingly ubiquitous assumption that large sites were the primary obsidian manufacturing and redistribution centers, presumably guided by elites residing in these centers. A brilliant exception to this trend is John Clark's (1986) recent critical review of Teotihuacan's role in Central Mexican obsidian production, in which that great center is viewed not as a producer of vast quantities of obsidian goods for export, as has been argued (Santley 1983; Sanders and Santley 1983; Spence 1981, 1986; Santley, Kerley, and Kneebone 1986), but rather as a voracious consumer of obsidian goods being produced locally and at nearby sources, such as the green obsidian source at Pachuca.

Closer to the subject matter of this volume, Joseph Michels (1976: 109)

## Analytical Approaches to Late Classic Maya Lithic Industries

has exposed the same problem in a study of Kaminaljuyu's role as the primary producer and exporter of El Chayal obsidian. Initially he states: "From the beginning of the Late Formative (500 B.C.) to the end of the late Classic (A.D. 1000) Kaminaljuyu was a principal center of both blade production and blade consumption." One might conclude from this statement that Kaminaljuyu acted both as an important regional or interregional producer of blades, and also as an important consumer of that production. Later in his paper, this observation is clarified: "This may imply that blade production within the site of Kaminaljuyu was intended almost exclusively for local consumption. And that, especially from Middle Classic times on, factory sites which produced blades for export remain to be found outside Kaminaljuyu, in the northeastern dependent territories" (Michels 1976: 117).

Thus it would appear that there is little evidence for Kaminaljuyu craftsmen having participated in long-distance obsidian trade with the lowlands. Rather, their production was directed toward local needs, mirroring Clark's (1986) Teotihuacan model. Instead, Michels proposed the existence of satellite factory sites that took prepared cores from the El Chayal quarry and produced blades for export. This model is troubling also, as these sites have not yet been archaeologically confirmed in the Guatemala Valley, and also because it seems unlikely that obsidian *blades* were the medium for long-distance exchange. If such was the case, it follows that obsidian blade-size distance/decay functions, such as those observed by Raymond Sidrys for the lowlands (1979), would not exist. Also, several obsidian workshops have now been located at lowland sites, and all reveal that El Chayal or Ixtepeque cores were present and were the basis for blade production (Woerner 1980; Neivens and Libbey 1976; Ford n.d.; Moholy-Nagy 1976). I am not arguing here that Kaminaljuyu had no control over El Chayal production and exchange. I am suggesting that, based on currently available data, the locus(i) of El Chayal export production has not been established. Therefore, archaeological evidence that confirms the hypothesized linkage between such production and the elite of Kaminaljuyu has yet to be produced.

Another weakness in our analytical approach to obsidian production and exchange has been a lack of integration between compositional fingerprinting and technological analysis. While we do have some technical indices with which to measure obsidian assemblages (such as the Cutting Edge to Mass Ratio or CE/M; Sheets and Muto 1972), in many cases these are not utilized in a complementary way with sourcing data.

Even very simple indices such as obsidian blade width, when coupled with source information, could provide valuable insight into Late Classic obsidian exchange patterns. Experimental studies by Clark (1988: 211–219) have demonstrated a strong correlation between prismatic blade width and parent blade-core size. In one such experiment, a sequence of eight complete "rings" of blade removals was accomplished before a replicated core was considered exhausted. Blades were measured and these measurements were averaged within each of Clark's sequential ring groups. Because each "ring" of blade removals reduced the size of the blade core, subsequent blades removed from the core were correspondingly narrower. Figure 1 illustrates this trend, graphing data from Clark's Zacualtipan core reduction experiment (1988: 218). Given this simple relationship, it should be possible to approximate the size of Late Classic parent cores by using obsidian blade width. Even when composed of fragmentary blades, which are far more common than complete ones at lowland sites, most obsidian blade assemblages should be sufficient to give the archaeologist a reasonable measure of core size. In turn, I would predict that in the Late Classic lowlands, spatial trends in core size will reflect the degree to which Late Classic polities could access the obsidian trade routes discussed above. Following Colin Renfrew (1975), what type of exchange system might characterize long-distance Maya obsidian trade? One can envision several possibilities. "Down-the-line," "Central place redistribution," "Central place market-exchange," "Emissary trading" or "Freelance (middleman) trading," or various combinations of the above are some of the conceivable models that might be applied. Our present data seem to be exhibiting a gradual distance-decay function in obsidian blade size (and CE/M ratios: Sidrys 1979). The existence of such a pattern, if accurate, suggests that a "Down-the-line," or "traveling craftsman" situation may have existed in the Late Classic. However, choosing between these or other competing exchange models will not be possible in the lowlands until adequate technical information is on hand to supplement our growing body of sourcing data.

*Chert*

As work in the Maya area has progressed, it has become clear that, unlike obsidian, cryptocrystalline silicate rocks (alternately termed flint, chert, or chalcedony, and henceforth called "chert") are distributed widely but intermittently across the lowland landscape. In addition to this patchy distribution, chert exhibits a great degree of spatial variability in terms of its color, grain, nodule form and size, and other characteristics that determine its general suitability for human utilization. For the purposes of this study, this suitability for human utilization can be referred to as chert "quality." It will be argued here that the patchy distribution and variable quality of lowland cherts acted as "limiting factors" in lowland Maya lithic economics. While we do not at present fully understand how Late Classic Maya economic systems were organized (See McAnany, Chap. 3), it is clear that lithic economies were conditioned in part by local and regional factors of demand, access, control, and utilization of lithic resources and lithic production.

One problem that has confronted lithic researchers in the Maya lowlands and elsewhere has been the difficult task of accurately establishing the source

*Analytical Approaches to Late Classic Maya Lithic Industries*

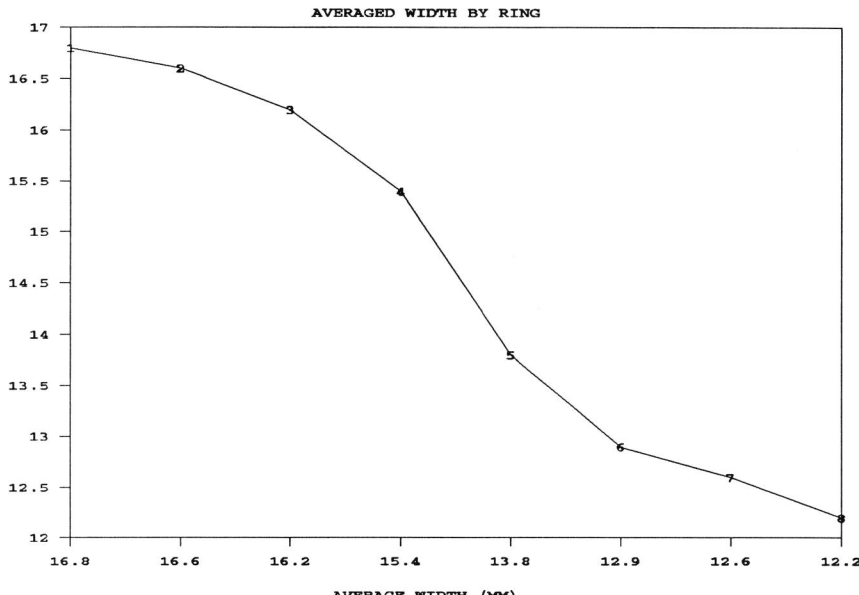

Fig. 1  Clark's Zacualtipan Core data; average blade width by ring number (width in mm).

of archaeological cherts from lowland sites. The ability to identify chert sources is, of course, particularly important when addressing the nature of Maya exchange. While visual distinctions exist between cherts from different localities across the lowlands and can be used with some success at a gross level, visual identification is subjective, not amenable to rigorous verification, and is therefore likely to produce rather untidy results. Frequently, researchers have described artifacts as being of "local" or "imported" origin, without any further definition or understanding of what either of these terms actually mean. Where do the fine-quality chert "imports" found at Late Classic sites come from? What is the range of variation in locally available cherts and what is their spatial distribution? Such questions have been nearly insurmountable in the past. Perhaps because of these conditions, the reconstruction of chert exchange patterns has been rather more difficult than those dealing with obsidian (Rovner 1981).

In this regard, Mark Tobey's (1986) study of chemical characterization of northern Belizean cherts based upon NAA is heartening and significant. Previous to Tobey's research, and as discussed previously in this chapter, chemical fingerprinting of archaeological materials through trace element analysis had been used widely and successfully on obsidian and ceramic artifacts. Attempts to apply these techniques to chert artifacts, however, had produced mixed results (Luedtke 1978), due to the greater chemical heterogeneity of the material.

In spite of these problems, Tobey has successfully isolated four distinct chert types/sources within the important northern Belizean chert-bearing zone. The site of Colha, an important tool-producing community during the eighth century A.D., was situated on two of these chert sources and Colha craftsmen utilized them heavily (Tobey 1986). Importantly, Tobey found that visual characteristics of northern Belizean cherts, such as color, fossil inclusions, etc., were not correlated with his NAA-defined groups.

Tobey's work has clearly demonstrated that lowland cherts can be geologically fingerprinted, allowing a new, more detailed look at Maya chert exchange. Several difficulties remain to be solved, however. Because the northern Belize chert samples analyzed by NAA produced groupings that are much less discrete than those of highland obsidian, it is likely that a very large number of samples will need to be processed in order to continue and expand on Tobey's analysis.

Susan Wurtzburg is also utilizing sourcing techniques (XRF and PIXE [proton induced x-ray emission]) in her ongoing study of Sayil lithics. PIXE has been found to be superior to XRF in distinguishing between chert types, and will be used to investigate differential residential access to imported vs. local cherts (Wurtzburg 1991). Although application of these techniques on a large scale will undoubtedly be a long and difficult effort, trace-element analysis of archaeological cherts now needs to be expanded to include assemblages from a wide range of sites throughout the lowlands. Sourcing studies will hopefully shed light on important regional and interregional trade patterns in this important resource, and will complement the technological studies now being pursued.

*Technological Analysis of Chert Assemblages*

Unlike earlier studies, which tended to be largely descriptive in nature and concerned with space/time systematics, recent lithic research has focused on a range of problems including lithic production strategies, the varying socioeconomic contexts in which lithic economies existed, functional analysis of tools, and replicative studies. Perhaps the most active and controversial of these topics relate to lowland lithic production systems. Such topics as degree of state control in production, the relationships between modes of production and the development of certain significant settlement forms ("Urban," etc.), and the degree of economic specialization represented by lithic remains and their contexts are involved here. I will touch upon this last point later in this paper, but first I would like to describe aspects of analytical and theoretical approaches to lowland lithic analysis. Historically, there is a long-standing descriptive tradition in lowland lithic

## Analytical Approaches to Late Classic Maya Lithic Industries

studies: Alfred Kidder's (1947) pioneering study at Uaxactun, Tatiana Proskouriakoff's Mayapan work (1962), Gordon Willey's (1965) analysis of the Barton Ramie lithic materials, and the work of William Coe (1959, 1965), are examples of this tradition, to list but a few. These studies outlined the distribution of major lithic tool forms across the lowland landscape and their occurrence within lowland prehistory. While lithic analysis has diversified in its scope and goals, descriptive studies remain an important pursuit, and are by no means complete as of this writing (cf. Sheets 1976; Hester 1976). Indeed, much remains to be worked out in the realm of time-space systematics across the Maya lowlands.

More recent analytical approaches include the typological and technological analysis of debitage (the residues of chipped-stone tool production) and manufacturing failures as revealing production sequences, or the technological trajectories employed by Late Classic stone tool makers. With this approach, we can now discern that significant differences existed in the ways Late Classic sites acquired and used chert tools. Recent analyses have provided considerable data on modes of tool manufacture at Colha (in Belize), Rio Azul (Peten), Becan (in the Rio Bec), and Xkichmock (in the Puuc region), all tool-producing sites. In addition, typological and technological analysis has revealed new information on conditions of tool use and recycling at *consumer* sites (sites that had no direct access to lithic resources). This approach is revealed in the separate studies of Harry Shafer (1983) and Patricia McAnany (1989) at Pulltrouser Swamp. In addition to analyses of archaeological assemblages, technological studies have been applied to modern Maya lithic assemblages with very significant results (Hayden 1987), and these contain important implications for any student of the Late Classic.

Functional analyses, including use wear and recycling studies, have been applied to assemblages with important results. Larry Kimball, Mark Aldenderfer, and April Hohol's (n.d.) microwear analysis of Maya lithics from the central Peten lakes region, Guatemala, and the work of Shafer (1983) and McAnany (1989) at Pulltrouser Swamp in Belize are examples. These analyses focus on how specific tool forms were used, what kinds of "contact" materials were being worked by stone tools, and how tool assemblages were maintained and curated. The former analytical goals of tool function and "contact material" allow us to at least partially reconstruct how the Maya interacted with their surrounding physical environment. The latter analytical goals of assemblage maintenance and curation inform us about the relative economic value chert possessed at varying times and places within lowland prehistory.

### THEORETICAL APPROACHES

If current theoretical approaches to Maya lithic assemblages can be characterized in such a brief treatment as this (a debatable undertaking), I would propose that current trends focus on the social correlates of Maya lithic economies. By far one of the most lively theoretical concerns in Classic Maya lithic studies in the last decade has been the measurement of economic specialization in lithic economies, and it is to this subject that we shall now turn.

Opinions vary markedly concerning the complexity of Classic Maya economic systems, and particularly to the degree of craft specialization present within these systems. Considerations of lithic economy have largely evolved within this debate. Shafer (n.d.: 12), Willey (1982: 215), and Shafer and Thomas Hester (1983: 539) have all advanced the idea that lithic craft specialization existed by Late Preclassic times and continued through the Classic period, at least in northern Belize. Their conclusions were largely based upon research at the site of Colha, northern Belize, where compelling evidence of specialized, intensive lithic tool production has been documented by Hester and Shafer (1983) and Irwin Roemer (n.d.). These and other authors have stressed the perception of Maya economies as complex regional or interregional systems, involving significant numbers of craft specialists.

Authors working in other lowland contexts have had strongly differing views. David Webster (1985: 389) has recently expressed the opinion that evidence for craft specialization has been so thin, this type of economy was simply not typical of the lowland Maya: "It is suggestive that . . . so few convincing data for any kind of specialization at all have emerged from excavations. The most plausible explanation is that there simply was not a great deal of highly organized economic specialization in Maya society." As with the authors of the Colha/northern Belize model, Webster's observations stem primarily from the intensive study of a single site, the great Late Classic center of Copan, and its surrounding settlement area. Here, convincing evidence for significant numbers of craft specialists has indeed been lacking (Mallory 1986: 152–157).

Which model is in fact representative of the Classic lowland Maya? The answer is both. As Sharer (Chap. 4) has stressed, "there is no such monolithic entity as 'Classic Maya social organization'—variation rather than uniformity characterized Classic Maya society." I believe this to be especially true of Maya socioeconomic organization. If Sharer's observation is correct—and I believe it is—it follows that data generated by any single site, such as Copan or Colha, cannot then be projected as a representative picture of panlowland Maya economy. It is only when a comparative approach is taken, and these sites are considered along with the numerous lowland economic studies now available (Turner and Harrison 1983; Turner 1983; Andrews 1983; McAnany and Isaac 1989, to name but a few), that we can begin to get an appreciation of the diversity of lowland Mayan economic structure. Thus, my intent here is to avoid the craft-specialization debate where possible. Since Maya economic systems were heterogenous, and not a single, homogenous system, it is conceivable that craft specialization was a significant economic factor in some contexts while in others it was not. I will present the Late Classic lithic evidence with an eye toward this potential regional variability. From this perspective, debate as to whether "The Maya Economic System" was capable of supporting substantial numbers of craft specialists simply ignores the reality of variable Maya economic systems.

I propose that three major factors caused this variable character of Classic Maya lithic economies. These include *demand, quality of resource,* and *manufacturing skills,* each of which will be briefly described here. Clearly, the strength and duration of demand will structure production and exchange rates, the intensity of assemblage curation and tool recycling. One condition influencing Late Classic lithic demand was a lack of raw material in certain parts of the lowlands. Pulltrouser Swamp is an example of this type of situation, as are the northern plains settlements of Dzibilchaltun (Rovner 1976) and Chichen Itza (Potter n.d.).

It also seems likely that intensification in separate but related cultural subsystems would have altered lithic demand rates: agricultural specialization, initiation or expansion of massive monumental construction activities, or population growth can be included here. Pulltrouser Swamp (Turner and Harrison 1983), of course, had a growing need for finished stone tools in order to build and maintain the extensive drained fields located there.

Lithic economy was also governed by the quality and quantity of the resource base. "Limiting factors" in terms of chert quality include nodule size, texture or grain size, and frequency of flaws, voids, or pre-fracturing within the material. Each of these factors effectively removed unsuitable portions of the potential resource base from development. The sites of Becan and Xkichmook provide good examples of Classic period lithic industries based on poor-quality resources, as will be described later in this paper.

Finally, technological and other social behaviors employed in the acquisition, production, and exchange of lithic implements require the effective transmission and preservation of certain skills and specialized knowledge concerning the resource and its utilization. In other words, sociocultural constraints and conventions would come into play in channeling knowledge concerning lithic procurement and manufacture, while socioeconomic and/or political networks would condition the flow of finished materials across the Maya landscape.

## LATE CLASSIC LOWLAND MAYA LITHIC ECONOMIES

In the light of the above discussion let us now look at some of the lithic evidence from the Late Classic Maya lowlands. I have included information from sites and regions which together form an approximate south-north transect across the lowlands. From south to north, these include northern Belize, the northeast Peten (Rio Azul), Becan in the Rio Bec region, and the southern Puuc region (Xkichmook).

Daniel R. Potter

*Colha and Northern Belize*

Located on the northern edge of the "Chert Bearing Zone" (CBZ) of northern Belize, the site of Colha was first investigated by Hammond's Corozal Survey (1973). Chert nodules outcrop at the site in abundance, with nodules up to 1 m diameter and 50 cm thick. CBZ cherts are of excellent quality for tool production, with colors including dark brown to honey-colored to gray, frequently banded.

Archaeological cherts at Colha appear in a number of primary and secondary contexts, but easily the most striking of these are the numerous chert workshops that occur throughout the site. More than twenty lithic workshops have been archaeologically verified as dating to the Late Classic (King, Hester, personal communications) out of the one hundred plus that are currently known to exist at the site. The term workshop is used to denote large, discrete concentrations of chert debitage, broken tools, etc., occurring as mounded accumulations, or as talus deposits associated with plazuelas. Workshops range up to 450 sq m in area and up to 1.75 m in thickness. It is important to stress that the workshops are not middens or soil deposits with high densities of debitage in them, as John Mallory seems to have interpreted them (1986). Rather, chert makes up over 99% of the matrix of these features (Shafer and Hester 1983, 1986).

Roemer (n.d.) has quantified debitage density in one Late Classic workshop (Operation 2007) to nearly five million pieces (larger than 3mm in size) per cubic meter. Also present within workshop fill are formal tools that have been broken in various stages of manufacture. During the Late Classic, these tool forms included the general utility biface, stemmed blades, bifacial celts, tranchet bit tools, and both bifacial and notched-blade eccentrics.

The workshops are thought to be the residues of standardized production techniques utilized by craft specialists. Evidence for these claims include standard recovery techniques from knapping errors, uniform reduction strategies, low incidence of errors, etc. (Shafer and Hester 1983, 1986; Roemer n.d.). In contrast to the Late Preclassic period, when workshop location seems weighted toward the site center, Late Classic workshops tend to be located across the entire Colha settlement zone. Other factors distinguish workshops of these two major periods at the site. These include a possible diminishing of overall production from Late Preclassic to Late Classic, a tendency for Late Classic workshops to be attached to residential architecture rather than standing alone, and importantly, the appearance of Late Classic workshops at other northern Belizean sites within the CBZ. While during the Late Preclassic workshops only occurred at Colha, Late Classic workshops are found at the small sites of Kunahmul and Chicawate, north of Altun Ha (Shafer and Hester 1983: 532–534). Shafer has suggested that these small sites, as well as Colha itself, fell under Altun Ha's political control during Late Classic times, but evidence for this intriguing possibility seems ambivalent at present.

A number of northern Belizean sites appear to have been consumers of Colha-produced stone tools. Hester and Shafer (n.d.) have referred to these sites as being located in Colha's "Primary Consumer Area." By far the best studied of these sites in Pulltrouser Swamp, a specialized settlement associated with a Y-shaped swamp system that feeds into both the New and Hondo Rivers. Survey and excavation at Pulltrouser in 1979 and 1981 confirmed the presence of drained agricultural fields associated with Preclassic and Late Classic Maya settlement (Turner and Harrison 1983).

Pulltrouser lies outside of the CBZ and thus is presumed not to have had direct access to this important resource. Excavations at Pulltrouser, however, have revealed the presence of chert tool forms that match exactly those being produced at Colha (Shafer 1983; McAnany n.d., 1989). However, the site's lithic assemblage differs significantly from Colha in that it is typified by a lack of primary production residues, including primary debitage, cores, manufacturing failures, etc. Rather, debitage from residences and field zones is associated with tool refurbishing (resharpening) and with the recycling of broken tools. Evidence for these activities includes heavy use wear on resharpening flakes and reworked or exhausted fragments of broken tools, primarily of the oval biface form that is so common at Colha. The presence of tools made on Colha/CBZ cherts, a complete lack of tool-production debitage at Pulltrouser, and an extreme degree of tool recycling within the Pulltrouser assemblage has led McAnany (1989: 341) to conclude that the site was a consumer of Colha lithics from Late Preclassic through Late Classic times.

Hester and Shafer (n.d.) have recently inventoried a number of additional Belizean sites that were also importing finished Colha tools. An abbreviated listing of these includes Nohmul, 38 km northwest of Colha, Santa Rita, 40 km northwest of Colha, where CBZ chert tools were likely imported from Late Preclassic through Early Postclassic times, and Sarteneja, 48 km northeast of Colha, where oval bifaces, macroblades, and general utility bifaces have been recorded. El Pozito, 31 km west of Colha, has revealed oval bifaces, general utility bifaces, tranchet tools, and blades, all with extensive evidence of recycling. At coastal sites on Ambergris Cay, 55 km northeast of Colha, general utility bifaces, stemmed blades, and recycled materials have been noted by James Garber. These data are presented in much fuller detail in Hester and Shafer (n.d.).

In most cases, northern Belizean sites possessing Colha/CBZ materials have revealed utilitarian tool forms, associated with land-clearing and soil-working tasks. At more distant sites outside of this zone, nonutilitarian artifacts of CBZ/Colha chert occur, with utilitarian forms rapidly dropping off in frequency. Nonutilitarian forms include stemmed macroblades and eccentrics of diverse form. I will briefly describe some of these contexts here, but for complete information, the interested reader is again referred to

*Daniel R. Potter*

Hester and Shafer (n.d.).

At Moho Cay, located at the mouth of the Belize River, Barton Ramie within the Belize Valley, and Ponce's site, central Belize, Late Classic stemmed macroblades, stemmed bifaces, and eccentrics of CBZ/Colha chert have been documented. In the Peten, at El Mirador, a blade core of CBZ material, as well as stemmed blades have been documented. At Tikal, stemmed macroblades of CBZ material are present, and within the Yaxha-Sacnab basins Aldenderfer and Rice have both noted CBZ chert artifacts. When viewed from the community and regional levels, Colha indeed appears to have developed methods of specialized production, the proceeds of which were exchanged with numerous sites within and beyond northern Belize.

*Rio Azul*

Within the greater Rio Azul settlement zone, workshops occur at El Pedernal, a very small satellite of Rio Azul less than a kilometer northeast of Rio Azul's monumental center (Black 1987). El Pedernal is notable for its evidence of a currently poorly understood form of intensive agriculture, for its large lithic workshops, and for its numerous chultuns. Black notes that chultuns (chultunob), presumably used for storage of agricultural produce, are much more frequent at El Pedernal than at the much larger site of Rio Azul, and that the latter site also completely lacks any type of lithic workshop. Time limitations prevent a detailed description of the agricultural evidence here, but Black suggests that the modifications involve some form of specialized preparation of the ancient ground surface for certain crop types, possibly cacao.

Although analysis of the El Pedernal data is incomplete, the workshops appear to be similar to those at Colha in size and depth. Five workshops have now been tested, all dating to Tepeu 2 times, with bifacial celts and adzes being the principal finished products. Little is currently known concerning the quality of the El Pedernal resource. Based upon my own observations of some of these workshop materials, I would characterize the resource as primarily light-colored, coarse-grained chalcedonies of intermediate quality. Raw nodule size is unknown at present. Interestingly, two of the five workshops directly overlie Late Preclassic deposits, in one case a Late Preclassic pyramid (possibly an elite mortuary structure?), and in the second, a workshop fills in a Late Preclassic limestone quarry. Presumably, these Late Preclassic features were part of a small, generalized Late Preclassic center. Black has proposed that during Late Classic times, El Pedernal settlement experienced a shift in function, probably initiated and controlled by Rio Azul. While in Preclassic times Pedernal had been a small center in its own right, in Late Classic times this general settlement picture changes into a specialized supporting community, geared toward intensive production of agricultural products and the tools needed for maintaining that production. Late Preclassic elite functions, represented by the small Late Preclassic pyramid noted above, were apparently centralized or absorbed by Rio Azul elites in the Late Classic, possibly in Tepeu 1 times. In summary, at Rio Azul, as we have seen at the sites of Colha and Pulltrouser Swamp in Belize, we see intensive production of stone tools in direct association with intensive agricultural practices.

Before turning to Becan, it should be mentioned that south of the site of Xpuhil, chert workshops were recorded by Jack Eaton (1982: 225) in 1971. The workshops apparently extend across a substantial area, within a CBZ extending to the Belize border. Although Eaton made a number of collections from these workshops, I have been unable to ascertain their current location. To my knowledge, Eaton's survey of nearly twenty years ago is the only work to be done on chert deposits south of the Rio Bec and north of Belize. It seems likely that this zone was an additional source of finished stone tools for an as-yet undisclosed area during Classic times.

*Becan*

Becan, of course, is well known, both in terms of its prehistory and the nature of its lithic resources. Here, chert nodules naturally occur in *bajo* settings, and in artificial chert rubble mounds of various forms. Prentice Thomas (1981) has recorded 155 chert mounds at the site, and these occur on ridgetops near *bajos,* usually in association with residential architecture. These features tend to occur within a kilometer of the defensive ditch surrounding the site center. The chert-mound features date primarily to the Bejuco (600–750 A.D.) and Chintok (750–850 A.D.) phases.

Marc Thompson's (n.d.) study of these features produced archaeological collections from half of these chert mounds, which he found to be composed primarily of unmodified nodules from 7 to 13 cm in diameter, with a mode of 8 cm. When we compare this nodule size with known Late Classic tool forms, it becomes quite clear that the bulk of these are simply inadequate for most formal tool types. Thompson also noted that "nearly half of the nodules were of insufficient quality for successful tool production" (n.d.: 34). Debitage collected from the same contexts, totaling 788 flakes, included a large proportion of decortication materials. Although Thompson proposes that the chert features and production residues indicate "mass production of stone tools at Becan" (n.d.: 71), and Rovner observes that there is a trend toward greater standardization in celt size and form in the Late Classic (1981: 173), such claims should be taken with caution. In my opinion, the low densities of production residues reported by Thompson suggest that the chert-mound features would be better described as loci of rather casual Late Classic quarry activities.

Both Thomas (1981) and James Stoltman (1978) have noted that tool-making occurred primarily in domestic contexts, especially within the hillside zone, presumably at rather unspecialized levels of production. Stoltman (1978: 24–25) also proposes that this is where the tools were primarily used, as more than half of the celts in his study were recovered from hillside houses or terraces, and "hoe-polish" was the most common wear pattern observed, suggesting soil-working was a primary task. Thus it seems likely that the terraced hillside settlement zone was the primary locus of tool manufacture, use, and maintenance, rather than the chert mounds themselves. As at Pulltrouser and El Pedernal, Becan exhibits a close relationship between local lithic industry and contemporary intensive agricultural system, in this case the extensive terracing within the Rio Bec region (Turner 1983: 96–97). As I have noted, however, intensity of production was limited at Becan, probably due to substantial amounts of poor quality chert, and the abundance of nodules of insufficient size.

*Xkichmook*

The small southern Puuc site of Xkichmook, which dates to the ninth century A.D. (Charles Lincoln, personal communication) is located approximately 50 km south of Oxkutzcab. Xkichmook's monumental center is situated on a small promontory surrounded by a deep-soiled, broad valley, which also contained scattered domestic settlement during the Classic. While the site was first investigated by E. H. Thompson nearly a century ago (Thompson and Dorsey 1898), Xkichmook was brought to my attention by Ruben Maldonado Cardenas, then Regional Director of INAH, Merida, Yucatan, after he and Beatriz Repetto-Tio had made a small collection of the site's plentiful lithic materials. Macroscopic examination of the Maldonado collection revealed close similarities with a significant amount of Charles Lincoln's excavated Chichen Itza lithic assemblage (Potter n.d.). Chichen Itza possesses no known locally available chert outcrops of any kind (Potter n.d.), and there is a strong possibility that the Puuc region supplied Chichen with this important resource. Investigations at Xkichmook by the author in 1986 and 1987 revealed a biface production workshop at Xkichmook, approximately 15 m in diameter, associated with a squared residential platform approximately 1.5 m high and 16 × 17 m in area. Surface collections of the workshop, collected in 1986, recovered a large number of manufacturing failures, primarily of very thin bifaces. The main cause of manufacturing failure appears to have been the presence of numerous calcitic impurities and empty cavities or "voids" within the material.

In 1987 research included test excavation within the known workshop and a survey and mapping program designed to locate and record any additional workshops at the site. Testing within the workshop revealed a depth of no more than 40 cm, and an estimated density of 850,000 pieces of macrodebitage (more than 1 cm diameter) per cubic meter. Note that unlike Roemer's work (n.d.), minimum size for the Xkichmook debitage count was set at 1 cm, rather than his 3 mm limit. Because this arbitrarily lowers the Xkichmook count when compared with Roemer's 5,000,000 pieces per cubic meter at Colha's Operation 2007, Xkichmook is at least roughly comparable to the recorded Colha densities (cf. Teotihuacan workshops at 10,000 for entire workshop; 500,000 for entire Tula excavated obsidian assemblage; 3,500 pieces per cubic meter in Mallory's Copan midden sample).

Examination of manufacturing failures from the excavation confirmed earlier impressions that considerable difficulties were encountered by flint-workers due to very frequent flaws and imperfections in the Xkichmook raw material. Manufacturing failures and debitage also gave some indication, albeit indirect, of raw nodule size. Inferred nodule sizes have not exceeded 12 cm in length from the workshop, and it is therefore likely that cobble size was probably prohibitively small for many tool forms. Although survey and mapping at the site revealed several blade production localities, these low-density lithic scatters are not classified as workshops and are primarily associated with small residences located on the valley floor. All remaining settlement at Xkichmook was devoid of substantial amounts of lithic production residues, and no additional biface workshops have been noted at Xkichmook.

A second workshop was encountered by the author and Pura Cervera Rivero at San Jose Xtunil, located about 4 or 5 km east of the small village of Salvador Alvarado. Here we recorded a talus workshop forming off the southwest side of two adjacent domestic platforms. The workshop was not tested, but measured 18 m in diameter, with an estimated depth of less than 50 cm. Debitage density appeared to equal that observed at Xkichmook. Several tool forms were represented by manufacturing failures, with the general utility biface form making up an estimated 75% of observed workshop production. As at Xkichmook, the workshop complex was located in an area of scattered domestic settlement. A brief inspection of this zone failed to produce additional workshops, or even appreciable amounts of debitage or other chart residues.

Additional sites within the Puuc chert-bearing area were also explored in 1987, but with no workshops (in sensu strictu) being recorded. Included here were the sites of Ucmil, approximately 8 km northwest of Becanchen with very large nodules outcropping nearby. Chert quarrying and reduction residues were extensive, but no workshops were encountered in our brief visit to the site. At San Martin Hili, very near Xkichmook, a large chert outcrop occurs within the valley bottom, with blade cores and blade production residues in profusion. No bifacing debitage was readily apparent, and no clearly defined workshops were noted. Chert outcrops are also known in the general area of Xkichmook at Hunto Chac, where large, unaltered chert nodules were encountered at considerable depths below the ground surface (Tomas Gallareta N., personal communication), and at Yalcoba Nuevo, a chert source of unknown character exists (Mario Magana, personal communication). These localities all demonstrate that chert resources are widespread in the southern Puuc, but that these display variable quality and nodule size. Despite the poor quality observed in much of the southern Puuc material, it is very likely that this is the region referred to by Landa as the "ridge of flint near the range of hills" in the quotation that opens this paper. The source Landa refers to presumably supplied much of the northern peninsula during Late Postclassic and early Colonial history. It is likely that the southern Puuc lithic sources also served the northern lowland plains centers during the Classic period as well. From the fragmentary evidence now at hand, however, it would appear that production at both the Xkichmook and San Jose Xtunil workshops was simply too low to supply the large consumer populations of the northern plain. Instead, these workshops primarily supported local consumption needs.

It is probable that the bulk of lithic production at both sites was localized to only one or perhaps a very small number of workshop/residences within each settlement. This latter suggestion is admittedly speculative at present, as our site samples are admittedly small, especially at San Jose Xtunil. As at Becan, production in the Xkichmook CBZ was probably hampered by small nodule size and abundant flaws within the raw material. However, so little is known about the surrounding region and its resources that better quality cherts may await discovery.

DISCUSSION

More than a decade ago, Payson Sheets wrote an article titled "Islands of Lithic Knowledge Amid Seas of Ignorance in the Maya Area," which gauged the status of lithic studies at that time. He noted of Mayan lithic studies that: "The needs for future research are numerous; in fact the needs are so vast and varied as to be discouraging, were it not for the fact that lithic analysis is rapidly becoming an integral component of Mesoamerican research programs" (Sheets 1976: 4).

Lithic studies have indeed expanded and diversified beyond the largely descriptive analyses so typical of earlier projects. Rather than offering broad generalizations concerning "The Maya Economic system" on a panlowland scale, economic studies (and particularly the analysis of lithic assemblages) are becoming increasingly sensitive to both natural variation in the character of critical resources, and to the varied social contexts in which these economies functioned. I have attempted here to present some of the variability within lithic economies of the lowland Late Classic period. My discussion has centered primarily upon such factors as the local or regional demand for lithic products, and the quality of available resources that were used to respond to that demand.

It is suggested that an important factor affecting demand rates (and therefore the intensity of production, exchange, and use of stone tools) is that of intensive agricultural subsistence strategies (Shafer and Hester 1983). This seems clearly to be the case in northern Belize, and at the diminutive Rio Azul satellite of El Pedernal, where intensive forms of agriculture and specialized lithic workshops occur in close juxtaposition.

Becan is an informative exception to the Belize/Rio Azul pattern. While the Rio Bec region is famous for its miles of agricultural terrace walls, claims of true Late Classic lithic "workshops" by Stoltman and Thompson remain unconvincing. I have suggested here that the reason for this seeming lack of production intensity at Becan is due to the lack of a quality resource base, both in terms of inadequate nodule size and a high frequency of poor quality native cherts.

Within the southern Puuc region surrounding the site of Xkichmook, very little is currently known concerning the intensity of Late Classic lithic economy. To my knowledge, the few data available to us presently have failed to indicate that intensive forms of agricultural economy were practiced here, although Nicholas Dunning (n.d.) notes that Puuc settlement was largely governed by the location of high-quality agricultural soils and may have exported agricultural surpluses to northern plains settlements. Our equally slim lithic data for the region suggest that the small workshops at the sites of Xkichmook and San Jose Xtunil represent the possibility of a minor form of specialized production, but not in a form comparable to Colha or Rio Azul. As at Becan, the poor quality of the chert resource at these two sites were clearly a major obstacle to successful fabrication of even modest quantities of finished tools.

An additional observation can be made concerning the relationship between more complex or specialized lithic economies and site size. Without exception, lithic workshops occurred during the Classic period at sites that were not occupying primary or even secondary positions within their regional settlement hierarchies. In Belize, Colha has been ranked by Richard Adams (1982) on the fifth of eight tiers of settlement rank in northern Belize. In the northeast Peten, El Pedernal, the diminutive satellite settlement less than 1 km from Rio Azul, fails to make it even to Adam's (1987) bottom rank of Peten settlement. Clearly this settlement was under the political sway of its much larger neighbor. In the southern Puuc, Xkichmook is tentatively assigned an intermediate but respectable third level rank by Dunning (n.d.). It is, however, dwarfed by the major northern Puuc centers such as Uxmal, Kabah, etc., and by no means can be considered a "large" center. San Jose Xtunil appears to be simply an area of domestic settlement without monumental architecture, and might mirror El Pedernal in its position within the regional settlement hierarchy.

To some, the association of small sites and intensive or specialized economies in a single phrase is contradictory. However, while it is undeniable that site size correlates with political importance, size was *not* the primary determinant of whether a settlement would develop a complex lithic economy. Thus, I suggest that the precondition of large site size as the primary locus of economic complexity needs close scrutiny. Such an approach may bias economic studies by understating the importance of smaller Late Classic Maya settlements (King and Potter n.d.) and of regional systems, which integrated large and small settlements alike.

In summation, new analytical techniques, applied to a large and growing data base are changing our perspectives on Classic Maya lithic economies. Trace-element studies and use-wear analysis are labor-, time-, and money-intensive forms of analysis, but hold great promise in the investigation of lithic production, exchange, and use patterns. As more lithic data become available, lowland Late Classic lithic economy is slowly being revealed at the levels of the household, the site, and also as a regional system, at times involving a number of functionally distinct settlements, as well as cross-cutting levels within regional settlement hierarchies. As this diversifying trend continues, we can expect that lithic research will provide both data and conceptual models with ever-widening applications to Maya studies.

## BIBLIOGRAPHY

ADAMS, R.E.W
- 1982 Rank Size Analysis of Northern Belize Maya Sites. In *Archaeology At Colha, Belize* (Thomas Hester, Harry Shafer, and Jack Eaton, eds.): 60–64. Center for Archaeological Research, The University of Texas at San Antonio, and Centro Studi e Ricerche Ligabue, Venice.
- 1987 *Rio Azul Reports, No. 3: The 1985 Season* (Ed.). Center for Archaeological Research, University of Texas at San Antonio.

ANDREWS, ANTHONY P.
- 1983 *Maya Salt Production and Trade*. University of Arizona Press, Tucson.

BLACK, STEPHEN L.
- 1987 Settlement Pattern Survey and Testing, 1985. In *Rio Azul Reports, No. 3: The 1985 Season* (R. E. W. Adams, ed.): 183–221. Center for Archaeological Research, University of Texas at San Antonio.

CLARK, JOHN E.
- 1986 From Mountains to Molehills: A Critical Review of Teotihuacan's Obsidian Industry. In *Economic Aspects of Prehispanic Highland Mexico* (Barry L. Issac, ed.): 23–74. *Research in Economic Anthropology: A Research Annual: Supplement 2*. JAI Press Inc., Greenwich, Conn.
- 1988 *The Lithic Artifacts of La Libertad, Chiapas, Mexico: An Economic Perspective*. Papers of the New World Archaeological Foundation, No. 52. Brigham Young University, Provo.

COE, WILLIAM R.
- 1959 *Piedras Negras Archaeology: Artifacts, Caches and Burials*. Museum Monograph Series. University of Pennsylvania, Philadelphia.
- 1965 Artifacts of the Maya Lowlands. In *Handbook of Middle American Indians, Vol. 3: Archaeology of Southern Mesoamerica, Part 2* (Gordon R. Wiley, ed.): 594–602. University of Texas Press, Austin.

DREISS, MEREDITH L.
- 1988 *Obsidian at Colha, Belize: A Technological Analysis and Distributional Study Based on Trace Element Data*. Papers of the Colha Project, Vol. 4. Published jointly by the Texas Archaeological Research Laboratory, University of Texas at Austin, and the Center for Archaeological Research, University of Texas at San Antonio.

DUNNING, NICHOLAS P.
- n.d. The Geography of Power in the Terminal Classic Northern Puuc, Yucatan. Version 2. Paper presented at the 54th Meeting of the Society for American Archaeology, April 1989.

EATON, JACK
- 1982 Chert Deposits and Lithic Workshops in the Rio Bec Region. In *Archaeology at Colha, Belize: The 1981 Interim Report* (Thomas Hester, Harry Shafer, and Jack Eaton, eds.): 225–228. Center for Archaeological Research, University of Texas at San Antonio, and Centro Studi e Ricerche Ligabue, Venice.

FORD, ANABEL
    n.d. The Economic and Political Implications of Long Distance Trade in the Central Maya Lowlands: Analysis of Obsidian from BRASS. Grant Proposal #47.051 to the National Science Foundation. University of California, Santa Barbara, 1986.

HAMMOND, NORMAN
    1972 Obsidian Trade Routes in the Maya Area. *Science* 178: 1092–1093.
    1973 British Museum-Cambridge University Corozal Project 1973 Interim Report. Cambridge University, Centre of Latin American Studies, Cambridge.
    1976 Maya Obsidian Trade in Southern Belize. In *Maya Lithic Studies: Papers from the 1976 Belize Field Symposium* (Thomas Hester and Norman Hammond, eds.): 71–82. Center for Archaeological Research, University of Texas at San Antonio.

HAMMOND, NORMAN, M.D. NEIVENS, AND G. HARBOTTLE
    1984 Trace Element Analysis of Obsidian Artifacts from a Classic Maya Residential Group at Nohmul, Belize. *American Antiquity* 49: 815–820.

HAYDEN, BRIAN
    1987 Past to Present Uses of Stone Tools in the Maya Highlands. In *Lithic Studies among the Contemporary Highland Maya* (Brian Hayden, ed.): 160–234. University of Arizona Press, Tucson.

HESTER, THOMAS R.
    1976 Belize Lithics: Forms and Functions. In *Maya Lithic Studies: Papers from the 1976 Belize Field Symposium* (Thomas Hester and Norman Hammond, eds.): 11–20. Center for Archaeological Research, University of Texas at San Antonio.

HESTER, THOMAS R., AND NORMAN HAMMOND (EDS.)
    1976 *Maya Lithic Studies: Papers from the 1976 Belize Field Symposium.* Center for Archaeological Research, University of Texas at San Antonio.

HESTER, THOMAS R., AND HARRY J. SHAFER
    n.d. The Ancient Maya Craft Community at Colha, Belize and its External Relationships. Paper presented at the 54th Annual Meeting of the Society for American Archaeology, Atlanta, 1989.

JOHNSON, JAY K.
    1976 Long Distance Obsidian Trade: New Data from the Western Maya Periphery. In *Maya Lithic Studies: Papers from the 1976 Belize Field Symposium* (Thomas Hester and Norman Hammond, eds.): 83–90. Center for Archaeological Research, University of Texas at San Antonio.

KIDDER, ALFRED
    1947 *The Artifacts of Uaxactun, Guatemala.* Carnegie Institute of Washington, Publication 576. Washington, D.C.

KIMBALL, LARRY R., MARK S. ALDENDERFER, AND APRIL S. HOHOL
    n.d. Microwear Analysis of Maya Lithic Artifacts from Rural/Center Contexts in the Central Peten Lakes Region, Guatemala. Paper presented at the 51st Meeting of the Society for American Archaeology, New Orleans, 1986.

KING, ELEANOR, AND DANIEL R. POTTER
    n.d.    Small Sites in Prehistoric Maya Socioeconomic Organization: A Perspective from Colha, Belize. (in press)

LUEDTKE, BARBARA E.
    1978    Chert Sources and Trace-Element Analysis. *American Antiquity* 43: 413–423.

MALLORY, JOHN K.
    1986    "Workshops" and "Specialized Production" in the Production of Maya Chert Tools: A Response to Shafer and Hester. *American Antiquity* 51: 152–157.

McANANY, PATRICIA
    1989    Stone-Tool Production and Exchange in the Eastern Maya Lowlands: The Consumer Perspective from Pulltrouser Swamp, Belize. *American Antiquity* 54: 332–346.
    1991    Structure and Dynamics of Intercommunity Exchange. In *Maya Stone Tools: Selected Papers from the Second Maya Lithic Conference* (Thomas R. Hester and Harry J. Shafer, eds.): 271–293. Prehistory Press, Madison.
    n.d.    Lithic Technology and Exchange among Wetland Farmers of the Eastern Maya Lowlands. Ph.D. dissertation, University of New Mexico, 1986.

McANANY, PATRICIA A., AND BARRY L. ISAAC
    1989    *Prehistoric Maya Economies of Belize.* Research in Economic Anthropology: A Research Annual. Supplement 4. JAI Press, Inc., Greenwich, Conn.

MICHELS, JOSEPH W.
    1976    Some Sociological Observations on Obsidian Production at Kaminaljuyu, Guatemala. In *Maya Lithic Studies: Papers from the 1976 Belize Field Symposium* (Thomas Hester and Norman Hammond, eds.): 109–118. Center for Archaeological Research, University of Texas at San Antonio.

MOHOLY-NAGY, HATTULA
    1976    Spatial Distribution of Flint and Obsidian Artifacts at Tikal, Guatemala. In *Maya Lithic Studies: Papers from the 1976 Belize Field Symposium.* (Thomas Hester and Norman Hammond, eds.): 91–108. Center for Archaeological Research, University of Texas at San Antonio.

MOHOLY-NAGY, HATTULA, FRANK ASARO, AND FRED STROSS
    1984    Tikal Obsidian: Sources and Typology. *American Antiquity* 49: 104–117.

NEIVENS, MARY, AND DAVID LIBBEY
    1976    An Obsidian Workshop at El Pozito, Northern Belize. In *Maya Lithic Studies: Papers from the 1976 Belize Field Symposium* (Thomas Hester and Norman Hammond, eds.): 137–150. Center for Archaeological Research, University of Texas at San Antonio.

NELSON, FRED W.
    1985    Summary of the Results of Analysis of Obsidian Artifacts from the Maya Lowlands. *Scanning Electron Microscopy* 2: 631–649.
    n.d.    Obsidian Exchange Networks in the Maya Lowlands. Unpublished paper on file with author, 1980.

POTTER, DANIEL R.
   n.d. Chichen Itza Lithic Project: Interim Report, March 15, 1987. Unpublished paper on file with author.

PROSKOURIAKOFF, TATIANA
   1962 The Artifacts of Mayapan. In *Mayapan, Yucatan, Mexico* (H. E. D. Pollock, ed.): 87–163. Carnegie Institute of Washington, Publication 619. Washington, D.C.

RENFREW, COLIN
   1975 Trade as Action at a Distance: Question of Integration and Communication. In *Ancient Civilization and Trade* (Jeremy Sabloff and C. C. Lamberg-Karlovsky, eds.): 3–59. University of New Mexico Press, Albuquerque.

ROEMER, IRWIN
   n.d. A Late Classic Maya Lithic Workshop at Colha, Belize. M.A. thesis, Texas A&M University, 1984.

ROVNER, IRWIN
   1976 Pre-Columbian Maya Development of Utilitarian Lithic Industries: The Broad Perspective from Yucatan. In *Maya Lithic Studies: Papers from the 1976 Belize Field Symposium*. (Thomas Hester and Norman Hammond, eds.): 41–54. Center for Archaeological Research, University of Texas at San Antonio.
   1981 Maya Lowlands Chert: Variations in Local Industries and Regional Exchange Systems. *Revista Mexicana de Estudios Antropologicos* 27: 167–181.

SANDERS, WILLIAM T., AND ROBERT SANTLEY
   1983 A Tale of Three Cities: Energetics and Urbanization in Pre-Hispanic Central Mexico. In *Prehistoric Settlement Patterns: Essays in Honor of Gordon R. Willey* (E. Z. Vogt and R. M. Leventhal, eds.): 243–291. University of New Mexico Press, Albuquerque.

SANTLEY, ROBERT S.
   1983 Obsidian Trade and Teotihuacan Influence in Mesoamerica. In *Interdisciplinary Approaches to the Study of Highland-Lowland Interaction* (Arthur Miller, ed.): 69–124. Dumbarton Oaks, Washington, D.C.

SANTLEY, ROBERT S., JANET M. KERLEY, AND RONALD R. KNEEBONE
   1986 Obsidian Working, Long-Distance Exchange, and the Politico-Economic Organization of Early States in Central Mexico. In *Economic Aspects of Prehispanic Highland Mexico* (Barry L. Isaac, ed.): 23–74. *Research in Economic Anthropology: A Research Annual: Supplement 2*. JAI Press Inc., Greenwich, Conn.

SHAFER, HARRY J.
   1983 The Lithic Artifacts of the Pulltrouser Area: Settlements and Fields. In *Pulltrouser Swamp: Ancient Maya Habitat, Agriculture, and Settlement in Northern Belize* (B. L. Turner II and Peter D. Harrison, eds.): 212–245. University of Texas Press, Austin.
   n.d. Maya Lithic Craft Specialization in Northern Belize. Paper presented at the 80th Annual Meeting of the American Anthropological Association, Los Angeles, 1981.

SHAFER, HARRY J., AND THOMAS R. HESTER
    1983    Ancient Maya Chert Workshops in Northern Belize, Central America. *American Antiquity* 48: 519–543.
    1986    Maya Stone-Tool Craft Specialization and Production at Colha, Belize; Reply to Mallory. *American Antiquity* 51 (1): 148–166.

SHEETS, PAYSON
    1976    Island of Lithic Knowledge amid Seas of Ignorance in the Maya Area. In *Maya Lithic Studies: Papers from the 1976 Belize Field Symposium* (Thomas Hester and Norman Hammond, eds.): 1–10. Center for Archaeological Research, University of Texas at San Antonio.

SHEETS, PAYSON, AND GUY MUTO
    1972    Pressure Blades and Total Cutting Edge: An Experiment in Lithic Technology. *Science* 175: 623–634.

SIDRYS, RAYMOND V.
    1976    Classical Maya Obsidian Trade. *American Antiquity* 41: 449–464.
    1979    Supply and Demand among the Classic Maya. *Current Anthropology* 20 (3): 594–597.

SPENCE, MICHAEL W.
    1981    Obsidian Production and the State in Teotihuacan. *American Antiquity* 46: 769–788.
    1986    Locational Analysis of Craft Specialization Areas in Teotihuacan. In *Economic Aspects of Prehispanic Highland Mexico* (Barry L. Isaac, ed.): 23–74. *Research in Economic Anthropology: A Research Annual: Supplement 2.* JAI Press Inc., Greenwich, Conn.

STOLTMAN, JAMES B.
    1978    *Lithic Artifacts from a Complex Society: The Chipped Stone Tools of Becan, Campeche, Mexico.* Middle American Research Institute, Occasional Paper 2. Tulane University, New Orleans.

THOMAS, PRENTICE M.
    1981    *Prehistoric Maya Settlement Patterns at Becan, Campeche, Mexico.* Middle American Research Institute, Publication 45. Tulane University, New Orleans.

THOMPSON, EDWARD H., AND GEORGE A. DORSEY
    1898    Ruins of Xkichmook, Yucatan. *Field Columbian Museum, Anthropology Series* 2: 209–229.

THOMPSON, MARC
    n.d.    Chert Mounds of Becan, Campeche, Mexico: Evidence of Intensive Stone Tool Production by Late Classic Maya. M.A. Thesis, University of the Americas, Cholula, Puebla, Mexico. 1981.

TOBEY, MARK HATHAWAY
    1986    *Trace Element Investigations of Maya Chert from Belize.* Papers of the Colha Project, Vol. 1. Center for Archaeological Research, University of Texas at San Antonio.

TOZZER, ALFRED M.
    1941    *Landa's Relacion de las cosas de Yucatan.* Papers of the Peabody Museum of Archaeology and Ethnology 28. Harvard University, Cambridge.

Turner II, B.L.
  1983  *Once Beneath the Forest: Prehistoric Terracing in the Rio Bec Region of the Maya Lowlands.* Dellplain Series in Geography. Westview Press, Boulder.

Turner II, B.L., and Peter D. Harrison
  1983  *Pulltrouser Swamp: Ancient Maya Habitat, Agriculture, and Settlement in Northern Belize.* University of Texas Press, Austin.

Webster, David
  1985  Surplus, Labor, and Stress in Late Classic Maya Society. *Journal of Anthropological Research* 41: 375–399.

Willey, Gordon R.
  1982  Maya Archaeology. *Science* 215: 260–267.

Willey, Gordon R., William R. Bullard, Jr., John B. Glass, and James C. Gifford
  1965  *Prehistoric Maya Settlements in the Belize Valley.* Papers of the Peabody Museum of Archaeology and Ethnology 54. Harvard University, Cambridge.

Woerner, Michael
  1980  Descriptive Analysis of the Obsidian from Operation 2012, 1980 Season. In *The Colha Project: Second Season, 1980 Interim Report* (Thomas Hester, Jack Eaton and Harry Shafer, eds.): 301–312. Center for Archaeological Research, University of Texas at San Antonio.

Wurtzburg, Susan
  1991  Applied X-Ray Fluorescence: Sourcing Chert Artifacts from Sayil, Yucatan. *Mexicon* 13: 92–95.

## 10

## *Architecture and Social Change in Late Classic Maya Society: The Evidence from Mundo Perdido, Tikal*

### JUAN PEDRO LAPORTE
UNIVERSIDAD DE SAN CARLOS, GUATEMALA

THE ARCHITECTURE OF LATE CLASSIC TIKAL is well known from archaeological studies conducted by several projects in different areas of the site. The best examples of the monumentality of Tikal are the North Acropolis—Great Plaza, Central Acropolis, several Twin-Pyramid Groups, and the temple pyramids that have defined architectural style of Tikal (Loten n.d.; Harrison n.d.; Jones n.d.; Coe 1963; Coggins n.d.; Dahlin 1986; Orrego and Larios 1983). This situation permits us to eliminate the description of the better known buildings and to analyze architectural compounds not studied before, focusing on their function in the eighth century, and looking for evidence of social and political change in the city during the period considered the most stable in the cultural history of the central Maya lowlands.

This analysis focuses more on the function of the architectural complexes than on stylistic modifications. In this functional analysis it is necessary to understand the structure of the sites in order to establish hierarchies between centers and to determine the changes in political affiliations that occurred over time.

For this analysis, data are presented from two recent archaeological projects in Peten. The first set of data is from the complex known as Mundo Perdido in Tikal (Laporte and Fialko n.d.), and the second, for comparative purposes, is from the program that is currently under way in the northern part of the Maya Mountains (Laporte and Torres n.d.).

### MUNDO PERDIDO DURING THE PRECLASSIC AND EARLY CLASSIC

Mundo Perdido is a ceremonial area in the southwest sector of Tikal (Carr and Hazard 1961; Fig. 1). The excavations carried out by the Proyecto

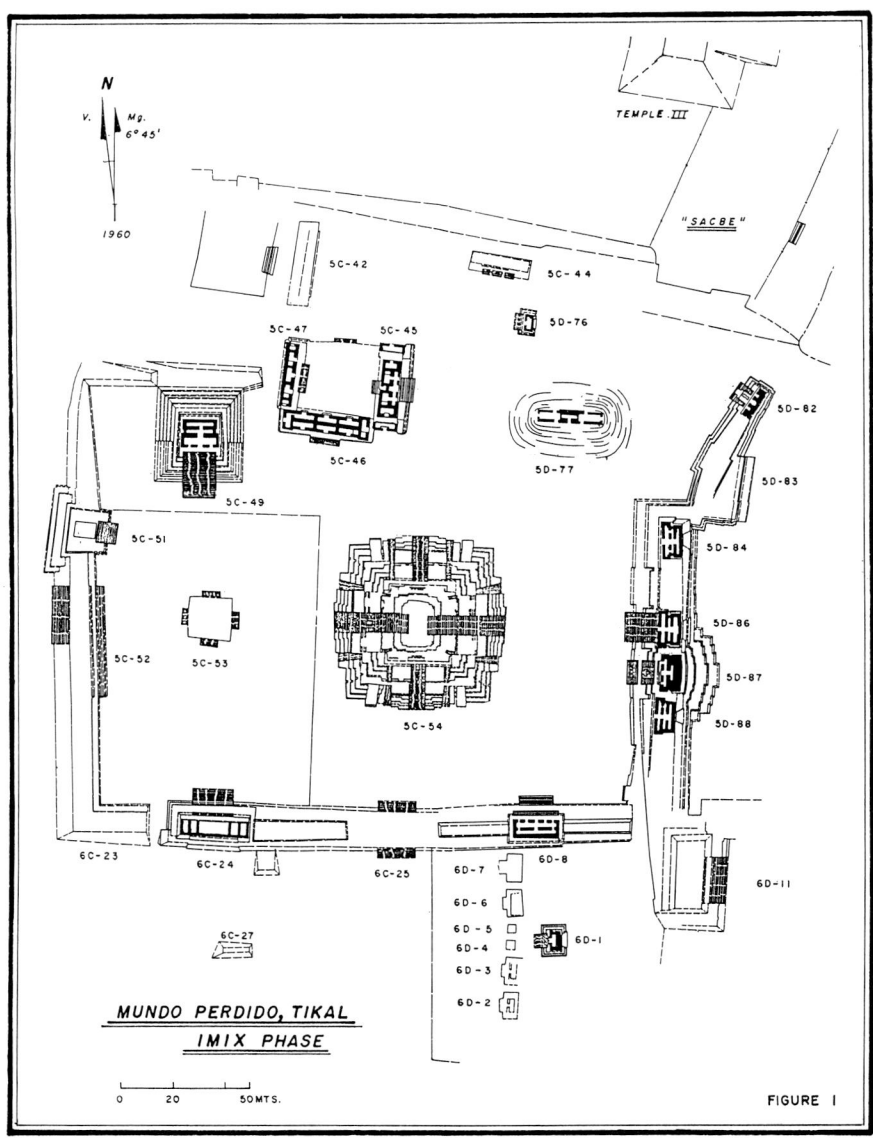

Fig. 1  Mundo Perdido during the Imix phase.

Nacional Tikal between 1979 and 1984 have shown it to have been utilized without interruption for twelve centuries, from the Middle Preclassic to the Terminal Classic, an aspect that permits the analysis of the character and function of this complex. The research demonstrates that its components form an astronomical complex, considered by Fialko (1988) as commemorative groups, revealing some of the ritual aspects related to them. Those complexes have their prototype in Group E of Uaxactun.

The layout of the astronomical complex is related to rituals associated with solstices and equinoxes in which the multidirectional quality of the radial pyramid was designed to express the cosmological symbolism in terms of spatial and temporal cycles that ruled Maya ritual (Cohodas 1985; Fialko 1988). In the beginning these complexes could have had a purely astronomical function. With time, however, they became symbols of lineage and ancestors, and, with this change, the related rituals became customary—formal but lacking a real function (Hartung 1968). It is important that the pattern adopted for these astronomical complexes was not influenced by topographical aspects of each site. Thus, the structural arrangement did not vary temporally or spatially in the various subregions of the central Maya lowlands.

Several studies have analyzed the architectural arrangement of the astronomical complexes (Blom 1926; Ruppert 1940; Rathje 1973; Fialko 1988). Other related elements besides the radial plan of the pyramid are the central stairway as the only access to the East Platform, the presence of radial platforms on the normative axis, and the close association of the complexes with causeways and ball courts.

The architectural development of Mundo Perdido was summed up by Fialko (1988) as follows. Its Preclassic history is one of continual growth. During the Tzec phase (500–300 B.C.) the pattern for this complex developed into a longitudinal platform and a radial pyramid (Fig. 2a), both aligned along an east-west axis that was ritually marked by the deposition of burials. This pattern would be used for the next millennium throughout the central Maya lowlands.

This situation is important in considering the possibility that the functionally ritual astronomical complexes predate the construction of their social and political counterpart, the triadic pattern complexes. Apart from Tikal, this situation is well documented in Uaxactun, where Group E developed earlier than the triadic Groups H and A (Valdés 1988). Other sites could well behave in the same manner, as in Nakbe, Seibal,[1] and Altar de Sacrificios.

---

[1] "Seibal" has been spelled with an "S" instead of a "C" throughout this volume as a result of an editorial decision. Such a spelling has been widely used for decades, particularly in North American publications, and a change now might cause considerable confusion. However, we should recognize that this spelling is the result of an early misspelling of *ceiba* and is incorrect in Spanish.

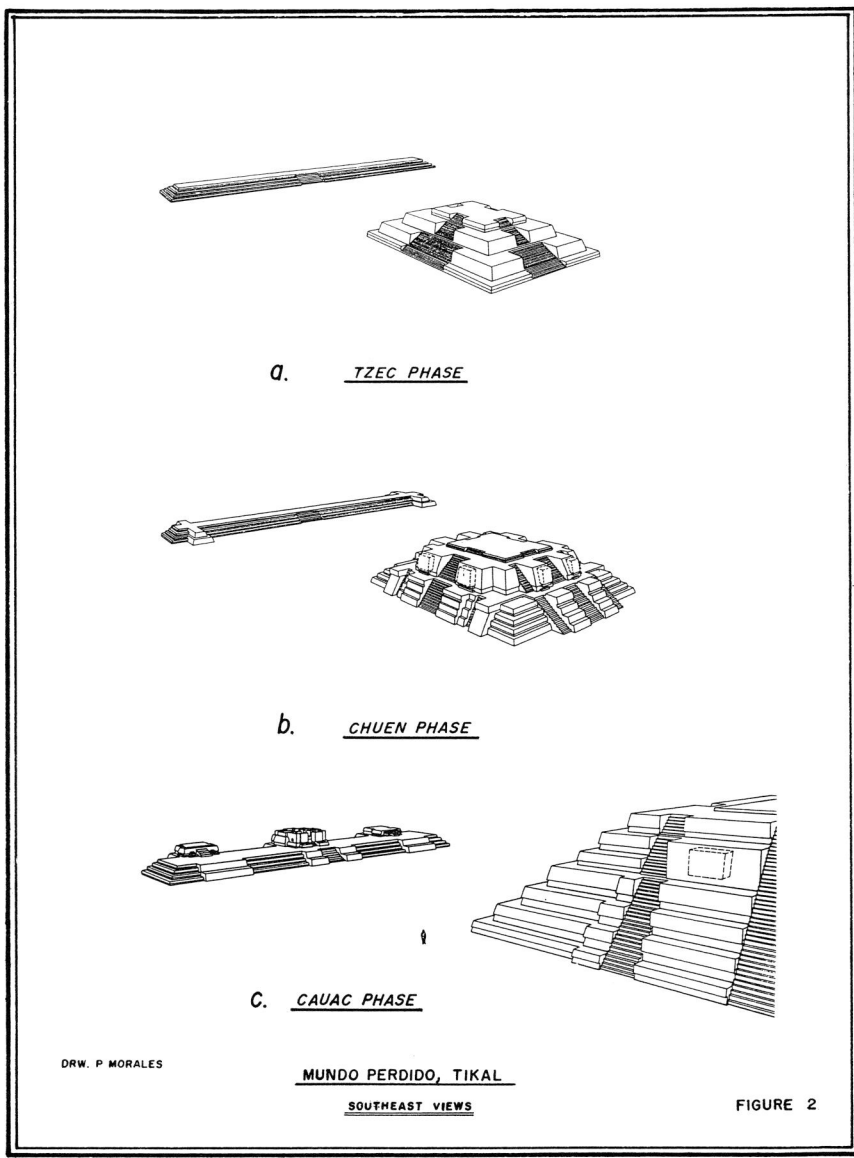

Fig. 2 Mundo Perdido during the (a) Tzec phase, (b) Chuen phase, (c) Cauac phase.

# Architecture and Social Change in Late Classic Maya Society

Fig. 3  Mundo Perdido during the Manik 3 phase.

This situation would emphasize that the earliest and original settlements in the lowlands are marked in the presence of the astronomical complexes.

New construction during the Chuen phase (300–100 B.C.) indicates the presence of a preestablished cyclical inauguration or completion ritual. The radial pyramid was enlarged and included masks framed by auxiliary stairways (Fig. 2b). During the Chuen phase, the formal position and orientation of the causeway that led to Mundo Perdido from the northeast was established, joining it with the first structures of the North Acropolis. Formal plazas were laid out in Mundo Perdido during the Cauac phase (100 B.C.–A.D. 250), enhancing the massiveness of the fourth version of the pyramid and the three temples that crowned the East Platform (Fig. 2c). Along the east-west axis two jaguar masks were modeled.

During the Early Classic, Mundo Perdido underwent a remarkable increase in size due to new construction and leveling, completing the slow process of enclosure. This activity was related to new versions of 5C-54, the Great Pyramid of Mundo Perdido, first built with eight, nine, and finally ten levels, when it reached 31 m in height, the tallest structure at that time in Tikal (Fig. 3). By the end of the Early Classic, Mundo Perdido had developed into a ceremonial compound enclosing 50,000 m, which in time would contain more than thirty structures.

Thus was Mundo Perdido at the beginning of the Late Classic, after ten centuries of development as one of the major public ritual compounds in Tikal (Coe and Haviland 1982). In spite of the changes in the political leadership of Tikal during the last part of the Early Classic (Manik 3 phase), in which Mundo Perdido played an important role, the function and importance of the complex was not altered.

Considering the temporal antiquity and stability of this complex in the ceremonial structure of Tikal, it is interesting that during the Late Classic, Mundo Perdido underwent a series of changes. These changes may reflect the social and political forces that caused the transformation of the ritual complex. In order to analyze these changes, the general scheme of the sixth and seventh century Ik phase (A.D. 550–650) and the seventh and eighth century Imix phase (A.D. 650–800) will be outlined.

### LATE CLASSIC MUNDO PERDIDO: THE CONSTRUCTION PROGRAM

During the Late Classic, the position of primary importance assigned to Mundo Perdido since the earliest times as a ceremonial area of Tikal continued without interruption. The construction process of Late Classic Mundo Perdido may have been contemporaneous with other changes in the nearby Plaza of the Seven Temples, Plaza of Temple III, and the Bats Palace (Palacio de las Ventanas).

*The Southern and Northern Sections of Mundo Perdido*

During the Ik phase, there were several important changes in the southern section of Mundo Perdido (Fig. 4). One of them was the construction of a building (Str.6D-8-4) with all five doorways oriented towards the north, thus limiting its function to the area of Mundo Perdido, and closing all access to the South Plaza, a space developed throughout the Early Classic. Some time later, during the Imix phase, seven small-sized structures were built in the South Plaza (Fig. 1), reinforcing the ceremonial character of Mundo Perdido. Since these structures are set apart from the main ceremonial compound their function is unclear, but we know that it was not funerary.

Other Late Classic additions enhanced the northern section of Mundo Perdido (Figs. 1,4). The plaza was extended northward, initially retaining the ancient causeway as a low platform, but it was not long before this was completely covered. New versions of the main structures (5D-77 and 5D-82) in this section were also built. An essential part of the construction program was the addition of a series of three large platforms in this section during the Ik phase (Fig. 4). One of these platforms (5C-47-3) covered several earlier architectural elements. The most interesting addition was a

*Architecture and Social Change in Late Classic Maya Society*

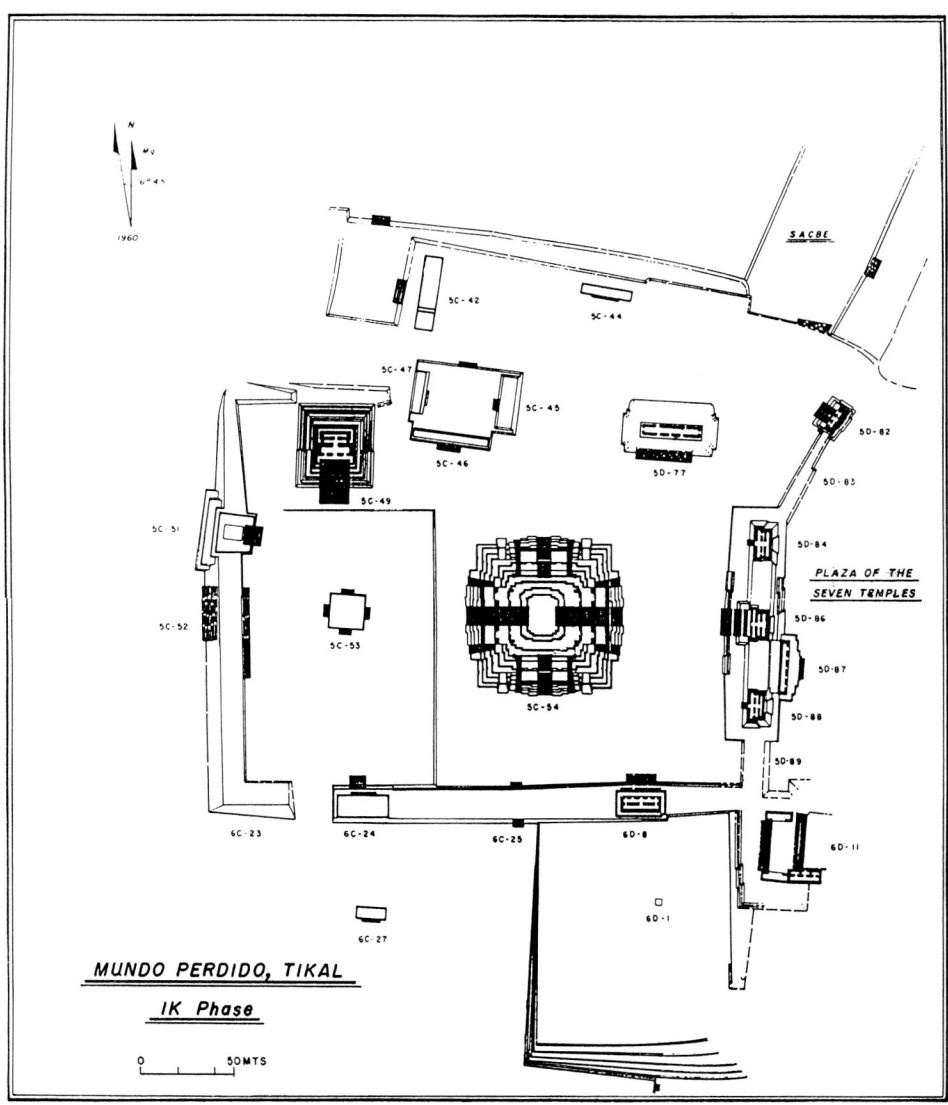

Fig. 4   Mundo Perdido during the Ik phase.

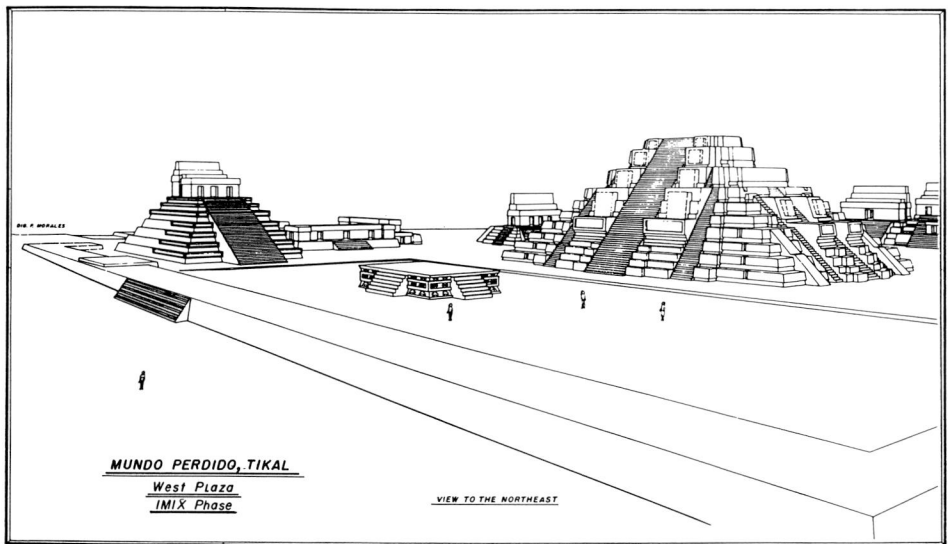

Fig. 5 Mundo Perdido during the Imix phase.

low basal structure that supported a decorated bench (5C-47-2A). No evidence of enclosing walls was found that would indicate that the bench was inside of a room. During the Imix phase, these three platforms would become multiroom structures (Figs. 1,5). Abundant internal modifications altered them over time by changing stairways, building benches, and putting decorative elements, including human figures, in the cornice.

It is important to note that these multiroom structures were the only major ones built in the ceremonial perimeter of Mundo Perdido whose function was not restricted to ritual aspects during the 1,500 years of its utilization. The construction of those buildings reflects a profound social change regarding Mundo Perdido and could be associated with the functional transformation of the compound. The group that built and used these structures was part of the elite of Tikal, as can be seen in burials, caches, ceremonial deposits, and other elements recovered during the excavations.

*The West Plaza of Mundo Perdido*

As the process of enclosure at Mundo Perdido continued in the Late Classic (Ik phase), the construction of new walls for the interior perimeter covered the *talud-tablero* elements that had been built during Manik 3 times. Nevertheless, several of those elements were still being used in the Late Classic, and new ones were built. Thus, it is evident that this construction program was not designed to cover all traces of the old style, and, therefore, the covering of these elements does not seem to be a fact of great social or political importance. Rather, the program just added new architectural styles or elements that were prevalent in Late Classic Tikal.

Covering an earlier low platform (5C-53-1), a new structure (5C-53-2) with a *talud-tablero* profile and peculiar decorative elements was built in the center of the West Plaza during the Ik phase (Rodríguez and Rosal 1987). Little is known regarding the exterior form of this platform since it was dismantled during the construction of the presently visible structure 5C-53-3 (Fig. 5). We do know that the second version of 5C-53 had a radial design and may have been decorated with butterfly symbols in the *talud* and with pairs of circles in the *tablero,* similar to that proposed for Structure 6E-144 (Puleston 1979). It should be noted that this platform was set on the normative axis of the astronomical complex, an indication that this position was still ritually important during the first part of the Late Classic (Ik phase).

The third version of 5C-53, also radial in design, was built near the end of the Ik phase, at the same time as 5D-43 in the East Plaza of Tikal. These are the best examples of the use of the trinomial profile (*atadura*), that is, the *talud-tablero* crowned with an outset cornice (*cornisa volada*). This trait could reflect special relations with the Gulf Coast of Mexico. The profile is found on all four sides and, as with the second version, it is decorated with butterfly symbols in the *talud* and cornice, and pairs of circles in each framed *tablero*.

The main alteration associated with the West Plaza during the Ik phase was the construction of the fifth version of 5C-49, the second highest building in Mundo Perdido (Fig. 5). At the end of the Early Classic (Manik 3 phase), the fourth version of 5C-49 consisted of four levels with *talud-tablero* architecture on the front and a portion of each side of the structure. On the remainder of each side and on the back, only the upper level carried the *talud-tablero* element. The stairway was framed by a balustrade (*alfarda*).

The construction of 5C-49-5 required the adding 4.6 m to the fourth version, which resulted in two new stepped levels. Both of the new levels were carried out with the *talud-tablero* element on all four sides. The increment in height of the structure made the construction of a new stairway necessary. This new stairway, built directly over the former one with very little fill, incorporated a different angle to reach the new temple. The old balustrade was covered, while at the same time reusing the same stair side. On top of this base, a three room temple with an elaborate roof comb was built. While the substructure of 5C-49-5 was not altered again, three clearly defined alterations to the temple were identified in its Late Classic evolution.

In contrast with the preceding versions of 5C-49, the fifth was the only one to have a funerary function. The principal tomb (Burial PNT-005), which had been looted, was placed under the bench of the final construction stage,

*Juan Pedro Laporte*

oriented along the north-south axis. Other burials (PNT-007 and PNT-009) were found, one over the other, along the axis of the second room.

## Late Classic Changes in the Astronomical Complex

In the eighth century, the ritual associated with the astronomical complex was still being practiced in Tikal, even though those activities did not include the cyclical renovation of structures as it had happened since the Middle Preclassic. By then, the Great Pyramid (5C-54) was the same ten-level, fifth version dating to the Early Classic. During the Late Classic, some consolidation was carried out to remedy structural problems that had developed in several of the levels in the centuries since its last renovation.

We have evidence of two incidents related to the use of the Great Pyramid during Ik phase, which should be mentioned. First, the presence of a slate stela in the upper section of 5C-54 was documented by small dispersed fragments and by the position of the base in the upper fill. The base indicates that this monument was small and thin. A single fragment of slate, perhaps associated with this stela, suggests that it could have been carved with some type of design (butterfly), similar to the ones in the *talud* and cornice of the central platform of the West Plaza (5C-53). The stela could also be related to a possible construction on the tenth level of the pyramid, but the extensive damage to this area does not permit this to be stated with any certainty.

The second evidence of Late Classic use is a limestone model that, due to its good preservation, seems to have been part of some type of cache. It was found out of context in the upper part of the eastern side of the pyramid. This model represents an architectural complex that has yet to be identified with one of the presently known groups at Tikal. Besides the various pyramidal structures, there is a ball court depicted, which establishes the north-south axis of this model.

In contrast, significant changes occurred during the Late Classic in the East Platform of the astronomical complex. In its original layout, the only evidence of late use of the temple that occupied the central position on top of the platform (5D-86) is the presence of the lower part of Stela 39, an Early Classic monument (8.17.0.0.0, A.D. 376), in the third room of the structure (Ayala 1987). The stela's original position might have been associated with the normative axis of the complex. Ayala (n.d.) suggests that the movement of this stela could have been ordered by Ruler C to commemorate katun 17 (9.17.0.0.0, A.D. 771). He used a monument from the same katun of Cycle 8, thus tying his lineage to that of Jaguar Paw. Some ritual offerings of polychrome vessels to the stela were done as late as the Eznab phase.

Another significant change in the east platform during the Ik phase was the construction of a structure with a single longitudinal room containing five entrances (5D-87-7), which opened onto the Plaza of the Seven Temples (Fig. 6). This structure was attached to the back of 5D-87-6 and formed

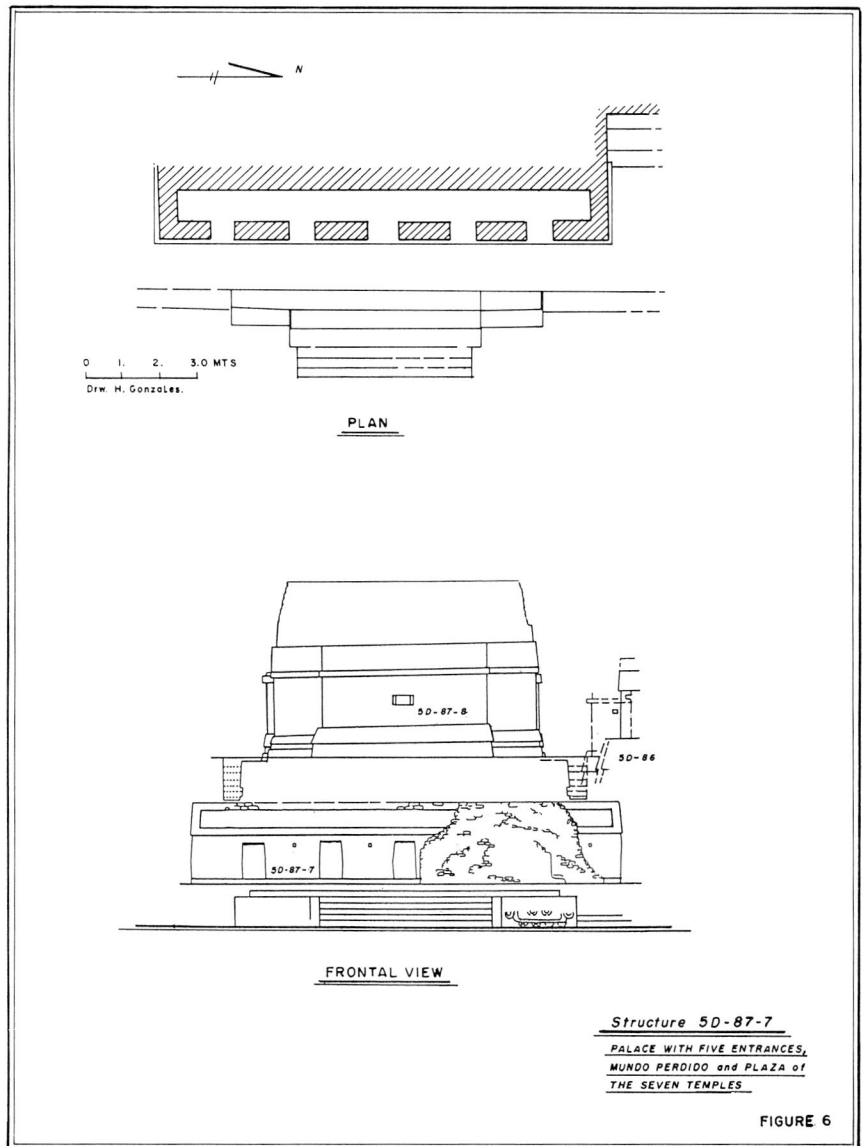

Fig. 6 Structure 5D-87-7, palace with five entrances, Mundo Perdido and Plaza of the Seven Temples.

the basis of a new axis that would later be part of a construction program in the Plaza of the Seven Temples (Fialko 1988). This building had an irregular vault and included some decorative elements in its platform. It was not used for long and was filled tightly with stones and mortar. No graffiti were discovered in its only room.

During the Imix phase, changes occurred in the general configuration of Mundo Perdido with the construction of a new structure on the East Platform (Fig. 1) that finally brought an end to the normative axis that had prevailed since the first version of the astronomical complex more than twelve centuries earlier. The third tallest structure in Mundo Perdido, 5D-87-8 is a temple whose pyramidal substructure is composed of four levels with moldings (Fig. 7). The stairway is divided by a vaulted niche that begins at the base of the first level. The niche was built on a small platform on which were carved three stone skulls, the lateral ones in profile and the central one in frontal view. This niche has a restricted interior space. This type of niche is a feature found in several buildings of the late period at Tikal, including another temple at the northeastern end of Mundo Perdido (5D-82-5) and structure 5E-38 in the East Plaza.

The temple at the top of 5D-87-8 has two rooms and three entrances. It is still possible to observe a graffito showing two human figures. Neither room had benches. A dedicatory cache (PNT-004) was found along the axis of the building. The contents of the cache may have been designed to reflect the underworld (shells), lineage blood (stingray spines), and the sky (jade) (Ayala n.d.); all were wrapped in a ritual paper bundle (*bulto*) given to the ruler as the representation of the cosmos.

*Mundo Perdido and the Funerary Activities*

Important changes in the pattern of funerary activities in Mundo Perdido were noted over time, maybe a reflection of differences in the social classes represented in them. During the Preclassic, burials were generally associated with propitiatory rituals and were located along the normative axis of the complex. In Early Classic times, Mundo Perdido was used for the deposition of burials of dynastic character, specifically connected to the Jaguar Paw lineage (Laporte and Fialko 1990). In the Manik 3 phase we found no evidence that the compound was used for funerary purposes.

During the seventh century, Mundo Perdido again became the focus of funerary deposition, mainly in the area occupied by the range structures described above. It is difficult to categorize the social position of these individuals due to the lack of research on the general Ik funerary tradition, apart from highly elite persons (Coggins n.d.). In the case of Mundo Perdido, the offering of polychrome vessels and other ornaments of exotic materials indicate its possible affiliation with the Tikal elites of the moment.

During the Imix phase it is evident that Mundo Perdido continued as an

# Architecture and Social Change in Late Classic Maya Society

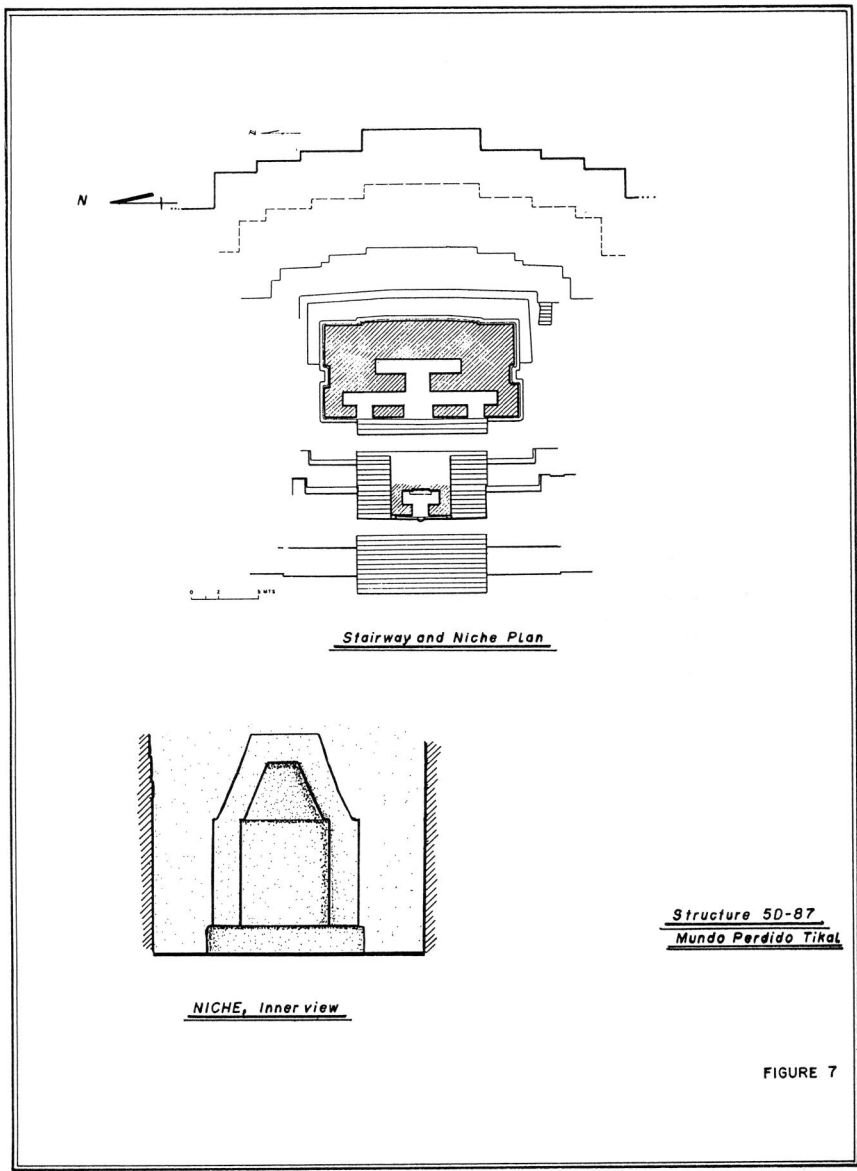

Fig. 7   Detail of niche, Structure 5D-87-8, Mundo Perdido.

important funerary location with the deposition of a number of tombs in temple 5C-49. The offerings, including a polychrome vase with a scene of a lady presenting the head of the sun god to the principal lord (Gallenkamp and Johnson 1985: 141), placed in Burial PNT-009, are important in determining social position. With the three vessels of this tomb were a series of small objects, including human figures, stars, shell and mother-of-pearl, and a turtle made of conch.

The occupation and architectural changes in Mundo Perdido did not stop with the Imix phase but continued well into the ninth century (Eznab phase) and are best known from the northern section of Mundo Perdido. During the Eznab phase, a dramatic change in the funerary pattern occurred with the interment of a larger number of burials whose offerings and ornaments do not indicate elite social affiliation. These were intruded into earlier architectural elements, such as stairways and floors, or were simply laid under the rubble of fallen buildings.

### THE TRANSFORMATION OF AN ANCIENT CONCEPT

The construction in the eighth century of a new temple on the East Platform (5D-87-8), which altered Mundo Perdido's normative axis and created a new one associated with the alignment of structures in the Plaza of the Seven Temples, was the most important change that occurred at Mundo Perdido during the Late Classic. This caused the transformation, if not the abandonment, of the ritual that was associated with the astronomical complex, mainly the archaic solar cult, for in no other compound of Tikal is there an architectural complex that could have replaced Mundo Perdido for the commemoration of solstices and equinoxes. This indicates a fundamental change in the ritual structure of Tikal, a change that may also be reflected in other regions of the central Maya lowlands.

Changes in the religious hierarchy and in calendrical ritual could be one cause of this discontinuity. It could also be the result of strains taking place in the social and political spheres and as such, be analyzed in relation to the importance of a one-person tradition in the site—a tradition of rulers who pushed the architectural development to new heights not seen before in Tikal, showing their power in the control of the labor needed for such a process. This process might have also occurred at other sites of Peten in the eighth century, in contrast with other sections of the central lowlands.

How did the other compounds of central Tikal respond to the changes mentioned for Mundo Perdido? Only two other ceremonial compounds have been dug in Tikal in a comparable manner: Central Acropolis and North Acropolis–Great Plaza. Other Late Classic groups have been tested and many details are known about them, but their architectural sequence and changes in function are not comparable.

Central Acropolis underwent continuous architectural changes during the

Late Classic, but these may not have modified its ascribed function in the structure of Tikal. For this reason it is difficult to observe the power concentration reflected in the functional change of Mundo Perdido.

North Acropolis–Great Plaza also shows important changes in the Late Classic. A new construction program was begun to close down the ancient North Acropolis by constructing several temples along its front. Finally the development of the two major temple pyramids of the Great Plaza may be the best symbol of the concentration of power at Tikal (Dahlin 1986). Paralleling the changes described for Mundo Perdido, the formation of the Great Plaza transformed North Acropolis, a compound that since the Late Preclassic (Chuen phase) had been the triadic group that represented the founding lineages of the site. The desire to dispose of all the remnants of the lineages and the old tradition to favor a more individual power is evident again.

It has been suggested that the abandonment of the astronomical complex at Tikal was associated with the development of the Twin-Pyramid Complexes in the Ik phase (seventh century; Group 5E-Sub.1; Jones n.d.). This is certainly not the case for other sites, since the Twin-Pyramid Complex is very restricted geographically, occurring only in Tikal and Yaxha, while being absent in nearby Uaxactun.

Variations in the arrangement of architectural traits of the astronomical complex may indicate some intrinsic form of change, either chronological or functional, in the associated ritual (Fialko 1988). The replacement in the Late Classic of the radial pyramid that defined the western position of the complex during the Preclassic and Early Classic, with a rectangular structure at Nakum, Xultun, and other sites, does not seem to have affected the original ritual scheme since the astronomical complex continued to be associated with the central sector of each site.

Among the northeastern Peten centers, data on changes of the function of ritual compounds are only available for Uaxactun, where Group E, the prototype for the astronomical complexes of the central Maya lowlands, was abandoned in the Late Classic (Ricketson and Ricketson 1937; Smith 1950), perhaps even earlier than Mundo Perdido. However, recent data from excavations in progress in Group D of Uaxactun (Renaldo Acevedo, personal communication, May 1989) seem to indicate that an additional astronomical complex was built during Tepeu 1. Unfortunately, information is not available at this time about the abandonment of this second complex. Late Classic development is strong in the groups located on the hill in the western section of the site (Groups A and B). Both groups developed during Late Preclassic and Early Classic periods with temples and range structures continuing until Tepeu 3. The periphery of Uaxactun has also been analyzed and all groups seem to have been occupied during the Late Classic. The process of transformation of the traditional rituals described for Tikal can be seen in Uaxactun in the abandonment of Group E and other ceremonial groups (astronomical complex and triadic group) located in the eastern section of the site (Groups D and H), and in the Late Classic modifications of Groups A and B.

ASTRONOMICAL COMPLEX AND TERRITORIAL DEFINITION

The astronomical complex may be useful for the definition of territorial units among analogous polities (Renfrew 1986), since this complex appears to be the nuclear foundation around which sociopolitical units developed. The association of the earlier carved stelae known in the central Maya lowlands with this type of architectural compound agrees well with this idea (Cohodas 1985; Fialko 1988). The best example of this is seen at Nakbe (Hansen n.d.), where Stela 1, the earliest monument (ca. A.D. 41), is found in the East Group (Strs. 47/53), a well-defined astronomical complex, intruding at least into two Preclassic floors and with a looted tomb in its front. At Uaxactun the early monuments were also erected in Group E, except for Stela 9 (ca. A.D. 328), probably moved from its unknown original position to one related with the causeway that developed in the Early Classic between Groups A and B. The situation at Tikal is more complex, the main problem being that Stela 29 (A.D. 292) was found dumped north of the plaza in front of Temple III (Jones and Satterthwaite 1982). Interestingly, the causeway that leads to Mundo Perdido comes from this point. The next monument known to have been erected at Tikal was Stela 39 (A.D. 376), found along the axis of Mundo Perdido.

Even if the above examples are not strong evidence to conclude that the original position to erect monuments was the astronomical complex plaza in most sites, there is no other reference to favor instead other types of plazas for this activity, including those that developed triadic architectural patterns around them. Even in later sites the monuments are generally found in association with the plaza of the astronomic complex, along the east-west normative axis or near it.

Due to the close relationship between the astronomic complex and dynastic affairs represented in the stelae noted in the north central Peten, their identification in other regions of the central Maya lowlands offers the possibility that this complex might reflect the relative sociopolitical position of each site in a regional basis. To illustrate this possibility and to understand the events that brought about the changes to Mundo Perdido, and Tikal in general, some preliminary observations will be drawn from the archaeological survey that is currently being conducted in the northwestern portion of the Maya Mountains (Laporte and Torres n.d.).

The Maya Mountains comprise a varied environment including mountains, valleys, and plateaus. The dominant topographic feature is the pres-

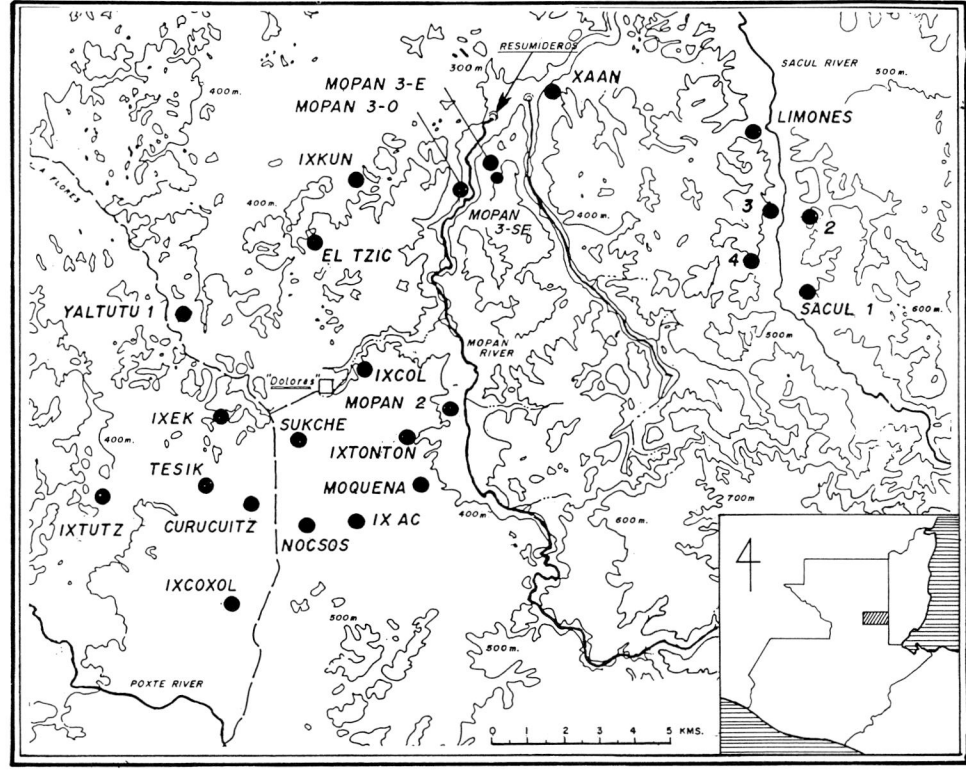

Fig. 8  Valley of Dolores, Maya Mountains, position of archaeological sites.

ence of karstic hills, the tops of which were used for settlement as seen in archaeological groups. The Valley of Dolores, located in the northwest part of the Maya Mountains, is a large plateau approximately 13 km long, north to south, and 8 km wide, which covers 100 sq km (Fig. 8). The valley, which is part of the upper Mopan River drainage system, is covered by pine trees in the southern section and by tropical forest in the northern section.

The survey of this area resulted in the identification of thirteen archaeological sites, with clear hierarchical distinctions evident between them. Chronologically, it is known that at least three sites, Ixtonton, Ixac, and Curucuitz, had been occupied since the Late Preclassic and that during the Late Classic all the sites in the Valley of Dolores were occupied. The carved stelae of the southeastern Peten cluster from 9.16.0.0.0 (A.D. 751) to 9.18.10.0.0 (A.D. 800), even reaching the third katun of Cycle 10 (Stela 1, Ixtonton; Escobedo n.d.).

In addition to the Valley of Dolores, two other sectors of the Maya Mountains are currently being surveyed: the Poxte River Valley to the west, which includes Ixtutz, and to the east, the Sacul River Valley, where in addition to the site of Sacul, with its well-known carved monuments, another four sites have been reported (Fig. 8).

Another group of sites, also in this mountainous region, were built in the same manner, according to the settlement pattern and to the presence of astronomical complexes, and thus can be used comparatively. These are the centers of the eastern margin of the Chiquibul River in Belize (Thompson 1931). There are two primary sites, each comprising several hills with groups on top of them: Cahal Pichik (including Cahal Cunil and Mountain Cow) and Hatzcab Ceel with the habitational sector known as Tzimin Kax.

While settlement density may reflect the importance of sites within each valley, it is not possible to rely only on population estimates. These tend to be subjective due to the fact that settlements are continuous and there is no clear spatial differentiation between sites. In the Valley of Dolores, the average distance between ceremonial groups is 4.4 km (Fig. 8), with ranges that vary between 2.2 km (Ixtonton-Ixcol) to 7.5 km (Ixcoxol-Ixcol).

To establish limits between sites and to develop hierarchies for the settlements, we have focused on complexes of a ritual character, in this case, the astronomic complexes. In addition, in forming hierarchies, the presence or absence of collateral elements such as ball courts, carved monuments, and causeways were analyzed.

The results of the archaeological survey of the northwestern Maya Mountains indicate a different situation from the one reported for the northern Peten, where the distance between sites is larger, possibly reflecting other sociopolitical conditions during the Late Classic. The northern sites show a stronger nucleation process than those of the Dolores region, which were more decentralized, perhaps with kin group or lineage segments occupying power positions in the secondary centers.

The population of the Valley of Dolores linked their origins with the development of their ceremonial and habitation sections around an astronomical complex, while reserving some highly specialized ceremonial functions, such as ball-game activities, the erection of stelae, and processions along causeways, for the regional centers that incorporated several lineages and exercised economic and political control. It has been argued that the subordinate towns and dependencies were often specialized, forming an economic interdependence within a province (Marcus, Chap. 5). Two regional centers have been defined for the Valley of Dolores: Ixtonton for the eastern sector and Ixkun for the northern sector.

According to this model, the association of the astronomical complexes with ancestors and lineages would have permitted the sharing of power manifest in the societies of the southeastern Peten. In contrast, the transformation of the astronomical complex of Tikal was significant for the action undertaken by the ruler at that moment (Ah Cacau) and not just for its calendaric and ritual implications, since it would not allow a continuation of the old tradition, which would have impeded the development of a more individual rule of the political system.

The sudden and radical change of Mundo Perdido, an astronomical complex that had been part of the ritual life of Tikal for the last thousand years, was an action to prove authority, and could reflect political and ideological problems in the government of the eighth century in Tikal.

# BIBLIOGRAPHY

Ayala Falcón, Maricela
    1987    La Estela 39 de Mundo Perdido, Tikal. *Memorias del Primer Coloquio Internacional de Mayistas:* 599–654. Centro de Estudios Mayas, UNAM, México.
    n.d.    El Bulto Ritual de Mundo Perdido, Tikal, y los Bultos Mayas. Paper presented at the Primer Congreso Internacional de Mayistas, San Cristóbal de Las Casas, 1989.

Blom, Frans
    1926    El Observatorio más Antiguo del Continente Americano. *Anales de la Sociedad de Geografía e Historia* 2 (3): 335–338. Guatemala.

Carr, Robert E., and James E. Hazard
    1961    *Map of the Ruins of Tikal, El Peten, Guatemala.* Tikal Reports No. 11. University Museum, University of Pennsylvania, Philadelphia.

Coe, William R.
    1963    A Summary of Excavation and Research at Tikal, Guatemala: 1962. *Estudios de Cultura Maya* 3: 41–64. UNAM, Mexico.

Coe, William R., and William Haviland
    1982    *Introduction to the Archaeology of Tikal, Guatemala.* Tikal Report No. 12. University Museum, University of Pennsylvania, Philadelphia.

Coggins, Clemency C.
    n.d.    Painting and Drawing Styles at Tikal: An Historical and Iconographic Reconstruction. Ph.D. dissertation, Harvard University, 1975.

Cohodas, Marvin
    1985    Public Architecture of the Maya Lowlands. *Cuadernos de Arquitectura Mesoamericana* 6: 51–68. Facultad de Arquitectura, UNAM, Mexico.

Dahlin, Bruce H.
    1986    Los rostros del tiempo: Un movimiento revitalizador en Tikal durante el periodo Clásico Tardío. *Mesoamérica* 11: 79–112. Centro de Investigaciones Regionales de Mesoamérica, Antigua, Guatemala.

Escobedo, Hector L.
    n.d.    Epigrafía e historia política de los sitios del noroeste de las Montañas Mayas durante el Clásico Tardío. Dissertation, Escuela de Historia, Universidad de San Carlos, Guatemala, 1991.

Fialko, Vilma
    1988    Mundo Perdido, Tikal: Un Ejemplo de Complejos de Conmemoración Astronómica. *Mayab* 4: 13–21. Sociedad Española de Estudios Mayas, Madrid.

Gallenkamp, Charles, and Regina Elsie Johnson (eds.)
    1985    *Maya: Treasures of an Ancient Civilization.* Harry N. Abrams, Inc., New York.

Hansen, Richard
    n.d.    Orígenes y Desarrollo: Nakbé. Report, Instituto de Antropología e Historia, Guatemala, 1987.

HARRISON, PETER D.
    n.d.    The Central Acropolis, Tikal, Guatemala: A Preliminary Study of the Functions of its Structural Components during the Late Classic Period. Ph.D. dissertation, University of Pennsylvania, 1970.

HARTUNG, HORST
    1968    Consideraciones Urbanísticas Sobre los Trazos de los Centros Ceremoniales de Tikal, Copán, Uxmal y Chichén Itzá. *37 Congreso Internacional de Americanistas* 1: 121–125. Buenos Aires (1966).

JONES, CHRISTOPHER
    n.d.    The Twin-Pyramid Group Pattern: A Classic Maya Assemblage at Tikal, Guatemala. Ph.D. dissertation, University of Pennsylvania, 1969.

JONES, CHRISTOPHER, AND LINTON SATTERTHWAITE
    1982    *The Monuments and Inscriptions of Tikal: The Carved Monuments*. Tikal Report No. 33, Part A. The University Museum, University of Pennsylvania, Philadelphia.

LAPORTE, JUAN PEDRO, AND VILMA FIALKO
    1990    New Perspectives on Old Problems: Dynastic References for the Early Classic at Tikal. In *Vision and Revision in Maya Studies* (F. Clancy and P. Harrison, eds.): 33–66. University of New Mexico Press, Albuquerque.
    n.d.    *Reporte Arqueológico: Mundo Perdido y Zonas de Habitación, Tikal*. 10 Vols. Instituto de Antropología e Historia, Guatemala, 1985.

LAPORTE, JUAN PEDRO, AND ROLANDO TORRES
    n.d.    El Proyecto Sureste de Petén: Resultados del Programa Regional 1985–1989. Paper presented at the III Simposio de Arqueología Guatemalteca, Museo de Arqueología y Etnología, Guatemala, 1989.

LOTEN, H. STANLEY
    n.d.    The Maya Architecture of Tikal, Guatemala: A Preliminary Seriation of Vaulted Building Plans. Ph.D. dissertation, University of Pennsylvania, 1970.

ORREGO, MIGUEL, AND RUDY LARIOS
    1983    *Investigaciones Arqueológicas en el Grupo 5E-II, Petén*. Instituto de Antropología e Historia, Guatemala.

PULESTON, DENNIS
    1979    The Discovery of Talud-Tablero Architecture at Tikal. *XV Mesa Redonda, Sociedad Mexicana de Antropología* 2: 377–384. Guanajuato (1977).

RATHJE, WILLIAM L.
    1973    Trade Models and Archaeological Problems: The Classic Maya and Their E-Group Complex. *40 International Congress of Americanists*: 223–235, Rome (1972).

RENFREW, COLIN
    1986    Introduction: Peer Polity Interaction and Socio-Political Change. In *Peer Polity Interaction and Socio-Political Change* (C. Renfrew and J. Cherry, eds): 1–18. Cambridge University Press, Cambridge.

RICKETSON, OLIVER G., AND EDITH B. RICKETSON
    1937    *Uaxactun, Guatemala, Group E, 1926–1931.* Carnegie Institution, Publication 477. Washington, D.C.

RODRÍGUEZ, ZOILA, AND MARCO ANTONIO ROSAL
    1987    La Plataforma 5C-53: Un Caso de Interpretación. In *Memorias del Primer Coloquio Internacional de Mayistas:* 319–330, Centro de Estudios Mayas, UNAM, Mexico.

RUPPERT, KARL
    1940    Special Assemblage of Maya Structures. In *The Maya and Their Neighbors* (C. Hay et al., eds.): 222–231. Appleton Century, New York.

SMITH, A. LEDYARD
    1950    *Uaxactun, Guatemala: Excavations of 1931–1937.* Carnegie Institution, Publication 588. Washington, D.C.

THOMPSON, J. ERIC S.
    1931    *Archaeological Investigations in the Southern Cayo District, British Honduras.* Field Museum of Natural History, Chicago.

VALDÉS, JUAN ANTONIO
    1988    Breve historia de la arquitectura de Uaxactún a la luz de nuevas investigaciones. *Journal de la Société des Américanistes* 74: 7–24. Paris.

11

*Historical Inscriptions and the Maya Collapse*

DAVID STUART

VANDERBILT UNIVERSITY

Only after a thorough understanding of the historical events which occurred in the late 9th and early 10th centuries A.D. in the Southern Maya Lowlands has been reached can the larger question of process be successfully broached. For if in our eagerness to change our goals from historical to processual ones, we relegate the reconstruction of historical events to a low priority role and ignore the importance of these events, then our efforts will be futile. (Sabloff and Willey 1967: 314)

What any given culture asks or fails to ask, records or fails to record, in itself offers an important clue as to the nature of that society. (M. I. Finley 1985: 105)

INTRODUCTION

MAYA HIEROGLYPHIC INSCRIPTIONS record ritual and political history. Yet within the vast assortment of ancient chronicles left to us, we seem to find little or no mention of one of the most momentous events of Maya civilization, namely the collapse of the southern cities during the late eighth and early ninth centuries. Certainly no one would expect to find hieroglyphic texts that explicitly discuss the abandonment of sites (who would read them?), but when considering the political and cultural background of the Maya collapse, the hieroglyphic record could potentially be very illuminating. Recent work in Maya decipherment has revealed a great many native documents concerning the histories of sites, their political structures, and the religious foundations of rulership. As a result, the window provided by historical texts allows us to analyze the nature of these cultural institutions that were the most obvious victims of the collapse.

Because many of these advances in hieroglyphic decipherment are very new, a great deal of historical and documentary evidence has yet to be fully utilized by Mayanists who are concerned with large questions of history and culture process. When using ancient texts to address broad issues of Maya history, we must keep important questions in mind: how should inscriptions be used in conjunction with archaeological data, and, more precisely, what questions can we realistically expect them to answer? Appreciating the value of textual sources hinges on our own ability to view them with a critical eye and to realize their advantages and inherent pitfalls. In general, then, Mayanists must now make proper use of documentary evidence in ways that have traditionally been the concern of Classicists and historical archaeologists.

Needless to say, texts are unique sources for the study of ancient history and culture. As more or less precise representations of language, written documents are direct reflections of the ancient mind. Nevertheless, the limitations of epigraphy in the study of all ancient societies are obvious. Our understanding of ancient literate cultures is bound by what ancient scribes and their patrons, for whatever reason, chose and chose not to record. As both an anthropologist and historian, the epigrapher constantly must beware of asking too much from the documents. We must try to acquaint ourselves with the purposes of texts and their points of view, or in other words, "to ask questions that the texts themselves do not pose and cannot answer directly" (Finley 1985: 105). Such a critical evaluation of Maya inscriptions has been slow in coming, simply because most recent efforts have centered on questions of what might be called "first-stage" decipherment.

Like other recent efforts (Culbert 1988; Houston 1989), this paper hopes to place some current advances in Maya decipherment into a larger historical and anthropological setting. Specifically, I will focus on the problem of the collapse and abandonment of large centers in the southern lowlands at the end of the Late Classic period. My aim is not to review and summarize the individual histories of sites leading up to the collapse, but rather to describe some of the telling characteristics of Maya social and political organization during the Late Classic period. I hope to demonstrate that hieroglyphic texts may have a special place in illuminating certain aspects of social and political process. However, as Marcus (Chap. 5) has also stressed, texts cannot stand alone in analyzing such broad issues. The trends that I shall describe must be evaluated together with broader archaeological perspectives on the collapse.

## WRITING IN LATE CLASSIC MAYA SOCIETY

Writing was a product and instrument of elite Maya culture. On the carved monuments, texts relate certain specialized themes revolving around the social, political, and ritual lives of rulers and others of elite standing. This narrowness in literary scope is sometimes exaggerated by Mayanists, however, due largely to our own narrow understanding of the contents of certain texts. Until very recently, after all, we could precisely identify (or "read") little more than hieroglyphic dates and the names of rulers. In the future, as we come to decipher more specific terms and, eventually, passages of texts that today remain enigmatic, we may encounter the treatment of unexpected subjects and themes. For this reason it is premature to claim that texts in general do *not* discuss certain subjects, especially in light of the thematic variations that exist among different sites. Indeed, it may even be premature to state that we should not expect the collapse to be mentioned explicitly in the inscriptions. As we shall see at the end of this essay, new decipherments may often surprise us.

To evaluate the usefulness of written texts, we must know something of their literary point of view. Who then was responsible for the composition of the inscriptions we see on carved monuments and painted vessels? Surely it is naive to assume that all monumental inscriptions were commissioned by Maya rulers as acts of self-advancing propaganda. More than a few royal inscriptions were probably composed under the direction of subsidiary nobles and functionaries (who will be described later). Moreover, many texts celebrate nobles of high rank, such as the *sahals,* who were not rulers.

Understanding the social position of Maya scribes becomes important when we try to confront questions of the viewpoint of Maya texts and the motives of their composition. Several recent decipherments have shed light on individual scribes and artisans and their place within Maya society (Stuart 1986, 1987, n.d.b). Here the personal signatures of individual pottery painters and stone sculptors are of special importance. Several ceramic vessels bear the names of painters (*ah ts'ib*), and numerous sculptors' names are found incised into the background of stone lintels and stelae from sites along the Usumacinta River. We know from these scattered examples that some Maya artisans, at least, were of very high status. As I have shown in previous studies (Stuart 1987, n.d.b.) the painter of a vessel from the area of Naranjo—a masterful scribe in his own right—was the son of the ruler of Naranjo and a royal lady from Yaxha. Several sculptors carry the title *ahaw,* "lord," making it fairly clear that at least some stone carvers were much more than humble laborers.

A term sometimes applied to both scribes and sculptors was *its'at,* "artist, wise man" (Stuart n.d.b.). The semantic range of this term is significant, since it seems to reflect an intimate interconnection between the sacred arts, writing, and intellectual advancement. Whereas in ancient Egypt we see a literate professional class of scribes, it seems evident that their Maya counterparts were much more closely tied to, if not participating members of, the priestly and ruling elite. This characterization agrees with the ethnohistorical sources from both the Maya area and central Mexico.

Interestingly, Early Classic sculptures and paintings lack artists' signatures. Artists' names appear only in the Late Classic period and become common at several sites in the Usumacinta region. With the collapse, signatures disappear altogether. The temporal pattern suggests that artists and craftsmen were becoming increasingly important as celebrated individuals during the Classic period. That is, we see a slightly broader spectrum of Maya society reflected in the writing of Late Classic times. Or, to interpret the pattern another way, it is possible that the Maya elite were gradually expanding their activity-base to include professions that were earlier reserved for lower- or middle-class specialists.

Recent archaeological research in the Copan valley lends support to assertions that elite craftsmen were becoming more conspicuous during the end of the Late Classic period. The so-called House of the Bacabs (Str. 9N-82) has been interpreted as the residence of a royal scribe or "calendar priest" (Webster 1989; Webster, Fash, and Abrams 1986; Fash 1986). The inscribed bench within names the "owner" of the structure, and relates him to the famous Copan ruler "Yax Pac." William Fash has pointed to this and other outlying elite compounds with inscribed benches as evidence of a growing diffusion of high-elite status toward the end of the Late Classic period. Several elite lineages seem to settle in residential zones throughout the Copan valley, expressing political ties to the main center. According to Fash's reconstruction of the events, the late Copan rulers were distributing royal symbolism and inscribed benches in an effort to consolidate their local base of power. While the mechanism for the diffusion of power may be different from the way Fash characterizes it, I feel that the rise of these secondary elite compounds, at least one of which is associated with scribes, represents a phenomenon strikingly parallel to the increased conspicuousness of artists (and as we shall see, other lesser elites) in the Late Classic hieroglyphic record.

### EPIGRAPHY AND POLITICAL ORGANIZATION

Many questions of the Maya collapse naturally revolve around political themes, and it is safe to say that ancient politics are best studied through epigraphic sources. Joyce Marcus (1973; 1976) was the first scholar to employ epigraphic data in the reconstruction of Maya political organization. In the present volume, however, Marcus moves away from the inscriptions and emphasizes parallels in Yucatec ethnohistory in order to reconstruct the political organization of the Classic southern lowlands. While I agree that the ethnohistoric data are relevant to the Classic period, I differ from Marcus' view of Postclassic Yucatec geopolitics as a model for the Late Classic southern lowlands. Even during the Late Classic, the character of Yucatec political organization seems to me to have been distinct from that of the southern lowlands. When we consider that several centuries of political upheaval elapsed before the emergence of the Late Postclassic Yucatec polities, we see that time and space set limits on the applicability of these models to the Late Classic period. In my view it seems more appropriate to make

 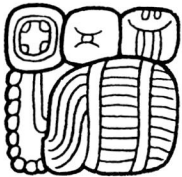

Fig. 1 The Emblem Glyph. These examples refer to the *k'ul ahaw*, or "holy lord," of the Petexbatun polity, which included the sites of Dos Pilas, Aguateca, and La Amelia: the left from Aguateca Stela 7, position D2; the right from Dos Pilas Stela 16, position C6 (redrawn after I. Graham 1967: figs. 17, 7).

use of the contemporary hieroglyphic records to address questions of political organization.

Emblem Glyphs, first recognized and discussed by Heinrich Berlin (1958), remain the principal epigraphic tools for reconstructing the Late Classic political geography of the southern lowlands. In his seminal study, Berlin found that a distinctive glyph appeared in the inscriptions, and that one of its three components varied, generally, in accordance with specific sites (Fig. 1). Berlin was noncommittal about the meaning of these "emblems," but suggested several possibilities: the variable signs could be actual place names, names or labels of ruling families, or perhaps names of tutelary deities. Later assuming that Emblem Glyphs were "geographical referents," Marcus (1976) noted the statistical frequencies of "foreign" Emblem Glyphs in various inscriptions, and from this posited certain hierarchical relationships among sites. In her own words, "if Site A was dependent on Site B, I expected Site A to mention (show the appropriate Emblem Glyph of) Site B more often than Site B mentioned Site A" (Marcus 1976: 10). Moreover, building upon earlier work by Thomas Barthel (1968), Marcus proposed that four Emblem Glyphs mentioned together on Copan, Stela A—those of Tikal, Palenque, Calakmul(?), and Copan—were the "four on high," or the four great regional capitals of the time. Another quartet of Emblem Glyphs—those of Tikal, Calakmul, Motul de San Jose (?), and Seibal—appears on Seibal, Stela 10 at a much later date. In Marcus' view this was an updated list of the four ruling centers of the Maya political landscape shortly before the collapse.

Marcus' 1976 book broke new ground in the effort to integrate hieroglyphic and archaeological data, but the epigraphic record does not support a quadripartite model. First, apart from viewing Emblem Glyphs as general referents to sites or political units, it is important that we understand that they are not simple place signs. Emblem Glyphs are above all *personal titles of*

*David Stuart*

*individuals.* As Peter Mathews and John Justeson (1984) point out, the one constant sign in all Emblem Glyphs—the so-called "ben-ich" or "ahpo" element—is read *ahaw,* "lord, noble," and can take several different graphic forms. Emblem Glyphs always accompany personal names or, on rare occasions, stand in place of them, referring to individuals as "lords" of specific places or areas. The frequent "water group" prefix, an abbreviated form of the God C glyph, is probably a representation of human blood (Stuart 1988), and is read *k'u* or *k'ul,* "god, holy, divine" (Barthel 1952; Ringle 1988). The addition of this prefix enhances the stature of the named individual to a *k'ul ahaw,* a "holy lord." This title refers to the supreme rulers, as distinct from the more general term *ahaw.* Some so-called Emblem Glyph titles at Chichen Itza and Uxmal lack the variable main element and seem to be read just *k'ul ahaw.* However, most examples of Emblem Glyphs are read *k'ul*-X-*ahaw,* where the central variable stands for a local reference, be it a place name or some other term. Evidently the same title exists in modern Tzotzil in the cognate form *ch'ul ohow,* "holy lord" (Guiteras-Holmes 1961: 334). The Mayan forms are literally equivalent to the Nahuatl *teoteuctli* ("holy lord"), glossed as "gran ministro, pontífice" (Siméon 1977: 489).[1]

Clearly this more personal interpretation of Emblem Glyphs has political implications. When one site mentions the Emblem Glyph of another, it refers primarily to a "holy lord," not to a place. For example, several monuments from Tonina record the Emblem Glyph of Palenque. Marcus earlier (1976: 109) had considered these references as evidence that Tonina was under the political dominion of Palenque. However, we now know that Tonina inscriptions occasionally mention Palenque *lords* without expressing any dependency relationship between the two sites. The references themselves may differ from case to case, and analyzing their individual contexts is, of course, especially revealing. To use one example, Monument 109 from Tonina carries an example of the Palenque Emblem, but it is inscribed upon the leg of the Palenque ruler "Kan-Xul," who is pictured on the stone as a bound captive. Clearly, then, we must have the sense of an entire monument before we can understand the nature of specific "foreign" references.

Epigraphic support for the "four capitals" model (see Marcus 1973, 1976, and Chap. 5) is also undermined by our ignorance of the full meaning of the

---

[1] The use of *ahaw* as a general title for Maya lords will become important in a later discussion of certain political offices mentioned in the inscriptions. Suffice it to say for now that in Mayan languages *ahaw,* "lord," is a widely applicable title. In colonial Tzotzil, *'ojov* means "king, lord, master of slaves, prelate" (Laughlin 1988, 1: 151). The Tzotzil entry continues (with my own translations in parentheses): "*'ojov* is universal for any individual of authority. They even call the alcaldes of their town, the prefects, and the provincial fathers *'ojov* in respect. When it is necessary to explain the difference between the king and the others, one must add to king *'sba 'ojov* (first lord), *muk' 'ojov* (great lord), *batz'i 'ojov* (true lord)." I believe that the title represented by Emblem Glyphs with the "blood" or God C prefix represents a similar elaboration of the basic title *ahaw.*

relevant passages. Stela A at Copan, for some unknown reason, mentions the *rulers* of four important cities. These rulers are indeed named in connection with the four cardinal directions, yet the surrounding text does not tell us why this is so, and many glyphs in this inscription still elude decipherment. It is equally risky to link the mention of four Emblem Glyphs at Copan with the Seibal example (Fig. 6), which lacks the "four on high" glyph (as Marcus reads a nearby glyph on Copan Stela A). The accompanying text on the Seibal monument tells us that the four rulers were "witnesses" of a single ritual event that took place at Seibal, so that contexts of the two references seem quite different. Thus, although we can now "read" certain texts with much greater certainty than in the mid-1970s, the literal hieroglyphic evidence we have so far does not itself support the model of a quadripartite political system.

It does support Mathews' (1985; n.d.) more recent idea of roughly egalitarian polities. Mathews sees every Emblem Glyph main sign as an indicator of a more or less autonomous political unit. In this scheme, no site with an Emblem was politically dominant over another during an extended period of time (with the exception of occasional "conquests," to be discussed below). Certainly there is as yet no *explicit evidence* of such domination relationships in the inscriptions. I had reached similar conclusions in my research of localized political structures (Stuart n.d.a.), but Mathews' broader arguments stand firmly on their own. Based on the epigraphic evidence currently at hand, therefore, we cannot posit the existence of political units above those defined by Emblem Glyphs. Mathews' polities are, following Renfrew's (1986: 4) definition, "the highest politically autonomous unit" we can identify with confidence from the inscriptions. If greater polities existed in Late Classic times, encompassing numerous sites with Emblem Glyphs, I would certainly expect them to be clearly documented in the historical texts, especially since politics and hierarchy were central themes in Maya inscriptions.

If we agree that individual Emblem Glyph main signs somehow refer to individual *political units,* then at about 9.18.0.0.0 (A.D. 790) we see at least twenty or so of these territories dotting the landscape of the southern lowlands (Mathews 1985), although perhaps several more have escaped our notice. Certain Emblem Glyphs are known only from texts of this late date, suggesting that some of these polities appear on the scene quite late in the course of Late Classic history. At the end of the eighth century, the central and eastern Peten region seems especially crowded with small polities, including a reduced area for Tikal's domain. In general, the peer-polity model agrees with recent evidence from archaeological sources (Demarest n.d.; Sabloff 1986).

Nevertheless a caution is in order. The epigraphic record still remains vague when it comes to illuminating the political and economic nuances of peer-polity relationships. Certainly such interactions among the various states differed considerably from center to center and may have changed over time, as Marcus (Chap. 5) also notes. Interestingly, however, economic control was never an explicit element in the presentation of Maya political and religious power. The relative political, military, and economic powers of the territorial units, different as they may have been, may be very difficult to reconstruct from the inscriptions for the very reason that these aspects of polity interaction were constantly changing during the Late Classic period. In any event, the nature of broader political and economic relationships will need to be investigated through several archaeological approaches.

Marcus and Mathews seem in agreement when it comes to arguing that Emblem Glyph main signs are actual place names. As Berlin long ago demonstrated, their specialized geographic distribution is clear enough, but questions still remain about their *specificity* as geographical references in the inscriptions. Since some Emblems are shared by two sites (Palenque and Tortuguero; Tikal and Dos Pilas), it would follow that these signs are somehow general references to large territorial units, and not necessarily to specific sites. Where, then, are the specific place names? David Kelley (1976: 215) once stated: "if Emblem Glyphs are not place names, then there seems no possibility that there is a major unexplored category of glyphs which could be place names." Recent decipherments show that this is not necessarily the case.

Stephen Houston and I have identified a number of glyphs that seem to name specific sites within the larger territorial units that appear to be named by Emblems (Stuart and Houston n.d.). We suggest that there exist actual place names or place glyphs corresponding to Palenque, Dos Pilas, Copan, Naranjo, and other sites. These designations are usually unrelated to the well-known Emblem Glyph main signs, but others, it seems, also serve as territorial glyphs.

One example is the place glyph of Aguateca, Guatemala (Fig. 2). Aguateca shares an Emblem Glyph with Dos Pilas, revealing that it is not specific as a locational reference. In contrast, at Aguateca we find a very distinctive glyph whose principal component is a *wits* or "hill" sign. The hill sign is cleft at its top, and takes the prefix *k'inich,* "sun-faced." "Sun-faced split hill" is an apt description of the physical setting of Aguateca: the site rests on a high hilltop that is literally split in two by a natural chasm or fissure up to 50 m in depth (I. Graham 1967). Cliffs on the eastern side of the hill stand out brightly in the morning sun, hence the *k'inich* designation (Houston, personal communication 1986). Thus, this glyph is a very precise place name—much more specific than the Emblem main sign used at Dos Pilas and distant Tikal. As it turns out, several other Classic period place names (not necessarily components of Emblem Glyphs) include the word "hill," as do many long-known toponyms of Postclassic central Mexico.

Other place glyphs seem more intimately related to Emblem Glyphs, but these are more general in scope. The site of Yaxha, for instance, has an

*Historical Inscriptions and the Maya Collapse*

Fig. 2  The place name of Aguateca, translatable as "Sun-faced Split Hill," from Aguateca Stela 1, position D10a (redrawn after I. Graham 1967: fig. 2).

Fig. 3  Two variants of the *sahal* title: the right from Kuna-Lacanha Panel 1 now at Dumbarton Oaks.

Emblem main sign that surely reads *Yaxha* (Stuart 1985a). Lake Yaxha ("clear water" or "blue/green water") is thus a very old name, and seems to have also been the designation for the local territorial unit. Evidently, at least some main signs of Emblem Glyphs function like place names, but the distinction between these Emblem main signs and the place names that Houston and I identify may be a matter of precision. We would argue that Aguateca's "split hill" glyph and the main sign of the Dos Pilas/Aguateca Emblem represent different *types* of place names, one being more geographically precise than the other. It is quite possible, we think, that the actual *site* known today as Yaxha had a different, more restricted designation in ancient times. Yaxha, as its meaning indicates, may have referred to the much larger area of the lake and its surroundings.

The size of political units, as well, can be studied using epigraphic sources. Palenque, Yaxchilan, Piedras Negras, and nearby centers all make reference to a certain subordinate political office or position that is often referred to as "cahal" (Stuart n.d.a, Mathews and Justeson 1984) (Fig. 3). This designation is a misnomer, though already widespread in the epigraphic and archaeological literature. I believe now that the true reading of the glyph is much more likely *sa-ha-la,* or *sahal*.[2] In Yucatec the root *sah*

---

[2] This revision is based upon assigning a new value to the so-called double-comb sign (T630 in Thompson's [1962] catalog). In several contexts I have found that the sign is best read as the syllable *sa*.

David Stuart

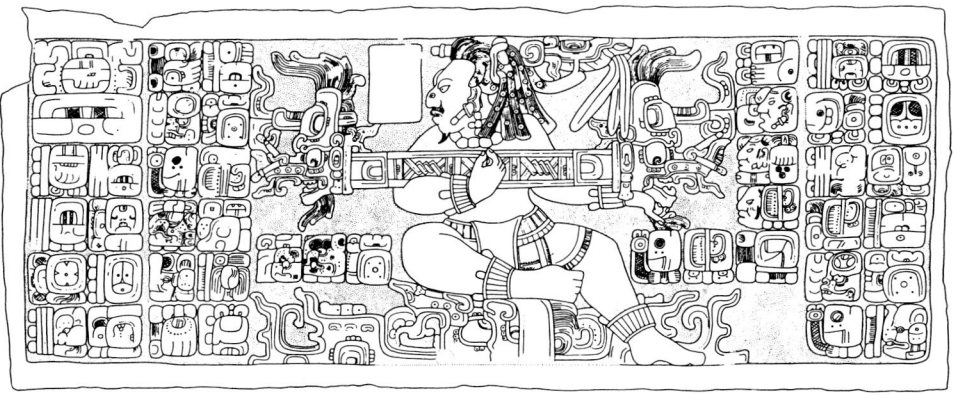

Fig. 4  Kuna-Lacanha Panel 1. Dumarton Oaks.

means "fear, terror." Michael Coe (personal communication, 1989) has pointed out to me that among the Aztec, "terror" and "fear" were the linguistic roots of regular epithets applied to rulers. The Nahuatl root *mahui,* "to be afraid," is found in *mahuiztli,* "a person worthy of being feared, an honorable person," and related terms (Andrews 1975: 450). The scowling countenance of the *sahal* on Lacanha, Panel 1 (Fig. 4) may lend some slight support to this reading. *Sahals,* as the possible translation might also indicate, often have an overtly military role in narrative scenes and inscriptions.

In any event, it is clear that these subordinate figures were, in some cases, rulers of small dependent sites within the larger polities of the western lowlands. Inscriptions from sites such as La Pasadita, a satellite of Yaxchilan, mention these subordinate figures in connection with the principal rulers (the *k'ul ahaw*). In several instances the texts explicitly state that a certain subordinate "is the *sahal* of" the ruler. These relationships allow us to define more clearly the political affiliations among small centers, thereby providing a more vivid picture of the relative sizes and frontiers of some territorial units (Fig. 5).

In a slightly different interpretation than that of Linda Schele and Mathews (1991), I feel that there was no inherent division between the titles *ahaw,* "lord, noble," and that given by the putative *sahal* glyph. Both represented the highest stratum in Maya society, and several *sahals* carry the *ahaw* honorific in their names. The real distinction was, rather, between the *sahal* nobility and the supreme ruler, the *k'ul ahaw,* or "holy lord."

Another title may shed further light on the constituents of nobility at Copan and other sites. As already noted, the hieroglyphic bench from Str. 9N-82 at Copan mentions a certain relationship between the noble "owner"

*Historical Inscriptions and the Maya Collapse*

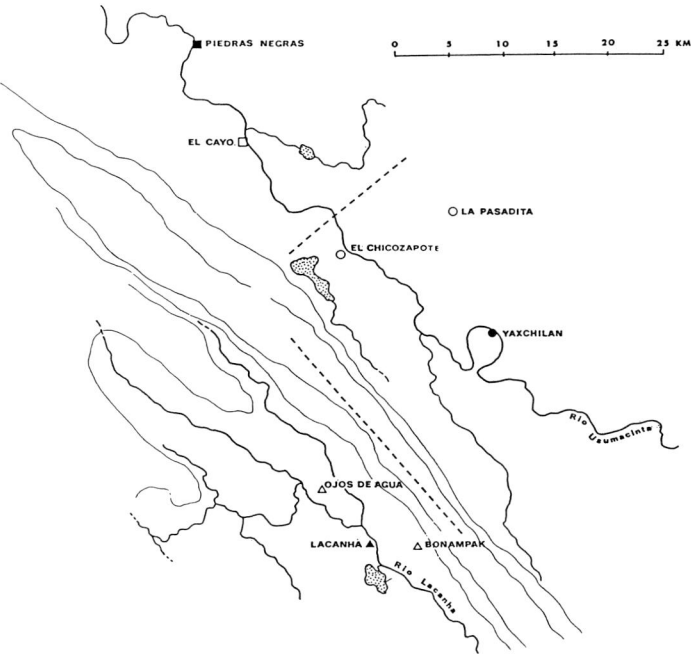

Fig. 5 Map showing posited frontiers (dashed lines) between three polities near the Usumacinta River. "Capitals" are indicated by solid symbols; satellite centers by open symbols.

of the building and the ruler Yax Pac (Webster 1989). The same relationship links the name of the owner of the so-called Harvard bench from Str. 9M-18 and Yax Pac's predecessor, "Smoke Shell." The relationship glyph is composed of three phonetic signs, *ya-k'u(l)-na,* which appear to constitute the possessed form of the common title *a-k'u(l)-na* (Houston, personal communication, 1989). This title appears throughout the Maya *corpus* of texts with several male individuals who are clearly not rulers. William Ringle (1988) has interpreted this as *ah k'una,* "He of the Temple," a decipherment that seems cogent in many instances, but an alternative reading may be possible. In Yucatec there exist a number of interesting titles based on the title *Ah K'ul* (from Martínez Hernández 1929: 93–94):

> *ah kul:* mandador a quien el cacique embia a que trate algo con la gente.
> *ah kulel:* cierto official de la república, menores que los *as cuch cabe,* mayores que los *tupiles.* Abogados, medianeros y terceros entre algunos.

331

David Stuart

> *ah kulem miatz:* doctor sagrado.
> "      "      *than:* lo mismo o gran theólogo
> "      "      *dzib:* escriptor sagrado que escrive cosas de dios y theólogo assi.

These titles might explain the context of the glyph under discussion, and seem especially fitting given the Copan evidence, both archaeological and epigraphic.

Along with *ah k'una* and *sahal,* we find in several inscriptions a subordinate title spelled *a-na-bi*. Unfortunately we have so far failed to find an adequate translation for this term. The title can be found with certain *sahals* (on Lacanha, Panel 1, for example), as well as with the names of sculptors and other artisans. The latter are often called the "*anabs*" of local rulers. This glyph also can be seen next to several figures portrayed in the murals at Bonampak, who Mary Ellen Miller (1986: 42) describes as "young princes training at the court of Bonampak." It seems entirely likely that more such specialized terms for political or social positions will be discovered with further epigraphic research.

The evidence for regional variation in Late Classic Maya geopolitics is striking. To my knowledge, the *sahal* title does not really occur to the east of sites on the Usumacinta River. The only other examples known to me come from the Classic period inscriptions of Xcalumkin and other sites far to the north in Campeche. No examples are known from the central Peten sites and the southeast. Even more interesting, I believe, is the fact that very few examples of the *sahal* glyph are known from before the eighth century. As the Classic period progressed, perhaps the complex political and economic strains were accompanied by a rising prominence of these political subordinates. If so, were the subordinate rulers partly a cause of pre-collapse tensions, or did their late appearance in the inscriptions reflect some attempt by the principal rulers to establish and strengthen the frontiers of their territories? Both of these scenarios might be partially true. These are difficult questions, but I would certainly think that they are vital for our understanding of the weak political situation of Maya polities at the end of the Late Classic.

### THE EPIGRAPHIC EVIDENCE OF MAYA WARFARE

Relationships among the various polities in Late Classic times are of great interest for the epigrapher and archaeologist alike. When we consider the issue of political interaction, we must often confront the many references to "war" in the inscriptions, which are certainly common yet poorly understood in any literal sense. Maya warfare in the southern lowlands has been the subject of considerable study (Webster 1976a, 1976b, 1977, 1988; Demarest 1978; Freidel 1986), and there still appears to be debate about the nature of these interactions. Was war a restrictive elite ritual designed primarily for captive-taking, or was it more conquest-oriented, and socially and politically disruptive? David Freidel (1986: 107) defines Maya warfare "as a prerogative of the elite and fought primarily by the elite, (and) the bulk of the population was neither affected by, nor participated in, violent conflict." In much the same vein, Richard Adams (1977: 153) earlier stated that "there is no indication of highly organized, state-level warfare with standing armies, sophisticated tactics, and anything approaching large-scale casualties or genocide. . . . Likewise, then, there is little indication that warfare was a socially disruptive activity." I would agree that warfare seems to have been primarily an elite enterprise, but, as we shall see, the epigraphy and archaeology may indicate that limited wars might have been more socially and politically disruptive than Adams and Freidel believe. Unfortunately, the inscriptions that we can read are not at all explicit about the motives for warfare, nor its character. Any discussion of Maya warfare must therefore rely on vague textual references to military events, and archaeological records that are largely unknown at many sites. It is possible to identify hieroglyphic events that seem to revolve around warfare, but, with the notable exception of the well-known "capture" glyph (*chu-ka-ha,* for *chuk-ah,* "was captured"), we are limited by our present inability to read these phonetically. However, even if in the most general terms, epigraphy provides a unique method for analyzing warfare in an ancient historical setting. It has been pointed out that hieroglyphic records of battles, captures, and raids appear more frequently in the late eighth century than at any time before (Rands 1973). This is especially true in the western lowlands. The last known inscriptions for Palenque, Yaxchilan, and Piedras Negras, not to mention the Bonampak murals, all revolve around military themes.

Hieroglyphic discussions of warfare are noticeably absent in the Early Classic period. I doubt that this is an effect of a limited sample of early inscriptions—the corpus of early inscriptions is, in fact, quite substantial (Mathews 1985). Rather, I believe that a discontinuity exists between the Early and Late Classic in the themes Maya lords chose to record on inscribed monuments. In positing such a shift, I must emphasize that warfare was not unknown in the political landscape of the Early Classic period. The great fortifications at Becan are clear testimony to the existence of war in the Late Preclassic and Early Classic periods (Webster 1976a). Moreover, we see militaristic iconography in the earliest stages of the Maya sculptural tradition, and captive and warrior portraits appear on very ancient monuments and artifacts of this time (the Leiden Plaque, for example). What is significant, I think, is that the inscriptions of this time lack the narrative discussions of warfare that so pervade the later historical records of Yaxchilan, Dos Pilas, and other centers. Instead, the texts of the Early Classic emphasize more localized ritual events, such as period endings, office-takings, and so on (see Willey and Shimkin 1973: 459). Military dress and captive portraits seem to have a more emblematic than narrative function during this period. Overall, warfare would not appear to play a prominent role in native histories of the Early Classic.

In making this claim, I must differ with Mathews (1985) in his identification of a war between Tikal and Uaxactun in 387 A.D., and the installation of one "Smoking Frog" as a new Uaxactun ruler under Tikal's dominion (see also Culbert 1988: 142). In keeping with the overall character of Early Classic inscriptions just described, I see no explicit evidence of this war in the hieroglyphic records of Tikal or Uaxactun.

I view the profound shift toward narrative records of warfare as a distinctive characteristic of the Late Classic inscriptions. The first explicit record of hostilities between sites occurs at Caracol, which apparently took military action against Tikal in 652 A.D. (S. Houston, personal communication, 1985). This event has been taken by some as an explanation of Tikal's famous monument hiatus at this time, but in reality we cannot yet know if this act of aggression was a causal factor in Tikal's temporary demise, or perhaps an example of Caracol kicking Tikal while it was already down. In any event, the epigraphy would seem to indicate that Caracol was precocious in its early textual concern with military events. The next known episode of war also appears at Caracol, this time being carried out against Naranjo at 9.9.18.16.3. Significantly, the dominance of Caracol over Naranjo is corroborated in the archaeological record of the defeated site, where a monumental inscribed stairway, carved in Caracol's distinctive style, was erected to exalt the ritual activities of the Caracol ruler and Naranjo's defeat.

As I have already stressed, Caracol's successful military exploits did not represent the advent of Maya warfare, but rather the advent of its detailed expression in the historical inscriptions. Many sites followed Caracol's lead. Soon after, Dos Pilas, located in the politically volatile Petexbatun region, begins its own historical record on Hieroglyphic Stairway 1 with a rich discussion of war and political interaction. Dos Pilas' sudden appearance on the Classic landscape seems to me to be linked with the instabilities we begin to find reflected in the inscriptions of this time. The local rulers make use of the Tikal Emblem Glyph as a title, and Dos Pilas' rise as a powerful dynastic center may be specifically linked to Tikal's own demise during the hiatus. The first documented ruler of Dos Pilas, Ruler 1 (Houston and Mathews 1985), appears to have defeated the Tikal lord "Shield Skull," the father of Ruler A. In any event, Dos Pilas went on to become one of the most militaristic centers of the Maya lowlands, perhaps second only to Yaxchilan in its epigraphic emphasis on war and capture.

At the same time, about 9.11.0.0.0 in Maya terms, we begin to see the rapid expansion of Yaxchilan on the Usumacinta River. Here the narrative record of warfare on sculpture and in texts becomes most explicit. In their day, the dynamic scenes and accounts of capture during the reign of Shield

Jaguar I must have made for some very novel monuments. To appreciate this shift, I need only point out that the "capture" glyph does not appear on contemporary monuments at Yaxchilan before his reign, well into the Late Classic period. Here and at other sites, we see Early Classic "capture" events cited in the local histories, but all are recorded on monuments of much later date. After the posited shift toward explicit militaristic narratives at the beginning of the Late Classic, rulers appear to have made some effort to manifest continuity between their own military ventures and the earlier traditions of capture and warfare. But the recording of such events in historical texts seems to me to be very different from Early Classic custom.

Militaristic themes continue unabated throughout the Late Classic period. One historical episode at Yaxchilan may illustrate this trend. Following the death of Shield Jaguar I after a long and productive reign, there is a long interregnum of ten years before the accession of his son Bird Jaguar IV. No other dynastic history records a gap of such length, and Tatiana Proskouriakoff (1963: 163) suggested that this period represented a time of political conflict in the Yaxchilan court. Her suggestion seems a cogent one, although no textual records directly support the hypothesis. We do see, however, that Bird Jaguar performed certain rituals and military raids during the interregnum. I find it significant that after his seating in office, Bird Jaguar emphasizes one particular title in his own inscriptions: "He of Twenty Captives" (Stuart 1985b). Bird Jaguar's successor, in turn, also uses the similar title, "He of Sixteen Captives." Before the interregnum, no "count of captives" title ever appears in the Yaxchilan inscriptions, but it is fairly common afterwards with other personages at Yaxchilan and other sites up to the end of the Classic period. These titles are reminiscent of the Aztec concern with captive counts (Sahagún 1950–82, bk. 8: 75–77). Aztec military status was often concerned with quotas of captives, and I would venture that the same concern was strongly felt by late Maya lords and military captains. Perhaps the interregnum at Yaxchilan saw a vying for power among certain claimants, as Proskouriakoff originally suggested, which may have been resolved somehow by taking a "captive count." In any event, unlike his predecessors, Bird Jaguar was certainly proud enough of his twenty prisoners to boast of it in every inscription he commissioned.

The late emphasis on warfare in Classic historical texts still requires explanation, and it must be viewed in the context of other trends we see reflected in the inscriptions before the collapse in the southern lowlands. Since we know that warfare was not unique to the Late Classic, the sudden explicitness in the later texts must reflect some new design in the historical messages that the Maya nobility took trouble to convey. While the motives and character of warfare may have changed over the Classic period, we see no direct indication of this in the hieroglyphic record. All that is left to us is a profound change in the "message" of Maya history.

By placing this thematic shift at the beginning of the Late Classic period, I would suggest that the geopolitical tensions that were no doubt important in the process of collapse had more time-depth in Maya history than is often claimed. At least in terms of warfare and its political repercussions, the collapse can perhaps be seen as gradually taking place throughout the Late Classic period. In a stimulating paper, Gordon Willey (1974) hypothesized that the Classic hiatus could be seen as a "rehearsal" for the collapse. I would agree with Willey in making a processual connection between the two events, but I would differ by characterizing the hiatus as a localized reflection of the inherent political instabilities that helped to "set the ball rolling" toward eventual political disintegration and abandonment of the southern centers. In my view, the whole Late Classic sees a single, long-term demise of the institution of southern lowland Maya rulership. This view contrasts with one advanced some years ago by Jeremy Sabloff and Willey (1967: 318) in a discussion of their "invasion hypothesis" of the collapse: ". . . we do not believe that the Maya were going 'downhill' at the time the Southern Lowlands were invaded by non-Classic peoples. All evidence points to the intrusion having occurred just before or by 9.19.0.0.0, a time when Maya civilization was still at its Late Classic peak."

External explanations for the collapse, such as foreign invasion, seem more attractive when the Late Classic is viewed as a cultural "peak." But the internal strife described above calls into question this assumption, and by extension weakens the case for an external explanation of the collapse.

## INSCRIPTIONS OF THE TERMINAL CLASSIC

So far, our discussion of epigraphy and iconography has centered on internal causes of the Maya collapse, specifically with regard to warfare between polities. As noted above, a traditional alternative to internal models of collapse (including ecological disasters) emphasizes external forces, namely an intrusion of outside "non-Classic" peoples into the Maya lowlands. The two alternatives are not unrelated, and most archaeologists would agree that political and religious changes occurred at this time alongside long-distance population movements within greater Mesoamerica. A largely unanswered question remains as to whether these real external factors were a cause or an effect of the sociopolitical instabilities that overran Late Classic civilization.

For many years, questions about a foreign role in the Maya collapse in the southern lowlands have centered on a number of late inscribed monuments that seem to show "Mexican" stylistic influences. The Terminal Classic monuments of Seibal, Guatemala, have received special attention for this reason (J. Graham 1973). Clearly there are new influences in this area around 800 A.D., not only in sculptural styles but also in the sudden appearance of fine-paste ceramics. Brief investigations at Seibal led to the conclusion that these new features were the direct result of a foreign invasion, probably by militaristic Putun Maya from the Campeche and Tabasco coastal area. It was believed that these outsiders forcibly took control over Seibal (Sabloff and Willey 1967).

Let us examine the sculptural evidence that is most often cited for the invasion hypothesis. In his analysis of the inscriptions and sculpture styles of Seibal, John Graham (1973) divided the monuments into two categories, the "A" and "B" groups. The identification of the A group "depends largely upon a physiognomy which suggests origins other than a purely local classic context" (J. Graham 1973: 211). Examples include Stela 10 (Fig. 6), whose finely carved portrait exhibits a moustache, a nose-plug, and long hair. Such traits, along with "non-Classic facial features and expressions" are thought to lie outside any Maya tradition of figural representation (see Sabloff 1973: 126). Graham's B group of monuments appear even more exotic:

> Figures of the group are especially to be recognized by their waist-length or longer hair, by absence, with minor exceptions, of elaborate Classic Maya attire and accoutrement, and by a constellation of traits which seem significant in their combination but are not all exclusive to the group: squared cartouche glyphs, non-Classic dates or an absence of Classic *hotun* dates, the large bead necklace, and other features (J. Graham 1973: 213).

The principal sculptural evidence of foreign intrusion therefore rests with facial features and details of attire.

I find the exotic or foreign characterization of Graham's A group particularly difficult to accept. The ceremonial costume and iconographic details of these monuments are firmly rooted in the greater Classic tradition. Moustaches and "facial features" like those displayed on Stelae 10 and 11 can be found on several earlier sculptures, such as Kuna-Lacanha, Panel 1, dated to 9.15.15.0.0 (Fig. 4), and Yaxchilan, Lintel 42. Graham's B group, which would seem to overlap chronologically with the other, is indeed more unusual. Differences in attire do not necessarily reflect distinct ethnicities, however. An equally likely interpretation might see the more simply dressed figures as members of a lower social or political status than the richly adorned rulers. Indeed, the two "types" are found together on the front of Stela 17 (J. Graham 1973: fig. 34). To me, this scene could simply represent a subordinate personage in the company of the ruler. As I have already noted, late inscriptions and art mention and portray a more diverse spectrum of political and social figures. The Seibal monuments may simply be a local reflection of this trend.

The interpretation of foreign intruders at Seibal is not substantiated by hieroglyphic evidence. Graham, Sabloff, and Willey understood the potential importance of the hieroglyphic evidence (J. Graham 1973: 210; Sabloff and Willey 1967: 317), but at the time Maya inscriptions remained largely

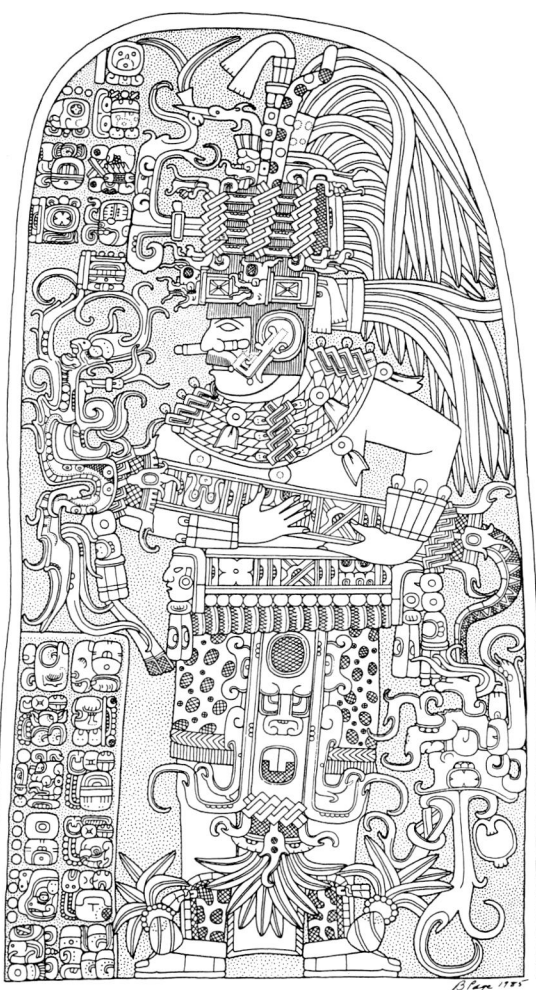

Fig. 6 Seibal Stela 10. Drawing by Barbara Page for the Peabody Museum of Archaeology and Ethnology, Harvard University.

undeciphered. Now, with considerable progress in this field, the hieroglyphic data can be used to help test the invasion hypothesis. The inscriptions at Seibal are generally restricted to stelae, and therefore are not of considerable length. One exception is the inscribed hieroglyphic stairway, from the middle of the Late Classic, which records certain ritual events performed by a local Seibal lord under the auspices of a Dos Pilas ruler. The texts associated with the Terminal Classic stelae, however, contain one or two passages at most. We see a single ruler featured on many of these monuments, including Stela 10 (Fig. 6). His hieroglyphic name is rendered by phonetic signs (*wa-ba-lu-k'a-?-le*) and he is called a *k'ul ahaw,* "holy lord," of Seibal. I do not offer any translation of the name, but Mathews and Willey (1991: 58) state that the compound of six phonetic signs indicates a foreign name. This is a puzzling claim. The frequency of phonetic signs in no way points to the spelling of foreign words—the Maya had a phonetic writing system, and could use it to spell any word or name they desired. It is worth noting here that the name glyph of one the most celebrated Maya rulers, Pacal of Palenque, is also known to be composed of six phonetic signs (*ha-na-bi-pa-ka-la*). The foreign name interpretation is in keeping with the invasion hypothesis, but it cannot stand on its own merits.

As for the Seibal inscriptions as a whole, there is absolutely no evidence for the presence of non-Maya terminology. The texts are well within the Peten mode of recording period endings and associated rituals, including the names of outside "witnesses" to these events on Stelae 8 and 10. In conclusion, there are no historical records of a Terminal Classic invasion. In the late records that do exist, we can see a strong continuation of Classic tradition and ritual practice.

This is not to say that outside influences were absent in Seibal's art and inscriptions. I would simply see these influences as considerably less dramatic and significant than Graham, Sabloff, and Willey have previously stated. The "non-Classic" label reflects a *temporal* distinction of this style, and there seems no reason to go beyond stylistic evolution to find an explanation for the slightly harsher effect of Seibal's late sculpture. We see that a similar style appears on late monuments from other Peten sites. At Xultun, the latest dated stela from the Maya lowlands (10.3.0.0.0) is iconographically identical to monuments that are considerably older, even though certain stylistic changes are clearly evident (Figs. 7, 8). At Tikal and the related site of Ixlu, a similar conservatism can be seen between monuments of the Late and Terminal Classic (Figs. 9, 10). No specific foreign influences can be pointed to on these later Peten stelae, but perhaps their overall stiff and simplistic artistic effect shows affinities to northern Mesoamerican traditions of representation. Seibal's own unique variety of sculpture stands out among other sites, I suggest, because of its relatively late beginning. No long-term sculptural tradition from the Classic period has survived there, and we are left to view its late monuments only in light of earlier traditions from Dos Pilas, Tikal, or other Peten sites.[3] Every Peten site has its own

---

[3] The earliest Seibal stelae with portraits are 5 and 7, dated to 9.18.10.0.0. These show an important ruler who is also named in the monuments of La Amelia, a small site on the Rio Pasion some distance downstream from Seibal. The style of these early Seibal and La Amelia monuments foreshadows a number of details seen in the Terminal Classic stelae at Seibal. If the Seibal monuments can be compared to any local "tradition," it is to these slightly earlier monuments.

David Stuart

Fig. 7   Xultun Stela 9. Drawing by Eric Von Euw (after Von Euw 1978: 35).

# Historical Inscriptions and the Maya Collapse

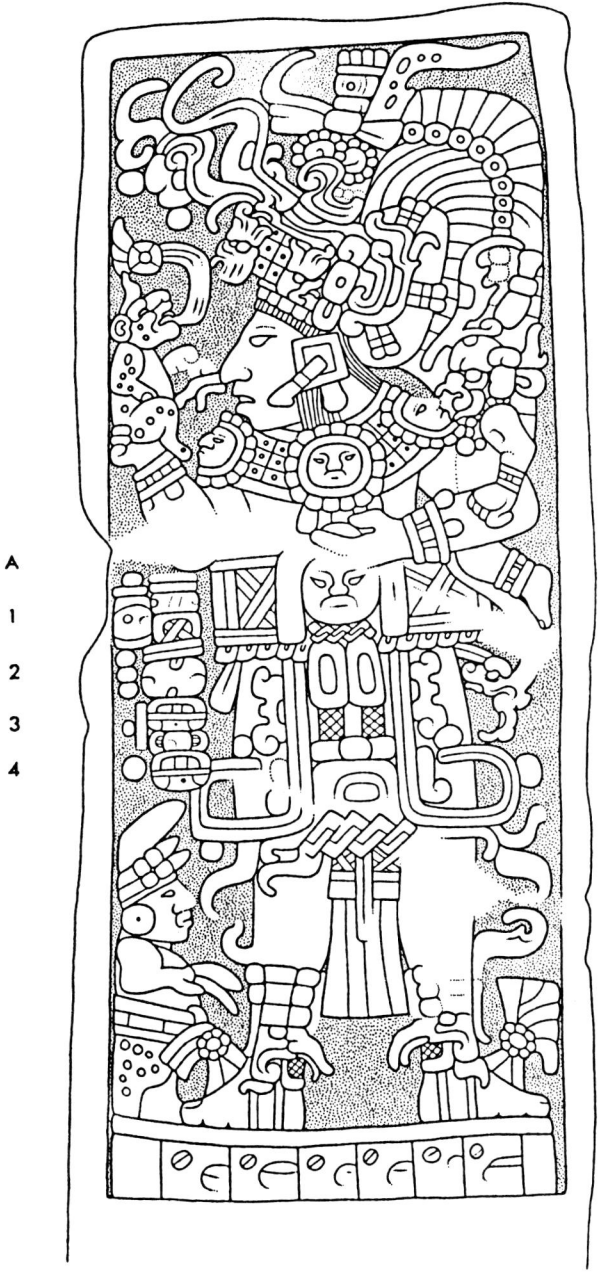

Fig. 8  Xultun Stela 10. Drawing by Eric Von Euw (after Von Euw 1978: 37).

Fig. 9 Tikal Stela 22. Drawing by William R. Coe (after Jones and Satterthwaite 1982: fig. 33).

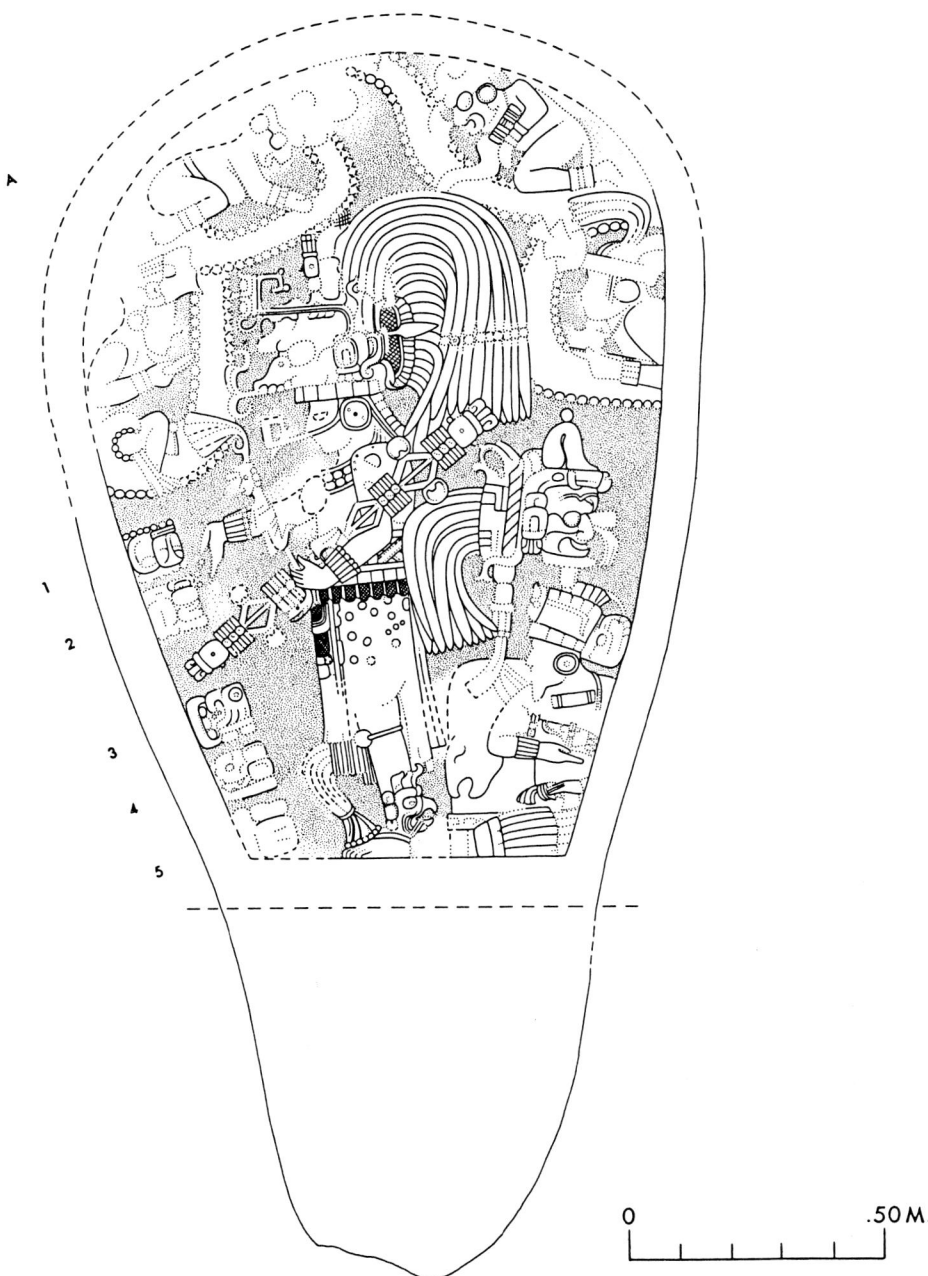

Fig. 10  Ixlu Stela 1. Drawing by William R. Coe (after Jones and Satterthwaite 1982: fig. 80).

*David Stuart*

idiosyncratic style of sculpture, and we must avoid comparing "apples and oranges."

The invasion hypothesis has remained a strong influence in general discussions of the Maya collapse in the southern lowlands. The discussions above have attempted to show that internal strife and political instability largely began within the Maya area at the onset of the Late Classic period, long before any of the so-called non-Classic influences came upon the scene. For this reason, I believe we must reevaluate the notion that foreign military invasions were directly responsible for the disintegration of the Maya elite. It seems more likely that these vaguely felt influences are part of a much greater interregional network of Mesoamerican contact that came about through the movement of peoples during Terminal Classic times, and that the Maya were more vulnerable to such influences and contacts as their political and social structures began to disintegrate.

## DYNASTIC COLLAPSE AT COPAN: AN EPIGRAPHIC CLUE

So far, the discussion of epigraphy's relevance to questions of the collapse has revolved around a recognition of certain thematic trends. These are, at best, indirect allusions to processual causes of the collapse. Now I move to a discussion of one inscription that is interesting in light of its possible bearing on the Maya's own views of the collapse.

Stela 11 from Copan—no more than a squat round column—is a very unimposing monument from a site known for its great sculptural tradition (Fig. 11). The upper fragment was discovered between Structures 16 and 17 during the first expedition of the Peabody Museum of Harvard University. The base of the column was found much later at the southeast corner of Structure 18, whence the monument originally fell (Becker and Cheek 1983: 491). The style of the monument suggests a date toward the end of the Late Classic. A figure of a standing lord graces the front of the stone, and a double-columned text consisting of eighteen glyphs runs down the opposite side. The inscription begins at block A1 with a probable date reference "on 8 Ahau." The inscription contains the names of two famous Copan rulers, *K'inich Yax K'uk' Mo'* (at A6–B6) and Yax Pac (at B7–A8). Clearly, the monument is associated with the later of the two kings, since *K'inich Yax K'uk' Mo'* was an Early Classic ruler who was the so-called founder of the Copan ruling line. Given this information, and assuming that the simple Ahau date records a period ending, we can assign with some assurance a more precise Long Count position of 9.19.10.0.0. This would make Stela 11 the latest known monument from Copan, and the general style of the carving perfectly fits such a date.

While the names are clearly legible, there are several trouble spots in the readability of the entire text. B2 through A5 are especially opaque, though we see a couplet structure that refers to obsidian and flint ("Obsidian is his ?;

## Historical Inscriptions and the Maya Collapse

Fig. 11  Copan Stela 11. Drawing by Barbara W. Fash (after Becker and Cheek 1983: fig. M-27).

Flint is his ?"). However, I find the first two glyphs after the date most interesting. It is here that we should expect to find the verb of event of the passage. B1 consists of three phonetic signs, *ho-mo-yi*. I suspect that the verb root is *hom,* and that the *yi* sign represents a final completive suffix. The next glyph, following the verb, is known from other inscriptions at Copan and other sites to be strongly associated with "founder" figures of local ruling lines (Schele n.d.; Grube 1988). Appropriately, the glyph often accompanies the name of *K'inich Yax K'uk' Mo'* in the Copan texts. The so-called founder glyph is difficult to read in full, but noteworthy is the suffix sign *nah,* which when found in this last position in other glyphs, seems to stand for *nah,* "house." It is therefore possible that the "founder" glyph refers to a house or type of structure directly associated with the founding ruling lines or dynasties. In this inscription, the "founder-house" glyph immediately follows the *hom* verb, and therefore seems to be its subject.

The verb root *hom* means "desplomar lo abovedado, desplomar techo, derribar edificios" in Yucatec Mayan (Barerra Vásquez 1980: 229). I have not found the same term in other languages. The Yucatec gloss is notably fitting in view of the "house" glyph that follows the verb in the inscription. If the reading is correct in this context, we would seem to have a literal reference to the destruction of the "founder's house," possibly a metaphorical statement of the end of Copan's ruling line. In support of this, it has been suggested that the portrait on the front of Stela 11 represents the deceased Yax Pac, the last documented Copan ruler (Schele, personal communication, 1988).

If these tentative conclusions contain any grain of truth, then it is possible to argue that Stela 11 holds a unique place as the only Maya inscription containing a direct reference to the collapse of a local political system. Sadly, the text of this monument tells us nothing of the specific circumstances of Copan's dynastic fall. Stela 11 seems to be a simple milestone of the event. Archaeological evidence suggests that Copan's population survived for a considerable period of time after the cessation of dynastic monuments (Webster 1989: 36–39), so at least there would have been an audience, short-lived as it was, for this historic marker.

### THE RULING BROTHERS OF CHICHEN ITZA?

Aside from this single monument at Copan, perhaps the most illuminating texts on political changes during the Terminal Classic come from Chichen Itza. Here there are no direct references to dynastic collapses or transformations, but rather intriguing descriptions of a very different political order than what we have seen in the southern sites discussed up to now. David Kelley (1968) made an important initial breakthrough in the study of Chichen's texts with his decipherment of the historical name K'ak'upakal (spelled *k'a-k'u-pa-ka-la*), the celebrated Itza military captain who is mentioned in the Books of Chilam Balam (Fig. 12). In 1987 I recognized another historical name at Chichen Itza, that of Hunpiktok' (Figure 12b), who according to Bernando de Lizana's history of Yucatan was an ancient Itza lord of Izamal (Lizana 1892). Extending this historical research, Nikolai Grube and I noted two instances in the inscriptions of the famous surname Cocom (Figure 12c) (Grube and Stuart 1987). The Cocoms are named in many Yucatec historical chronicles as the ruling family of Mayapan. All these identifications have provided an important link between Maya hieroglyphic decipherment and the traditional ethnohistorical "reality" of ancient Yucatan.

Several other historical names appear together in the Chichen Itza inscrip-

## Historical Inscriptions and the Maya Collapse

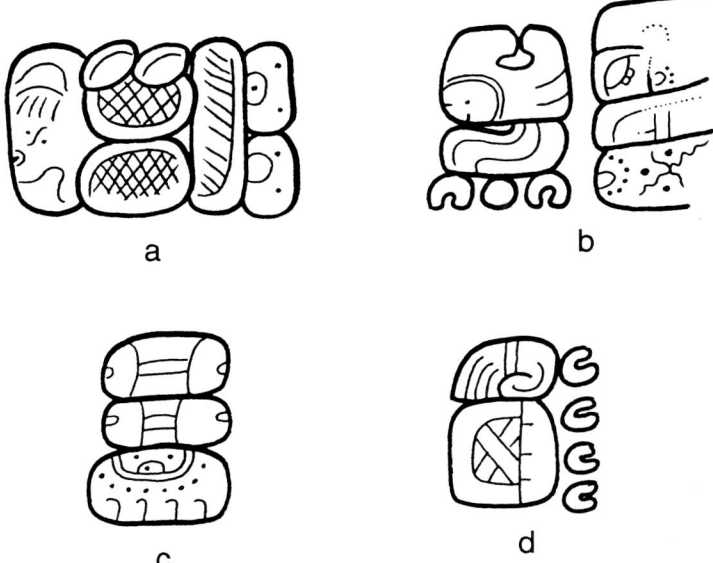

Fig. 12 Selected glyphs from the inscriptions of Chichen Itza: (a) K'ak'upakal, from Monjas Lintel 4, at Y3; (b) Hunpiktok', from Halakal Lintel at G4b, G5; (c) Cocom, from Akab Dzib Lintel, a, at E2; (d) *y-itah,* "sibling of . . ." (?), from Temple of the Four Lintels, Lintel 2, at G1.

tions, but these cannot yet be connected directly with known figures mentioned in the native chronicles. What is most important, however, is a certain relationship glyph that links several of these names (Figure 12d). I suggest that this glyph is to be read *y-itah,* probably signifying "sibling of."[4] If this reading is correct, then at least three sets of brothers can be isolated from the Chichen texts. No one figure stands out among these, suggesting to me a much different political organization than any we have previously seen in Maya history.

On noting these possible sibling references at Chichen, I immediately

---

[4] The "sibling" reading, first suggested by the author in a letter circulated in February, 1988, has happily gained acceptance among several colleagues. I caution, however, that questions of its precise phonetic reading remain to be resolved, and that the reading requires some testing before it may be added to the growing list of solid decipherments. Nonetheless, the painted texts at Najtunich offer perhaps the best contextual evidence for the "sibling of" interpretation, since there it links the names of two nobles who are called "elder brother" and "younger brother."

recalled the "Episode of the Three Brothers" recorded by Landa (in Tozzer 1941: 177):

> Chichen Itza is a very fine site, ten leagues from Izamal, and eleven from Valladolid, in which, as the old men of the Indians say, three lords who were brothers ruled, who as they remember to have heard from their ancestors came to that country from the west, and brought together in those localities a great population of towns and peoples; whom they governed in great peace and justice for some years. There were devoted worshippers of their god; and so they erected many and magnificent buildings, and especially one, which was the largest, of which I will here give a sketch, as I drew it when I was there. . . .

According to this legendary history, the three brothers from the west were responsible for the construction of the "Castillo" at Chichen Itza. No inscription accompanies that "Toltec" structure—rather, those texts that mention the sibling relationships come from the buildings of "Old Chichen," traditionally believed to be earlier than edifices of the "Toltec" style. I do not wish to enter into a complex and debatable discussion of Chichen Itza's chronology, but there now seems to be considerable doubt as to the exclusivity of these two periods, defined principally by art styles (Lincoln 1986). The ethnohistorical mention of the brothers' rule accords with the "group" effect of the Chichen inscriptions mentioned above. In any case, the fact that the names in these inscriptions may be linked by the term "sibling" is perhaps more than suggestive.

I posit that the Chichen Itza inscriptions may be a more appropriate place to discuss an "invasion," for we appear to see the introduction of a political order that differs radically from any other known to have existed before in Yucatan. This possibility must be contrasted with the invasion hypothesis used in models for the southern Peten area, for at Seibal and elsewhere, as I have suggested above, the indicators of political and religious structure accord with the Classic period traditions of that area.

## CONCLUSIONS

The present review of the epigraphic evidence has raised some broad questions about the nature of Classic Maya society, and particularly some of the dynamic changes the elite culture underwent before the collapse. It is hoped, therefore, that the relevance of native historical texts to larger processual questions has been made clear. I have stressed particularly the thematic shifts we find in inscriptions at the beginning of the Late Classic period. These changes are twofold: first, the conspicuous appearance of lesser political officeholders and elite craft specialists, and, second, a new explicitness in records of warfare. The two developments are, I believe, closely linked.

As noted above, a platitude in our field holds that the Late Classic was the apogee of lowland Maya civilization. However, the unilinear evolutionary models that have traditionally been used to arrive at such a view have changed radically in recent years with the study of Preclassic urban centers such as El Mirador (Matheny 1980). Many of the qualitative traits so often used to characterize Late Classic society could just as easily describe the elite society of El Mirador. The conspicuous monumental and artistic achievements of the Late Classic long ago gave rise to subjective views of its greatness, but I feel that this is chiefly a result of a shallow perspective in the archaeological record. By restricting such descriptions to the Late Classic, we make trouble for ourselves by having to confront a great—and possibly false—irony: why did the southern lowland Maya collapse at their height?

Perhaps they did not. Over the last fifteen years, the view of the Classic as a period of great internal instability has gained considerable favor. This has come not only as a result of archaeological groundwork (Webster 1976a, 1976b), but also due to important art historical and epigraphic studies (Miller 1986). We see from such evidence that the collapse of the southern lowlands may not be so sudden from a historical, or at least textual, perspective.

Does the evidence we have discussed pertain to broad societal changes, or just a new textual *emphasis* on long-held institutions such as warfare, artists, and subsidiaries? The question is difficult to answer given the present evidence. I feel, however, that any new thematic emphasis or concern in the native historical record reveals a profound societal change in itself. Either way, the hieroglyphic record shows us that Classic Maya society was anything but static.

Processual perspectives on the Classic Maya, and the collapse in general, have been the subjects of many diverse articles in recent years. The culture-historical foundations upon which any such models must rely are only now becoming realized in the inscriptions. Perhaps this brief review of the textual evidence will demonstrate the usefulness of epigraphy not only as a purely historical tool, but also, in building upon the historical base, its importance as a source for understanding questions of historical and cultural evolution.

# BIBLIOGRAPHY

ADAMS, R. E. W.
1977 *Prehistoric Mesoamerica.* Little, Brown and Company, Boston.

ANDREWS, J. RICHARD
1975 *Introduction to Classical Nahuatl.* University of Texas Press, Austin.

BARERRA VASQUEZ, ALFREDO
1980 *Diccionario Cordemex: Maya-Español, Español-Maya.* Cordemex, Mérida, Yucatan, Mexico.

BARTHEL, THOMAS S.
1952 Der Morgensternkult in den Darstellungen der Dresdener Mayahandschrift. *Ethnos* 17: 73–112. Stockholm.
1968 El Complejo "Emblema." *Estudios de Cultura Maya* 7: 159–193. Universidad Nacional Autónoma de México, Mexico.

BECKER, MARSHALL J., AND CHARLES D. CHEEK
1983 La Estructura 10L-18. In *Introducción a la arqueología de Copán, Honduras:* 382–500. Secretaria de Estado en el Despacho de Cultura y Turismo, Tegucigalpa.

BERLIN, HEINRICH
1958 El glifo "emblema" en las inscripciones mayas. *Journal de la Société des Américanistes,* n.s. 47: 111–119. Paris.

CULBERT, T. PATRICK
1988 Political History and the Decipherment of Maya Glyphs. *Antiquity* 62: 135–152.

DEMAREST, ARTHUR
1978 Interregional Conflict and "Situational Ethics" in Classic Maya Warfare. In *Codex Wauchope: A Tribute Roll* (M. Giardino, B. Edmonson, and W. Creamer, eds.): 101–111. Human Mosaic, Tulane University, New Orleans.
n.d. Ideology and Ancient Maya Cultural Evolution: The Dynamics of Galactic Polities, 1987. Manuscript in author's possession.

FASH, WILLIAM L.
1986 La Fachada Esculpida de la Estructura 9N-82: composición, forma e iconografía. In *Excavaciones en el area urbana de Copán,* Tomo I. Instituto Hondureño de Antropología e Historia, Tegucigalpa.

FINLEY, M. I.
1985 *Ancient History: Evidence and Models.* Penguin Books, New York.

FREIDEL, DAVID A.
1986 Maya Warfare: An Example of Peer-Polity Interaction. In *Peer Polity Interaction and Sociopolitical Change* (C. Renfrew and J. F. Cherry, eds.): 93–108. New Directions in Archaeology. Cambridge University Press, Cambridge.

GRAHAM, IAN
1967 *Archaeological Explorations in El Petén, Guatemala.* Middle American Research Institute, Publication 33. Tulane University, New Orleans.

GRAHAM, JOHN A.
    1973  Aspects on Non-Classic Presences in the Inscriptions and Sculptural Art of Seibal. In *The Classic Maya Collapse* (T. Patrick Culbert, ed.): 207–219. University of New Mexico Press, Albuquerque.

GRUBE, NIKOLAI
    1988  Städtegrunder und "erste Herrscher" in Hieroglyphentexten der Klassischen Mayakultur. *Archiv für Völkerkunde* 42: 69–90.

GRUBE, NIKOLAI, AND DAVID STUART
    1987  Observations on T110 as the Syllable *ko*. *Research Reports on Ancient Maya Writing* 8. Center for Maya Research, Washington, D.C.

GUITERAS-HOLMES, C.
    1961  *Perils of the Soul: The World View of a Tzotzil Indian*. The Free Press of Glencoe, New York.

HOUSTON, STEPHEN D.
    1989  Archaeology and Maya Writing. *Journal of World Prehistory* 3 (1): 1–32.

HOUSTON, STEPHEN D., AND PETER MATHEWS
    1985  *The Dynastic Sequence of Dos Pilas, Guatemala*. Pre-Columbian Art Research Institute, Monograph 1. San Francisco.

JONES, CHRISTOPHER, AND LINTON SATTERTHWAITE
    1982  *The Monuments and Inscriptions at Tikal: The Carved Monuments*. Tikal Report No. 3, Part A. The University Museum, University of Pennsylvania, Philadelphia.

KELLEY, DAVID H.
    1968  Kakupakal and the Itzas. *Estudios de Cultura Maya* 7: 255–268.
    1976  *Deciphering the Maya Script*. University of Texas Press, Austin.

LAUGHLIN, ROBERT M. (WITH JOHN B. HAVILAND)
    1988  *The Great Tzotzil Dictionary of Santo Domingo Zinacantán, with Grammatical Analysis and Historical Commentary*. Smithsonian Contributions to Anthropology 31. Smithsonian Institution Press, Washington, D.C.

LINCOLN, CHARLES E.
    1986  The Chronology of Chichen Itza: A Review of the Literature. In *Late Lowland Maya Civilization: Classic to Postclassic* (J. A. Sabloff and E. W. Andrews V, eds.): 141–196. University of New Mexico Press, Albuquerque.

LIZANA, FR. BERNANDO DE
    1892  *Historia Conquista Espiritual de Yucatan*. Museo Nacional de Mexico, Mexico.

MARCUS, JOYCE
    1973  Territorial Organization of the Lowland Classic Maya. *Science* 180: 911–916.
    1976  *Emblem and State in the Classic Maya Lowlands: An Epigraphic Approach to Territorial Organization*. Dumbarton Oaks, Washington, D.C.

MARTÍNEZ HERNÁNDEZ, JUAN
    1929  *Diccionario de Motul, Maya-Español*. La Compañia Tipográfica Yucateca, Mérida, Yucatan, Mexico.

MATHENY, RAY
    1980   *El Mirador, Peten, Guatemala: An Interim Report*. Papers of the New World Archaeological Foundation 45. Provo, Utah.

MATHEWS, PETER
    1985   Maya Early Classic Monuments and Inscriptions. In *A Consideration of the Early Classic Period in the Maya Lowlands* (G. R. Willey and P. Mathews, eds.): State University of New York 5–54. Institute for Mesoamerican Studies, at Albany, Albany.
    n.d.   The Sculpture of Yaxchilan. Ph.D. dissertation, Department of Anthropology, Yale University, 1988.

MATHEWS, PETER, AND JOHN S. JUSTESON
    1984   Patterns of Sign Substitution in Mayan Hieroglyphic Writing: The Affix Cluster. In *Phoneticism in Mayan Hieroglyphic Writing* (J. S. Justeson and L. Campbell, eds.): 185–231. Institute for Mesoamerican Studies, Pub. 9. State University of New York at Albany, Albany.

MATHEWS, PETER, AND GORDON R. WILLEY
    1991   Prehistoric Polities of the Pasion Region: Hieroglyphic Texts and their Archaeological Settings. In *Classic Maya Political History* (T. Patrick Culbert, ed): 30–71. School of American Research and Cambridge University Press, Cambridge.

MILLER, MARY ELLEN
    1986   *The Murals of Bonampak*. Princeton University Press, Princeton.

PROSKOURIAKOFF, TATIANA
    1963   Historical Data in the Inscriptions of Yaxchilan, Part I. The Reign of Shield-Jaguar. *Estudios de Cultura Maya* 3: 149–167.

RANDS, ROBERT L.
    1973   The Classic Maya Collapse: Usumacinta Zone and the Northwestern Periphery. In *The Classic Maya Collapse* (T. Patrick Culbert, ed.): 165–206. University of New Mexico Press, Albuquerque.

RENFREW, COLIN
    1986   Introduction: Peer Polity Interaction and Sociopolitical Change. In *Peer Polity Interaction and Sociopolitical Change* (C. Renfrew and J. F. Cherry, eds.): 1–18. Cambridge University Press, Cambridge.

RINGLE, WILLIAM M.
    1988   Of Mice and Monkeys: The Value and Meaning of T1016, the God C Hieroglyph. *Research Reports on Ancient Maya Writing* 18. Center for Maya Research, Washington, D.C.

SABLOFF, JEREMY A.
    1973   Continuity and Disruption during Terminal Late Classic Times at Seibal: Ceramic and Other Evidence. In *The Classic Maya Collapse* (T. Patrick Culbert, ed.): 107–131. School of American Research, University of New Mexico Press, Albuquerque.
    1986   Interaction among Classic Maya Polities. In *Peer Polity Interaction and Sociopolitical Change* (C. Renfrew and J. F. Cherry, eds.): 109–116. Cambridge University Press, Cambridge.

SABLOFF, JEREMY A., AND Gordon R. Willey
    1967    The Collapse of Maya Civilization in the Southern Lowlands: A Consideration of History and Process. *Southwestern Journal of Anthropology* 23 (4): 311–336.

SAHAGÚN, BERNARDINO DE
    1950–82    *General History of the Things of New Spain* (Arthur J. O. Anderson and Charles E. Dibble, trans. and eds.), 12 bks. in 13 vols. School of American Research and the University of Utah Press, Santa Fe.

SCHELE, LINDA
    n.d.    The Founders of Lineages at Copán and Other Maya Sites (Copan Note 8), 1986. Manuscript in the author's possession.

SCHELE, LINDA, AND PETER MATHEWS
    1991    Royal Visits and Other Intersite Relationships among the Classic Maya. In *Classic Maya Political History* (T. Patrick Culbert, ed): 226–252. School of American Research and Cambridge University Press, Cambridge.

SIMÉON, REMI
    1977    *Diccionario de la Lengua Nahuatl o Mexicana.* Siglo 21 Editores, México.

STUART, DAVID
    1985a    The Yaxha Emblem Glyph as *Yax-ha. Research Reports on Ancient Maya Writing* 1. Center for Maya Research, Washington, D.C.
    1985b    The "Count-of-Captives" Epithet in Classic Maya Writing. In *Fifth Palenque Round Table, 1983* (M. G. Robertson and V. M. Fields, eds.): 97–101. The Pre-Columbian Art Research Insitute, San Francisco.
    1986    The Lu-Bat Glyph and Its Bearing on the Primary Standard Sequence. Paper presented at the Primer Simposio Sobre Epigrafía Maya, Guatemala City.
    1987    Ten Phonetic Syllables. *Research Reports on Ancient Maya Writing* 14. Center for Maya Research, Washington, D.C.
    1988    Blood Symbolism in Maya Iconography. In *Maya Iconography* (E.P. Benson and G.G. Griffin, eds.): 175–221. Princeton University Press, Princeton.
    n.d.a    New Epigraphic Evidence of Political Organization in the Classic Maya Lowlands. Manuscript in the author's possession, 1984.
    n.d.b    *The Maya Artist: An Epigraphic and Iconographic Study.* A.B. Thesis, Department of Art and Archaeology, Princeton University, 1989.

STUART, DAVID, AND Stephen D. Houston
    n.d.    Classic Maya Place Names, 1987. Manuscript submitted for publication to Dumbarton Oaks, Forthcoming.

THOMPSON, J. ERIC S.
    1962    *A Catalog of Maya Hieroglyphs.* University of Oklahoma Press, Norman.

TOZZER, ALFRED M. (ED. AND TRANS.)
    1941    *Landa's Relacion de las Cosas de Yucatan.* Papers of the Peabody Museum of Archaeology and Ethnology 18. Harvard University, Cambridge.

VON EUW, ERIC
    1978    *Corpus of Maya Hieroglyphic Inscriptions, Volume 5, Part 1: Xultun.* Pea-

body Museum, Harvard University, Cambridge.

WEBSTER, DAVID
- 1976a *Defensive Earthworks at Becan, Campeche, Mexico: Implications for Maya Warfare*. Middle American Research Institute, Publication 41. Tulane University, New Orleans.
- 1976b Lowland Maya Fortifications. *Proceedings of the American Philosophical Society* 120 (5): 361–372.
- 1977 Warfare and the Evolution of Maya Civilization. In *The Origins of Maya Civilization* (R. E. W. Adams, ed.): 335–372. University of New Mexico Press, Albuquerque.
- 1989 *The House of the Bacabs, Copan, Honduras* (Ed.). Studies in Pre-Columbian Art and Archaeology 29. Dumbarton Oaks, Washington, D.C.

WEBSTER, DAVID, WILLIAM L. FASH, AND ELLIOT M. ABRAMS
- 1986 Excavaciones en el Conjunto 9N8: Patio A (Operación VIII). In *Excavaciones en el Area Urbana de Copán, Tomo I*. I.H.A.H., Tegucigalpa.

WILLEY, GORDON R.
- 1974 The Classic Maya Hiatus: A Rehearsal for the Collapse? In *Mesoamerican Archaeology: New Approaches* (N. Hammond, ed.): 417–431. University of Texas Press, Austin.

WILLEY, GORDON R., AND Dimitri B. Shimkin
- 1973 The Maya Collapse: A Summary View. In *The Classic Maya Collapse* (T. Patrick Culbert, ed.): 457–501. University of New Mexico Press, Albuquerque.

12

# On the Eve of the Collapse:
# *Maya Art of the Eighth Century*

MARY ELLEN MILLER

YALE UNIVERSITY

INTRODUCTION

Most Maya art and architecture that we can see dates to the eighth century, the final era of Classic flowering, and so the works of that era have generally informed our notions of what Maya art is: we think of towering Tikal temples, Yaxchilan lintels, elegantly painted pottery, ranging palace complexes. The works of the eighth century have generally determined the standard against which all other Maya art has been judged. Many works of art made before this era have often been understood to form the basis on which the eighth century is built; later art, made after the eighth century, is called decadent or simply Postclassic, but the very idea of succeeding a "classic" suggests a one-way ticket to an aesthetic wasteland.

To Sylvanus Morley, Maya civilization at the beginning of the eighth century was about "to come into the full enjoyment of its artistic and intellectual inheritance. It was at the threshold of its Golden Age" (1920: 217). Morley recognized "a brilliant cultural florescence, a tremendous outburst of art and architecture" that ran from 9.15.0.0.0 to 9.19.0.0.0, or 731 to 810, and he called this flowering the "Great Period." In 1946 Carnegie Institution of Washington archaeologists were apparently the first to use the term "Classic" to describe the "flowering of Mesoamerican civilization."[1] In 1950 Tatiana Proskouriakoff gave prominence to the term Classic when she used it to refer to the period in the southern lowlands when the "Classic motif," the depiction of a single individual on the front of stone monu-

---

[1] A. V. Kidder went on: "It is marked by elaboration of arts and crafts; by intensified regional specialization; most strikingly by a tremendous development of religious architecture, implying the growth of a rich ceremonialism; by the attainment of economic conditions sufficiently favorable to permit diversion of great amounts of labor to nonessential activities; and, in order to recruit and direct that labor, by a close meshing of religious and civil authority" (Kidder, Jennings, and Shook 1946: 3).

ments, flourished (1950: 1). The terminology of "Classic" was adopted by Mayanists and is used in this essay to refer to the period of roughly A.D. 200–900. Proskouriakoff broke the Late Classic into several periods. She termed 9.8.0.0.0–9.13.0.0.0, or 593–692, the "Formative" period of Late Classic development; she called 9.13.0.0.0–9.16.0.0.0 (692–751) the "Ornate" phase, and in her schema it was followed first by the "Dynamic" phase (9.16.0.0.0–9.19.0.0.0, 751–810) and then by the "Decadent" phase (810–889). By means of these terms, whether intentionally or not, art is linked to the state of society and assumed to be a reflection of it. When art is "formative" or "decadent," then society is often assumed to be "formative" or "decadent" too, even when not specified as such. As if to make the connection explicit, J. Eric S. Thompson wrote, "The art of the Initial Series Period reflects cultural tranquility as clearly as the restless art of the Mexican Period mirrors the turbulent, extrovert influences of that epoch" (Thompson 1950: 15). The term Classic has always seemed to suit the eighth century of Maya art best, when forms are standardized, rather than, say, any moment in the Early Classic at all, when Maya elite imagery is first codified. In short, scholars have often viewed art of the eighth century as the pinnacle of Maya achievement and its art the very reflection of the high cultural achievement of the civilization.

Because of the use of the similar term "classical" to refer to the high civilizations of Greece and Rome, the word Classic has sometimes seemed to Mesoamericanists to carry with it connotations of the idyllic and the ideal, of humanism and democracy, worthy predecessors to ourselves, or so we have liked to imagine. We now know that the Classic period no longer can be equated with Thompson's era of "cultural tranquility." These Classic Maya practiced war, and certainly during the eighth century they practiced war incessantly. But as I am reminded by my art historian colleagues, the classical world was fraught with warfare, and the very Greek art that we think of as most "classic" was made during the Peloponnesian Wars.

Under the influence of modern views of material culture, we could consider the art of the Maya just one more artifact of their history, but it is, in fact, *the* artifact that makes the Maya of such compelling interest to modern man. Maya art frequently includes Maya writing, and images rarely appear without words. Without Maya art and writing, Maya archaeology would be fundamentally different. Both the art and writing reveal the history of the Maya, as they conceived it in images and wrote it down in a writing system that represented spoken language. Because of Maya art and writing, Maya archaeology can move beyond the study of prehistory to the study of history itself. Historical reconstruction is particularly significant in the eighth century, when a ten-year time period is unobservable in archaeological time but critical in historical time. In ten years, the Yaxchilan realm can crumble and Shield Jaguar II's historians may tell us the tale; in ten years a system of government and administration may change or the meaning of warfare shift—all of which may only be discerned in the archaeological data with a clue from the inscriptions. If art and writing appear to tell a different story from one another or one that differs from the archaeological record, we may have some of the texture and complexity of a broader history. Contradictions, as we know from modern historical studies, do not obviate one point of view at the expense of another but reveal the richness of past life. From Maya writing, we learn one story at a time, the official story at any one moment and place.

It is the special characteristic of writing that sets the Maya apart from all other Mesoamerican peoples. It is probably the technology of writing itself that enabled them to be what they were. Had the Maya flourished at a single center, say, at Tikal, as Teotihuacan civilization had done at Teotihuacan or Zapotec civilization at Monte Alban, it would not seem so extraordinary to us. But it is the ability to communicate across distance and through time, to remember a particular history and to write for posterity, that allowed dozens of cities and towns to subscribe to a single reigning belief system.

By the eighth century both the art and the writing had reached full maturity. More of both was made than at any other time (perhaps more than half of all known Classic Maya art was made in the eighth century), and many of the longest texts survive from this period. As the final and most obvious level in Classic stratigraphy, the eighth century frequently is given as an archetype, even when we know it to be derived from earlier models. Given the presuppositions that have been held in the past, it seems useful to examine the nature of eighth-century art. Is it more brilliant or is it just more abundant? Is it better, or is it just better preserved and better known? And how do we make such judgments? What relationship does the history of art have to the history of a civilization? What relationship does southern lowland Maya art of the eighth century bear to Maya art of the ninth at Chichen Itza and elsewhere? In a single study it would be foolhardy to tackle the entire scope of Maya art, so I will begin by considering examples from the tradition of stone sculpture at a series of Maya sites: Tikal, Yaxchilan, Piedras Negras, Palenque, and Copan, and briefly, the paintings at Bonampak. Also, for the purpose of this essay, I have chosen to define the eighth century in Maya katuns, 9.13.0.0.0–9.19.0.0.0, the six katuns that run from 692 to 810.

### EIGHTH-CENTURY ART: TIKAL

Three powerful kings ruled Tikal in this era, beginning with Ruler A, for whom Stela 16 is the sole surviving stela. Ruler B is commemorated on Stelae 5, 20,[2] and 21, and Ruler C on Stelae 19 and 22. The monuments all celebrate

---

[2] As Christopher Jones has pointed out, this stela may celebrate the reign of the 28th *hel*, the ruler for whom the only clear record is on the roofcomb of the Temple of Inscriptions (Jones

period endings of one sort or another, from 9.14.0.0.0 to 9.18.0.0.0, that is, 711 to 790, and all were once associated with carved altars which vary much more than the stelae. At Tikal, of course, there was a rich Early Classic tradition on which later eighth-century sculptors could draw, but there was no more recent tradition: Ruler A's accession in 681 was the first dynastic event to be publicly commemorated there in generations, and there is no sculpture that can be securely placed between 9.7.0.0.0 and 9.13.0.0.0: essentially, there is no surviving record of the seventh century at all. Tikal's Late Classic tradition of stone sculptures begins late, first with Stela 30 and its mate, Altar 14, in 9.13.0.0.0, and then with Stela 16, in 711 (Fig. 1).

Like all Late Classic Tikal stelae, Stela 16 is carved in very low relief. Ruler A stands in a frontal pose, with his head turned in profile. From head to toe, ritual paraphernalia adorn his body. With his fingers making the same gesture as the glyphic hand that indicates the completion of 14 katuns, he holds a triangulated ceremonial bar with the Perforator God attached. Had he been portrayed frontally, the cutaway mask shown in profile with mouthpiece and Venus sign would have blocked his face. Ruler A has wrapped his lower torso with a hipcloth marked by crossed bones and trimmed with feathers and extruded eyeballs.

About twenty-five years later in 736, Ruler B erected Stela 21 in commemoration of his own accession to kingship (Fig. 2). For the depiction, Ruler B stands in profile, sprinkling droplets of blood. Part of the monument is badly broken off—making it impossible to determine whether a mask is worn, for example—but one can nevertheless recognize that the new king wears his father's hipcloth and belt assemblage; he bears the same triangulated ceremonial bar, although the Perforator God heads have been replaced with split spondylus shells. Seen as a mass of feathers on Stela 16, the backrack on Stela 21 can be recognized as the sort of assemblage worn by so-called Holmul Dancers—that is, Maize Gods—on painted ceramics.

Just 8 tuns later, Ruler B erected Stela 5, this time in front of the North Acropolis, where it was set in the company of many Early Classic monuments (Fig. 3). Although the monument incorporated many archaistic details, as noted by Morley (1937–38, 1: 343) and Proskouriakoff (1950: 125), it is perhaps even more striking for its repetition of the human figure on Stela 21. Although the Stela 5 figure bears different ritual paraphernalia and is somewhat differently attired, the human figures on the two stelae are so identically proportioned that the later one may well have been made from a tracing of the first. Stela 5, the later stela, also incorporates a captive that closely resembles the captive figure described on the upper surface of Altar

---

and Satterthwaite 1982: 46). Ruler B is named as the 27th *hel* and Ruler C as the 29th. The period ending 9.16.0.0.0 is not known to have been celebrated by Ruler B, but B's own date of death remains unknown.

# On the Eve of the Collapse: Maya Art of the Eighth Century

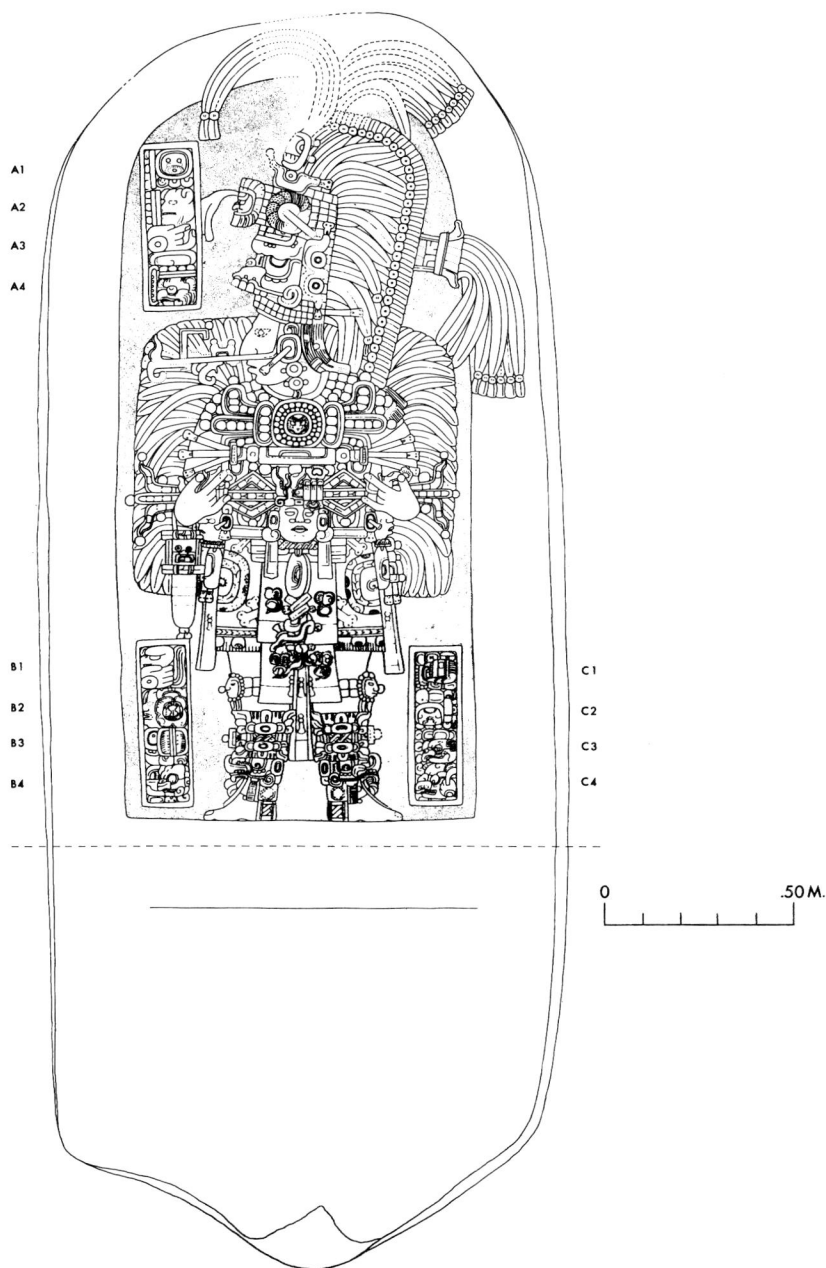

Fig. 1 Stela 16, Tikal. Drawing by William R. Coe (after Jones and Satterthwaite, 1982: fig. 22).

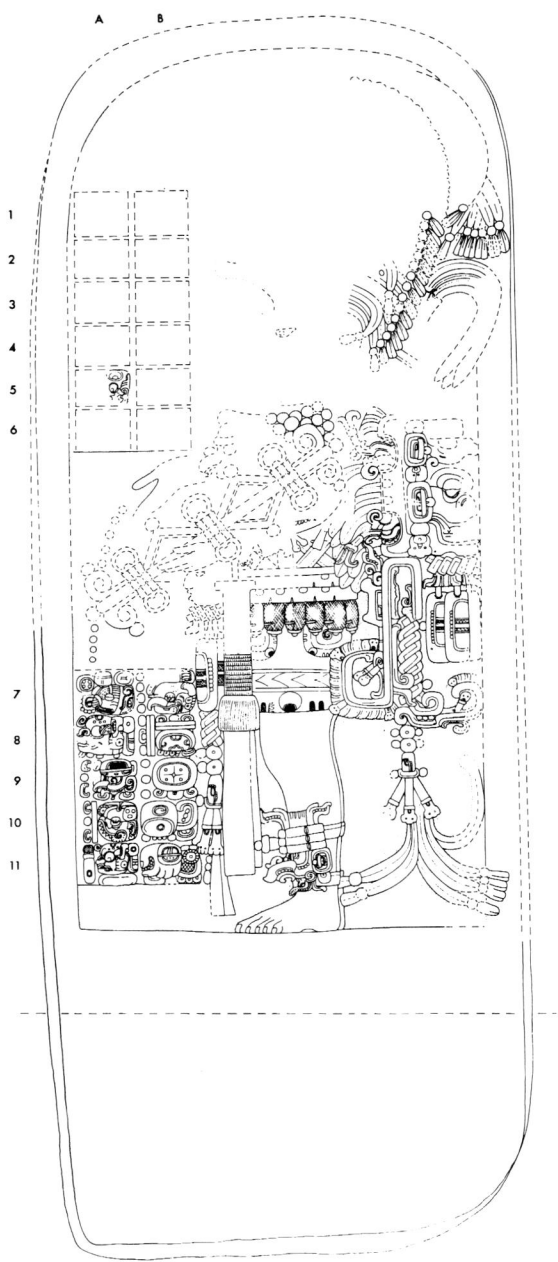

Fig. 2 Stela 21, Tikal. Drawing by William R. Coe (after Jones and Satterthwaite 1982: fig 31).

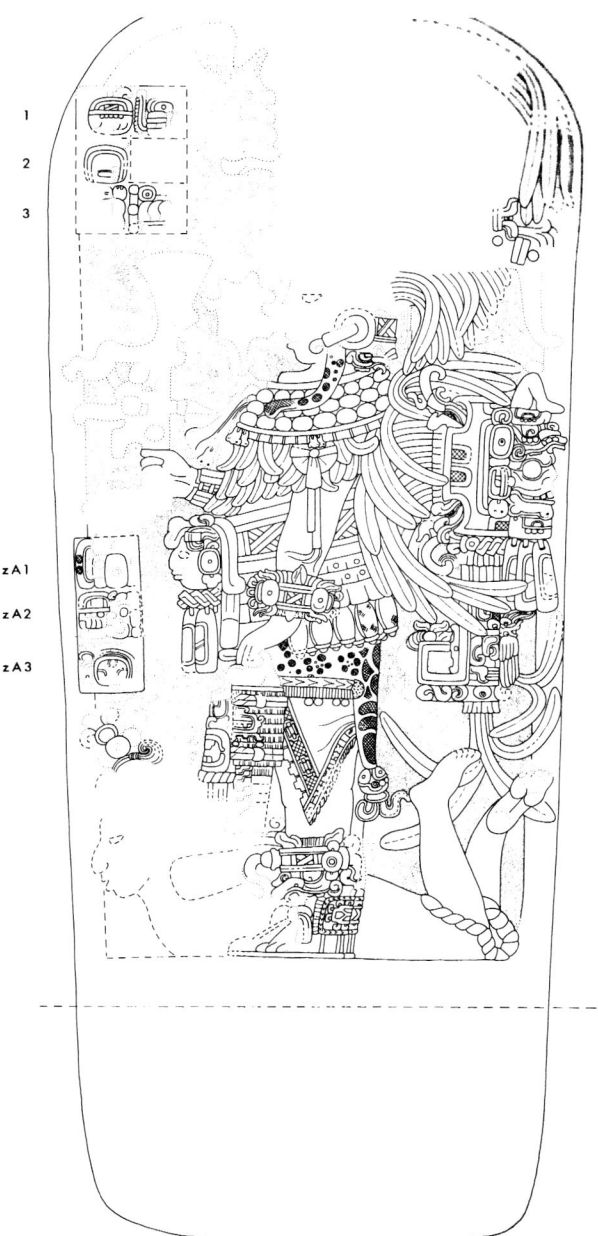

Fig. 3 Stela 5, Tikal. Drawing by William R. Coe (after Jones and Satterthwaite 1982: fig. 7).

9, which was once paired with Stela 21, thus economically conflating the imagery of two older sculptures into a single new one. So whoever carved Stela 5 drew on the entire previous corpus of stone monuments commemorating the ruling sovereign when he set about to put a new monument on the Great Plaza.

As Jones and others have pointed out, Stela 20 may celebrate the reign of Ruler B's successor, the 28th *hel,* or member of the succession, at Tikal, but the name is not clear on the monument, and it might be another monument of Ruler B (Fig. 4). Although bearing many similar ornaments to his predecessors, including the cutaway mask with Venus sign of Stela 16, the backracks of Stelae 5 and 21, and the pouch held on Stela 5, this stela figure is dressed for war and captive sacrifice. He stands in front of a Waterlily Jaguar throne. In both proportion and scale, the figure is unlikely to have been drawn directly from any other surviving monument.

After Ruler C became king in 768, he commissioned—along with other works—stelae that commemorated the katun endings 9.17.0.0.0 and 9.18.0.0.0, in 771 and 790. He returned to the model of Stela 21, which had been made by his father thirty-five years earlier. On Stela 22 Ruler C was depicted in the same posture as his father, making the same offering, in almost identical garb, rendered with only slight differences (Fig. 5). The hipcloth, for example, is now turned to show the finished corner of cloth, shell noisemakers have multiplied, and Ruler C has retained the jaguar pelt wrap that his father wore on Stela 5. Like his grandfather, Ruler A, Ruler C's face is seen through a cutaway mask; he has also adopted his grandfather's loincloth and worked beads like those of his grandfather into his long hair. Ruler C, however, may have been the first Tikal king to put the Paddlers in scrolls of blood at the upper margin of the stela. Emblematic of ancestors and ancestral blood (Stuart 1988: 189), the Paddlers may also recall early monuments where ancestors were set in the upper margins of stelae. A katun after Stela 22, Ruler C was rendered on Stela 19 (Fig. 6) in a nearly identical fashion to Stela 22. From toes to belt and from head to ceremonial bar, the proportions and scale are almost identical: the Stela 22 figure may have been traced and transferred from one monument to the other with the image compressed at the waist, yielding a smaller human figure on what is also a smaller stela altogether.

The stela tradition at Tikal, then, is a conservative one, with one ruler carefully retaining the costume, paraphernalia, and posture of another. Thus Ruler C appears in 790 much the way his grandfather did eighty years earlier. At Tikal, the longevity of repeated sculptural representations combined with limited attention to portraiture and poor preservation of human faces undoubtedly contributed to the notion that these stelae depicted anonymous calendar priests, one following another in a succession as relentless as the court of katuns itself. When art is seen as a reflection of society or society a reflection of art, then Tikal can be perceived as static and conservative.

# On the Eve of the Collapse: Maya Art of the Eighth Century

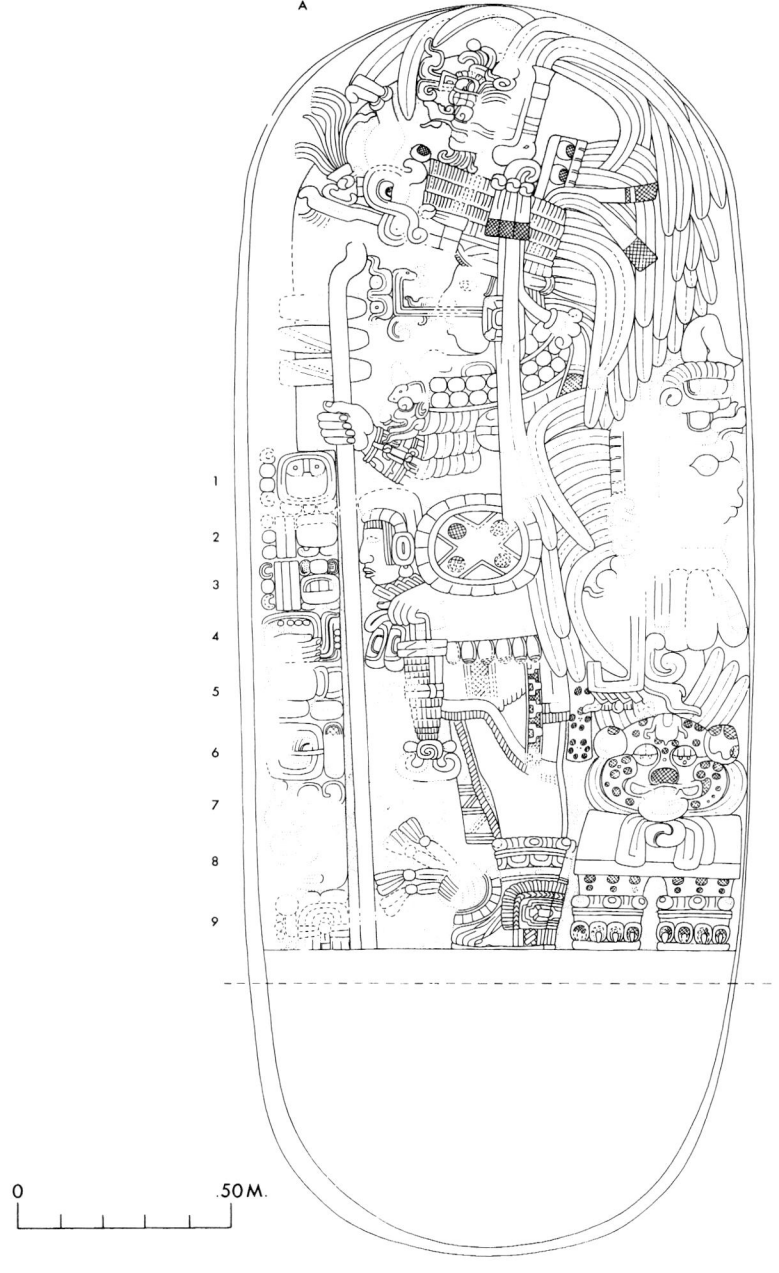

Fig. 4 Stela 20, Tikal. Drawing by William R. Coe (after Jones and Satterthwaite 1982: fig. 29).

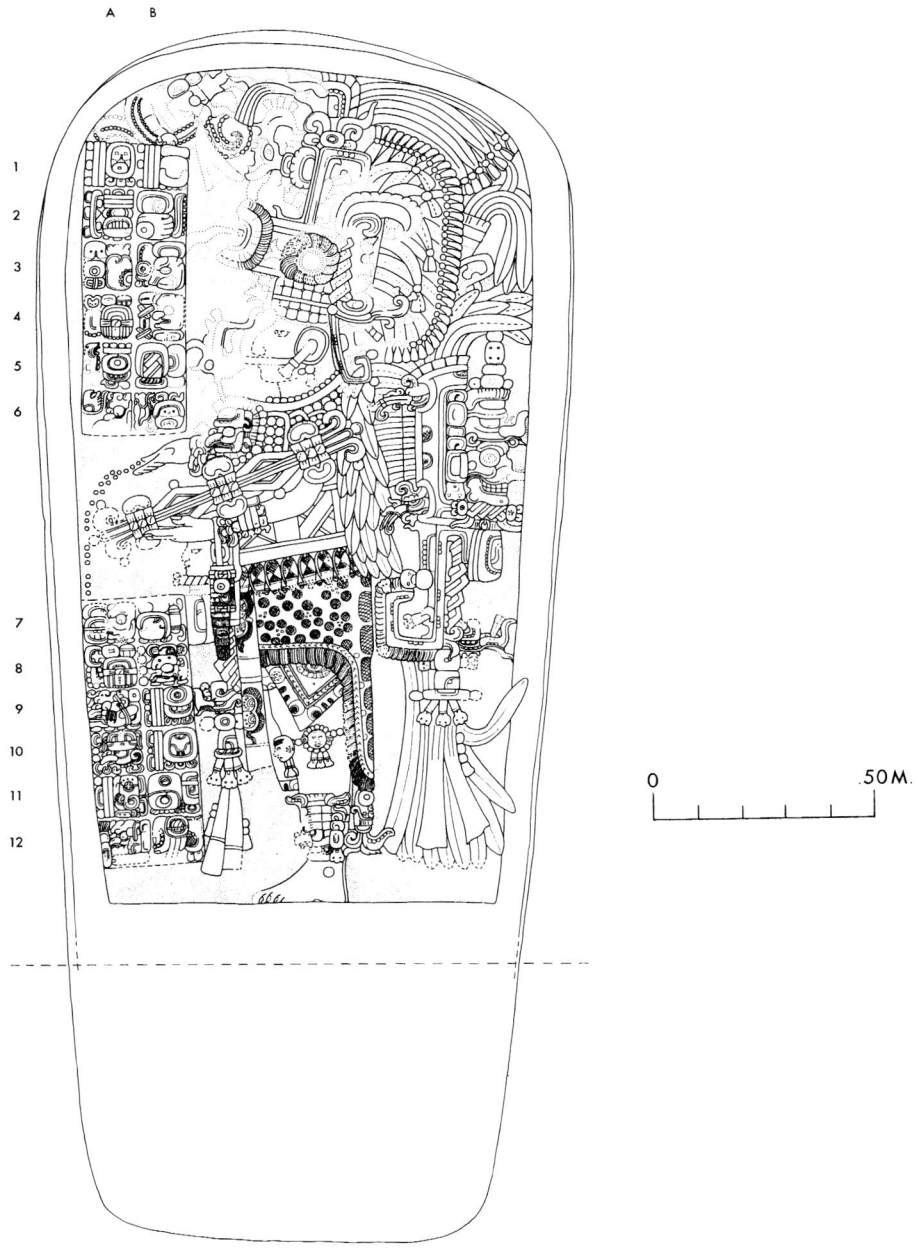

Fig. 5 Stela 22, Tikal. Drawing by William R. Coe (after Jones and Satterthwaite 1982: fig. 33).

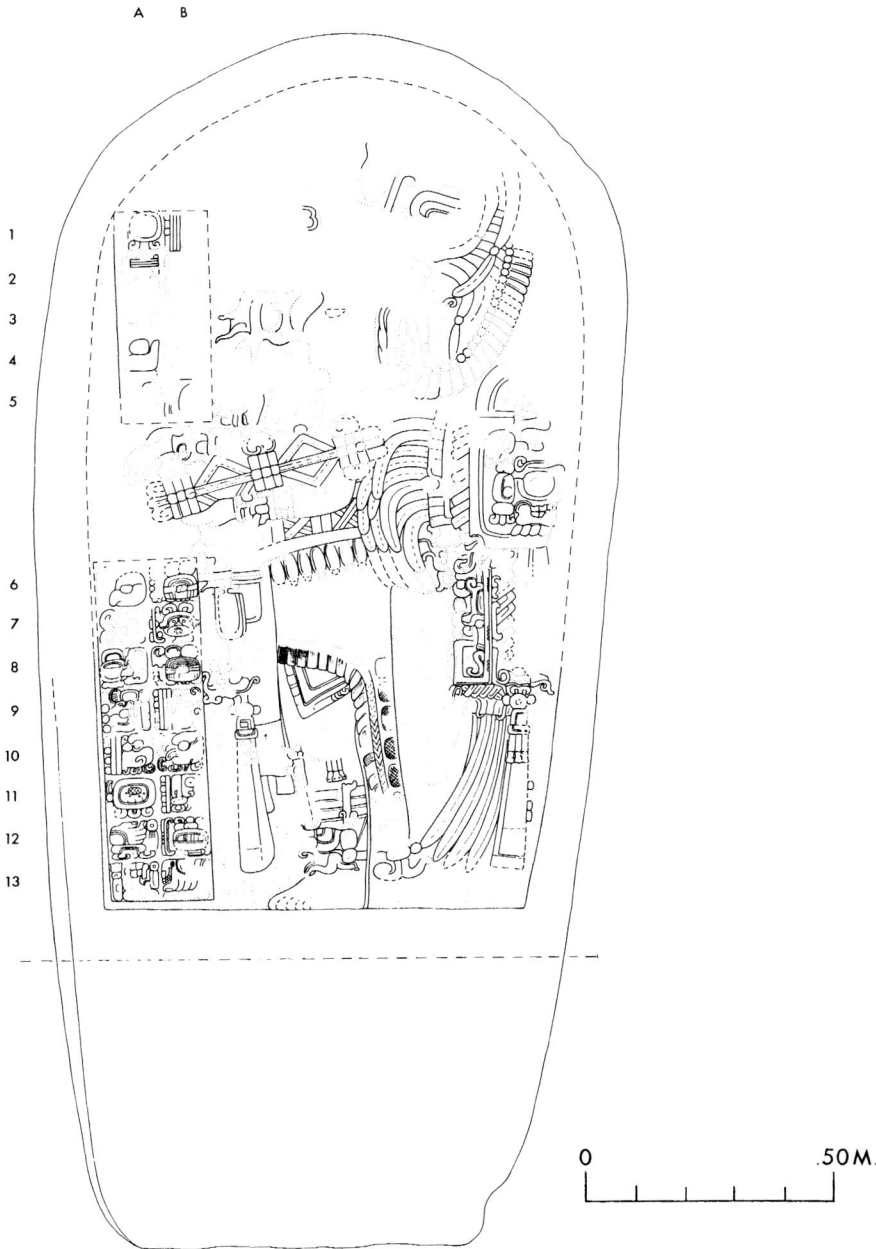

Fig. 6  Stela 19, Tikal. Drawing by William R. Coe (after Jones and Satterthwaite 1982: fig. 27).

Mary Ellen Miller

## PALENQUE

The perfect foil to Tikal's sculptural trajectory of the eighth century is Palenque, for at Palenque, the seventh century was the time of artistic developments. Enormous amounts of carved and stucco sculpture can be dated to the seventh century there, including the programs of Pacal and his son, Chan Bahlum. Pacal's second son, Kan-Xul, became king in 702, but just nine years later, in 711, Kan-Xul fell prey to the king of Tonina. Palenque never recovered its grandeur. The recovery of Tikal at just this moment may not be coincidental, although we know of no specific connection between the two sites at this time. At Palenque, we know of only a small amount of sculpture that was completed later. After a brief reign by a lesser lord, the Palenque dynasty was reestablished with Chaacal III and K'uk, but except for a date on a pot, nothing more is known of the family after 785.

Pacal and Chan Bahlum had directed innovative programs of art and architecture. They borrowed old forms and broadcast them in new ways; they took the iconography of Maya religion and made it more public than it had ever been. Kan-Xul drew upon the innovations of his predecessors— and apparently had the same extraordinary economic wherewithal—but unlike his older brother, Kan-Xul sought to emulate and honor his father above all else. First, in honor of accession, he refurbished House E in the Palace, the site of commemoration of his father's accession. Around the Oval Palace Tablet, the record of Pacal's accession, Kan-Xul added stucco ornament and replaced an old throne with one that acknowledged his own rise to power (Fig. 7). He may very well have directed massive additions to the Palace, and certainly no later than his reign, all the galleried colonnades that frame the Palace were completed.

As a commemoration of his accession, Kan-Xul commissioned a large sculpture to be set in the gallery framing the north end of the Palace. Perhaps the most beautifully carved of all Palenque tablets, the Palace Tablet depicts Kan-Xul seated on a throne in front of an oval jaguar cushion— perhaps as he appeared for his own accession in the refurbished House E— and framed by his dead parents who offer him the regalia of office (Fig. 8). All three sit amid one of the longest Maya texts to be incorporated with figurative sculpture, and the Initial Series takes the form of full-figure glyphs. Most of the text treats Kan-Xul and his father Pacal. The composition was planned with attention to both symmetry and balance, and the figures at top were once balanced by a small throne set within the opening at the bottom. The edges of figures and glyphs have been carefully worked to achieve the soft, buttery appearance of the carving, and the background has been meticulously smoothed of all chisel marks. The adroit full-figure glyphs provide a humorous subtext for both the literate and the nonliterate.

As on some other Palenque sculptures, the text on the Palace Tablet has been crowded at the end in order to accommodate a denser inscription than

Fig. 7 Palace Throne, House E, Palenque. Reconstruction drawing by Merle Greene Robertson.

might have originally been planned, for the last column of text records the accession of yet a third son of Pacal, known as Xoc, on 9.14.8.14.15, or 10 August 720.³ The captions, too, speak of this Xoc, and relate his birth and heir designation. But whose monument is this, after all? The text mainly deals with Kan-Xul and begins with his birth and its auguries and leads to his accession. Kan-Xul, however, receives his last notice not at Palenque but at Tonina, where he is depicted as a captive and where Palenque is named as defeated on 9.13.19.13.3, or 26 August 711. After a disruption of some nine years, Kan-Xul's brother Xoc must have then taken some sort of office. He

³ Correlations are based on Thompson's 584,284 number (Thompson 1950) and are given here in the Julian calendar.

*Mary Ellen Miller*

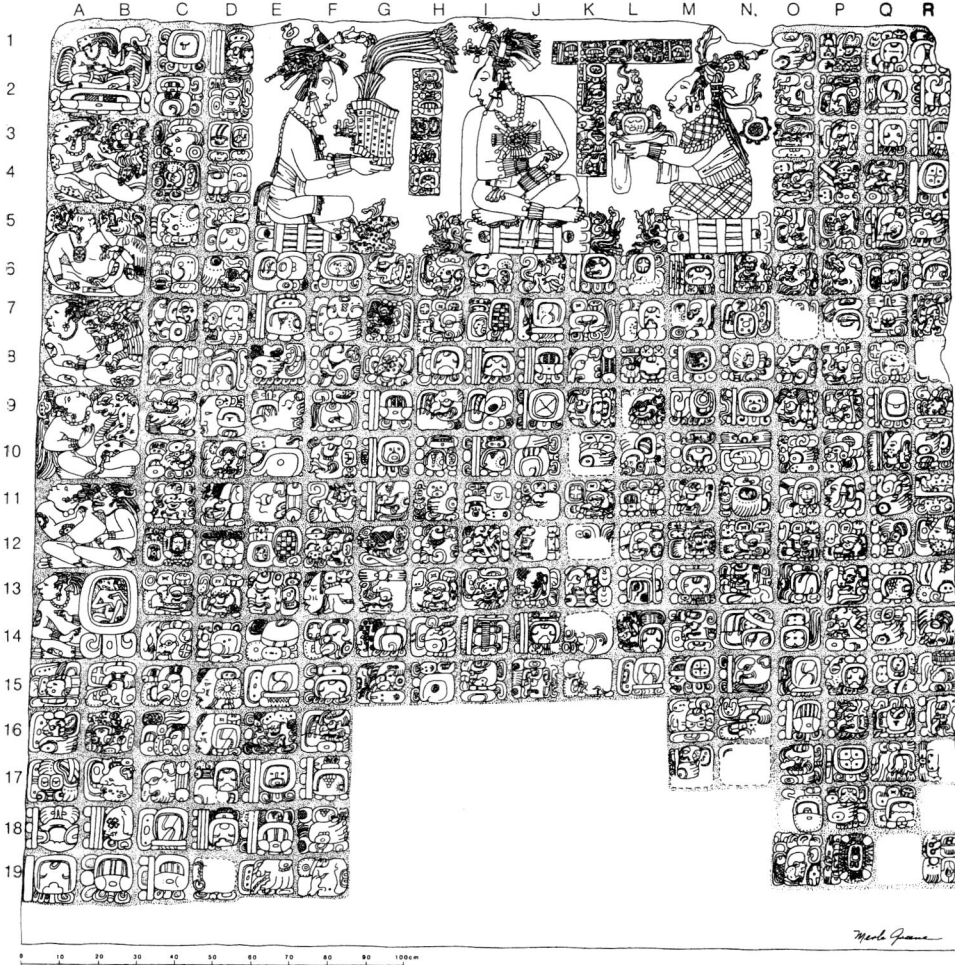

Fig. 8   Palace Tablet, Palenque. Drawing by Merle Greene Robertson.

commissioned the completion of the Palace Tablet, but with his own role appended to the main text and other particulars added to the captions.

Given what we know of Palenque sculpture prior to the reign of Kan-Xul, the Palace Tablet represents yet another phase of innovation in stone sculpture at that site. During the reigns of Pacal and Chan Bahlum, compositions generally included only two human figures, the ruler (sometimes depicted twice, as on the Cross Group panels) and his mother. Kan-Xul, however, favored a trifigural composition in which a ruler would be depicted with two subsidiary figures, generally the late parents, as on the

Palace Tablet itself. This pattern was sustained on the Palace piers as well, where the stucco sculptures of House D incorporate two figures and those of House A three figures (Figs. 9 and 10). Although both programs may be attributed to Kan-Xul's reign,[4] the format of the stuccoes suggests to me that the House D piers precede those of House A. In adopting the trifigural composition, the carved or stuccoed image achieved structural unity and harmony with the text, as, for example, it is written on the Palace Tablet, in which both parents are acknowledged. With the commission of the Palace Tablet, Kan-Xul established a new format.

Even after Kan-Xul's presumed sacrifice at Tonina, his descendants retained the trifigural program. On the Dumbarton Oaks panel, Kan-Xul is remembered after his death, framed by his mother and father, recapitulating the format of the Palace Tablet (Fig. 11). Given the last date on the Dumbarton Oaks panel, the sculpture must have been carved during the reign of Chaacal III, Kan-Xul's son and eventual successor, who sought to commemorate his father's reign. Although beautifully drawn, the monument appears to have been hastily carved, and perhaps barely finished. Sculptors finished the glyphic text and portraits, but chisel marks remain on the background and the feet of all three protagonists are poorly worked and clumsily carved.

Chaacal III became king in 722, but we know of only glyphic jamb panels from Temple 18 that record his accession. One year later in 723, Chac-Zutz' was seated as a *sahal*,[5] a regional governor or a lord of the second tier, and by the circumstances of preservation and discovery, we happen to know more of his reign than Chaacal's, although Chaacal probably ruled for many years. Although lords of the title *sahal* had been referred to at Yaxchilan and Piedras Negras by this time, this is the first reference to such a person at Palenque. At least nine attendant lords of such title appear together in the Bonampak murals, for example, and they may have been warlords, rich merchants, or administrators of high rank. The Tablet of the Slaves (Fig. 12) records Chac-Zutz's elevation to power on a trifigural panel designed to emulate the Palace Tablet. Chac-Zutz wears Kan-Xul's pendant, and his attendant parents—neither of whom appears to have been Palenque royalty, according to their captions—offer him the same regalia offered to Kan-Xul. The symmetry and balance achieved in the Palace Tablet are set askew by the inscribed captions and are only roughly recalled here, however. The quality of carving itself is very like that of the Dumbarton Oaks panel.

---

[4] Merle Greene Robertson has raised various possibilities in attributing these stuccoes, and the solution I favor is one of them, although she would prefer to order the House A piers before those of House D (Robertson 1985).

[5] David Stuart discussed both the pattern of use of this glyph and offered the reading *cahal* (n.d.a). He subsequently retracted the reading of *ca* for the first syllable of this word (1987). The term *cahal* has now entered the literature of Maya studies, but it is probably not correct. Stuart and Houston have now proposed *sa* for this syllable (personal communication 1990), yielding a reading of *sahal* for this widespread title.

Mary Ellen Miller

Fig. 9  Pier D, House D, Palace, Palenque. Drawing by Merle Greene Robertson.

During the eighth century, many kings shared power with *sahals,* although the meaning of such a relationship at Palenque and elsewhere remains essentially unknown. Chaacal and Chac Zutz' apparently shared power in some fashion. They are each depicted, for example, on a pair of panels (the so-called Orator and Scribe tablets) that once flanked the base of the Palace Tower, but with so little differentiation that it could be a double portrait of a single man (Fig. 13). These panels are also very similar to the Temple 21 *alfarda* sculptures. With their rich drapery and elegant gestures, these two pairs of sculptures are the finest known works of the Chaacal-Chac Zutz' era. Carved in shallow relief, they are also more compelling to

Fig. 10  Pier C, House A, Palace, Palenque. Drawing by Merle Greene Robertson.

us today as drawings than as sculptures, and they lack the commanding visual power of the Palace Tablet.

Finally, in 764, after a period of more than thirty years had passed for which we have no historical information written by the Maya at Palenque themselves, Chaacal's son Kuk became king. A katun later, in honor of that event, he commissioned a small carving known to us as the Tablet of the 96 Glyphs, rebuilt the south stairs of the Palace Tower for the Tablet to be set in place, and covered it with a jaguar pelt (Fig. 14). (The jaguar pelt throne mentioned in the text may be the Tablet of the 96 Glyphs itself.) Although the works of sculpture following Kan-Xul's ignominious defeat by Tonina

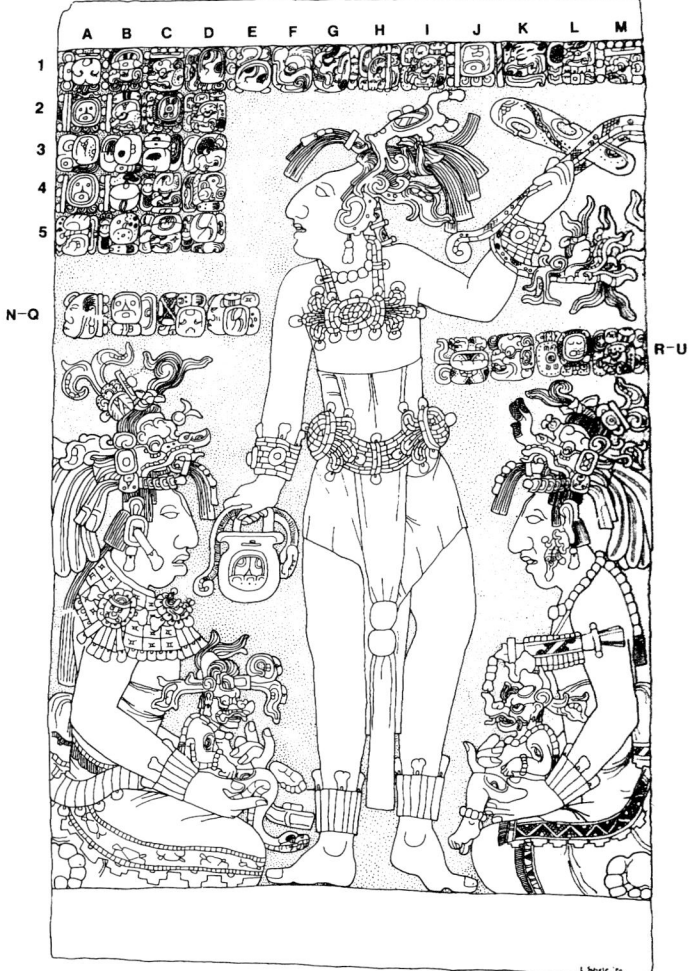

Fig. 11  Dumbarton Oaks Tablet, from Palenque. Drawing by Linda Schele.

are characterized by skilled draftsmanship and drawing, most are not as well executed as the works of the previous generation. But the Tablet of the 96 Glyphs is drawn and executed with great skill, and it would be hard for me to believe that the entire sculpture was not the work of a single artist. The sculptor has worked in both thick and thin incision, driving his chisel or burin to produce lines usually achieved only with a brush.[6] The text is

[6] A similar effect is achieved on the Creation Tablet, which is probably also the work of this same sculptor.

## On the Eve of the Collapse: Maya Art of the Eighth Century

Fig. 12  Tablet of the Slaves, Palenque. Drawing by Linda Schele.

creatively and imaginatively configured: as an example, one might consider just the distance number introducing glyphs, each of which is a paired opposition, of light and dark, fleshed and skeletal, and so forth. At Palenque, there is no known sculpture after the Tablet of the 96 Glyphs.

At Palenque, then, during the eighth century, little sculpture was made after 711 and none after 783. Some works suffered in the quality of execution, but the last dated sculpture displays technical finesse that exceeds all other sculptures at Palenque and perhaps anywhere in the Maya area.

### YAXCHILAN AND PIEDRAS NEGRAS

If Palenque and Tikal provide dramatic contrasts, Yaxchilan and Piedras Negras offer interesting comparisons. Both thrived for roughly the same period of time, from the fifth century to the beginning of the ninth. Both occupied what seems to have been a similar geographical and ecological niche at strategic points on the Usumacinta River. At both cities, prominent women appear to have held some power at the end of the seventh through the beginning of the eighth centuries. The histories of Yaxchilan and Piedras

Mary Ellen Miller

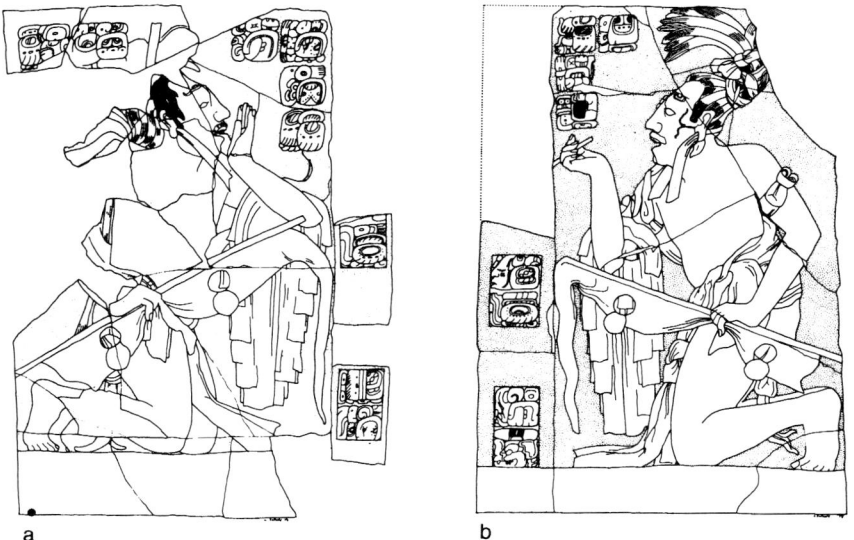

Fig. 13  Tablet of the Orator and Tablet of the Scribe, Palace, Palenque. Drawing by Linda Schele.

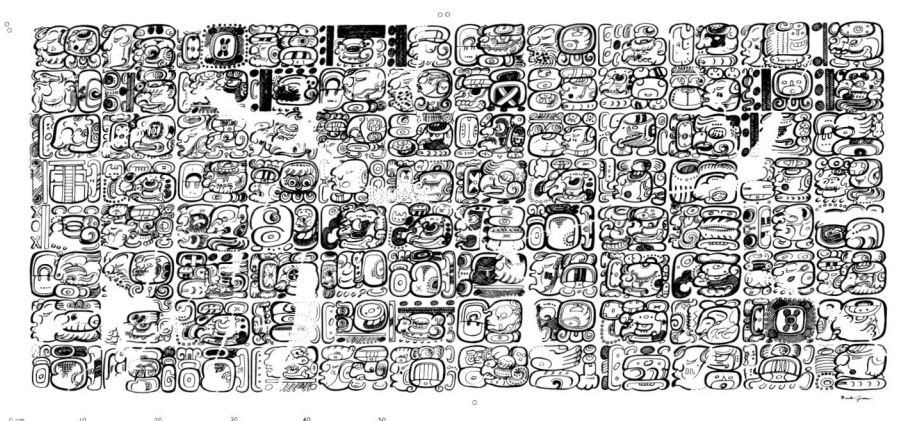

Fig. 14  Tablet of 96 Glyphs, Palenque. Drawing by Merle Greene Robertson.

Negras intertwine, and from their respective positions a one or two day trip up- or downstream and on opposite sides of the Usumacinta River, they must have always kept an eye on the other's affairs.

Intermarriage between the royal families of Yaxchilan and Piedras Negras is not known, but both royal visits and warfare between the two cities are recounted. A Yaxchilan text mentioned Piedras Negras during the Early Classic; then an Early Classic Piedras Negras ruler claimed victory over a Yaxchilan foe. Before the rise of King Shield Jaguar at Yaxchilan at the end of the seventh century, Yaxchilan may have suffered because once again it had fallen prey to Piedras Negras. Although there is no corroborating record at Yaxchilan, in 624 Ruler 1 of Piedras Negras proclaimed his victory in shell/star was over the king of Yaxchilan, probably Knot-Eye Jaguar, who, indeed, was on the throne at this time, and who, in turn, promoted his own victories over Bonampak (Fig. 15). On the one katun anniversary of Ruler 1's death in 658, several young soldiers from Yaxchilan and Bonampak came to Piedras Negras—not only, as I previously suggested, for some sort of young men's initiation ritual led by Ruler 2 (Schele and Miller 1986: 136)—but also, as I now believe, to reinforce a political hierarchy in which Piedras Negras dominated Yaxchilan, which in turn dominated Bonampak. For most of the seventh century, then, Piedras Negras may have held some sort of upper hand over other cities of the Usumacinta-Lacanha drainage.

When Ruler 2 died in 686, he had reigned over a powerful, successful, and conservative Piedras Negras for over 48 tuns—nearly half a century. At the time of Ruler 2's death, however, his descendants were finding that the configuration of Maya power along the Usumacinta River was changing, and the political relationships established by Rulers 1 and 2 of Piedras Negras were no longer secure. In 683, after an even longer reign of sixty-eight years, King Pacal of Palenque died, perhaps further unsettling a political equilibrium. Ruler A of Tikal came to power in 681. At Yaxchilan, Shield Jaguar had become king in that same year, and just a few months before his accession, he took the most important captive of his life, an *ahau* known in the Yaxchilan inscriptions as Ah Ahaual and probably the king of the "serpent-segment" site (Stuart 1985), a place that seems to have been somewhere along the Usumacinta River between Yaxchilan and Piedras Negras (Fig. 16). Shield Jaguar seized the opportunity opened by the aging Ruler 2 to capture a lord who may traditionally have been within the Piedras Negras sphere of influence. With this act, he asserted his own independence from Piedras Negras and may have ensured his own prosperity.

In 674, a princess, Lady Ahau Katun, was born at the "serpent-segment" site, possibly a daughter of Ah Ahaual, Shield Jaguar's hapless captive (Fig. 17). On 13 November 686, under the auspices of the ailing Ruler 2, this princess, then twelve years old, came to Piedras Negras and married Ruler 3. Ruler 2 died three days later, having united his son and Lady Ahau Katun.

Mary Ellen Miller

Fig. 15 Stela 26, Piedras Negras. Drawing by John Montgomery.

Meanwhile, at Yaxchilan, Shield Jaguar began to erect monument after monument that proclaimed his victory over Ah Ahaual, and he had perhaps physically overtaken the "serpent-segment" site (Fig. 18). Piedras Negras partisans at that place may have spirited the young woman down river to unite her noble blood with the Piedras Negras ruling family, the traditional guardians and dominators of the river up until this point. Like Eleanor of Aquitaine, Lady Ahau Katun held a powerful claim to territory and title all her life, and like Eleanor, her lands were sought by neighboring kings through marriage or conquest. With the arrival of Lady Ahau Katun in Piedras Negras and her marriage to his son, Ruler 2 offered Lady Ahau Katun protection and prestige, but he could no longer dominate the entire Usumacinta River. Lady Ahau Katun's homeland, the "serpent-segment" site, had probably been an independent city between the two great Usu-

Fig. 16  Lintel 45, Structure 44, Yaxchilan (after Graham 1979, 3: 99).

macinta powers, but there were increasingly little room for such buffers. Shield Jaguar of Yaxchilan was carving a powerful empire of his own in the Upper Usumacinta, and along its main tributaries, the Pasion and Lacanja Rivers, Dos Pilas and Bonampak lords too began to consume small sites and build centralized powers.

At about the same time, Lady Xoc, wife of Shield Jaguar, began to be celebrated in Yaxchilan monuments as well (Figs. 19, 20, 21). The depiction of such prominent women at both Piedras Negras and Yaxchilan often draws modern attention, and their portrayal often makes us imagine a more egalitarian life for women along the Usumacinta than at say, Tikal, where they figure more rarely as protagonists. The appearance of women is sudden and without precedent at both sites, and then, in subsequent generations, women generally return to more traditional roles as wives and mothers and occur less frequently as protagonists in texts. As we have seen, the rise to prominence of Lady Ahau Katun at Piedras Negras may be one response to Yaxchilan's efforts to consolidate the Usumacinta; the rise of Lady Xoc may have occurred for similar reasons. Shield Jaguar may have brought Lady Xoc to Yaxchilan in order to incorporate her home into his realm. Within a

*Mary Ellen Miller*

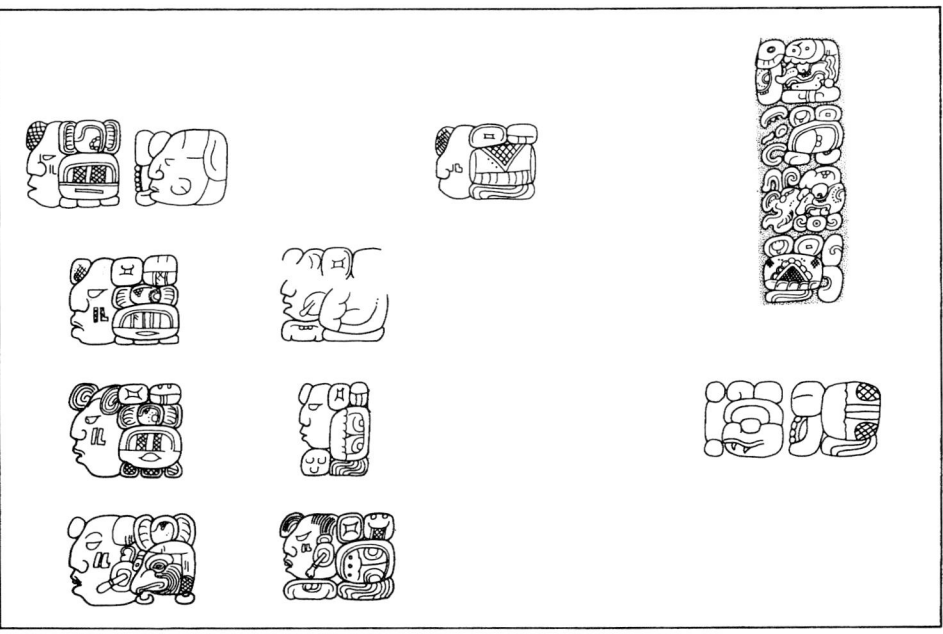

Fig. 17  Parallel texts of Lady Ahau Katun and captive Ah Ahaual, both of the "serpent-segment" site. Composite drawing by David Stuart; Lintel 45 text by Ian Graham.

generation, however, the lands were incorporated; individual women may no longer have held the independent power and status granted them during the era of empire building.

Given so many political connections over such a span of time, one might anticipate shared characteristics in the artistic record, but such is not the case. In format, style, and iconography both Piedras Negras and Yaxchilan follow independent patterns, some of which were established in Early Classic times. Although stelae are important at Yaxchilan, lintels are the most abundant surviving surfaces for artistic expression. The absence of Long Count dates long stalled decipherment even of calendrical matter in the inscriptions, and only after the historical hypothesis had been advanced could the Yaxchilan sculptures be grouped by protagonist and dated.[7] At Piedras Negras, clusters of stelae (the monuments originally identified as lintels at Piedras Negras

[7] In fact, Proskouriakoff's own style dating placed Lintels 15, 16, and 17 ten years *earlier* than Lintels 24, 25, and 26 (1950: 199), roughly at 9.17.0.0.0 and 9.17.10.0.0. In Proskouriakoff's subsequent historical analysis, she *reordered* the completion of the monuments, with Lintels 24, 25, and 26 at 9.14.15.0.0.0 and Lintels 15, 16, and 17 at roughly 9.17.0.0.0 (Proskouriakoff 1963; 1964).

On the Eve of the Collapse: Maya Art of the Eighth Century

Fig. 18 Stela 20, Yaxchilan. Drawing by Carolyn Tate (after field drawing by Ian Graham).

were exterior wall panels) celebrate an individual ruler and his family, as Herbert Spinden first recognized in 1916; the continuous record of Long Count dates led the University of Pennsylvania to conduct excavations there for most of the 1930s. Both Piedras Negras and Yaxchilan thrived during the eighth century, and far too much sculpture survives at both for it all to be considered here, so I will examine it selectively.

For the first thirty years after his installation in 681, King Shield Jaguar set up one monument after another in front of Structure 41, each with the same program: on the front, Shield Jaguar as victor, enemy noble a humbled captive; on the reverse, Shield Jaguar performing bloodletting (Fig. 18). Then, after 9.14.10.0.0 (721) or so, the Yaxchilan royalty commissioned two extraordinary programs that engaged many more artists than any previous efforts: in them they transformed the nature of Yaxchilan art. The two

Mary Ellen Miller

Fig. 19  Lintel 24, Yaxchilan (after Graham 1977, 3: 53).

themes of Yaxchilan sculpture, captive sacrifice and personal bloodletting, were separated and each treated programmatically in its own building.

On the West Acropolis Structure 44 went up, and its carved lintels and steps glorified Shield Jaguar as a warrior. On the main plaza, almost due north of Structure 41, builders laid out Structure 23 and artists began to carve its lintels. Lady Xoc, Shield Jaguar's main wife, dominates the lintels of Structure 23 (Figs. 19, 20, 21) and she may even have been responsible for the commission of the building. Both sculptural programs introduced new formats, new techniques, and new configurations of Maya sculpture: from their completion until the abandonment of the site, other kings and artists at Yaxchilan measured their own works against these two masterpieces. During the creation of the buildings, new artists may have come to Yaxchilan or new students may have been trained. The sculptures of these two buildings are among the finest Maya carvings known, and, as if to lay claim to the merit, some artists signed their works. Although there was a Yaxchilan tradition before these two structures were built, by the time of their completion there was an identifiable Yaxchilan school, characterized by both style of carving and a vivid iconography.

### On the Eve of the Collapse: Maya Art of the Eighth Century

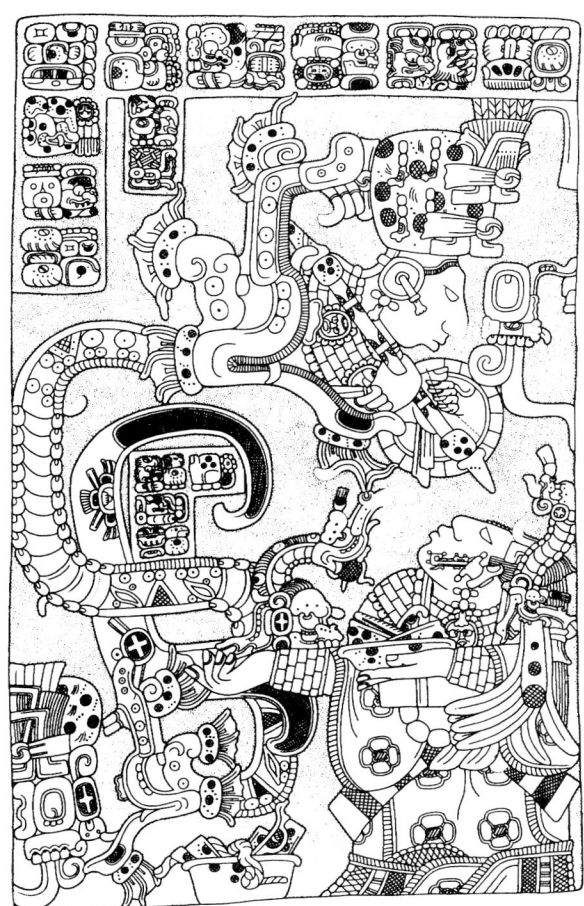

Fig. 20 Lintel 25, Yaxchilan (after Graham 1977, 3: 55).

Shield Jaguar died in 742, and after a ten-year interregnum, his son Bird Jaguar became king in 752.[8] With Bird Jaguar's accession, new programs of sculpture and building were initiated all over the site. He closely emulated some of his father's works and set some programs beside those of his father; he added sculptures to some of his father's buildings; and he developed new programs, such as Structure 33, to promote his own reign. But from the beginning there were several fundamental differences between the art of father and son. Perhaps most fundamental, Bird Jaguar's depiction rarely occurs alone. The first monument of his reign may very well be Stela 11, and on its front, Bird Jaguar faces his late father (Fig. 22). Subsequently,

[8] The many political implications of this interregnum cannot be considered in this essay.

Mary Ellen Miller

Fig. 21  Lintel 26, Yaxchilan (after Graham 1977, 3: 57).

Bird Jaguar shared his monuments with his wives, his *sahals*, and his son, as well as captives. Shield Jaguar had commissioned many monuments, but Bird Jaguar was responsible for many more than his father, although the father ruled for sixty years and the son for twenty. It is not surprising, then, to find that the quality of execution diminished in many instances, although not in all.

To take an example: Lintels 15, 16, and 17 of Bird Jaguar's reign emulate Lintels 24, 25, and 26 of his father's (Figs. 23, 24, 25). Both sets illustrate the same ritual cycle of bloodletting, vision quest, and warfare. The earlier set is larger and carved on two sides of the stone prism as well as in much greater detail. Artists executed the carving on two levels, and the back was sharply cut away. Although of equally fine stone, the later set is smaller, more sketchily carved, and lacking the unusual configurations (the mirror writing or the x-ray mask of Lintel 25, for example) that characterize the larger set. When the first set was made, there was just one other major building program under construction at Yaxchilan, Structure 44—but at the time of the making of the second set, there were perhaps as many as seven programs of art and architecture under way. In what we might call artistic inflation, much artistic effort appears to have been diluted through the volume of

# On the Eve of the Collapse: Maya Art of the Eighth Century

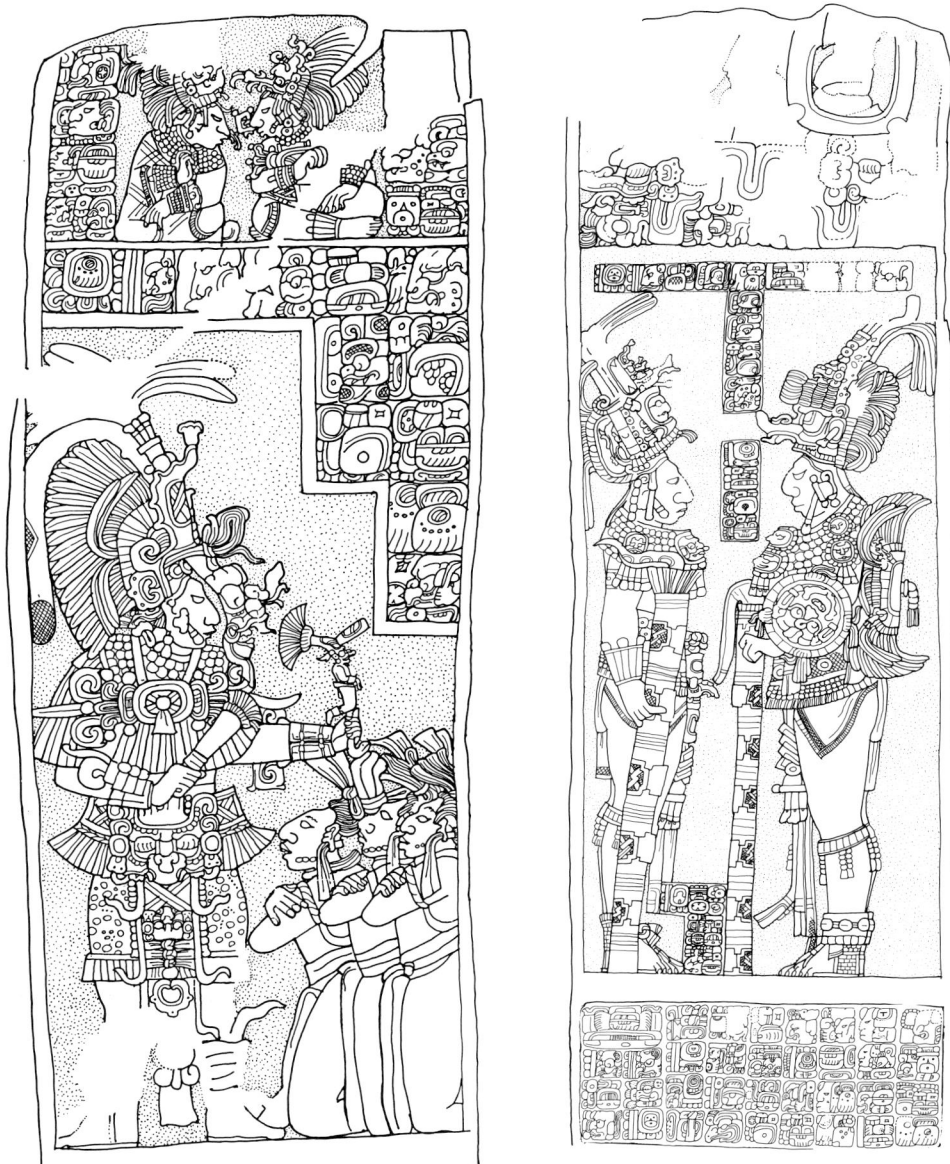

Fig. 22   Stela 11, Yaxchilan. Drawing by Linda Schele.

Fig. 23   Lintel 15, Yaxchilan (after Graham 1977, 3: 39).

Fig. 24   Lintel 16, Yaxchilan (after Graham 1977, 3: 41).

Fig. 25   Lintel 17, Yaxchilan (after Graham 1977, 3: 43).

Fig. 26   Lintel 8, Yaxchilan (after Graham 1977, 3: 27).

output, although there are individual sculptures of the Bird Jaguar reign—say, Lintel 41 or Step 7 of Structure 33—that are indeed extraordinary.

During Bird Jaguar's reign, both the pictorial content and the hieroglyphic narrative changed at Yaxchilan. Bird Jaguar shared the depictions with his wives, children, and *sahals,* the regional governors of Yaxchilan, and the texts emphasize the same point. Typical representations of his era depict shared and exchanged ritual paraphernalia. Not only do *sahals* appear at Yaxchilan, but Bird Jaguar is also depicted with the *sahals* at their regional centers up and down the Usumacinta. Because of the importance of Lintel 8 to modern scholarship, we may think of Bird Jaguar as a greater warrior than his father, but one significance of Lintel 8 is that it shows Bird Jaguar *sharing* his military success (Fig. 26).

Shield Jaguar II became king around 770, although neither the date of his accession nor his father's death is known. He inherited a large domain, one that stretched up and down the Usumacinta River, encompassing La Pasadita, Lastunich, and other stations. But toward the end of the eighth century, the Maya realm was a troubled place, and the management of this small empire must not have been an easy task. Shield Jaguar II soon found that he was constantly at battle. No longer always the aggressor, Shield Jaguar II found it necessary to fend off enemies and to use force to contain the Yaxchilan realm.

Shield Jaguar II undertook only one major building program, Structure 20 and the ceremonial space it encompassed: Hieroglyphic Stairs 5 and Stelae 4, 5, 6, and 7. In this single complex, Shield Jaguar II condensed the programs of his forebears: warfare, conquest, humiliation of captives, the joint celebration of rituals with allies and wives, bloodletting, and the celebration of the period endings are all honored. Accession, now lost, may have once been recorded on at least one of the now-fragmentary stelae and is certainly suggested in the eroded enthroned stucco figures set on the exterior of Structure 20. The Lintels 12, 13, and 14 of Structure 20 (Figs. 27, 28, 29) recall the program of Lintels 24, 25, and 26 of his grandfather (Figs. 19, 20, 21). Although rich in detail, the carvings are imprecise and hard to read; laconic texts refer back to the birth of Shield Jaguar II and the time before Bird Jaguar the Great became king.

In front of Structure 20, Shield Jaguar II set a series of stelae. Stela 7 was once one of the most graceful monuments of the plaza. No dates survive on it, but on the preserved face (Fig. 30), Shield Jaguar II carries the names of many captives as his own titles. The monument surely commemorates a period ending, perhaps as early as 9.17.10.0.0, or perhaps, given the many captives, as late as 9.18.10.0.0.

Stela 7 was carved in the style of ancestral stelae on the plaza, among them Stelae 1, 11, and 3. Morley thought Stela 7 so fine that he refused to assign a late date (1937–38, 2: 573). Proskouriakoff plotted its style chart and evaluated its date at 9.15.10.0.0 plus or minus 2 katuns (1950: 199). Sharply cut into the stone, with attention to rigid vertical and horizontal axes, symmetry, balance, and human proportions, these monuments retain the proportions characteristic of the early eighth century. What are often considered late—and even "degenerate" details in Proskouriakoff's system—are completely absent here, even at the same time that the lintel program of Structure 20 exhibits just such details: what Proskouriakoff called the "effect of restless motion" and careless execution (1950: 147), the substitution of x's for spaceholders in number glyphs, and compositions in which repeated details cover all surfaces, giving emphasis to pattern over form. Even as this new style proliferated, other artists at Yaxchilan returned to an older style for Stela 7—much in the way that classicizing, Hellenic forms persisted in Rome for centuries after their heyday. Such disparate currents in Yaxchilan as a political and social entity may have led to the juxtaposition of styles within the Structure 20 complex.

Late in his reign, Shield Jaguar II set a carved riser in front of Structure 20. Rediscovered in 1980, the carved stairs are fragmentary and eroded, but they enunciate a single theme: war. The dates and names of Shield Jaguar II's defeated enemies are recorded, a relentless litany of conquest, all between 9.18.5.0.0 and 9.18.10.0.0 (795–800). He set Stela 21 in front of his grandfather's war memorial, Structure 44, and that monument, too, enumerates one victory after another.

Finally, by 9.18.17.0.0 (10 July 807), we hear no more of Shield Jaguar II. Shield Jaguar II completed his staircase of conquest at home, but, embroiled in so many battles, he may have at last fallen from his throne. King for about thirty-seven of his fifty-seven years, he had held together a besieged realm, particularly in his last ten years. His successor created a tiny building, Structure 3, beside Structure 20 on the plaza, and placed a single carved

Fig. 27   Lintel 12, Yaxchilan
(after Graham 1977, 3: 33).

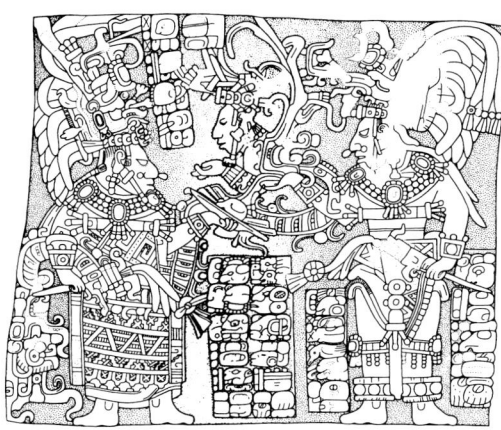

Fig. 28   Lintel 13, Yaxchilan
(after Graham 1977, 3: 35).

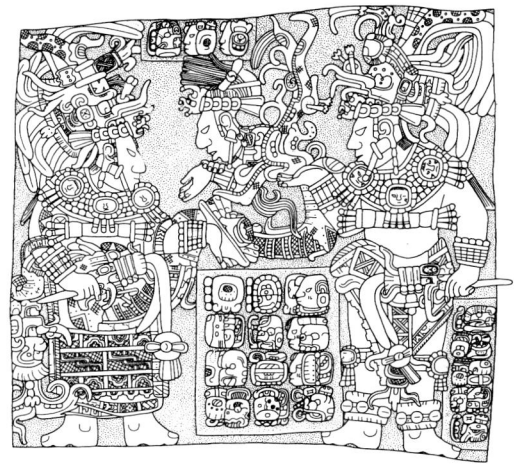

Fig. 29   Lintel 14, Yaxchilan
(after Graham 1977, 3: 37).

Mary Ellen Miller

Fig. 30  Stela 7, Yaxchilan. Drawing courtesy of Ian Graham.

## On the Eve of the Collapse: Maya Art of the Eighth Century

Fig. 31   Lintel 10, Yaxchilan (after Graham 1977, 3: 31)

monument over its doorway, Lintel 10 (Fig. 31). A list of claimed battle victories, the lintel is really the record of a lost cause. From left to right across Lintel 10 the glyphs grow more and more compact, as the sculptor tried to jam in yet more information as it became available to him. Cramped and dense, the text is the final word surviving from Yaxchilan: ostensibly a boast of conquest, it can be read by us as the message of a dying city.

Shortly after Shield Jaguar had become king at Yaxchilan, Ruler 3 took the throne at Piedras Negras. From 692 to 726, he commemorated every five-tun ending with a stela set in front of the West Acropolis. He followed the patterns established by his father and grandfather, thus beginning with an inaugural stela (Stela 6), followed by a scattering stela five years later (Stela 2), then a stela on which he wears a mosaic mask (Stela 4). Unlike his predecessors, however, he commissioned stelae that were carved on all four sides. Stelae 6, 2, and 4 all fell foward, thus preserving the front face. The next two stelae to be erected, Stelae 1 and 3, fell backward, with only the rear faces preserved. The backs of these two stelae show Lady Ahau Katun, the lady of the serpent-segment site, wife of Ruler 3. Subsequently, Ruler 3 appears within a supernatural frame on Stela 5, an image for which there is no prototype. Finally, like his father and grandfather, Ruler 3 is arrayed as a warrior on his last two monuments, Stelae 7 and 8. His grandfather's program was just two stelae, the first an inaugural niche monument and the second a warrior stela; his father's program was more extensive; Ruler 3's expands and builds upon the standard repertoire but opens and closes with the monuments most fundamental to the Piedras Negras tradition.

The rear faces of Stelae 1 and 3 offer the most unusual presentations of Ruler 3's sculptural program. Stelae 1 and 3 were the first monuments at Piedras Negras to feature a woman so prominently (Figs. 32, 33). Artists portrayed Lady Ahau Katun in the same full-frontal view, with face carved in higher, nearly three-dimensional bas-relief, that characterizes the most important representations of kings, that is, upon inauguration and as warriors. Lady Ahau Katun was the only woman at Piedras Negras ever to be depicted as if she were a man.

Ruler 4 succeeded his father in 729. Like his father, he commissioned monuments for the West Acropolis. Where the father's were to the right of the palace chambers, Ruler 4 set monuments in a row to the left. In 731 he dedicated a niche stela to commemorate his accession, and the carving recapitulates moments of that event: a slain captive lies at the base of a scaffold that supports the niche, and bloody footprints lead along the draped cloth that connects the sacrifice and the niche (Fig. 34). Three figures on the sides of the monument face forward and frame the niche scene, as if to observe it. Their attire suggests a foreign origin. In spangled pillbox headdresses at right and with a single feather in a headband at left, they most closely resemble Toltec Maya at Chichen Itza. Unfortunately, these individuals do not appear as protagonists of the Stela 11 texts.

After erecting a warrior monument, Ruler 4 commissioned two successive monuments that focused on ancestor worship. On Stela 10, the king sits under the great Waterlily Jaguar. On Stela 40 (Fig. 35), as Norman Hammond has aptly pointed out, the subject of this stela is not the "sowing of corn" to some "chthonic deity," as Morley, its discoverer, thought, nor the temporary delegation of power, as Proskouriakoff suggested: rather, the upper figure is Ruler 4, sprinkling offerings down into a temple pyramid, where an ancestor rises up from his sarcophagus in a chambered tomb in order to communciate with the living world by means of a twisted cord that runs up the left-hand side of the monument (Hammond 1981). As we learn from a monument made twenty-five years after the fact, Ruler 4 himself died on 26 November 757, and was buried three days later.

Let us move on, at this point, to the reign of the last king of Piedras

Negras, Ruler 6, a man of thirty-one years at his accession in 781.[9] Unlike his contemporaries at Yaxchilan or Palenque or Tikal, whose reigns seem wracked by economic poverty and a poverty of creativity, Ruler 6's reign ushered in creativity, a revival of the past, and if abundant, well-crafted sculpture are an indication, some economic well-being. Exuberant sculptures celebrate his reign, and many of them seem to introduce new types of sculpture to Piedras Negras. A handful of principal sculptors worked on the monuments of his reign over a period of about thirty-five years and guided Piedras Negras through this period of creativity (Stuart n.d.b). Ruler 6's accession monument, for example, was the first in Late Classic Piedras Negras history to eschew the niche: on Stela 15, Ruler 6 stands erect, in the simple garb and with the incense bag characteristic of niche figures (Fig. 36). The entire figure is worked in high relief, nearly in the round. His left (viewer's right) arm has been freed from the stone, and his feet are at a natural, oblique angle to the ground line. As a sculpture, Stela 15 has more in common with the works of Copan or Tonina than it does with previous accession monuments at Piedras Negras.

Throne 1 was built for the niche in J-6, the west colonnade of Court 1 (Fig. 37). It had only front legs, its heavy rear screen supported by the architectural niche. Both the wedge legs and the front of the seat were carved. The throne back is worked in the shape of a giant Cauac Monster without lower jaw: as at Temple 22, Copan, the lower jaw may have been the surface of the chamber itself, so that when seated on the throne, one was in the maw of the Cauac Monster, a cave, the very heart of the earth. Artists chose smooth, fine-grained limestone for both this throne and Stela 12 and worked its surface as if it were soft butter. When they completed Throne 1, they gave it a coat of red paint, and the sculpture still sparkles today from metals in the paint.

More than any other Piedras Negras king, Ruler 6 lived by the stars, timing nearly every moment of his regime to the patterns of Venus. According to the texts on the throne, he took captives just sixty-three days before his accession—possibly to expedite his kingship—and also proclaimed himself the victor in shell/star warfare. That day marked Venus' departure from maximum eastern elongation, and then, sixty-three days later, on his accession, Venus rose as morning star. No other point in Venus' cycle was so auspicious for warfare and sacrifice as the heliacal rising, and so, on the morning of his accession, Ruler 6 may very well have sacrificed the captives taken sixty-three days before. Finally, as its own text indicates, the throne was set in place on 9.17.15.0.0, or 2 November 785.

---

[9] Stephen D. Houston has demonstrated that Proskouriakoff's Ruler 6 of Piedras Negras was in fact an El Cayo *sahal* whose installation was celebrated at Piedras Negras under the auspices of Ruler 5 (Houston 1983). Accordingly, I have renumbered the Piedras Negras Late Classic kings Rulers 1–6; Proskouriakoff's 1960 designations remain for Rulers 1–5; Proskouriakoff's Ruler 7 is now Ruler 6.

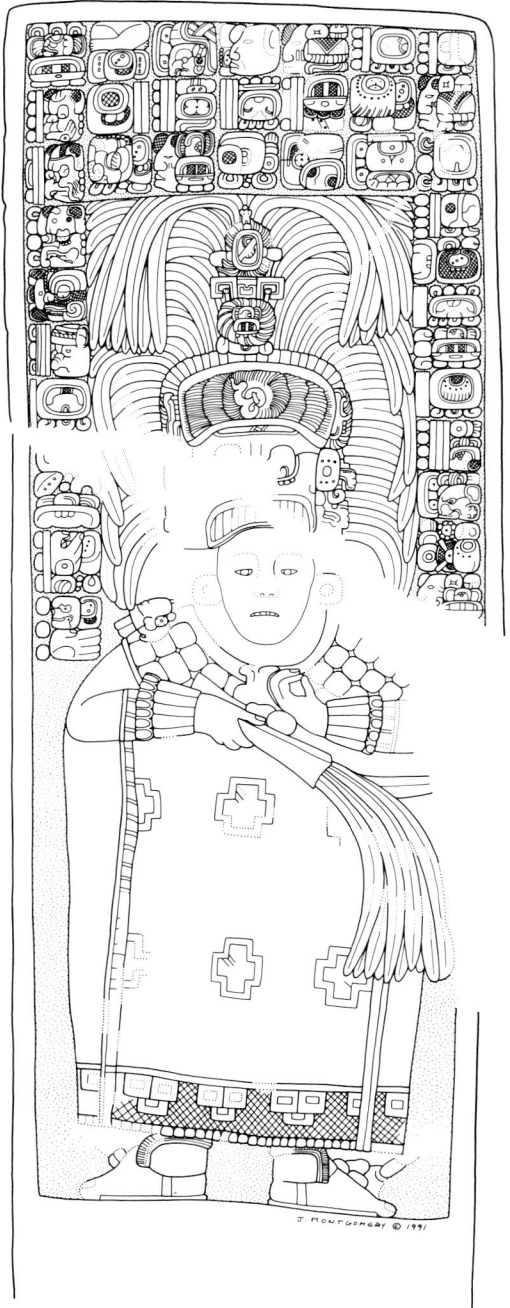

Fig. 32 Stela 1, Piedras Negras. Drawing by John Montgomery.

## On the Eve of the Collapse: Maya Art of the Eighth Century

Fig. 33 Stela 3, Piedras Negras. Drawing by John Montgomery.

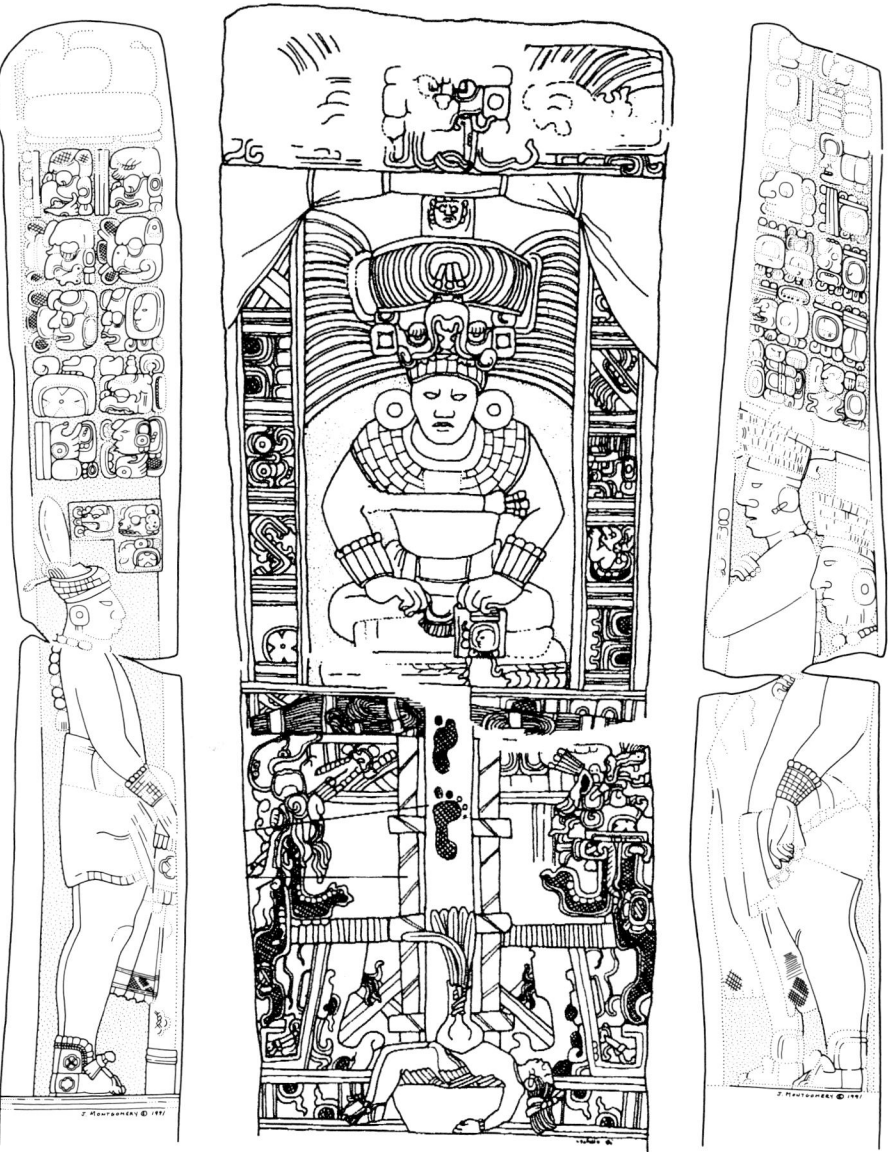

Fig. 34  Stela 11, Piedras Negras; front, sides. Front, drawing by Linda Schele. Sides, drawings by John Montgomery.

# On the Eve of the Collapse: Maya Art of the Eighth Century

Fig. 35 Stela 40, Piedras Negras. Photograph courtesy of The University Museum, University of Pennsylvania, Philadelphia.

Mary Ellen Miller

Fig. 36 Stela 15, Piedras Negras. Photograph courtesy of the Carnegie Institution of Washington.

At Palenque, the last known monument recites Kuk's direct ancestors in a line back to Pacal. Shield Jaguar II of Yaxchilan commissioned monuments that recreated and commented on moments in the past, particularly the years before the accession of his father, and his monuments to the past may have been actively revisionist. Ruler 6, the Piedras Negras contemporary of Shield Jaguar II, also referred back to earlier times. He commissioned Panel 3 to portray the Piedras Negras court during the days of the one-katun ceremony of Ruler 4, an occasion attended by the king of Yaxchilan, other members of the royal family, and loyal *sahals* (Fig. 38). Why would the last king of Piedras

## On the Eve of the Collapse: Maya Art of the Eighth Century

Fig. 37   Throne 1, Piedras Negras. Photograph copyright Justin Kerr, 1991.

Negras commission such a monument? The scene itself seems to have nothing directly to do with his own rule: instead, it captures the heyday of his grandfather's reign, when even the great Bird Jaguar of Yaxchilan came as a visitor. With Wall Panel 3 he not only honored his grandfather but also the time of his own birth (he had been conceived at about the same time of the one-katun anniversary party) and the memory of his youthful days, before the Usumacinta was convulsed in war and retribution.

Through balance, symmetry, and the use of the two registers, Wall Panel 3 achieves greater unity of composition than any other Maya carving, and there may well be no other indigenous sculpture of the New World that so captures a "naturalistic" grouping that can be read as such in Western terms. It was dedicated on 9.17.15.0.0, the same day as Throne 1, and in all likelihood, on that day, Throne 1 replaced the throne depicted on Panel 3.

Ten years later, in 795, Ruler 6 dedicated Stela 12, which was set on an upper terrace of Structure 0-13, the great ancestral shrine built and then refurbished by Rulers 4, 5, and 6. Stela 12 (Fig. 39) depicts three registers of figures on stepped risers, perhaps 0-13 itself: Ruler 6 at top, two war cap-

Fig. 38  Wall Panel 3, Piedras Negras. Photograph copyright Justin Kerr, 1991.

tains and a noble captive at middle, and eight more captives tied together in a heap at bottom, almost like some modern sociological chart of class and status. Ruler 6's reign had already seen some changes in styles of carving: he had not commemorated his accession with a niche stela, for example, and both Throne 1 and Wall Panel 3 are unusual monuments. With Stela 12, another standard was violated: this time, the warrior monument did not include the frontal, larger-than-life warrior in War Serpent or Balloon headdress, and from certain points of view, the captives are more prominent than the ruler himself.

According to the text on Stela 12, a battle in 794 and Ruler 6's forty-six-tun birthday in 795 were the two most notable events of the recent past when Stela 12 was set up a few days later in 795. Now this "shell/star" battle of 794 had been waged against Pomona, far downstream and inland from the Usumacinta River. From the fragmentary sculptures known from Pomona (Fig. 40), however, a little-known, badly looted Maya site, one can easily see that its works resembled more those of Palenque than those of Piedras Negras: fine, buttery limestone was carved with elegant, supple, two-dimensional figures in profile. A surviving wall panel from 771 depicts four seated lords, at least two of whom bear a glyph reading "Pauahtun," a title also borne by scribes and masters of courtly arts.[10] Although we know

---

[10] See, for example, the so-called Teaching Vase (Kerr #1196), where God N, Pauahtun, teaches counting and writing to his students (Kerr 1989). The great Monkey Scribe excavated in Structure 9N-82 at Copan is also Pauahtun (Schele and Miller 1986: pl. 46).

On the Eve of the Collapse: Maya Art of the Eighth Century

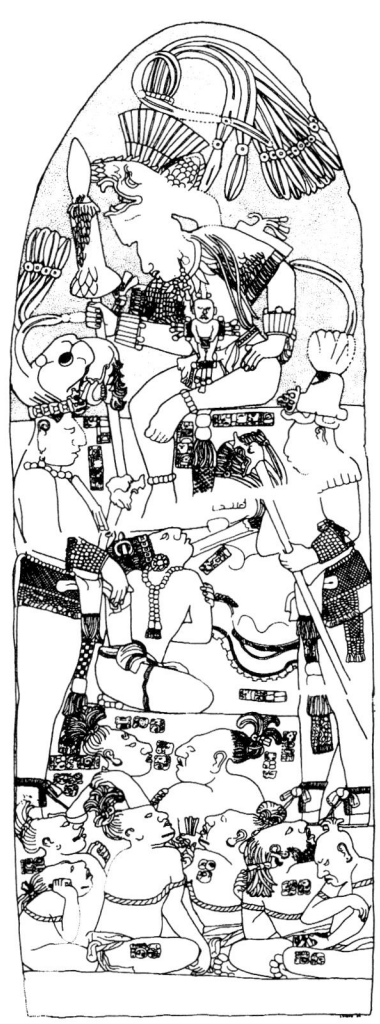

Fig. 39   Stela 12, Piedras Negras. Drawing by Linda Schele.

little of Pomona, from this panel we know that artists were depicted in carvings, and we can recognize something of the style of carving.

Strikingly, Stela 12, which so prominently claims victory over Pomona, is worked in the style of that city. With their graceful, profile postures, elegantly worked as very low bas-relief on limestone, the captives of Stela 12 may very well be from Pomona, commemorated in the style of their home. When the Piedras Negras lords defeated Pomona in the "shell/star" battle, they may have demanded tribute, and although some of the principal

Mary Ellen Miller

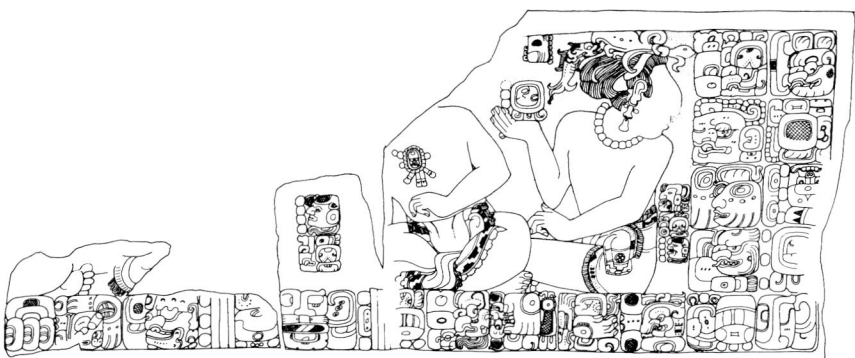

Fig. 40  Wall Panel, Pomona. Drawing by Linda Schele.

artists of this monument had made other Piedras Negras works (Stuart n.d.b), yet others may have been Pomona captives, who represented their own demise with unsurpassed empathy. If such elaborate works of art were being made as a sort of tribute art, we may well want to ask ourselves what other sorts of tribute flowed from defeated sites. Foodstuffs? Building materials? Less skilled labor?

Stela 12 is the last known figural monument at Piedras Negras. It proclaims victory, but the absence of further notice of the royal family suggests that someone else may have then claimed a victory over Piedras Negras. Throne 1 was ripped from its niche and smashed on the steps in front, where it appears to have remained undisturbed until the University of Pennsylvania recovered it in the 1930s. Along the Usumacinta, both Yaxchilan and Piedras Negras claimed victory as their last events, but the subsequent silence suggests that they, too, were subsumed by war.

## Copan

Now let us take a quick look at the sculpture of Copan, where ongoing excavations continue to change our notions of Copanec art. In the seventh century, under King Smoke Imix, a series of stelae were erected to commemorate his reinvigorated reign. In many ways, these stelae establish a pattern that later rulers would follow: all four sides of the prism are carved, with frontal figures on the front and sometimes front and rear faces. This form may have achieved its greatest success under his son and successor, 18 Rabbit (acceded in 695), who populated the Great Plaza with rich three-dimensional images at the beginning of the eighth century.

In 737, however, the king of Quirigua, Cauac Sky, took 18 Rabbit captive—and that fact became the single most recorded event in Quirigua's history. Until he died, Cauac Sky promoted and recalled his victory over Copan on every monument he commissioned. Such defeats often seem to have impoverished Maya sites: Palenque, for example, seems to have suffered after its defeat at the hands of Tonina. But Copan barely skipped a beat: a new king was inaugurated and new programs of art and architecture were begun, including the Hieroglyphic Stairs. All across the Maya realm, hieroglyphic staircases generally commemorate victory and were used for rituals reenacting military success. But following its defeat by Quirigua, Copan constructed its staircase to celebrate all victories of its dynasty. Interposed among lengthy texts, five three-dimensional Copan kings reign over two-dimensional captives at their feet. Conspicuously, 18 Rabbit *is* on the stairs, reigning victoriously at Copan in the official record. At Copan, the response to military defeat appears to have been the creation of a permanent memorial that promoted revisionist history.

The last Copan king, Yax Pac, took office in 763. He refurbished much of the Main Acropolis, starting with Structure 11, which was rededicated as the shrine to his reign. Although two-dimensional figures had been carved before at Copan, now, under Yax Pac's direct reign and at outlying noble palaces, two-dimensional carvings of figures in profile became widespread. Under the influence of his mother, a woman from Palenque, Yax Pac may have become more familiar with a two-dimensional style, but Yax Pac may have turned to this format for his own purposes. He was particularly keen to cast himself in Copan history, as he did on Altar Q (Fig. 41) or on his own accession bench. To do so visually required multiple depictions fixed in space—an effect difficult to achieve with three-dimensional sculptures. In the art at the end of the eighth century of Copan, Yax Pac rarely appears alone: he is in the company of ancestors and subservient lords. This shift would appear to be analogous to what happens at Yaxchilan, where Bird Jaguar rarely appears alone, and even at Piedras Negras or Palenque, where the last rulers recalled specific moments in the past. More than at any other time, late eighth-century Maya rulers explicitly and publicly commemorated their present existence in light of past experience.

### BONAMPAK

As one final stop at the end of the eighth century, we turn to the Bonampak paintings (Fig. 42). As Clemency Coggins pointed out some time ago, a stuccoed pot (Fig. 43) in Ruler A of Tikal's tomb bears figures nearly identical to those in the Bonampak murals (n.d.: 504–510). But because of its archaeological context, we know that the pot was made by 727 at the latest—and the Bonampak paintings no earlier than 790. That means that for sixty-five years at the very least, a stucco painting tradition preserved a rigid canon. In the history of art, sixty-five years can be a long time. Styles can and do often change dramatically in less than a century, but

Mary Ellen Miller

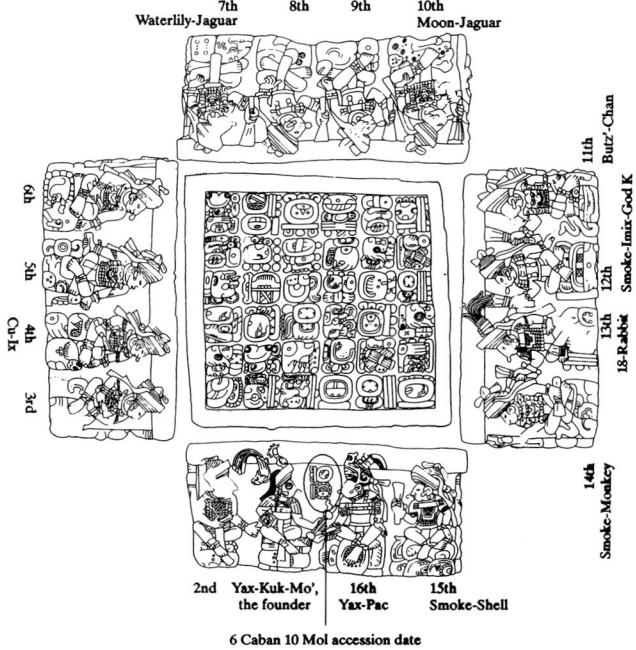

Fig. 41  Altar Q, Copan. Drawing by Linda Schele.

apparently among the Maya they did not, even along the Usumacinta, the region generally considered to exhibit the most stylistic evolution.

In fact, much of the Bonampak mural program seems to have been formulaic. For example, around 760 or so, an artist carved La Pasadita Lintel 1 and portrayed a kneeling captive unlike any other previous depiction, with frontal torso and profile legs and head (Fig. 44). Thirty years later, a different artist rendered an almost identical but reversed figure in Room 2 of the Bonampak murals (Fig. 45), perhaps based on direct observation of the former, but in all likelihood, from a common model. The central confrontation of the great battle itself would seem to be drawn from Yaxchilan Lintel 8 or a similar model, slightly rephrased (Figs. 26 and 46). The comparison between Yaxchilan Lintel 8 and the Bonampak paintings is also chilling: should we imagine such large-scale warfare every time we see a scene of capture? At Bonampak, the battle is specifically named as shell/star warfare, or, that is, a battle timed to coincide with the movements of Venus and other planets. I suspect that most shell/star records do denote massive battles.

Perhaps no other work of art would seem to provide such a window on late eighth-century life as do these murals of the 790s. They are yet one

On the Eve of the Collapse: Maya Art of the Eighth Century

Fig. 42  South wall, Room 1, Structure 1, Bonampak. Reconstruction painting by Felipe Dávalos.

more final monument of the Maya region that celebrates warfare. Although the subject of the paintings is the ritual surrounding the presentation of a young heir, warfare and sacrifice dominate the program. King Chaan-muan rules and presides, but not without great support, including foreign dignitaries and at least fourteen *sahals*. The program was never completed, and the celebrated little heir probably never became king. Even before the paintings were finished, the building fell into disrepair and the cap of calcifications that preserved them for the future began to grow over them.

DISCUSSION

Now what have we learned from this quick tour of the eighth century? There certainly is no uniform artistic development of the era, except that by 9.19.0.0.0, that is, A.D. 810, only a very few sites would continue to make monuments. Palenque, Piedras Negras, Yaxchilan, Bonampak, and Copan

403

Fig. 43   Stucco pot, Burial 116, Temple I, Tikal. Drawing by William R. Coe (after Coe 1967: 102).

Fig. 44   Lintel 1, La Pasadita. Drawing courtesy of Ian Graham.

Fig. 45 Detail, North Wall, Room 2, Structure 1, Bonampak (copyright 1975 by the President and Fellows of Harvard College).

had all finished, although Tikal had dated monuments through 869. Artistically, the end can appear to fizzle out, as it does at Yaxchilan, where the quality of monuments declines over several generations, or it can be a dramatic cessation, as it is at Piedras Negras and Copan, where the final monuments are of extraordinary quality and detail. At Tikal, monuments become smaller and more conventional generation after generation, but at Palenque, the last carved stone is an innovative, exciting piece of work. Late monuments, such as the Structure 20 complex at Yaxchilan, may include many styles, a seemingly conscious eclecticism that undermines style dating and baffles us in our attempts to create convenient stereotypes.

Surely it is also the very abundance of eighth-century art that continues to draw us back to it. Its very richness and diversity make it the best laboratory for any study of Maya elite culture—their writings, their religion, their relationships with each other—and even, as I have tried to show, their different responses in the generation before the Classic Maya collapse. The great volume of eighth-century art is also no archaeological accident: there simply was more of it. More nobles received fine burials with elaborate offerings; more kings responded to difficult political situations with complicated artistic programs of justification. Where Ruler 1 at Piedras Negras had commissioned two stelae, Ruler 3 commissioned eight; where Shield Jaguar of Yaxchilan

*Mary Ellen Miller*

Fig. 46 Detail, South Wall, Room 2, Structure 1, Bonampak. Reconstruction painting by Antonio Tejeda (copyright 1975 by the President and Fellows of Harvard College).

had commissioned the lintels for three or four buildings at most, Bird Jaguar sought them for ten or twelve. It is no longer fashionable for art historians to focus exclusively on issues of quality, but even such notions follow no standard guidelines, for one might well argue that Ruler 3's stelae are greater achievements than his predecessor's, while Bird Jaguar's lintels are not.

Archaeological data that exclude art and inscriptions may give us an altogether different view into these last decades of Maya art. For one thing, both art and inscriptions offer a precision of dating beyond the reach of archaeology: a series of events may be spelled out across days; a series of images may be dated to five-year intervals that could only be grossly lumped together archaeologically. If we talk about archaeological data of a one hundred-year period, say 750–850, it can tell us about the before and after, of physical changes wrought upon landscape, skeletons, or pottery, but without art and inscriptions it can provide little insight into the thinking of the humans who endured or wrought such changes.

If art were a mirror of historical events and processes, then we might expect the eighth-century art of the Maya to trudge down a steady path to decadence, impoverishment, and change. But it doesn't. There is no uniform pattern of artistic response to the eighth century. The only sure response is the final one, the cessation of Classic art.

## On the Eve of the Collapse: Maya Art of the Eighth Century

Because some Maya formal portraiture and stone sculpture resisted change, we often tend to think that the fabric of Maya society was also unchanging. But here is where we ought to distinguish between history of Maya art and the history of the Maya. Some Maya art did change: new representations were added, as at Yaxchilan, where the eighth century scenes of two, three, or more individuals seem to occur at the same time as change in administration of that site. The art *does* reflect that change, particularly as more individuals gained the right to be portrayed in stone sculpture. But equally frequently, the change is not reflected in the representations of human individuals. At Tikal, for example, the portrayals of the king suggest, if anything, the absolute absence of societal change. How can we tell when the art, like Shakespeare's lady, doth protest too much?

Across the Maya area, the inscriptions of the eighth century *do* reveal ever-increasing numbers of successful captures of other Maya nobles. Here is where the history of art and history itself begin to diverge, creating dissonance. Shield Jaguar boasts of four captives; his son calls himself the captor of twenty; the reign, in turn, of his successor and son Shield Jaguar II, reads like a litany of warfare with at least ten noble captives taken over a period of only five years. Unsuccessful battles, of course, were not recorded by the losers, so it is hard to know how many other battles there were in addition to those proclaimed by the victors. The Maya used the shell/star glyph to record their greatest battles. Up until the end of the seventh century only a handful of shell/star events were recorded anywhere, but from about 9.13.0.0.0 (692) until the end of the baktun at the beginning of the ninth century, the numbers of shell/star battles, captures, and other war events multiply. If a battle of the scale of the one depicted in Room 2 of the Bonampak murals is considered each time that a shell/star war event is recorded or even a capture enumerated, then the Maya area was convulsed by warfare during the eighth century.

Throughout this era, the art does not necessarily change: after all, King Cauac Sky of Quirigua captured King 18 Rabbit of Copan and hauled him to Quirigua for sacrifice, but the nature of representations did not change at either site. This capture and sacrifice was a fundamental rent in the fabric of Maya society, but the art is seamless, as if no change had occurred. Throughout the Maya area, as more and more of it during the eighth century convulsed in warfare according to the inscriptions, there was little change in the art at most places, which, if anything, clung more desperately to established traditions that they sought to emulate. What reveals the change are the inscriptions. The inscriptions recorded the deeds of the Maya nobility in the Maya language. These deeds did indeed change as the role of king became more that of warlord, and, with pride, the deeds are recorded. So we reach a point in the history of Maya art where the narrative reveals a change not clearly reflected in the art. One might say even the rigid copying among

Tikal stelae of the eighth century reflects a tough determination to deflect change—and even to appear as if there is no reason for change. In this case, we may want to consider the static image as an artifact that can only make sense when juxtaposed against a more dynamic narrative text. The dissonance between the two begins to yield the stuff of true history.

Although the inscriptions carry the story of eighth-century chaos, they are rendered in the Classic format, usually beginning with an Initial Series or a calendar round date. If one cannot read their narrative, they seem, then, not to have changed from earlier texts. To Morley and Thompson, the first signal that something was amiss with the Classic Maya was the sudden absence of art and inscriptions altogether, not the tale of chronic warfare woven by the historical texts. In fact, to Thompson the katun ending 9.13.0.0.0 (in 692) was the initiation of a period of Maya glory, not the beginning of the end, as in many ways it sadly seems to me. Inscriptions grew long at that point, paeans and invocations to gods and spirits, Thompson thought, but now recognized as boasts of conquest and victory. The art itself seems not to yield to the change and transformation in society until its demise altogether.

As the Leiden Plaque (ca. 320) and other early monuments indicate, the Maya took at least occasional captives from the beginning of the Classic period. Sacrificial victims and their blood had also been offered to seal sacred moments. Why did the pace of warfare increase so dramatically for the eighth-century Maya? In Central Mexico, warfare has long been tied to the economic gain one would accrue in battle. Tribute was exacted; land titles of the vanquished were held by the victorious. Through ethnographic analogy, similar economic goals of warfare have been imputed to the Toltecs and Teotihuacanos, but ironically, not to the Maya. Despite the embrace of the historical interpretation of Maya art, it has been hard to shed many of our notions about the Classic Maya. Because of the elegant, courtly art made by the Maya, it has been difficult to accept their cruelty, their warfare, even what may have been crass economic patterns. Maya warfare, too, was probably waged for economic gain and not only to gain sacrificial victims. No written tribute document exists, nor any treaty by which lands were ceded by one city-state to another, but we can expect that such records may have existed; in fact, the depiction of Bird Jaguar with his regional governors may be just such records, although no one has yet interpreted them in that light.

Caracol may be the first Maya city to boast of besting its neighbors in outright war. In 562 Caracol claimed victory over the king of Tikal; about seventy years later, Caracol added Naranjo to its list of fiefdoms. Arlen and Diane Chase now demonstrate that archaeology amplifies and confirms the textual record: the years of claimed political expansion are in fact accompanied by unprecedented growth of the city and its resources (Chase and Chase 1989). In all likelihood, such sudden wealth results from the direct

## On the Eve of the Collapse: Maya Art of the Eighth Century

transfer of Tikal and Naranjo resources and people in Caracol. In this first explicit test case of the material consequences of war, the Chases have shown that warfare provided the Maya victors with prosperity, if only temporarily.

How did this transfer occur? When a king or an important lord was captured, he was apparently carried off to the victor's city. There, alive, he and other members of the nobility made perfect hostages. There are no records of the movement of ordinary commodities, probably paid in regular installments, although such records probably existed. If Caracol exacted tribute from Tikal and Naranjo, both the taxers and the taxed must have kept careful track of the exchange.

One particular commodity whose movement can be observed following warfare, however, is art. In some instances, it is clear that the victors erected monuments at the home of the defeated.[11] At other sites, however, the style of the defeated site became the style of the victors. For example, the capture of Kan-Xul of Palenque by Ruler 3 of Tonina introduced the style of Palenque to Tonina. Piedras Negras Stela 12, the record of victory over Pomona, is characterized by the fine low relief typical of Pomona. The captives are vividly depicted, with an eloquence perhaps attributable to their having made the sculpture that recorded their demise.[12] This pattern may also help explain the beauty of the captives at Bonampak and Cacaxtla: in all likelihood, these paintings too were made by tribute labor of the defeated city.[13]

In this view of the era, then, the eighth century was a world of widespread, near-constant warfare—of which I suspect the inscriptions are only the tip of the iceberg—accompanied by burdensome tribute that emptied the cities of both skilled artisans and supplies. Whereas the centralization of tribute by the Mexica may have made the system work smoothly, among the Maya several city-states may have demanded tribute from vulnerable border populations, increasing the instability of such a system. Although tribute was a wracking economic burden among the Maya, it may nevertheless be in part responsible for the enormous quantity of rich goods made in the eighth century. But warfare not only depleted the resources and supplies

---

[11] Caracol, for example, promoted its victory over Naranjo with a carved staircase in Caracol style at Naranjo; much later, when Naranjo defeated Ucanal, a piece of what must have been the hated staircase was hauled to Ucanal, a symbol of its humiliation. The Hieroglyphic Stairs at Seibal that record the demise of Paw Jaguar, their defeated king, were worked in the style of Dos Pilas.

[12] The eloquence of the captives has long been noted. Herbert J. Spinden, for example, in 1916 wrote of one captive: "the most marked individuality is seen in the downcast old man at the observer's right, and in the heavily bearded person who sits next to him" (1916: 444).

[13] Nine captives—perhaps a symbolic number—appear both on Piedras Negras Stela 12 and on the north walk of Bonampak. Nine is also the number of sacrificial victims interred in several Early Classic tombs (See, for example, Tomb A-1, Kaminaljuyu (Kidder, Jennings, and Shook 1946: 444).

of society, it also removed young men from circulation, both by their loss in battle and by tribute.

The description of the world that had been given centuries before, in which the blood of the divine king united upper- and underworlds, nurtured by a small amount of sacrificial blood, was beginning to cease to describe the world as it was. The conservative representations characteristic of some Maya sculpture may have been generated out of little more than habit. By the end of the eighth century, the disjunction between what was known of the cosmos and what was happening may have been so profound that faith ebbed among the Maya. If the example of Caracol proves to hold true elsewhere, then thousands of Maya may have been taken by victors from one city to another. To avoid the carnage of battle, to avoid conscription, to avoid paying the tribute, or to escape from forced labor at another city, many Maya may have fled into the jungle, abandoning the cities where they were the obvious targets of their enemies. The Maya did not vanish from their homeland altogether, but they may well have "melted" away into the tropical rain forest.[14] Classic art ceased to be made altogether.

For the Classic Maya lowlands, and for the Chol and Chorti Maya, the ethnic groups of power during the Classic, there was little reprieve for their culture: their cities did not revive. Their abandonment of the cities, however, left a power vacuum by the onset of the ninth century, and there were other Maya willing to move into it—and whose presence may well have exacerbated the eighth-century ferment. Yucatec Maya, in nothern Yucatan, maintained their developmental trajectory for at least another century or two. Chontal Maya, also known as the Itza, began to dominate the Usumacinta and Pasion drainages, and they took over Seibal.[15] Prominent as warriors, these Itza were probably also aggressively picking at Classic Maya territory during the difficult eighth century. They may be the foreigners depicted on Piedras Negras Stela 11 (Fig. 34). As Jeff Kowalski and others have argued, after A.D. 869, they simultaneously became the dominant Maya group at Chichen Itza (Kowalski 1989). An out-group throughout the Classic, the Itza were nevertheless Maya, and they used and understood Classic Maya hieroglyphs and iconography. More familiar with and receptive to the imagery both of Central Mexico and that of the Gulf Coast, they readily incorporated it into their own vocabulary of power.

Chichen Itza, in the ninth century, was the greatest Mesoamerican metropolis of its time.[16] Ideas, forms, and probably even peoples from through-

---

[14] The ability of native Mesoamericans to do so is well documented. In the 19th century, for example, during the Caste War of Yucatan, the Maya almost vanished as targets. They retreated to the jungle, retaining the ability to fight a guerrilla war but preventing their own isolation by regular troops in major population centers (Reed 1964).

[15] Thompson called these Maya the Putun (1970: 41–45).

[16] Few large cities existed at that time for comparison; among Xochicalco, Cholula, Tula, or Uxmal, Chichen Itza was probably the greatest.

out Mesoamerica contributed to its success. The importance of Central Mexican imagery at Chichen Itza has led many Mesoamericanists to suspect outright conquest of Yucatan by Toltecs from Tula, Hidalgo. The use of chronological terminology separating Chichen Itza from its Maya predecessors has made it difficult to see continuity with its Maya past.[17] The elements cited by Proskouriakoff as the intrusive non-Maya ones that distinguished Chichen Itza from its predecessors (1950: 157) can now be shown to occur widely during the eighth century, in contexts that are completely consistent with Classic Maya art and that do not indicate foreign domination, although some of them characterize minor arts more than the major ones. Despite the different appearance of Yucatan art of the ninth century and beyond, it is a development out of eighth century art, and its makers may have been some of the very persons whose presence speeded the demise of eighth-century cities.

For forty years we have worked with the notion of a Classic period defined essentially by art and writing that could not be understood at the time that the definition came into general use—and then applied to other contemporary flowerings in Mesoamerica. Now that we can read and understand both the writing and the art, this Classic world no longer seems so ideal. The eighth-century materials that have defined the very nature of Classic art seem to predict the demise of Classic society. The Postclassic civilizations that once seemed so culturally distant from the eighth-century Maya now seem to grow directly from them. The eighth century can be seen now to be a time of transformation for the Maya, the end of one sort of world in the southern lowlands and the introduction of another to the north.

---

[17] In 1950, evaluating the relationship between Chichen Itza and Tula, Proskouriakoff wrote that "if, subsequently, some of the components designated non-Classic or non-Maya prove to be native to Yucatan, a rearrangement of our present concepts would become necessary" (1950: 157).

# BIBLIOGRAPHY

CHASE, ARLEN, AND DIANE Z. CHASE
    1989    The investigation of Classic Period Maya Warfare at Caracol, Belize. *Mayab* 5: 5–18.

COE, WILLIAM R.
    1967    *Tikal: A Handbook of the Ancient Maya Ruins.* University Museum, Phildelphia.

COGGINS, CLEMENCY CHASE
    n.d.    *Painting and Drawing Styles at Tikal: An Historical and Iconographic Reconstruction.* Ph.D. dissertation, Harvard University, 1975.

GRAHAM, IAN
    1977–79    *Corpus of Maya Hieroglyphic Inscriptions,* 3. Yaxchilan. Peabody Museum, Harvard University, Cambridge, Massachusetts.

HAMMOND, NORMAN
    1981    Pom for the Ancestors: A Reexamination of Piedras Negras Stela 40. *Mexicon* 3 (5): 77–79.

HOUSTON, STEPHEN D.
    1983    On "Ruler 6" at Piedras Negras, Guatemala. *Mexicon* 5 (5): 84–86.

JONES, CHRISTOPHER, AND LINTON SATTERTHWAITE
    1982    *The Monuments and Inscriptions of Tikal: The Carved Monuments,* Tikal Report 33a. University Museum, University of Pennsylvania, Philadelphia.

KERR, JUSTIN
    1989    *The Maya Vase Book: A Corpus of Rollout Photographs of Maya Vases,* vol. 1. Kerr Associates, New York.

KIDDER, ALFRED V., JESSE D. JENNINGS, AND EDWIN SHOOK
    1946    *Excavations at Kaminaljuyu, Guatemala.* Carnegie Institution of Washington, Publication 561. Washington, D.C.

KOWALSKI, JEFF KARL
    1989    'Who Am I among the Itza?': Links between Northern Yucatan and the Western Maya Lowlands and Highlands. In *Mesoamerica after the Decline of Teotihuacan A.D. 700–900* (Richard A. Diehl and Janet Catherine Berlo, eds.): 173–185. Dumbarton Oaks, Washington, D.C.

MORLEY, SYLVANUS G.
    1937–38    *The Inscriptions of Peten,* 5 vols. Carnegie Institution of Washington, Publication 437. Washington, D.C.

PROSKOURIAKOFF, TATIANA
    1950    *Classic Maya Sculpture.* Carnegie Institution of Washington, Publication 593. Washington, D.C.
    1960    Historical Implications of a Pattern of Dates at Piedras Negras, Guatemala. *American Antiquity* 25 (4): 454–475.
    1963    Historical Data in the Inscriptions of Yaxchilan, Part I. *Estudios de Cultura Maya* 3: 149–167.

    1964    Historical Data in the Inscriptions of Yaxchilan, Part II. *Estudios de Cultural Maya* 4: 177–201.

REED, NELSON
    1964    *The Caste Wars of Yucatan.* Stanford University Press, Palo Alto.

ROBERTSON, MERLE GREENE
    1985    *The Sculpture of Palenque: The Late Buildings of the Palace,* vol. 3. Princeton University Press, Princeton.

SCHELE, LINDA, AND MARY ELLEN MILLER
    1986    *The Blood of Kings: Ritual and Dynasty in Maya Art.* Kimbell Art Museum, Fort Worth, and George Braziller, New York.

SPINDEN, HERBERT J.
    1916    Portraiture in Central American Art. In *Holmes Anniversary Volume: Anthropological Essays* (F.W. Hodge, ed.): 434–450. Smithsonian Institution, Washington, D.C.

STUART, DAVID
    1985    The Inscriptions on Four Shell Plaques from Piedras Negras, Guatemala. In *Fourth Palenque Round Table, 1980,* 5 (Elizabeth P. Benson and Merle Greene Robertson, eds.): 175–183. Pre-Columbian Art Research Institute, San Francisco.
    1987    *Ten Phonetic Syllables.* Research Reports on Ancient Maya Writing 14. Center for Maya Research, Washington, D.C.
    1988    Blood Symbolism in Maya Iconography. In *Maya Iconography* (Elizabeth P. Benson and Gillett G. Griffin, eds.): 175–221. Princeton University Press, Princeton.
    n.d.a    Epigraphic Evidence of Political Organization in the Usumacinta Drainage. Unpublished manuscript, 1983.
    n.d.b    The Maya Artist: An Epigraphic and Iconographic Study. Senior thesis, Princeton University, 1989.

THOMPSON, J. ERIC. S.
    1950    *Maya Hieroglyphic Writing.* Carnegie Institution of Washington, Publication 589. Washington, D.C.
    1970    *Maya History and Religion.* University of Oklahoma, Norman.

# 13

# The Study of Maya Warfare: What It Tells Us about the Maya and What It Tells Us about Maya Archaeology

DAVID WEBSTER

PENNSYLVANIA STATE UNIVERSITY

## INTRODUCTION

Had a symposium on the eighth century Maya been held twenty years ago, discussions of Maya warfare would have been conspicuous by their absence. In our symposium, by contrast, the issue of Maya warfare and the evidence for it was raised in several papers, most notably those of Joyce Marcus, Mary Ellen Miller, and David Stuart (Chaps. 5, 12, and 11, respectively). This proliferation of interest in Maya warfare is also reflected in much of the recent literature, most conspicuously in *The Blood of Kings* (Schele and Miller 1986) and *Forest of Kings* (Schele and Freidel 1990), but also in many less popular, more technical works.

Two recurrent themes of both the symposium papers and discussants were the variation and political fragmentation now apparent among the Classic Maya, particularly during the eighth century. The issue of warfare relates to both themes. Among the various forms of regional interaction characteristic of the Maya, such as elite economic exchanges, intermarriage, and visitation, warfare is the only process that emphasizes disequilibrium and competition. It thus draws our attention to stresses in Maya society that were difficult or impossible to resolve, and to variations inherent among lowland Maya regional sociopolitical systems that have been obscured by our traditional perspective, which overstates the monolithic nature of elite Maya culture. I have long believed that the evidence for Maya warfare, comprehensively examined within the context of robust anthropological models, has great potential for investigating sociopolitical and socioeconomic structures and dynamic processes. Maya warfare is a particularly important subject because evidence for it may be recovered using both epigraphic/iconographic and traditional archaeological approaches.

David Webster

I have been studying Maya warfare intermittantly since 1970. At first this paper seemed to me to be a good opportunity to review recent developments in our understanding of it. But I soon became convinced that the way we think about Maya warfare is as interesting and revealing as what we actually know about it, and is in fact a kind of barometer of the manner in which Maya scholarship has developed during the last 150 years. Consequently, what I offer here is a critique of our current understanding of Maya warfare from an anthropological perspective. In the last sections of the paper I will particularly address a subtheme of the symposium—the relationship of warfare to the Classic/Postclassic transition.

### MAYA WARFARE AND THE MYSTIQUE OF THE MAYA

In 1970 when I was excavating the fortifications at Becan, a tourist flew in who was one of that not uncommon breed, an amateur Maya enthusiast—in fact the president of a Maya club in the Midwest. As I showed him around the defensive system he became visibly agitated, and at the end of the tour asked me beseechingly if I was sure that these were fortifications. I had already pointed out all of the compelling reasons for believing so, and asked him why he doubted their function. His response was "Dammit, somewhere in the world there has got to have been a peaceful civilization!"

The attitude of this visitor exemplifies the extremely powerful notion, prevalent among both the general public and, more to the point, professional archaeologists, that the Maya were a "special" people—that their social institutions and cultural accomplishments were unique. This is what Gordon Willey once referred to as the "mystique of the Maya"—a mystique that seriously undermines our efforts to evaluate Maya culture from the perspective of comparative anthropology. Major elements of this mystique syndrome are:

(1) a romantic fascination with the dramatic, impressive, elite level of Maya society, and the tendency to conceive of Maya elites in monolithic terms.
(2) emphasis on the aesthetic, intellectual, and ideological aspects of Maya culture.
(3) the idea that the Maya—and especially the Classic Maya—were somehow mysterious, different, or unique, especially in their sociopolitical arrangements (no one ever writes a book called *The Mysterious Mixtecs*). This, the most pernicious element, might be characterized as the "suspension of uniformitarianism."
(4) The idea that Classic Maya society abruptly and inexplicably collapsed for highly idiosyncratic reasons.
(5) The notion that there is a major fault in cultural continuities between the Classic and the Postclassic.

One of the early "mystiques" which developed, traceable to Alfred P. Maudslay and Alfred Tozzer and especially to J. E. S. Thompson, was that the Maya—and especially the Classic Maya—were not plagued by the warfare and militarism that characterized other complex societies; that somehow they, with their special genius, had developed modes of interaction that stressed amicable cooperation while somehow avoiding serious competition and aggression (see Miller 1986: 5–8 for a convenient overview). A review of the older literature—especially the writings of S.G. Morley and Thompson—reveals that these scholars did not actually deny the presence of warfare among the Classic Maya. Rather they brusquely dismissed it in a somewhat embarrassed manner as generally unimportant, or alternatively tried to explain it away as an occasional, regrettable, and unaccountable aberration of ritual. According to these scholars, warfare, to the extent that it eventually became an obtrusive and significant component in Maya behavior, was introduced by militaristic outsiders and was largely motivated by the need to acquire sacrificial victims for the gods (sometimes themselves characterized as bloodthirsty foreign deities), although in Late Postclassic times it also had a political dimension during struggles for power in northern Yucatan. This new "foreign" pattern was symptomatic of the degeneration of the old theocratic, intellectual, peaceful Classic system.

It was this Classic "peaceful Maya" mystique that my tourist acquaintance had internalized and so obviously valued. Given the lack of scholarship concerning Classic Maya warfare in 1970 (Michael Coe was one of the few Mayanists to recognize its presence and possible importance), his attitude is understandable.

Since 1970 the situation has changed markedly, as much evidence for warfare in the Maya lowlands has accumulated. Unfortunately the residual effects of the "peaceful Maya" mystique are still with us, even among informed non-Mayanist scholars who work on the fringes of our field, much less the general public: "Perhaps we culturally prefer to associate ourselves with the peaceful and enlightened Mayas, rather than the bloodier and more aggressive ways of the Aztecs" (Ingle 1984: vi). Much more unfortunately, however, the mystique still operates, in a somewhat altered form, among Mayanists themselves in ways that inhibit or trivialize our understanding of the role that warfare may have played in the prehistoric Maya lowlands.

This statement might surprise anyone perusing the Maya literature over the last decade, for both overall summaries and specialized papers are often filled with references to Maya warfare or even treat it as a specialized topic in its own right. This is in marked contrast to the early 1970s, when one had to seek diligently for any sort of discussion of the topic, apart from superficial and often dismissive references, especially for the Preclassic and Classic periods. As one who has long been concerned with the effects of warfare on evolving cultural systems, I find this hypertrophied interest gratifying in general terms. On the other hand I am unconvinced that our understanding of warfare has increased proportionately to the pages devoted to it or that current research efforts and conceptual models are leading to the kinds of productive conclusions that we need. In particular, I think we have done little to develop systematic concepts of what warfare is, in behavioral terms, what it does, in processual terms, and how to perceive it archaeologically.

Also disturbing is the lack of the broad, comparative, ethnographic approach that is essential to the enterprise of anthropology (although there are a few exceptions to this—e.g., Ball 1977, Demarest 1978, Cowgill 1979, and Webb 1973), and the increasing focus on ideological or mentalist models that, by themselves, seem to me to have very limited value, as well as being curiously retrograde in their implications. Scholars from many disciplines, including art historians, epigraphers, and ethnohistorians, have contributed to our current understanding of Maya warfare. My own comments here are directed primarily to those trained as anthropologists, and particularly anthropologists who espouse a scientific approach to archaeology.

## THE CONCEPT OF WARFARE

Conspicuously rare in the Maya literature is any sort of definition of warfare as a general mode of human behavior and interaction, particularly from a comparative ethnographic perspective (see Haas 1990). One can hardly fault Mayanists too much for this, since numerous cultural anthropologists who have observed warfare at first hand have tried to define it without notable consensus. Rather than venture a strict definition myself, I would like to make a few general observations about that complex set of behaviors we call warfare. First, following Keith Otterbein (1970) and R. Berndt (1964), warfare involves planned confrontations between organized groups of people who conceive of themselves as members of political communities. By political communities I mean groups whose members possess and recognize a high level of common interest and who are prepared to defend their interests, or augment them, through the use of violence. Second, warfare is armed conflict or confrontation that the combatants recognize may involve deliberate killing. Third, warfare consists of contests organized to maintain a status quo or to bring about a shift of power relations, usually the latter.

A basic problem in defining warfare is that there are so many levels of behavior that can be associated with it. Andrew Vayda (1976) has sidestepped this definitional problem by emphasizing warfare as a long-term, graded process with a series of distinct but related phases. Such a process might begin with very simple confrontations (e.g., between feuding individuals), then escalate through a series of more serious, lethal phases, eventually culminating in all-out, deadly conflict resulting in considerable mortality and redistributions of population on the landscape. A very important point is that this escalation is not inevitable. It may be short-circuited at any

## The Study of Maya Warfare

level, and alternative solutions to the stresses that generated conflict in the first place may be sought. The process thus generates at each level information in the sociocultural system(s) concerning the efficacy of warfare as a solution to problems for any particular political group or the advisability of pursuing some other course. Warfare in this scheme is "about" many things on many levels. Robert Carneiro (1970) has made much the same point—resource limitation does not necessarily cause warfare (it can be of variable origins), but under certain conditions stimulates specific forms of warfare which have new evolutionary effects.

Vayda's model possesses the advantage of incorporating a wide range of behaviors visible in both the ethnographic and archaeological records, including low-level feuding and raiding, ritualized conflicts, and what we would all recognize as outright war. It reminds us that these may all be associated, and unless sorted out may cause confusion. A relevant case here is Landa's comments on the purposes and functions of endemic contact period Maya war, as well as Tozzer's glosses on Landa derived from other contemporary documents (see especially Tozzer [1941] 41, 217). These comments are too sketchy to be very revealing, and refer to such varied phases (and motivations) of the warfare process that one can make up any sort of explanatory scenario one likes, depending upon which passages one chooses and how one interprets them. Vayda's model also cautions that even very general propositions about warfare, such as those given above, must be used carefully. For example, some levels of warfare may not be highly organized and planned by combatants, or highly lethal. Finally, the model also suggests that confusion results if we focus too intensively on one particular phase of the warfare process.

Otterbein (1970) makes the important distinction between internal war (contests between culturally similar groups) and external war (contests between culturally dissimilar groups). This distinction, as we shall see later, has important implications for Maya warfare and has figured in certain recent conceptualizations of it.

### ISSUES

In order to build useful models and comprehensively understand warfare in any context, ethnographic or archaeological, we must discriminate between, and effectively investigate, the following:

### Presence of Warfare

To avoid confusion we must properly identify those behaviors or attributes related to the warfare process, as opposed to those which are not. For example, a defensive wall should not be confused with one built solely to emphasize the social exclusivity of an elite component of a community.

cussed above, and which, as we shall see, may be useful in sorting out patterns of prehistoric war among the Maya.

*Fortifications*

Formal constructions relating to boundary maintenance or defense of human populations and/or strategic sites are often conspicuous in the archaeological record. Such constructions best contribute to our understanding of arena, scale, and strategy/tactics, and to a lesser degree organization and entities.

*Epigraphy*

The presence of comprehensible texts adds an historical dimension to studies of warfare. Texts, at least of the kind available for the Maya, contribute to our understanding of phase, intensity, arena, organization, entities, and to some degree purpose/motivation and function.

*Art*

To the extent that artistic themes and representations actually relating to the warfare process can be identified, as opposed to those that may be superficially militaristic but are merely metaphorical, they inform us about purpose/motivation, phase, organization, entities, tactics, and possibly arena.

*Weaponry*

By weaponry I mean the physical remains of military equipment of all kinds. The existence and use of such equipment may be portrayed artistically, but physical remains and especially their distributions offer information on arena, scale, entities, tactics, and possibly strategy.

*Paleopathology/Paleodemography*

In this category of evidence I would include all information on trauma recoverable from human skeletal materials that might relate to the warfare process, and also distinctive paleodemographic patterns (e.g., in life tables) that might be produced by warfare. This class of evidence most strongly bears on phase, organization, scale, intensity, arena, entities, and tactics.

*Violent Destruction*

Occasionally archaeological contexts may yield signs of destruction that are plausibly related to warfare, informing us about purpose/motivation, function, phase, scale, arena, entities, strategy, and tactics.

*Disruption of Pattern*

By this I mean any rapid, drastic, and unexpected alteration in fundamental patterns of an archaeologically known cultural sequence that might be related to war or conquest. Such disruptions might include sudden abandonment of sites and/or shifts in settlement pattern, abrupt replacement of traditional patterns of ceramics, art, or architecture by "foreign" ones, etc. This kind of information is extremely informative about function, and to a lesser extent purpose/motivation and virtually all of the other issues concerning warfare.

Clearly these classes of evidence vary considerably in ease of recovery and, if properly interpreted, exactly what issues they tell us about. The important point is that any research focused on warfare is weakened to the extent that some are neglected at the expense of others, although it is also true that the pragmatics of research make some much more accessible than others, as well as more dramatic and exciting.

*Negative Evidence*

Warfare, in general, and particularly certain patterns or phases of warfare are difficult to detect in the archaeological record, as I pointed out earlier (Webster 1976a). We must consequently be very careful about what we assume on the basis of the apparent absence of evidence presumed characteristic of the warfare process. On one level, the problem may be simply finding or recognizing features for what they are, and here fortifications provide a good example. Mary Miller (1986: 6) points out that early Mayanists such as Maudslay and Thompson partly embraced the "peaceful Maya" mystique because of the assumed absence of fortifications associated with Classic Maya sites (one can see how this would especially have impressed Thompson, with his penchant for European medieval analogues). Even if this absence of obvious fortifications had turned out to be correct—as it certainly did not—the equation fails. Maya centers might have been defended in ways not easily recoverable at all (Webster 1976a: 94–95), but even discounting this possibility we must remember that in many cultural traditions violent, conquest-motivated warfare is carried out in the absence of effective defensive systems. Japanese feudal warfare prior to the mid-sixteenth century is a case in point. Interestingly, in this tradition a fairly dispersed settlement pattern of agricultural villages was also maintained in the context of incessant war.

Also frequently cited as an argument against "conquest" models of Maya warfare is the apparent absence of signs of large-scale destruction at Maya centers (Miller 1986: 99; Demarest 1978). One wonders exactly how much damage one would expect to the stone-built palaces and temples of the elite, even if centers were fiercely defended. But this is beside the point. In many cultural traditions conquest did not generally involve the physical destruction of defeated centers. For example, I think it would be very difficult to find such evidence in centers in the Basin of Mexico subjugated by the Aztecs, who seem to have reserved ferocious destruction only for particularly recalcitrant opponents. Even the ritual razing of temple superstructures might be difficult to detect.

David Webster

In making these observations about negative evidence I am not implying that we have a license to make up any stories we wish about Maya warfare and not worry about empirical verification. Rather we must do enough research so that as much potential evidence for warfare as possible is recovered, develop plausible models, and then make our assumptions about what is missing or unrecognized in the archaeological record.

RECENT INVESTIGATIONS OF MAYA WARFARE

The following comments on recent investigations of Maya warfare are not meant to be a comprehensive review. Instead, I summarize only briefly some recent developments, first in terms of substantive evidence, and second in terms of concepts concerning the nature of Maya warfare.

*Evidence*

Since my own review article on lowland Maya fortifications (Webster 1976b) a significant number of new or suspected defensive arrangements—specifically walls—have been identified at such sites as Mirador, Muralla de Leon, El Paar, Calakmul, Oxpemul, Ek Balam, Chunchucmil, Yaxuna, and Uxmal (Demarest 1978; Rice and Rice 1981; Robles and Andrews 1986: 83; Freidel n.d.). The assumption that all these functioned mainly for defensive purposes is still open to question, since most have only been casually investigated, although a considerable amount of work has been, or is, being focused on a few, such as the walls at Mirador (Beth Chambers, personal communication), Ek Balam (William Ringle, personal communication), and the newly discovered fortifications at many Petexbatun centers now being studied by Arthur Demarest and Stephen Houston. Significantly, these provisionally identified new defensive systems span the temporal range from the Late Preclassic to the Early Postclassic.

Maya art, and especially Late Classic Maya art in the eighth century, is replete with themes of war and its concomitants, capture and sacrifice (see Miller, Chap. 12). As Linda Schele and Miller (1986: 14–15) have recently observed: "Among the most common events recorded on Maya monuments are war and capture. . . . Warfare . . . gave rise to more varied depictions than any other theme." Just how ironic and revealing this undoubtedly valid comment is in terms of the mystique of the Maya becomes obvious when we remember that much, or perhaps even most, of the iconography on which it is based was available before World War II (only Herbert Spinden, among early Mayanists, was impressed by this evidence). Thus the current obtrusiveness of warlike themes is not so much a product of the recovery of the images themselves, but rather our willingness to recognize them for what they are.

Since 1959–60, and especially during the last decade, epigraphic evidence for warfare and its closely associated themes of death and sacrifice has proliferated. Particularly important is the identification of glyphs, and sometimes multiple glyphs, for conquest, capture, and sacrifice, the recognition of the linkage of these glyphs to the careers of rulers as expressed on political monuments, and to specific sites or dynasties as represented by Emblem Glyphs (for general discussions see Schele 1984; Schele and Miller 1986; Miller 1986; also the papers by Marcus [Chap. 5], Miller [Chap. 13] and Stuart [Chap. 11]). It is fair to say that inscriptions, together with associated iconography, have recently provided some of the best evidence for some levels of Maya warfare and for some historical processes of conflict. One has only to contrast references in the recent literature to the glyphs now recognized as associated directly or indirectly with warfare with such references in earlier standard works (e.g., Thompson's [1971] update of his catalogue of Maya hieroglyphs) to appreciate the change in our perspective.

Unfortunately none of the other lines of evidence for warfare has been nearly as productive as those just mentioned, although a great deal of possibly relevant information on pattern disruption can be mined from the many settlement-system studies published in the last two decades (see Miller's comments in this volume). We still lack large-scale, well-controlled Maya paleopathological and paleodemographic studies, although some will shortly become available (e.g., for Copan). There are, nonetheless, tantalizing bits of skeletal evidence that may reflect warfare. An example is the apparent mass human sacrifice of young men from Late Preclassic contexts at Chalchuapa reported by William Fowler (1984). I know of no specialized studies at all of Mayan weaponry, though it is sometimes treated as a minor subject (e.g., Miller 1986).

On a strictly empirical level our understanding of Maya warfare, and especially warfare prior to the Postclassic, is still hampered by the general paucity of evidence, and much of what has come to light remains to be effectively studied. The exceptions are the categories of art and epigraphy, in which great progress has been made. Also conspicuously absent are large-scale field projects that have singled out warfare as a dominant research concern (I do not include here projects aimed particularly at recovering only glyphic and iconographic information). The one exception is the Petexbatun project recently begun by Demarest and Houston, which has the scope to provide unparalleled information on the nature of war and its political effects for a series of Late Classic/Early Postclassic Maya kingdoms. This project has already turned up hitherto unexpected Terminal Classic fortifications at several sites, such as Punta de Chimino, which I visited with Demarest in the summer of 1989; the lesson once again is that an apparent absence of evidence often reflects only a lack of research.

Since such integrated projects have not been completed, we still lack the variety of data necessary to build convincing synthetic models of Maya warfare by addressing all of the issues discussed above. In part this is a result

David Webster

of the difficulties inherent in acquiring various categories of data. It is much easier to find a new piece of iconography (or recognize something previously misinterpreted in an old piece) than to recover and properly analyze a reliable sample of burials that might show signs of war-related trauma. This kind of problem will sort itself out over the long run, but precisely because of the disjunctive nature of data accumulation, at any given time we tend to see (and more importantly interpret) the complex process of Maya warfare through a tiny window of archaeological visibility. Currently the clearest part of the view is provided by art and epigraphy; paradoxically, I believe that it is our preoccupation with these catagories of evidence that distorts our conceptualizations of Maya warfare as a form of interaction.

*Critique of Recent Research and Models of Maya Warfare*

There seem to me to be three recent currents in research on Maya warfare, although they necessarily overlap because of the evidence on which they are based.

*The Culture History of Maya War*

The first current, which is presently dominant but rather unobtrusive, is the reconstruction of the culture history of Maya war. By this I mean the identification of those centers involved in something we might reasonably call warfare, the accurate determination of the dates of conflicts, the military roles of elites—particularly royalty—at contending centers, and, to some degree, the large-scale effects of such conflicts on the particular sociopolitical systems involved. Virtually all of the direct evidence utilized in such reconstructions is artistic/epigraphic, although some use settlement and artifactual data (mainly ceramics). A good case in point is the recent work of Fernando Robles and Anthony Andrews (1985) on the postulated Postclassic Coba-Chichen Itza standoff. Classic/Terminal Classic examples would include the Quiriqua-Copan conflict at ca. A.D. 738 (if indeed it was a war), the warfare between Dos Pilas and Tikal and among the Petexbatun centers themselves, and the series of conflicts involving Caracol, Tikal, and Naranjo.

By my count we now have records for about twenty such episodes, many from the eighth century. While basically particularistic, such culture-historical reconstructions are absolutely essential, bearing as they do on the issues of arena, entity, intensity, scale, purpose/motivation, and function. The danger lies in getting stalled on the culture-historical level and failing, ultimately, to develop broader comparative models and explanations of what is going on. We have already been through the culture history vs. culture process wrangle with regard to Maya warfare once before (Binford 1968), and there is no sense in rehashing it.

Reconstruction of specific episodes of conflict also contribute to our understanding of the variation inherent in Maya warfare and its archaeological expression. The major axis of variation long emphasized in the literature is diachronic—the supposed Classic/Postclassic discontinuity. That an important discontinuity in the existence of warfare characterizes this juncture of Maya culture history is now doubted by most Mayanists. However, many identify new Postclassic patterns of warfare based on the intrusions of upstart ruling groups not ethnically enculturated to the more (supposedly) formalized Classic Maya military traditions, carried out in the context of new, "internationalized" commercial routes and exchange networks (Sabloff and Andrews V 1986). Except for the recognition that Postclassic warfare has continuities with Classic war there seems little new in it, apart from a more comprehensive and accurate analysis of the arenas, entities, and functions involved. My own feeling is that the discontinuities between Preclassic and Classic warfare were more structurally profound than those of the Classic-Postclassic, although for obvious reasons they are much harder to investigate.

Although seldom discussed, there must have been enormous synchronic variation as well. Certainly the sociopolitical environment for warfare would have been very different in the socially circumscribed northeastern Peten, the Petexbatun region, and the Usumascinta drainage (during the Late Classic or earlier) than it was in western Honduras, where Copan is located. Not unexpectedly, the glyphic and iconographic evidence for warfare reflects these differences. At Usumacinta sites such as Piedras Negras and Yaxchilan, military/sacrificial themes are much more numerous and explicit that they are on the southeastern Maya frontier. As I have maintained elsewhere (Webster 1988), our fascination with the (purported) monolithic nature of Classic Maya elite culture, and especially its ideological components, frequently distracts us from a necessary multilinear view of many things Maya, including warfare.

Recently several models of Maya warfare have emerged that have special relevance for our understanding of Maya warfare, particularly during the eighth century and Classic/Early Postclassic transition. Two related ones are the "situational ethics" model of Demarest, and a similar model developed by David Freidel and colleagues.

*The "Situational Ethics" Model*

In 1978 Demarest published a paper titled "Interregional Conflict and 'Situational Ethics' in Classic Maya Warfare," which is important in its own right and particularly because of one of its intellectual offspring. In his paper Demarest accepts, but offers some refinements of and significant additions to, a series of earlier systemic/competition models of Maya warfare, including in particular my own. He begins by hypothesizing two patterns of Classic (and possibly Late Preclassic) warfare. One, following earlier suggestions made by Richard Adams (Demarest 1978: 101–102), is a pattern of elite warfare which, despite its violence, has only low-level effects (e.g., in terms of destruction or conquest of political centers, territorial aggrandizement, demographic shifts) and is mainly reflected in art and inscriptions. The second pattern, evidenced in particular by impressive fortifications (as at Becan), is carried out in a much more massive, disruptive, and probably lethal fashion.

Demarest feels that the explanation for these two patterns lies in the relatedness of the antagonists. In the first, warfare is controlled or limited in its goals and effects by common understandings—what Demarest calls "situational ethics" but which might be better conceived of as cultural etiquette—because contending entities are ethnically similar. In the second, warfare is "open" or "unlimited" because enemies lack these shared conventions and values. Such (presumed) aberrations as the Becan fortifications are thus caused by conflicts on ethnic (linguistic) boundaries between groups lacking the means to limit them. Here Demarest is making the same distinction made earlier by Otterbein, as we have already noted, between "internal" and "external" war. In essence, Demarest is arguing that there are two distinct warfare situations of very different character in the Late Preclassic/Classic periods, and very different military ethics or "rules" associated with each. We thus do not have to see the levels of conflict implied by the fortifications at Becan (and elsewhere) as the most complex phases of a general model of Maya warfare (a la Vayda), but rather as the final phases of a particularistic and idiosyncratic kind of war ("unlimited" or "total" war). The other kind, "limited war" between closely related rivals, does not escalate to these levels at all. This distinction allows Demarest to accept the previously unacceptable evidence for large-scale warfare, but still preserve the notion of more homeostatic, gentlemanly, ritualized Maya conflicts.

Demarest's paper is thoughtful and thought-provoking, and presents a clear hypothesis about the variable nature of Maya war. One of its strengths is its use of ethnographic examples to defend its main point, the limited character of "conventionalized" war between ethnically and culturally similar groups. My own understanding of situational ethics and my own reading of the ethnographic and historical records, however, lead me to different conclusions.

One definition of situational ethics is that one differentially perceives, and applies, one's ethical standards depending upon the situation one finds oneself in—particularly with regard to the assessment of self-interest. This definition is consistent with Vayda's general model of warfare discussed above. Its implication is that, especially in warfare, behaviors of all kinds—conventionalized or not—may be flexibly adapted to circumstances. This, despite Demarest's implication that my own models imply constrained violence, has always been the way I understand the process of warfare (and especially internal war).

## The Study of Maya Warfare

The ethnographic or historical records provide many accounts of conventionalized warfare carried out between culturally similar groups. As I noted earlier, such phases of conflict may be the most common and easiest to observe. Karl Heider (1970: 118) found that frequent ritual encounters among the Dani have a sporting, tournamentlike quality, but that there occur very occasional conflicts that are "short, treacherous, bloody, and with major economic effect." Although the ritual (emic) aspects of Dani war could be observed and elicited from informants, the more unlimited episodes were difficult to investigate, even though they had important etic consequences. Normally in archaeological contexts the ritualized levels of war would be less visible, as I have argued, than the more large-scale, lethal phases; the Maya, however, express the conventionalized level in inscriptions and iconography.

Medieval European warfare was, of course, full of episodes of conventional regulation and even ritualization of warfare between ethnically similar (and even dissimilar) groups (in this case reinforced by the influence of a dominant "international" religious institution, the Catholic Church), but these frequently escalated into levels involving conquest as well as considerable destruction and mortality. Feudal Japanese warfare offers an even better example. It was fought between political groups of exactly the same cultural background (antagonists were even often from the same families) and was heavily conventionalized on the elite level. It was also characterized by some of the most ruthless destruction and savagery for purposes of territorial gain in the annals of history (Sansom 1961). The Late Postclassic Mexica were certainly ethnically and culturally similar to most of the other inhabitants of the Basin of Mexico, and Demarest himself has written on the highly ritualized dimensions of Mexica war (Conrad and Demarest 1984). Yet this did not stop them from politically subjugating or destroying other similar polities, seizing territory to enrich their own elites, and imposing heavy demands on conquered people for labor, tax, and tribute. One may also turn the argument topsy-turvy. On the northwest frontier of the British Raj, as late as the 1930s, many British officers felt it was cheating and ungentlemanly to use airplanes, which only they of course had, against fractious hill tribesmen; here we have limitation in "external" war.

I agree with Demarest that in many of its contexts and phases war is limited by commonly understood conventions and even ritualized, and that such limitations are probably most frequent and effective among culturally similar peoples. But having said this, where does it get us in evaluating particular sequences of warfare, since such conventionalizations are often accompanied by, or fail to preclude, war's most destructive phases? The problem is to determine under what circumstances warfare is limited by convention and under what circumstances such limitations break down. This we have not done for the Maya, leaving unresolved implications for conflict models such as Demarest's. For example, many Maya archaeolo-

David Webster

gists believe that a few large-scale, multicenter polities (especially one dominated by Tikal) emerged during the Classic period, even though they did not long endure. Might not these be situations in which, for a variety of reasons, the proposed homeostatic nature of conventionalized Maya war broke down? Demarest also notes (1978: 108) that there seems to be increased fragmentation even within subregions of the Maya lowlands (e.g., the northeastern Peten) as the late Classic wears on, with a corresponding widening of "unlimited war." To the extent that this is a real contrast with the Early Classic (for which, after all, we have comparatively sparse data), it is just as plausible that these are patterns partly produced by war that never was effectively conventionalized in the first place, and which became more severe as the political and economic problems of the Maya intensified.

Another dimension of Demarest's argument, following earlier suggestions by Adams, is that the limited form of Maya warfare is essentially elite warfare (Demarest 1978: 102). This is a truism. From at least Late Preclassic times on, Maya polities were dominated by elites. Under the circumstances, what is the alternative to elite warfare (unless we fall back on Thompson's old argument in which rebellious peasants might constitute a political group)? Clearly, whatever form it took, Maya warfare was initiated by elites, led by elites, carried out for elite purposes, and elites reaped most of the rewards of success (though not necessarily most of the consequences of failure). In this sense Maya warfare was similar to that associated with ranked and stratified societies in general.

My own models (1975, 1977), as well as Carneiro's (1970), to which they are related, emphasize warfare as competition in terms of its basic systemic functions. By competition I mean the active demand on the part of two or more entities (however these are defined) for a common vital resource that is in short supply. Many phases of the warfare process, of course, are not directly related to competition in this sense, although from an evolutionary perspective the process as a whole must be. Demarest seems to accept competition models for warfare for the Preclassic, and for warfare along ethnic boundaries in the Classic (the unlimited war syndrome). It is difficult to determine the role of competition, however, in his limited-war syndrome, a problem I would like to enlarge upon since it relates to the crucial issue of the entities involved in Maya war.

I think Maya warfare was fought by, and in the interest of, several entities, and that the mix of such entities changed through time. On the most fundamental (and probably earliest) level, the entities involved were territorial teams. By this I mean that the combatants represented territorially or residentially defined political groups—we might call them communities or polities—regardless of their degree of ethnic/cultural relatedness. It is this sort of entity which I believe was dominant in the highly competitive warfare involving basic resources, such as agriculturally productive land, throughout most of the Preclassic, and perhaps in the very turbulent times of the Terminal Classic. Such competing entities were typically closely juxtaposed in spatial terms and were probably culturally very similar in any particular region, because competition is most severe between entities with the most overlapping common vital resources. Success broadly advantaged the members of political groups. This sort of competition (among other things), I have argued, stimulated effective ranking or early forms of economic stratification (Webster 1975).

The Late Preclassic and the Early Classic saw the demographic infilling of many of the richest zones of the Maya lowlands. The possibilities for major territorial aggrandizement were accordingly lessened. With the emergence of hierarchically structured, centralized political systems, there appeared a new potential resource—systems of new political positions, titles, or offices at particular centers that conferred upon their occupants (along with their families and retainers) very real, material advantages, as well as political authority and prestige. Since these positions were by definition limited, they themselves provided additional incentives for conflict. To the territorial entities were now added entities that might be called simple intrapolity factions (which I think were often ranked kin groups). Conflict among these factions had two motivations: (1) intrapolity competition over possession of a particular existing set of positions, titles, and offices (these being the ideologically valued, symbolic keys to access to power, labor, and tribute or taxes); or (2) the opportunity to escape, or secede from, an existing polity and form a new one with its own hierarchical structure. The latter process, of course, could engender new cycles of territorial team competition elsewhere as the political landscape continued to fill in. Simple interpolity conflict is a kind of dynastic warfare.

Eventually some Maya political systems, at least for a time, became multicentered polities with a superordinate center dominating subordinate ones. The latter may have been attached through conquest, colonization, elite intermarriage and alliance, or any combination of these. Such systems stimulated what I will call complex intrapolity competition, which involved attempts by subordinate centers to become independent of dominant ones, or perhaps in some instances to usurp their positions. Here the entities involved are once again territorial in one sense, but also intrapolity factions in another. This is mature dynastic warfare. Marcus (Chap. 5) plausibly argues that most warfare episodes of the eighth century reflect this pattern.

A good example is the conflict in A.D. 738 between Cauac Sky of Quirigua and 18 Rabbit of Copan, the apparent eventual loser (see Miller, Chap. 12). This has always been a confusing military episode for a number of reasons. It is hard to see it as a territorial conflict, given the distance between the two centers. Copan, demographically larger and at least as politically centralized, is the loser. Neither side, to my knowledge, shows associated damage or destruction, and Copan thereafter experiences at least fifty to sixty years of unusual vigor during which many monuments were built, including the Hieroglyphic Stairway which celebrates the very conflict in which a Quirigua ruler was the ostensible victor. None of this makes much sense as a "territorial team" kind of struggle, but can easily be reconciled to the complex dynastic one. As I understand the glyphic evidence for this episode, in fact (it seems to relate mainly to the decapitation of the Copan king), it might not even have been a war at all. Copan rulers, including Smoke Imix, are known to have carried out ceremonies at Quirigua. Conceivably 18 Rabbit was lured to his client center of Quiriga and then killed. This would simply be an elite coup.

Finally, there may indeed, as Demarest suggests, have been rivalries between ethnically and culturally dissimilar groups (e.g., those of the Rio Bec zone against those of the northeastern Peten) involving large alliances of polities and warfare of an unusual intensity and scale.

The cautionary tale here is that Classic Maya warfare was probably very complex, and that "conquest," when it occurred, probably meant many things. It might sometimes have involved significant territorial aggrandizement, but dynastic war no doubt had many perfectly real political or material goals even in its absence. Schele (1984: 44) notes the paucity of place names in Maya inscriptions related to warfare, although illustrious personal names and titles abound, and concludes that ". . . this deemphasis of place reflects the nature of Maya warfare; I do not think it was territorial for the most part." Here there seems to be the tacit assumption (in the context of her article) that if war is not fought for territory, the only other motivations involve ritual and public prestige. The emphasis on elite titles and names is certainly consistent with elite dynastic warfare, and practitioners of this kind of conflict have historically been competitors in the strict sense—that is, successful acquisition of titles and positions provides not only prestige, but access to the scarce vital resources (from the elite perspective) of retainers, taxes, labor, and strategic geographical position.

I see all of these things as overt, emic purposes of Maya warfare. Given the density of population and political units on the Classic Maya landscape, it is no wonder that much, if not most, elite warfare was inconclusive, especially from our perspective, but lack of success should not be taken to mean lack of motivation or attempt.

The foregoing is essentially an additive model of the entities and motivations of Maya war in the sense that new levels are added to old ones and perhaps become more systemically significant and obtrusive. My own opinion is that there was a wide variety of behaviors related to each of these levels, and that to the extent that there were limitations, these were not primarily limitations of convention, but rather of goals, means, and opportunities. Despite these reservations, the situational ethics hypothesis is a stimu-

## The Killer King Complex

The concept of Maya warfare critiqued in the rest of this paper might, in its more extreme manifestations, be labeled the Killer King Complex (hereafter KKC). This concept emphasizes warfare as a kind of royal sport in which powerful kings engage in ritualized royal hunts for illustrious rivals, whose eventual sacrificial deaths not only legitimize and reinforce the roles of the captors and their dynasties, but also nourish and maintain the great cosmological processes and personalities, especially ancestors, of the Maya universe. It mainly pertains to the eighth-century Maya, but has larger diachronic implications as well, particularly the Late Classic/Early Postclassic transition. The concept seems to stem from the situational ethics model, coupled with new inscriptional and iconographic reconstructions, and a model of ritual regulation suggested by Roy Rappaport (1971a, 1971b). KKC-related interpretations of Maya warfare have proliferated over the last five years. While they are still secondary as important research currents to cultural historical reconstructions (although closely related to these), they are highly visible and popularized and rapidly gaining prominence and acceptance, and they wrongly reinforce the Maya mystique.

The most important source of KKC interpretations is the burgeoning corpus of glyphic and iconographic texts in which war-related symbols are being discovered and interpreted; most such work is being done by art historians, iconographers, and epigraphers, some of whom are also anthropologists. In one respect their work constitutes a real revolution in our understanding of Maya war since they are providing a whole new dimension of data. In another sense it is a revolution unnecessarily delayed because it is often based upon raw data long available, but ignored or wrongly interpreted by scholars laboring under the old intellectual/priest/theocrat conception of Classic Maya culture. What is especially interesting about this dimension of information is not only its specificity (e.g., in terms of arena, entities, frequency, phase) but also its unique ability to provide insights into that most obdurate issue for the prehistoric archaeologist, purpose/motivation—the emic perspective.

A package of associated Maya behaviors involving warfare and sacrificial ritual has been well documented by the glyphic and iconographic evidence, leading to the general conclusion that: "War, human sacrifice, and personal bloodletting seem to have composed a major part of Classic life" (Schele 1984: 45). This comment would have made Morley and Thompson decidedly uncomfortable, but most Mayanists today, myself included, would agree with it.

A more specific conclusion relates to the issue of the purpose or motivations of Maya war. "Commemorations of war activity in Maya art show that . . . the capture of sacrificial victims was its fundamental goal. . . ." (Schele and Miller 1986: 220). "It doesn't appear that their wars were for territory because they don't record the capture of cities on their monuments. What they do record is the capture of high-ranking individuals who would later be sacrificed. War was the way you got gifts for the gods and kept the universe running" (Schele, quoted in Morell 1986: 59).

Here a sharp conceptual dichotomy is drawn between war as either territorial or as related to prestige and ritual; the emphasis is on elite purposes and goals, and emic cosmological functions, as opposed to more fundamental etic, systemic functions. This perspective is apparent in more recent work: "From the Maya vantage, warfare explicitly served to prove the charisma of kings and high nobility" (Schele and Freidel 1990: 441). Schele and Freidel also postulate the beginnings of "conquest" warfare at the end of the fourth century A.D. (1990: 441). Given the scale of the fortifications at Becan, and the occurrence of other possible fortifications at Preclassic centers such as Mirador, I would place such warfare considerably earlier.

Among anthropologists the KKC concept has been most developed by Freidel (1986, n.d.). His is primarily an interaction model with emphasis on the Classic period, but with diachronic implications as well.[1]

Freidel's interest is the relationship between warfare on the one hand, and what he sees as an apparent contradiction on the other—the lack of effective, overall Maya political integration (at least through Classic times), at the same time that there is an essential similarity of Maya sociocultural systems (at least on the elite level). Here there is a clear relationship to Demarest's situational ethics model.

Freidel asserts that beginning in the Late Preclassic and continuing throughout the Classic there was a ". . . cohesive and pervasive charter of political power which is replicated and displayed at every major center" (1986: 93). This charter was essential to the Maya conception both of rulership and of polity and provided for predictable interaction among independent elites. It was mainly derived from the myth of the Hero Twins and their "First Father," which provided the great cosmological themes of conflict (especially related to ball-game imagery), bloodletting, and human sacrifice (Freidel n.d.). Acceptance and dissemination of this common charter formally defined the principle of "peer polity" as the Late Preclassic

---

[1] He begins his most specific argument (Freidel 1986) by contrasting two models of warfare, one of my own and one of Cowgill's (1979), and concludes that neither explains the peculiar sociocultural patterns characteristic of the Classic Maya. I will not review these models here, but I do want to clarify one point. Freidel mistakenly states that Cowgill's model is different from mine in that "He [Cowgill] reasons that warfare among the Maya was probably guided by the same motivations found worldwide: power and aggrandizement at the expense of neighbors" (Freidel 1986: 94). However much Cowgill and I may differ on many things, we could not be closer on this issue (although I would restate it somewhat to read "aggrandizement at the expense of others").

Maya made the "breakthrough" to "civilized life." Its pervasive acceptance validated a distinctly nonegalitarian intrapolity hierarchical structure, but at the same time preserved interpolity equality among royalty. Thus ". . . the myriad kings of the Maya formed a brotherhood of equals" (Freidel 1986: 93), because despite the obvious variation in the sizes of their political domains and the scope of their authority, all were bound by the same ideological conventions.

While Demarest is specifically concerned with patterns of warfare, Freidel is mainly trying to explain the nature of Classic Maya politics and elite solidarity, and especially the ideological nature of the postulated shared elite charter that perpetuated independent polities as well as the common understandings that facilitated elite interaction of whatever kind. Simply put, his main theme is royal/elite sameness. This charter is expressed principally in iconography and inscriptions in which, as Schele and Miller point out, war-related themes are so common. Since war is usually considered to signal at least rivalry and disruption, if not outright competition, the problem is to show how warfare contributes to parity and effective levels of homeostasis.

The solution is, in large part, the KKC concept. Warfare is interpreted as highly conventionalized—one might say choreographed—ritual conflict essential to the concept of Maya kingship. It is both a regulated and regulating mechanism. On the level of purpose/motivation it is royal contests in which elite territorial teams (e.g., from Bonampak) seek to acquire elite captives (preferably royal ones) for ritual sacrifice. Such sacrifices are one form of the bloodletting considered essential to honor deified ancestors and nourish cosmological processes. Schele (1984: 95) would add that Maya human sacrifice, like that of the Aztecs, brought social prestige and merit to donors of victims. Although there were many sacrificial occasions, elite human sacrifices were particularly necessary at life-crisis ceremonies of royalty, such as accession to kingship or heir-designation.

Freidel recognizes that occasionally during the Classic the conventions of elite war were violated, as major centers such as Tikal attempted to assert their royal power over formerly independent centers. But such attempts were short-lived and ineffective precisely because they violated the political charter. This created a "structural impasse" (Freidel 1986: 108)—the peer-polity ideology was so powerful that no alternative political charter sanctioning such dominance emerged, and without ideological justification the emergent large-scale polities collapsed. Under the stresses of the Terminal Classic another such impasse occurred more widely, and there was an overall failure of the traditional charter, signaling the collapse of the Classic peer-polity pattern and setting the stage for the more secular, competitive warfare and empire-building of the Postclassic.

Because of my own lack of experience I cannot critically evaluate the validity of the iconographic and glyphic analyses on which the identification of the war/captor/human sacrifice complex is based nor the evidence from such analyses for the existence of the larger peer-polity charter. It certainly has not been demonstrated, though, that such an ideological charter, if it existed, was "replicated and displayed" at all major Maya centers as Freidel asserts, and it is probably not even demonstrable. Many large centers (as well as many small ones) lack inscriptions entirely. Becan is a good example; without inscriptions the charter must be inferred from art alone, which is much more difficult.

The argument tends to reinforce the old notion of a monolithic Maya elite, although Maya research in the last three decades has increasingly revealed the variety of Maya culture on all levels, both in diachronic and synchronic terms. Demarest's situational ethics model recognizes important dimensions of this variation, which Freidel would eliminate entirely. As E. W. Andrews V took pains to point out during the symposium, we have real difficulty in documenting any historical episodes or conventions in northern Yucatan because of the general lack of inscriptions there.

Given the history of Maya scholarship (Sanders and Webster n.d.), the KKC concept seems reactionary. Its perspective is entirely on Maya elites, particularly Maya royalty, as the only entities involved in conflict, and entirely upon elite emic purposes/motivations rather than systemic function. It sees warfare as ". . . a perogative of the elite and fought primarily by the elite. . .and the bulk of the population was neither affected by, nor participated in, violent conflict" (Freidel 1986: 107). Such a sweeping conclusion is based upon a particular view of Maya warfare, rather than any comprehensive evidence.

The concept also leaves much unexplained. It does not specify, for example, how teams of elite warriors structured their ritualized combats, both spatially and temporally. It does not show how presumably closely juxtaposed centers captured and sacrificed each other's important men without wider political or economic effect. To the extent that the concept addresses function, it sees warfare as preserving "boundary maintenance" (i.e., the spatial integrity of the peer polities) and as contributing to the public prestige of elite warriors. Freidel's model sees territorial expansion or appropriation of resources as having occasionally occurred, but as being incidental to the overall process, rather than having important systemic functions, since such things are not celebrated in inscriptions (1986: 107). Here the conclusion is that if it isn't written down it isn't important. By this criterion we might then have to assume that royal economic exchanges were unimportant, as were the size of a king's subject population or the taxes and tribute he extracted from them. Although advances in deciphering Maya inscriptions have been spectacular, it is increasingly obvious that the Maya recorded a very restricted set of themes. We may understand these themes in ever greater detail, but we must also reconcile ourselves to the fact that there were important things—important both to them and to us—that the Maya simply were not interested in recording.

There are two basic problems with the KKC model. First, if war is seen as a process at all, in Vayda's sense, analysis is confined to the elite ritual level of conflict. The possibility that war had other important levels or functions is insufficiently considered, although many fascinating possibilities are present. For example, phases of ritualized elite warfare, like the "nothing fights" of New Guinea, may have generated information about the military capabilities of particular entities (e.g., quality of leadership, numbers of combatants fielded, number and resolve of allies, etc.) and thus regulated the escalation (or not) of the larger warfare process. Another possibility is that raiding was a source of slaves who provided labor for royal captors, adding a new dimension of economic power to the establishment of kings and increasing stratification (something like this, of course, occurred in Postclassic times). A second problem is that one class of evidence—art and epigraphy—is used virtually to the exclusion of others. In saying this, I do not deny the many and important insights that such evidence has given us, especially in the last decade. My point is rather that all classes of evidence are in themselves limited and inconclusive. Overemphasis on one not only yields only partial information, but also distorts our perceptions of a complicated process such as warfare.

The KKC model assumes that elite interactions such as intermarriage, visitation, pilgrimage, and especially exchange of highly valued items were incompatible with highly competitive warfare. Diego Durán's (1964) accounts of the interactions between, and common understandings among, antagonistic elites in the aggressive political environment of Central Mexico show how oversimplified this notion is. Consider another example. Having placed an embargo on salt, cotton, and cacao trade with Tlaxcala, the Mexica elite apparently supplied these commodities to their noble Tlaxcalan counterparts: "During the short intervals of war, it is said, the Aztec nobles, in the spirit of chivalry, sent supplies of these commodities as presents, with many courteous expressions of respect, to the Tlascalan chiefs" (Prescott 1955: 225, citing Camargo). This is a perfect example of solidarity among antagonistic elites. Elite antagonism is one thing; elite deprivation quite another. Few would disagree that there is an elite facade to Classic Maya culture (although it is variably expressed and participated in), and that a shared elite culture serves to structure and regulate interactions of all kinds, including warfare. Such elite subcultures have crosscut political boundaries throughout human history without notably restraining warlike territorial, economic, and political aggrandizement among their members. Thus I cannot believe that the Maya alone were able to devise a political charter that, for a thousand years, so effectively ritualized conflict that war was virtually eliminated as a form of competition, but paradoxically glorified as a kind of elite drama.

David Webster

Freidel sees ideology as the dominant variable in this equation: "Maya religion and political ideology, then, provided a charter for the creation of peer polities, and only peer polities, throughout the history of the civilization" (Friedel 1986: 93).

This brings us to the final issue—ideology as an independent, or at least preeminent, variable in cultural evolution. This, I think, is the thrust of Freidel's argument. Whatever its origins, the political charter was able, by itself, to constrain competition, either by eliminating it entirely or by frustrating its effects when renegade members of the Maya brotherhood of kings dared, on the basis of political ambition and power, to carve out larger realms.

In this model, a "structural impasse" was reached when conquering Maya kings were unable to accommodate their thought processes to new political contingencies and opportunities, and when defeated royalty were unable to realize that the old days of fraternal, ritual jousting were over. Freidel (n.d.: 7) asserts that "The absence of the stable consolidation of large states in the southern Lowlands cannot be attributed to the lack of attempts, and hence must be attributed to a lack of effective means." If this refers to the inability to overcome the "structural impasse" of the ideology of the political charter, rather than the lack of the demographic strength, military skill, and organizational and logistical capability necessary to create new levels of political complexity, then Freidel is seeing ideology as an independent variable.

Freidel clearly links his model to the larger issue of culture as an adaptive system (1986: 108). Among anthropologists Rappaport has developed the theme of cybernetic ritual regulation most comprehensively (1971a, 1971b). For Rappaport, sanctity and rituals associated with it generate information in cultural systems, which regulate other subsystems. Rappaport's abstract model is elegantly presented, and he convincingly argues that sanctity and ritual have important homeostatic functions. His discussion of the origins of new patterns of sanctification and ritual (i.e., the evolution of these elements of larger cultural systems) is much weaker, although he recognizes that sanctity and ritual themselves evolve to accommodate new stresses or opportunities. One of his comments on systems that become "oversanctified" has particular relevance for Freidel's model: "Ultimate sacred propositions cannot adaptively be irrevocably associated with anything more specific than the extremely unspecified goal of the social aggregate: survival. To bind them irrevocably to particular social forms . . . is to overspecify the terms under which the society may survive, i.e. to reduce its adaptiveness" (Rappaport 1971a: 41). This corresponds to what Freidel means by a structural impasse in the political charter.

If the point Freidel is making is that humans generally are constrained in terms of innovation by valued mental habits, traditions, and structures acquired from their cultural milieu, and that evolutionary models that include these components are richer than those without them, then I am in complete agreement with him. But this is a commonplace observation. Despite such constraints, systems (including their ideological and ritual components) do evolve and usually without extreme crises. Dimensions of mentalism can be included in a systemic model of evolution only after one investigates, in a detailed fashion, why such constraints operate the way they do in particular sequences. This linkage of ideology to systemic adaptation is Rappaport's valuable contribution. But the problem here is not to state the argument in abstract terms, but to operationalize it in methodologically effective ways. A concept such as "structural impasse," cut loose from its materialist underpinnings and the other components of the Maya sociocultural system, is an insufficient explanation.

### IMPLICATIONS FOR THE MAYA COLLAPSE

Both the situational ethics and KKC models implicitly or explicitly assert that Maya warfare was more frequent, more intense, more lethal, and less constrained by political/ideological conventions during the Terminal Classic/Early Postclassic than it had ever been before. Both models, but most surely that of Freidel, single out political/ideological stresses as the fundamental causes of the Terminal Classic/Early Postclassic transformations of much of Maya society. My own discomfort with political/ideological explanations of the Maya "collapse" stem not from an inability to discern political (and related ideological) stresses at the end of the Classic; these were clearly present, however clouded our current understanding of them may be. It is the conception of political/ideological factors as independent variables in a complex system of interacting causes that bothers me. The assertion that the Maya had "political problems" relating to warfare at the end of the Classic period is both true and trivial, in the sense that it is not useful. Why did the Maya have more intractable problems then than during Late Preclassic or the Early Classic? What had changed in the sociopolitical lowland Maya environment?

Freidel and Schele (n.d.) have recently gone so far as to assert that a "warring-states phase" of Maya warfare was the "brainchild" of a particular Tikal ruler, Great Jaguar Paw. This ruler, having assimilated Teotihuacan religious ideology and weaponry (the atlatl), embarked upon a successful career of conquest, beginning the "warring-states phase" of Late/Terminal Classic Maya civilization. They interpret change as having been introduced into the system by diffusion, which I see as historical particularism.

My own opinion is that we do not need to fall back on particularistic explanations. We know that throughout the Classic period there was both a proliferation of population in the Maya lowlands and a corresponding proliferation of autonomous or dependent elite centers. We know that where we can phase settlement with some accuracy, as at Tikal or Copan, population densities were extraordinary by the eighth century, eventually degrading the landscape and causing severe internal problems for rulers (Webster and Freter 1990). If significant political/ideological changes took place in southern Maya society during the Late and Terminal Classic, they must be related to, and in some sense caused by, these larger stresses. As archaeologists we do not disagree that a multiplicity of causes, including warfare, is needed to explain the so-called collapse, but only about the comparative weighting of factors in a hierarchy of causes. In my opinion the political/ideological model is not reductionist enough. By itself it leaves too many things unexplained.

An anonymous critic of this paper accused me of "epigraphy-bashing." I have made my own position about the relationship of epigraphy (and iconography) to the larger enterprise of Maya archaeology explicit elsewhere (Webster 1989: Introduction) and will not repeat it here. Readers can make up their own minds about the charge. As I have tried to point out, epigraphy and associated iconography are important elements in our reconstruction of Maya warfare, and never more so than today. But as an anthropological archaeologist, I regard glyphs and icons in much the same way I regard buildings, or charred seeds, or burials, or bits of pottery and stone. They are simply two more components of a potentially infinite suite of data sets that we can use to reconstruct any sort of past behavior, and that we must use *en suite*, along with robust behavioral models, if we are to accurately reconstruct any kind of past behavior. All sets of data have their limitations and their particular strengths. What I have criticized here is not epigraphy, but rather particular inferences drawn from it which I believe to be weak and unconvincing. We all have the obligation to criticize such inferences no matter what data sets they derive from.

### CONCLUSIONS

So where does all this leave us from the perspective of Maya warfare as a process of interaction? On the plus side, we now have a great deal more evidence for Maya warfare than ever before. Just as importantly, our grasp of the cultural/historical framework of Maya war is becoming much richer. On the negative side, we have not yet gathered enough evidence of all kinds to build convincing synchronic and diachronic models.

But most disturbingly, the "mystique of the Maya" is still insidiously with us. All of its elements still operate powerfully. The increasingly visible and popular KKC concept emphasizes the elite perspective of Maya rulers as a monolithic brotherhood of kings—clients of the gods, or deities themselves—acting out rituals of cosmic renewal through highly conventionalized and ideologically motivated warfare. This is, I submit, not very far from the peaceful, theocratic Maya concept of Maudslay, Morley, and Thompson. The work of Tatiana Proskouriakoff and others ultimately necessitated the rejection of this model of Maya society, and the acceptance that the Maya had dynasties of secular rulers just as worldly as those associated with other great ancient civilizations. Ironically, our success in deciphering texts has strengthened our preoccupation with Maya elites, and our penchant for elite perspectives of what Maya society was like. Texts mainly relate to ritual or religion, and the theocratic aura of Maya rulership is still strong.

Maya warfare is often conceived of only in terms of its dramatic, textual expressions because many Mayanists have become constrained by, and addicted to, the historical data that provide such detailed insights about culture history and emic elite (actually royal) behavior. There is still a powerful feeling that the Maya were somehow different, special, unique. We can no longer deny that they had kings, but Maya kings, unlike those elsewhere, devised ideological charters which, uniquely in human history, defused the terror of war, making of it a special and noncompetitive royal display that kept universe and polities in harmonious balance. Yet these innovative rulers eventually fell victim to their own oversanctified ideologies, and were unable to adapt them to new social, political, and economic realities. The mystique of the Maya continues to be the mistake of Maya scholarship. Certainly the Maya are unique. So are the Eskimo and the Kwaikutl. Documenting such uniqueness is one of the tasks of anthropology, but another is developing general, comparative models of structure and change. What we are experiencing here is the same tendency more widely abroad in anthropological archaeology—the proliferation of mentalist models that are not only epistemologically flawed, but which lead us down sterile paths of cultural particularism and relativism, eventually to the mystification of not only the Maya, but of all prehistoric cultures.

## BIBLIOGRAPHY

BALL, JOSEPH
    1977    The Rise of the Northern Maya Chiefdoms: A Socio-Processual Analysis. In *The Origins of Maya Civilization* (R. E. W. Adams, ed.): 101–133. University of New Mexico Press, Albuquerque.

BERNDT, R.
    1964    Warfare in the New Guinea Highlands. *American Anthropologist* 66 (4, 2): 183–302.

BINFORD, LEWIS R.
    1968    Some Comments on Historical versus Processual Archaeology. *Southwestern Journal of Anthropology* 28 (2): 267–275.

CARNEIRO, ROBERT
    1970    A Theory of the Origin of the State. *Science* 169: 733–738.

CONRAD, GEOFFREY, AND ARTHUR DEMAREST
    1984    *Religion and Empire*. Cambridge University Press, Cambridge.

COWGILL, GEORGE L.
    1979    Teotihuacan, Internal Militaristic Competition, and the Fall of the Classic Maya. In *Maya Archaeology and Ethnohistory* (Norman Hammond and Gordon Willey, eds.): 51–62. University of Texas Press, Austin.

DEMAREST, ARTHUR
    1978    Interregional Warfare and Situational Ethics. In *Codex Wauchope: A Tribute Roll* (M. Giardino, B. Edmonson, and W. Creamer, eds.): 101–111. Human Mosiac, Tulane University, New Orleans.

DURÁN, DIEGO
    1964    *The Aztecs: The History of the Indies of New Spain*. Orion Press, New York.

FOWLER, WILLIAM
    1984    Late Preclassic Mortuary Patterns and Human Sacrifice at Chalchuapa, El Salvador. *American Antiquity* 49 (3): 603–618.

FREIDEL, DAVID
    1986    Maya Warfare: An Example of Peer Polity Interaction. In *Peer Polity Interaction and Socio-Political Change* (Colin Renfrew and John Cherry, eds.): 93–108. Cambrige University Press, Cambridge.
    n.d.    Children of First Father's Skull. Expanded version of a paper delivered at the Meeting of the American Anthropological Association, Chicago, November 1987.

FREIDEL, DAVID, AND LINDA SCHELE
    n.d.    Tlaloc-Venus Warfare and the Triumph of the Confederacy at Chichen Itza. Paper presented at the 54th Annual Meeting of the Society for American Archaeology, Atlanta, 1989.

HAAS, JONATHAN (ED.)
    1990    *The Anthropology of War*. Cambridge University Press. Cambridge.

HEIDER, KARL
    1970    *The Dugum Dani*. Viking Fund Publications in Anthropology, No. 49.

New York: Wenner-Gren Foundation for Anthropological Research, Inc.

INGLE, MARJORIE
 1984 *Maya Revival Style*. Peregrine Smith Books, Salt Lake City.

MILLER, MARY
 1986 *The Murals of Bonampak*. Princeton University Press, Princeton.

MORELL, VIRGINIA
 1986 The Lost Language of Coba. *Science* 86, March: 48–59.

MORELY, S. G., GEORGE BRAINERD, AND ROBERT SHARER
 1983 *The Ancient Maya*, 4th ed. Stanford Univeristy Press, Stanford.

OTTERBEIN, KEITH
 1970 *The Evolution of War: A Cross-Cultural Study*. Human Relation Area Files Press, New Haven.

PRESCOTT, WILLIAM
 1955 *History of the Conquest of Mexico*. New York: Random House.

RAPPAPORT, ROY
 1971a The Sacred in Human Evolution. *Annual Review of Ecology and Systematics* 2: 23–44.
 1971b Ritual, Sanctity, and Cybernetics. *American Anthropologist* 73 (1): 59–76.

RICE, DON, AND PRUDENCE RICE
 1981 Muralla de Leon: A Lowland Maya Fortification. *Journal of Field Archaeology* 8 (3): 271–288.

ROBLES, FERNANDO, AND ANTHONY ANDREWS
 1985 A Review and Synthesis of Recent Postclassic Archaeology in Northern Yucatan. In *Late Lowland Maya Civilization* (Jeremy Sabloff and E. Wyllys Andrews V., eds.): 53–98. University of New Mexico Press, Albuquerque.

SABLOFF, JEREMY, AND E. WYLLYS ANDREWS V (EDS.)
 1986 *Late Lowland Maya Civilization*. University of New Mexico Press, Albuquerque.

SANDERS, WILLIAM T., AND DAVID WEBSTER
 n.d. The Conjunctive Approach Revisited: The Archaeology of Copan in the 1980s. Paper presented at the 54th Annual Meeting of the Society for American Archaeology, Atlanta, 1989.

SANSOM, GEORGE
 1961 *A History of Japan, 1334–1615*. Stanford University Press, Stanford.

SCHELE, LINDA
 1984 Human Sacrifice among the Classic Maya. In *Ritual Human Sacrifice in Mesoamerica*. (Elizabeth Boone, ed.): 6–48. Dumbarton Oaks, Washington, D.C.

SCHELE, LINDA, AND MARY ELLEN MILLER
 1986 *The Blood of Kings*. Kimbell Art Museum, Fort Worth.

SCHELE, LINDA, AND DAVID FREIDEL
 1990 *Forest of Kings*. William Morrow and Company, New York.

is needed is a new conceptualization of the entire Maya cultural tradition.

THOMPSON, J. ERIC S.
    1971   *Maya Hieroglyphic Writing: Introduction.* University of Oklahoma Press, Norman.

*John S. Henderson and Jeremy A. Sabloff*

Freter 1990), and as Tourtellot indicates, in general scholars really don't control the relevant variables—especially chronology—very well.

    A recent (and very controversial) study (Pope and Dahlin 1989) emphasizes the restricted distribution and early dates of wet-field systems and the limited evidence, especially quantitative data, for such subsistence strategies as terracing (particularly inconspicuous small systems), tree cropping, kitchen gardens, and reliance on animal protein. These contentions have yet to be demonstrated empirically, of course (cf. Adams et al. 1990 for a strong counterargument), so that it would be premature to generalize from the limited data reported so far. Should these arguments prove correct, however, and should accumulating data confirm the apparent indications of population peaks, the traditional dilemma of Maya ecology would be revived: how were so many people fed? Tourtellot points to the most obvious possibility, a reassessment of the importance of swidden cultivation (see Killion et al. 1989).

## SOCIAL ORGANIZATION

    Social organization, central to the functioning of ancient Maya societies, is in many ways the most difficult cultural realm to reconstruct. In large part, this difficulty reflects the weak development of unambiguous material signatures for features of social organization in archaeology at large. At the most basic level, in the Maya world the correspondence of mound clusters to extended families—or any other kinship unit—is not well documented by excavation except at Seibal, Tikal, Copan, and a few other centers. The expectation of household diversity within regions and centers—in general, Mesoamerican cities were thoroughly cosmopolitan places—and variability across regions complicates matters considerably. Data like those from recent work at Copan, emphasizing rural and low-status residences as well as palaces and public facilities (Webster and Gonlin 1988), though still comprising limited samples, are beginning to rectify the situation. Recent excavations in the Sepulturas residential zone adjacent to the center of Copan (Webster 1989) provide a particularly well-documented case of functional diversity and social and cultural heterogeneity.

    Given the dearth of relevant data on commoner households and social organization, Robert Sharer's (Chap. 4) essay inevitably falls short of resolving all the issues, but it certainly focuses on critical problems. Here, too, regional variation is the most striking pattern in the data; Sharer's call for delimiting the variability in Maya social groups serves as a reminder that we still cannot define "Maya" culture and plot its distribution with sufficient rigor. Local and regional variability offset similarities in language and most other cultural spheres, and diachronic variation balances continuities from the Classic period into the post-Conquest era.

    Sharer's reminder that reconstructing social organization is not fundamentally an epigraphic problem, but one that demands reference to the full array of archaeological data (Hammond 1991), is particularly timely in light of the elite bias that lingers on in our perspectives on Classic Maya civilization. Yet in archaeological terms, Maya elites are surprisingly poorly defined. Tourtellot (Chap. 7) rightly notes that despite vast amounts of settlement pattern research it is even hard to get a quantitative picture of such a fundamental data category as elite residences. Access to labor (Marcus 1983b; Sanders 1989), however, is one approach with considerable potential for improving intuitive definitions. Elliot Abrams (n.d.; Webster 1989: 30) estimates, for example, that 180 workmen could have completed the House of the Bacabs, the most impressive structure in the Copan valley outside the civic core, in sixty days.

Epigraphic data do, of course, lend themselves to exploring such issues as internal differentiation within elite groups, through titles that may reflect native categories, for example. Hieroglyphic texts are rarely straightforward though, and far from evenly distributed across the Maya lowlands, so that the precise meaning and social implications of many titles are not clear.

David Stuart (Chap. 11), echoing Nicholas Hopkins (1988), is probably correct about royal patrilineality, although bilateral descent principles may sometimes have been operative as well. James Fox and John Justeson's (1986) case for matrilineality is quite tenuous, but their fundamental skepticism about the degree to which actual patterns in hieroglyphic texts match assumptions derived from Tatiana Proskouriakoff about dynastic organization is a healthy approach. Patrilineal principles do not always indicate corporate kin groups, or even unilineal descent. Quiche lineages, for example, were corporate at several levels of segmentary linkage. Copan Altar Q provides a striking case: it surely does illustrate dynastic succession (Schele and Miller 1986; Stuart and Schele 1986; Riese 1988), but not necessarily patrilineality. In fact, a father-son relationship is not explicitly alleged for every pair (let alone documented). It is also important to keep in mind that the monument reflects Yax Pac's version of history, not necessarily "objective truth." Sharer's suggestion that elites reckoned descent bilaterally has the virtue of resonating with the importance of both male and female connections in royal genealogies, although it is clear that patrilineal principles were important as well.

The possible existence of endogamous social strata is another key issue in the reconstruction of the social organization of Classic Maya societies. The class concept is certainly appropriate, taken in its ordinary sense: a form of ranking involving economic and status factors, both achieved and ascribed; compared with castes, classes are relatively flexible in terms of considerations like social mobility. Endogamy is a separate issue. It is part of the more general question raised by both Joyce Marcus (Chap. 5) and Patricia administrative than commercial cities in overall character. Ball's analysis likewise suggests that the regal-ritual model is the best fit with ceramic data. Here we want to emphasize two points that have been made about regal-ritual centers: they have been viewed as expanded rulers' households (Sanders and Webster 1988), and they have been linked with segmentary states (R. Fox 1977; Sanders 1989). Whether or not one accepts these arguments, the attempts to test an abstract model against real data are important.

It is equally important to try to elucidate native Mesoamerican concepts of territoriality. In general, Mesoamerican societies of the Conquest period tended to be eclectic, nonexclusive; that is, they were tolerant of linguistic and cultural differences. In the same way, Mesoamerican territories were often discontinuous. The Triple Alliance, for example, not only controlled outlying provinces not contiguous with the central territory, but also had the politically independent and hostile Tlaxcalan state embedded within its core. The relevance of concepts like boundaries or borders becomes doubtful in cultural traditions with this pattern of territoriality (Hammond 1991). In fact, in Mesoamerica there is no very strong evidence for the importance (or even the existence) of borders except where they are provided by topography, as in the case of the peten ("island, territory, province") noted by Marcus. In terms of political and economic power, of course, the critical issue is not territory, but the size of the group who owed allegiance to a particular lord (Marcus 1983b).

POLITICAL ORGANIZATION

Marcus (Chap. 5), like most interpreters of Maya civilization, emphasizes that powerful nonegalitarian, centralized states were distributed throughout the lowlands in the eighth century. It should also be emphasized that many of these states were apparently unstable, never completely counterbalancing inherent tendencies toward fission that reasserted themselves when the original stimulus toward centralization evaporated. Thus, continuing resistance to institutionalization of centralized power, and to centralized control by a rigid hierarchy, may have been quite common. In Laporte's analysis, the noncentralized pattern of the Valley of Dolores would represent the norm, the process of centralization visible at Tikal in the Late Classic period the exception. Certainly the enormous size of Tikal and its state was atypical; the absolute scale of most Maya polities was relatively small. Although the Copan state controlled a large area during some periods, its permanent core comprised a single small valley with a total population on the order of 20,000 to 25,000.

Classic Maya centers, as Marcus notes, certainly reflected a hierarchy, but identifying the relative positions of centers in the hierarchies is not always straightforward. Stuart's suggestion that titles such as *sahal* (formerly read *cahal*) and *k'ul ahau* can be used to delineate hierarchical relations of centers and polities points to an important area for research; realizing the full interpretive potential of this strategy, though, will require further exploration of the semantic domains of these titles. *Sahal,* for example, might signify subordinate, vassal, tributary, ally, governor, or any one (or more) of a series of similar statuses. In addition, as Stuart indicates, there is both regional and diachronic variability in the use of these titles. Settlement data are equally critical for reconstructing political organization, but it is difficult to identify polities and determine their limits as well as to develop detailed interpretations of political orders (de Montmollin 1989).

Marcus (Chap. 5) echoes an important recent trend (Marcus 1976; Mathews 1985) in her attempt to use patterns of occurrence of Emblem Glyphs to delineate Classic Maya political geography. Although Stuart and Mathews argue convincingly that Emblem Glyphs normally serve as titles (lord of + place), the primary referent of the main signs is still unresolved. Emblem Glyphs are not place names per se, but they do designate the lords of powerful centers, and the main signs do somehow refer to polities, perhaps by referring to their ruling lineages. Emblem Glyphs consequently correlate, at least in an indirect way, with geography. As Marcus points out, Conquest period references to the towns of Ah Canek's realm in terms of the names of their *batabob* suggest considerable overlap between the designations of towns and territories and the names and titles of their rulers. It is now clear that Marcus' (1976) initial formulation—that subordinate centers are likely to refer to dominant centers in their political inscriptions, but not the reverse—does not hold without exception. Major centers certainly mentioned other major centers, and centers might refer to less powerful places in a few circumstances—when they held special prestige or when they were defeated in battle, for example. Nonetheless, Marcus' (1976) analysis had enough statistical validity to provide a useful first approximation of the political landscape of the southern lowlands. Even with the radical recent improvements in our ability to decipher texts, the details of political relationships among centers and polities remain obscure, and patterns of Emblem Glyph citation do reflect, in a very general way, the hierarchical relationships among them.

Whether or not the polities associated with Emblem Glyphs were autonomous is, of course, a quite separate issue (Hammond 1991). It is important to remember that the texts in which the Emblem Glyphs appear were produced at the behest of rulers, so that autonomy might well be the ideal of a center boasting its own Emblem Glyph, even if the implied claim of sovereignty were fictive in reality. There is no need to assume centers without Emblem Glyphs had no rulers; they may simply have had no occasion (or no authority) to erect stelae on which to record their names and titles.

In general, the role of kinship, and of lineages in particular, in the political organization of Classic Maya states needs more emphasis, although kinship is an important principle in at least one of Roys' types of political order discussed by Marcus. By analogy with the Quiche state, the best documented Maya polity (Carmack 1981), royal lineage would have provided the basis for state structure. In addition, kinship probably always provided a web of social obligations linking centers. Internal organization within centers is an area that has been almost ignored by students of Maya political organization, though some attention has been paid to economic and social facets of internal organization—especially craft production, organization of the aristocracy, and, to a lesser degree, family and household organization. The implications of public architecture for municipal organization—apart from general indications of the scale and centralized power of political systems—demand serious exploration.

With respect to the need to develop general anthropological models of Maya polities, the segmentary state model (Southall 1978; de Montmollin 1989) recently used by John Fox (1987) to interpret Postclassic Maya societies has great potential, although many of the specifics of his reconstructions are open to dispute. In general, the segmentary state is not really a very well-defined type of society, and some of Fox's African analogical material comes from societies that are not at all statelike and quite different in sociopolitical complexity from Classic Maya societies (particularly the Nuer).

We propose to emphasize the importance of the *process* of segmentary linkage, rather than focusing exclusively on the fission. This process of situationally specific alliance between comparable entities can be seen as an adaptive response to particular historical situations. It was particularly advantageous in "managing" internal diversity. Focusing on the process rather than on a putatively homogeneous class of polities called a segmentary state has the advantage of emphasizing the inherently dynamic nature of Maya political organizations as Marcus enjoins us to do. In this view of unstable polities characterized by resistance to permanent institutionalized centralization and stratification, the Maya world and its regions emerge as a kaleidoscopic array of alliances continuously forming, dissolving, and re-forming, as suggested by Marcus' model of alternating peaks and troughs. This view also emphasizes that segmentary linkage can occur in many kinds of sociopolitical contexts, that is, at various levels of sociopolitical complexity, not just in state contexts. Lineages are often, but not always, important to the mechanism of linkage, which can involve other kinds of social segments. This kind of flexible model is especially appropriate for a cultural tradition as diverse (and embracing as much evolutionary change) as the Maya tradition.

Patterns of variability in Emblem Glyphs are perfectly consistent with the notion of polities as coalesced segments: for example, the sharing of Emblem Glyphs among several Petexbatun sites and between Palenque and Tortuguero; Yaxchilan's double Emblem Glyph; and Palenque's variants. By the same token, the segmentary linkage model clarifies a variety of particular institutional arrangements and historical episodes including:

(1) the Triple Alliance
(2) the relationship betwen Tikal and Uaxactun
(3) the Early Classic hiatus
(4) the shared power of Chaacal and Chac Zutz at Palenque
(5) the collapse
(6) the formation of a large state centered at Chichen Itza
(7) the collapse of the Chichen Itza polity
(8) the formation of the Mayapan "confederation"
(9) Mayapan's collapse
(10) Roys' three kinds of organization in Yucatan, reflecting different alliance patterns produced by the same process of segmentary linkage
(11) the joint rule of Ah Canek and Kin Canek in the Itza polity centered on Tayasal. The situation of a *halach uinic* "subject" (in some sense) to Canek would not be surprising under a segmentary linkage model, since such an arrangement would not necessarily be institutionalized in terms of a "higher" title for Canek. His residence on the main island might reflect a situation in which provincial lords maintained establishments in the capital either as hostages for the good behavior of their provinces, or perhaps to create a "microcosm" of the whole polity within the capital, as at Mayapan.

Invoking a process of segmentary linkage doesn't explain these cases, but it does represent a useful first step in developing a model to be tested. In sum, it leaves us with a much improved but still sketchy anthropological understanding of the highest-level political units of the Classic Maya.

Epigraphic data have enormous potential to provide insights into political organization, permitting the formulation and testing of intricate models, and enriching reconstructions of particular polities with important details. Mary Ellen Miller (Chap. 12) rightly calls attention to the rapid and tremendously exciting advances in our understanding of Classic Maya civilization that have resulted from recent epigraphic and iconographic work. These advances are, of course, still in progress; as Stuart notes, whole new subject areas in the texts may still be unrecognized, and it is certain that most nuances are unappreciated. These advances are also not all cumulative, in the sense that new work has invalidated some earlier "advances," as with revision (Stuart 1988; Houston 1989: 12–13) of Michael Coe's (1973, 1978) interpretation of mortuary polychromes as a Maya "book of the dead." Rigorous epigraphic work demands a continuous reevaluation of conventional wisdom like the healthy skepticism of Fox and Justeson (1986) noted above. Literal interpretation is seductive, but poses many pitfalls. Stuart illustrates some of the very exciting interpretive avenues opened by the *linguistically* literal readings that are now possible—using textual clues to enhance our interpretation of architectural function, for example—but he also emphasizes the critical need to explore the semantic domains of the lexical items in question.

As Miller points out, other kinds of literal interpretation are dangerous. Inscriptions record what the rulers called for, which was not necessarily objective reporting. It is essential to remain aware of and continually reevaluate the many assumptions embedded in interpretations that new insights are making possible: interpretations involving posthumous monuments; multiple figures with the same names; retrospective monuments, sometimes incorporating revisionist history and involving namesakes.

The very touchy issue of unprovenienced (or anecdotally provenienced) objects arises here. One problem is straightforward: geographic origin and chronological placement are unknown (except by indirect inference). Besides the difficulties raised by stylistic conservatism, archaisms, or forgeries, unprovenienced objects lack the full information that context can give. Another problem, perhaps the thorniest, is the relationship between scholarly use of unprovenienced objects and the continuing destruction of archaeological sites; the archaeological record is, of course, not just an academic resource but the cultural heritage of millions of modern Mesoamericans.

A critical issue, as Stuart indicates, is to make our use of various classes of archaeological data genuinely complementary (Marcus 1983a; Houston 1989; Webster 1989a). In meeting this challenge, it is difficult to overemphasize the importance of confirmation, although we should also bear in mind Miller's admonition that differences in the apparent implications of different classes of data are sometimes best interpreted as reflections of the richness and complexity of the past rather than as irreconcilable alternatives. Just as interpretations based on settlement patterns, or artifact distributions, or mortuary remains, or any other type of material evidence need to be tested against the evidence of epigraphy, so interpretations derived from hieroglyphic texts need to be assessed in terms of the indications provided by other classes of archaeological data. For instance, Stuart argues that from hieroglyphic and iconographic viewpoints, the tenth cycle monuments from Seibal do not provide evidence for a "foreign" intrusion. Yet recent burial analyses (Tourtellot 1990), as well as inferences from archaeological data classes such as settlement, ceramics, and architecture (Sabloff 1973, 1975), all point to an intrusion (also see Willey 1990). Clearly, varied interpretations such as these need to be jointly examined in further detail.

Warfare provides another good example. As Stuart indicates, most epigraphic references to warfare are not well understood. The Bonampak murals obviously reflect armed conflict along the Usumacinta during the Classic period, but they do not indicate the scale of that warfare. The apparent capture of Copan's 18 Rabbit by Cauac Sky of Quirigua has no direct archaeological corroboration: Copan initiated an ambitious new program of art and architecture and installed a new king, but only after the brief, murky reign of Smoke Monkey (Fash 1988). Explaining the Hieroglyphic Stair as fictive claims compensating for defeat at the hands of Quirigua is plausible, but requires a fairly convoluted argument. If confirmed, this case would provide a nice illustration that art need not reflect political events.

ECONOMIC ORGANIZATION

As we indicated above, understanding economic organization must be a critical part of any processual model of the growth of Maya civilization. Unfortunately, until recently, this aspect of Maya studies has been sadly neglected. Moreover, reconstructions of Classic Maya economic organization, like those of social organization, have traditionally suffered from an excessively narrow concentration on aristocracies. McAnany's focus (Chap. 3) on household and polity balances this elite bias. However, at the same time, we cannot let this long-needed change cause a subsequent underemphasis on interpolity and interregional aspects of economics.

McAnany's important paper provides a timely reminder of the need to avoid ethnocentric assumptions about Mesoamerican economies based on implicit Western capitalist models. It is still useful to consider such issues as markets vs. redistributive systems, even at the risk of resurrecting some of the rhetoric of formalist/substantivist debates. Insofar as markets correlate with the scale of sociopolitical entities and with community or regional specialization, they make much more sense in Central Mexico than in the Maya world. As McAnany says, a focus on monopoly control of exotics like jade may very well reflect more about analysts than about the Maya, but her own argument that exotics do not create wealth may invoke an inappropriate analytical concept. In the same way, boundaries may well impede the flow of goods, but it is not clear that boundaries of this (Western) sort existed in Pre-Columbian Mesoamerica.

McAnany's emphasis on the need to frame better questions about issues like economy and polity and their links and the need to integrate perspectives on political economy, social organization, and production is well placed. We need a far more rigorous exploration of production and distribution if we are to evaluate such issues as the true value of exotics.

Ball (Chap. 8) puts the key questions well in his discussion of ceramics, directing our attention to "the social and economic circumstances of pottery manufacture . . . the contexts and mechanisms of pottery distribution at both the local and regional levels, . . . and [the implications for] socioeconomic structure and political organization." His arguments are exemplary in their attention to the relations between data and issues.

Ball's own data from the upper Belize Valley give the best, albeit tentative, current picture of ceramic production. These data suggest local production involving multiple individuals working in close proximity to the palace and under its direct influence. Thus, palace styles correspond to specific centers. Ceramic systems (Henderson and Agurcia 1987)—sets of types with the same surface treatment, decorative techniques, and basic design structure, but not necessarily paste and temper—reflect networks of alliance among centers. Stylistic analysis of elite wares suggests multiple artists, which may imply multiple workshops; manufacture and decoration may be partially (or even entirely) separate processes. Elite wares are not just mortuary in function, and, by and large, they are not well defined—we need far better distributional data than we now have to actually demonstrate their elite associations (Henderson n.d.). At Copan, for example, no locally made pottery is as carefully decorated or as well manufactured as Ulua polychromes imported from areas to the east. Ulua polychromes occur in high-status burials and in other elite and public contexts, but in lower frequencies than Copador pottery; the highest frequencies of Ulua polychromes are in an architecturally modest sector of the Sepulturas residential complex, perhaps occupied by foreign retainers of the local lord (Gerstle 1987). In the lower Ulua valley, locally made Ulua polychromes occur in substantial quantities in tiny rural dwellings with no other indications of high status or wealth.

In a few cases—for example, Palenque (Rands and Bishop 1980) and Copan (Beaudry 1987)—the distinction between emic conceptualization and production categories can be recognized in archaeological distribution patterns. Potters may conceptualize in terms of categories that reflect complex interaction between form and function as Stephen Houston, Stuart, and Karl Taube (1989) have shown, but their repertoire is far more likely to correspond to surface-finish categories (e.g., Reina and Hill 1978). Household and/or community output most closely corresponds to ceramic groups; in fact, "workshop" output is probably a better (more neutral) characterization, since we rarely have archaeological data adequate to actually demonstrate the nature of the producing entity.

Stuart's argument for the elite, even royal, status of some sculptors and vase painters is an intriguing insight into the social contexts in which certain elite goods were produced. The painting of a polychrome from Naranjo by the son of the ruler and a royal woman from Yaxha is particularly interesting (assuming that the genealogical claim in the text is true). As Stuart notes, the combination of epigraphic, iconographic, and material evidence—as in the case for elite scribes at the House of the Bacabs at Copan (Webster 1989a)—provides for much stronger arguments than could be marshaled on the basis of any single category of data alone.

Ball's summary (this volume) is very well put, although economic and political networks need not be coterminous, so the landscape may not have been as highly fragmented politically as he implies: "Distinct decorated fineware systems . . . represent numerous discrete palace schools of production. Their existence and the dendritic networks of their distribution imply a highly fragmented sociopolitical landscape characterized by great need to symbolize local identities and signify formal ties of relation. The palace school style-groups emblematize specific centers: the ceramic systems identify their networks of dependence and alliance."

Powerful centers may have had important roles in the distribution of "elite" ceramics, but they had no obvious impact on that of other kinds of ceramics. For these classes of pottery, factors other than the state were at work—such as social considerations and resource availability—and assemblages are generally community-specific. Although political centralization need not imply economic centralization, ceramic data patterns are nonetheless, as Ball notes, more consistent with chiefdoms or segmentary states than with centralized states, and they are inconsistent with the mercantile city model.

Potter (Chap. 9) raises the same issues of variability in relation to resources, production, distribution, and consumption patterns in the context of lithic manufacture. Here, too, the focus of analysis is shifting from traditional preoccupations with description and typology toward a greater concern with production, utilization, recycling, and especially toward a generally intensified interest in social contexts in which the economics of lithic resources is relevant. With respect to the level at which specialization occurs, Potter provides examples of community specialization in lithic production, heavily conditioned by resource availability.

Ultimately, the kinds of reconstructions of Classic Maya economies that we wish to achieve—specifying such things as the roles and value of exotic goods and whether obsidian was a luxury or a utilitarian commodity—demand far better data on the economic nature of various goods: especially better contextual data and more detailed distributional data.

### BELIEF SYSTEMS

Most considerations of Classic Maya religion have focused very closely on inferences based on temples and hieroglyphic texts—that is, on state religion, mainly in its public aspects. Gary Gossen and Richard Leventhal (Chap. 6) deal with this sphere, but in the context of an interesting use of insights from modern ethnographic work, which necessarily focuses on "folk" rather than state religion. They recast the traditional folk religion vs. elite cults dichotomy in terms of complementary peripheral (female, domestic, egalitarian) and central (male, public, ranked) contexts. The center is, in effect, the periphery writ large, suggesting that elite organization was not very different from that of the rest of society. This perspective provides a clean-cut charter and framework for their attempt to relate the structural importance of women in modern Maya belief, especially in transitional (liminal) situations, to the appearance of women in Classic dynastic political affairs.

One very interesting facet of religion that has never been adequately explored is the implication of zoomorphic architecture and even furniture. To enter Temple 22 at Copan and a host of structures in the Chenes zone is to step into the mouth of an immense supernatural beast; Throne 1 from Piedras Negras, noted by Miller, with its back in the form of a Cauac monster without a lower jaw, seems to embody a parallel concept in that a figure seated upon it may have been meant to be conceptualized as being in the monster's maw. This situation may simply be another facet of a basic Maya world view in which virtually every component of the natural and cultural environment is animate—imbued with some aspect of a diffuse, pervasive supernatural force. In the same way, the Maya supernatural is much better conceptualized in terms of nondiscrete bundles of context-specific supernatural symbols and emblems. The "deities" that reappear in sculpture and painting correspond, in this view, to recurrent contexts rather than to discrete entities.

Miller points to another critical issue about the religion of Classic Maya aristocracies: the striking similarities among the many polities across the Maya lowlands. Some of these features are part of a pan-Maya (and pan-Mesoamerican) heritage, but she is fundamentally correct, we believe, in attributing many of the relationships to the Maya writing system that facilitated communication across space and through time, although other factors—relating to the varied social, economic, and political alliances that were simultaneously operative across the Maya world—were assuredly at work as well. At the same time, elite and state religion were not uniform. Laporte's analysis indicates considerable differences in architectural reflections of public solar ceremony from region to region and through time, even within the Peten.

## THE "CLASSIC COLLAPSE"

The new perspectives on the Classic Maya world embodied in the syntheses in this volume also afford new perspectives on the ninth century decline of many southern lowland centers. Marcus' "uniformitarian" view of Classic to Postclassic continuities is particularly helpful in demystifying a process that, until recently (see Sabloff 1985; Sabloff and Andrews V 1986), has been seen as a nearly inexplicable cultural catastrophe. As Tourtellot suggests, we need to revise our basic approach to the problem in light of new information. Recent settlement data from Copan (Webster and Gonlin 1988; Webster 1989a), for example, suggest that initially the decline, at least at that center, was essentially an elite and state phenomenon with a very modest impact on the rural population. The chapters by Rice, Stuart, Miller, Laporte, and David Webster highlight the importance of new indications of demographic stress, environmental degradation, political instability, and conflict. Solid empirical evidence for a variety of factors contributing to a widespread process of decline in reconstructable cultural systems is beginning to replace abstractions about multifactor causation. Marcus' graph (Chap. 5) provides a useful perspective here too: perhaps what we once called a collapse is best conceptualized as a set of very deep troughs that overlap to an unusual degree, though they are not perfectly synchronized.

PROGRAMMATIC IMPLICATIONS

Some of the most obvious implications of the new perspectives on Maya civilization presented in this volume relate to research design. There is a desperate need for verified archaeological signatures for such features as stratification, elite statuses, and full-time specialization (see, among others, Sabloff 1983, 1986; Freidel and Sabloff 1984; Arnold 1990; Killion 1990; Moholy-Nagy 1990; Smyth 1990). What does a workshop look like on the ground? A market (Sabloff 1990)? How can archaeologists consistently identify evidence for a standing army? Civil servants? Particular attention is needed to address the question of specialization, because without the means to verify craft production and its development through time or the mode(s) of distribution of products and foodstuffs, it will not be possible to examine and test hypotheses about the changing political economies of the ancient Maya in a rigorous manner.

Developing better signatures will require rethinking some long-established field strategies and refining analytical units to make them appropriate to the analytical and interpretive tasks at hand. As Ball indicates, to resolve questions of social context and economic significance of ceramic production, as well as to permit the identification of ceramic signatures for political and social segments, we need analytical units that clearly segregate variability dependent on local resources from variability conditioned by other social factors. Such analytical units would permit detailed plotting of the distribution of the products of particular workshops, palace schools, and the like. As noted above, Ball's methodological focus is important in making explicit the putative social and behavioral correlates of his analytical constructs. In addition, Laporte indicates an important stragegy for improving our reconstructions of social and political organization: more extensive excavation of complete architectural complexes as a basis for reliable inferences about building functions. Distinctions like that between status and wealth that McAnany calls for are essential to explore possibilities like the multiple hierarchies (political, economic, social, religious, etc.) proposed by Marcus (1983a).

The importance of more rigorous settlement data is evident for general societal models, as well as for evaluating organizational complexity, for more realistic assessments of demographic variables, and for relating settlement hierarchies to administrative hierarchies. Marcus' proposal that research design focus on secondary and lower-order centers is appealing and, as

Tourtellot suggests, there is a pressing need for more attention to the lower end of the range of site hierarchies. Moreover, as Potter rightly points out, site size is not an infallible indicator of economic complexity or importance.

Mayanists have now acknowledged the importance of variability not only in the natural environment and ecological relationships, but in virtually every cultural sphere as well. The most basic task before us is documenting that variability and plotting its distributions with a view toward finding patterns with significance for understanding Maya economic, political, and social organization. This work will require an operational definition of Maya civilization, which in turn implies an explicit view of Classic southern lowland societies within the larger Maya and Mesoamerican cultural traditions. Only this kind of perspective can provide an appropriate context for using richly documented Postclassic and highland societies as sources of models for reconstructing Classic lowland societies.

The "uniformitarian" approach takes us in the right direction, but we can be bolder. Maya scholars need to break out of their Classic *southern* lowland fixation to consider issues in the larger arena of the Maya lowlands and highlands as a whole, and they need to stop assuming that the "collapse" was a process of utter transformation. Such a perspective will allow us to look—with measured and balanced care—to Postclassic societies for models for understanding their predecessors. In the same way, we must expand our routine frame of reference to include the Maya highlands. The highland-lowland transition does not correspond to a vast cultural gulf, and highland societies, especially the Quiche, can certainly provide useful models for examining lowland groups.

Defining the Maya cultural tradition inevitably raises the issue of its relationships to the rest of Mesoamerica. Just as Marcus (Chap. 5) argues "that some patterns only become clear when the whole of the northern and southern lowlands are combined," so an understanding of other patterns requires that we broaden our perspective to include the highlands, and still others demand a yet broader perspective that embraces all of Mesoamerica. The ninth century decline of southern lowland centers, for example, now appears to be part of an array of larger processes at work also in the dissolution of the Teotihuacan polity in the seventh century (Ball and Taschek 1989). At the same time, as Stuart reminds us, earlier views of foreign military incursions as the primary causal factor in the collapse are no longer tenable.

Developing an operational definition of key facets of the Maya cultural tradition is an undertaking that raises fundamental theoretical and methodological questions about the relationships among the data, analytical categories, and interpretive constructs of archaeology and those of social anthropology (e.g., Shennan 1989). It is far more difficult to envision a satisfactory approach than simply to reject pointless tinkering with trait lists. The standard list of archaeological markers for Classic Maya civilization—ball courts

*Reconceptualizing the Maya Cultural Tradition*

with markers, stelae with inscriptions, corbeled vaults, and a specific art style—obviously represents a very impoverished conceptualization of Mayaness dominated by traditional elite bias and Peten-centrism. This definition focuses on traits whose centrality is far from uniform; it does not acknowledge the geographic and chronological variability of the features, nor does it take account of their functions. Stelae, for example, were erected largely in response to needs for political legitimation that were met in other ways in other societies.

It is nonetheless essential that we find more useful ways to tackle the issues underlying the problem of definition, particularly that of cultural identity. If we accept the obligation of communicating with a nonprofessional audience, we must certainly develop better basic definitions; even specialists are sometimes hard-pressed to determine precisely what Mayanists mean to imply when they use the term "Maya." Greater clarity of expression will undoubtedly enhance the clarity of our thought and the logic of our inferences as well. Moreover, cultural identity is a basic dimension of public curiosity about the past, so it is an issue we must address explicitly.

Language is probably the foremost dimension of lay understanding of cultural identity. Language can be a very useful marker of differences, for actors as well as for ethnographic analysts, but identity often cuts across language distributions, and it is an archaeological truism that material culture and language correlate poorly. The noncoterminous distributions of Yucatec and Cholan speech on the one hand, and of architectural, sculptural, and ceramic styles on the other afford an obvious illustration of the difficulty of determining material correlates of language. In most archaeological contexts, interaction among groups (and the resulting similarity of overall cultural patterns) is really more relevant to identity than language affiliation. The Huastecs, for example, are not normally part of Mayanists' analytical field, except perhaps in connection with very old features conserved since before their initial separation from the rest of the Mayan language family. The typically multicultural and polyglot character of states and communities is, in fact, an important mechanism for interaction among Maya societies, highland and lowland, and between them and other Mesoamerican peoples.

In another sense, however, language is an inescapable dimension of Maya identity. Since reliably deciphered hieroglyphic texts document the use of identifiable Mayan languages, at least by elites, in several lowland centers, it is difficult to imagine a purely archaeological definition of Maya culture with no linguistic implications.

Assumptions about identity structure all description, analysis, and interpretation. In connection with many issues—relationships between Quirigua and its hinterland (Ashmore 1986; Schortman 1986), cultural links between Copan's elite and the populations of the valley and areas to the east

465

(Ashmore 1987; Gerstle 1987; Urban and Schortman 1988; Webster 1989: 15), the impact of Gulf Coast groups on the emergence of the Quiché ruling elite (Carmack 1981, J. Fox 1987), the relationships of Itza (Ball and Tascheck 1989)—the centrality of identity is obvious, and most interpreters have made inferences explicit. Interpretations of other processes of interaction in the Maya world do not address the issue of identity directly, though it is very difficult to see how to deal with any kind of interaction without implying some view of identity (Schortman 1989).

Developing truly useful new perspectives of archaeological markers of Maya-ness will require more and better archaeological signatures for key institutions and social groups. In general, the challenge is to sort out functional, social (e.g., status), and cultural dimensions of variability (Collier 1975).

The fundamental issue in considering identity in an archaeological context is whether it is useful to define multiple archaeological aspects of identity to parallel social anthropological usages (Barth 1969; Cohen 1978). In ethnographic analysis it is often useful to distinguish a more generic "culturality" from "ethnicity," which is context-specific. Ethnic dimensions of identity tend to be ambiguous, and it is not always critical to resolve the ambiguity. In the most basic sense, ethnicity is a survival strategy that secures access to resources and to social support networks; in this sense, ethnicity is itself a resource. Identity is also linked to place through noneconomic factors. In terms of material markers of identity, the sharpest distinctions might occur within fairly restricted social fields where cultural, social, and ethnic distinctions are of greatest immediate importance (C. J. Greenhouse, personal communication). That is, the clearest contrasts may be at the center rather than on the peripheries.

Intuitively, belief seems a particularly good cultural realm in which to locate basic cultural identity since it is not sharply constrained by environmental features. Iconography, particularly as it reflects religion and world view, would constitute the most relevant data class.

Domestic organization also seems fundamental to identity, so the household is a key analytical unit for recognizing cultural differences (Stanish 1989). The household represents a context that is minimally susceptible to the confusing effects of elite status goods and other exotic artifacts that do not reflect differences in cultural identity in any straightforward way. At the same time, households themselves constitute an important data set. Domestic architecture and the arrangement of features within houses reflect the size and composition of family units as well as general social, economic, and political features of the larger social context. These features should correlate with cultural identity.

The problem of identity implies the issue of frontiers. In Mesoamerica, where sharply defined political borders rarely, if ever, existed, frontier zones would have been characterized by complex blending of households and communities of varied cultural affiliations (Henderson 1978).

Conceptualizing the Classic lowland Maya in terms of a hierarchy of cultural definitions is an important part of putting Maya civilization in a broader anthropological perspective. The concept of culture defines fields of analysis in anthropology; it constrains the kinds of analyses that are done and the way they are done. Specifically, cultural traditions bound fields for analogy. For example, the inference that exchange took place often depends upon recognition of objects that are not part of a local style (which is an important part of a cultural tradition). Continuity is always a question, not an assumption, and we cannot simply project ethnographic information back to the Classic period. We can, however, extract "models" of organizational features and, avoiding circularity as much as possible, test them against available data (a procedure that will help to define what data are needed for better reconstructions).

The new syntheses in this volume and the new perspectives they embody leave us with a much improved, but still imperfect, anthropological perspective on Maya societies, particularly on their more complex political organization and institutions. Again, Marcus' discussion of archaic states and Webster's analysis of Maya warfare call attention to the appropriate theoretical and comparative realm. The challenge now is to move our consideration of Classic Maya civilization into this intellectual arena.

We do not suggest that the syntheses and perspectives in this volume constitute a genuinely new theoretical perspective on Classic Maya civilization. The field of Maya studies is sophisticated enough to eschew the all too common attempt to elaborate a radically new perspective solely for the sake of self-conscious innovation. In some sense, older syntheses, though badly outdated by new information, and not very sophisticated methodologically, are not really *conceptually* obsolete. Rather than high-level theoretical abstractions, we now need sustained attention to "middle-range" theory (Sabloff 1983, 1986). Maya studies, like archaeology in general, stands in desperate need of verified material signatures for key social groups, institutions, and features of social organization: elites, commoners, nuclear and extended families, lineages, guilds, households, palaces, state-level organization, kingship, political domains, redistribution, markets, economic spheres, occupational specialization, ranking and stratification, to name but a few. We also need standardized scales for assessing such factors as social and economic status. These signatures and scales cannot be developed simply by reexamining the literature on the ancient Maya; they will require significant reorientation of research designs, in terms of field and excavation strategies as well as analyses, and an expansion of focus to Mesoamerica as a whole and to other relevant preindustrial civilizations.

The particular constellation of emphases embodied in this volume's essays has much productive potential. Their eclectic approach to relevant data, methods, and theoretical perspectives and their recognition of the importance of a broad anthropological perspective are departures from tradition. The clear recognition of variability and the generally greater inclination to document it have put the field in a position finally to break away from the constraints of Peten-centrism. The recognition of the importance of validating interpretations empirically, of developing archaeological signatures for key institutions and social segments, of posing issues more precisely, and of developing analytical techniques appropriate to these questions all suggest that the field may be ready to enter a period of methodological rigor and theoretical sophistication. We may finally be positioning ourselves to *evaluate* models with data, rather than simply proposing them and admiring their elegance.

*Acknowledgements* We would like to thank Elizabeth Boone, Joyce Marcus, Carol Greenhouse, and two anonymous reviewers for their insightful comments on earlier drafts of this essay. They have improved the final version greatly; we retain responsibility for its shortcomings, many of which probably are the result of not always following their advice.

# BIBLIOGRAPHY

ABRAMS, ELLIOT M.
    n.d.    Systems of Labor Organization in Late Classic Copan, Honduras: The Energetics of Construction. Ph.D. dissertation, Department of Anthropology, Pennsylvania State University, 1984.

ADAMS, RICHARD E. W., T. PATRICK CULBERT, WALTER E. BROWN, JR., PETER D. HARRISON, AND LAURA J. LEVI
    1990    Rebuttal to Pope and Dahlin. *Journal of Field Archaeology* 17: 241–244.

ARNOLD III, PHILIP J.
    1990    The Organization of Refuse Disposal and Ceramic Production within Contemporary Mexican Houselots. *American Anthropologist* 92: 915–932.

ASHMORE, WENDY
    1986    Peten Cosmology in the Maya Southeast: An Analysis of Architecture and Settlement Patterns at Classic Quiriguá. In *The Southeast Maya Periphery* (Patricia A. Urban and Edward M. Schortman, eds.): 35–49. University of Texas Press, Austin.
    1987    Cobble Crossroads: Gualjoquito Architecture and External Elite Ties. In *Interaction on the Southeast Mesoamerican Frontier: Prehistoric and Historic Honduras and El Salvador* (Eugenia J. Robinson, ed.): 28–48. BAR International Series 327. Oxford.

BALL, JOSEPH W., AND JENNIFER T. TASCHEK
    1989    Teotihuacan's Fall and the Rise of the Itza: Realignments and Role Changes in the Terminal Classic Maya Lowlands. In *Mesoamerica after the Decline of Teotihuacan, A.D. 700–900* (Richard A. Diehl and Janet Catherine Berlo, eds.): 187–200. Dumbarton Oaks, Washington, D.C.

BARTH, F.
    1969    *Ethnic Groups and Boundaries: The Social Organization of Cultural Difference*. Allen & Unwin, London.

BEAUDRY, MARILYN P.
    1987    Interregional Exchange, Social Status, and Painted Ceramics: the Copán Valley Case. In *Interaction on the Southeast Mesoamerican Frontier: Prehistoric and Historic Honduras and El Salvador* (Eugenia J. Robinson, ed.): 227–246. BAR International Series 327. Oxford.

BINFORD, LEWIS R.
    1968    Some Comments on Historical Versus Processual Archaeology. *Southwestern Journal of Anthropology* 24: 267–275.

BOONE, ELIZABETH H., AND GORDON R. WILLEY (EDS.)
    1988    *The Southeast Classic Maya Zone*. Dumbarton Oaks, Washington, D.C.

BROWN, KENNETH L.
    1987    Core or Periphery: The "Highland Maya" Question. In *Interaction on the Southeast Mesoamerican Frontier: Prehistoric and Historic Honduras and El Salvador* (Eugenia J. Robinson, ed.): 421–434. BAR International Series 327. Oxford.

CARMACK, ROBERT M.
    1981    *The Quiche Mayas of Utatlan: The Evolution of a Highland Guatemala Kingdom.* University of Oklahoma Press, Norman.

COE, MICHAEL D.
    1973    *The Maya Scribe and His World.* Grolier Club, New York.
    1978    *Lords of the Underworld: Masterpieces of Classic Maya Ceramics.* The Art Museum, Princeton.

COHEN, R.
    1978    Ethnicity: Problem and Focus in Anthropology. *Annual Review of Anthropology* 7: 379–403. Annual Reviews, Inc., Palo Alto.

COLLIER, GEORGE A.
    1975    *Fields of the Tzotzil: The Ecological Basis of Tradition in Highland Chiapas.* University of Texas Press, Austin.

DEETZ, JAMES
    1988    History and Archaeological Theory: Walter Taylor Revisited. *American Antiquity* 53: 13–22.

DE MONTMOLLIN, OLIVIER
    1989    *The Archaeology of Political Structure: Settlement Analysis in a Classic Maya Polity.* Cambridge University Press, Cambridge.

FASH, JR., WILLIAM L.
    1988    A New Look at Maya Statecraft from Copan, Honduras. *Antiquity* 62 (234): 157–169.

FOX, JAMES A., AND JOHN S. JUSTESON
    1986    Classic Maya Dynastic Alliance and Succession. *Handbook of Middle American Indians,* Supplement 4 (Munro Edmonson and Victoria R. Bricker, eds.): 7–34. University of Texas Press, Austin.

FOX, JOHN
    1987    *Maya Postclassic State Formation: Segmentary Lineage Migration in Advancing Frontiers.* Cambridge University Press, Cambridge.

FOX, RICHARD G.
    1977    *Urban Anthropology: Cities in Their Cultural Settings.* Prentice-Hall, Englewood Cliffs, N.J.

FREIDEL, DAVID A., AND JEREMY A. SABLOFF
    1984    *Cozumel: Late Maya Settlement Patterns.* Academic Press, New York.

GERSTLE, ANDREA
    1987    Ethnic Diversity and Interaction at Copan, Honduras. In *Interaction on the Southeast Mesoamerican Frontier: Prehistoric and Historic Honduras and El Salvador* (Eugenia J. Robinson, ed.): 328–356. BAR International Series 327. Oxford.

GLASSIE, HENRY
    1975    *Folk Housing in Middle Virginia.* University of Tennessee Press, Knoxville.

HAMMOND, NORMAN
    1991    Inside the Black Box: Defining Maya Polity. In *Classic Maya Political*

History (T. Patrick Culbert, ed.): 253–284. Cambridge University Press, Cambridge.

HELLMUTH, NICHOLAS M.
1972  Excavations Begin at Maya Site in Guatemala. *Archaeology* 25: 148–149.

HENDERSON, JOHN S.
1978  El noroeste de Honduras y la frontera oriental maya. *Yaxkin* 2: 241–253.
1981  *The World of the Ancient Maya.* Cornell University Press, Ithaca.
1992  Variations on a Theme: A Frontier View of Maya Civilization. In *New Theories on the Ancient Maya* (Elin C. Danien and Robert J. Sharer, eds.): 161–171. University Museum, University of Pennsylvania, Philadelphia.
n.d.  Elites and Ethnicity. In *Mesoamerican Elites: An Archaeological Assessment* (Arlen Chase and Diane Z. Chase, eds.). University of Oklahoma Press, Norman. (in press)

HENDERSON, JOHN S., AND RICARDO AGURCIA F.
1987  Ceramic Systems: Facilitating Comparison in Type-Variety Analysis. In *Maya Ceramics: Papers from the 1985 Maya Ceramic Conference* (Prudence M. Rice and Robert J. Sharer, eds.): 431–438. BAR International Series 345. Oxford.

HOPKINS, NICHOLAS
1988  Classic Mayan Kinship Systems: Epigraphic and Ethnographic Evidence for Patrilineality. *Estudios de Cultura Maya* 17: 87–121.

HOUSTON, STEPHEN D.
1989  Archaeology and Maya Writing. *Journal of World Prehistory* 3: 1–32.

HOUSTON, STEPHEN D., DAVID STUART, AND KARL A. TAUBE
1989  Folk Classification of Classic Maya Pottery. *American Anthropologist* 91: 720–726.

JUSTESON, JOHN S., WILLIAM M. NORMAN, AND NORMAN HAMMOND
1988  The Pomona Flare: A Preclassic Maya Hieroglyphic Text. In *Maya Iconography* (Elizabeth P. Benson and Gillett G. Griffin, eds.): 94–151. Princeton University Press, Princeton.

KILLION, THOMAS W.
1990  Cultivation Intensity and Residential Site Structure: An Ethnoarchaeological Examination of Peasant Agriculture in the Sierra de los Tuxtlas, Veracruz, Mexico. *Latin American Antiquity* 1: 191–215.

KILLION, THOMAS W., JEREMY A. SABLOFF, GAIR TOURTELLOT, AND NICHOLAS P. DUNNING
1989  Intensive Surface Collection of Residential Clusters at Terminal Classic Sayil (A.D. 800–1000), Yucatan, Mexico. *Journal of Field Archaeology* 16: 273–294.

MARCUS, JOYCE
1976  *Emblem and State in the Classic Maya Lowlands: An Epigraphic Approach to Territorial Organization.* Dumbarton Oaks, Washington, D.C.

1983a   Lowland Maya Archaeology at the Crossroads. *American Antiquity* 48: 454–488.
1983b   On the Nature of the Mesoamerican city. In *Prehistoric Settlement Patterns: Essays in Honor of Gordon R. Willey* (Evon Z. Vogt and Richard M. Leventhal, eds.): 195–242. Peabody Museum, Harvard University, Cambridge, and University of New Mexico Press, Albuquerque.
n.d.    Royal Families, Royal Texts: Examples from the Zapotec and Maya. In *Mesoamerican Elites: An Archaeological Assessment* (Arlen Chase and Diane Z. Chase, eds.). University of Oklahoma Press, Norman. (in press)

MATHEWS, PETER
1985    Maya Early Classic Monuments and Inscriptions. In *A Consideration of the Early Classic Period in the Maya Lowlands* (Gordon R. Willey and Peter Matthews, eds.): 5–54. Institute for Mesoamerican Studies, Publication 10. State University of New York at Albany, Albany.

MOHOLY-NAGY, HATTULA
1990    The Misidentification of Mesoamerican Lithic Workshops. *Latin American Antiquity* 1: 268–279.

POPE, KEVIN O.
n.d.    Paleoecology of the Ulua Valley, Honduras: An Archaeological Perspective. Ph.D. dissertation, Department of Geology, Stanford University, 1986.

POPE, KEVIN O., AND BRUCE H. DAHLIN
1989    Ancient Maya Wetland Agriculture: New Insights from Ecological and Remote Sensing Research. *Journal of Field Archaeology* 16: 87–106.

PYBURN, ANNE
1987    Settlement Patterns at Nohmul, a Prehistoric Maya City in Northern Belize, C.A. *Mexicon* 9: 110–114.

RANDS, ROBERT L., AND RONALD L. BISHOP
1980    Resource Procurement Zones and Patterns of Ceramic Exchange in the Palenque Region, Mexico. In *Models and Methods in Regional Exchange* (R.E. Fry, ed.): 19–46. Society for American Archaeology Papers 1, Washington, D.C.

REINA, RUBEN E., AND R.M. HILL II
1978    *The Traditional Pottery of Guatemala*. University of Texas Press, Austin.

RIESE, BERTHOLD
1988    Epigraphy of the Southeast Zone in Relation to other Parts of Mesoamerica. In *The Southeast Classic Maya Zone* (Elizabeth H. Boone and Gordon R. Willey, eds.): 67–94. Dumbarton Oaks, Washington, D.C.

RENFREW, COLIN, AND JOHN F. CHERRY (EDS.)
1986    *Peer Polity Interaction and Socio-Political Change*. Cambridge University Press, Cambridge.

ROBINSON, EUGENIA J. (ED.)
1987    *Interaction on the Southeast Mesoamerican Frontier: Prehistoric and Historic Honduras and El Salvador*. BAR International Series 327. Oxford.

SABLOFF, JEREMY A.
- 1973 Continuity and Disruption during Terminal Late Classic Times at Seibal: Ceramic and Other Evidence. In *The Classic Maya Collapse* (T. Patrick Culbert, ed.): 107–132. University of New Mexico Press, Albuquerque.
- 1975 *Excavations at Seibal: Ceramics.* Peabody Museum of Archaeology and Ethnology, Memoirs 13 (2). Harvard University, Cambridge.
- 1977 Old Myths, New Myths: The Role of Sea Traders in the Development of Ancient Maya Civilization. In *The Sea in the Pre-Columbian World* (Elizabeth Benson, ed.): 67–97. Dumbarton Oaks, Washington, D.C.
- 1983 Classic Maya Settlement Pattern Studies: Past Problems, Future Prospects. In *Prehistoric Settlement Patterns: Essays in Honor of Gordon R. Willey* (Evon Z. Vogt and Richard M. Leventhal, eds.): 413–422. Peabody Museum, Harvard University, Cambridge, and University of New Mexico Press, Albuquerque.
- 1985 Ancient Maya Civilization: An Overview. In *Maya: Treasures of an Ancient Civilization* (Charles Gallenkamp and E. Johnson, eds.): 34–46. Harry Abrams, New York.
- 1986 Interaction among Classic Maya Polities: A Preliminary Examination. In *Peer Polity Interaction and Socio-Political Change* (Colin Renfrew and John F. Cherry, eds.): 109–116. Cambridge University Press, Cambridge.
- 1990 *The New Archaeology and the Ancient Maya.* Scientific American Library, W.H. Freeman, New York.

SABLOFF, JEREMY A., AND E. WYLLYS ANDREWS V
- 1986 *Late Lowland Maya Civilization: Classic to Postclassic.* University of New Mexico Press, Albuquerque.

SABLOFF, JEREMY A., AND GORDON R. WILLEY
- 1967 The Collapse of Maya Civilization in the Southern Lowlands: A Consideration of History and Process. *Southwestern Journal of Anthropology* 23: 311–336.

SALMON, MERRILEE H.
- 1978 What Can Systems Theory Do for Archaeology? *American Antiquity* 43: 174–183.

SANDERS, WILLIAM T.
- 1989 Household, Lineage, and State at Eighth-Century Copan, Honduras. In *The House of the Bacabs, Copan, Honduras* (David Webster, ed.): 89–105. Studies in Pre-Columbian Art and Archaeology 29. Dumbarton Oaks, Washington, D.C.

SANDERS, WILLIAM T., AND DAVID WEBSTER
- 1988 The Mesoamerican Urban Tradition. *American Anthropologist* 90: 521–546.

SCHELE, LINDA, AND MARY ELLEN MILLER
- 1986 *The Blood of Kings: Dynasty and Ritual in Maya Art.* Kimbell Art Museum, Fort Worth.

SCHORTMAN, EDWARD M.
    1986    Interaction between the Maya and Non-Maya along the Late Classic Southeast Maya Periphery: The View from the Lower Motagua Valley, Guatemala. In *The Southeast Maya Periphery* (Patricia A. Urban and Edward M. Schortman, eds.): 114–137. University of Texas Press, Austin.
    1989    Interregional Interaction in Prehistory: The Need for a New Perspective. *American Antiquity* 54: 52–65.

SHENNAN, STEPHEN (ED.)
    1989    *Archaeological Approaches to Cultural Identity*. Unwin Hyman, Boston.

SMYTH, MICHAEL P.
    1990    Maize Storage among the Puuc Maya: The Development of an Archaeological Method. *Ancient Mesoamerica* 1: 51–70.

SOUTHALL, A.W.
    1978    *Alur Society: A Study in Processes and Types of Domination*. W. Heffer & Sons, Cambridge.

STANISH, CHARLES
    1989    Household Archaeology: Testing Models of Zonal Complementarity. *American Anthropologist* 91: 7–24.

STUART, DAVID
    1988    The Rio Azul Cacao Pot: Epigraphic Observations on the Function of a Maya Ceramic Vessel. *Antiquity* 62: 153–157.

STUART, DAVID, AND LINDA SCHELE
    1986    Yax-K'uk-Mo': The Founder of the Lineage of Copán. *Copan Notes* 6.

TOURTELLOT, GAIR
    1990    *Excavations at Seibal; Burials: A Cultural Analysis*. Peabody Museum of Archaeology and Ethnography, Memoir 17 (2). Harvard University, Cambridge.

TRIGGER, BRUCE
    1970    Aims in Prehistoric Archaeology. *Antiquity* 44: 26–37.

URBAN, PATRICIA A., AND EDWARD M. SCHORTMAN
    1988    The Southeast Zone Viewed from the East: Lower Motagua-Naco Valleys. In *The Southeast Classic Maya Zone* (Elizabeth H. Boone and Gordon R. Willey, eds.): 223–267. Dumbarton Oaks, Washington, D.C.

URBAN, PATRICIA A., AND EDWARD M. SCHORTMAN (EDS.)
    1986    *The Southeast Maya Periphery*. University of Texas Press, Austin.

WEBSTER, DAVID
    1989    The House of the Bacabs: Its Social Context. In *The House of the Bacabs, Copan, Honduras* (David Webster, ed.): 5–40. Studies in Pre-Columbian Art and Archaeology 29. Dumbarton Oaks, Washington, D.C.
    1989a    *The House of the Bacabs, Copan, Honduras* (Ed.). Studies in Pre-Columbian Art and Archaeology 29. Dumbarton Oaks, Washington, D.C.

WEBSTER, DAVID, AND ANNCORRINE FRETER
   1990    The Demography of Late Classic Copan. In *Precolumbian Population History in the Maya Lowlands* (T. Patrick Culbert and Don S. Rice, eds.): 37–62. University of New Mexico Press, Albuquerque.

WEBSTER, DAVID L., AND NANCY GONLIN
   1988    Household Remains of the Humblest Maya. *Journal of Field Archaeology* 15: 169–190.

WHITTINGTON, STEVEN
   n.d.    Characteristics of Demography and Disease in Low Status Maya from Copan, Honduras. Ph.D. dissertation, Department of Anthropology, Pennsylvania State University, 1989.

WILLEY, GORDON R.
   1990    *Excavations at Seibal: General Summary and Conclusions.* Peabody Museum of Archaeology and Ethnography, Memoirs 17 (4). Harvard University, Cambridge.

# Index

Ac Kan, 205
Acalan, 132–133
Agriculture, 27, 32–39, 69, 220–222, 234–235, 286–287, 291, 450
    channelized/raised fields, 23, 33, 38–39, 44, 221, 283
    degradation due to, 25. *See also* Environment
    gardens, 35, 221, 222, 231
    multiple cropping, 32–33
    orchards, 35, 65
    swidden/milpa, 32, 33, 66, 220–221, 223
    terraces, 36–38, 221
Aguateca, 328–329
Ah Canek, 123–125, 132, 133, 134, 142, 445, 457
Ahau, 95, 118, 123, 130, 137–138, 140, 145, 164, 323, 326, 330, 375, 454
Ahuitzotl, 142
Alliances, 39–40, 44, 138, 141–142, 148–149, 204, 223, 225, 375–378, 415, 431, 437, 456, 460
    *See also* Diplomacy
Altar de Sacrificios, 5, 42
Altun Ha, 163, 284
Analogy, 4, 91–92, 100, 185, 186, 456, 457
Architecture, 6, 27, 73, 165–166, 299–317, 448, 450, 463
    ball court, 308, 316, 463–465
    causeway, 228, 229, 231, 303, 304, 314, 316
    kinship and, 97, 101
    palace, 115, 116, 138, 230, 231
    range structure, 230–231
    status/wealth and, 94–95, 101, 306, 310, 312
    talud-tablero, 306, 307, 308
    temple, 138
    vault, 231, 310, 465
Avendano y Loyola, Fray Andrés, 122, 123, 124, 125, 132
Azcapatzalco, 169
Aztec, 142, 169, 192, 330, 335, 417, 423, 435, 437

Bajo, 17, 25, 287
Basin of Mexico, 169, 423, 429
Bat Jaguar, 144
Batab, 118, 120, 123, 124, 126, 130, 131, 137–138, 142, 145, 148, 157, 164, 170, 455
Becan, 135, 136, 155, 206, 281, 287–288, 291
    war, 333, 416, 428, 434
Bird Jaguar, 335, 381–386, 397
Bloodletting. *See* Cosmology
Bonampak, 155, 206, 375, 401 ff, 458
    war, 333
Bourbons, 201
Buenavista, 75, 275
Burials, 74, 75, 96, 310, 312, 458

Cacao, 5, 70, 73, 131, 437
Cahal, 95, 329. *See also* Sahal
Calakmul, 149, 150, 151–152, 154, 162, 164, 424
Calendrics, 188–192, 196, 207
    architecture and, 301 ff
    Calendar Round, 188, 189, 191
    Sacred Round, 191
    Long Count, 188, 191, 192, 344, 378
    Lord of Night cycle, 191
Calpulli, 77, 80
Cannibalism, 124
Captives, 145, 170, 326, 333, 335, 358, 367, 375, 379–380, 382, 386, 390, 391, 397, 400, 402, 408, 417, 424, 433, 434, 435, 436

477

## Index

glyphs, 333, 334–335
Caracol, 167, 229
   epigraphy, 334, 408
   war, 424, 426
Cauac Monster, 211
Cauac Sky, 148, 400–401, 431–432
Celestial Monster, 211
Cenote, 16, 126
Central Place model, 113, 138, 153–154, 163, 250, 452–453
Ceramics, 80–81, 226, 243–272, 459
   distribution, 245–254, 258–260, 263–264
   production, 244–254
   schools of, 250, 258–264
Chaan Muan, 403
Chac Zutz, 369–370, 457
Chacaal, 366–367, 369, 457
Chalchuapa, 425
Chamber pot, 219
Chamula Protestant movement, 194, 197, 201
Chan, 133
Chan Bahlum, 366–367, 368
Chan Kom, 133
Chenes, 150, 162, 462
Chert, 16, 18, 81–82, 274–275
   production, 145, 280, 281, 288
   sources, 278–280, 283, 284, 285, 286, 289, 290
   trade, 285, 290
   use-wear analysis, 281
   workshops, 284, 285, 286, 288–290
Chiapa de Corzo, 192, 193
Chichen Itza, 5, 117, 120, 121, 135, 136, 148, 167, 390, 457
   rulers, 346–348, 410–411, 426
   Sacred Cenote, 135
Chilam Balam, 126, 132, 346
Chol Maya, 410
Chontal Maya, 100, 131, 133, 410
Chorti Maya, 100, 410
Chultun, 286
Coba, 45, 135, 136, 229, 426
Cocom, 113, 117, 135, 346
Colha, 81, 145, 163, 276, 280, 281, 282, 284–286, 291
Collapse, 5, 43, 44–45, 167–168, 220, 225, 232, 321, 322, 323, 336, 344, 346, 349, 411, 416, 439, 440, 462–463
   dynastic, 226

*See also* Foreign influences; Political organization, fragmentation of
Copan, 5, 73, 144, 164, 289, 449, 452, 462, 465
   art, 400–401
   epigraphy, 133
   population, 224, 225–227, 230, 234, 439
   rulers, 98–99, 148, 226, 281, 324, 330–331, 344–346, 400–401
   war, 148, 149–150, 151–152, 425, 426, 431–432
Cosmology, 69–70, 74, 113, 115–116, 185–218, 301 ff, 410, 433–434, 440, 462
   ancestor worship, 210–212, 301, 362, 386, 397, 433, 435
   bloodletting, 206–207, 379–380, 382, 385, 410, 433
   completion rituals, 191, 303, 308, 357–358, 362, 385
   sacrifices, 113, 193, 390, 391, 408, 417, 424, 425, 433–434, 435, 436
   territory and, 125–128, 132–133, 149–150
Cotton, 73, 437
Cozumel, 136, 228, 230

Debitage, 281, 285, 287. *See also* Chert; Obsidian
Diplomacy, 144, 164, 165–166, 260–264, 403, 417, 437
Dos Pilas, 145, 328–329, 333, 334, 338–339, 426
Dresden Codex, 132
Dual residence, 228–229
Dzibilchaltun, 13, 135, 283

Earthquake, 15–16
Economy, 69, 115–116, 163, 282–283, 448, 451–452, 463
   ceramic, 243 ff
   control of, 39–40, 44, 72, 73, 131–132, 145
   elite/wealth/prestige, 69, 71, 73, 74, 75, 94–95, 98, 101, 247, 248, 255, 264
   feudal model, 67
   lithic, 273 ff
   models, 68–69
   production: attached, 70, 263–264, 323, 348, 380, 398, 463; craft, 145,

## Index

223, 277 ff, 323, 348, 380, 409;
household, 71, 72, 81–82, 250–253, 284, 289, 460. *See also* Agriculture; Ceramics; Chert; Obsidian
trade/exchange, 31, 42, 44, 72, 73
Eight-Deer "Tiger Claw," 134, 138
Eighteen-Jog, 148, 149, 150, 151, 152
Eighteen-Rabbit, 400, 401, 431, 432
El Chayal, 274, 275–276, 277
El Mirador, 145, 229, 349
 war, 424, 434
El Pedernal, 286, 291
Elites, 6, 71, 74, 94, 125, 164, 287, 322, 324, 330, 332, 348, 356, 375–378, 415, 419, 426, 427, 429, 432, 435, 437, 440, 441, 451, 452, 463
Emic, 420, 429, 433, 436, 441, 460
Environment, 448–450
 climate, 18–23, 44
 diversity, 31, 44, 45
 geological, 11–18
 soil fertility, 29–30, 33–34, 221
 vegetation, 23–26
Environmental change, 22, 26–30, 44–45, 449
 deforestation, 23, 27, 31
 degradation, 25, 73, 336, 439
 erosion, 29, 31, 449
Epigraphy, 73, 95, 133, 149 ff, 249, 253, 321–349, 410, 422, 424–425
 capture glyphs, 333–335
 Emblem Glyphs, 113, 140–144, 152, 155, 157, 159, 164, 165–166, 259, 325–329, 334, 425, 455–456
 propaganda, 323
 Toothache glyph, 138, 140, 141, 142, 144
 Seating glyph, 141, 142
Ethnocentrism, 68, 356, 416, 417, 459
Etic, 420, 436

Faunal resources, 13, 26, 36, 131
 animal husbandry, 13, 36
Feathers, 74
Floral resources, 26, 28. *See also* Agriculture; Environment
 forest resources, 24–26, 28–29, 31, 36, 131
Foreign influences, 336, 339, 344, 348, 410, 411, 417, 423, 458, 466
Forest of Chiefs, 159

Gods, 211, 250, 312, 358
Grabens, 15

Halach Uinic, 118–120, 123, 124, 126, 130, 131, 148, 457
Hapsburgs, 201
Health. *See* Skeletal analysis (nutrition and conflict)
Hero Twins, 204, 434
Honey, 131
Household, 76–83, 96–97, 101, 226, 232, 288, 289, 450 ff
Huastec, 465

Iconography, 249
 slaves, 72
Ideology, 27, 247, 317, 427, 435, 438–439, 440, 441
Itza, 117, 120–122, 133, 410, 448, 457, 466
Itzcoatl, 169
Ixtepeque, 274, 275–276, 277
Izapa, 192

Jade, 70, 71, 74
Jaguar God, 211
Jaguar Paw, 308, 310, 439
Juárez, Benito, 201

Kabah, 135
Kaminaljuyu, 277
Kan-Xul, 326, 367–371
Karst, 14, 16
Kekchi, 101–102
Kinship, 69, 96–100, 115–116, 205–206, 301, 448, 451, 455, 467
 ancestor, 301, 362, 386, 397, 433, 435
 clan, 97–98
 household composition, 97, 101
 lineage, 70, 73–74, 76–77, 97–100, 117, 118, 120, 121, 126, 135, 192–193, 196, 204 ff, 301, 324, 346, 431, 450–452, 456
 marriage, 74, 94, 96–97, 125, 139, 142, 164, 167, 204, 223, 378, 415, 431, 437, 451–452
Kuk, 366–367, 371, 396
Kul Ahau, 95

La Mojarra, 192, 193
Labna, 135

Labor, 69, 72, 73, 131, 312, 313, 429, 432, 451
Lacandon, 100, 122, 133
Lady Ahau Katun, 375–377, 390
Lady Kanal-Ikal, 205
Lady Six, 206
Lady Xoc, 377, 380
Lady Zac-Kuk, 205
Lamanai, 5
Land tenure, shortage and alienation, 34, 42, 66, 71, 76–78, 83, 408
Land Treaty of Mani, 126
Landa, Fray Diego de, 97, 132–133, 135, 273, 290, 348, 419
Legitimacy, 188, 190–196, 207
Lineages. *See* Kinship
Lithic resources, 16, 18, 81–82, 275–281, 284, 287, 289–290. *See also* Chert; Jade; Obsidian
Lord of Night cycle, 191

Magnetite, 74
Maize, 27, 42, 131
Maize God, 211, 358
Malinche, 210
Mam, 187, 190
Mani, 126, 157
Maya Mountains, 15, 314–316
Mayapan, 5, 117, 120, 121, 132, 133, 135, 157, 167, 346, 467
Mechanical solidarity, 111
Mexica, 169, 409, 429
Mixtec, ruler, 134, 138
Mixteca, 169
Monte Alban, 117, 145, 157, 357
Mopan, 122, 133
Motul de San Jose, 152
Myths, 189, 191, 197–198, 204–205. *See also* Cosmology

Nahuatl, 330
Naranjo, 138, 141–143, 152, 154, 159, 167, 206, 334, 408, 426
rulers, 206, 260
Nohmul, 5, 276, 285, 449
Nutrition. *See* Skeletal analysis (nutrition and conflict)

Oaxaca, 145, 157
Obsidian, 80–81, 226, 234, 255–256, 274, 275–278
sources, 275
trade, 275, 277–278
Olmec, 192
Organic solidarity, 111, 113

Pacal, 205, 339, 366–367, 368, 396
Pachuca, 276
Pajarito movement, 197, 201
Palenque, 141, 144, 149, 150, 152, 154, 164, 457
art, 366–373
rulers, 205–206, 326, 339
war, 333
Pepet Tsibil (native maps), 125–128
Perforator God, 358
Peten, 15 ff, 34, 40, 44–45, 121–125, 449
population, 155
Peten-centrism, 445, 465, 468
Petexbatun, 334
agriculture, 222
confederacy of, 145, 147–148, 152, 164
forts, 424–425, 426
Piedras Negras, 138, 144, 206, 376–400, 462
war, 333
Political organization, 39, 69, 113, 117–121, 145, 165–166, 170, 247–248, 254, 256, 260, 264, 324, 420, 430, 431, 434, 448, 454–459
archaic state, 115–116, 134–139, 145, 148, 451
capitals, 129, 159, 162, 164, 169, 325–326
chiefdom, 115, 156, 159, 192–193, 264
confederacy, 147–148, 164, 167, 169
dynasty, 335, 346, 358, 366, 425, 431, 432, 451
ethnographic/historic models, 114–115, 116 ff, 448
feudal model, 67
formation of, 136–137, 156, 167–169, 377, 431, 456
fragmentation of, 121, 134, 136–137, 153, 156, 157–158, 164, 167–169, 257, 263, 336, 415, 435, 456
officials, terms for, 95, 130, 331–332. *See also* Ahau; Batab; Catal; Halach Uinic; Sahal
peer-polity model, 74, 156, 264, 327, 434–435, 438

# Index

quadripartite model, 149–150. *See also* Territory; Cosmology)
segmentary state, 254, 256, 264, 454, 456
succession/accesion, 97 ff, 118, 144, 164, 165–166, 358, 366, 397, 435
*See also* Diplomacy; individual rulers by name
Popol Vuh, 204
Population, 6, 40–43, 45, 73, 76, 316
   agricultural production and, 40, 44, 45, 222, 223–227
   density, 40, 155, 222, 439
   growth, 39–40, 223, 224–225, 283, 316, 431
   problems estimating, 221, 226, 228–229, 232, 233–234
Pulltrouser Swamp, 38, 79, 235, 281, 283, 285
Putun Maya, 337
Puuc, 5, 76, 135, 136, 148–149, 164, 169, 281, 288, 289, 290, 291
   agriculture, 221–223, 229, 234–235

Quiche, 187, 190, 447, 451, 456, 464, 466
Quirigua, 16, 81, 465
   art, 400–401
   rulers, 148, 400–401
   war, 148, 149, 152, 164, 426, 431–432

Ramon, 42
Rank-size analysis, 159–162
Religion. *See* Cosmology
Rio Azul, 38, 75, 79, 167, 281, 286–287, 291
   epigraphy, 133
Rio Bec, 150, 162
Rio Pasion, 162
Root crops, 42
Rosario phase (Oaxaca), 157
Ruler A (Tikal), 334, 358, 401
Ruler B (Tikal), 357, 358
Ruler C (Tikal), 308, 362
Ruler 1 (Dos Pilas), 334
Ruler 3 (Piedras Negras), 389–390
Ruler 4 (Piedras Negras), 390
Ruler 6 (Piedras Negras), 390–398

Sahal, 323, 329–330, 332, 369, 370, 382, 385, 396, 403, 454. *See also* Cahal

Salt, 13, 131, 437
San Gervasio, 228
Sayil, 135, 221, 230, 280
Sea level, 22, 23, 44, 45
Seibal, 5, 79, 94, 95, 96, 97, 101, 136, 138, 145, 148, 152, 162, 230, 234, 336–338, 410, 450, 453, 458
   territory of, 158
Settlement, 34, 44–45, 76–77, 97, 101, 219–235, 423, 462
   concentric zonation model, 72, 228
   hidden structures, 221, 229, 233–234
   hierarchies, 115–116, 117–121, 130, 138, 144–145, 153–154, 155, 159, 162, 163, 165–166, 291–292, 314, 316, 431, 463
   relocations of, 76–77, 225, 336, 409, 410, 418, 422–423
   ribbon/floodplain, 228
   site type/function, 131–132, 227–230, 235, 247–248, 254, 256, 260, 264, 280, 292, 316, 453–454, 460–461
   structure type/function, 229–231
   *See also* Central Place model; Site organization; Territory; Thiessen polygon
Shell, 70, 71, 74
Shield Jaguar I, 334–335, 356–357, 375–377, 379–382
Shield Jaguar II, 385–389, 396
Shield Skull, 334
Sierra Madre de Chiapas, 12
Sierra Madre del Sur, 12
Site organization, 72, 130, 133, 135, 230–231, 299–317, 450–452
Skeletal analysis (nutrition and conflict), 42–43, 422, 425
Slaves, 72, 135, 437
Smoke Imix, 400
Smoke Shell, 331
Smoke Squirrel, 206
Social organization, 93–96, 115, 448, 450–454, 459
   authority/power, 69–70, 73–76, 145, 170, 312, 313, 462
   gender relations, 190, 200, 461. *See also* Women
   status/prestige, 74, 80, 94–95, 101, 247, 248, 255, 337, 398, 430–432, 451, 463
   *See also* Elites; Kinship

481

Storage, 223, 286
Subsistence, 26, 30–42. *See also* Agriculture
Sun God, 211, 312

Tayasal, 121, 168, 457
Tenochtitlan, 169
Teotihuacan, 68, 72, 169, 191, 357, 408, 439, 464
  obsidian, 276, 277, 289
Territory, 74–75, 314, 327–329, 332–336, 357, 408, 428, 436, 452–454, 466–467
  historical terms for, 128–132
  quadripartite model, 125–128, 132–133, 149–150, 228–229, 325, 326, 327, 453
  *See also* Settlement; Thiessen polygon
Texcoco, 169
Thiessen polygon, 113, 154–156, 163, 453
Tibaat, 81
Tihoo, 126
Tikal, 5, 13, 42–43, 73, 79, 95–96, 101, 137, 159, 162, 163, 167, 169, 230, 275, 426, 450
  architecture, 299–317
  art, 356–365, 377, 401, 408
  epigraphy, 138, 140–144, 334
  fortifications, 113
  population, 113, 154, 223, 439
  territory, 154, 157, 159, 162, 327
  warfare, 439
Tlacopan, 169
Tlaxcala, 437, 454
Toltec, 169, 348, 408, 411
Toltec Maya, 390
Tomaltepec, 145
Tonina, 152, 154–155, 326, 366, 369, 371
  territory, 158
Trend surface analysis, 152
Tres Zapotes, 192, 193
Tribute, 66, 73, 130, 131, 135, 223, 231, 399–400, 408–410, 429, 432
Triple Alliance, 169, 454, 457
Tro-Cortesianus Codex, 132
Tula, 169, 289, 411
Turkeys, 131
Twin Monkey God, 250
Tzeltal Revolt, 197, 201
Tzotzil, 187, 196, 201, 326

Uaxactun, 137, 154, 159, 167, 191
  architecture, 301, 313, 314
  epigraphy, 334
Uaymil, 157
Usumacinta, 373, 375, 385, 397, 410, 427
Uxmal, 135, 230
  fort, 424

Venus, 204–205, 358, 362, 391, 402
Villagutierre Soto-Mayor, Juan, 123, 124, 125, 132

War of Santa Rosa, 193, 201, 205
Warfare, 39, 74–75, 113, 148, 153, 164, 167, 207, 223, 225, 327, 332–336, 339, 349, 356, 371, 375, 376, 382, 385, 386, 389–390, 391, 397, 402–403, 407, 417–446
  circumscription and, 419, 427
  definition of, 418–419
  ethnographic/ethnohistoric evidence, 120, 135, 418–419, 423, 429
  fortifications, 113, 124, 333, 416, 419, 422, 423, 424, 425, 428, 434
  historic terms for leaders, 130
  Killer King Complex model, 433–439
  Situational Ethics model, 427–433
  types of evidence for, 421–424
Waterlily Jaguar, 362, 390
Women
  political roles of, 201, 204–206, 210, 375–378, 380, 382, 385
  religious roles of, 196 ff, 206–207, 208
  rulers, 205, 375–377, 380, 390
  social movements by, 201–203

Xiu, 113, 117, 120, 126, 132, 135
Xoc, 367

Yax Pac, 98, 99, 324, 331, 401, 451
Yax Kuk Mo, 98, 99
Yaxchilan, 144, 150, 162, 164, 206, 334, 356–357, 375–400
  rulers and art, 373–400
  territory, 157–158
Yucatan, 11, 117–121, 131, 157, 448

Zapotec, 117, 142, 357